"Reading *Invitation to Christian Ethics* is like taking a course with a favorite professor, one who is immensely knowledgeable, unusually wise, and unexpectedly warm. Dr. Magnuson writes with refreshing clarity—both moral and stylistic. I have rarely seen such sound, thorough Christian teaching rendered so compelling and so beautiful. This is the kind of robust Christian ethics needed by the church and the world right now."

—Karen Swallow Prior;
author of *On Reading Well* and *Fierce Convictions*

"Magisterial in its scope and account of Christian ethics, Ken Magnuson has offered us the benefits of his years of thoughtful analysis and faithful teaching in a seminary context. Rich in biblical exposition and practical application, the volume is more than an invitation to Christian ethics, it is an immersion. Magnuson makes his case elegantly and treats his opponents respectfully. This is a model of irenic pastoral ethical reflection on some of the pressing moral issues of our day."

—C. Ben Mitchell;
Graves Professor of Moral Philosophy;
Union University

"The importance of Christian ethics was underscored while I was reading this book for the first time. Medical doctors battling the raging Covid-19 epidemic in Italy were being forced to decide which patients to condemn because essential ventilators were scarce. Meanwhile, cities in the United States were burning with racial protests over yet another Black man killed in police custody. A Christian ethical view of both issues was covered deftly in Dr. Magnuson's book along with a biblical perspective on other vital topics such as abortion, sexual identity, and creation care. Written with the wisdom of a Cambridge scholar, yet in a language welcoming to pastors and university students, this book is a wonderful guide for developing moral reasoning. The very title of this book invites the reader to explore Christian ethics and sets an irenic tone to consider thoughtful arguments from Scripture. Relentlessly biblical and readily accessible, every pastor should have this book on the shelf to help Christians navigate some of the hardest issues in life."

—Dr. David Kotter;
professor of New Testament Studies;
Dean of the School of Theology;
Colorado Christian University

INVITATION TO THEOLOGICAL STUDIES SERIES

INVITATION TO
CHRISTIAN
ETHICS

Moral Reasoning and Contemporary Issues

KEN MAGNUSON

KREGEL
ACADEMIC

Invitation to Christian Ethics: Moral Reasoning and Contemporary Issues
© 2020 by Ken Magnuson

Published by Kregel Academic, an imprint of Kregel Publications, 2450 Oak Industrial Dr. NE, Grand Rapids, MI 49505-6020.

The Hebrew font, NewJerusalemU, and the Greek font, GraecaU, are available from www.linguistsoftware.com/lgku. htm, +1-425-775-1130.

ISBN 978-0-8254-3445-7

Printed in the United States of America

20 21 22 23 24 / 5 4 3 2 1

To Katherine

Contents

PREFACE

This book project has been long in the making and has been shaped by many influences. For more than two decades, I have had the privilege of teaching Christian ethics to seminary students. This volume reflects these years of engaging with students about moral reasoning and contemporary moral issues, seeking to apply a biblical worldview to many of the matters of our day, and to understand what it means to walk in a manner worthy of the Lord (Col. 1:10). Student questions and perspectives have been challenging and refreshing, and have had a significant impact on this work and on my life as a fellow disciple of Jesus. I am grateful for each of the amazing students I have had the privilege of teaching.

Through the years, I have appreciated many contributions to the discipline of Christian ethics, which have been required reading for my students. Some focus on the theoretical, emphasizing either philosophical approaches or a biblical framework, or a combination of the two. Many others mainly attend to moral issues of the day. A few address both foundations and issues. In this volume, I seek to strike a balance, providing both foundations and a discussion of some key issues in Christian ethics. Part 1 (chaps. 1–2) surveys philosophical frameworks for ethics. Part 2 (chaps. 3–5) examines biblical foundations and some themes in biblical ethics. Parts 3–5 examine moral issues, including marriage and human sexuality (chaps. 6–9), the sanctity of human life (chaps. 10–13), and social order and the environment (chaps. 14–17). I hope that the structure of the book, moving from foundations and moral reasoning to moral issues, serves teachers and students well. However, the latter chapters can be understood without having read earlier chapters, and some readers may want to jump around based on their particular interests.

I have written this book with the hope that it will be of service in introductory courses in ethics for a college or seminary, and also for readers interested in a biblical perspective on a number of current and perennial issues. As reflection on the issues in this book makes clear, Christian ethics involves the intersection of a number of disciplines, including theology, biblical studies, philosophy, history, law, sociology, and science, as well as pastoral care, counseling, and preaching. I am by no means an expert in each of these disciplines, but I am an interested reader, and I seek to bring important pieces of these disciplines together as I examine the issues. I hope that the discussion in this book is a helpful guide for students, pastors, counselors, and "lay" readers.

Though this book is significant in size, it is not exhaustive by any means. Many of the chapters deserve a book-length treatment of their own, and there are many moral issues that are not addressed here, though they are of immense interest to me. This treatment of ethics is written from the perspective of a biblical worldview within the evangelical tradition, though I engage with a broad range of scholars, and I hope it will be useful for readers from a variety of traditions who wish to engage with a biblical perspective on the moral life. It is grounded in the trustworthiness and authority of the Bible as God's Word and applied to our lives by the work of the Spirit, and it ultimately seeks to understand the lordship of Jesus Christ over all things for the glory of God.

Many texts in Scripture, and Scripture as a whole, have shaped my life and thinking

about ethics, my teaching, and the writing of this book. I seek to give attention to the whole canon of Scripture, including the Old Testament and New Testament—the Scriptures of Jesus! This incorporates the Decalogue, the Sermon on the Mount, the books of history, poetry, prophecy, and the Gospels and letters to the churches. It is not a full work of biblical ethics (a project that is waiting for a new treatment!), though it is intended to be biblically saturated. In addition to the Bible as a whole, some of the texts that profoundly shape my thinking include Genesis 1–2; Exodus 20:1–17; Deuteronomy 5:1–21; Micah 6:8; Psalm 19:7–10; Matthew 5–7; 22:36–40; 28:19–20; Romans 12:2; 2 Corinthians 10:3–5; Colossians 1:9–10; 2 Timothy 3; and Titus 2:11–13.

I am grateful to many people who have made this book possible. The outline and the first chapters were completed during a sabbatical granted by the trustees and administration of The Southern Baptist Theological Seminary. I am thankful for that opportunity, and for more than two decades of teaching at Southern. As indicated already, countless students over the years have influenced this work through their questions in class, and also through feedback on chapter drafts. Parts of the section "Moral Reasoning and Decision-Making" in chapter 2 were previously published in Kenneth Magnuson, "Ethical and Moral Reasoning," in *Faith and Learning: A Handbook for Christian Higher Education*, ed. David S. Dockery (Nashville: B&H Academic, 2012), 51–71. "Sources of Ethics" in chapter 3 is expanded from Kenneth Magnuson, "Sources for Ethics," in *The*

Worldview Study Bible (Nashville: B&H, 2018). I cannot begin to thank enough the editors at Kregel, especially Robert Hand, Jeffrey Reimer, Shawn Vander Lugt, and Laura Bartlett, for their careful reading of the manuscript and their corrections and suggestions. They have definitely made this a better book! Thanks also goes to my PhD student and teaching assistant, David Closson, who helped put together the index. I deeply appreciate the formative influence of Bob Rakestraw, professor of theology and ethics at Bethel Theological Seminary, who was my first ethics professor, and who invested in me as a research and teaching assistant. I am also ever grateful to Michael Banner, my doctoral supervisor at Cambridge University. He was far more patient than I deserved in his critique of my work as a student, and I am ever struck by his keen and probing analysis of ethics and contemporary issues, in dialogue with towering figures of the past. Other influences—college and seminary professors, authors from across the ages, friends who have asked for and given counsel on moral issues—are far too many to name. To these and more, I owe a great debt in helping to bring this book together, though I take full responsibility for it, especially its weaknesses.

My wife, Katherine, and our four children (Karl, Haaken, Hannah, and Broder) have been an encouragement and blessing to me through the years. Time with them has been a distraction in the best possible sense from long hours of teaching, research, and writing!

Most of all, I am grateful to God, in whom we live and move and have our being. His grace is beyond comprehension. I encourage anyone reading this book to consider how the Triune God has conspired for our good, loving the world in such an immeasurable way that the Father gave his only begotten Son, that anyone who believes in him will have eternal life (John 3:16). As the apostle Paul asks, "If God is for us, who is against us? He did not even spare his own Son but gave him up for us all. How will he not also with him grant us everything?" (Rom. 8:31–32). How can we not give ourselves to such a God as living sacrifices?

(Rom. 12:1). Consider this book an attempt to consider how we might live before such a gracious God, to walk worthy. *Soli deo gloria!*

PART 1

PHILOSOPHICAL FOUNDATIONS

CHAPTER 1

AN INVITATION TO CHRISTIAN ETHICS

Listen closely, pay attention to the words of the wise,
and apply your mind to my knowledge.
For it is pleasing if you keep them within you
and if they are constantly on your lips.
I have instructed you today—even you—
so that your confidence may be in the LORD.
                                    —Proverbs 22:17–19

Let your light shine before others, so that they may see
your good works and give glory to your Father in heaven.
                                    —Matthew 5:16

Many people are interested in moral issues, but not so many want to read a book about ethics. Similarly, many people want to play a sport, but not so many people want to practice. Perhaps some are reluctant to read books about ethics because they believe that ethics is all about religious, civic, or institutional policies, rules, regulations, or laws, all of which (they may believe) limit freedom and deny us pleasures in life. Why would they want to read a law code? It may be important, but surely it is boring. There may be a few people who like that kind of thing, and we may need people who do that work, but you don't want to be one of them, and you don't want to read their reports. Moral issues may be interesting, but reading about ethics seems abstract, boring, and difficult.

Yet ethics can't be boiled down to a list of rules and regulations. This book is an invitation to understand ethics, particularly *Christian* ethics, differently. Ethics is worth reading, in short, because it is about things that are worthwhile, like faith, family, friendship, love, the purpose of life, choices we make and how we make them, and so on. Yes, rules play a role too, as we will see, but they must be understood in relation to everything else. They are not the essence of ethics.

Readers are invited to think about what ethics is all about, and to consider what makes Christian ethics distinct from other ethics; to ask, for instance, what the gospel has to do with ethics. Readers who are not convinced that Christianity is true, and may be opposed to many positions that Christians take on moral issues, are invited to consider the issues discussed in this book as part of a worldview, or view of reality, that is represented here. Positions on moral issues should not be taken up buffet style, picking and choosing according to what we prefer with each issue. Rather, we should understand particular issues, moral principles and rules, right and wrong, virtues and values, and all other aspects of ethics, in relation to a comprehensive worldview. In turn, it is important to weigh carefully any worldview, both in terms of its overall view of reality and its moral claims. Before looking more closely at what Christian ethics is all about, it might be good to ask why you should want to study it.

First, properly understood, ethics is a central concern of Scripture, from beginning to end. Genesis describes the order and design of God in creation, God's relationship to his creation, responsibilities given to human beings, as well as the problem of sin and rebellion in the fall, creating disorder and death. These are all part of a moral framework to unpack. The Mosaic law establishes parameters to uphold justice and prevent harm, to promote love in relationship with God and others, and to structure Israel's society. Old Testament narratives portray examples of good and evil, faithful and unfaithful people, and God's faithfulness to his covenant promises. The wisdom literature presents paths of life and death, extols the wisdom of living according to God's law, and teaches how to respond appropriately to God through worship. The prophets condemn the immorality of Israel and its neighbors, and call for repentance and justice, especially for the weak and powerless.

Ethics is no less a concern in the New Testament. At the cosmic level, the Gospels and the Epistles declare Jesus to be the Son of God and true human, who came to reconcile human beings to God and to one another through his death on the cross, to defeat evil and death, and to inaugurate the kingdom of God on earth. These things are part of the gospel, within which ethics must be understood. At the level of everyday living, the New Testament gives attention to actions and motives, to virtues and vices, and to what it means to be a follower of Jesus and to walk in a manner worthy of the Lord. When Jesus met with his disciples for the last time, he gave them a charge that we refer to as the Great Commission, to make disciples, "teaching them to observe every-thing I have commanded you" (Matt. 28:19–20). The failure to make disciples and, yes, to teach ethics, is sometimes the great *omission* of the church. The biblical resources for Christian ethics are not limited to Jesus's teaching, either. Second Timothy 3:16–17, often quoted to emphasize the authority of Scripture, also speaks to the concern for ethics in the whole of the Bible: "All Scrip-ture is inspired by God and is profitable for teaching, for rebuking, for correcting, for training in righteousness, so that the man of God may be complete, equipped for every good work." Our lives are important to God, and he takes great care to teach us how to live. We should be concerned to live in a manner that pleases God, and to teach others to do so as well.

Second, it follows, then, that we ought to study ethics because it is important. In a fre-quently cited statement, Socrates says, "The discussion is not about an incidental matter, but about the way we ought to live."[1] Ethics has to do with how we live our lives. Many people prefer not to think too deeply about life, perhaps for fear that something they love will need to be sacrificed, that there are things that may need to change. They prefer the distractions of sports, movies, televi-sion, music, and other entertainment. Or they prefer to peer into other people's lives through social media, and to present the mundane things of their own lives to others. Though entertaining for a time, such things

are empty, and life may seem to be mean-ingless—a despairing thought that is some-times encouraged by song lyrics that say as much. Entertainment and mundane things in life need not be eliminated. They are part of life, along with big decisions about faith, education, marriage and children, friends, work, where to live, and many other impor-tant choices. The big issues, and countless decisions that we make every day, all reflect and mold our character, and they are all meaningful as they are shaped by our basic orientation in life and our understanding of the purpose of our life. In turn, sorting out the orientation and purpose of our lives will affect our decisions about the big, and even the mundane, things in life. Thinking about ethics will help us to sort out how we live our lives.

Third, it is worth thinking about ethics in order to improve our moral reasoning. How we live our lives involves our basic alignment and intentions, about who we are and how we act. Moral reasoning concerns how we make such decisions. It is something that we develop by observing others, by thinking about how to do it, by practicing it, by engaging with the people of God, and being saturated with the Word of God. I will devote some time later to the process of moral reasoning, involving especially moral reflection and deliberation. For now, it can simply be said that we need to understand issues well through careful reflection, and not simply act or judge by impulse (though

---

1.   Plato, *Republic* 1.352, eds. Chris Emlyn-Jones and William Preddy, Loeb Classical Library (Cambridge, MA: Har-vard University Press, 2013), 109.

our impulses can also be shaped). We should go beyond simply articulating our position on a given matter, to offer a reasonable and compelling rationale for our position that flows out of a biblical worldview. That is, we ought to articulate not just what we believe but also why we believe it.

One of the fruits of careful reflection is better decision-making or moral deliberation. We want to be able to apply a biblical worldview properly to contemporary, concrete, and often complex matters, in order to make decisions or offer counsel about such things as dating, marriage and family, contraception, politics, economics, the environment, assisted reproductive technology (e.g., *in vitro* fertilization), stem-cell research, and many more issues. It is easy to feel overwhelmed by some decisions. It is often difficult to access and assess all the facts, to know how to weigh competing moral claims, or even to have time to think things through when it seems like decisions have to be made at once. All these things and more can make moral reasoning difficult. Yet it is a skill that can be developed. This book may help you with moral reasoning in two ways: by proposing a model for moral reasoning and by working through a number of issues. If you don't agree with what is proposed, your reasons for disagreement and thinking about alternatives will be part of the development of your own skill.

Fourth, studying ethics can help us to understand and engage with people around us, and to share with them reasons for our beliefs. We do well to try to understand better why other people think and act the way they do. We may disagree, but we ought to listen and engage with others, to take an interest in them, rather than simply reject them out of hand. This does not mean affirming each person's view as legitimate, or "true for them." Many views are not legitimate, or justifiable; some are repugnant. Many attitudes and actions ought to be resisted and rejected, or repudiated. Yet that can be done with genuine care and concern for the person. From a Christian point of view, how we respond to others is important, and is an opportunity to witness to them about Christian faith.

Many people are not interested in talking about "religion," but they are interested in what is going on in the world around them. Ethical issues are in the news every day, and some who would close the door to direct talk about faith (yours or theirs) may be willing and eager to talk about current issues. Ultimately, such conversations will lead back to matters of faith, since what we believe determines what we do, though they might not have initially thought in such terms. Making those connections may provide the opportunity to explain why you believe (and act) as you do, and perhaps even to make a compelling case for faith in God and following Jesus. There are opportunities with neighbors, coworkers, someone sitting in the adjacent seat on a plane, or other parents whom you sit with for hours at your kids' sporting events, to name a few. Christians have, or should have, much to say to make sense of the world and of difficult issues, including the mundane (but extremely important and relevant) ones. Indeed, the Christian worldview is the only one that can make full sense of what is happening in our world. We ought to engage people.

Fifth, ethics is important to think about as a preparation for ministry. So many issues in ministry and pastoral counseling have an ethical dimension. Consider a relatively brief, yet diverse, sampling of matters that people in the church (and outside of it) might bring to their pastor (or seminary-educated friend):

- Someone asks, "What are the most important issues that should be considered when deciding who to vote for, and how should we think about such things as care for the poor, national security, immigration, the economy, marriage and family issues, abortion?"
- A newly married couple wonders whether there are any moral considerations related to birth control.
- A married couple desiring children recently found out that they are infertile, and they desire to know whether there is anything wrong with using *in vitro* fertilization. What if they find out it is only possible with the use of a donor sperm or egg, or a gestational surrogate?
- A group of singles in their twenties would like you to talk about whether it is legitimate, or perhaps even preferable, for them to remain single. Some of them wonder whether it is a calling. Others want to avoid marriage because the divorce rate is so high.
- A friend who is a member at a megachurch has discovered that a couple at the church are cohabiting, and that they

say there are many other couples in the same situation. Further, they are convinced that there is nothing wrong with it biblically, as long as they are faithful to one another. Marriage is just a piece of paper. How do you respond?
- An elderly man at the hospital is on life support. The family is told that there is no brain activity and he has no chance of recovery. Yet they are hoping for a miracle, and they believe that if they "pull the plug," it would be killing him, so they are fighting the hospital to prevent them from doing that. They want to know what you think.
- A woman tells you that her husband is addicted to pornography. She is disgusted by his behavior and feels betrayed. She wants to know whether she is justified in pursuing a divorce. He says he knows that it is wrong, feels terrible after he succumbs to the temptation, and has tried for years to stop viewing pornography; but he can't control his desires. What can he do? What should she do?
- A young woman tells you that she is confused about her sexuality. She has come to realize that she is attracted only to other women. She was recently pursued by another woman, and it ended in a sexual encounter. She felt guilty, but also thrilled by it. She always thought homosexuality was wrong, but now she is not sure. She didn't choose to be attracted to women; it is just the way she is "wired." Can she be in a faithful relationship with a woman and be a member at her church?

Each one of these scenarios are matters involving pastoral care, as well as matters of ethics and moral reasoning. Each involves understanding people and their situation, considering relevant facts, helping them to discern what the Bible has to say about the situation and what is God's will for them; that is, what is the right thing to do? Each person must examine who they are and how they ought to respond to the situation. In addition, what is sometimes missed is a consideration of how the community plays a role in each situation.

Sixth, it is worth thinking about Christian ethics in order to combat false teachings and destructive behavior in society and the church and to offer a coherent and compelling moral vision for all of life, which flows out of the Bible and our theological convictions. For some, the message of the Bible is that there is good news and bad news. The good news is that you can have eternal life. The bad news is that you have to give up all the good things in this life. It just doesn't seem worth sacrificing a life of pleasure, especially if they don't find the appeal to eternal life compelling (due perhaps to an impoverished understanding or an impoverished vision cast by Christians). Christians, they think, are suspicious of all of life's pleasures. They are all about rules, and they want to tell everyone else how to live. Why live by somebody else's rules? Why not go for the gusto, experience everything that life has to offer, and do things my way? These things deserve an answer, and Christians can offer a coherent moral vision that challenges the

presuppositions and conclusions suggested by such critics.

Indeed, Christians must challenge the view of autonomous individualism that is so prevalent—not because self-interest is simply wrong, but because it is so often misguided and detrimental, and lacks a proper understanding of human sociality and community. Christians must challenge the way that pleasure is made to be the highest goal, not because the pursuit of pleasure is wrong, but because it is so often misplaced and destructive, and too many people simply don't know where or how to look for the greatest pleasures. And Christians must challenge the notion that the Christian life is all about rules, not because rules are wrong, but because they are misunderstood by those who reject all rules and by those who think that rules are the essence of ethics. Finding one's identity in God and in a community, pursuing and enjoying life's greatest pleasures, and experiencing the liberating reality of God's commands—all these things (and more) are part of a robust vision of Christian ethics, of living in glad obedience to a good Creator.

Ours is an increasingly secular world, which calls evil good and good evil (see Isa. 5:20). It relativizes things that are absolute and absolutizes things that are not. It profanes what is holy and worships what is mundane. It minimizes what is truly significant and maximizes what is small. It rejects what is honorable and celebrates what is dishonorable. It conceals what is true and proclaims what is false. It is tempting to go along. It seems normal. It is, after all, the world we have always known and so it is comfortable to us. Paul wrote to Christians in Rome who, no doubt, experienced the same thing. Yet Paul reminds them that they had experienced "the depth of the riches both of the wisdom and the knowledge of God!" (Rom. 11:33). In light of this, he exhorts them to give themselves fully to God in worship, and then says, "Do not be conformed to this age, but be transformed by the renewing of your mind, so that you may discern what is the good, pleasing, and perfect will of God" (Rom. 12:2).

This is why we ought to be concerned about ethics, for it is where our theology and our doxology spill over into the way we live our lives. It is an arena where you may "let your light shine before others, so that they may see your good works and give glory to your Father in heaven" (Matt. 5:16).

CHAPTER 2

ETHICS AND MORAL REASONING

That you may be filled with the knowledge of his will in all spiritual wisdom and understanding, so as to walk in a manner worthy of the Lord, fully pleasing to him: bearing fruit in every good work and increasing in the knowledge of God.

—Colossians 1:9–10 ESV

Now if any of you lacks wisdom, he should ask God—who gives to all generously and ungrudgingly—and it will be given to him.

—James 1:5

So, whether you eat or drink, or whatever you do, do everything for the glory of God.

—1 Corinthians 10:31

Introduction

Before we look more closely at Christian ethics, it will be helpful to understand something of ethics in more general terms. What is ethics? When asked that question at the beginning of a new term, students in an introductory ethics course give a broad range of answers. They say ethics is about the following things:

- What you do when no one is looking
- Right and wrong
- Moral values
- Moral rules
- Doing justice .
- Doing the right thing
- Doing what God commands
- Duties and obligations
- Virtues
- Treating other people the way you want to be treated
- Making the right decisions

These responses, and more, point to some of the things that are concerns of ethics. They tend to cluster around concepts of right and wrong, and things we should and shouldn't do. As we look to sort out what ethics is all about, we could first add to these responses some possibilities offered by theologians, philosophers, ethicists, and others. For some, ethics is about the following:

- Seeking the good
- Pursuing pleasure
- Doing your moral duty

- Applying moral principles to concrete decision-making
- Trying to ensure the best results for as many people as possible
- Being a good person
- Discovering and living by the moral or natural law
- Doing the loving thing in each situation
- Having integrity, defined by when your actions match your attitude
- Simply a description of the way a person or group does things
- A description of the things we like and don't like

Some of these notions are incompatible with others, and we may ask which ones represent legitimate aspects of ethics, and how all the right pieces fit together in our understanding of ethics. To understand better what ethics is—that is, to see how it all works—it will be helpful to compare major approaches to ethics. These are attempts to offer a structure for ethics that prioritizes what is thought to be most important, and seek to bring together different aspects of ethics within that structure. First, I will briefly describe these approaches by sketching some of their key features and suggesting some strengths and weaknesses of each. This will not be an attempt to offer a full summary of these positions, or to capture all the nuances that may be added to this description. Rather, what follows will simply sketch the basic patterns of thought in these accounts of ethics, in order to compare and contrast them with each other. Then I will evaluate them from the perspective of a Christian account of ethics, and consider how they compare to the shape of Christian ethics with a biblical framework.

Major Approaches to Ethics

Deontology

> Act only according to that maxim by which you can at the same time will that it should become a universal law.
> —Immanuel Kant[1]

Immanuel Kant (1724–1804) articulates a deontological approach to ethics, which is brought into focus in what he calls a categorical imperative, an example of which is cited above. Deontology is oriented to duty, from the Greek word δέον. Other approaches, such as consequentialism (see below), may emphasize duty as well. However, in deontology, or at least Kant's version of it, duty is central, for it not only demands that we do the right thing but also serves as the proper motive for an act to be considered right. Moral obligation is not derived from intended results or from desire, but from the binding character of universal moral norms, which, properly understood, are considered objective and absolute. For some deontologists, including Kant, as well as some **natural law** thinkers, these norms, which are expressed as principles or maxims, are discovered by reason, while for others they are known by revelation. Thus, as Kant's statement shows, deontology understands ethics to be objective and universal. A right moral act is one that is derived from or is in accord with a universal principle. It is the principle, not necessarily the particular act, that applies to everyone. Different situations may require different acts, but those acts are grounded in the same moral principles. In other words, to test whether an act is right, we are to ask whether it is based on a moral principle that all people should follow. Moral reasoning involves discerning these moral principles, and determining acts that corresponds to a proper principle in a particular case.

The affirmation that moral decisions must be based on universal principles involves a rejection of the view that our choices are determined by the consequences of an act. If an act is right, it is not made wrong by a potential—or actual—negative outcome of the act. Conversely, if an act is wrong, it is not made right by a positive result. For instance, if lying is wrong, it is not made right simply because it seems necessary to avoid some harm or bring about some positive result. The deontologist asks whether we want lying to be universal. Since that would lead to a breakdown in trust and communication in society, the answer must be no. Therefore, we are not justified in lying, even to produce a good result or to prevent harm.

---

1. Immanuel Kant, *Foundations of the Metaphysics of Morals*, trans. Lewis White Beck (New York: Bobbs-Merrill, 1959 [1785]), 39.

In other words, deontologists deny that the ends justify the means. That is, a good result does not justify a bad act. It may be granted that a good act will sometimes produce tragic results, and an evil act may sometimes produce positive results. Yet, deontologists say, the tragic result does not make the good act wrong and the positive result does not make the bad act right. This does not mean that deontologists necessarily ignore the consequences of acts. They may consider consequences to be important, but not determinative, for deciding what is right. In any case, we cannot possibly know in advance all the consequences of our acts, and results may only appear to be negative or positive in the short term, while rejecting moral principles, a deontologist believes, is always wrong.

Consequentialism

> Actions are right in proportion as they tend to promote happiness, wrong as they tend to produce the reverse of happiness.
>
> —John Stuart Mill[2]

John Stuart Mill (1806–1873), whose perspective on ethics sharply contrasts with deontology, promotes **utilitarianism**, which is a form of a broad framework for ethics called **consequentialism**. What consequentialists have in common is that they believe ethics should be oriented to the results or consequences of our actions. In particular, acts are judged to be right or wrong, good or evil, only in view of the consequences that are produced. A bad act is one that produces, on balance, undesirable consequences. Conversely, a good act is one that produces or maximizes desirable consequences. Moral reasoning is based on utility, or what works, so the task is to determine how to act so as to bring about desired results. For consequentialists, moral obligation is derived not from objective, universal moral norms, but rather from the necessity of producing, or at least attempting to produce, good results.

There are many different forms of consequentialism. Some are narrow in scope, such as **ethical egoism**, where moral reasoning is based on an individual's self-interest, and an act is right that maximizes desirable results for oneself. The most prominent form of consequentialism is **utilitarianism**, which is broad in scope, seeking to act so as to bring about the greatest good for the greatest number of people. (See below under evaluation for the distinction between **act-utilitarianism** and **rule-utilitarianism**.) For consequentialists, since acts are evaluated morally only in terms of results, acts themselves do not have intrinsic moral value—that is, they are not intrinsically good or evil.

---

2. J. S. Mill, *Utilitarianism* (New York: Bobbs-Merrill, 1957 [1861]), 10. Mill's work built on the thought of Jeremy Bentham (1748–1832), especially his *An Introduction to the Principles of Morals and Legislation* (New York: Hafner, 1948 [1789]), and many other editions.

The consequentialist holds that the ends do justify the means, at least to a point. Few consequentialists would justify *any* means to *any* good end, for the means used will depend on the end that is pursued. The phrase "the ends justify the means" serves its purpose as a general summary of this perspective, even if it might be more accurate to say that acts that produce a balance of desirable over undesirable results are right, while acts that produce a balance of undesirable over desirable results are wrong.

In moral philosophy, especially from the eighteenth century to the middle of the twentieth century, much of the discussion focused on a debate about how acts are justified and evaluated morally, how to resolve moral conflicts, and so on. Moral philosophy has been dominated by deontology and consequentialism, as the two main frameworks for ethics. It has seemed that either ethics is about doing the right thing, regardless of the consequences, or doing whatever it takes to make sure things turn out right. In many cases, adherents of each view have defined their understanding of ethics not only by what they affirm but also by what they deny, particularly in relation to what the other view affirms; that is, some might adopt deontology primarily because they reject consequences as determinative for ethics, while others have found

deontology and its commitment to inflexible moral principles to be inadequate, and so have turned to consequentialism. Of course, this is something of an oversimplification, and there have been other options. Yet, while recognizing that a number of smaller trails have been made, two of the main paths have been the deontological commitment to principles and rules, and the consequentialist focus on results.

However, during the latter half of the twentieth century, dissatisfaction with these two options grew, due in part to the impasse between these seemingly incommensurable views, a growing breakdown of moral consensus, and a fragmentation of morality that retained certain rules and customs but lost a rationale for them. What was lost, some argue, was a fuller account of ethics that recognizes the significance of virtue, character, and community in the moral life. In recent years, due in no small part to the work and influence of the philosopher Alasdair MacIntyre and the theologian Stanley Hauerwas, virtue ethics (also called *aretaic* ethics, from the Greek ἀρετή, for virtue) has challenged both deontology and consequentialism, and has provided a major alternative to those views as an approach to ethics.[3]

---

3. See, e.g., Alasdair MacIntyre, *After Virtue: A Study in Moral Theory*, 3rd ed. (Notre Dame, IN: University of Notre Dame Press, 2007 [1981]); MacIntyre, *Whose Justice? Which Rationality?* (Notre Dame, IN: University of Notre Dame Press, 1988); MacIntyre, *Three Rival Versions of Moral Enquiry: Encyclopaedia, Genealogy, and Tradition* (Notre Dame, IN: University of Notre Dame Press, 1990). Among Hauerwas's voluminous works, see Stanley Hauerwas, *Character and the Christian Life: A Study in Theological Ethics* (Notre Dame, IN: University of Notre Dame Press, 1994 [1975]); Hauerwas, *A Community of Character: Toward a Constructive Christian Social Ethic* (Notre Dame,

Virtue Ethics

> Once we resist the temptation to abstract "situations" and "cases" from their narrative context, we can begin to appreciate the testimony of many, both Christians and non-Christians, that in matters of significance even involving the "hardest choices" there was no "decision" to be made. Rather, the decision makes itself if we know who we are and what is required of us.
>
> —Stanley Hauerwas[4]

One way of getting at the contrast between virtue ethics and both of the other views already surveyed is through the statement above from Hauerwas. Many people, considering decisions they have made, do not seek to justify them by analyzing moral principles or consequences. Rather, they testify that they simply knew what they had to do. This highlights one of the main characteristics of virtue ethics, that it is oriented primarily to the moral agent (rather than the moral act), which directs attention to the agent's character and to the community (or communities) to which the agent belongs. It is not the decisions we make, but rather knowing who we are and who we should be, that matters most in ethics. Or, as it is sometimes put, it is about *being* more than *doing*.

The emphasis on the agent in virtue ethics means that moral reasoning is not focused so much on decision-making as on the nature of virtue, reflection on what makes for the good life, the values and priorities of a community, and so on. Nevertheless, decisions *are* made, and something can be said about how moral decision-making works in virtue ethics, in order to compare it with deontology and consequentialism. Even if a virtue ethicist is reluctant to put it this way, it seems fair to say that moral decision-making is based on the demands arising from one's character or community. In relation to Hauerwas's statement above, instead of saying that *the decision makes itself* we might say that *we know what we must do* "if we know who we are and what is expected of us," for we still must make a decision. The point remains, however, that the decision flows from the demands of character (who we are) or of the community to which we belong (what is expected of us).

When faced with the temptation to lie, presumably for some desirable goal, Susan knows that she "cannot" do so because she has formed the virtue of truthfulness, which "demands" that she tell the truth. She also "cannot" do so because she has learned from the community to which she belongs that she must always be truthful, and that expectation carries significant weight. She does not even think of it as making a

---

IN: University of Notre Dame Press, 1981); Hauerwas, *The Peaceable Kingdom: A Primer in Christian Ethics* (Notre Dame, IN: University of Notre Dame Press, 1983).

4. Hauerwas, *The Peaceable Kingdom*, 128–29.

decision, for her action often simply flows from a source of which she is not consciously thinking when she acts. That is important, for she makes such decisions many times each day, without pausing in each case to analyze what she ought to do. When she does stop to think about it, perhaps because she is tempted to do something that has caused her conscience to be troubled, she is engaging in moral reasoning. In that case, she might consider what truthfulness demands or what the expectations of her community are; or, conversely, she might think about what effect her action will have on her character or her standing in the community. Or she might ask herself what the virtuous person would do in her situation. Each of these possibilities is a way of getting at how we act based on who we are and what is expected of us. Thus, rather than speaking of our duty to a universal moral principle or of the responsibility to make sure things turn out right, we might say that moral obligation is derived from the nature of virtue (what virtue demands) or from community expectations (what a virtuous community demands).

We may understand virtue ethics a bit more clearly by highlighting contrasts between it and both deontology and consequentialism. I have suggested that each of those perspectives has been defined, both by its adherents and its opponents, largely in contrast to the other. Recent virtue ethics, on the other hand, by focusing on moral agents more than moral acts, has been developed in contrast to both of those perspectives.

- Instead of focusing on how to make the right decision, virtue ethics focuses on character, which is necessary for choosing well.
- Instead of emphasizing the development of intellectual skills aimed at knowing and weighing moral principles or consequences, with a view to making the "right" decision, virtue ethics emphasizes the importance of family and community, which are essential for the development of virtue and character.
- Instead of thinking in terms of a manual or rule book, which outlines moral principles or provides a way to measure consequences, and perhaps even offers a step-by-step guide for reaching ethical decisions, virtue ethics thinks in terms of a narrative that tells stories of virtue and shows how virtuous people live.
- Instead of focusing on "quandary ethics," in which ethics is understood largely as resolving moral dilemmas, virtue ethics focuses on preparing people to do what we know we ought to do. Virtue ethics tends to downplay moral dilemmas, suggesting instead that ethics has more to do with plain and clear decisions. Put another way, while deontology and consequentialism imply that the primary problem of ethics is intellectual (solving difficult cases), virtue ethics implies that the primary problem of ethics is the will, or doing what we know we ought to do. This is important, for the way that we understand the problem plays a critical role in how we understand the solution

(and how we teach ethics!). If every difficult decision in ethics is thought of as a moral dilemma, it distorts our understanding of the situation.[5]

Evaluation of the Major Approaches to Ethics

Strengths and Weaknesses of Each Approach

Strengths of deontology

Deontology has a certain appeal. First, it recognizes that means are important, and not only ends. This recognition resonates with a sense that certain moral principles are true, and that some acts are right or wrong intrinsically, not simply because of their results. Second, by grounding the morality of particular acts in objective, universal moral norms, and having moral agents base their actions on principles that apply to everyone, it guards against acting merely out of self-interest. This is not a strength in some people's view, such as an ethical egoist, but then **ethical egoism** (see below) is not a particularly persuasive view, and hopefully the problems with acting merely from self-interest are self-evident. Third, by denying

that moral decisions should be determined or evaluated by results, deontology controls the impulse to make things right. It is not bad to desire that things turn out right. Yet it is an impulse that is readily susceptible to rationalizing all kinds of illicit activities.[6]

Weaknesses of deontology

There are some weaknesses with deontological ethics, especially as a unifying theory— for example, when it tries to bear the load of ethics by itself. First, in spite of the sense of certainty often projected by deontologists, since they are confident that they are dealing in objective, universal moral norms, its certainty is tenuous at points. The confidence in reason to establish universal moral norms seems clearly to be challenged by significant moral disagreements, at least in the application of those norms. For instance, both reason and revelation may teach us that truth-telling is a universal moral norm that governs human speech. Yet, how is the norm to be applied in a difficult case, as when Kant considers whether it is proper to lie to a murderous perpetrator who seeks the location of an innocent person? Kant answers that we must tell the truth, even if there are evil consequences. Such is the

---

5. For instance, the vast majority of cases concerning the morality of abortion do not involve a moral dilemma. Rather, a large number of those cases involves a crisis pregnancy, in which the pregnancy was not planned and it presents some hardship. To think of it as a moral dilemma is to indicate that it is difficult to know whether it is better to have an abortion or allow the baby to live. But, in most cases, it is a moral wrong to kill the child; what makes the choice difficult is not a matter of *understanding* what is right, but of *doing* what is right.
6. Chuck Colson and others in Richard Nixon's administration justified breaking into Watergate offices, and lying to cover up the break-in, because it was thought that the fate of the republic was at stake in the cause of getting Nixon re-elected. Colson later recognized, and often wrote and talked about, the moral bankruptcy in that "ends-justify-the-means" thinking. See, for instance, Chuck Colson, *Born Again* (Old Tappan, NJ: Chosen, 1976); Colson, *Life Sentence* (Old Tappan, NJ: Fleming H. Revell, 1987); and Colson, *Loving God* (New York: HarperPaperbacks, 1990).

binding nature of the moral law. We cannot take the path of the consequentialist, and decide when and for what results we are justified in disregarding moral principles. A healthy society operates on the expectation that the truth will be told, and heard. (Notice, however, that this rationale could itself be construed as consequentialist!) Yet, even if we hold that both reason and revelation teach us that truthfulness is demanded of us, how do we know that this absolute demand does not include within it the provision that we are not to give information knowingly to someone who intends to use it to harm an innocent person?

Second, rules or laws, which tend to feature prominently in deontology, are sometimes given unwarranted absolute status. The problem here is not with the idea of absolutes as such, or with moral rules. Rather, it is that moral rules, which are applications of moral principles in a particular context, are themselves treated as absolutes. There may be nothing wrong with the rules, but when they are multiplied and absolutized, and we fail to distinguish between the rules and the principles from which they flow, the rules can smother people. Put differently, the focus on rules can easily lead to a disregard for the true meaning of the moral principle, and thus for people and their well-being, which the moral principle is meant to protect. As an example, in Jesus's day, the religious leaders' rules for keeping the Sabbath were not necessarily bad as such, but they were wrongly made absolute, and so

actually worked against the true meaning of the Sabbath (see Mark 3:1–6). Deontological ethics, in this way, may be construed and experienced in a legalistic manner, which often causes people to reject moral rules and principles altogether.

Third, by itself, deontology is a truncated perspective on morality, including moral formation, and on what constitutes a good act. In the Kantian version, for instance, a good act is one that conforms to a universal moral principle and is done for the sake of duty. To be sure, duty is a good thing, but is it the only, or even the most important, *motive* for moral action? Kant fails adequately to correlate duty with positive desires, and thus indicates that there is no moral virtue in desiring what is good. Indeed, it may seem to count against the virtue of duty, for if we desire to do what is also demanded of us, it seems to be less virtuous than if we do our moral duty in spite of the fact that we do not desire it, thus overcoming a significant obstacle.

For instance, Kant considers people who are "so sympathetically constituted that without any motive of vanity or selfishness they find an inner satisfaction in spreading joy, and rejoice in the contentment of others which they have made possible." Is this other-centeredness a virtue to be praised? Apparently not, in Kant's view, for he says, "however dutiful and amiable it may be, that kind of action has no true moral worth."[7] While Kant may rightly seek to secure the importance of doing our duty no matter what our inclinations are, and to guard

---

7.   Kant, *Foundations of the Metaphysics of Morals*, 14.

against self-deception when it comes to our inclinations, his argument is troubling. Moral formation should not only encourage doing one's duty, even when we are not so inclined, but it should also encourage the development of virtues that incline us to do our duty, to love others, and to be delighted in doing so. Deontology, with its focus on moral principles and rules, at least by itself, tends not to deal adequately with the inner life in its moral framework.

Strengths of consequentialism

For many people who think of ethics in terms of moral principles, there may seem to be nothing good about consequentialism as a moral framework. To dismiss this perspective out of hand, however, would be to overlook what it is about consequentialism that is appealing to so many people, or why it has staying power. One of the obvious strengths of this view is that it takes consequences seriously, especially in terms of a concern for people and how they are affected by our acts. Utilitarianism, in its modern iteration, was advanced by Jeremy Bentham (1748–1832) and John Stuart Mill, British legal and social reformers interested not only in ethical theory but also in economics, law, and legislation.[8] It is not difficult to see the appeal of utilitarianism, or at least one of its principles, for legislative purposes. When considering tax laws or economic policies or traffic ordinances, for instance, it makes sense to ask what will most likely produce the greatest good for the greatest number of people. There is no absolute moral principle at stake in many cases, such as deciding whether the speed limit on the highway ought to be fifty-five or sixty-five miles per hour, or another speed. Rather, a balance of human needs and interests are in view, and considerations may include public safety, fuel economy, and time efficiency (especially for trucking goods and materials). Consequences matter, and are rightly given significant consideration in legislation and in other areas of decision-making, including morality.

Second, consequentialism is goal oriented—that is, it has a *telos* or aim. This strength can also be a weakness, but it is important to note here why it is a strength. Really, it is simple: any valid ethical perspective must have an orientation toward some goal (a point that will be developed below). Consequentialism brings the goals of ethics into sharp focus, and though, as we shall see, it suffers from the manner in which it emphasizes goals, the problem is not found in being goal-oriented in itself.

A third strength of consequentialism, which is perhaps too quickly dismissed by many deontologists, has to do with its pursuit of happiness, for there is an echo of truth in ordering human life toward happiness. Granted, it is not difficult to see why those who are serious about ethics dismiss happiness—measured in terms of pleasure—as an end in itself (rather than, say, the by-product of a life well lived), for it is the pursuit of philosophical hedonists and ethical egoists,

---

8. See, e.g., Bentham, *An Introduction to the Principles of Morals and Legislation*; Mill, *Utilitarianism*.

whose slogan is "eat, drink, and be merry." Yet the problem with such hedonists is not that they pursue pleasure, but that they miss the mark, by aiming in the wrong direction and falling short. Human beings pursue happiness; we seem to be wired that way. So Blaise Pascal (1623–1662) says, "All men seek happiness, without exception; they all aim at this goal, however different the means they use to attain it." Yet, he continues, "never has anyone, lacking faith, reached the mark at which all continually aim."[9] Even Kant says that "to secure one's own happiness is at least indirectly a duty," and that happiness is an end of all rational beings "by a necessity of nature," though he notes that those who devote themselves to happiness will fall short of "true contentment."[10] All this is not to say that consequentialists generally get it right when they focus on happiness as the goal of ethics, as we shall see. But neither are they completely mistaken.

Weaknesses of consequentialism

If consequentialism has certain strengths, it nevertheless fails as a moral theory in its central claim, that consequences are *determinative* for moral evaluation. That is, the problem is not the claim that consequences *matter*. As Michael Banner says, "It would be a very unusual account of ethics which overlooked or denied this claim." But, he continues, "consequentialism does not consist in the straightforward and uncontentious claim that consequences matter in the making of moral judgment, but rather in the doctrine that consequences are the *only* things that matter (and that if anything else matters, it is somehow because of its consequences)."[11] The focus on consequences as determinative for moral action makes this view, in its various forms, problematic—indeed, fatally flawed—as a moral theory, for several reasons.

First, the consequences of our actions, especially in the long term, are difficult to predict, and decisions aimed at some good result often produce unintended negative consequences. Thus the pragmatic moral reasoning of consequentialism gets bogged down by unmanageable complexities. For a given situation, moral reasoning requires that we consider every reasonable act and the possible consequences for each act, including the number of people affected positively and negatively, and the intensity and duration of both the positive and negative consequences, and so on. Beyond that, it is necessary to consider the subsequent actions and consequences produced by those people affected by the initial act, as far out as we can predict. Human knowledge is limited. We simply do not have every relevant fact that we need, or the proper vantage point, to make certain judgments. We are left with a paralyzing problem, for we cannot possibly know in advance that we are doing the right thing. Views that stress universal moral

---

9. Blaise Pascal, *Pensées*, trans. H. F. Stewart (New York: Pantheon, 1950), 143.
10. Kant, *Foundation of the Metaphysics of Morals*, quotations from pages 15, 33, 11.
11. Michael Banner, *Christian Ethics: A Brief History* (Chichester, UK: Wiley-Blackwell, 2009), 119–20.

principles at least avoid this problem, as they focus on doing what is right, and they trust the laws of reason, or nature, or the divine will to maintain a balance of justice.

Second, the difficulty in predicting consequences also brings in a serious problem with moral evaluation, by potentially calling the same act right and wrong, depending on whether we are making our judgment before or after the completion of the act. In making a moral evaluation, should we put greater weight on the intention of the act, or the actual result? Let's say, after careful reflection and deliberation, including consulting the wisest advisors available, you make a decision that is praised as a morally good one because it is sure to bring about the greatest good for the greatest number of people. Yet, at some later date, it is clear that it did not bring about a balance of good, but rather it produced significant harm, and so in the end it is judged to have been the wrong decision. The same decision is judged as both the right act and the wrong act, depending on the vantage point, and it is difficult to make a final judgment, for the result could change for better or worse at some point. According to its own logic, consequentialism cannot escape contrary judgments of at least some acts. Any moral framework that produces such a contradiction is bound to create great uncertainty, even moral paralysis, and is unsustainable.

A third problem for consequentialism concerns moral reasoning in a situation where a particular course of action will result in a state of affairs in which a few are made to suffer, but many are made happy.

In practical terms, consider the process of creating laws. Legislators should consider which laws will bring about the greatest good. Most laws produce some mix of desirable and undesirable consequences, protecting one person's rights or liberties while constraining others, or providing some with certain benefits that others must pay for. However, legislators and other authorities should not act only on pragmatic grounds; they must be constrained by *moral* considerations, or they are liable to act wrongly toward some citizens. What is true about legislation is certainly true of moral reasoning. The principle of utility itself does not teach us proper limits. If cutting off the hands of a few thieves will effectively end theft, creating order and happiness for the vast majority, is there a convincing argument against doing so, based on consequences alone? If the goal is big enough, what *consequentialist* principle will keep us from doing great harm to some to achieve the goal? This is the deontologist's concern about the impulse that may lead us to do virtually anything to make sure things turn out right.

A fourth problem also has to do with moral reasoning, and it may be raised by asking how, on consequentialist terms, we are to weigh things such as pleasure and pain, health and sickness, or strength and weakness. It may be possible to offer a scale measuring things such as the intensity and duration of pleasure on an individual and collective basis, against the intensity and duration of pain. But any such scale is subjective, as some will determine that the pain is worth it, while others will think otherwise. On the basis of pleasure and pain or costs and benefits alone, it is difficult to know what ought to be done, and such consequences alone may lead us to do what we would otherwise question morally.

Fifth, consequentialists have really given away *moral* language—that is, the language of good and evil, virtue and vice, and right and wrong—altogether. There are no *moral* principles, only the principle of utility. There are no intrinsically good or evil acts or motives. There are only desirable and undesirable results. In a sense, it is like emotivism, which claims that moral language only expresses our preferences. The emotivist claims that the statement "Lying is wrong" simply expresses the sentiment "I don't like lying" or "I don't like being lied to." For the consequentialist, the statement "Lying is wrong" means that lying—in a particular case for the act-utilitarian, or in general for the rule-utilitarian—will produce undesirable consequences. In the end, consequentialists cannot make *moral* judgments without borrowing something from outside their own framework.[12] Thus, while legislation may rightly use a utilitarian *formula* (the greatest good for the greatest number of people), it cannot simply use a utilitarian

framework (only results matter). It must be grounded in a larger moral framework.

A sixth problem with consequentialist reasoning is related to some of the problems already mentioned. It doesn't adequately provide a way to coordinate the good things in life, the things that really matter. Or, as one author puts it, rather starkly (before qualifying his criticism), "Consequentialism is a shallow and lazy approach to life. It's very important for a consequentialist not to think about anything other than the goal he seeks."[13] The problem isn't merely that it seeks to accomplish certain goals; we ought to be concerned with goals, and how to weigh proper from improper goals, and how to achieve proper goals. The problem is that everything is simply a means to something else. There is no virtue that is good in itself. There is no act or rule that is good unless it brings about some desirable result. Consequentialism may be driven by admirable motives, such as making life better for those in need. But by not attending to intrinsic goods, it is unable to secure what it seeks, because it "fails to notice that its own real consequences are more likely to be the dissolution of the structures, habits and practices that makes life in society worth living." For instance, "I lie to get ahead but find that once 'ahead,' I'm lonely, because good

---

12. When the judgment is made that the speed limit in a residential community should not exceed thirty miles per hour, the utilitarian may say that it is the greatest good for the greatest number of people. It may slow some people down and make them late for work, but it will protect children, pedestrians, and bicyclists from harm, and it is therefore in the interest of public safety. But that judgment is not made merely on the basis of consequences. Ultimately it is based on an intrinsic moral good, expressed as the value or sanctity of human life, which is more significant than arriving at our destination sooner, which we might call a "pragmatic" good.

13. Andrew J. B. Cameron, *Joined-Up Life: A Christian Account of How Ethics Works* (Nottingham, UK: Inter-Varsity Press, 2011), 42.

relationships need trust, and trust needs honesty." Or "I refuse to 'complicate' my relationship to a partner with any promises, but then find we cannot prosper, because we needed assurances of fidelity all along."[14] These examples of ethical egoism, which concerns itself only with consequences that advance self-interest, serve well as a critique for consequentialism in general. Many will be quick to dismiss egoism (though in practice it is probably the most common ethical framework), yet broader views, like utilitarianism, share the problems of ethical egoism on a larger scale.

The amount of space given to this critique of consequentialism may seem disproportionate, but there are reasons for this. One is that although it is commonly criticized, particularly within theological traditions, it is nevertheless widely followed in practice. In addition, some of its fragments make their way into other ethical perspectives, and it is important to recognize when they do. (Again, it is not the concern for consequences, but rather framing moral reasoning around consequences, that is the problem.) Finally, it is given more space here because it will not be engaged to the same extent as the other perspectives in the following chapters.

Strengths of virtue ethics

The strengths of virtue ethics should be evident in the description above, but they can be drawn out here. First, virtue ethics provides an important reminder that the moral life must involve thinking about who we are and who we should be, and not only about what we do. In this way, moral theologians and philosophers who focus on the themes of virtue ethics provide an important corrective to views that focus on acts alone. Any adequate approach to ethics must relate what we do to who we are, discussing not only personal virtues and character but also the relationships within which they are formed, including families and broader communities to which we belong. Our actions arise from what is in our hearts, whether manifested as virtues or vices (for example, Matt. 5:21–48; 15:19).

Second, virtue ethics deals with many of the moral decisions that we make better than approaches focused on moral dilemmas. Consider the following:

- Some people do face dilemmas, such as having to decide whether to lie to save a life or preserve some other significant good. Yet everyone needs to develop the virtue of honesty, and to learn to speak the truth even when it is costly (Ps. 15:4).
- Someone may have to decide whether it is justifiable to steal a loaf of bread in order to feed a child who is starving. Yet we all need to learn what it means to be content with what we have, not to envy or take what belongs to others, and even to delight in the material blessings that our neighbor has received while we have many wants and needs.
- Some women will be confronted with a crisis pregnancy in which their health

---

14. Cameron, *Joined-Up Life*, 43.

or even their very lives are threatened. But many simply need moral resources such as courage—and support—to face a pregnancy that is difficult because there is no stable relationship, or because finances are tight, or life already feels overwhelming, or simply because it is unexpected and not desired.

- Some may have to decide whether to take the life of a person who threatens violence to them or to someone they are called to defend. All of us need to know how to respond to an angry or unreasonable person with love, to be peacemakers, and to leave vengeance to the Lord.

- Some will have to decide whether to remove medically assisted nutrition and hydration from a loved one when the doctor says that there is no brain activity. But all of us need to know what it means to prize human dignity and the sanctity of human life, and to have compassion and to provide care for those who are sick and suffering.

Examples such as these could be multiplied indefinitely. Virtue ethics deals better with the majority of ethical choices in part because such everyday situations are more common than quandaries, and require virtues that direct the will to do what we ought to do, rather than intellectual problem-solving skills that settle moral dilemmas. Further, it deals with such choices better because it draws on role models, stories, and other powerful tools for teaching and motivation, engaging the moral imagination. In addition, as we learn what to do in everyday situations, we develop

virtue and character, along with wisdom, that helps to prepare us even for moral quandaries.

Third, by providing a narrative account of morality, virtue ethics not only demonstrates who we are to be and how we are to live but also deals with the issue of fragmentation in moral reasoning. That is, it shows that acts and decisions are not things that can be cut off from a larger framework, as though our worldview commitments and "histories" (not to mention intentions and motivations) do not matter. We can only know who we ought to be and what we ought to do in relation to a grand narrative that provides meaning and coherence to the moral life (which may cause us to wonder why the atheist and theist agree on many moral commitments, and whether one of them is borrowing from the other). In another sense, it suggests that our being and our doing are intertwined with relationships that form us, reminding us that the moral life is not simply about abstract or isolated acts but rather is about our being and doing in relationship with God and others.

Weaknesses of virtue ethics

While virtue ethics does have a number of strong points, and makes up for some blind spots shared by deontologists and consequentialists, it is also prone to certain weaknesses. First, while virtue ethics reminds us of the importance of being, and not simply doing, there is a tendency to neglect the importance of acts and decision-making. Perhaps it is inevitable, as it offers a corrective to the act-oriented tradition(s) in ethics, that the case is sometimes overstated. In any event, acts are important, even as they relate to virtue and character, for acts not only reveal a person's character but also shape character. A person's character cannot be judged apart from the fruit of that character, which we observe in the acts that issue from it (Matt. 7:17–18). Further, while it is significant to recognize that acts flow from the reservoir of who we are (character), and the groups and expectations that shape us (community), decisions don't make themselves, even if it is rhetorically powerful to say that they do. Training in virtue is crucial, and it will provide resources for acting well, but we also must *decide* to do what we ought to do, often battling the temptation to do other than what we ought to do, and we must reflect on what is the right course of action.

Second, there is a strong tendency in virtue ethics to deny or diminish too greatly the notion of moral principles, especially universal moral norms, no doubt because of the focus on the moral agent rather than the moral act. The aversion to talking about moral norms or principles may also reflect a belief that they do not exist; or, if they do exist, that we cannot know them, or at least that we cannot agree on them. Or it may be that moral principles are considered too abstract, and that focusing on them leads to the quandary ethics that virtue ethicists disavow. If these concerns suggest some problematic tendencies with deontological

approaches to ethics, they do not justify a neglect of moral principles altogether.

Finally, while virtue ethics reminds us of the importance, indeed the indispensability, of community for ethics, this emphasis can lead to certain problems. If moral identity and responsibility, and even moral "norms," are considered to be products of the communities to which we belong, rather than related in some way to objective moral standards, then particular communities may be seen to function as autonomous authorities. A community can be understood to be determinative of the moral life for its members, and without some kind of access to objective moral norms, however imperfect that access might be, it is difficult to challenge the norms of the community, particularly from outside of the community. We are left with subjective communities that can only claim to "regulate" their own members, unable to shape those outside or to be criticized significantly from within.

Put another way, if each community operates by its own tradition and narrative, and there is no grand narrative that speaks to all communities and presents a moral vision (including moral norms) by which to evaluate human actions across communities, then there is no significant dialogue between communities and no firm ground on which to call others to account. A Christian, for example, cannot appeal to principles that other groups, or society as a whole, should be expected to follow, but can only expect to hold other Christians to account.[15] In practice, virtue ethicists do, in fact, speak prophetically and seek not only to influence those inside but also to call others outside to account on the basis of some objective standard. It seems that this is an appeal made in relation to something like moral norms that cut across communities, even if they do not say so.

Toward a Framework for Christian Ethics

Inadequate Perspectives

Each of these views has merit, but each on its own represents an inadequate account of ethics, presenting aspects of ethics that are necessary but not sufficient as a moral framework. The discussion of strengths and weaknesses above highlighted the shortcomings of any single approach on its own. This can be further illustrated by considering how moral reasoning or decision-making works in each view. Below we will look specifically at the process of moral reasoning. For now, I will simply show how a truncated view of ethics, which focuses on any one of the approaches to ethics to the exclusion of the others, fails to deal adequately with all the various aspects of ethics and the complexity of moral reasoning.

The complexity of ethics and moral reasoning may seem daunting at times, impossible for many people to figure out. However, as Andrew Cameron notes, "everyday people do complex things all the time"[16]—like walking, which is learned early and for life with a good bit of effort at the beginning; or playing a musical instrument, which takes a bit more work, with ongoing practice; or a movement in sports, like a serve in tennis or a golf swing. A framework that takes into account more elements of moral reasoning will better equip us to address moral issues, especially if practitioners are well trained and keep working at it.

Three Parts of Morality: A Moral Framework for Christian Ethics

Deontology and virtue

If each of these perspectives is inadequate on its own, what is the way forward, particularly in an account of Christian ethics that is grounded in the Bible? Christians tend to gravitate toward some form of deontology as a necessary component of Christian ethics, for the Bible presents certain commands as universal moral norms, applicable to all people at all times. At the

---

15. Note Hauerwas's testimony concerning a Christian view of IVF before the Ethics Advisory Board of what was then called the Department of Health, Education, and Welfare, where he said, "By speaking from a theological perspective I do not pretend to speak from principles that are or should be shared by everyone in our society." Stanley Hauerwas, "Theological Reflection on *In Vitro* Fertilization," in *Suffering Presence: Theological Reflections on Medicine, the Mentally Handicapped, and the Church* (Notre Dame, IN: University of Notre Dame Press, 1986), 142. Part of his point is that many in society do not share a Christian worldview and thus will reject its "recommendations." Of course, that is true; however, it does not follow that we cannot advocate certain moral principles for everyone (knowing that they may be rejected). If we believe that we have knowledge of the truth, even if imperfectly, we may expect that it will resonate with many people, even if they reject the foundations of that truth.

16. Cameron, *Joined-Up Life*, 19.

same time, virtue ethics has firm footing in Scripture, with an emphasis on the heart, motives, virtue and character, relationships in community, and a narrative that defines one's identity as a follower of Jesus. Some form of virtue ethics is indispensable for an account of Christian ethics.

Rejection of consequentialism

If the moral framework of Christian ethics is in significant ways compatible with deontology and virtue ethics, the same cannot be said of consequentialism. Of course, Christian moral reasoning must take *consequences* very seriously. However, it diverges significantly from consequentialism, which grounds ethics *solely* on consequences, while denying universal moral norms and the intrinsic morality of acts, which are significant aspects of Christian ethics. Thus a Christian moral framework will include a concern for consequences, and also for ends, in a manner that is consistent with key concerns of deontology and virtue ethics, but is distinguished from consequentialism in crucial ways, especially its view that results are the determinative factor in moral reasoning. That is, it will include a form of teleology (as described below), a concern for ends or goals, but in a way distinguished from how they are conceived by consequentialists. A building metaphor may be used to illustrate a framework for Christian ethics that incorporates key elements of deontology, virtue ethics, and teleology. It will also illustrate why each of those approaches is inadequate in itself.

The framework of Christian ethics: a structural analogy

Deontological principles may be thought of as something like the pillars of an ancient building. They are integral to the building, but they are not built to stand on their own. Indeed, if you see freestanding pillars, you assume that either the building has not been completed or the rest of the structure has eroded. An architectural plan that included only the pillars or the frame of the building would be incomplete. Further, it is critical that the structure have a foundation that supports the pillars, or they will collapse when the ground shifts or is saturated with water. Virtue ethics represents that foundation. The foundation is not poured to remain on its own; it is a critical part of a larger structure, in part as it anchors and provides stability for the pillars. Finally, the foundation and the pillars support and point to something else, which is represented by the roof of the structure. The role for each part of the building is coordinated with the others. Without the roof, the other parts of the building would be incomplete and lacking in purpose. At the same time, it would be an absurd architectural plan that called for a roof to be constructed without a structural framework and a foundation to support it. Without the other parts in place, there would be no roof. But what part of ethics does the roof represent? Isn't that consequentialism, or at least consequences?

Teleology

The third part of morality is teleology, which is critical to any moral framework. Here it is necessary to recognize a significant distinction between teleology and consequentialism, with which it is often identified. It is sometimes said that teleology is a consequentialist perspective, or that consequentialism is a teleological perspective. In other words, they are more or less equated with one another.[17] This is a mistake with significant implications, for while consequentialism is problematic in principle, some form of teleology is essential for ethics, particularly a biblical framework for ethics. If this is so, why are they equated? It seems to be because there is overlap between these two perspectives, especially in terminology, though in many cases the overlap is superficial.

Teleology comes from the Greek term τέλος, which means "end" (in the sense of goal or purpose). Teleological ethics is concerned with the goals, purposes, or "ends" of human life, terms that can also be used to express the concerns of consequentialism. Yet each of these terms has nuances, as we will see, so the use of the same terms does not mean that the perspectives are equivalent. In addition, both perspectives are interested in how human actions relate to and are derived from ends or goals, which makes it easy to equate them. Indeed, it is possible to understand consequentialism as a form of teleology. However, it is unhelpful and misleading to understand teleology as a form of

consequentialism. Teleology concerns the ends or goals or purposes for human life in general and for human action in particular, but its concerns need not be in the form of consequentialism.

Indeed, teleology is indispensable for ethics; every ethical framework has some element of teleology, some end or purpose that is its aim. What is critical is how its ends are understood, and how means are related to ends. For utilitarianism, the end or goal is the greatest good for the greatest number of people. For ethical egoism it is one's own interests. For philosophical hedonism it is pleasure. For Plato it is the Good. For Aristotle it is a sense of human well-being or flourishing. And so on. The relationship between ends and means may move in either direction. In the above cases, the ends—whether chosen or perceived—direct the means. For consequentialists, means are chosen that are aimed at producing the greatest good or some other goal. For Plato and Aristotle, the ends are given, and the means to the end is something to be discerned, and not simply chosen. In other cases, the means (e.g., acts or principles) are understood to be given, and directed to some end, whether or not the end is clearly understood. For instance, in a divine-command perspective, which is deontological, the commands (or means) are usually presented clearly, whether or not

17. Examples include James H. Burtness, *Consequences: Morality, Ethics, and the Future* (Minneapolis: Fortress, 1999), 77; Joe E. Trull, *Walking in the Way: An Introduction to Christian Ethics* (Nashville: Broadman & Holman, 1997), 28; David K. Clark and Robert V. Rakestraw, *Readings in Christian Ethics*, vol. 1, *Theory and Method* (Grand Rapids: Baker, 1994), 20; Stanley J. Grenz, *The Moral Quest: Foundations of Christian Ethics* (Downers Grove, IL: InterVarsity Press, 1997), 33, 36; John S. Feinberg and Paul D. Feinberg, *Ethics for a Brave New World* (Wheaton, IL: Crossway, 1993), 27; Norman L. Geisler, *Christian Ethics: Options and Issues* (Grand Rapids: Baker, 1989), 24; William K. Frankena, *Ethics*, Foundations of Philosophy (Englewood Cliffs, NJ: Prentice-Hall, 1963), 13.

their purpose is given. Yet there is a purpose (or end) for which the command is given, whether it is articulated or not, and whether it is perceived or not. Thus deontology, too, is teleological. There is a teleological dimension to every ethical system.

It may be helpful to think of teleology as a category that is concerned with ends, within which consequentialism is a subcategory concerned with a particular type of ends. Note how the concepts of goals, purposes, and ends can be understood within each perspective. Consequentialism is a subjective perspective, in the sense that its ends are chosen by the individual or the ethicist, or some other person or group, and the work of ethics is to *choose* acts that are intended to bring about those ends. Yet, while a teleological perspective may be subjective, it can also be objective, where its ends are understood to be "given" (in nature or revelation, for instance), and the work of ethics is to *perceive* acts that are most in line with those given ends. Aristotle's ethics and natural law ethics are teleological in this sense, based on a confidence that the world has an objective order to it and that human beings ought to live in accordance with that order.

Thus consequentialism may be considered a form of teleology, but not the other way around; for consequentialism is a subjective perspective, while teleology can take subjective or objective forms. That is, consequentialism is a subjective system in which both the ends or results and the means are determined or chosen by the agent(s). By contrast, an objective teleology is interested in *perceiving* purposes in terms of the *ends for which we exist* and/or in terms of the norms by which we are commanded to live. An objective teleology gives confidence that there is purpose to human life, established by God or found in nature, that a good life is one that is aligned with those purposes, and further, for Christian ethics, that God's commands are purposeful. Thus, while there is some overlap between these views, at least with respect to certain terms, and consequentialism may be considered a subcategory of teleology, they can be sharply distinguished, and it is important to see that teleology is not a subcategory of consequentialism.

Oliver O'Donovan presents a form of teleology in Christian ethics that is captured in his statement, "The order of things that God has made is there. It is objective, and mankind has a place within it. Christian ethics, therefore, has an objective reference because *it is concerned with man's life in accordance with this order.*"[18] This form of teleology does not impose order by choosing certain ends and the actions to achieve them. Rather, it is confident that there is a God-given order, which can be perceived—even if only dimly at times—and with which we ought to align our lives. Natural law is consistent with this perspective. However, O'Donovan outlines ethics in a way that is dependent on God's revelation of himself and his created order,

---

18.   Oliver O'Donovan, *Resurrection and Moral Order: An Outline for Evangelical Ethics*, 2nd ed. (Grand Rapids: Eerdmans, 1994), 17 (emphasis added).

and while it may be called a "natural ethic," it is nevertheless distinguished from natural law, which often is presented as independent of revelation.

It remains to see how teleology functions in Christian ethics, and how it is related to deontology and virtue ethics.

Acts, Agents, and Ends in Christian Ethics

We may now summarize and attempt to bring together what has been said to this point. Given the different perspectives, and arguments made for each, what does a biblical framework for ethics look like, and where should emphasis be placed in a Christian ethical perspective? Deontology rightly draws attention to moral acts that are grounded in moral principles. Virtue ethics rightly draws attention to moral agents, and to the communities to which they belong, and the narratives—and grand narrative—that provide the context or story of the moral life. Teleology rightly draws attention to the end or purpose of our lives, which orders and provides meaning for both acts and agents. So how are these different perspectives in ethics related and prioritized in Christian ethics, and in Christian moral reasoning? In the remainder of this chapter we will look at the relationship between these perspectives in a biblically based Christian ethics, and at the end of the chapter we will discuss how they are related and function in moral reasoning.

Acts and commands

Some combination of or relationship between a form of deontology, virtue ethics,

and teleology is critical for understanding the shape of biblical Christian ethics. Commands feature prominently in Scripture, and at least some are presented as (or point to) universal moral norms. To be sure, we need to have a nuanced view of the Bible's commands, determined by the Bible itself. This will be discussed later. For now it can be said that, like the pillars of a building, moral norms or commands are integral to Christian ethics as it is grounded in the Bible. Yet they do not stand alone, and an ethical system that focuses exclusively on commands, moral norms, or principles will seem to be rigid, legalistic, and even arbitrary, at least to some, and will eventually collapse. They will appear like the remaining columns of a Roman building whose walls and ceiling are long gone: interesting perhaps, and clearly purposeful at one time, but now they are simply the remains of an ancient civilization. In Christian ethics, commands are part of a larger structure. Understanding that structure better will help us to understand the commands better. Conversely, attention to the commands will help us to understand the overall structure.

Agents and virtue

In the building metaphor, virtue ethics was compared to the foundation that undergirds the commands. This can be understood in at least two ways. First, attending to the narrative of Scripture provides the foundation for understanding the commands. This includes the grand narrative that describes the relationship between God and his people. This may be articulated in various ways but must have redemptive history in view, including creation, fall, redemption and reconciliation, and the end or consummation to which everything is directed. This grand narrative provides the broad context within which to understand God's commands—for example, a command may serve to accomplish a creation purpose, or to restrain sinful desires after the fall. Further, biblical commands must also be understood within the immediate context within which they appear. For example, the Mosaic law, including the Ten Commandments, is given in the context of God's covenant relationship with Israel. The Gospels and Epistles in the New Testament, on the other hand, instruct Christians who live in relation to one another in the church in the new covenant, but also under a secular governing authority, in light of Jesus's life and teachings, sacrificial and atoning death, resurrection, ascension, and the sending of the Spirit. In both the general and more immediate perspectives, the narrative structure not only provides a context for understanding biblical commands but also shapes the identity of a people in relation to God, one another, and strangers, both for Israel and for the church.

It should be noted that narrative works in another way to support moral principles or commands. An example of this is the parable of the good Samaritan. A lawyer, recognizing that he must keep the command to love God and neighbor, asks Jesus, "Who is my neighbor?" He wants to know what he owes to whom—that is, What is the obligation of the law concerning love for neighbor? He might expect Jesus to explain this moral principle by quantifying who is his neighbor (which we may be tempted to do ethnically, religiously, geographically, and so on), and then to say just what love owes to the neighbor. Instead, Jesus tells the story of one who loved even his enemy with extravagant love (as Jesus himself does), demonstrating what it means to be a neighbor, and adds that the lawyer should do likewise (Luke 10:25–37). The approach of virtue ethics uses narrative to engage our imagination and help us to see how the law is fulfilled, not by mere external conformity, but by understanding and pursuing something of its deeper purpose.

A second way that virtue ethics undergirds commands is by its attention to the character of the moral agent, which provides the foundation for keeping the commands. Commands call for obedience, yet obedience is not an automatic or natural response to a command, regardless of how "reasonable" or "universal" the command, or even how authoritative the commander. Further, obedience requires more than rational assent to the command. It requires character that is trained to respect authority and is inclined to respond to (proper) authority with obedience. An elementary school teacher receives students each year who have learned to respect authority and rules, and some who have not. The teacher may like to think that simply by posting classroom rules on the board, everyone will follow them. However, it quickly becomes evident which children have a respect for authority and follow rules and which don't.

Of course, character is more than that, but that is one way that virtue undergirds commands. It might be added that the relationship between virtue and commands works the other way as well, for learning to follow appropriate commands works to build character and virtue.

A third and slightly different way that virtue functions in an ethical framework is that it draws our attention to features of ethics that are particularly important in a biblical Christian ethics. At least two problems arise when ethics is primarily concerned with right acts, and how moral principles and commands dictate our actions. One is that that ethics becomes concerned largely with the intellectual problem of solving difficult cases and trying to figure out what we ought to do when moral principles conflict. By contrast, giving significant attention to virtue highlights the fact that, more often than not, moral problems have to do with the will rather than the intellect. That is, the primary question is often not concerned with what we should do; rather, we know what we should do, and the primary question is whether and how we will do what we know is right. A second problem with centering on acts is that it easily can lead us to become self-justified and concerned with performance, forgetting that we depend from first to last on God's grace to live according to his will. Attention to virtue reminds us not only that good acts flow from virtue but also that true virtue is made possible only by the transformation of the heart by the work of the Spirit.

The point of it all

Moral principles and virtues represent significant aspects of Christian ethics. They do not stand alone, or even together in relation only to one another. Rather, they have a point or purpose beyond themselves, and thus can be related to a teleological perspective, which is critical to complete a Christian ethical framework. As indicated earlier, it makes no sense to talk about ordered ends or purposes in ethics without the corresponding structures of moral virtues and moral rules. In Christian ethics, commands are not simply arbitrary statements of the will, even of the divine will, as ethical voluntarism suggests. Rather, at least where they have the force of universal moral norms, divine commands are grounded in the divine nature and the moral order, and they have a purpose beyond themselves. Note the components of these three perspectives in ethics in this view: the nature and character of God (corresponding to virtue ethics) is the source from which God's commands are given (corresponding to a form of deontology), and God's purposes or ends (corresponding to teleology) flow from his character and are indicated by his commands. Likewise, a person's character (virtue ethics) provides the foundation for keeping God's commands (deontology), which work together to fulfill the purposes for which human beings are created (teleology).

A nonconsequentialist teleological perspective is based on a confidence in an ordered and purposeful world, which discerns purpose and meaning for human action. Moral commands are understood to be not only deontological but teleological as well. Jesus underscores this purpose of obedience when he says, "Let your light shine before others, *so that* they may see your good works and give glory to your Father in heaven" (Matt. 5:16). Paul echoes this teleological principle of action in his discussion of Christian liberty, when he says that, "whether you eat or drink, or whatever you do, do everything for the glory of God" (1 Cor. 10:31). The Westminster Shorter Catechism offers this teleological perspective as the reason for which we are created: It asks, "What is the chief end of man?" The answer: "To glorify God, and to enjoy him forever."[19]

Recognizing the teleological principle in a command sometimes helps us to understand the command better, as when Jesus says, "The Sabbath was made for man and not man for the Sabbath" (Mark 2:27). Thus, if Sabbath regulations are inherently burdensome rather than liberating, they stand in tension with the purpose of the command, and the particular application ought to be questioned.

One last point can be made about a teleological perspective in Christian ethics, in response to the consequentialist pursuit of happiness. As stated earlier, in looking at its strengths, there is an echo of truth in ordering life toward human happiness. It seems that we are wired to do so, though sin has made a mess of the business of pursuing pleasure. It is, in fact, a theme in the Bible

and in Christian theology, though perhaps one that has received less attention than others. As Psalm 16:11 puts it,

> You reveal the path of life to me;
> in your presence is abundant joy;
> at your right hand are eternal pleasures.

So Augustine described the sinful pleasures that he pursued prior to his conversion as bonds—"delightful trifles"—from which God freed him. He discovered that genuine happiness is found in God, who is "the true and highest joy." That happiness is found in God, and in his good gifts, Augustine explains when he says, "You have made us for yourself, and our hearts are restless till they find their rest in you."[20]

C. S. Lewis argues that if there is an aversion to seeing pleasure as a proper goal of ethics, it does not come from biblical thought. Rather, "if there lurks in most modern minds the notion that to desire our own good and earnestly to hope for the enjoyment of it is a bad thing, I submit that this notion has crept in from Kant and the Stoics and is no part of the Christian faith." The problem is not that our desires are too strong, but that they are too weak, and that we look for satisfaction in the wrong places. Lewis continues, "We are half-hearted creatures, fooling about with drink and sex and ambition when infinite joy is offered us, like an ignorant child who wants to go

---

19. "Shorter Catechism," in *Westminster Confession of Faith* (Glasgow: Free Presbyterian Publications, 1990 [1646]), q. 1.
20. Augustine, *Confessions* 9.1; 1.1. These translations are taken from *The Confessions of Augustine in Modern English*, ed. Sherwood E. Wirt, Clarion Classics (Grand Rapids: Zondervan, 1971).

on making mud pies in a slum because he cannot imagine what is meant by the offer of a holiday at sea. We are far too easily pleased."[21] That human beings pursue happiness in the wrong things does not mean that the pursuit itself is mistaken, any more than the inability to follow a map to a destination means that the map is mistaken, or that the destination must be wrong. On the other hand, seeking pleasure wherever we may find it is like insisting that there is no destination and thus no route to look for, so we may just as well abandon the map and go wherever we please.

Reflection on biblical commands, including the Ten Commandments, demonstrates how aspects of deontology, virtue ethics, and teleology are related; indeed, it is essential to see this relation in order to understand the nature and function of the commands. For instance, the seventh commandment, prohibiting adultery, is not merely an arbitrary statement of the divine will or simply a test of obedience, so that God could just as easily have given a command to commit adultery.[22] Rather, it is grounded in God's nature (and sustains rightly ordered human nature) as an expression of his will, for his purposes. In other words, adultery—and sex outside of marriage more generally—is prohibited in part because it is contrary to the nature of marriage and human sexuality as God designed them, to be ordered by faithfulness and love that reflects God's own nature. Sex outside of marriage robs human beings of a significant good, and it destroys human fellowship and community. One purpose or *telos* of the command against adultery, then, is that it serves human good as it protects marriage and sexual integrity. Further, it promotes stability in families and society, which in turn promotes human happiness. Its ultimate purpose is that God is glorified through faithful human relationships, which represent God's faithfulness and love. Sex outside of marriage robs God of the glory that is meant to be displayed in human marriage; since marriage is meant to reflect God's faithfulness, sex outside of marriage misrepresents God. In addition, faithfulness or fidelity is the virtue necessary to keep the command against adultery (and lust, as Jesus claims, Matt. 5:27–30). Further, keeping the command, by guarding against adultery and lust, builds the virtue of fidelity.

Conclusion: The three parts of morality

The conclusion reached in the above examination is that the three perspectives on ethics discussed in this chapter—deontology, virtue ethics, and teleology (rather than consequentialism)—are best understood as complementary aspects of ethics,

---

21. C. S. Lewis, *The Weight of Glory and Other Addresses* (Grand Rapids: Eerdmans, 1965), 1–2. The good of pursuing pleasure in God is advanced by John Piper in *The Dangerous Duty of Delight* (Sisters, OR: Multnomah, 2001), and more fully in his *Desiring God: Meditations of a Christian Hedonist* (Portland, OR: Multnomah, 1986).

22. As strange as this may seem to some readers, this is precisely the point that some have made, who hold that morality is grounded solely in the will of God, so that God could have commanded the opposite of the Ten Commandments and that is what would be right.

rather than being complete and rival ethical systems in themselves. Lewis articulates this point nicely in *Mere Christianity*, as he describes the three parts of morality. Morality is concerned with "fair play and harmony between individuals"—this is the deontological perspective. It reminds us that moral principles and rules serve to regulate human behavior and interaction with one another in order that we will not harm one another, and our lives and relationships can flourish. Further, morality is concerned with "harmonising the things inside each individual"—this is a concern of virtue ethics. It reminds us that ethics is concerned with more than external behavior, for good acts flow from good character, and moral agents matter. Finally, according to Lewis, morality has to do with "the purpose of human life as a whole"—this is the concern of a teleological perspective.[23]

Lewis offers an analogy to make the point about these three essential parts of morality. Imagine a fleet of ships commissioned to sail from Southampton, England, to New York. First, for the journey to be successful, each vessel must be seaworthy, or it will risk sinking. If one sinks, the problem is not limited to that one vessel, but involves the entire fleet, for the welfare of one is intertwined with the others. Already it is possible to see that ethics is never merely an individual matter. The second factor for the individual ships and the fleet to sail successfully is that they sail in proper formation, following certain rules that prescribe a set course for all the ships to follow. If a ship veers off course, it may endanger itself, or it may collide with another ship, causing a serious or even fatal problem. Finally, it is not enough simply that each vessel is seaworthy and that the ships sail in formation. The destination matters as well. If the destination of the fleet is New York and it ends up in Calcutta, it is not a successful journey, for it did not follow the prescribed course or reach its destination.[24]

A similar analogy may be made with motor vehicles, and it perhaps discloses better one of the tensions in contemporary ethics, for we tend to think of ourselves in relation to others less like a ship that is part of a fleet on a common journey, and more like a vehicle that interacts with but is not traveling with them or dependent on others. Many journeys are taking place at the same time. The three parts of morality emerge:

- "Harmonising the things inside each individual": It is important that each vehicle is in good condition. Loose steering, bad breaks, worn tires, and many other things can create problems for the vehicle itself as well as for others. A vehicle that breaks down may involve others in an accident, and will often impede the flow of traffic (and a driver stalled on the side of the road may need help from a friend or even stranger, and not only from a professional driving an emergency vehicle).

---

23. C. S. Lewis, *Mere Christianity* (New York: Macmillan, 1952), 3.1.
24. Lewis, *Mere Christianity*, 3.1.

- "Fair play and harmony between individuals": Roadworthy vehicles are important, and so are traffic rules. Speed limits, stop signs and lights at intersections, navigational signs, rules about passing, right of way, and so on are critical if we are to avoid unnecessary and unwelcome disruptions, injuries, and fatalities. They promote safe and efficient transportation; good traffic life, if you will. In addition, since the rules cannot cover every contingency, it is important that drivers learn to respond instinctively to events that occur, including potholes, hazardous weather conditions, and reckless drivers who disregard traffic rules. Some are ignorant of the rules, while others see them as a nuisance. Then there are those who carry on as if they make the rules, and all other drivers are in their way. (Driving habits do have a way of revealing moral character!)
- "The purpose of human life as a whole": Vehicles in good condition that follow traffic laws are important. But where are we headed? Everywhere, it seems! Someone might want to use the traffic analogy to say that everyone has to choose their own destination and the path to get there. Here is where this analogy is less useful, for while it highlights the importance of virtues and moral rules, it does not convey as well the ultimate purpose of the moral life. Nevertheless, it does illustrate the correlation between our destination and our path in some sense. Some may know where they need to go and have some idea of how to get there, but ignore their navigational system (or map). They get off track and head in the wrong direction. Others may be heading in the wrong direction because they have the wrong information—they did not know the right destination and did not have the right directions.

Of course, an analogy isn't meant to be a complete representation—vehicles and roads were not built for the purpose of replicating the moral life! As we explore Christian ethics, however, we will pay attention to the way in which the three parts of morality converge, which will help us to see how laws function, why virtue matters, and the point of it all. What remains in this chapter is to move from thinking about the parts of morality, or what ethics is, to how moral reasoning works.

Moral Reasoning and Decision-Making

Two Main Aspects of Moral Reasoning: Reflection and Deliberation

O'Donovan asserts that "Christian moral reasoning involves the exercise of two kinds of thought together: 1. reflection; and 2. deliberation. Reflection is thought *about* something; when we reflect, we ask 'What is the truth?' Deliberation is thought *toward action*; when we deliberate, we ask, 'What are we to do?'"[25]

In seeking to know the truth about something, moral **reflection** is concerned with understanding a situation and its context rightly. For moral theology, according to Bernard Haring, the basic task is "to gain the right vision, to assess the main perspectives, and to present those truths and values which should bear upon decisions to be made before God."[26] The Bible describes an order to reality that must be received and perceived in order to make proper sense of human action and moral decisions. Some acts do not require prolonged reflection to discern what is true and to form a moral judgment. For instance, we have a clear conviction (and a command!) that murder is wrong. Yet, whether certain acts constitute murder, such as abortion or euthanasia, is a judgment shaped by our worldview. In a Christian perspective, all human beings are created in the image of God and are therefore worthy of protection, and God has prohibited the unauthorized taking of human life.

The prohibition of murder is straightforward enough, but what about a different case, such as torture? It may be argued that torture is wrong for the same reason that murder is wrong—namely, that God has created human beings in his own image and has deemed human life to be sacred, so that the abuse of any human being is an attack on God and is therefore wrong. Yet some might defend torture—even if wrongly so—on the basis that they do not believe human life is sacred, or because they think that it is permitted to treat the person who would be tortured inhumanely because that is the way he or she has treated others. Or because they believe that there is an exception to the general prohibition against torture when certain conditions apply—for example, when a terrorist involved in a plot to kill thousands of innocent people has information that can save lives, and it seems the information can only be attained through torture.

These examples illustrate the relationship between reflection and **deliberation**. First, it can be seen that moral deliberation is grounded in moral reflection. Indeed, according to O'Donovan, "deliberation cannot happen at all without reflection" for it "depends on a reflective grasp of some truth."[27] Deliberation is concerned with possible alternatives for action that are available to us, which are clarified and limited through moral reflection. Deliberation may follow immediately on a period of reflection. Or it may flow from reflection that has taken place long before, or from beliefs that are held not because of extended reflection but because they are revealed (by God or another authority) and accepted as such, or there is a large degree of consensus on the matter.

---

25. O'Donovan, "Christian Moral Reasoning," 122, in *New Dictionary of Christian Ethics and Pastoral Theology*, eds. David J. Atkinson, David F. Field, Arthur Holmes, and Oliver O'Donovan (Downers Grove, IL: InterVarsity Press, 1995).

26. Bernard Haring, *Free and Faithful in Christ* (New York: Seabury, 1978), 1:6.

27. O'Donovan, "Christian Moral Reasoning," 122.

Another point that underscores the significance of moral reflection is this. If deliberation depends on a grasp of some truth, then where truth is grasped inadequately—or not at all—the deliberation that follows will be lacking, often leading to immoral action. For instance, someone might defend torture based on faulty moral reflection. Perhaps the fault is in failing to understand that human beings bear God's image. Or the fault may be in failing to grasp that even suspected terrorists are human beings who must be treated with dignity—even though they may have denied others their dignity—otherwise the would-be torturer may commit the very evil that he is fighting against. Another insight of reflection may be to note that torture is often ineffective for gaining reliable information.

In some cases, deliberation may be problematic because little or no moral reflection has preceded it. Consider a case in which Susan, a single woman, finds herself in a crisis pregnancy, and without reflecting significantly on her situation, she thinks about how to deal with her crisis. She contemplates all the options, which include (1) having the baby, marrying the father, and raising the baby together; 2) having the baby and raising the baby by herself; 3) having the baby and raising the baby with help from her family; (4) having the baby and placing the baby with an adoptive family; (5) having an abortion. The very nature of a crisis is that there typically are no easy solutions, and abortion may have previously seemed unthinkable to her. Yet there it is as an option, and Susan may consider it, not because she defends abortion in principle, but because it may seem to her now to be the "lesser of two evils." Her doubts about that choice may be alleviated by thinking that the fetus is merely a potential human being, not a human being in its own right, as she has previously thought.

It is possible to understand the deliberation in this example to be faulty at least in part because Susan has not attended adequately to moral reflection. We may, for instance, ask what it means to say that she "found" herself in a crisis pregnancy, and whether thinking in such terms is a subtle way of evading moral responsibility for her actions. The way we articulate a situation shapes our understanding, for it may reveal or conceal what is true. Often we first need to articulate better—more truthfully—the situation, and that is part of the task of moral reflection. In this respect, we might also question whether we ought to think of this crisis merely as *her* crisis. For there is, or was, a man involved, David, who bears responsibility as the father of the child, so that if there is a crisis, it is his crisis too. It may also be understood as a crisis for the families of Susan and David, and even for the community to which they belong, which also bears responsibility.[28]

Another and more obvious effect that moral reflection will have on this case has to

---

28. This is a point made by Dietrich Bonhoeffer, *Ethics*, trans. Neville Horton Smith, ed. Eberhard Bethge (New York: Macmillan, 1955), 175–76.

do with the child in Susan's womb. For if it is perceived that the child is a human being, who must therefore be treated with dignity, then the options for deliberation will not include abortion. Abortion will not be considered the *lesser of two evils*, giving it a certain degree of credibility, for other options available are not evil, though they may be difficult or inconvenient. Again, it is the work of reflection both to grasp and to articulate things truthfully. For that reason, we might seek to clarify one or two other things. We might ask, for example, whether the use of the term *fetus* is sometimes a way of obscuring the identity of the child, and point out that the term is simply Latin for "offspring," used in medical terminology to denote the stage, not the status, of the human being to which it refers. Finally, our reflection might clarify what it means to refer to the unborn child as a *potential* human being. Such language conceals the reality that the unborn child is not merely a *potential* human being, but an *actual* human being, who is simply in an early stage of development in comparison to the newborn or the child in school or the adult human being whom the unborn child has the potential to become.

Some of these points need to be developed if they are to stand up to scrutiny, and, from a Christian perspective, they need to be tested biblically and theologically. Here the purpose is simply to demonstrate the significance of adequate reflection, and to show

how moral deliberation depends on reflection, for better or for worse. Moral reasoning is a skill that involves learning to grasp what is true about the world, and to understand how moral decisions relate to and flow from the truth that has been grasped. Whether and how that skill is developed, and just how reflection and deliberation are understood and related depends on the way that ethics in general is conceived.

A Model for Moral Decision-Making

In *Moral Choices*, Scott Rae provides a model for making ethical decisions, which he applies to several case studies to show how it works. He lists, explains, and applies seven elements in his model:[29]

1. Gather the Facts.
2. Determine the Ethical Issues.
3. Determine What Virtues/Principles Have a Bearing on the Case.
4. List the Alternatives.
5. Compare the Alternatives with the Virtues/Principles.
6. Consider the Consequences.
7. Make a Decision.

My purpose here is not to examine Rae's work, though his discussion of case studies nicely demonstrates examples of moral reasoning. Rather, I will propose a model that is similar in substance, but which seeks to integrate key elements of moral reasoning

---

29. Scott B. Rae, *Moral Choices: An Introduction to Ethics*, 4th ed. (Grand Rapids: Zondervan, 2018), 111–13. Rae, in turn, indicates that he has adapted his model from a course taught by William W. May at the University of Southern California.

discussed above. The elements in the model that I propose are as follows. *virtue ethics*

Pre-reflection signifies that even prior to our reflection on a particular case, we have a worldview through which we interpret what we see. This is analogous to the way we speak in hermeneutics of presuppositions that we bring to a reading of any text, which affect our understanding of the text. Pre-reflection involves who we are and how we think, shaped by our upbringing and education. Virtue and teleological dimensions are central here, for how we interpret a situation is particularly affected by the virtues that we possess or lack, and the purposes that we perceive in the world. Ultimately, in biblical perspective, it is determined by our relation to God, for we are either enlightened or darkened in our understanding, depending on whether we acknowledge God or turn away from him (e.g., Rom. 12:1–2; Eph. 4:17–24). Of course, inasmuch as the deontological perspective is closely related to the other two, it will operate in our pre-reflection as well, though it may not be as pronounced.

To place the **situation** in this model is simply to recognize that moral decision-making takes place in relation to some situation, real or hypothetical.

The central task of moral reasoning, as discussed earlier, involves reflection and deliberation. We need only make a few comments here to place these elements in the decision-making process. It is significant to note, first, that while deliberation follows on and is shaped by reflection, it does not stand apart from it, or follow on reflection in a strict chronological sense, as if it is a task performed only after reflection has been completed. There is influence in both directions, as indicated by the arrows in the diagram. Second, this model may be related to the one presented by Rae as follows: The first three elements of Rae's model are part of reflection (gathering facts, determining ethical issues, and discerning what virtues and principles relate to the case), while the next three elements are part of deliberation (listing alternatives, comparing the alternatives with virtues and principles, and considering the consequences), followed by actually making a decision.

Third, in both reflection and deliberation, while we may consider a situation distinctly from the perspective of teleology, virtue, or deontology, they belong together and influence each other. In reflection, our understanding of moral norms arises from and is shaped by our understanding of purpose and virtue—for example, if we discern God's purpose for speech and communication and what is entailed by the virtue of truthfulness, we may better grasp what is demanded by the prohibition of false witness. At the same time, attention to moral norms helps to shape our understanding of virtue and purpose—for example, the prohibition of false witness indicates what is entailed by the virtue of truthfulness and of the purpose of speech and communication. This shows how difficult it is to separate the three aspects of ethics. In deliberation, the three aspects influence each other as well. As we consider alternatives, we may ask how the alternatives relate to ultimate purposes, how they flow from and shape our character, and to what extent the best alternative is determined by a particular moral norm. Finally, while considering the alternatives, it is important to take into account anticipated consequences, which will play a role in narrowing the options, other things being equal.

At some point, a **decision** is made, even if the decision is not to act at all. Yet moral reasoning does not end even when the decision has been made, for it is then open to **evaluation** by the moral agent and others, which is critical to maintaining perspective and sharpening our skills. This is a particularly important aspect of the process because moral decisions are made frequently without opportunity to engage in sustained reflection and deliberation, and it is then left to the task of evaluation to sharpen the mind and will for the ongoing process of moral reasoning. Finally, it should be recognized that as we engage in moral reasoning, whether spontaneously or with a great deal of thought, we are shaped so that we arrive at a new place of pre-reflection, which is a product, for better or worse in both our will and intellect, of our cumulative moral decisions. As Lewis wrote, "Every time you make a choice, you are turning the central part of you, the part of you that chooses, into something a little different from what it was before. And taking your life as a whole, with all your innumerable choices . . . all your life long you are slowly turning this

central thing into a Heavenly creature or into a hellish creature."[30] Moral reasoning matters.

---

30. Lewis, *Mere Christianity*, 3.4.

Select Resources

Bentham, Jeremy. *An Introduction to the Principles of Morals and Legislation*. New York: Hafner, 1948 (1789).

Feinberg, John S., and Paul D. Feinberg. *Ethics for a Brave New World*. 2nd ed. Wheaton, IL: Crossway, 2010.

Frankena, William. *Ethics*. Englewood Cliffs, NJ: Prentice-Hall, 1963.

Hauerwas, Stanley. *The Peaceable Kingdom: A Primer in Christian Ethics*. Notre Dame, IN: University of Notre Dame Press, 1983.

Holmes, Arthur. *Ethics: Approaching Moral Decisions*. 2nd ed. Downers Grove, IL: InterVarsity Press, 2007.

Kant, Immanuel. *Foundations of the Metaphysics of Morals*. Translated by Lewis White Beck. New York: Bobbs-Merrill, 1959 (1785).

Lewis, C. S. *Mere Christianity*. New York: Macmillan, 1952.

MacIntyre, Alasdair. *After Virtue: A Study in Moral Theory*. 3rd ed. Notre Dame, IN: University of Notre Dame Press, 2007 (1981).

Mill, J. S. *Utilitarianism*. New York: Bobbs-Merrill, 1957 (1861).

O'Donovan, Oliver. *Resurrection and Moral Order: An Outline for Evangelical Ethics*. 2nd ed. Grand Rapids: Eerdmans, 1994.

Rae, Scott B. *Moral Choices: An Introduction to Ethics*. 4th ed. Grand Rapids: Zondervan, 2018.

PART 2

BIBLICAL FOUNDATIONS

CHAPTER 3

THE BIBLE AND CHRISTIAN ETHICS

*Blessed is the one
who does not walk in step with the wicked
or stand in the way that sinners take
or sit in the company of mockers,
but whose delight is in the law of the LORD,
and who meditates on his law day and night.*

—**Psalm 1:1–2 NIV**

*How can a young man keep his way pure?
By keeping your word.*

—**Psalm 119:9**

Introduction

We have seen that Christian ethics is concerned with the proper aims, behavior, and character for human life, which focuses our attention on how human beings are to live in relation to God, one another, and the world. Those things have to do with the *framework* of Christian ethics. Part 2 of this book will highlight certain aspects of the specific *content* of Christian ethics, by examining a number of contemporary ethical issues. Before we get there, it is important to lay some additional groundwork, by addressing key questions, especially the question of *authority* for Christian ethics, and the structure of authority in relation to the Bible.

The question of authority is closely related to the question of *claim*. Moral claims are statements about the kind of person we should be, the way we ought to live, and the purpose of life, each of which derives from and advances a particular vision of the world. Such claims can take different forms: "euthanasia is wrong"; "greed is good"; "don't bully your sister"; "copyright infringement is stealing"; "do everything for the glory of God"; "eat, drink, and be merry." Some are general or specific statements of right and wrong; others are value judgments; others are direct commands; still others express some sense of purpose in life or vision of the world. Inevitably, when moral claims are made, they raise questions of authority: Who says? Why should I do what you say? How do you know? Questions like these are concerned with who is making the claim, and on what basis they have the right to do so. Anyone can make a moral claim, but why should I consider a given claim to be compelling or have authority in my life? These questions do not necessarily spring from a challenge to authority. Rather, they are important if we are to be morally responsible, for there are competing visions of the world and competing moral claims. Some claims may be immoral, even deadly, and moral responsibility may necessitate resisting or rejecting such claims.

Christian ethics examines and presents moral claims about who we are and how we are to live, which raises the question of where its claims are drawn from, or what is the source of authority behind those claims. The obvious answer is that the Bible is the primary source of authority for Christian ethics. However, when it comes to delineating the significance of biblical authority for contemporary Christian ethics, and applying the teaching of the Bible to our day, scholars raise a variety of challenges. These include the relation of the Bible to other sources of authority, such as tradition, reason, and experience; the significant gap between biblical times and ours, in terms of years, culture and customs, knowledge, and moral values; and what is said to be an irreducible diversity of teaching within the Bible itself, owing to its many human authors and their particular interests and perspectives.

The bottom line is that many people see the Bible as authoritative in some sense, but an authority whose claims must be tested by contemporary thought and experience and, at times, challenged.[1] Its basic function is said to be its witness to God, and while appeals to specific teachings are often contested, its general moral values and unifying themes, such as love and justice, are considered relevant and authoritative. In this chapter, challenges that are brought against the authority and relevance of Scripture will be examined, and we will consider how Christian ethics springs from the Bible.

---

1. For a discussion of some of the challenges with respect to biblical authority and ethics, see Joel B. Green et al., eds., *Dictionary of Scripture and Ethics* (Grand Rapids: Baker Academic, 2011).

The Bible and Christian Ethics

Challenges to the Authority and Relevance of the Bible for Christian Ethics

Challenges to the authority of the Bible

It is uncontroversial to assert that the Bible is an authoritative source for the work of Christian ethics. For many scholars, however, there is uneasiness or dis-ease when it comes to affirming the authority of the Bible and its relevance to contemporary life. This uneasiness relates to the nature of biblical authority, the relevance of this ancient text to our contemporary situation, and its significance in relation to other sources of authority. For instance, Bruce Birch writes,

> The Christian moral life must include the Bible and its interpretive traditions as authoritative *in some manner*; otherwise, there is no basis on which to label our ethics as Christian. However, in Christian ethics the Bible, though always primary, is never self-sufficient. The Bible cannot be the sole source of authoritative influence, and thus it is never the exclusive authority for the moral life. Nevertheless, the Bible is indispensable for ethics to be labeled as Christian because it places us in a common tradition with other varieties of Christian experience throughout history and in today's world.[2]

By saying that the Bible is not self-sufficient, or the sole or exclusive authority, Birch is asserting that there are other sources of authority that inform us and that are operative even in our understanding and application of Scripture. Few would deny that; the question is how various authorities or sources of knowledge are weighted, and where ultimate authority lies.

Birch asserts that the Bible is primary and indispensable, yet his affirmation is cautious. For instance, he says the Bible is authoritative *in some manner*, and rather than appealing to the source of the Bible or the truth of the Bible as the reason for its authority, he simply concedes that it is necessary to affirm its authority if what is being done is to be called Christian ethics. In addition, his statement that the Bible is primary is not so much an assertion as it is a concession, his main point being that the Bible is not self-sufficient. Likewise, he suggests that the Bible is indispensable, not in itself, but because it connects us (albeit at times only very loosely) with "other varieties of Christian experience." None of this instills confidence in the authority of Scripture itself; the real operating authority seems to lie elsewhere. Allen Verhey, who shares Birch's basic perspective, offers a stronger statement of the general point that Birch is making: "There is no 'Christian Ethics' that would deny the authority of the Bible, *for apart*

---

2. Bruce C. Birch, "Scripture in Ethics: Methodological Issues," in Green et al., *Dictionary of Scripture and Ethics*, 31 (emphasis added).

from scripture the Christian church has no enduring identity."[3]

Elsewhere Birch and Larry Rasmussen affirm that "the Bible is *somehow* formative and normative for Christian ethics."[4] The critical issue is how and why the Bible is formative and normative. They argue that "authority is not a property inherent in the Bible itself."[5] Rather, its authority is recognized by the Christian community, for it witnesses to God's activity and thus is a source of empowerment. Further, they suggest, "the end result toward which we should strive is a deabsolutized canon which allows for the honoring of ancient witness *to the degree that it reveals to us the basic truths of our faith* while at the same time honoring *the power and authority of our own experience of God.*"[6] Again, Birch says, "What the canon represents is the judgment of generations of faithful communities that have found these texts worthy of moral contemplation and ethical reflection"; and, "The moral authority of these texts is foundational for the moral character and conduct of contemporary communities of faith, but only in dialogue with the traditions that passed on these texts and with the best critical understanding of our own experience of God and

the world we live in now."[7] It is not clear how such statements might distinguish the Bible from a canon of other great literature. It appears that the authority of Scripture actually resides in the community of faith and its interpretation, not in the Bible itself.

Paul Jersild also voices caution about the authority of the Bible for contemporary ethics. In his discussion of moral decision-making, he argues that "appeal to the Bible as an authority for the moral life never takes place in a vacuum. There are too many dimensions to the process of making moral decisions to think that any one source can function exclusively."[8] Alongside Scripture, he asserts, attention must be given to the church's tradition, the experience of the Christian community, normative patterns of thought in society, and the facts and circumstances of the case, all of which need to be taken seriously. This basic point is fairly uncontentious, as it is affirmed in some way by the vast majority of biblical scholars. The question is how various sources of authority and knowledge are related to one another. For Jersild, Scripture is primary as it conveys the message that forms the identity of the Christian community. However, when it comes to particular moral judgments

---

3. Allen Verhey, "The Bible in Christian Ethics," in *The Westminster Dictionary of Christian Ethics*, eds. James F. Childress and John Macquarrie (Philadelphia: Westminster, 1986), 60 (emphasis added). See also Verhey, "Ethics," in *Dictionary for Theological Interpretation of the Bible*, eds. Kevin J. Vanhoozer et al. (Grand Rapids: Baker Academic, 2005), 199–200.
4. Bruce C. Birch and Larry L. Rasmussen, *Bible and Ethics in the Christian Life*, rev. ed. (Minneapolis: Augsburg Fortress, 1989), 14 (emphasis added).
5. Birch and Rasmussen, *Bible and Ethics in the Christian Life*, 142.
6. Birch and Rasmussen, *Bible and Ethics in the Christian Life*, 157 (emphasis added).
7. Birch, "Scripture in Ethics: Methodological Issues," 29.
8. Paul Jersild, *Spirit Ethics: Scripture and the Moral Life* (Minneapolis: Augsburg Fortress, 2000), 79.

and decisions, "it is generally the case that the ethical witness of the Bible is neither sufficiently clear nor consistent to give it a blanket hermeneutical primacy."[9]

Verhey sums up the contemporary perspectives on the authority of the Bible well when he says, "With virtually one voice the churches have declared that the Bible is an authority for moral discernment and judgment. . . . That single voice, however, becomes many voices when Scripture is *used* as an authority. To affirm the authority of Scripture is to invoke the use of the Bible in moral discernment and judgment, but it is not to prescribe how the Bible is to be used."[10]

Challenges to the relevance of the Bible

Another challenge to the authority of Scripture has to do with the question of relevance. Here the challenge comes in several forms.[11]

- There is diversity within Scripture, in terms of historical periods and cultures, literary genres, and multiple human authors, as well as in its moral teaching, at least with regard to its specific commands. Thus not *all* of the Bible can be taken to be relevant and authoritative for us. Attention tends to focus on general principles such as love and justice, and the overarching biblical narrative of redemption.
- The gap between the Bible and our contemporary context, in terms of time,

culture, knowledge, and moral values, means that the Bible is not morally relevant for us in a simple and immediate way. Indeed, some of the moral values and instructions found in the Bible are unacceptable in an age of science, technology, and contemporary knowledge, which produce a moral sensibility that is foreign to biblical writers.

- The Bible is the product of fallible human authors, and while it is "inspired," its teaching cannot be accepted uncritically. Its testimony is not to be treated as authoritative truth claims, but rather as a witness to God's faithfulness and ongoing activity in the world.

Given these issues, it is argued that no simple application of the text to our contemporary circumstances is possible. Charles Cosgrove sums up the view of biblical authority for ethics in contemporary scholarship:

> By the close of the twentieth century, the role of the Bible in Christian ethics had become a highly complex theological and intellectual problem. . . . The diversity of moral perspectives in Scripture and the epochal difference between antiquity and modernity (or postmodernity) made it difficult to conceive the Bible as a direct source of Christian ethics. . . . By the dawn of the twenty-first century, almost all participants in the discussion

---

9. Jersild, *Spirit Ethics*, 80.
10. Verhey, "Bible in Christian Ethics," 57.
11. A survey of some of these challenges is found in Charles H. Cosgrove, "Scripture in Ethics: A History," in Green et al., *Dictionary of Scripture and Ethics*, 21–24.

agreed that the Bible is in some sense an authority for Christian ethics, but conceptions of that authority—its force and scope—continued to vary widely.[12]

If confidence in the authority and relevance of Scripture has declined, what authority has taken its place? The answer to that question is not particularly new, though perhaps some contemporary scholars are more candid in asserting what has been true in the past: that experience or reason (perhaps especially derived from physical and social sciences) are granted increased authority, and serve to challenge the authority and relevance of the Bible, especially by seeking to qualify or undermine particular biblical texts and affirmations. The resulting challenge to the relevance of Scripture often amounts to an exertion of human autonomy against the authority of Scripture. For instance, Cyril Rodd contends that "the first requirement is to abandon the propositional view of revelation, and *with it the belief in the Bible as an external authority.* We need to leave the Old Testament where it is, in its own world—or rather worlds, for it stretches across different periods of history and contains the ethics of many different human groups."[13]

This raises an obvious question: What sort of authority does the Bible present to us, if not an external one? Perhaps what

Rodd intends is expressed more clearly, or pragmatically, by Robin Scroggs. He notes reasons for what he understands to be the progressive erosion of biblical authority, including unacceptable ethical prescriptions in Scripture. His summary of the process of erosion is revealing:

> To oversimplify, it seems that where biblical culture has influenced the contours of the contemporary society, the biblical injunctions have been held to be authoritative—that is, they "fit" the present culture. Where the injunction does not seem to relate to a society's reality, the injunction is blithely ignored. The biblical injunction is then branded as "outmoded," fitting perhaps the context of its times, but not that of the contemporary society. *Thus, it is the mood of the contemporary society that judges what is held to be suitable* and, therefore, perhaps authoritative.[14]

Given this situation, Scroggs argues, the Bible does not in fact function as authoritative, which might as well be acknowledged: "What we need is a new understanding of the role of the Bible in the church today that acknowledges the actual reality of our situation—an understanding that takes the Bible as a foundational document but not as authoritative."[15] Others have stated the

---

12. Cosgrove, "Scripture in Ethics: A History," 24.
13. Cyril Rodd, *Glimpses of a Strange Land: Studies in Old Testament Ethics* (Edinburgh: T&T Clark, 2001), 327 (emphasis added).
14. Robin Scroggs, "The Bible as Foundational Document," *Interpretation* 49, no. 1 (January 1995): 18.
15. Scroggs, "The Bible as Foundational Document," 19. The quote continues, "that is, an understanding that does not assume that the Bible determines all that we are to think and do." If that is how he means to define "authoritative," it is a very narrow definition, seldom used in practice. (How many people suggest that the Bible should determine

case even more bluntly. Jack Sanders argues that Scripture "must not be allowed to stand in the way of what is humane and right."[16] Writing much earlier, C. J. Barker says that an appeal to Scripture is merely to "acknowledge the source that inspired the idea set down [rather] than to produce corroborative evidence." He continues, "No supposed exegesis must ever be allowed to force upon man a doctrine repugnant to his moral and religious convictions." Rather, we must simply apprehend "the spirit breathing through the text."[17]

Response to the challenges

A full discussion of these challenges lies beyond the scope of this book.[18] Several brief comments will be made here, and later chapters on particular issues will suggest how the Bible determines the shape and content of Christian ethics and moral reasoning. Some of the concerns raised by the challenges outlined above are valid, and serve as a reminder that we cannot interpret and apply the Bible in a simplistic way. However, often the question at stake in contemporary moral debates is whether presuppositions and conclusions will be based on widely held cultural views or on Scripture. In some cases, it is clear that

human autonomy and judgment trumps the authority and teaching of Scripture. In other cases, there is an acknowledgment of the authority of Scripture, yet often the difficulties are magnified even as the moral authority and relevance of the Bible are relativized.

For example, Birch affirms that the Bible is relevant and authoritative, yet he argues it is not a "prescriptive code of conduct" in part because "biblical texts do not speak with a single voice." As evidence, he offers two examples: "The commandment says, 'Do not kill,' but other laws in the Pentateuch allow capital punishment and waging of war. The teachings of Jesus include those often called his 'hard sayings,' radical demands of the kingdom that few can meet."[19] Granted, he could presumably offer more examples in a fuller treatment of the issue than in a relatively brief article. However, we can assume that in his concise treatment he is offering what he considers to be among the more significant examples. The problem for Birch seems to lie in the particular directives of Scripture, for he suggests that the way the Bible serves as a moral authority and resource is in its "clear broad moral imperatives that frame our moral decisions." These include a "concern for those marginalized

---

how to solve math problems, or establish building codes, or specify traffic laws?) In any case, the point seems to be to escape the authority of the Bible over or against us.

16. Jack T. Sanders, *Ethics in the New Testament: Change and Development* (Philadelphia: Fortress, 1975), 130.

17. C. J. Barker, *The Way of Life: A Study in Christian Ethics* (London: Lutterworth, 1946), 12, 14.

18. For a much more extensive discussion, see Green et al., *Dictionary of Scripture and Ethics*; Brian Brock, *Singing the Ethos of God: On the Place of Christian Ethics in Scripture* (Grand Rapids: Eerdmans, 2007); Richard B. Hays, *The Moral Vision of the New Testament: Community, Cross, New Creation; A Contemporary Introduction to New Testament Ethics* (San Francisco: HarperSanFrancisco, 1996); and Christopher Wright, *Old Testament Ethics for the People of God* (Downers Grove, IL: IVP Academic, 2004).

19. Birch, "Methodological Issues," 30.

in human community," as well as "images that challenge our moral imagination," and "important principles, norms, and standards that can guide our decisions in particular contexts: justice, love, compassion, righteousness."[20]

Birch is representative of many scholars who appeal to the general message of the Bible while eliminating what they believe to be its inconsistencies and, for some, unacceptable teachings. The problem is that, often, by rejecting the particular teachings of the Bible, the broad moral principles lose much of their biblical meaning. The broad moral principles then are shaped by contemporary judgments more than biblical examples. Yet, just as we know God—not fully, but truly—by how he is revealed in Scripture, our knowledge of Jesus and his teaching, our understanding of love, justice, compassion, grace, and forgiveness, are derived from the Bible, and not apart from it. That is, our knowledge of moral principles and norms must be derived from Scripture, and not just in a general way, which can easily be loosed from or antithetical to the way they are illustrated and given concrete expression in Scripture. If we are not constrained by what the text actually teaches us about these things, our conclusions are liable to be at odds with the will of God. This easily happens when judgments and decision-making are based on a general (and vague) sense of the teaching of Jesus, or on very broad moral principles, without attention to the

way the Bible actually delineates those principles. For instance, some reject the Bible's prohibition on divorce or homosexuality on the grounds that those prohibitions are unloving, which may simply reflect how the interpreter understands love, not how the Bible teaches what love is and entails.

Indeed, it is not uncommon to justify actions that are condemned in Scripture on the basis of love, bolstered by an appeal to Jesus's double love command (Matt. 22:37–40), and Paul's command that says, "Do not owe anyone anything, except to love one another, for the one who loves another has fulfilled the law" (Rom. 13:8). In the extreme, Joseph Fletcher defends his situation ethics on this basis, saying that it "goes part of the way with Scriptural law by accepting revelation as the source of the 'norm' while rejecting all 'revealed' norms or laws but the one command—to love God in the neighbor. The situationist follows a moral law or violates it according to love's need. . . . Only the commandment to love is categorically good."[21] Yet love is not an empty concept to fill with what we think it means. Rather, attention to Scripture will teach us what it means. Indeed, Paul frames the command to love by referring to the law, asserting that the prohibitions of adultery, murder, theft, coveting, and other commands are summed up in the command to love one's neighbor as one's self (Rom. 13:9). In other words, by absolutely prohibiting certain behaviors that are intrinsically unloving—declaring what

20. Birch, "Methodological Issues," 30.
21. Joseph Fletcher, *Situation Ethics: The New Morality* (Louisville: Westminster John Knox, 1966), 26.

love is not—biblical commands help us to understand the meaning of love.[22] To affirm broad moral principles while rejecting particular mandates undermines biblical teaching and authority. It makes those principles, now filled out by our conception of love or justice, and not the Bible itself, our primary source. Our appeal to the authority of Scripture is really an appeal to our own (or our culture's) authoritative judgment.

In Birch's case, his appeal to broad principles and norms in Scripture is substantial, often moving and prophetic.[23] Yet the examples (noted above) that he suggests in some way challenge the consistency, relevance, and moral authority of the Bible are unconvincing no matter how often they are repeated. As we have seen, one example Birch offers to indicate that biblical texts do not speak in a unified voice is the fact that the Bible prohibits killing in the sixth commandment, yet approves of killing elsewhere (such as in capital punishment and war). If valid, this would be a serious problem to those who hold to the unity of the Bible's moral teaching. Indeed, this involves not a comparison of the Old

Testament teaching with the New, or even a comparison of the Old Testament Law and the Prophets. Rather, this example suggests not only diversity but also conflicting views *within* the Pentateuch and, more specifically, within the law code. Presumably, we are to believe that this obvious inconsistency was not noticed by the scribes, judges, and people of Israel. Anyone sentenced to the death penalty would have had fairly strong grounds for appeal, since the Decalogue, which is the very summary of the covenant with God and Israel's highest legal standard, prohibits killing!

In fact, the people of Israel did not miss such a major inconsistency, and the resolution to the "problem" in this case is not difficult. While some translations use the term "kill" in the sixth commandment, it is not a precise translation for the Hebrew term that is used (רָצַח). Thus other translators use the more precise term "murder."[24] In reality, the term is narrower in meaning than "kill" and broader than "murder," signifying something like "reckless manslaughter." Conceptually, even without a study of the Hebrew term, it is not difficult to understand how

---

22. Besides the problem of his subjective view of love, Fletcher does not adequately justify the choice to reject all norms or laws but one. Further, he shifts the love command from loving God with your whole being and loving your neighbor as yourself to loving God in the neighbor, a move with significant consequences.

23. See, e.g., Bruce C. Birch, *Let Justice Roll Down: The Old Testament, Ethics, and the Christian Life* (Louisville: Westminster John Knox, 1991).

24. Hence, the KJV and RSV use the translation "kill," while the NASB, the NIV, the ESV, and the CSB use the term "murder." Neither term captures the Hebrew precisely. Though there may not be an exact English equivalent, examples in the law indicate that what is prohibited is causing the death of an innocent human being where it is intentional or even foreseeable. A rough equivalent in English might be "you shall not commit reckless manslaughter." Examples in Exodus 21:12–24 are instructive (cf. Num. 35). See R. Laird Harris, Gleason L. Archer, Jr., and Bruce K. Waltke, eds., *Theological Wordbook of the Old Testament* (Chicago: Moody Press, 1980), 2:860. Thus, for instance, it seems to me that the sixth commandment could be applied to prohibit someone from driving a vehicle after consuming enough alcohol to impair judgment, since it is foreseeable that such an act endangers lives.

killing in cases of capital punishment or war could be consistent with the prohibition found in the sixth commandment. Therefore, it is curious that the unity of the Bible's moral teaching would be called into question on this point, especially since this particular example would represent a problem of inconsistency for modern justice systems as well, which prohibit killing in most forms while justifying killing in some cases of war, capital punishment, or self-defense. To respond, as some might, that no killing can be morally justified is not itself convincing evidence that the Mosaic law (or modern law) is inconsistent on this point.

Notice what is happening here. By pitting the general principle (do not kill) of the Bible against its own specific teaching, which justifies certain instances of killing, Birch makes it appear that there is an internal conflict, and does not allow the Bible to determine how the general moral principle is to be understood and applied. When this happens, it is the interpreter's presuppositions or moral values that determine how the general principle is filled out. One of the dangers in this is that by shifting the application of the general principle away from the Bible's internal teaching to that of the interpreter's moral values, it is not only the application but the general principle itself that changes. For it is then the interpreter's understanding of love or justice that defines what the commandment prohibits or allows,

rather than a biblical understanding, which defines or illustrates general principles by specific commands. The same thing happens when, for example, the principle of fidelity is embraced, but the specific teaching against divorce is rejected as stifling or unloving, and is presumably replaced with alternative concepts of fidelity.

Birch's example from the teaching of Jesus is equally unconvincing, at least for the purpose of showing inconsistency or disunity in the Bible. There is no doubt that we find "hard sayings" in the Sermon on the Mount and elsewhere. Indeed, Birch *understates* the difficulty when he claims that there are radical demands that "few can meet," for *no one*—other than Jesus himself—can meet these demands perfectly. Thus Christians through the centuries have struggled with how to understand Jesus's moral teaching: perhaps the demand of the law is made even more stringent, to prepare the way for grace; or perhaps Jesus intended it to be followed only for the short term, believing in his own imminent return, so that we cannot expect to follow such radical demands over the long haul; or perhaps—since it is clearly impossible to fulfill at present—it is a portrait of the future kingdom, when evil and sin are vanquished; or perhaps Jesus is simply using hyperbole; or perhaps there is another explanation.[25] Understanding the intention of Jesus, and how his teaching relates to the Old Testament, and the rest of the New

---

25. Books and interpretations of the Sermon on the Mount abound. For a survey of its treatment by a variety of significant interpreters through the ages, see Jeffrey P. Greenman, Timothy Larsen, and Stephen R. Spencer, eds., *The Sermon on the Mount through the Centuries: From the Early Church to John Paul II* (Grand Rapids: Brazos, 2007).

Testament, is not simple.[26] Yet it is not clear why the radical demands of Jesus call into question the Bible's unity and consistency or imply that the Bible doesn't present us with a prescriptive code.

Jesus himself challenges such a perspective when he introduces his radical demands in the Sermon on the Mount by saying that he came not to destroy but to fulfill the Law and the Prophets (Matt. 5:17), and he expects his followers to obey his teaching (Matt. 5:19–20; 7:24; 28:20). It seems best to understand what follows as Jesus's interpretation of the law, showing its inner logic and meaning, though perhaps in some cases he heightens its demands for his disciples, in light of the dawning of the kingdom. But even if one interprets the text differently, it must be shown why the radical nature of the teaching, or even the shift that takes place from the Old Testament, indicates inconsistency or a rejection of a code of conduct. For even though it is right to say that the Bible— even its moral teaching—is not *merely* a code of conduct, it is wrong to conclude that the Bible includes *no* moral code of conduct.

The movement from Scripture to Christian ethics should not be simplistic; indeed, there is no application of the text without interpretation, and it is important to recognize what is taking place when we interpret Scripture. However, neither should we presuppose an irreducible diversity, or a gap in knowledge and customs so great

that the Bible is allowed to speak only in the most general terms, effectively disregarding its particular relevance and muting its authority. Emphasizing the gap between the biblical world and ours can be simply a thinly veiled attempt to challenge the authority of Scripture. Brian Brock argues, "Attempts to dismiss the Bible's moral relevance with the claim that its authors 'couldn't have known' about our moral dilemmas or conceptual distinctions are sure signs that the Bible has ceased to be Scripture for that interpreter, for whom some other text or group of texts has become Scripture, against which the Bible must now be justified."[27] Barker, cited earlier, reflects this perspective when he rejects biblical teaching that is "repugnant" to our convictions. Yet he does not wish to dismiss the Bible entirely, arguing that we are to sense "the spirit breathing through the text."[28]

Barker's view illustrates what it means to reject the Bible as an *external* authority, and to assert human autonomy, often by means of some cultural consensus. Those who reject its external authority in reality empty the Bible of *its* authority entirely. What is left, after removing what they find to be repugnant, is what they approve. They do not walk, or stand, or sit under the authority of the Bible. To accept what the Bible says, they must first filter it so that it can pass the test of experience or contemporary reason, even of those who reject its most basic truth

---

26. For a helpful perspective, see Jonathan Lunde, *Following Jesus, the Servant King: A Biblical Theology of Covenantal Discipleship* (Grand Rapids: Zondervan, 2010).
27. Brock, *Singing the Ethos*, 247.
28. Barker, *Way of Life*, 14.

claims. The moral authority of the Bible is challenged and often rejected because of the fallibility of its human authors (a claim made by moderns whose own fallibility is evidently not a great obstacle to asserting moral authority). The broad principles of Scripture such as love and justice and compassion are accepted, for they are easily shaped to fit contemporary notions of love and justice and compassion. In a candid statement, in which the veil is removed completely, Scroggs articulates and approves of a pattern that exists in relating the Bible and contemporary perspectives, indicating why the Bible should be understood as "a foundational document," but not authoritative:

> If assessments about biblical faith and ethics are made from contemporary sensitivities about what is right and wrong, *then it is our contemporary perspectives that are authoritative.* Where the Bible agrees with those sensitivities, it is invoked to support what one already knows to be correct. Where the Bible disagrees, it is relegated to its historical context and becomes something we have overcome in our struggle for the truth.[29]

In this view, one might appeal to the Bible for insight or inspiration—concerning a perspective that is already known—much like one might cite other sources for support. In that case it is a corroborating witness, not an external authority, and its insight is only as strong as current opinion on the matter at hand. If the Bible is rejected as an external authority, and its teaching is divided into what is approved by contemporary readers and what is repugnant, then the "spirit breathing through the text" is not the Holy Spirit, but simply the spirit of the age.

This survey shows a range of perspectives that challenge biblical authority for Christian ethics, from those who acknowledge its authority but are uneasy with how it functions, to those who effectively reject it altogether. One of the underlying questions in this discussion concerns sources of ethics, and how the Bible relates to other sources.

Sources of Ethics

When we consider sources for ethics, we may distinguish first between an ontological aspect (the source or ground of ethics itself) and an epistemological aspect (the source of knowledge of ethics), each of which has implications for ethical authority. The ontological question has to do with the nature of morality. One common view is moral relativism, which understands morality to be subjective and "created" by human beings. In this view, ethics is established in order to create a civil society and avoid anarchy, to establish and protect individual rights, and so on. Knowledge is derived from a variety of sources, including reason (which especially considers data from the physical and social sciences), experience (many varieties, including conscience, intuition, desire and emotion, and simply what "works"), and tradition. Even though morality is considered

---

29. Scroggs, "The Bible as a Foundational Document," 19 (emphasis original).

to be subjective, it involves reflection on the world, which exerts itself as objective—a relativist may wish the world were different, and try to live as though it were, only to find that it goes against the grain of the universe. Further, when a relativist asserts moral authority, which may lie in the will of the community or the individual, it is often made to seem objective.

In contrast to subjective perspectives, Christian ethics holds that morality is objective and revealed. The ultimate source of morality is God, who created the universe with moral order—determined by his character, purposes, and will—and graciously reveals to human beings not only the reality of that order but also how to live according to that reality. This perspective is one of moral realism. Knowledge is derived primarily from the Bible, but it also includes a range of secondary sources, including reason, tradition, and experience. Thus a key question for Christian ethics concerns how these sources are coordinated or related. The Reformation appeal to *sola Scriptura* (Scripture alone) is relevant here. What is meant by *sola Scriptura* is not a denial of all other sources, for other sources have validity. But those sources must be tested by and subordinated to Scripture as the primary source (the "norming norm"). Brock affirms that "*sola scriptura* does not mean that we know nothing but the Bible: it means that the key to Scripture is Scripture, and that this key comprehends and criticizes all that is, including our interpretive schemas."[30] It would be naive to

ignore or deny other sources, for they are inescapable, and will influence or determine moral judgments whether acknowledged or not. More importantly, Scripture affirms other sources, even if it qualifies them. Consider these sources briefly.

Tradition, understood in Christian ethics first as the practices and teachings of the church, shapes believers and our understanding of God and Scripture. We must not affirm tradition uncritically, for sometimes it develops in ways that are unfaithful to God and his revelation in Scripture. Yet the problem is not tradition itself. While Jesus condemned human traditions that stood in opposition to God's commandments (Matt. 15:3), he taught the people to follow the teaching (tradition) of the scribes and the Pharisees—though not their actual practice (Matt. 23:1–3). In addition, God's people are called to pass on the teaching and commandments that we have received in Scripture (e.g., Deut. 6:1–9; Matt. 28:18–20; Jude 3). The test for tradition is its fidelity to Scripture.

Reason is also necessary to understand and apply the truth of God's Word, and to convey it to others (Acts 17:17; 1 Pet. 3:15). However, the Bible warns that human reason is prone to suppress the truth, so that human minds are darkened and foolish (Rom. 1:18, 21), unable to discern the things of the spirit (1 Cor. 2:14). Yet God's will is accessible to Spirit-filled reason (Rom. 12:1–2; Col. 1:9–10). Thus the mind must be renewed by God's Spirit, and human reason must submit to and be tested by Scripture.

---

30. Brock, *Singing the Ethos*, 252–53.

In the discussion of reason as a source of ethics, a word should be said about **natural law**. This is a perspective, grounded in reason, which affirms that there is a moral order revealed and perceptible in creation. Scripture testifies that, alongside Scripture, creation stands as a witness to God's goodness and glory (Ps. 19), by which human beings are held accountable, for it reveals something of God's divine nature and power (Rom. 1:18–20). Consistent with this, natural law asserts that morality is objective and accessible to all, for human reason is able to discern proper conduct in accordance with nature. Natural law appeals to some Christians because it is consistent with a biblical perspective without requiring an appeal to revelation for authority, so it can be a starting point for discussions of morality in the public square. However, its usefulness is limited. Paul's appeal to nature in Romans 1 does not prove the effectiveness of natural law as a source of morality. Instead, it highlights the depth of human sin and rebellion, which has corrupted even human desires and the ability to reason. This is particularly true when it comes to moral matters, because human beings pursue and justify their own desires. For this reason, apart from God's grace manifested in the gospel, human beings are in a hopeless situation. Natural law is not therefore useless, but it depends on and must be coordinated with revelation. Reason must be transformed, not merely applied, to understand God's will (Rom. 12:2). Thus Michael Banner asserts the maxim "that the claims of natural law are, where uncontroversial, uninteresting and where interesting, controversial."[31] That is, natural law may be accepted where it confirms people's presuppositions, but it will often be rejected or revised where it is said to challenge them.

Experience is another source of knowledge, though it is looked on with great suspicion by many, and for good reason: human beings are very often self-deceived, and personal experience is a dubious authority to which to appeal, for it lacks accountability. On the other hand, human experience is significant, and it would be a strange view of ethics to insist on the veracity of a given claim against all experience. Instead, we are invited to "Taste and see that the LORD is good" (Ps. 34:8). The faithful ought to be able to confirm by their experience that God's Word is true and his will is good (Rom. 5:5, 12:2). Conscience is related to experience. On the one hand, a well-formed conscience may "accuse or even excuse" a person (Rom. 2:15). On the other hand, by rejecting truth a person's conscience will become seared and untrustworthy (1 Tim. 4:1). The test for conscience, and experience in general, is the Word of God. Any claim of authority based on personal experience that contradicts the Bible itself should be rejected.

In short, we depend on tradition, reason, and experience, and they inform our ethics in helpful and necessary ways. Sometimes, as Verhey notes, they even "challenge and disrupt a conventional understanding and

---

31. Michael Banner, *Christian Ethics: A Brief History* (Chichester, UK: Wiley-Blackwell, 2009), 51.

use of Scripture and force a new examination of what it requires of the believing community." Yet the Bible will also "challenge and disrupt conventional moral certainties and securities," and "biblically based identity must limit, corroborate, and transform appeals to reason and to group interests."[32] Other sources may be distorted by sin, and so they are not fully trustworthy. They should be recognized as important but secondary, to be tested by Scripture within the community of believers. The Bible itself is the only fully reliable source for ethics, and thus our understanding of the Bible should not be conformed to other sources, but those sources must conform to the authority and teaching of the Bible.

After examining closely how several interpreters engage Scripture in relation to other sources for developing moral judgments, and laying groundwork for his own engagement with the New Testament, Richard Hays draws the following conclusion:

> Extrabiblical sources . . . are not independent, counter-balancing sources of authority. In other words, the Bible's perspective is privileged, not ours. However tricky it may be in practice to apply this guideline, it is in fact a meaningful rule of thumb that discriminates significantly between different approaches to New Testament ethics. This guideline by no means excludes exceedingly

> serious consideration of other sources of wisdom, but it assigns those sources an explicitly subordinate role in normative judgments. They function instrumentally to help us interpret and apply Scripture. They must not, however, be allowed to stand as competing sources for theological norms.[33]

To privilege the Bible's perspective is to affirm its authority, to resist the temptation toward self-rule, and to humble ourselves, grappling with its strangeness to us. Its strangeness should itself be taken seriously, rather than simply used as evidence against its relevance. As Brock writes, "If those who take the Bible's moral strangeness seriously look quixotic from the vantage point of modern readers, they in turn see modern readers as self-insulated travelers who . . . are impoverished by reading everything through the categories and perceptions of their home culture."[34] We might even recognize that the gap between us and the people(s) and culture(s) of the Bible is not as deep and wide a chasm as is sometimes supposed. Indeed, readers in modern Western societies may fail to recognize that much of the world in the twenty-first century is able to identify with the peoples and cultures of the Bible more than with modern Western societies and their values. Further, the primary issues with which the Bible is concerned, including a diagnosis of the human condition, our alienation from God and

32. Verhey, "Bible in Christian Ethics," 60.
33. Hays, *Moral Vision*, 296 (emphasis original).
34. Brock, *Singing the Ethos*, xii.

others, and the effects of sin on our minds and affections, on individuals and institutions, speaks to all people. Brock asserts, "In the final analysis, it is not our historical or moral distance from the Bible that renders it foreign to us, not the gap between time and eternity, but the gap between the ways of God and those of humanity."[35]

The authority and relevance of Scripture, as it is understood in the Protestant confessional tradition, is summarized in the following statements. The Westminster Confession of Faith says, "The whole counsel of God, concerning all things necessary for his own glory, man's salvation, faith, and life, is either expressly set down in scripture, or by good and necessary consequence may be deduced from scripture."[36] Similarly, the Baptist Faith and Message affirms, "The Holy Bible . . . is a perfect treasure of divine instruction. . . . [A]ll Scripture is totally true and trustworthy . . . the supreme standard by which all human conduct, creeds, and religious opinions should be tried. All Scripture is a testimony to Christ, who is Himself the focus of divine revelation."[37] These are reflections of the Bible's own claims. Second Timothy 3:16, often cited to show the claim of divine inspiration, also points to its

moral relevance: "All Scripture is inspired by God and is profitable for teaching, for rebuking, for correcting, for training in righteousness."

The "Use" of the Bible in Christian Ethics?

It has been noted that while there is widespread agreement that the Bible is authoritative, it is not clear how its authority applies in contemporary life. This tension was summarized earlier by Allen Verhey: "With virtually one voice the churches have declared that the Bible is an authority for moral discernment and judgment. . . . That single voice, however, becomes many voices when Scripture is *used* as an authority. To affirm the authority of Scripture is to invoke the use of the Bible in moral discernment and judgment, but it is not to prescribe how the Bible is to be used."[38] In recent decades, much scholarly attention has been given to discussion of how the Bible is to be used in Christian ethics.[39] The relation between the Bible and Christian ethics is important to discern, and there has been significant insight and clarification in the discussion, as well as some helpful interdisciplinary interaction between biblical scholars and ethicists. Yet it is necessary to assess critically the framework of the discussion and its operating

---

35. Brock, *Singing the Ethos*, xv.
36. *Westminster Confession of Faith* (Glasgow: Free Presbyterian Publications, 1990), 1.6.
37. Southern Baptist Convention, *The Baptist Faith and Message* 2000, 1: The Scriptures. http://www.sbc.net/bfm2000/bfm2000.asp.
38. Verhey, "Bible in Christian Ethics," 57.
39. A flurry of publications in this area began in the 1960s. See, e.g., Edward LeRoy Long Jr., "The Use of the Bible in Christian Ethics: A Look at Basic Options," *Interpretation* 19, no. 2 (April 1965): 149–62; James M. Gustafson, "The Place of Scripture in Christian Ethics: A Methodological Study," *Interpretation* 24, no. 4 (October 1970): 430–55; Bruce C. Birch and Larry L. Rasmussen, *Bible and Ethics in the Christian Life*, which first appeared in

premise, for to speak of use of the Bible in Christian ethics may itself be problematic.

First, we ought not to think in terms of the "use" of Scripture for Christian ethics as if we are engaged in a project for which the Bible provides some service. The problem with framing the question in this way is to turn things around, suggesting that we set the agenda for Christian ethics and the Bible is engaged to contribute to our agenda. That is not humility before the Word of God, which sets the agenda and judges human action and ways of thinking. It is perhaps to be expected in an academic setting, which purports to approach the Bible objectively, setting standards by which to test it. In such a setting, where one attempts to be detached rather than engaged, the Word of God may be analyzed and yet not understood, studied and yet not obeyed.

However, we do not lay claim on the Bible; it lays claim on us. That is, through Scripture God lays claim on us. Instead of being used to contribute to an agenda, where the Bible is affirmed or rejected based on whether it conforms to widely held opinions, the Bible ought to shape our minds and wills so that our opinions conform to the Bible. The Bible "does not confirm and complete human thought, but challenges it. The Word of God does not base itself on human culture, self-understanding, and consciousness, but instead judges culture, self-understanding, and consciousness. Certainly it does not satisfy criteria of reasonableness stipulated by its critics. And the task of theology is certainly not to justify the Word of God, let alone to judge it. Its task is to expound and explicate it."[40] Rather than using Scripture to complete a task for Christian ethics, the task of Christian ethics is to engage the Bible continually, in order to facilitate "God's claiming of human thoughts, passions, and actions through Scripture."[41]

Another reason that the "use of the Bible" is problematic is made clear in the discussion itself. It is often said that the Bible should not be used merely as a moral rule book. This is true, though not necessarily in the sense intended. Where the assertion is stated in order to silence certain commands of Scripture, parts of the Bible that are unpalatable to modern ears, or to indicate that the Bible does not provide moral claims in the form of rules at all, the statement is problematic. On the other hand, it is true that the Bible is not merely a rule book, and it should not be used as if it were. To

---

1976, was later revised and expanded (Minneapolis: Augsburg Fortress, 1989); Allen Verhey, "The Use of Scripture in Ethics," *Religious Studies Review* 4, no. 1 (January 1978): 28–39; Thomas W. Ogletree, *The Use of the Bible in Christian Ethics: A Constructive Essay* (Philadelphia: Fortress, 1983). Jeffrey S. Siker provides an overview of key figures in *Scripture and Ethics: Twentieth-Century Portraits* (New York: Oxford University Press, 1997). For recent discussions, see Hays, *Moral Vision*, part 3, "The Hermeneutical Task: The Use of the New Testament in Christian Ethics," 207–312; Jersild, *Spirit Ethics*; Charles H. Cosgrove, *Appealing to Scripture in Moral Debate: Five Hermeneutical Rules* (Grand Rapids: Eerdmans, 2002); Brock, *Singing the Ethos*, part 1, "Learning about Reading the Bible for Ethics," 3–98; and Green et al., *Dictionary of Scripture and Ethics*.

40. Banner, *A Brief History*, 107, summarizing Karl Barth's view.
41. Brock, *Singing the Ethos*, 244.

take the Bible seriously, we do not "use" it by simply mining it for an appropriate command that fits our current situation. To reduce the moral relevance of Scripture to its list of commands fails to account for the significance of the whole of Scripture for ethics. Consequently, while those who use the Bible this way assert the importance of the Bible, in fact they do not take it seriously enough: like an instruction manual for an appliance, too often it remains on the shelf until a problem arises and it is needed.[42] If the Bible is to be taken seriously, if it is to determine the framework and substance of Christian ethics, and not be determined by some other existing framework, it must be read continually. More than that, as the Bible itself indicates, we must meditate on it—it is not merely to be read, but "sung" and *lived*.[43] In this way, the application of Scripture involves far more than relating its commands to situations we face (though it will include that). Rather, as we encounter situations in our contemporary context, we return to Scripture again and again, with new questions for which we may gain fresh insight from an encounter with God's living Word. This repeated encounter with God, and especially a reflection on his grace, effects a transformation of our minds, with the result that we are able to discern God's will (Rom. 12:2).

That is not to say, as some might be tempted to say, that the Bible does not speak to us in the mode of rules or commands that are relevant to our situation. If it is not to be seen merely as a book of commands, neither should its commands be silenced. The basic point being made—that the Bible should not be treated merely as a rule book—should be taken further: the Bible should not be appropriated merely in any single mode.[44] To do so is to blunt part of its overall witness. We may outline several features of a biblical Christian ethics that takes the Bible to be its primary source of authority and knowledge.

The Bible as a Source of Knowledge in Christian Ethics

Hays offers helpful guidelines for how Christian ethics can be developed and evaluated in relation to the Bible. First, he discusses tasks for New Testament ethics, which can easily be extended to the task of a biblical Christian ethics:[45]

1. The descriptive task: we need to read the Bible carefully to see what it actually says.
2. The synthetic task: particular texts need to be considered within the context of the whole Bible. Hays rejects claims that the New Testament is irreducibly diverse, arguing instead for a coherent unity. On the other hand, he argues that the unity

---

42. Banner, *A Brief History*, 21.
43. This is a significant emphasis of Brock, *Singing the Ethos*, that he underscores by examining the engagement of the book of Psalms in the work of such theologians as Augustine, Luther, and Bonhoeffer.
44. Hays, *Moral Vision*, 208–9, 294.
45. Hays, *Moral Vision*, 3–7. Compare Wright, *Old Testament Ethics*, 442–44, where he discusses the descriptive question, the canonical question, and the normative question.

should not be artificial, and that there may be tensions that must be allowed to stand. This is reasonable to a point, but Hays assumes too high a degree of diversity and disunity, which is unnecessary and which undermines the basic unity and coherence that he affirms.

3. The hermeneutical task: this involves relating the Bible to our situation, bridging the "temporal and cultural distance between ourselves and the text."[46]

4. The pragmatic task: this is what Hays calls the "fruits test" (Matt. 7:18–20), testing what kind of community is produced by our moral judgments and reading of the Bible.

In addition to these tasks, Hays describes four modes of appeal to Scripture in ethics:[47]

1. Rules: "direct commandments or prohibitions of specific behaviors," such as Jesus's prohibition of divorce (Mark 10:2–12 and parallels).

2. Principles: "general frameworks of moral consideration by which particular decisions about actions are to be governed," such as the double love commandment given by Jesus (Matt. 22:37–40 and parallels).

3. Paradigms: "stories or summary accounts of characters who model exemplary conduct (or negative paradigms: characters who model reprehensible conduct)." Hays offers the story of the good Samaritan (Luke 10:29–27) and the example of Paul (1 Cor. 10:31–11:1) as positive examples, and the example of Ananias and Sapphira (Act 5:1–11) as a negative example. It might be added that many times characters are simply presented without comment on what kind of example they are, in which case it is best to judge their behavior by other clear examples or commands if possible.

4. A symbolic world: "the perceptual categories through which we interpret reality," including "representations of the human condition" (e.g., Rom. 1:19–32) and "depictions of the character of God" (e.g., Matt. 5:43–48).

Conclusions

Hays's framework, or something like it, serves as a helpful guide. Any helpful framework for engaging with Scripture will not simply be developed and then brought to the Bible, but will develop out of the engagement with the Bible. While some of the pattern that Hays prescribes is taken into account in this book, it will be evident that there are deviations at points. Part of the framework that will be used has emerged by interaction with alternative viewpoints above. Other aspects will be presented in the following chapters. What remains at present is simply to summarize a few key points.

First, it is worth repeating that the whole of the Bible serves as a source for Christian ethics (2 Tim. 3:16–17). If we engage the Bible

---

46. Hays, *Moral Vision*, 5.
47. Hays, *Moral Vision*, 208–9.

as God's Word, we will take seriously its commands, but we will do more than that. We will be transformed as we enter into its world, and find ourselves in its description of God, creation, humanity, sin, brokenness and alienation, reconciliation and redemption, eschatological hope, and so on. What Banner says about the centrality of the Bible and its function in the Rule of Benedict offers something of an outline of this pattern of transformation. It is "from the Bible that they must learn to order reality, and they must constantly return to this text to understand themselves and others. They are to allow the Bible, with its confusing mix of chronicles, laws, poems, letters, and stories, to form their imaginations, affections, hopes, and desires."[48] Moral rules will help to order reality, to understand ourselves and others, and—if they are received from a gracious lawgiver—they may even help to form imaginations, affections, hopes, and desires. Yet they cannot do so fully. To engage the complexity of human understanding, including the will, thoughts, and emotions, the Bible offers not only laws but also chronicles, poems, letters, and stories, each of which serves as a source for Christian ethics.

Second, and related to the first point, the Bible defines the "moral field" for ethics, which includes God as Creator (and his character, purposes, and will), human beings, and the world created by God and inhabited by human beings. In particular, the Bible presents a metanarrative that is critical for Christian ethics, which depicts a redemptive

history that profoundly shapes our understanding of what is right and what is wrong with the world. The basic outline of redemptive history may be characterized as follows:

- The world is created good by a gracious God, infused with moral order and marked by harmonious relationships, a universe that is purposeful, not fragmented or chaotic.
- The original goodness of the world is now disordered because of human sin, and marked by broken relationships and violence.
- In the midst of this disorder, God reveals his steadfast love, which seeks to redeem and reconcile sinful human beings, to re-order and repair broken relationships, and to establish justice and peace, which God calls and commands a people to embody.
- Beyond the present, God gives hope for a future that surpasses even the original goodness of creation.

This is all part of the metanarrative that represents a biblical worldview—that is, a lens that sharpens our vision so that we can interpret and understand the world more clearly. This is important for ethics because our worldview (what we think about God, the world, and human beings, etc.) determines our ethics, and is contrasted with alternative worldviews and ethics. The Bible is not simply a textbook about God or the moral law, which we study. It is Scripture, God's living Word, which we must enter

---

48. Banner, *A Brief History*, 21.

into, adopt, and live out—even sing, as indicated in Colossians 3:16 (cf. Eph. 5:19) and demonstrated throughout the Psalms![49]

Ultimately, moral responsibility is not to a command or a moral principle, but to a personal God. However, that does not lessen the importance of commands and principles in the Bible, since it is God who gives them. If they are understood rightly, commands are something to delight in, for they come from a gracious God, they light the path of life, and they keep us from destruction (Deut. 30:11–20; Ps. 119). They are structured by love (Matt. 22:37–40) and involve the whole self, for Jesus reveals that true righteousness is not mere outward conformity to the law but an inward reality as well (Matt. 5–7). Commands in themselves do not fully reveal the will of God, but Jesus declares to his disciples that after he leaves, he will send the Spirit to guide them into all truth, including the knowledge of God's will (John 16:13; Rom. 12:1–2; Col. 1:9–10).

Third, we may distinguish between particular commands in the Bible, limited to a particular person or people in a particular situation, and universal or general commands, which apply to all people at all times. We ought to be able to offer some reason why God's command to Israel, "Love the LORD your God with all your heart, with all your soul, and with all your strength" (Deut. 6:5) is universal, while his command to Hosea, "Go and marry a promiscuous wife" (Hosea 1:2

HCSB), or his command to Abram, "Go out from your land . . . to the land that I will show you" (Gen. 12:1 HCSB), are not. O'Donovan offers criteria for determining which type of command we encounter, which are to be found within the context that the command is given.[50] Particular commands are justified by the particular goal or situation for which they are given. Universal commands are justified by some universal principle. Some conclude that all biblical commands are particular, as Karl Barth insisted, so that their function is to witness to the God who commands, and perhaps to teach us something about God's will. However, Barth's own example in his *Church Dogmatics* seems to contradict his principle, for he repeatedly applies biblical commands directly and with moral force to his own day. More specifically, as O'Donovan observes, Barth finds it difficult to be consistent when he examines the Decalogue: "When Barth finally declares the Decalogue to be a collection of 'summaries,' he effectively admits, with more good sense than consistency, that the particularist approach cannot be carried through, for a 'summary' is nothing if not the universal generalization which he sought so hard to exclude."[51]

Again, the judgment concerning whether a given command is particular or universal may at times be contested, but that should not lead to the conclusion that such judgments are impossible or hopelessly subjective. These examples suggest that there are some

---

49. Brock brings this point to the forefront of Christian ethics in *Singing the Ethos*.
50. Oliver O'Donovan, "Towards an Interpretation of Biblical Ethics," *Tyndale Bulletin* 27, no. 1 (1976): 62–63.
51. O'Donovan, "Towards an Interpretation," 62. See Karl Barth, *Church Dogmatics* II/2, trans. Harold Knight (Edinburgh: T & T Clark), 673, 681–83.

basic principles that operate when moving from the Bible to Christian ethics. Of course, there are those who are quick to raise objections to any given principle, or to the entire proposal of moving from the text to our situation, and some objections are not easily settled. However, that does not preclude us from making moral judgments that are grounded in the Bible, and offering principles for how to move from the Bible to Christian ethics. The next two chapters will examine the Old and New Testaments and the pattern of ethical teaching and worldview perspective that emerges in each. Later chapters will apply the biblical worldview and teaching to contemporary issues.

Select Resources

Birch, Bruce C., and Larry L. Rasmussen. *Bible and Ethics in the Christian Life*. Rev. ed. Minneapolis: Augsburg Fortress, 1989.

Brock, Brian. *Singing the Ethos of God*: *On the Place of Christian Ethics in Scripture*. Grand Rapids: Eerdmans, 2007.

Green, Joel B., Jacqueline E Lapsley, Rebekah Miles, and Allen Verhey, eds. *Dictionary of Scripture and Ethics*. Grand Rapids: Baker Academic, 2011.

Gustafson, James M. "The Place of Scripture in Christian Ethics: A Methodological Study." *Interpretation* 24, no. 4 (October 1970): 430–55.

Hays, Richard B. *The Moral Vision of the New Testament: Community, Cross, New Creation; A Contemporary Introduction to New Testament Ethics*. San Francisco: HarperSanFrancisco, 1996.

Jones, David W. *An Introduction to Biblical Ethics*. Edited by Daniel R. Heimbach. B&H Studies in Biblical Ethics. Nashville: B&H Academic, 2013.

Murray, John. *Principles of Conduct: Aspects of Biblical Ethics*. Grand Rapids: Eerdmans, 1991.

Ogletree, Thomas W. *The Use of the Bible in Christian Ethics: A Constructive Essay*. Philadelphia: Fortress, 1983.

Verhey, Allen. "Bible in Christian Ethics." In *Westminster Dictionary of Christian Ethics*. Philadelphia: Westminster, 1986.

CHAPTER 4

ASPECTS OF BIBLICAL ETHICS:
OLD TESTAMENT

*He has told you, O man, what is good;
and what does the Lord require of you
but to do justice, and to love kindness,
and to walk humbly with your God?*

—Micah 6:8 ESV

*All Scripture is God-breathed and is useful
for teaching, rebuking, correcting and
training in righteousness, so that the servant
of God may be thoroughly equipped for every
good work.*

—2 Timothy 3:16–17 NIV

Introduction

In *The Year of Biblical Womanhood*, Rachel Held Evans writes about an experiment in which she seeks for one year to apply what she takes to be a very literal interpretation of teaching about women in the Bible.[1] So, for example, she stood at the edge of town holding a sign praising her husband as an application of Proverbs 31:23, and she spent time on her roof as a sign of contrition when she was contentious, to keep Proverbs 21:9 and 25:24 (cf. 21:19). To be fair, her book is not a work of serious scholarship, yet it does raise questions about the relevance and authority of the Bible for today, and how it should (and should not) be applied. Before discussing Old Testament ethics, several brief comments are worth making about Evans's book. First, her experiment illustrates that neglecting basic rules of biblical hermeneutics leads to an unwarranted (and trivial) understanding and application of Scripture. For instance, we ought not to mistake descriptive accounts (or narratives) as prescriptive or normative. In addition, we need to recognize different genres in the Bible, and what those differences convey, which will help to avoid wrongful applications based on misinterpretation.

Second, Evans is a talented writer, and her book gained popularity and influence.[2] Unfortunately, it creates or reinforces a view that biblical commands, especially Old Testament ones, are difficult to keep or don't apply to Christians, or are really out of step with modern sensibilities and basic common sense. Those who are concerned to show the relevance of Scripture attempt to clarify rather than confuse, by presenting or illustrating basic principles of interpretation. It is not always clear how to apply Scripture in our lives, but we ought to avoid exaggerating the difficulties, making the task seem impossible. Evans' conclusion, that it is always necessary to pick and choose, and that interpreters simply need to decide how to do so, doesn't reflect the kind of nuance required for adequate interpretation and application of Scripture, and it makes it seem to be a highly subjective process. That fails to do justice to the way in which the Bible itself teaches how it applies for followers of Jesus, and to the centuries of reflection by the church on the question, which, in spite of debate, has produced significant agreement. One of the difficult questions has to do with the relevance of the Old Testament for Christian ethics.

In the previous chapter I discussed the authority and relevance of the whole Bible for Christian ethics. Its moral commands help us to understand the will of God, but the Bible provides much more than commands for Christian ethics. Narratives portray the relationship between God and his people, and indicate what his people are to be like. It is noteworthy that even the books

1. Rachel Held Evans, *A Year of Biblical Womanhood: How a Liberated Woman Found Herself Sitting on Her Roof, Covering Her Head, and Calling Her Husband "Master"* (Nashville: Thomas Nelson, 2012).
2. At the time of this writing, the author's website indicated that the book was a *New York Times* best seller, and that it had been featured in popular newspapers and magazines, and on popular television programs. See also "A Year of Biblical Womanhood," Rachel Held Evans's personal website, http://rachelheldevans.com/biblical-womanhood.

of the Law are largely in the form of narrative. The wisdom literature develops many aspects of ethics, including the pursuit and application of wisdom and, in the Psalms especially, the significance of remembering the character and works of God and participating as a community in singing his praise.[3] The Prophets offer penetrating insight into Israel's failure to keep the law, the hypocrisy of external conformity without internal reality, the emptiness of religious practices without concern for justice and mercy, and so on.

In addition, the Bible provides a worldview and a moral field within which human beings—and biblical commands—are situated. Without this larger field of vision—its metanarrative—appeals to biblical commands represent a truncated view of Christian ethics, focused on acts and duties without reference to character, and the purpose of life, corresponding to God's character and purposes. Even more, its metanarrative, and redemptive history in particular, is crucial for interpreting the place of law in Scripture as a whole, and in the Christian life.[4] It will not be possible in this chapter to offer a comprehensive treatment of the contents of biblical ethics. Such a task would require a full volume in itself, and there are several volumes that offer significant treatments.[5] Instead, this chapter will look at a few representative aspects of Old Testament ethics that are critical for Christian ethics. The next chapter will examine aspects of New Testament ethics.

Biblical Commands, the Gospel, and Christian Ethics

Even though biblical commands and law represent only one aspect of biblical ethics, it is necessary to offer particular reflection on their significance for Christian ethics, for they play an important role. If it is true that they have been emphasized at times to the exclusion of other important aspects, it is also true that they are sometimes marginalized in favor of attention to things like narrative and virtue, community, and the worldview of the Bible. It is important to understand the nature, purpose, and function of biblical commands.

The Old Testament law presents a challenge for Christian ethics. It is important

---

3. The significance of the Psalms for Christian ethics is nicely presented by Brian Brock, *Singing the Ethos of God: On the Place of Christian Ethics in Scripture* (Grand Rapids: Eerdmans, 2007). Many aspects of the Psalms, including worship, singing, memory, community, and repetition, are neglected in accounts of Christian ethics.

4. A helpful guide for understanding the law and its relevance for Christians, with attention to the historical-redemptive perspective, is Thomas R. Schreiner, *40 Questions About Christians and Biblical Law* (Grand Rapids: Kregel, 2010).

5. John Frame, *The Doctrine of the Christian Life* (Phillipsburg, NJ: P&R, 2008); Richard B. Hays, *The Moral Vision of the New Testament: Community, Cross, New Creation; A Contemporary Introduction to New Testament Ethics* (San Francisco: HarperSanFrancisco, 1996); Walter C. Kaiser Jr., *Toward Old Testament Ethics* (Grand Rapids: Zondervan, 1983); T. B. Maston, *Biblical Ethics: A Guide to the Ethical Message of the Scriptures from Genesis through Revelation* (Macon, GA: Mercer University Press, 1982 [1967]); Wolfgang Schrage, *The Ethics of the New Testament*, trans. David E. Green (Philadelphia: Fortress, 1988); Christopher J. .H. Wright, *Old Testament Ethics for the People of God* (Downers Grove, IL: IVP Academic, 2004).

to get this right, for "the foundations of Christian ethics must be evangelical foundations; or, to put it more simply, Christian ethics must arise from the gospel of Jesus Christ. Otherwise it could not be *Christian* ethics."[6] To put it another way, Christian ethics is only *Christian* "insofar as [it is] an expression of the good news."[7] Surely, some will say, an ethical system that places too much emphasis on law cannot be gospel, or an expression of good news, so it must be sub-Christian. If Christian ethics is grounded in the gospel, does it exclude the law? If an account of ethics is constructed on the Ten Commandments, is it to be considered sub-Christian or legalistic?[8] Alternatively, if all of Scripture is applicable, how is the Mosaic law to be applied? Did Jesus affirm or abolish the law? What did he teach his followers about the law? Such questions are significant for Christian ethics because they arise from reflection on the gospel and on the whole Bible. Some representative texts from the New Testament illustrate the challenge:

• "Don't think that I came to abolish the Law or the Prophets. I did not come to abolish but to fulfill. For truly I tell you, until heaven and earth pass away, not the smallest letter or one stroke of a letter will pass away from the law until all things are accomplished. Therefore, whoever breaks one of the least of these commands and teaches others to do the same will be called least in the kingdom of heaven. But whoever does and teaches these commands will be called great in the kingdom of heaven" (Matt. 5:17–19).

• "For the law was given through Moses; grace and truth came through Jesus Christ" (John 1:17).

• "For sin will not rule over you, because you are not under the law but under grace" (Rom. 6:14).

• "So then, the law is holy, and the commandment is holy and just and good" (Rom. 7:12).

• "For Christ is the end of the law for righteousness to everyone who believes" (Rom. 10:4).

• "Before this faith came, we were confined under the law, imprisoned until the coming faith was revealed. The law, then, was our guardian until Christ, so that we could be justified by faith. But since that faith has come, we are no longer under a guardian, for through faith you are all sons of God in Christ Jesus" (Gal. 3:23–26).

• "For freedom, Christ set us free. Stand firm, then, and don't submit again to a yoke of slavery" (Gal. 5:1).

---

6. Oliver O'Donovan, *Resurrection and Moral Order: An Outline for Evangelical Ethics*, 2nd ed. (Grand Rapids: Eerdmans, 1994 [1986]), 11.
7. Brock, *Singing the Ethos*, xvii.
8. Reformed teaching has often structured Christian ethics this way, out of a sense of the abiding validity of the Ten Commandments as an expression of God's moral law. See the Westminster Confession of Faith; also Frame, *Doctrine of the Christian Life*.

These texts must be interpreted, of course, in terms of both the immediate context and the larger biblical paradigm within which they appear. Yet, when the context is considered, there is still much disagreement about how to understand the law and its function, and these verses do indicate something of the tension concerning the law within the New Testament. They indicate some key issues with the law, including its abiding relevance, the sharp distinction between law and grace, some role for the law in redemptive history, some sense in which Christian freedom includes freedom from the law, and so on. One question that emerges has to do with how Jesus's followers should understand and relate to the Old Testament law.

The Traditional Three-Part Distinction

One traditional strategy for applying the law to Christian ethics is that we may draw a distinction within the Mosaic law between the ceremonial, civil, and moral law, along lines something like these:

- **Ceremonial law** (also called cultic law) refers to laws of sacrifice, dietary laws, ritual cleanness, calendar days and festivals, and other aspects of Israel's religious practices. Among other things, such laws serve to set Israel apart from other nations, to establish and maintain Israel's distinct identity as the people of Yahweh, to indicate the need for the Messiah, and to foreshadow the coming Messiah.

- **Civil law** (also called judicial law) refers to commands that govern civil order for the nation of Israel, including punishments for lawbreaking.

- **Moral law** refers to those laws that are considered to have universal application. The Decalogue is considered the primary body of these laws, which serve as the basis for case laws. Unlike ceremonial and civil laws, moral laws are not distinct for Israel, but are understood to apply to all people everywhere. In the language of ethics, they are considered universal moral norms. The category of moral law does not mean that ceremonial or civil laws are not also moral, or that they have no moral component, but rather that they are not universal moral norms—that is, they may be changed or abrogated.

Something like this distinction is mentioned at least as early as Justin Martyr, who writes to Trypho, a Jew, that "some injunctions were laid on you in reference to the worship of God and practice of righteousness; but some injunctions and acts were likewise mentioned in reference to the mystery of Christ"; it is developed by Thomas Aquinas, and is fairly standard at the time of the Reformation.[9] The general purpose of

---

9.   See Oliver O'Donovan, "Towards an Interpretation of Biblical Ethics," *Tyndale Bulletin* 27, no. 1 (1976): 59. The citation of Justin Martyr is from his *Dialogue with Trypho* 44, in *The Ante-Nicene Fathers*, vol. 1, *The Apostolic Fathers with Justin Martyr and Irenaeus*, eds. Alexander Roberts and James Donaldson (Grand Rapids: Eerdmans, 1996 [1885]), 217. For a discussion of Aquinas, see David Clyde Jones, *Biblical Christian Ethics* (Grand Rapids: Baker, 1994),

this paradigm is to identify and offer a rationale for why certain Old Testament laws only applied to God's people under the Mosaic covenant, while others continue to be in force beyond the Mosaic covenant, to be kept by Jesus's followers, and, for that matter, all people everywhere. Or, to put it another way, it is to explain why some Old Testament laws are reaffirmed in the New Testament while others are either not reaffirmed or clearly taught to be no longer practiced in light of Jesus the Messiah.

Is this traditional paradigm valid? At the risk of oversimplifying the issues that this paradigm raises, I will summarize one or two common objections to this view, with a response to the objections. The purpose is not to consider all the issues involved in the debate, or necessarily to resolve them. Rather, the discussion about the model provides an opportunity to draw out certain relevant points about the law, and in particular the Ten Commandments, with respect to both the Old Testament and Christian ethics. Even if the paradigm is not finally persuasive to some, it does provide insight, and it is not easily dismissed, as it is "the most remarkable, perhaps the only attempt ever made to find general and non-arbitrary grounds on which to say that some Old Testament commands do, and others do not, lay claim on Christians."[10]

Objections to the Traditional Threefold View of the Law

Perhaps the primary objection to the threefold distinction is that it does not do justice to the original context in which the Mosaic law was given. That is, the Mosaic law is a body of legislation, and it is anachronistic to differentiate between ceremonial, civil, and moral categories. Israel did not understand the law that way, so it is not valid to read back into the law such an understanding. It is a paradigm that is imposed on the text. The law was given to Israel as a whole, and it all functions within Israel's particular political-religious structure, so it is misguided to single out certain laws as moral and argue that they transcend that structure, while others do not.[11] Put another way, since the whole law belongs to the Mosaic covenant, and that covenant is no longer in force, it is not legitimate to try to enforce part of the Mosaic law. It might be added that the New Testament does not identify the three categories as such, and it is sometimes difficult to determine which category most appropriately applies to certain laws. For example, "love your neighbor as yourself" in Leviticus 19:18 is surely considered to be a moral law. Yet it is immediately followed, in verse 19, by a law that prohibits the crossbreeding of two different kinds of livestock, the planting of two different kinds of seed in a field, and

---

111. See Thomas Aquinas, *Summa theologiae*, trans. David Bourke and Arthur Littledale (New York: McGraw, 1969), 1a2ae.99, 4; cf. John Calvin, *Institutes of the Christian Religion*, ed. John T. McNeill, trans. Ford Lewis Battles, Library of Christian Classics 21 (Philadelphia: Westminster, 1960), 4.20.14–15 (2:1502–4). Note its use in the Westminster Confession of Faith, chap. 19, and in the Anglican Thirty-Nine Articles of Religion, article 7.

10.   O'Donovan, "Towards an Interpretation," 60.

11.   O'Donovan cites these objections without affirming them. O'Donovan, "Towards an Interpretation," 60.

the wearing of a garment made of two kinds of material. There is no distinction made between these laws, as far as categories. They are simply woven together in the text.

The challenge to the traditional view is clear enough. The conclusion reached by many is that the attempt to distinguish moral laws from ceremonial or civil, asking which laws still apply to us, is not very fruitful, and does not adequately reflect a biblical perspective on the law. Thus, for instance, Thomas Schreiner writes, "Even though it has some elements of truth, it does not sufficiently capture Paul's stance toward the law."[12] Christopher Wright suggests that the traditional view is not helpful, and that a legitimate classification of Old Testament laws serves a different purpose, to help us "discern the ethical relevance of the whole range of Israel's law by first understanding its function and purpose in its own context."[13] By implication, one of the risks with the threefold classification is that the ethical relevance of the "nonmoral" laws will not be recognized.

Response to the Objections

On the one hand, these objections are significant, and raise important considerations. On the other hand, as a critique of the traditional view, they may miss the mark in part perhaps because they do not address the purpose of the traditional view. For instance, the threefold distinction is not intended to describe how Israel understood the law as such (though attention to the function of the law in its original context is important). Rather, it represents an attempt to understand the relevance and application of various laws from a Christian perspective. As Oliver O'Donovan suggests, such categorization can be compared to the way modern scholars identify various literary genres: "Israel, I take it, never dreamed of the distinction between Wisdom literature and priestly code, royal psalms and psalms of lament; and yet such categorisation is not only convenient for us, but may claim a fair amount of objectivity."[14] The traditional distinction developed as an attempt to understand the law in light of Christ, explaining why certain laws were set aside in the New Testament, while some were repeated and urged on followers of Christ. Thus, right or wrong, the traditional distinctions are made based on a redemptive-historical perspective that is grounded in New Testament teaching.

In particular, in light of the person and work of Jesus, the inclusion of the Gentiles in the people of God, and specific teaching about food laws and sacrifices, for example, the so-called ceremonial or cultic laws were fulfilled by Jesus in a way that they should no longer be practiced. Further, in light of the expansion of the people of God from the nation of Israel to the nations, the so-called civil laws that governed Israel no longer function in the same way. The use of the term

---

12. Schreiner, *40 Questions*, 89–90.
13. Wright, *Old Testament Ethics*, 288.
14. O'Donovan, "Towards an Interpretation," 60–61.

moral law, then, applies to those commands that are considered universal (rather than meaning simply that these laws have a moral dimension). It is not meant to imply that part of the Mosaic covenant is carried forward while other parts are not, but that some of its commands articulate abiding moral norms, which are then repeated in the New Testament. As an attempt to understand the whole law, and each law, in light of Christ, the charge that the traditional paradigm is arbitrary is not as strong as it first appears. In the text from Leviticus 19 mentioned above, it is a valid point that one would not expect the people of Israel to have found in the command to love their neighbor a moral law that stood out from the rest in its context. Yet Jesus points to that very command and distinguishes it as the second greatest commandment (Matt. 22:39; Mark 12:31)! By the critics' reasoning, it seems that Jesus could be charged with arbitrariness. The key to evaluating the threefold distinction is not whether Israel understood the law in such a way, but whether some such view of the law is drawn from or consistent with the teaching of the New Testament.

That is not to argue that the distinction between ceremonial, civil, and moral laws is adequate. Yet, even if the traditional view is judged to be inadequate, it may provide some insight into universal moral norms in the law that are otherwise missed, or even dismissed. Clearly there has been some reason for the appeal of the traditional view, and it is doubtful that it is as simplistic and as easily rejected as some would suggest. In

what follows, my purpose is not to advocate the traditional view as a necessary paradigm for understanding the moral law, but simply to offer some insights gained from engaging the logic of the traditional view.

Insights Gained by Reflection on the Traditional Distinction

Universal norms and particular laws

Wright's argument against the threefold view highlights a potentially significant problem, which is that the description of some Old Testament laws as moral could imply that other laws have no moral relevance. He rightly urges that we should seek to understand the function and purpose, and thereby the moral relevance, of each law in the context in which it appears. However, while Wright's point is an important reminder, it raises an issue that is not necessarily a problem for the threefold view, since those who assert that there are distinct moral laws also seek to discern the moral significance of the rest of the law. John Calvin makes this clear when talking about the traditional distinctions, for instance, when he says, "We must consider each of these parts, that we may understand what there is in them that pertains to us, and what does not. In the meantime, let no one be concerned over the small point that ceremonial and judicial laws pertain also to morals. For the ancient writers who taught this division, although they were not ignorant that these two latter parts had some bearing upon morals, still, because these could be changed or abrogated while morals remained untouched, did not call them moral laws."[15] The issue is not moral versus nonmoral laws, but *universal* versus *particular* laws, which is a common distinction used in ethics. The two goals—discerning distinct universal moral laws as well as the moral significance of all laws—are compatible. Wright's own categories are helpful for understanding the law, as he discusses criminal law, case law, family law, cultic law, and compassionate law.[16] Yet it seems to work against some criticisms of the traditional view, since his categories overlap with it (e.g., criminal and case laws, cultic laws) and since Israel did not neatly organize their laws along Wright's categories either.

Schreiner articulates an appreciation for the traditional view, noting that it is "appealing and attractive" and has "elements of truth," but he argues that it is inadequate.[17] For instance, he notes that "it is quite difficult to distinguish between what is 'moral' and 'ceremonial' in the law," supported by the fact that "the law forbidding the taking of interest is clearly a moral mandate" (Exod. 22:25).[18] This is a fair test case, for this command is not considered part of the moral law,[19] and yet there is a clear moral mandate or principle. In response, the meaning of *moral law* does not imply that other laws have no moral mandate. Rather, *moral law* refers to one that is a universal moral norm. A law that is not part of the moral law may still be a moral mandate, based on a deeper moral principle, but since the command could be changed or abrogated, it is not part of the moral law.

That is, while it is based on a moral principle, the law itself is a particular moral rule rather than a universal moral norm. Schreiner even provides the rationale that would justify changing the law, for while he says it is "clearly a moral mandate," he adds that "this law was addressed to Israel as an agricultural society in the ancient Near East."[20] As such, the principle behind the law might be applied differently in an industrial society. It is generally not too difficult to perceive that certain laws are applications of moral principles that are bound to a cultural context in ways that others are not. To take another example, the universal command "Do not steal" (Deut.. 5:19; 19:11) can be distinguished from a particular application, "The wages due a hired worker must not remain with you until morning" (Lev. 19:13), which may not apply in an economic system that pays workers on a weekly, biweekly, or monthly basis. The particular law is grounded in a universal moral norm and it has a moral mandate, but it is one that can change. Schreiner recognizes something

---

15. Calvin, *Institutes* 4.20.14 (2:1502–3).
16. Wright, *Old Testament Ethics*, chap. 9.
17. Schreiner, *40 Questions*, 89.
18. Schreiner, *40 Questions*, 90. Schreiner references David A. Dorsey, "The Law of Moses and the Christian: A Compromise," *Journal of the Evangelical Theological Society* 34, no. 3 (1991): 329–30.
19. It seems to me that it would be classified as a civil law rather than a ceremonial law, under the threefold rubric, but that does not significantly alter the assessment.
20. Schreiner, *40 Questions*, 90.

like this when he says of certain Old Testament laws that are affirmed and applied for believers that "it seems appropriate to designate such commands as moral norms," and that some of the laws of the Old Testament "express transcendent moral principles."[21]

A similar point can be made with respect to our twenty-first-century law code. Even though we may not express it in these terms, it is possible to distinguish within our law code those laws that have universal moral claim and those that do not. "Do not murder" has universal claim, while "Speed Limit 30 MPH" does not. There is a moral principle behind the speed limit (e.g., protection of life), but the particular speed limit could be changed. To take another example, "Do not steal" has universal claim, while particular regulations concerning the use of copyright material does not. Copyright laws are based on a moral principle, but they can be adjusted. In other words, laws against murder and stealing are appropriately called moral laws, while laws governing speed limit and copyright infringement could reasonably be called civil laws. The point is not whether we actually refer to them as such, or whether there is overlap. Rather, it is that such an explanation makes sense, and it helps to clarify the nature and purpose of our laws. Likewise, even if the people Israel did not understand the law in terms of the threefold distinction, they could presumably make sense of a rationale given for it. In spite of the inadequacies with the traditional view, including issues raised by Wright and Schreiner, it does provide insight into a distinction between universal and particular laws.

The basis for discerning civil and ceremonial laws

Not only does the traditional view distinguish between moral laws and other laws, but it also uses categories of civil and ceremonial to identify significant features or functions of the law. It is a fair criticism to point out that the categories are not easily discerned with respect to each and every law. Nevertheless, it is not difficult to perceive that various laws fall under different human authorities, and some apply to religious practices while others apply to the marketplace and civic life; some carry civil punishments for disobedience, while others do not.[22] The traditional view recognizes, for instance, that because of Jesus's death on the cross, as a perfect sacrifice for sins, laws of sacrifice are fulfilled in Christ, so they are no longer necessary. That is, the New Testament highlights the cessation of Old Testament sacrificial laws in light of Jesus's person and work (Heb. 9:25–26; 10:1–12). In a similar way, Old Testament dietary laws are distinguished and set aside, no longer marking a boundary between Jews and Gentiles (Mark 7:19; Acts 10:15, 11:9; cf. Heb. 9:10). Even though there is no particular category within which these laws are formally

---

21. Schreiner, *40 Questions*, 93–94.
22. Allen Verhey offers a modest affirmation of the traditional "rubrics" because of such distinctions. Verhey, "Ethics," in *Dictionary for Theological Interpretation of the Bible*, eds. Kevin J. Vanhoozer et al. (Grand Rapids: Baker Academic, 2005), 197.

listed in the Old or New Testament, it is not unreasonable to group them together and to recognize that they no longer apply today as they did for Israel. There is New Testament precedence for doing so.

It is also possible to talk about "civil ordinances," even though there is less direct evidence in the New Testament. In terms of distinctions within the Old Testament law, at least in general terms, the civil law falls under the authority of judges and other civil magistrates rather than under the authority of priests, and is not directly part of Israel's religious practices. Further, from a New Testament perspective, the people of God are no longer identified with the nation-state of Israel, as in the Old Testament, but now are identified as the church, which is spread among the nations. These nations are ruled by secular authorities, which are recognized as legitimate by Jesus (Mark 12:17; John 19:11),[23] Paul (Acts 25:11; Rom. 13:1–7), and Peter (1 Pet. 2:13–14). There is no indication that they are to enforce specific Mosaic statutes, though the Bible makes clear that their authority is not only granted by God but limited by God as well, and they are held accountable to standards of justice (John 19:11; Acts 5:29; 22:25; Rom. 13:3–4; 1 Pet. 2:14).

The moral law, then, is used to refer to laws that articulate moral norms that remain in force after the Mosaic covenant. They may be known because they are reaffirmed in the New Testament, which signifies that there is some underlying basis or moral norm that can be discerned or assumed. Or they could refer to Old Testament laws that are not revoked, though that perspective is less convincing, particularly if there is a compelling biblical and theological argument for claiming that the Mosaic law as a whole is no longer in force.[24] To put it slightly differently, as indicated above, the moral law refers to Old Testament commands that are not simply particular, but universal. If there are no "universal" laws within the law, the New Testament would not uphold any of them, nor would it be necessary to repudiate any particular laws, since none would apply.[25] There may be difficulties and disagreements over how to identify the moral law, but the point is that if we can identify something that makes claim on all people, we have discerned the moral law.

The traditional view may not be adequate, but it is at least reasonable, and not as readily dismissed as some opponents seem to suggest. That is, there is a reasonable

---

23. Mark 12:17, "give to Caesar the things that are Caesar's," at least appears to accept Caesar's authority to collect taxes; John 19:11 is astounding in that Jesus acknowledges Pilate's earthly authority over him, though he tells Pilate that his authority is granted from God.

24. Douglas Moo has published insightful arguments for understanding the Old Testament law to be fulfilled in Jesus in such a way that "it does not seem that any Mosaic commandment can be assumed to be directly applicable to the believer." Douglas J. Moo, "Jesus and the Authority of the Mosaic Law," *Journal for the Study of the New Testament* 7, no. 20 (1984): 29. Moo argues against the threefold distinction, saying that "the *whole* law came to culmination in Christ" (29). Nevertheless, it does not seem that his arguments unravel the traditional view, though they may correct and qualify it at important points.

25. O'Donovan, "Towards an Interpretation," 63.

basis for identifying different aspects of the law and for judging that some are universal (the moral law), while the specific requirements of others are limited to the people of Israel under the Mosaic covenant (civil and ceremonial laws). Further, it is not arbitrary, in that it distinguishes certain patterns in the law and seeks to understand the law in light of Christ. The usefulness of the categories can be seen in that a similar pattern is identified by scholars who reject the traditional threefold distinction. For instance, referring to the use of the law in James, Schreiner comments, "James never mentions circumcision, Sabbath, or food laws. The ceremonial dimensions of the law are entirely absent."[26] Likewise, he recognizes something like the category of civil law, even if not for the same purpose, when he comments that "'an eye for an eye' is found in civil contexts, where governing authorities are given instructions about the penalties that are fitting for those who have committed crimes (Exod. 21:22–25; Lev. 24:17–22; Deut. 19:21)."[27] Although Wright rejects the traditional view, his appeal to categories such as criminal law and case law, as well as family law, on the one hand, and cultic law, on the other, suggest that he sees a similar pattern, even if for a different purpose.[28] Charles Scobie does not advance the traditional view as such, but when noting the various types of laws, he refers to civil, social, moral, and cultic.[29]

The Decalogue as the heart of the moral law

A significant part of the traditional distinction is that the Decalogue is identified as the primary block of the moral law. This is because, depending on one's interpretation, all or most (90 percent!) of the Decalogue is repeated in the New Testament, and because it is said to have special standing within the Old Testament. Earlier, the objection was raised that the traditional view is anachronistic because Israel did not distinguish a moral law apart from the rest. One response to that objection was noted, which is that the traditional view does not suggest that Israel saw the law that way, but that it seeks to understand the law in light of Jesus. A different type of response, however, is to say that Israel could and should have perceived some distinction in the law, or among the laws. Whether or not it is considered to be the moral law of the Old Testament, the Decalogue is easily distinguished from the rest. Consider the following brief points:

- Perhaps most significant is the reference to the "Ten Commandments" (or, better, "ten words," or *Decalogue*). Exodus 34:28 says, "He wrote the Ten Commandments, the words of the covenant, on the tablets." The term translated "Ten Commandments" is עֲשֶׂרֶת הַדְּבָרִים, the "ten words" (from which we get *Decalogue*, from δέκα = ten and λόγος = word/s)

---

26. Schreiner, *40 Questions*, 200.
27. Schreiner, *40 Questions*, 168.
28. Wright, *Old Testament Ethics*, chap. 9. He also identifies "compassionate law."
29. Charles H. H. Scobie, *The Ways of Our God: An Approach to Biblical Theology* (Grand Rapids: Eerdmans, 2003), 749.

(see Deut. 4:13; 10:4). The very reference to "ten words," and the fact that these, and not all the law, were written on the tablets, demonstrates their unique place. They were clearly distinguished from other laws.

- Remarkably, in the text of Exodus 34:28 just cited, and in Deuteronomy 4:13, the Decalogue is identified with the covenant!
- The events leading up to the giving of the Decalogue, described in Exodus 19 (cf. Deut. 5:22), culminating in thunder and lightning, fire and smoke, and the violent shaking of the mountain, mark out both the event and the Decalogue as unique.
- In addition, there is special emphasis placed on the Decalogue as having a direct imprint of God: "inscribed by the finger of God" (Exod. 31:18; cf. 32:16; 34:1, 28; Deut. 4:13; 9:10).
- The tablets on which the Decalogue is inscribed are placed in the ark (Deut. 10:1–5), further signaling its importance.
- In the New Testament, both Jesus and Paul make direct appeal to the Decalogue (Matt. 19:18–19; Rom. 13:8–10) as a summary of the law. There are further allusions and appeals to the Decalogue in the New Testament as well (Matt. 5:21, 27; 15:19; Rom. 2:21–24; Eph. 6:1–4; 1 Tim. 1:8–11).

This broad recognition of the Decalogue within both the Old and New Testaments is one reason why it is identified as the primary representation of the moral law. In addition, the commands of the Decalogue are set apart by the type of claims they make, and the way they function within the Mosaic law as a whole. Many have viewed the Decalogue as the general standard, while detailed laws with particular situations and penalties represent "case law," or the application of the Decalogue to specific situations. Thus the detailed laws can be related back to one of the Ten (see below the example from Calvin, which, even if one wishes to challenge the details, illustrates the point clearly enough):[30]

The Relation of the Decalogue to the Rest of the Law in Calvin

Example of the eighth commandment: "Thou shall not steal."

"Exposition" (laws that clarify or apply the commandment):

- Prompt payment of wages (Lev. 19:11, 13; Deut. 24:14; 25:4)
- Care and impartiality for aliens (Exod. 22:21–24; Lev. 19:33; Deut. 10:17–19)
- Honesty in weights and measures (Lev. 19:35; Deut. 25:13–16)
- No removal of boundary markers (Deut. 19:14)

---

30. Calvin, *Commentaries on the Four Last Books of Moses Arranged in the Form of a Harmony*, vols 1–4 (Edinburgh: Calvin Translation Society, 1852–1855). See the discussion in C. J. H. Wright, *Walking in the Ways of the Lord: The Ethical Authority of the Old Testament* (Downers Grove, IL: InterVarsity Press), 78.

- Duties in respect of pledges for loans (Exod. 22:26–27; Deut. 24:6, 10–13, 17–18)
- Laws against taking interest (Exod. 22:25; Lev. 25:35–38; Deut. 23:19)
- Recovery of lost possessions (Exod. 23:4; Deut. 22:1–3)
- Restitution for theft (Num. 5:5–7)
- Denunciation of bribery and corruption (Exod. 23:8; Lev. 19:15; Deut. 16:19)
- Prohibition on partiality, for or against the poor (Exod. 23:3, 6)

"Political supplements" (civil or ceremonial aspects for Israel):

- Gleanings for the poor (Lev. 19:9, 23:22; Deut. 24:19–22)
- The sabbatical year (Exod. 21:1–6; Deut. 15:1–18)
- The jubilee and redemption regulations (Lev. 25)
- Ban on destroying fruit trees in war (Deut. 20:19)
- Exemptions from military service for certain categories of people (Deut. 20:5–8)
- The levirate marriage duty (Deut. 25:5–10)

The general nature and universal application of the Decalogue has been noted by various scholars. Geoffrey Bromiley asserts that the detailed rules of the law, along with the penalties attached to them, "apply strictly and properly only to the Old Testament period when God's people is also a nation with its own legal and social institutions. In this regard, the detailed rules differ from the ten commandments. The commandments do not deal with individual situations or prescribe penalties (apart from the general judgment of God). They have a more general character and describe the conduct which God wills or does not will for the human creature."[31] David Clyde Jones agrees that the Decalogue, with its broad moral scope, has universal application: "The Ten Commandments are universal moral norms because they represent the will of God for human nature as he has created it—to be fulfilled through his ordinances of worship, rest, authority, life, sex, property, and communication; they are grounded in his purposes and instructions for human beings always and everywhere."[32] John Murray also emphasizes the centrality and abiding validity of the Decalogue, by noting that the moral responsibility that they entail does not begin and end with the giving of the Mosaic law. He asserts three significant points about the Ten Commandments: that they "furnish the core of the biblical ethics"; that they were "but the concrete and practical form of enunciating principles which did not then for the first time come to have relevance but were relevant from the beginning"; and that "as they did not *begin* to have relevance at Sinai, so they did not cease to have relevance when the Sinaitic economy had passed away."[33] In other words, Murray claims that the

31. Geoffrey W. Bromiley, *God and Marriage* (Grand Rapids: Eerdmans, 1980), 18.
32. Jones, *Biblical Christian Ethics*, 116.
33. John Murray, *Principles of Conduct: Aspects of Biblical Ethics* (Grand Rapids: Eerdmans, 1957), 7.

commands in the Decalogue articulate universal moral norms that were true before the Mosaic covenant and remained true after the Mosaic covenant ceased.[34]

There is not a lot of direct textual evidence supporting Murray's argument that the moral law predates the giving of the law at Sinai. It may be taken by some as an obvious inference, given the nature of the commands. (False worship and murder, for instance, were wrong before they were declared to be wrong at Sinai.) For others, there are earlier texts that at least hint at a universal moral law. The devastating judgment of God to send a flood to wipe out all inhabitants on earth in Genesis 6 suggests that people ought to have known God's moral law. The prohibition of murder, enforced by penalty of death, is given to Noah with application to all people, grounded in the creation norm that human beings are made in God's image (Gen. 9:6). Further, God makes a striking statement made to Isaac when he confirms to him the promise made to Abraham, that "all the nations of the earth will be blessed by your offspring, because Abraham listened to me and kept *my mandate, my commands, my statutes, and my instructions*" (Gen. 26:4–5, emphasis added). This suggests something beyond the particular command of God given to Abraham alone, instead

using terminology reflective of the law given at Sinai, the whole Mosaic code, and the Pentateuch.[35] Indeed, it looks enough like a reference to a knowable and known set of laws that critical scholars presume that it must be the insertion of a redactor who is obsessed with the law. Against such an assumption, Wright asserts that "taken with proper theological seriousness (and crediting the editor of Genesis with being just as aware as we are that his text was located chronologically before the giving of the Sinai law) this text suggests that the basic content and thrust of the law, though not yet given in detail as it was at Sinai, was in principle available to and observed by Abraham."[36]

Whether or not the Decalogue is identified as the moral law, it has proved to have a unique place for Christian moral reflection, teaching, and preaching. Some accounts of Christian ethics have been framed by the Decalogue, without neglecting the gospel, or the person and work of Jesus, or the teaching of Jesus and the rest of the New Testament. So, for various reasons, and regardless of whether it is identified as the moral law of Old Testament law, it is worth considering the form and substance of the Decalogue. First, though, it is important to note challenges to an exposition of the Decalogue, biblical law, and commands generally.

---

34. Some may see merit in Murray's point but reject the conclusion on the basis that the Sabbath command does not appear to claim the same universal application as the others. It is not possible here to discuss the Sabbath in detail, but as a general point, it can be said that one's view of the Sabbath will affect how one views the Decalogue in general. The reverse is also true, that one's view of the Decalogue will affect how one views the Sabbath, and in particular whether there is a universal moral norm articulated in the Sabbath command. I will make further comments on the moral principles of the Sabbath below.
35. John H. Walton, *Genesis*, NIV Application Commentary (Grand Rapids: Zondervan, 2001), 552.
36. Wright, *Old Testament Ethics*, 283n2.

The Decalogue and the Problem of Law

The Law in a Negative Light

One challenge for any account of Christian ethics that expounds the Decalogue is that laws are viewed mostly negatively, particularly in contemporary Western cultures, in which freedom is often identified as personal liberty and autonomy, which the law constrains. Naturally this view is associated with laws or commands in Scripture, and it is incorporated into a theological framework by appeals to the New Testament. Paul declares, "you are not under the law but under grace" (Rom. 6:14), and, "For freedom, Christ set us free. Stand firm then and don't submit again to a yoke of slavery" (Gal. 5:1). Peter declares that the yoke of the law is one that "neither our fathers nor we have been able to bear" (Acts 15:10 ESV). By contrast, Jesus says, "My yoke is easy, and my burden is light" (Matt. 11:30 ESV). A quick glance at Galatians 3 seems to show the law in a negative light, saying that "we were confined under the law, imprisoned until the coming faith was revealed" (v. 23). Paul adds that the law "was our guardian until Christ," but "since that faith has come, we are no longer under a guardian" (vv. 24–25). It is not difficult to see why some would understand that an affirmation of the gospel implies a rejection of the law. The whole package of law, requirements, obedience, and more is associated with the burden of legalism that some Christians experience.

The Law in a Positive Light

Yet the biblical understanding of law is more nuanced than the brief account just outlined, and it is helpful to get a fuller picture of law before considering the Decalogue further. However one understands legalism in the context of the gospel, it cannot be said that the law itself is the problem. If a reading of the law codes in Exodus, Leviticus, and Deuteronomy leaves some modern readers with a negative impression, perhaps due to their presuppositions about law in general, it might be challenged by a reading of the Psalms. There the law is something to delight in (Ps. 1:2), a delight that overflows with celebration in Psalm 19:7–10. Using a full range of terminology for the law, it is described as "perfect," "trustworthy," "right," "radiant," "reliable," and "altogether righteous." The attitude toward the law is also emphatically positive, as it "renews one's life," "makes wise," "makes the heart glad," "makes the eyes light up," is "more desirable than gold" and "sweeter than honey." Psalm 119 echoes and expands on that description, using eight different Hebrew terms for the law, translated in the CSB as "instruction," "decrees," "ways," "precepts," "statutes," "commands," "judgments," and "word." In addition to its delight in the law, a significant emphasis in this psalm is the sense of gratitude to God for his provision of the law, which reveals sin and death, and also righteousness and life, guiding God's people on the path of life. For example:

- "How can a young man keep his way pure? By keeping your word" (v. 9).

- "I am a resident alien on earth; do not hide your commands from me" (v. 19).
- "Your decrees are my delight and my counselors" (v. 24).
- "Turn my eyes from looking at what is worthless; give me life in your ways" (v. 37).
- "Instruction from your lips is better for me than thousands of gold and silver pieces" (v. 72).
- "May your compassion come to me so that I may live, for your instruction is my delight" (v. 77).
- "I will never forget your precepts, for you have given me life through them" (v. 93).
- "Your word is a lamp for my feet and a light on my path" (v. 105).
- "Make your face shine on your servant, and teach me your statutes" (v. 135).
- "Your compassions are many, LORD; give me life according to your judgments" (v. 156).

As Wright says, commenting on Psalms 19 and 119,

The least one can say about people who express such enthusiastic sentiments for the law is that they were not groveling along under a heavy burden of legalism. They were not anxiously striving to earn their way into salvation and a relationship with God through punctilious law-keeping. They were not puffed up with the claims of self-righteousness or exhausted with the efforts of works-righteousness. They did not, in short, fit into any of the caricatures that have been inflicted upon the Old Testament law by those who, misunderstanding Paul's arguments with those who had *distorted* the law, attribute to the law itself the very distortions from which Paul was seeking to exonerate it.[37]

The psalmist can delight in the law, love the law, learn from the law, seek diligently to keep the law, warn others not to break the law, and urge them to keep it without a hint of legalism, because it is the law of God. Far from being oppressive, Wright continues, Israel saw the law as a "national treasure," a "gift of God's grace and token of God's love," which was given for their good (Deut. 4:1, 40; 6:1–3, 24). It was a "blessing in itself, and the means of enjoying God's continued blessing (Deut. 28:1–14)." To receive the law from God was "a unique privilege, granted to no other nation (Deut. 4:32–34; Ps. 147:19–20)." Israel was urged to obey the law, "not in order to get saved, but because God had already saved them (Deut. 6:20–25)."[38] It is important to recall that in the Old Testament, "law" refers not only to commandments and legislation but to the Pentateuch as a whole, with its narrative as well, all of which served as instruction.[39] Nevertheless, within this

---

37. Wright, *Old Testament Ethics*, 282.
38. Wright, *Old Testament Ethics*, 282.
39. Wright, *Old Testament Ethics*, 283. In this vein, consider many New Testament references to "the Law and the Prophets," denoting two major blocks of Old Testament writings (e.g., Matt. 5:17; 7:12; 11:13; 22:40; Luke 16:16; 24:44; John 1:45; Acts 13:15; 24:14; 28:23; Rom. 3:21).

larger framework, there are large blocks of law in the legal sense of the word, and these were embraced as part of the whole.

The New Testament itself does not disparage the law. Jesus upholds and fulfills the law (Matt. 5:17–20). However his words are interpreted—even if his fulfilling of the law means that his followers no longer "practice" some of it—it is not a rejection of the law. Echoing the psalmist, Paul says that the law is holy and just and good, and even spiritual (Rom. 7:7, 12, 14). Indeed, Paul's argument in Romans 7 demonstrates that the law is not the problem. Sin is the problem, and the law exposes sin. The problem for human beings before the law is that it "pronounces" judgment, yet it is powerless to redeem the sinner. The contrast between law and gospel is that the gospel effects what the law is unable to do (Rom. 8). Those who trust in Jesus and put their faith in him are thus not under the law and fear of its judgment. Again, the law is not the problem. Seeking to keep the law is not the problem. The problem with those in Israel who pursued righteousness through the law is that "they did not pursue it by faith, but as if it were by works" (Rom. 9:32).

The Contrast between Law and Grace

In John Murray's discussion of law and grace, he attempts to describe the contrast between them. First, he notes a sharp distinction between the two, for we are not under the law but under grace (Rom. 6:14). Yet, he argues, that does not mean we are not obligated to keep the commandments of God. To get at the antithesis between law and grace, Murray discusses what the law can and cannot do. It can command and demand, express the will of God, "pronounce" approval for conformity and judgment for infractions, expose and convict of sin, and it "excites and incites" sin. However, the law can do nothing to justify the person who has broken it and has "come under its curse," or "to relieve the bondage of sin." So the one who is "under law" is the one "upon whom only law has been brought to bear."[40] By contrast, the power of the gospel is that it can do precisely what the law could not do, by the grace of God through faith in Jesus Christ and his atoning sacrifice for the forgiveness of sin, to reconcile sinners to God. Thus, for one who already knows the grace and forgiveness of God, the law can be a source of delight.

Further Perspective on the Law

The following brief summary will give some perspective on understanding the purpose and function of law, and help to place the Decalogue, and the law in general, within a framework of Christian ethics.

Uses of the law

Classic treatments note three uses of the law. First, the law convicts of sin and leads the sinner to Christ. Second, the law is able to restrain sin, a function that law serves in society, not only for a person who is inclined to follow the law, but also for the one who would readily break the law if not for the threat of penalties. Third, the law gives

---

40. Murray, *Principles of Conduct*, 184–85.

instruction concerning the will of God. This "third use of the law" is commonly associated with Calvin, in part because Martin Luther only explicitly emphasizes the other two uses. However, practically speaking, Luther also sees the law as fulfilling this function, since he appeals to it regularly in his catechism and other writings. These uses of the law are described in a slightly different way by Bromiley, who asserts that the law is given to Israel to guide the newly liberated people (instruction in the will of God); as a protection against disintegration through self-interest, force, and violence (to restrain sin); and teleologically in relation to the gospel (to point to the need for Christ and to lead people to Christ).[41]

Laws and the law of love

When Jesus is asked which commandment in the law is the greatest, he answers, "Love the Lord your God with all your heart, with all your soul, and with all your mind. This is the greatest and most important command. The second is like it: Love your neighbor as yourself. All the Law and the Prophets depend on these two commands" (Matt. 22:37–40, citing Deut. 6:5 and Lev. 19:18; cf. Mark 12:29–30). It is significant that Jesus offers two commandments, not one. The second is like the first, it is linked to it, as if you cannot have the one without the other, or the first produces the second. What ties the two commandments together is love: love for neighbor flows out of love for God. Further, it is love that ties all the

commandments together; they all depend or hang on love. It is interesting to note that when Jesus identifies the two great commandments, he cites not the Decalogue but Deuteronomy 6:4–5 and Leviticus 19:18. However, that does not diminish the Decalogue. Rather, it reflects its vertical and horizontal dimensions, which outline what love for God and love for neighbor entail (see below). Elsewhere the command to love one's neighbor is tied to the horizontal dimension of the Decalogue. When Jesus is asked which commandments to keep, he cites the fifth through the ninth commandments, and then adds, "and love your neighbor as yourself" (Matt. 19:18–19). Likewise, Paul connects the second half of the Decalogue to love for neighbor (Rom. 13:8–9). What is perhaps surprising in Jesus's teaching is the statement that all the Law and the Prophets depend or hang on love. If love for God and neighbor is evident in the Decalogue, it is not so obvious in some laws. But here Jesus gives us something of an interpretive device. In looking at any given law, we ought to be able to perceive how it depends on love. If the connection is not evident, perhaps the law has not yet been understood. It is the law of love that not only holds together but also produces the other laws.

Discerning the purpose and function of the law

It is not always a simple task, but it is possible, in most cases, to understand the function of a given law in its setting, which

---

41. Bromiley, *God and Marriage*, 18–20.

makes it possible to relate it to our contemporary situation. Laws are not arbitrary tests of obedience, but are given for a reason, and the reason for a given law may be seen by asking questions about how it functions: What conditions does the law promote or prevent? Whose interests does the law protect? Whose power does it restrict? What rights and responsibilities are implied? What behavior does it require? What character trait does it encourage or discourage? What principle does the law embody? Is the law grounded in a particular rationale?[42] In addition to questions like these, we might ask whether the Prophets and other writings clarify or illustrate the purpose of the law. Finally, as we have seen above, it can be asked how the law encourages or protects love for God or neighbor.

By looking carefully at laws in their context, we can begin to see how they might apply in our own context. This task requires seeing analogies between the two contexts. Sometimes the analogy is not immediately clear, due to significant cultural differences. Other times it is fairly direct, because there is a close parallel between the two contexts. Specific laws are often not universal, but may be based on a universal principle. Consider Deuteronomy 22:8, which requires building a "parapet" (ESV, NASB, NIV, RSV) around the roof when a new house is built. What sort of law is this, and what is its moral significance? Houses in the ancient Near East, like many today in parts of the world, had flat roofs, with access to the roof, which was useable space. The parapet is a wall or "railing" (CSB) to protect people from falling off the roof. Thus the text gives the reason for the command: "so that you don't bring bloodguilt on your house if someone falls from it." It is a particular application of the requirement to protect human life, based on the universal principle of the sanctity of human life in the sixth commandment. In places today that have flat roofs that are used by people, it is reasonable to assume that this command has direct application. It makes no sense, however, to require a parapet where roofs have a slope and are not used as living space.

It is not difficult to see other applications. In 1984, while spending some time in Palm Springs, California, I read an article in the paper about a new law that was being debated. It required California residents who owned a pool to build a fence around the pool. The law was the result of the fact that a number of young children had drowned by falling into swimming pools. The law was especially pertinent to Palm Springs residents, since they had among the highest number of pools per capita in the United States. The paper featured a debate about the law. Some thought it was a reasonable measure, to protect human lives that were at risk. Others were upset that they would be forced to build a fence at their own expense on their private property. If they had no children, some felt that it was unfair to

---

42. These are the types of questions offered by Wright in his insightful chapter "Law and the Legal System" (chap. 9) in *Old Testament Ethics*, 323.

require them to protect other people's children, who should not be on their property in the first place. In some cases, in order to meet zoning specifications, the fence could be very expensive. The newspaper noted that there were competing rights, the protection of human life verses the right to privacy and the right for people to do what they want with their own property. In my judgment at the time, both sides made a compelling case, and I was unsure about which side should prevail. It was later that my attention was drawn to the example of the parapet around the roof. The parallel was direct, and in thinking about it, it seemed clear that building a fence around the pool was a reasonable requirement to protect human life.

The Decalogue

One of the reasons for this extended discussion of law in the Old Testament is to appreciate better the nature and function of the law, against the tendency to bristle at the notion of law in contemporary culture. Even the Decalogue, which has special standing not only in biblical ethics but also in the legal tradition of Western civilization is perceived by many as representing the antithesis of grace and freedom. One likely reason for this perspective is that, like much of the law, it is expounded largely in the form of prohibitions. "Thou shall not" is a phrase that often incites a rebellious will. Whatever follows must be oppressive, or at least have the effect of suppressing freedom and joy. In the following pages, I hope to challenge such perceptions of the law by looking more closely at the Decalogue.

Grace precedes the law

Israel's law is given by a gracious, liberating God, and its requirements are part of the covenant relationship between God and Israel (Exod. 34:28). In the giving of the law at Sinai, God reminds Israel of his grace before articulating Israel's obligations, saying, "I am the LORD your God, who brought you out of the land of Egypt, out of the place of slavery" (Exod. 20:2; cf. Deut. 5:6). Israel can trust that God's laws are not oppressive, for God has already shown his grace in rescuing his people: God has not delivered Israel from slavery in Egypt only to enslave them to the law. What is true for Israel is true in general: God's will, expressed in his commands, promotes freedom, not oppression.

The law is grace

In spite of the contrast that is rightly drawn between law and grace, there is a sense in which law itself is grace, or an expression of grace.[43] We have seen how various psalms express this, not only because the law gives necessary instruction for life, but also because Israel was privileged to be given the law among all the nations (Deut. 4:32–34; Ps. 147:19–20). God gives Israel the law not to oppress but to sustain human life and

---

43. John 1:17, "for the law was given through Moses, grace and truth came through Jesus Christ," does not contradict this. Verse 16 says, "we have all received grace after grace." The contrast is that the grace of God in Jesus is superior to the grace in the law, not that the law is without grace. See Schreiner, *40 Questions*, 190.

welfare by restraining sin and encouraging holiness. In a similar way, loving parents give their children rules out of love for them, to protect them from danger. Instead of being a burden, the law establishes conditions in a sinful world within which freedom can be experienced. Jesus said to the teachers of the law, who laid a burden on the people with their Sabbath regulations, "The Sabbath was made for man and not man for the Sabbath" (Mark 2:27). Their regulations had become oppressive, but the Sabbath itself is given for rest and enjoyment.

Prohibitions are least restrictive

Though it is easy to respond negatively to the words "you shall not," in fact, prohibitions are typically less restrictive than positive requirements. In spite of the sometimes negative association of the Decalogue with prohibitions, the restriction on human freedom is minimal. For instance, the "horizontal" dimension demands that we do not murder, commit adultery, steal, bear false witness against our neighbor, and covet. These require a basic minimum, and they restrict freedom very little, in a way that protects human dignity. By contrast, if God had commanded positive requirements toward one's neighbor, to demonstrate love or act toward their good, the list could be endless and thus exceedingly burdensome, fostering resentment rather than love.

Boundaries within which to live and love

Another way to look at it is to see that these commands do not define loving action, but rather set boundaries that mark violations

of love very clearly. It is possible to keep the commandments, as far as external acts are concerned, without truly loving God or neighbor. Consider the seventh commandment, "You shall not commit adultery" (Exod. 20:14 ESV). To break the command is to violate the marriage covenant and break faith with one's spouse. It is an inherently unfaithful and unloving act. However, to keep the command in a minimal way is not to demonstrate love. You cannot be a faithful spouse and commit adultery; on the other hand, you can refrain from adultery and yet be an unfaithful and unloving spouse. In other words, the commandment is not an expression of love so much as a boundary within which to express love. It is possible to keep this and other commands in a formal way without loving God or neighbor. Thus, when the wealthy young man tells Jesus that he has kept the commandments (Matt. 19:20), Jesus does not challenge him on that point. Rather, by telling the young man to give all he has to the poor and follow him, Jesus tests whether he truly loves God (in Jesus) and neighbor, and he exposes the young man's failure on that point. He does not wish to give up what he has to follow Jesus.

Positive (or negative) corollaries of the command are implied

The commands of the Decalogue are minimalist, in themselves requiring very little in terms of specific action. They can be kept formally without actually loving God and neighbor. Indeed, those who truly seek to keep these commands will look beyond (or behind) the explicit statements to the implications for loving God and neighbor. For instance, love for God isn't simply a matter of declaring that there is one God, or refusing to bow before idols, or avoiding the frivolous use of God's name. It leads us to prize God above anything else, to center our lives on God, and to honor and fear God and glorify him in all that we do. To keep the Sabbath (and work) command isn't simply to punch the time clock during the work week and rest and go to church one day a week. It suggests that we are to be industrious, but not a slave to work, to give rest to those in our care, and to trust fully in God by resting in him with confidence that he will provide all of our needs. To honor our parents isn't simply to do what they demand whether we want to or not, but to resist the urge to rebel against them and to respect their authority in our lives and the wisdom that they offer, in spite of their imperfections. Love for neighbor isn't demonstrated merely by refraining from murder, adultery, theft, false witness, and covetousness. Otherwise these commands could be fulfilled by "sheer inactivity," which is "not moral at all."[44] Rather, these commands, driven by love, direct us to protect and promote our neighbor's life and well-being, to be devoted to our spouse and honor other marriages, to work and give to others, to defend and protect the truth and our neighbor's reputation, and to be content with what we have and to delight in the blessings that God has given to others. Specific application and illustration of the broad commands of the Decalogue, in the form of Mosaic case laws, help us to see the particular scope of the commands.

Overarching categories of moral responsibility

To appreciate the Decalogue is to recognize how its minimalist demands on the surface represent vast and broad categories of moral responsibility. David Clyde Jones recognizes and articulates this well. To repeat part of a quotation cited above, he states that the Decalogue represents the will of God concerning "his ordinances of worship, rest, authority, life, sex, property, and communication" (to this list we might add work and desires).[45] These categories represent virtually every area of moral responsibility. It is for this reason, and not because of an emphasis on law, that many Christian ethicists have continued to appeal to the Decalogue in setting out the structure of ethics.

Basic structure of the Decalogue (vertical and horizontal)

As we have seen already, like the double love command of Jesus, the Decalogue has a basic shape that is vertical (love for God) and horizontal (love for neighbor). This shape has long been noticed and exposited. A few examples will serve to draw out certain features of the Decalogue. As illustrated below, Philo understands the first five commandments to be a summary of our service to God, with the last five representing our

44. Kaiser, *Toward Old Testament Ethics,* 83.
45. Jones, *Biblical Christian Ethics*, 116.

service to others. The Westminster Catechism, on the other hand, presents the first four commandments as our duty to God, with the last six representing our duty to others.

Philo

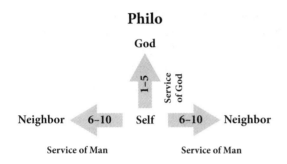

The Westminster Larger Catechism

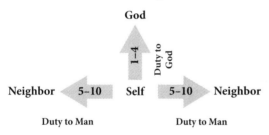

The difference in these two accounts is only slight. Philo may have thought it right to have an equal number of commands governing human relations with God and others. In any case, the command to honor parents seemed fitting to him as a vertical command, for parents reflect God's nature "by begetting particular persons."[46] In the

Westminster Catechism, on the other hand, the fifth command seems rightly placed with the horizontal commands, as parents and children are close "neighbors."

A slightly different version of note is offered by Old Testament scholar Walter Kaiser. Kaiser maintains the basic vertical and horizontal pattern, but shifts the emphasis somewhat by taking note of the grammatical form of the Decalogue as a way of understanding its structure. Including the prologue, he notes, there are three positive statements in the Decalogue, each of which governs what follows:[47]

- Prologue: "I am the LORD your God," therefore, (1) do not worship other gods; (2) do not make idols; (3) do not take God's name in vain.
- (4) "Remember the Sabbath," therefore, do not work on the Sabbath.
- (5) "Honor your father and mother," therefore, (6) do not murder; (7) do not commit adultery; (8) do not steal; (9) do not bear false witness against your neighbor; (10) do not covet.

As a result of following the grammatical structure, the fourth command is distinguished from the first through the third (the vertical dimension) and the fifth through the tenth (the horizontal dimension), though Kaiser does not discuss it in those terms. He does draw attention to the fact that the

---

46. Philo, *On the Decalogue, On the Special Law, On the Virtues, Books 1–3*, trans. H. Colson, Loeb Classical Library (Cambridge, MA: Harvard University Press, 1937), 51.
47. Kaiser, *Toward Old Testament Ethics*, 84. On this structure, Kaiser follows John J. Owens, "Law and Love in Deuteronomy," *Review and Expositor* 61 (1964): 274–83.

fourth command calls people first to rest and cease from work, and then to worship. As such, it seems to point in both horizontal and vertical directions, serving as something of a hinge between the two (see diagram below).

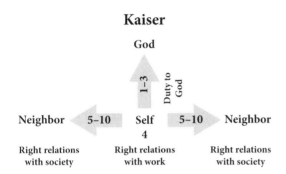

Kaiser

Kaiser's proposal is insightful, particularly if we read into it that the fourth command points in both the vertical and horizontal directions, which I will comment on further below. One of the weaknesses is the way that he casts the commands in terms of "right relations." This is unsatisfying for two reasons. First, "right relations with work" is insufficient for describing the purpose of the fourth commandment. In one sense, this is because it seems to use the term *relation* in a way that is different from the other commandments, which govern personal relationships—that is, relations with some*one*, not a relation to some*thing*. For that reason, "right relations with society" as a heading for the sixth through the tenth commandments is too abstract and thus also insufficient, since

it is not society but people with whom we have relationships. In another sense, "right relations with work" is insufficient because the fourth commandment governs much more than work (though Kaiser should be commended for drawing attention to the fact that work, and not merely Sabbath rest, is addressed in this command). Even if rest, which is most prominent in the commandment, is seen necessarily in relation to work, the heading "right relations with work" does not do justice to the implications for worship or the care for those around us, which are addressed in the fourth commandment.

Second, in more general terms, "right relations" does not quite capture what the commandments establish, even if they are kept formally. As we have seen, to refrain from adultery is a condition necessary to love one's spouse, but it is not sufficient to establish or demonstrate right relations. So, too, not to murder one's neighbor is necessary but not sufficient to have right relations with them. Similarly, it is possible to keep the first three commandments, at least formally, and yet not have right relations with God. Jesus's attacks on the scrupulous religious teachers of his day indicate as much. In fairness, Kaiser might reply that the commandments establish right relations because of all that they imply, in terms of the necessary positive actions and heart condition.[48] Nevertheless, in my view, "right relations" does not best describe what the commandments themselves establish.

---

48. Kaiser, *Toward Old Testament Ethics*, 83.

Spheres of moral responsibility in the Decalogue

If the commandments do not establish right relations, they do establish boundaries that make right relations possible, by guarding personal relationships, and thus communities as well. They are general moral norms, in the form of prohibitions and positive mandates, which govern overarching categories of moral responsibility. The moral norms and boundaries provide conditions within which human beings are called to love God and neighbor, and to discern God's will and purposes for human life. What follows is an account of the structure of the Decalogue and its spheres of moral responsibility, with slight modifications of the above accounts, which describes both a narrow and broad scope for each command.

Vertical dimension—commandments 1–3: establishing spiritual foundations and boundaries within which to love God

First commandment: "Do not have other gods besides me" (Exod. 20:3; cg. Deut. 5:7). The narrow scope here is the object of worship—that is, who or what we worship. This is the internal aspect of worship. Broadly, it is the sphere of ultimate allegiance, or what we prize most in our lives, demonstrated in part by our stewardship of time, money, and talents. It is also demonstrated by what we think about most, about who or where we turn to in our need, and even about what causes anxiety and fear.

Second commandment: "Do not make an idol for yourself" (Exod. 20:4; cf. Deut. 5:8–10). The narrow scope here concerns our manner of worship, or how we worship. It is the external aspect of worship. The broad scope of this commandment concerns God's identity, or how he is represented. God is Creator and Lord, above all creation and material things. To worship created things, or to use them to represent God is to misrepresent God and rob him of the glory that is due God alone.

We ought not to make too sharp a distinction between the internal and external aspects of these two commandments. In the end, if we do not have any god besides God, we will not worship idols, and if we do not worship idols (in the broad sense), we will not have any god besides God. That is why the Jewish, Catholic, and Lutheran understanding of the Decalogue counts these together as one commandment without seeing any difficulty.[49]

Third commandment: "Do not misuse the name of the Lord your God" (Exod. 20:7; cf. Deut. 5:11). Narrowly, this commandment concerns verbal worship,[50] prohibiting frivolous and false invocations of God's name, as implied by the gravity and truth by which God demands his name be invoked (e.g., Deut. 6:13; Ps. 63:11; Jer. 12:16). The broad sphere in this commandment is reverence

---

49. On different accounts, see Ronald Youngblood, "Counting the Ten Commandments," *Biblical Review* 10, no. 6 (December 1994): 30–35, 50, 52; also Jones, *Biblical Christian Ethics*, 104.
50. Kaiser, *Toward Old Testament Ethics*, 87.

for God, his person and authority. This is reflected not merely in speech but also in who we are and what we do. God's people are identified with him—they bear his name—and are called to be holy as he is holy (Lev. 11:44). To act immorally is thus to bear his name falsely and to profane his name (Lev. 18:21; 21:6).

Intersection—commandments 4–5: keeping relationships aligned

Fourth commandment: "Remember the Sabbath day, to keep it holy: You are to labor six days and do all your work, but the seventh day is a Sabbath to the Lord your God" (Exod. 20:8–11; cf. Deut. 5:12–15). This command includes several related areas, and is not easily summarized in the pattern that I have been using. The narrow sphere concerns rest, work, and worship— that is, to expand slightly, it involves our use of time and balance of activities. The broad sphere concerns faith and worship. God prohibits labor on the Sabbath not only for the sake of physical rest (though that is a significant aspect of it), and not even solely for the sake of worship (though that too is significant). There is a vital element of faith in God and his provision that is demonstrated through rest, as the people of Israel learned with God's provision of manna (Exod. 16:11–30). The reason given for the Sabbath in Exodus is that it is a reflection of God's own rest in creation, after he had completed his work (Exod. 20:11). In Deuteronomy, it is grounded in God's

act of liberating the people of Israel from bondage (Deut. 5:15), which may emphasize the aspect of the Sabbath command that requires giving rest to subordinates. The implications of the command to keep the Sabbath are broad, but connected by faith in God: trusting God to provide, not being a slave to work or wealth gained from work, or to building our own kingdom.

Fifth commandment: "Honor your father and your mother" (Exod. 20:12; cf. Deut. 5:16). In this command, the narrow sense is the sphere of family and the integrity of the family structure, including its authority. The broad sphere has to do with authority in a more general sense. A significant aspect of honoring parents has to do with their authority in our lives, and respecting their authority as God-given. Beyond that, just as the command concerns parental authority, it extends to other authorities, such as judges, priests, kings/magistrates, and prophets. As Kaiser notes, "All divinely ordered structures of authority were meant to be embraced in the command to honor one's father and mother."[51]

As indicated by the headings above, I have grouped the fourth and fifth commandments together. One reason for this is that, as already noted, the grammatical structure of the Decalogue includes a shift from prohibitions (1–3), to positive mandates (4–5), back to prohibitions (6–10). There is another reason to group these two commands together. The first three prohibitions relate directly to the vertical dimension of

---

51. Kaiser, *Toward Old Testament Ethics*, 134.

morality—that is, our relationship to God. The last five prohibitions relate directly to the horizontal dimension of morality—that is, our relationships with one another. What about the two mandates in the middle? We have seen that Philo places both with the vertical commands, while the Westminster Catechism considers the fourth to be vertical and the fifth horizontal. Kaiser separates out the fourth commandment, due to the grammatical construction of the Decalogue. It was noted above that the fourth commandment has both vertical and horizontal dimensions. It is vertical in the sense that it is "a Sabbath to the LORD your God," a day for rest and worship, and by ceasing from work it is a demonstration of faith in God and rest in him. It is horizontal in the sense that it prescribes six days of work, and also in that it requires "employers" or heads of households to rest those who work for them, including slaves, and even livestock (Exod. 20:10; Deut. 5:14)!

The fifth command, honoring parents, shares with the fourth not only the positive mandate but also distinct vertical and horizontal dimensions. The horizontal is clear, as parents and children are near neighbors, so it is often placed with the horizontal prohibitions. On the other hand, Philo placed it with the vertical dimension—as service to God. He reasoned that it belongs with the vertical commandments because parents reflect God's nature by begetting children. But there is more to its vertical aspect than that. There is a sense in which this command is vertical because parents are placed by God as authorities in their children's lives *on God's*

behalf. They are appointed by God to teach and discipline their children (Deut. 6; Eph. 6:4) in the ways of the Lord. God is the ultimate authority in our lives, but he has entrusted human beings with carrying out his authority as the direct and immediate source of authority, beginning with parents, who are called to convey and mediate his authority.

Accordingly, the fourth and fifth commandments have in common not only that they both are positive mandates, rather than prohibitions, but also that they have distinct vertical and horizontal dimensions. In this way, the structure of the Decalogue may be seen as follows: commandments 1–3 pertain primarily to the vertical dimension, 6–10 pertain primarily to the horizontal dimension, and 4–5 serve as an intersection between the vertical and horizontal, keeping the two perspectives aligned. This model can be seen like this:

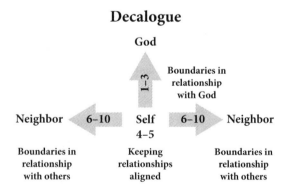

Decalogue

This is simply a way of highlighting certain features of the Decalogue. As with other models, it is not meant to suggest that this is how the people of Israel would have articulated their understanding of the Decalogue (though they may have recognized the features that are highlighted by this model). In addition, it should be said that, as with the other models, this should not be taken to say that the distinction between vertical and horizontal dimensions is rigid. There is a sense, for instance, in which all the commands of the Decalogue are vertical in orientation! To break any of the commands is to sin against God, as Joseph and David both confess (Gen. 39:9; Ps. 51:4). Yet, at the same time, it is consistent with the particular commands to see how they relate directly to one dimension or the other.

Horizontal dimension—commandments 6–10: establishing social foundations and boundaries within which to love[52]

Sixth commandment: "Do not murder" (Exod. 20:13; cf. Deut. 5:17). The narrow sphere of this command is the sacredness of human life and its protection. The keeping of this commandment is necessary for the enjoyment of all God's blessings and purposes in creation. More broadly, it enjoins us to care for and do good to our neighbor.

Seventh commandment: "Do not commit adultery" (Exod. 20:14; Deut. 5:18). Narrowly, this is the sphere of marriage. The prohibition of adultery is a necessary boundary for marriage to serve its God-given purposes. More broadly, this commandment is about the sphere of sexuality in general. The integrity of marriage and of sexuality is broken by adultery and all sexual immorality. The seventh commandment serves as a heading for particular commands governing sexuality, including prohibitions of fornication, incest, rape, and homosexuality.

Eighth commandment: "Do not steal" (Exod. 20:15; cf. Deut. 5:19). The narrow sphere of this commandment governs property rights, affirming and protecting ownership. The broad sphere concerns economics, for the prohibition of theft extends beyond personal property rights to the integrity of trade and commerce, and work itself. It is the norm that grounds specific laws regarding payment of wages (Lev. 19:11–13), just weights (Deut. 25:13–16), boundary markers (Deut. 19:14), loans (Deut. 24:10–13), interest (Exod. 22:25), and other economic activities.[53]

Ninth commandment: "Do not give false testimony against your neighbor" (Exod. 20:16; cf. Deut. 5:20). The narrow sphere of this commandment is the sanctity of truth. Telling the truth is necessary if we are to have integrity of speech. This reality highlights the broader sphere of the ninth commandment, which is communication. The ability to communicate (through speech, writing, or other forms) is precious, and it depends on the expectation that the truth is told. Any falsehood or deception breaks down communication and community. Thus Jesus says simply, "let your 'yes' mean 'yes,' and your 'no' mean 'no'" (Matt. 5:37). This is

---

52. What follows is a very brief exposition, aspects of which will be developed in more detail throughout the rest of this book.
53. For further examples, see the figure above, on Calvin's exposition of the eighth commandment.

particularly significant when it comes to an accusation or defense of one's neighbor.

Tenth commandment: "Do not covet" (Exod. 20:17; cf. Deut. 5:20). Narrowly, this command concerns the sphere of desire. As such, the tenth commandment is much more personal and private than the other horizontal commands (since desires, unlike overt acts, cannot be observed), though it has clear implications for the others, since wrongful acts are preceded by wrongful desires. The broad sphere of the tenth commandment relates to contentment, for coveting springs from dissatisfaction with God's provision in our lives. While the New Testament gives greater attention to desire, as we shall see, it is extremely significant that the prohibition of wrongful desires occurs here in the Decalogue. It is part of the covenant between God and Israel.

Conclusion

Much more could be said about each of the individual commands in the Decalogue than is possible in the brief survey above. The goal has been simply to describe something of its overall structure and its broad (and narrow)

scope. If we can get beyond a distaste for commands, perhaps we will be able to appreciate the Decalogue more fully, without the worry that such an appreciation will drag us back under the law. We may be able to see beauty in the remarkable scope of human life that is taken up in this succinct covenant code with its overarching categories of moral responsibility. We may even be taken further. Far from being a set of repressive laws, it may be possible to see the Decalogue as liberating. As a gracious and loving Father, God commands a sinful people to abstain from acts and attitudes that are destructive of self and others. Indeed, each of the commandments governs and protects precious gifts from God: supremely, God himself, followed by gifts of work, rest, family/leaders, life, sex/marriage, property, communication, and desires. To abuse these gifts by disregarding God's commandments for their use is to become enslaved. To protect these gifts and to use them properly is to experience the blessing of God and to avoid disintegration of the communities to which we belong. It is also to glorify God as his image bearers, and to bring God's blessing to others.

Select Resources

Cameron, Andrew J. B. *Joined-Up Life: A Christian Account of How Ethics Works.* Nottingham, UK: Inter-Varsity Press, 2011.

Frame, John. *The Doctrine of the Christian Life.* Phillipsburg, NJ: P&R, 2008.

Jones, David Clyde. *Biblical Christian Ethics.* Grand Rapids: Baker, 1994.

Kaiser, Walter C., Jr. *Toward Old Testament Ethics.* Grand Rapids: Zondervan, 1983.

Rooker, Mark F. *The Ten Commandments: Ethics for the Twenty-First Century.* NAC Studies in Bible and Theology 7. Nashville: B&H Academic, 2010.

Schreiner, Thomas R. *40 Questions About Christians and Biblical Law.* Grand Rapids: Kregel, 2010.

Wright, Christopher J. H. *Old Testament Ethics for the People of God.* Downers Grove, IL: IVP Academic, 2004.

CHAPTER 5

ASPECTS OF BIBLICAL ETHICS: NEW TESTAMENT

Then Jesus came near and said to them, "All authority has been given to me in heaven and on earth. Go, therefore, and make disciples of all nations, baptizing them in the name of the Father and of the Son and of the Holy Spirit, teaching them to observe everything I have commanded you. And remember, I am with you always, to the end of the age."

—Matthew 28:18–20

Love the Lord your God with all your heart, with all your soul, and with all your mind. This is the greatest and most important command. The second is like it: Love your neighbor as yourself. All the Law and the Prophets depend on these two commands.

—Matthew 22:37–40

Introduction

In their book, *Kingdom Ethics*, Glen Stassen and David Gushee assert that Christian ethics has too often neglected or diminished its most obvious resource: the teachings of Jesus himself, particularly in the Sermon on the Mount, which is the largest block of Jesus's teaching.[1] If their assessment is correct, this is indeed a critical exclusion. In Matthew's Gospel, Jesus's parting charge to his disciples—the Great Commission—is to make disciples, *teaching them to observe everything that he commanded*. Surely the teaching of Jesus must not be neglected in Christian ethics. There may be various reasons for such neglect: an interest in the philosophical or doctrinal elements of Christian ethics, or in the teaching of Paul, or one of the other New Testament writers. It may be valid for a particular study of Christian ethics to focus on one of these, even over a focus on the Sermon on the Mount or other teachings of Jesus. However, Stassen and Gushee are right to call attention to this Great Omission, for the person, work, and teaching of Jesus must be central to Christian ethics, and other interests must not take precedence over Jesus himself.

On the other hand, there are several caveats that should be made with regard to focusing on the teaching of Jesus. First, it is possible to focus on the person and teaching of Jesus yet in the process distort Christian ethics by pitting Jesus against Paul, for example (or against the Old Testament), asserting that we must follow Jesus (instead of Paul). To do so is to create a false opposition between Jesus and Paul, and it typically distorts Jesus's teaching. Someone might argue that Paul condemns homosexuality, but nowhere does Jesus do so; instead, Jesus preaches love and forgiveness, and he accepts everyone just as we are. Therefore we ought to reject Paul's view and accept homosexuality. Yet this is a distortion of Jesus's teaching, and of biblical teaching as a whole, and thus of Christian ethics. It represents an inadequate view of biblical theology and hermeneutics, leading to a truncated view of Christian ethics.

This raises a second point: it is possible to focus on Jesus's teaching and yet distort Christian ethics by effectively creating a canon within a canon, neglecting large swaths of biblical teaching.[2] What Jesus has to say is critically important. Yet he did not say everything that needs to be said in Christian ethics, or about being his disciple. For one thing, he did not intend for us to discard the Old Testament— the entire Scriptures that he knew and taught—and we must consider its teaching carefully, especially since Jesus does not address every issue in the Old Testament. In addition, Jesus declares that, after he is gone, he will send the Spirit to remind

---

1. Glen H. Stassen and David P. Gushee, *Kingdom Ethics: Following Jesus in Contemporary Context* (Downers Grove, IL: InterVarsity Press, 2003), xi–xii.
2. Stassen and Gushee do not commit this error; while centering on Jesus's teaching, they utilize a broad spectrum of Scripture, both Old and New Testaments.

the disciples what he has said and to teach them all things (John 14:26). The writings of Paul, Peter, James, and other New Testament letters are part of the outworking of Jesus's promise, as the Holy Spirit brings the teaching of Jesus to bear on the growing church. This is necessary, in part, because Jesus taught primarily within a Jewish context, as reflected in the Gospels, while New Testament writers address a wide variety of situations in which the Holy Spirit instructs the church, including understanding Jewish laws in relation to gentile believers. What is implicit in Jesus's teaching is made explicit elsewhere in the New Testament. Both the Old Testament and the letters of the New Testament help to clarify and fill out Jesus's teaching. This is similar to the way that Christian doctrine, such as Christology, the Trinity, ecclesiology, or eschatology, must attend carefully to Jesus's teaching but will necessarily incorporate the teachings of the Bible as a whole. Christian theology and ethics are developed by attention to all of Scripture, and not only by the words Jesus spoke in the flesh. As 2 Timothy 3:16–17 declares, "All Scripture is inspired by God and is profitable for teaching, for rebuking, for correcting, for training in righteousness, so that the man of God may be complete, equipped for every good work."

Third, it is possible to focus on Jesus's teaching and yet distort Christian ethics by neglecting the moral implications of Christian doctrine. We may draw ethical conclusions from the doctrine of creation, or of sin, or of the incarnation, or the cross, or eschatology, which are not explicit in Jesus teaching. Of course, the doctrine itself will (or ought to be) shaped by Jesus's teaching, and thus incorporate what Jesus said, yet biblical theology will shape our view of many things that Jesus never spoke about, such as reproductive technology, cloning, contraception, transgender surgery, and so on. In many cases, Jesus's own teaching on creation or sin or other doctrines provides a pattern to follow. Yet, in other cases, we may need to draw implications from Christian doctrine that Jesus's teaching does not clearly address. Whether or not we recognize it, theology determines ethics. Christian ethics must seek to clarify what otherwise might be neglected if it is derived from Jesus's teaching alone.

In this chapter, I will highlight a select number of important themes from New Testament ethics. In order to constrain the length, these themes will focus primarily on the teaching of Jesus in the Gospels and the teaching of Paul. Other New Testament writings are also important, and some will be touched on in this chapter and elsewhere in this book, but Jesus and Paul represent the largest blocks of ethical teachings in the New Testament, so it is proper to give particular attention to what they have to say. In addition, as indicated above, it is instructive to include Paul because he brings the gospel to bear on relationships within the new Gentile churches, and what it means to live in a manner worthy of the Lord.

Jesus's Person, Work, and Teaching: The Center of New Testament Ethics

The Person and Work of Jesus in Relation to Ethics

The teaching of Jesus is central for Christian ethics not simply because Jesus was a great teacher. There are other great teachers, others who can captivate audiences with their stories, others who command a certain authority by their manner and their message. Yet none can claim what is true of Jesus. The reason that the teaching of Jesus is central is because of his identity: the Christ, the Son of God (Matt. 16:16 and parallels; cf. Matt. 3:17, 17:5; Luke 3:22); the Son of Man (Mark 14:62); the Word of God (John 1:1); the Bread of Life (John 6:35); the Light of the world (John 8:12); the I Am (John 8:58); the Good Shepherd (John 10:11); the Resurrection and the Life (Jn11:25); Teacher and Lord (John 13:13); the Way, the Truth, and the Life (John 14:6); the True Vine (John 15:1). The authority of Jesus and his teaching is grounded in his person and work. Here it is possible only to outline a few key aspects of Jesus's person and work, with implications for ethics.[3]

A Christocentric universe

The christological hymn in Colossians 1 makes staggering claims about Jesus:

He is the image of the invisible God,
the firstborn over all creation.
For everything was created by him,
in heaven and on earth,
the visible and the invisible,
whether thrones or dominions
or rulers or authorities—
all things have been created through him
    and for him.
He is before all things,
and by him all things hold together.
He is also the head of the body, the church;
he is the beginning,
the firstborn from the dead,
so that he might come to have
first place in everything.
For God was pleased to have
all his fullness dwell in him,
and through him to reconcile
everything to himself,
whether things on earth or things in heaven,
by making peace
through his blood, shed on the cross. (Col. 1:15–20)

Jesus Christ is not merely the long-awaited Messiah anticipated by Israel. He is the very image of God, Creator and Lord of the universe, who holds all things together. He is the head of the church. He is the firstborn from the dead, in whom the fullness of God dwells, and through whom God has acted to reconcile everything to himself and make

---

3. For a significant treatment of the theological and christological basis for Christian ethics centered on the resurrection of Jesus, see Oliver O'Donovan, *Resurrection and Moral Order: An Outline for Evangelical Ethics*, 2nd ed. (Grand Rapids, Eerdmans, 1994 [1986]). For a recent work in Christian ethics that centers on the person, work, and teaching of Jesus, see Andrew J. B. Cameron, *Joined-Up Life: A Christian Account of How Ethics Works* (Nottingham, UK: Inter-Varsity Press, 2011).

peace. This description of Jesus is "breath-taking," as Andrew Cameron puts it, for "it pictures a 'Christ-powered' planet, where 'everything' and 'all things' find a secure home in one who cares for everything and for all things—including *people like us*, who once were alienated and alone (Col. 1:21–22)."[4]

Such a description of the Messiah was not obvious from the Old Testament and its prophecies. It was revealed to Jesus's followers gradually through their experience with him in his authoritative teaching, claims about himself, authenticating miracles, sacrificial death, and especially by his resurrection, all of which were finally realized through the witness of the Holy Spirit. The New Testament writers make it clear that such claims about Jesus are not simply a set of new religious dogma but a startling message of good news that completely transforms perspectives, hearts, minds, and the way those who understand the good news will live. Jesus is not merely to be added to an existing ethical system to make it better, like icing on a cake. He is not simply an element that is added to the environment; he holds the environment together. Jesus is at the center of Christian ethics because Jesus is the center of everything.

More than followers

Jesus calls people to follow him in radical obedience, in some cases leaving behind their families, their occupations, and their comfort. The Gospel of Mark especially highlights the unequivocal call of Jesus. He calls Simon and Andrew as the two brothers are casting their net into the sea, and *immediately* they leave their nets and follow Jesus (Mark 1:16–18). Similarly, he calls the brothers James and John, sons of Zebedee, who leave their father and his servants in the boat and *immediately* follow Jesus (Mark 1:19–20). To follow Jesus is costly, for he takes priority over human relationships and life itself (Matt. 10:34–39; 8:21–22). Dietrich Bonhoeffer challenges an easy discipleship characterized by cheap grace that requires merely believing certain things and accepting God's favor, saying, "When Christ calls a man, he bids him come and die."[5] Following Jesus requires total commitment. Many follow Jesus when it suits them, but fall away or even turn against him when it does not. Indeed, many people "follow" a leader, a teacher, a coach, or a sports team with much enthusiasm, as long as it serves their purposes. Following Jesus means something more than that. Cameron points out that the metaphor of following Jesus is not used by later New Testament writers. Perhaps it is because being a follower is "an *insufficient* metaphor to describe Christ's impact upon our identity. The apostles prefer to describe people as being 'in Christ.'"[6] To be "in Christ" is to be identified with him in his life, death, and resurrection. It is to be

---

4. Cameron, *Joined-Up Life*, 84.
5. Dietrich Bonhoeffer, *The Cost of Discipleship* (London: SCM, 1959), 79. The title in the original German for this work translates simply as "Discipleship."
6. Cameron, *Joined-Up Life*, 95.

connected to Jesus as a branch to a vine, and without such a connection it is impossible to bear fruit (John 15:4–5). It is not merely to call Jesus "Lord," but to do God's will (Matt. 7:21); yet it is not merely to keep certain commandments, in order to secure favor for oneself, but it is to treasure Jesus above all earthly things (Matt. 19:16–22).[7]

The cross and resurrection

The cross is central for Christian ethics, as it is central to the mission of Jesus. So, Richard Hays contends, it is one of the focal images that emerges in the New Testament, calling Christians to sacrificial service and suffering for others.[8] Christian ethics cannot simply be the affirmation of contemporary culture with the adornment of Christian theology. The cross challenges human thinking, inverts power structures, and transforms religion and morality. The cross confronts human beings with the seriousness of sin and challenges complacency with (sinful) human nature. "The death of Christ rejects our regular way of being human," Cameron argues, such as the destructive patterns of behavior described by Paul in 1 Corinthians 6:9–11, including greed, drunkenness, and sexual immorality, which are normative in our culture. He continues, "I may view these practices as routine; but the immensity of Christ's action against them alerts me that in fact, all is not well."[9]

On the cross, Jesus condemns not only sinful behavior but also any attempt at self-justification through a moral life (Eph. 2:8–10). Moreover, rather than putting sinful human beings in a hopeless situation, the cross is a noticeboard on which is posted a cancellation of the debt that was owed as a legal demand because of sin (Col. 2:14). Jesus makes true life and freedom possible through his death on the cross, reconciling people to one another and to God (Col. 1:20; cf. Eph. 2:11–22). That new life and freedom purchased on the cross produces a transformation and new patterns of behavior, calling for humility, service to others, kindness, compassion, forgiveness, and reconciliation.[10] The cross does not stand alone, but is closely tied to the resurrection, for Jesus's mission, and in particular his death on the cross for human sin, is vindicated by his resurrection, the defeat of death itself. Those who identify with Jesus in death, and die to sin, are raised to new life on the basis of Jesus's resurrection (Rom. 6:5; cf. Phil. 3:10–11). Christian hope is grounded in the resurrection (1 Cor. 15:17), and that hope transforms our perspective and our action now. For instance, Paul reasons that if God has purchased human beings by the death of Jesus on the cross, and if God will raise up those who identify with Christ in his death and resurrection, then it matters what we do

---

7. On the theme of treasuring Jesus above all else, see John Piper, *What Jesus Demands from the World* (Wheaton, IL: Crossway, 2006).
8. Richard B. Hays, *The Moral Vision of the New Testament: Community, Cross, New Creation; A Contemporary Introduction to New Testament Ethics* (San Francisco: HarperSanFrancisco, 1996).
9. Cameron, *Joined-Up Life*, 103.
10. Such themes are prevalent in the New Testament, grounded in the cross. See, e.g., Phil. 2:1–11; Eph. 4, esp. v. 32.

with our bodies now (1 Cor. 6:12–20; cf. 1 Cor. 15:12–34; Col. 3:1).

The Teaching of Jesus in Relation to Ethics

The authority of Jesus and his teaching

The issue of authority is central to ethics. Ethical authority may be grounded in the person or office of the one who commands, or in the veracity of the teaching itself, or all of these. Each of the Gospels, and the rest of the New Testament, makes it clear that Jesus has authority and that he teaches with authority. Note several aspects of Jesus's authority. First, the authority of Jesus is unique. As the text from Colossians declares, Jesus has authority over all dominions and rulers and lesser authorities because he created all things, he existed before all things, and he holds all things together (cf. Eph. 1:20–23). The authority of Jesus is unique because, as the Son of God and Messiah, Jesus is unique. He is thus able to make astounding, yet legitimate, authoritative claims. At the beginning of his ministry, Jesus enters the synagogue in his home town of Nazareth, and reads from Isaiah, claiming that the Spirit has anointed him in fulfillment of Isaiah's prophecy (Luke 4:16–21). Toward the end of his ministry, he tells his disciples that after the great tribulation, the Son of Man will come "with great power and glory" (Mark 13:26). No one else could legitimately claim the authority that Jesus does. Jesus claims to fulfill the Law and the Prophets (Matt. 5:17), and to offer a definitive interpretation of the law and tradition by saying, "You have heard . . . but I tell you" (Matt. 5:21–48). He claims to be Lord of the Sabbath (Matt. 12:8; Mark 2:28; Luke 6:5), and even to have the authority to forgive sins (Mark 2:10). The uniqueness of Jesus is also attested at the transfiguration, when the disciples hear a voice from heaven saying, "This is my beloved Son. . . . Listen to him" (Matt. 17:5; cf. Luke 9:35; Mark 9:7). His power as the Son of God gives him authority over nature (Mark 4:41 and parallels), and authority to raise the dead (Jairus's daughter, Mark 5:21–23, 35–42; the son of a widow in Nain, Luke 7:11–17; and Lazarus, John 11:38–44).

Second, Jesus grounds his authoritative teaching in Scripture. Against those who might have charged him with undermining the authority of Scripture, Jesus declares that he has not come to abolish the Law and the Prophets but to fulfill them (Matt. 5:17). When the Pharisees and scribes ask why Jesus breaks with their tradition—again, an issue of authority—Jesus answers with an appeal to Scripture itself, asking them why they break God's commandments for the sake of their tradition (Matt. 15:1–6). He challenges traditions and teachings that undermine Scripture. As another example, some Pharisees test Jesus by asking him whether divorce is lawful (Mark 10:2–12; cf. Matt. 19:3–9). The ensuing debate is about how to interpret Scripture. The Pharisees assert that Moses permitted divorce (Mark 10:4). Jesus acknowledges that, but declares that it was because of their hardness of heart. He then appeals to Genesis 1–2 to demonstrate the will of God in creation, and his purpose for marriage, which is permanence (Mark 10:6–9; Gen. 1:27; 2:24)—that is, he appeals to Scripture to answer the question about divorce in the law.

Third, the authority of Jesus and his teaching is recognized by the crowds and even, implicitly, by the teachers who were opposed to him. Early in his ministry when Jesus taught in the city of Capernaum on the Sabbath, Luke comments that the people "were astonished at his teaching because his message had authority" (Luke 4:32). There was something about Jesus's teaching that resonated deeply with the people. Luke's comment implies that it was something they were not accustomed to. What Luke implies Matthew and Mark make plain. At the end of the Sermon on the Mount, Matthew comments, "When Jesus finished these sayings, the crowds were astonished at his teaching, for he was teaching them as one who had authority, *and not as their scribes*" (Matt. 7:28–29 ESV, emphasis added; cf. Mark 1:22, 27). John draws this point out further. After Jesus taught in the temple area, John writes, "Then the Jews were amazed and said, 'How is this man so learned, since he hasn't been trained?'" (John 7:15). Jesus responds by telling them that his teaching is not his, but it comes from God (John 7:16–17).

Fourth, Jesus grounds the commissioning of his disciples in his authority. At the end of Matthew's Gospel, Jesus tells his disciples that he is sending them out to "make disciples of all nations," a daunting task for this small group of followers, which includes teaching new disciples to obey everything Jesus commanded them. Thus, to strengthen them for the task, Jesus tells them that "all authority has been given to me in heaven and on earth" (Matt. 28:18), and he promises them that he will be with them to the end of the age (Matt. 28:20). That is, it is on the basis of Jesus's authority, and his continuing presence with them, that he sends them into the world to make disciples and to teach them to obey.

The kingdom of God

The kingdom of God is a central focus of Jesus's teaching, with significant application and implications for ethics. The Gospel of Mark tells us that at the start of his ministry, Jesus announced that "the kingdom of God has come near. Repent and believe the good news" (Mark 1:15), connecting the coming of the kingdom with the gospel. Of course, God is already king, and his reign is over all creation. Yet there is a future sense of the fulfillment and consummation of God's kingdom, since those who reject his reign remain in the present age. In the Old Testament, for example, it is clear that God is ruler over all (e.g., Ps. 22:28; 103:19), and yet his comprehensive reign can still be anticipated as a future, longed-for event (Zech. 14:9). Thus, when Jesus announces that the kingdom of God has come near, he may be understood to be declaring that the God who is sovereign over all of creation is "about to establish that sovereignty in a newly effective way."[11]

---

11. R. T. France, "Kingdom of God," in *Dictionary for Theological Interpretation of the Bible*, eds. Kevin J. Vanhoozer et al. (Grand Rapids: Baker Academic, 2005), 421.

That the kingdom of God (or heaven, used by Matthew) has come near in the teaching and work of Jesus doesn't mean that it has come in its fullness; though it is present in a new way, there remains a "not yet" aspect. In Jesus's ministry, the kingdom of God has come, illustrated by Jesus driving out demons by the power of the Spirit (Matt. 12:28). His death and resurrection mark the certain and decisive victory over sin and death, yet the complete and total reign of God and the elimination of those who reject his reign remains to be realized in the future.

Several things stand out about the kingdom in Jesus's parables. First, it is of utmost value, worth giving up everything else for it (Matt. 13:44–46). Second, the message of the kingdom evokes a response either of acceptance or rejection (Matt. 13:3–9, 18–23), and there is a secret quality to it, so that Jesus's parables are understood only by those with eyes to see and ears to hear (Matt. 13:10–17). Third, in the present age, while the kingdom is "now and not yet," heirs of the kingdom and rebels are intermixed, like wheat and weeds (Matt. 13:24–29, 36–43), or "good" and "worthless" fish that are caught in a net (Matt. 13:47–49). In the end they will be separated, and the weeds or worthless fish will be thrown out. Fourth, the kingdom is small, but it is growing and it has a permeating effect, like the tiny mustard seed that grows into a large tree (Matt. 13:31–32), or like a small amount of yeast that spreads through a large amount of flour (Matt. 13:33). Though God has given people the responsibility to plant the seed, it is God who causes the seed to grow, "secretly away from human observation."[12] (Mark 4:26–29).

The Sermon on the Mount: the Kingdom of God and Righteousness

Jesus taught about the kingdom not only in parables but also in the Sermon on the Mount, which could be described as "a manifesto for life in the kingdom of heaven,"[13] as long as that does not signify that the way of life described by Jesus is meant only or primarily for the future kingdom. In this block of Jesus's teaching, certain aspects of the kingdom stand out, including an inversion of the significance of social status, God's concern for the downtrodden, and a call to true righteousness. The significance of the Sermon on the Mount for Christian ethics is difficult to overstate. Indeed, as one New Testament scholar put it, "No other short section of the Bible has been more prominent in theological discussion and in the general life of the church."[14] Even more strongly put, "It is quite simply the most celebrated discourse by Jesus of Nazareth, the incarnate Word. . . . Its influence runs through the centuries like a majestic

12. France, "Kingdom of God," 421.
13. France, "Kingdom of God," 421.
14. G. N. Stanton, "Sermon on the Mount/Plain," in *Dictionary of Jesus and the Gospels*, eds. Joel B. Green, Scot McKnight, and I. Howard Marshall (Downers Grove, IL: InterVarsity Press, 1992), 735.

river, giving life to new crops everywhere it goes."[15] As such, the points highlighted below are only a few of the key themes for ethics that are representative of Jesus's teaching, and additional aspects will be discussed as they relate to relevant issues in the chapters that follow.[16]

The Beatitudes

The Sermon on the Mount begins with a declaration of good news for the downtrodden, for its first section—the Beatitudes—opens and closes with the announcement that the kingdom of heaven belongs to the most unlikely candidates: the poor in Spirit (Matt. 5:3; "poor" in Luke 6:20), and those who are persecuted for righteousness (v. 10). Rather than belonging to those with honor, position, and wealth, the kingdom of God belongs to those who know their need of God and are humble before him. It belongs to those who mourn, the gentle, those who hunger and thirst for righteousness, the merciful, the pure in heart, the persecuted. Its message is captured in Luke 4:18–19, where Jesus announces the fulfillment of Isaiah's prophecy, that he is anointed by the Spirit to "preach good news to the poor . . . to proclaim release to the captives and recovery of sight to the blind, to set free the oppressed, to proclaim the year of the Lord's favor" (cf. Isa. 61:1–2).

The Beatitudes show vividly that God's kingdom is countercultural. Those who are blessed by God do not pursue the things that are valued by others. The Beatitudes emphasize the formation of virtue and true righteousness, a theme that Jesus develops throughout the sermon, something for which his followers should hunger and thirst (Matt. 5:6), and for which they will be persecuted and insulted (vv. 10–11). The Beatitudes thus acknowledge the suffering that Jesus's followers will experience. Yet, in spite of their hardships, Jesus calls them blessed. How is it that those who are downtrodden and persecuted can be considered blessed? It is because they know God and are the heirs of God's kingdom. As Paul says of sufferings, this "momentary light affliction is producing for us an absolutely incomparable eternal weight of glory" (2 Cor. 4:17). Elsewhere he declares that his *goal* is "to know him and the power of his resurrection *and the fellowship of his sufferings*," so that he will "reach the resurrection from among the dead" (Phil. 3:10–11).

Hence, the Greek term μακάριοι, sometimes translated "happy," carries a sense of blessing, as it "expresses the happiness which is the result of God-given salvation."[17] The Beatitudes reveal God's concern for the downtrodden, with the comfort that God will reverse their position and they will

---

15. Timothy Larsen, introduction to *The Sermon on the Mount through the Centuries: From the Early Church to John Paul II*, eds. Jeffrey P. Greenman, Timothy Larsen, and Stephen R. Spencer (Grand Rapids: Brazos, 2007), 13.
16. For fuller development, see Stassen and Gushee, *Kingdom Ethics*; Bonhoeffer, *Cost of Discipleship*; Greenman, et al, *Sermon on the Mount*; Charles Quarles, *The Sermon on the Mount: Restoring Christ's Message to the Modern Church* (Nashville: B&H Academic, 2011); D. A. Carson, *The Sermon on the Mount: An Exposition of Matthew 5–7* (Grand Rapids: Baker, 1978).
17. Stanton, "Sermon on the Mount/Plain," 741.

be rewarded in heaven. They highlight the fact that God's kingdom is so valuable; it is worth giving up everything to obtain it (cf. Matt. 13:44–46). The blessings of the Beatitudes are grounded in an eschatological perspective, for while Jesus's followers belong to God's kingdom even now, their full inheritance awaits a future fulfillment. That is something on which Jesus's disciples are to set their hope (cf. Col. 1:5).

Salt and light: metaphors of impact

Following the Beatitudes, Jesus says that his disciples are the salt of the earth (Matt. 5:13) and the light of the world (v. 14). It is not something they are becoming; they *are* salt and light, which has implications for their mission.[18] As salt, they are to have a profound influence on society, to be a preservative. Though they are small and weak and powerless by the world's measure, they have an influence on all of society, just as a small amount of salt seasons and preserves. To be heralds of God's kingdom and bring the good news to all people, Jesus's followers must be the sort of people Jesus describes in the Beatitudes. If they fail to be God's people and to do God's will, they are like salt that has lost its taste, and thus its purpose, and is "no longer good for anything but to be thrown out and trampled under people's feet" (Matt. 5:13).

Similarly, by virtue of who they are, their actions and their message, followers of Jesus are light in a dark world. This metaphor works slightly differently. The salt metaphor

indicates that Christians are to be a part of society, mixing with and influencing all those around them, almost without notice. The light metaphor indicates that there is clarity and purpose in the mission of those who follow Jesus, something that is clearly noticed by others. "A city situated on a hill cannot be hidden" (Matt. 5:14). Jesus's followers are light, and light cannot be hidden, especially in the darkness. What is more, to hide the light is to deny its very purpose, which is why "no one lights a lamp and puts it under a basket" (v. 15). In this sense, Jesus's followers cannot just "blend in" and go unnoticed in a world that is hostile to God, whether to avoid persecution or to pursue worldly pleasures. Instead, just as a lamp is set up to give light to everyone around, Jesus says, "let your light shine before others, so that they may see your good works and give glory to your Father in heaven" (v. 16). That is, as people see Jesus's followers practicing true righteousness, they will be blessed and they will glorify God. Thus Jesus lays out the tension that comes with the gospel: as the Beatitudes indicate, some will despise and persecute Jesus's followers, and ultimately reject God; yet others will rejoice and glorify God. In either case, Jesus's followers are to be salt and light.

Righteousness and the law

The large middle block of the Sermon on the Mount, from 5:17 to 7:12, opens and closes with references to the Law and the Prophets.

---

18. Bonhoeffer, *Cost of Discipleship*, 105–6; Christopher Bryan, "Sermon on the Mount," in Vanhoozer et al., *Dictionary for Theological Interpretation*, 737.

From 5:17 to 6:18, emphasis is given to true righteousness. The section from 6:19 to 7:11 may roughly follow the Lord's Prayer, guiding disciples in faithful living.[19] Space does not allow an exposition of the entire sermon; instead, it will only be possible to highlight some key features of 5:17–6:18 as it pertains to Christian ethics, highlighting the nature of righteousness and obedience to God's will to which Jesus calls his disciples.

Jesus fulfills the law

Against those who might charge him with disregarding the law, Jesus says, "Don't think that I came to abolish the Law or the Prophets. I did not come to abolish but to fulfill. For truly I tell you, until heaven and earth pass away, not the smallest letter or one stroke of a letter will pass away from the law until all things are accomplished" (Matt. 5:17–18). It is clear enough that the law matters to Jesus, and that it has lasting significance. It is not as clear what Jesus means by saying that he came to fulfill the law. On the one hand, some argue that Jesus's emphasis on the smallest letter or even stroke of a letter means that he affirms the law completely. Others, though, argue against such a view on the basis of Jesus's own actions and teaching, the place of the law in biblical theology, and especially Paul's statements on the law. In this view, the law is fulfilled in Jesus himself, so that "the law remains valid only *until all things come to pass* [or "all things are accomplished"] in

Jesus' coming and ministry."[20] An extended discussion of this challenging issue cannot be pursued here. However, it does not seem best to interpret Jesus's fulfillment of the law to mean that it is no longer valid after Jesus's ministry. While that could fit with "until all things are accomplished," there seems to be emphasis on the enduring validity of the law, in some way, beyond Jesus's ministry. First, Jesus says that the law remains, "until heaven and earth pass away." Second, he says, "whoever breaks one of the least of these commands and teaches others to do the same will be called least in the kingdom of heaven. But whoever does and teaches these commands will be called great in the kingdom of heaven" (v. 19). There is no indication that this applies only during his ministry, and it does not appear to refer to Jesus's own teaching in contrast to the law. Rather, in Matthew 5:21–48 (and following), Jesus contrasts external "righteousness" with true righteousness, which shows the intention of the law.

You have heard ... but I tell you: beyond "righteous acts" to true righteousness

A high demand. Just before Jesus begins a series of contrasts, teaching the way of righteousness for his followers (Matt. 5:21–48), he says to his disciples, "Unless your righteousness surpasses that of the scribes and Pharisees, you will never get into the kingdom of heaven" (v. 20). This is a difficult saying, for more than one reason. First, the stakes

19. Cf. Stanton, "Sermon on the Mount/Plain," 740.
20. Robert A. Guelich, *The Sermon on the Mount: A Foundation for Understanding* (Waco, TX: Word, 1982), 148.

are very high—entrance into the kingdom of heaven. Second, the requirement is very high—Jesus refers to the scribes and Pharisees not because they were pretentious snobs (though some may have been). That would render his statement unremarkable and set the bar low, effectively saying, "Don't be pompous and you will enter heaven." Rather, he uses the scribes and Pharisees as a standard because of their reputation for scrupulous righteousness in relation to the law. Whatever else might be said about them, they were keepers and enforcers of the law. Jesus's statement is striking particularly because he declares that the righteousness required for entrance into the kingdom of heaven is greater than that of the very people whose righteousness is seemingly impeccable.

The disciples and the listening crowd—including perhaps some scribes and Pharisees—must have wondered how the demand for righteousness could be more stringent. Having created a seemingly impossible demand, and having gained everyone's attention, Jesus goes on to show that their righteous acts are not sufficient to fulfill the requirement of righteousness that God seeks. The Pharisees are concerned to impress people (and perhaps God) with their righteous acts and adherence to the law, but they are hypocrites (Matt. 6:2, 5, 16). They look good on the outside, and they sound impressive, but inside they are corrupt and full of greed, hypocrisy, and lawlessness (cf. Matt. 23:5, 25–28). In their detailed casuistry, they fail to keep what the law truly demands (Matt. 13:3–6; 23:16–24). Jesus's demand that the righteousness of his followers exceed that of the scribes and Pharisees requires not only that their acts be righteous but also that their desires and motivations be consistent with righteous acts. In essence, Jesus calls for what God promised through Jeremiah, that he would write his law on their hearts (Jer. 31:33), that they will fulfill the commands to love God and love one another.

Jesus and the law: six "antitheses"? In a series of statements in Matthew 5:21–48, Jesus repeats the phrase, "you have heard . . . but I tell you" (vv. 21–26, 27–30, 31–32, 33–37, 38–42, 43–47; v. 48 summarizes the series). In these six sayings, often referred to as antitheses, Jesus demonstrates the demand of true righteousness. He is not merely contrasting his teaching with tradition, for he is engaged in a discourse about the "Law and the Prophets" (Matt. 5:17). Further, though some see these statements as evidence that the law no longer applies, or that Jesus has authority over the law and can set it aside, such a view does not fit well with the earlier statements in Matthew 5:17–20.[21] The idea of "antitheses" is thus not the most helpful. Rather, Jesus demonstrates what it looks like to fulfill the law, by going beyond a "mere" (even if strict) external conformity to the law to an inner conformity of the heart. He shows that it is possible to "keep" the law externally yet be guilty of violating it in internally. Moreover, Jesus later declares that the law is fulfilled by the Golden Rule (Matt.

---

21. Cf. Stanton, "Sermon on the Mount/Plain," 742.

7:12: "this is the Law and the Prophets") and by the double love command (Matt. 22:37–40: "All the Law and the Prophets depend on these two commands"), illustrating what is at the heart of the law. Jesus seeks not only to show the way of righteousness by exposing unrighteous attitudes, but in doing so, he seeks to transform the heart. The following is a brief overview of the six sayings.

In the first saying, Jesus declares, "You have heard that it was said to our ancestors, Do not murder, and whoever murders will be subject to judgment. But I tell you, everyone who is angry with his brother or sister will be subject to judgment. Whoever insults his brother or sister, will be subject to the court. Whoever says, 'You fool!' will be subject to hellfire" (Matt. 5:21–22). In effect, Jesus teaches that it is possible to keep the sixth commandment outwardly but violate it inwardly, to not murder anyone yet to be guilty of murderous hatred and violence. Jesus does not condemn every kind of anger, but rather ungodly anger (though even godly anger must be dealt with or it can easily lead to sin; see Eph. 4:26–27). Hatred for another person is the inner dimension and violation of God's command not to murder. Words of contempt are verbal expressions of that wrongful inner disposition. Or, to put it another way, murder does not come out of nowhere; it is preceded by the wrongful desire or emotion of hatred (cf. James 4:1–2). Yet the problem with wrongful desire is not simply that it may lead to wrongful action. The desire itself is murderous and subject to judgment. So, against those who would say that only

actions, not desires, can be commanded, Jesus prohibits wrongful desires.

In addition, he goes beyond a bare command and gives instruction for overcoming hostilities that lead to hatred and murder by giving two examples of reconciliation. In the first, you (Jesus makes it personal) are offering a gift at the altar and remember that someone has something against you. Reconciliation is so important that you ought not only to be open to reconciliation but also to pursue it, and even to interrupt worship to go and be reconciled. In the second example, Jesus exhorts you to settle with your adversary on the way to court, so that it doesn't reach the point of being decided by a judge, in which case the judgment may not go in your favor. Jesus does not indicate clearly who is at fault, though in each case the person seems to have a claim against you, indicating that you have done wrong and need to seek forgiveness and reconciliation. In any case, the emphasis is on transforming the heart, so that instead of harboring anger and resentment that escalates all the way to murder, you (we) would seek to deescalate the situation. The pattern is clear: the law means not simply, "Do not murder," but "Do not foster hatred for your brother, and instead seek reconciliation." That is love. That is what you would want someone to do to and for you.

The second saying is similar: "You have heard that it was said, Do not commit adultery. But I tell you, everyone who looks at a woman lustfully has already committed adultery with her in his heart" (Matt. 5:27–28). Again, Jesus teaches that outward conformity to the commandment does not demonstrate that the commandment has been kept, to obey the prohibition of adultery and yet be guilty of adulterous desire. Thus Jesus teaches that desires are not innocuous. He claims more than simply that lustful desire is wrong because it *leads* to adultery. That is true, for the act of adultery does not just happen, but it is the consequence of nurturing wrongful desire. Yet Jesus goes beyond that, claiming that lust *is* a form of adultery and the one who lusts is subject to judgment. The issue is not to be taken lightly. To avoid the sin of lust, Jesus says, you must take serious action: put an end to whatever is causing you to sin. Gouge out your eye or cut off your hand—that is, take radical action, for the consequences of not doing so are deadly, and "it is better that you lose one of the parts of your body than for your whole body to be thrown into hell" (v. 29). In other words, the law does not mean simply, "Do not commit adultery," but "Do not allow lust to take root in your heart, and do whatever it takes to prevent or remove it." As much as a marriage and a community are ruptured by adultery, a person's character is ruptured by lust. Transformation of acts and desires begins with resisting evil desires and forming proper desires and behavior. To protect marriage, community, and character, lustful desires need to be dispatched, not indulged. That is love. That is what you would (or should) want someone to do for you and your marriage.

It is not necessary to develop each of the remaining four sayings, on divorce, taking oaths, retribution, and love. Having outlined what the pattern looks like, it will be sufficient simply to summarize the pattern. In the third saying, on divorce, the law does not simply mean that if you divorce your wife, you should do so righteously by giving her a certificate of divorce, but rather that you should preserve your marriage. In the fourth saying, on oaths, the law does not simply mean that you should tell the truth when you are bound by the proper oath, but rather that you should tell the truth in all things (Matt. 5:33–37). In the fifth saying, on retribution, the law does not simply mean that you should not exceed just punishment for wrong,[22] but rather that you should be forgiving and merciful, willing to be wronged so that violence will not escalate (Matt. 5:38–42). In the last saying, on love, the law does not simply mean that you should love your neighbor and hate your enemy, practicing "love" in a selective and sinful way, but rather that you should love and do good to all, for that is what your father in heaven does (Matt. 5:43–47).

The demands of true righteousness. At the end of the six sayings is the summary statement in Matthew 5:48: "Be perfect [τέλειοι], therefore, as your heavenly Father is perfect." This command well displays the tension that arises from what precedes it. It seems to be an impossible demand, leading

---

22. "An eye for an eye and tooth for a tooth" represents the *lex talionis* (cf. Exod. 21:23–25; Lev. 24:19–20; Deut. 19:21). This required proportionate punishment, no more or less than what was deserved, but it could easily be employed in a spirit of vengeance.

some to conclude that Jesus presents not a requirement for all, but a way of "perfection" for those who are ready to pursue it.[23] Yet this does not fit with several key aspects of the Sermon on the Mount. First, Jesus addresses both his disciples and the listening crowd (Matt. 5:1; 7:28–29). Second, Jesus introduces the difficult sayings by a general statement on the law and its demands (5:17–20). He indicates that the demand for anyone who would follow him is that their righteousness must surpass that of the scribes and Pharisees, who would most likely be thought of as the few who were pursuing perfection. That is, the law applies to all, and Jesus teaches what it requires. This is further supported in 6:1–18, where Jesus teaches how to practice righteous acts such as giving, praying, and fasting, in contrast to the way that the hypocrites do these things (certainly referring to the religious leaders). Third, when Jesus begins his summary of the Sermon on the Mount, he says, "therefore, *everyone* who hears these words of mine and acts on them will be like a wise man who built his house on the rock" (Matt. 7:24).

In addition, it is instructive to consider the place of the Sermon on the Mount in Matthew's Gospel, and how it functions. Christopher Bryan claims, "What precedes it prepares us to know who Jesus is and what grace he brings (1:1–4:25). Now we hear his first major teaching, wherein he begins to tell us of life in that sphere of grace, and the part we are called to play."[24] This is an important reminder. Jesus's "stringent" demands are not meant for the select few pursuing perfection, and neither are they meant to lay an impossible burden on those who would follow him (cf. Matt. 11:29–30). Rather, they represent the way of life that will be pursued willingly and gladly by all of those who have experienced God's grace. It is the way of love and peace, grounded in God's own character, and thus a necessary and "natural" characteristic of God's children.

Practicing righteousness

In Matthew 6:1–18, Jesus continues his teaching on true righteousness by describing how righteous acts are characterized. Like his teaching on the law in 5:21–48, Jesus here indicates that righteousness is not displayed merely by meeting a formal, external requirement. That is the way of the scribes and the Pharisees, who he now describes as hypocrites (6:2, 5, 16). The three acts that Jesus highlights—giving alms, praying, and fasting—are basic moral and religious acts. They are all good things to do, but to do them is not praiseworthy in and of itself, for true righteousness goes beyond the "right act" and includes the motive for the act. Several brief comments will highlight what Jesus emphasizes concerning "practicing righteousness."

The main point that Jesus makes is that acts of righteousness are not to be done in order to impress people or to try to make ourselves look good. Such acts are not pleasing to God—he does not reward them.

---

23. Bryan, "Sermon on the Mount," 737, points to Bonaventure and Maldonatus as two such examples.
24. Bryan, "Sermon on the Mount," 737.

Thus Jesus says, "Be careful not to practice your righteousness in front of others to be seen by them. Otherwise, you have no reward with your Father in heaven" (Matt. 6:1). To impress others and to look good is what motivates hypocrites. They do righteous acts, but for their own benefit rather than out of love for God and others. When they give to the poor, Jesus says, they sound a trumpet, so that people will applaud (v. 2). When they pray, they stand in a prominent place so that they will be seen and heard (v. 5). And when they fast, they become gloomy and make themselves look disfigured, so that it is obvious what they are doing (v. 16). These are "good acts," but they are done for the wrong reason. Hypocrites do not give out of gratitude to God or because they care about the poor. They simply care about themselves and their reputation. Their act is empty and thus not praiseworthy, even if it may do some good. If that is true about giving to the poor, how much more about praying and fasting, for the nature of these acts is more internal, between God and the individual. That is, they are acts that involve communion with God, so that if they are done to impress people, they are completely empty and useless.

A second observation is that Jesus does not discourage his followers from doing these acts of righteousness. Instead, he is concerned to teach them how to do them. He says, "when you give" (v. 2), "pray" (v. 5), "fast" (v. 16). Third, Jesus says that there is reward in doing these acts. If they are done for the praise of other people, the reward is the praise of other people ("they have their reward," repeated in vv. 2, 5, 16). But if the acts are done out of a heart of thanksgiving and devotion to God, or genuine love for others, they are rewarded by God ("and your Father who sees in secret will reward you," repeated in vv. 4, 6, 18). Fourth, when Jesus urges his followers to do these things "in secret" (vv. 4, 6, 18), it should not be taken in a literal sense to mean that they should make sure no one knows what they are doing. It may appear that way at first, since he emphasizes the point strongly: "when you give to the poor, don't let your left hand know what your right hand is doing" (v. 3); "when you pray, go into your private room, shut your door, and pray to your Father who is in secret" (v. 6); and "when you fast . . . don't show your fasting to people but to your Father who is in secret" (vv. 17–18 HCSB). However, the point that Jesus is making has to do more with taking care to have proper motives than with hiding all such acts from public view. He has already said that good works done by his followers and seen by others bring glory to God (Matt. 5:16). In addition, elsewhere Jesus and other New Testament writers do not seek to hide such acts: Mark and Luke record Jesus commending the poor widow for her gift at the temple treasury, deliberately calling attention to it (Mark 12:41–44; Luke 21:1–4); Paul encourages giving to the church in Jerusalem in a public way (1 Cor. 16:3; 2 Cor. 9:5); though Jesus goes to pray alone, he also prays publicly (at least not in "private," Matt. 19:13; John 17); Jesus refers to the temple as a house of prayer (Matt. 21:13 and parallels); and the early church is referred to positively in Acts for their prayers together (Acts 1:14; 2:42; 6:4; 12:5). Many other examples could be given.

To take Jesus literally by doing "acts of righteousness" only in private would effectively mean that his followers would try to look as if they were not his followers! Instead, Jesus reinforces that God is not pleased merely by the external act. Emphasis is placed on a person's motivation, whether an act is done for reasons that are self-serving, primarily to be seen and commended by other people, or out of love for God and others. As a practical implication, it seems, Christians should not establish practices that draw attention and praise to "righteous acts" in a way that is likely to encourage others to do those acts in order to receive praise for them.

Conclusion: do these things

The Sermon on the Mount has obvious significance for Christian ethics. Yet its particular significance has been widely debated. Given its difficult demands, some conclude that it is impossible to follow, at least in the present day before Christ returns. Perhaps it is intended only to be an "interim ethic"— that is, a radical way of life for followers of Jesus to follow until he returns, which was believed to be very soon. It is too radical to practice for the long haul. Or it must be— at least primarily—a statement of life in the future kingdom of God (though it is something to strive for now). Or it may be that all should seek to follow Jesus's teaching, but that the more difficult demands are simply counsels for those who would seek perfection. Or the radical demands may be a way of revealing sinful human hearts and the impossibility of keeping the law, preparing sinners to understand the need for God's grace. Or it may be that Jesus holds up an ideal that, while it is impossible to perform, we are to try to approximate as well as we can. On the other hand, there are many, including the majority of early Christian commentators, who deduce that a straightforward reading of the Sermon leads to the conclusion that Jesus presents a way of life that those who are faithful to God will seek to follow.[25]

How should the teachings of Jesus in the Sermon on the Mount be understood? In the first place, it is true that sinful human beings cannot keep the requirements in the Sermon perfectly. Yet Jesus indicates simply that he intends for his listeners to do what he says. If the "not yet" aspect of the Sermon suggests that the vision laid out by Jesus will not be fully realized until the consummation of the kingdom, he nevertheless urges listeners to obedience now. Allowing for devices of speech, such as hyperbole, Jesus exhorts listeners throughout the Sermon to act on his teaching. Indeed,

---

25. For a history of interpretation of the Sermon on the Mount, see Quarles, *Sermon on the Mount*, 4–11; D. H. Field, "Sermon on the Mount," in *New Dictionary of Christian Ethics and Pastoral Theology*, eds. David J. Atkinson et al. (Downers Grove, IL: InterVarsity Press, 1995), 777–78; Douglas J. Moo, "Sermon on the Mount," in *Encyclopedia of Biblical and Christian Ethics*, ed. R. K. Harrison (Nashville: Thomas Nelson, 1987), 373–76; Greenman et al., *Sermon on the Mount*.

as we have seen, he gives very specific examples and practical counsel for fulfilling his commands. He acknowledges the difficulty of his teaching, saying, "How narrow is the gate and difficult the road that leads to life, and few find it" (Matt. 7:14), yet he urges listeners to "enter through the narrow gate" (v. 13). In addition, as the Sermon nears the end, Jesus declares that those who actually do God's will, and not those who simply pay him lip service (or display merely external obedience), are the ones who will enter the kingdom of heaven. "Not everyone who says to me, 'Lord, Lord,' will enter the kingdom of heaven, but only the one who does the will of my Father in heaven" (Matt. 7:21). Finally, in the conclusion of the Sermon, Jesus says, "Therefore, everyone who hears these words of mine and acts on them [ESV: "and does them," καὶ ποιεῖ αὐτούς], will be like a wise man who built his house on the rock" (Matt. 7:24). By comparison, "Everyone who hears these words of mine and doesn't act on them [ESV: "does not do them," καὶ μὴ ποιῶν αὐτοὺς] will be like a foolish man who built his house on the sand" (Matt. 7:26).

That is, it is clear that Jesus expects faithful listeners to do what he has taught them. Dietrich Bonhoeffer asserts that Jesus gives the answer to the question of how the Sermon on the Mount ought to be understood: "He does not allow his hearers to go away and make of his sayings what they will, picking and choosing from them whatever they find helpful, and testing them to see if they work. . . . Humanly speaking, we could

understand and interpret the Sermon on the Mount in a thousand different ways. Jesus knows only one possibility: simple surrender and obedience, not interpreting it or applying it, but doing and obeying it."[26]

Thus there is a tension between seemingly impossible exhortations and the expectation that those exhortations be followed. The tension is resolved in two ways. First is the realization that there is a "now and not yet" aspect to the kingdom. That doesn't mean that Jesus desires something less than obedience to his commands, or even less that it is a picture of the future kingdom. Rather, it means that it will not be realized perfectly until the kingdom of heaven is fully realized. Second, and more pertinent, is that there is a hint that only Jesus can fulfill the law as he teaches it (Matt. 5:17). Further, only those who are "connected" to him are able to do what he says. Jesus hints at this later in Matthew, when he says, "Come to me, all of you who are weary and burdened, and I will give you rest. Take up my yoke and learn from me, because I am lowly and humble in heart, and you will find rest for your souls. For my yoke is easy and my burden is light" (Matt. 11:28–30). In John's Gospel, Jesus further indicates the relationship between obedience and being connected to Jesus when he says, "Remain in me, and I in you. Just as a branch is unable to produce fruit by itself unless it remains on the vine, neither can you unless you remain in me" (John 15:4). In other words, obedience to Jesus's words is possible only through dependence on

---

26. Bonhoeffer, *Cost of Discipleship*, 175.

God and his grace, experienced through a relationship with Jesus.[27] That is how transformation occurs, reforming the heart and will to be conformed to God's will (cf. Rom. 12:1–2), and empowering the will to act in obedience. Again, Bonhoeffer asserts, "The command of Jesus is hard, unutterably hard, for those who try to resist it. But for those who willingly submit, the yoke is easy, and the burden is light. . . . Jesus asks nothing of us without giving us the strength to perform it. His commandment never seeks to destroy life, but to foster, strengthen and heal it."[28]

Ethics and the Christian Life in Paul's Letters

The significance of the writings of the apostle Paul for Christian ethics is difficult to overstate. He engages moral questions in the newly formed churches, working through the implications of the gospel for the Christian life on diverse issues, including an understanding of the law, relationships among believers (especially between Jews and Gentiles), sexual morality, marriage and singleness, and many others. He offers strong moral exhortation, but avoids legalism or mere external conformity; he proclaims liberty, but avoids libertinism. In the brief space that follows, we will look at aspects of Paul's thought as it pertains to ethics, considering some general patterns here, while engaging with his views on some specific issues in the relevant chapters that follow.

Sources of Paul's Ethics

The gospel in Paul's ethics

The gospel is central for Paul's ethics. Allen Verhey asserts that "within Paul's churches moral reflection is to be radically affected by the works and way of God made known in the gospel (Rom. 12:1). The power of God enables and requires a response, a life and a common life 'worthy of' or fitting to the gospel (Phil. 1:27)."[29] For Paul, the gospel is central not only theologically and missionally, but morally, and for all of life, as Richard Hays observes: "Paul is driven by a theological vision of extraordinary breadth: everything is brought under scrutiny of the gospel, and the attempt is made to speak to all pastoral problems in light of the gospel. Meat offered to idols, proper behavior at church potluck dinners, speaking in tongues, or sex counseling for married couples: Paul has something to say on every topic that comes up."[30]

How does moral discernment work in relation to the gospel? Paul draws on various sources for ethics,[31] including three prominent ones, each of which stands in significant relation to the gospel.

27. See Jonathan Lunde, *Following Jesus, the Servant King: A Biblical Theology of Covenantal Discipleship* (Grand Rapids: Zondervan, 2010).
28. Bonhoeffer, *Cost of Discipleship*, 31.
29. Allen Verhey, "Ethics," in Vanhoozer et al., *Dictionary for Theological Interpretation*, 198.
30. Hays, *Moral Vision*, 18.
31. See Eckhard J. Schnabel, "How Paul Developed His Ethics: Motivations, Norms and Criteria of Pauline Ethics," in *Understanding Paul's Ethics: Twentieth Century Portraits*, ed. Brian S. Rosner (Grand Rapids: Eerdmans, 1995), 294–95.

Jesus's teaching and work

One obvious source is Jesus himself, though not all scholars think so. Verhey claims that "the Epistles of Paul make little use of the tradition of Jesus' words and deeds."[32] Against this claim, Paul's thought and life are profoundly shaped by Jesus, and he makes reference to Jesus's life and teaching with normative force (Acts 20:35; 1 Cor. 7:10; 9:14; 11:23; 1 Thess. 4:2, 15).[33] Indeed, he defends his understanding of the gospel in the Galatian controversy by claiming that he received it directly from Jesus by special revelation (Gal. 1:12, 16–17). Further, his own teaching and exhortation closely echoes Jesus on important matters: compare, for example, their teaching on retribution and love for enemies (Matt. 5:38–48 and Rom. 12:14–21); commands in the Decalogue and love for neighbor (Matt. 19:18 and Rom. 13:9); love as the fulfillment of the law (Matt. 22:37–40 and Rom. 13:8–10; cf. Gal. 5:14); anxiety (Matt. 6:25–34 and Phil. 4:6); being wise and innocent (Matt. 10:16 and Rom. 16:19); the return of the Lord like a thief in the night (Luke 12:39–40 and 1 Thess. 5:2). Jesus's "words and deeds" serve as a source for Paul's own teaching, in specific texts like these, and in more general terms, since the implications of the gospel cannot be separated from Jesus himself.

The Old Testament

Another significant source for Paul is the Scriptures he studied—namely, the Old Testament.[34] Paul is deeply shaped by the moral norms of the Old Testament Law and the Prophets. Rather than portraying the gospel and Old Testament as opposing ethical sources and norms, for Paul the Old Testament provides the contours of the manner of life worthy of the Lord. Some would suggest that Paul's ethics is not dependent on the Old Testament, offering as an example a passage like 1 Corinthians 5–7, which is full of moral exhortations without directly citing the Old Testament for support. However, Paul's dependence on the Old Testament is apparent even in this passage. For instance, Brian Rosner contends that Paul's exhortation to the Corinthians, who have tolerated sexual immorality in their congregation, to "put away the evil person from among yourselves" (1 Cor. 5:13 HCSB), draws on Deuteronomy (13:5; 17:7; 19:19; 21:21; 22:21; 24:7), and 1 Corinthians 5:1–13 as a whole draws heavily on Scripture, especially on Deuteronomy. In fact, Rosner argues, "the investigation of this link not only unveils Paul's profound indebtedness to the Scriptures but also opens up a fuller understanding of the reasons for the expulsion in 1 Corinthians 5."[35] He notes numerous other examples in 1 Corinthians 5–7.

---

32. Verhey, "Ethics," 198.
33. Schnabel, "How Paul Developed His Ethics," 295.
34. Schnabel notes how Paul makes use of Old Testament texts very naturally to make his point, citing as examples Gal. 6:1; Rom. 8:1–4; 1 Cor. 7:19; 5:13; 6:12–20; 2 Cor. 8:15; 9:9. Schnabel, "How Paul Developed His Ethics," 294.
35. See Brian Rosner, *Paul, Scripture, & Ethics: A Study of 1 Corinthians 5–7* (Grand Rapids: Baker, 1994), 63. Rosner reviews the literature on sources of Paul's ethics, and argues that Paul is dependent on the Old Testament even in ethical passages where he does not directly cite it.

The created order

A third source of ethics for Paul is the created order, properly perceived. Though human understanding of creation, and creation itself, is adversely affected by the fall, nevertheless, "Paul is convinced that God's salvific action in Jesus Christ makes the *cosmos* recognizable again as God's creation."[36] The prime example of Paul's appeal to creation is found in Romans 1, where Paul sees God's creation pattern of sexuality as normative and as evidence against homosexual union.

The Foundation of Pauline Ethics

God-glorifying

Simply put, the foundation of Paul's ethics is God, who reveals himself in Scripture and supremely in Jesus Christ, through the gospel and by the power of the Spirit. The foundation of Paul's ethics is thus threefold. In the first place, it has as its purpose to glorify God. Just as Jesus exhorts his disciples to good works so that others will glorify God the Father (Matt. 5:16), Paul prays for believers in Rome to "live in harmony with one another, according to Christ Jesus, so that you may glorify the God and Father of our Lord Jesus Christ with one mind and one voice" (Rom. 15:5–6). This is a key purpose or *telos* of the Christian life, a point that he presses home to the Corinthians on more than one occasion. In one instance, Paul argues that what we do with our bodies is important. It is inconceivable

that the one who is united with God will indulge in sexual immorality. Rather, the goal of glorifying God entails that we abstain from sexual immorality, reinforcing clear moral prohibitions of sexual immorality. "Don't you know that your body is a temple of the Holy Spirit who is in you, whom you have from God? You are not your own, for you were bought at a price. So glorify God with your body" (1 Cor. 6:19–20). The broad application of this principle is asserted later in the same letter, after a discussion of what might be considered morally neutral matters, beginning in chapter 8. The presenting issue is whether it is acceptable to eat meat that has been sacrificed to idols, which raises other issues, such as conscience, freedom in Christ, personal "rights," unity, and the gospel itself. After working through various considerations, Paul presents a basic principle for discernment in matters where there is no clear moral norm: "So, whether you eat or drink, or whatever you do, do everything for the glory of God" (1 Cor. 10:31). Disciples of Jesus will humbly place others ahead of themselves, for the sake of the gospel, for it is not our desires, but God's glory, that we should seek.

Christ-centered

Second, for Paul and other New Testament writers, ethics is centered on Jesus Christ. This goes far beyond adopting Jesus's teaching, as one might embrace a school of thought, such as Aristotle, Aquinas, Kant,

---

36. Schnabel, "How Paul Developed His Ethics," 295. For a substantial development of the notion that the work of Jesus reestablishes the significance of the created order for ethics, see O'Donovan, *Resurrection and Moral Order*.

Buddha, or Marx. It also goes beyond adhering to a particular way of life, though it includes that. Even "following Jesus," while an appropriate and significant expression, is "an *insufficient* metaphor to describe Christ's impact upon our identity."[37] Instead, Paul and other New Testament writers frequently use the phrase "in Christ." There are Aristotelians and Kantians and Marxists who are profoundly influenced by those teachers, but they do not speak of being *in* Aristotle or Kant or Marx.[38] This phrase speaks to a profound unity with Christ, and with others who are in Christ, such that one's identity is changed and the benefits of Christ are realized by grace through faith.[39] Perhaps most striking is 2 Corinthians 5:17. A typical translation of this verse asserts that if anyone is in Christ, that person is a new creation (CSB, ESV, RSV). However, in Greek the sentence does not have a subject or verb, and thus might simply be translated, "If anyone is in Christ— new creation!"[40] This is more than personal transformation. To be sure, one of the implications of the exclamation is that those who are "in Christ" undergo "a fundamental shift in their identity."[41] Yet it goes beyond that, and includes a proclamation of "the apocalyptic message that through the cross God has nullified the *kosmos* of sin and death and brought a new *kosmos* into being."[42]

The declaration—"new creation!"—is a reminder that Jesus Christ is at the center of God's purposes of redemption, for human beings and the cosmos. If anyone is in Christ, it is true that there will be a transformation of that person, including their moral life (e.g., 1 Cor. 6:9–11). Yet it is also a reminder of God's proclamation, through the cross and resurrection, that "the old has passed away; behold, the new has come" (2 Cor. 5:17 ESV), a guarantee that awaits an eschatological completion. The implications for ethics are profound. It involves not only personal transformation and a new identity but also a new community and sense of inclusion, an undoing of pride and performance, a sober consciousness of the reality of sin and sinful desires, a new "way of being human," a new sense of purpose in life, a new sense of love and justice in relationships, and so on.[43]

Spirit-filled

Third, Pauline ethics is grounded in the work of the Spirit. This is often a neglected reality in the Christian life and in Christian ethics. Jesus promised his disciples that, after he left, the Father would send "another Counselor," the "Spirit of truth" (John 14:15–16), who would guide them into all truth (15:13), the same Spirit who through conversion caused them to be born again (John 3:5–6). Paul is

---

37. Cameron, *Joined-Up Life*, 95.
38. Cameron, *Joined-Up Life*, 95.
39. A sampling of the variety of uses: Rom. 8:1; 16:7, 9, 10; 1 Cor. 1:2, 30; 4: 10; 15:18; 2 Cor. 5:7; Gal. 1:22; 2:17; 3:28; Eph. 1:1, 3; 2:6, 10; Phil. 2:5; 3:9; 4:21; Col. 1:2; 1 Thess. 4:16;
40. Hays, *Moral Vision*, 20.
41. Cameron, *Joined-Up Life*, 96.
42. Hays, *Moral Vision*, 20.
43. Such things are nicely developed by Cameron, *Joined-Up Life*, 94–114.

keenly aware of the work of the Spirit, and the dependence of Jesus's disciples on the Spirit. Briefly, the following are among the works of the Spirit in relation to ethics.

The Holy Spirit creates new life. Apart from Jesus, human beings are dead in trespasses and sins (Eph. 2:1). Jesus says that it is necessary to be born again in order to enter into God's kingdom (John 3). Paul makes a similar point in Romans 8. "Those who are in the flesh cannot please God" (v. 8). But those who are united with Christ are not in the flesh because "the Spirit of God lives in you" (v. 9). The one who was dead because of sin, by being united with Christ, is brought to life by the Spirit (vv. 10–11; cf. 2 Cor. 5:17; Gal. 4:29; 6:15; Eph. 2:4–5).

The Holy Spirit liberates. Those who are "in Christ" are not condemned by the law of sin and death, but have been set free by the law of the Spirit of life (Rom. 8:1–2). To be born of the Spirit is to be freed from the bondage to sin, a freedom for true obedience: "in order that the law's requirement would be accomplished in us who do not walk according to the flesh but according to the Spirit" (v. 4).

The Holy Spirit creates a new community. Ephesians makes this point clear. In chapter 4, immediately after urging his readers to "live worthy of the calling you have received" (v. 1), Paul commends dispositions that foster relationships: humility, gentleness, patience, and loving acceptance (v. 2). The purpose is to maintain the unity of the Spirit (v. 3). That unity is underscored by the reminder that there is one body, one Spirit, one hope, one Lord, one faith, one baptism, and one God and Father of all (vv. 4–6). The Holy Spirit unites Christians, working against conflict and the tendency to divide, promoting fellowship (Phil. 2; 2 Cor. 13:14).

The Holy Spirit transforms the mind and will. Paul knows well that Christians will sin, yet he boldly declares that the Spirit is a reality in the life of those "in Christ" in a way that is transformative for both understanding the will of God, and being oriented to God's will (Rom. 12:1–2; 1 Cor. 2:12–16; 6:9–11). This is in clear contrast to those who do not know God, whose minds and desires are hostile to God (Rom. 1:18–32; 8:6–7; Col. 1:21; 3:5–11; cf. Eph. 4:17–19).

The Holy Spirit battles against the "flesh." The flesh represents not our physical bodies or desires as such; the incarnation of Jesus challenges such gnostic ideas (John 1; 1 John 4:2; 1 Tim. 3:16). Rather, the flesh signifies ungodly desires and temptations that wage war against the spirit and keep people in bondage (Rom. 7:5). "For the flesh desires what is against the Spirit, and the Spirit desires what is against the flesh" (Gal. 5:17). The Spirit's rejection and defeat of ungodly desires is not repressive but liberating (John 6:63; Rom. 8:12–13; Gal. 6:8). It is liberating because the Spirit takes up the battle against desires that the will, drawing on the flesh alone, is powerless to defeat, and because "we're no longer forced to view ourselves as powered by the immediate demands of bodies, brains and social collectives."[44]

---

44. Cameron, *Joined-Up Life*, 118.

The Holy Spirit produces fruit in the life of the Christian. It is a process rather than an instantaneous event, but Spirit-filled Christians will grow in the fruit of the Spirit (Gal. 5:22–23; cf. John 15). This challenges those Christians who rationalize their lack of love or peace or patience or kindness because that is simply not their disposition. For Paul, such a person is living by the flesh, not the Spirit.

The Holy Spirit reveals God's will. God's will is revealed in Scripture, yet the Holy Spirit is necessary for understanding God's will, in part because Scripture does not explicitly address many concrete situations in contemporary life, and also because sin distorts and blinds human beings to God's revelation in Scripture. Paul declares that the Spirit reveals God's wisdom (1 Cor. 2:10). The Spirit does not work in a vacuum, or reveal God's will to the individual in some subjective way. As Hays reminds us, "There are instruments and mediating structures through which the Spirit works," which include Scripture, Paul himself and other apostles and emissaries, and the Christian community.[45] Concerning the community, it is notable that in Romans 12:1–2 it is the community with whom Paul pleads to present their bodies (plural) as a living sacrifice (singular), and it is the community within which God's will is discerned.

There is an important principle here. On the one hand, the Spirit is necessary for understanding God's will and interpreting Scripture rightly. On the other hand, a test of whether discernment is truly of the Spirit is that it does not contradict Scripture, and it is confirmed by the community of those who are faithful in Christ.

The Holy Spirit empowers the Christian to obey the will of God. On their own, human beings are powerless to do God's will. Yet, joined to Christ, believers are enabled by the Holy Spirit to overcome desires of the flesh and do God's will (Gal. 5:16–26; Col. 1:9–10; Phil. 2:12–13; cf. Rom. 1:5).

Aspects of Paul's Ethics

This survey of Pauline ethics will be concluded with a brief summary of significant aspects of ethics in his letters.

Indicative and imperative

The relationship between theology and ethics in Paul is often expressed by the terms *indicative* and *imperative*.[46] In short, these terms summarize the view that Christian ethics is determined by what God has done in Jesus Christ. This relationship between the indicative and the imperative is indicated, in part, by the structure of several of Paul's letters, composed of two main sections. The beginnings of these letters describe what

---

45. Hays, *Moral Vision*, 45.

46. Cf. Wolfgang Schrage, *The Ethics of the New Testament*, trans. David E. Green (Philadelphia: Fortress, 1988), 167. For a discussion of this theme in Paul, see Thomas R. Schreiner, *Paul: Apostle of God's Glory in Christ* (Downers Grove, IL: InterVarsity Press, 2001), 253–61; Schrage, *Ethics of the New Testament*, 167–72; and essays by Rudolf Bultmann, "The Problem of Ethics in Paul" (195–216), and Michael Parsons, "Being Precedes Act: Indicative and Imperative in Paul's Writing" (217–247), in Rosner, *Understanding Paul's Ethics*.

God has accomplished in Jesus Christ, a rich theological exposition of the gospel. The latter parts of the letters describe the ethical implications of the gospel, typically introduced by "therefore" (Rom. 12:1; Eph. 4:1; Col. 3:1; 1 Thess. 4:1). The indicative points to the Christian's status in Christ—who we are—while the imperative declares how we ought to live. This pattern is illustrated in several texts. Paul urges Christians not to let sin reign in their bodies (imperative: Rom. 6:12) because they are dead to sin and alive to God in Jesus (indicative: Rom. 6:11), and have been freed from sin (indicative: Rom. 6:22). In 1 Corinthians 5:7, Paul exhorts the Corinthians to cleanse out the old leaven (imperative) because they are unleavened (indicative). Paul's demand to the Colossians not to lie to one another (imperative) is grounded in the fact that they have put off the old self and put on a new self (indicative; Col. 3:9–10). To the Galatians, he reasons, "If we live by the Spirit, let us also keep in step with the Spirit" (Gal. 5:25). The indicative is the basis for the imperative. So too in Ephesians 5:8: "For you were once darkness, but now you are light in the Lord. Walk as children of light."

The imperative is not the basis for the indicative: living in a manner worthy of the Lord is the result, not the basis, of a right relationship with God through faith in Jesus Christ (Eph. 2:8–10). The gospel logic is that justification grounds and leads to sanctification. Those who have experienced forgiveness and have been brought into right relationship with God are no longer enslaved to the passions of the body and mind but are transformed in mind and will so that they are free to become what God has created them to be. The eschatological tension between the "now" and the "not yet" appears here, for the indicative is certain by the completion of Christ's work on the cross, yet the imperative is not fulfilled automatically, immediately, or completely in this life. Rather, believers are *being* conformed to the likeness of Christ as we "await the redemption of our bodies and the complete extinguishing of sin."[47]

Christian freedom

Freedom is important to Paul, and he defends it vigorously in his Letter to the Galatians, for it is bought by Jesus in his death, and it is being threatened. "For freedom, Christ set us free. Stand firm then and don't submit again to a yoke of slavery" (Gal. 5:1). To reject the freedom that Christ has made possible is to reject God's grace. Freedom in Christ is rejected by those who place themselves under the stipulations of the law (Gal. 5:4). Yet freedom in Christ isn't freedom from all law (antinomianism), but freedom from the requirements of the law as a means of justification, an impossibility that provokes the fear of judgment and condemnation, and sometimes produces a slavish legalism. Further, freedom in Christ is not for indulging the desires of the flesh (Gal. 5:13). Quite the opposite, the Spirit brings a freedom from the tyranny of

---

47. Schreiner, *Paul*, 254.

the desires of the flesh (Rom. 8:12–13). It is also a freedom for glad obedience and good works with service to God and others produced by a lavish love. As Martin Luther famously put it, "A Christian is a perfectly free lord of all, subject to none. A Christian is a perfectly dutiful servant of all, subject to all."[48] In essence, how Christians use their freedom indicates something of their level of Christian maturity.

Absolute freedom, which moderns may sometimes think they have achieved, or at least can achieve, is an illusion. Those who think they are absolutely free, or who think they are their own masters, are often enslaved to their immediate desires, or to an image they wish to convey, or to people's opinions of them, or to power, money, sex, or various substances. In Paul's view, we are either slaves to sin and the passions of the flesh, or we are slaves to God and righteousness, which is liberation (Rom. 7:15–23). Thus the freedom that we are called to involves obedience to God and a rejection of all other masters, including ourselves. True Christian freedom includes several other characteristics:

- It is not used to gratify the flesh (Gal. 5:13a).
- It is used in the service of others, produced by love (Gal. 5:13b).
- It does not hinder the weak (1 Cor. 8:9).
- It seeks the good of others (1 Cor. 10:24).

- It is consistent with a good conscience (1 Cor. 10:24–33).
- It is directed to the glory of God (1 Cor. 10:31).

Eschatological perspective

An eschatological perspective is significant for Paul's ethics.[49] It is not a triumphalist perspective, based on an over-realized eschatology. Nor is it a rigorous ascetic lifestyle, grounded in the imminent return of Christ. Further, it does not entail a futuristic focus that renders mundane worldly activities meaningless. Rather, Paul's ethics is shaped by an eschatological perspective on the kingdom of God that maintains the tension between the "now" and "not yet." Because the kingdom has come and the decisive work of Christ on the cross is complete, there is a certainty about the future that grounds both a sure hope in the future and confident moral action in the present. Because the consummation of the kingdom is awaited, and the powers of this world still rage, there is seriousness with respect to moral action (see Rom. 13:12). The tension between the "now" and "not yet" in the present age includes world-affirming and world-denying elements, and precludes both "pure passivity" and "alienation" with regard to the present world.[50]

Eschatology and ethics both feature prominently in Paul's first letter to the Thessalonians. In the opening chapter he

---

48. Martin Luther, "The Freedom of a Christian," In *Martin Luther's Basic Theological Writings*, ed. Timothy F. Lull, 2nd ed. (Minneapolis: Fortress, 2005), 393.
49. See Hays, *Moral Vision*, 19–27; Schrage, *Ethics of the New Testament*, 181–86.
50. Cf. Schrage, *Ethics of the New Testament*, 181.

recalls how they turned from idols to "serve the living and true God" (v. 9), even as they "wait for His Son from heaven" (v. 10). In the "eschatological interval" between the resurrection and return of Jesus, Christians are called to serve God and one another (cf. v. 3). Ethics is grounded in eschatology: "The future-directed hope is directly connected with a transformation of the Thessalonians' lives in such a way that they are, according to Paul, engaged in active works of love as a means of serving God."[51] Later in the letter, Paul's explicit eschatological teaching about the coming of the Lord (in 4:13–5:11) is woven seamlessly into his moral exhortations (especially 4:1–5:24). The eschatological teaching serves as a motivation and encouragement for action, to be alert and practice self-control (4:13, 18; 5:6–8, 11, 23–24).

An eschatological perspective also grounds Paul's teaching on marriage, divorce, and singleness in 1 Corinthians 7. The eschatological emphasis in this text is easily overlooked, since it appears late in the discussion, and even then Paul refers to the "present distress," which hardly seems to be an eschatological reference. Paul cites the "present distress" as a reason for not getting married (yet for not separating from one's spouse either). For a time of hardship, be it war or famine or the like, is not an opportune time to marry. The urgency of the distress requires attention and energy that cannot be devoted to family. Yet Paul moves quickly from the present difficulty

to a much broader principle: "This is what I mean, brothers and sisters: *The time is limited*, so *from now on* those who have wives should be as though they had none, those who weep as though they did not weep, those who rejoice as though they did not rejoice, those who buy as though they didn't own anything, and those who use the world as though they did not make full use of it. *For this world in its current form is passing away*" (vv. 29–31, emphasis added). The urgency of the "present distress" is a reminder of a much greater urgency, which is the work that must be done in the service of God during the interval between Jesus's resurrection and return. To remain unmarried in this interval is not mandated, as Paul makes clear (vv. 7, 9, 25, 28, 35, 36, 38, 39–40). Rather, it is a matter of expedience, in order to be "devoted to the Lord without distraction" (v. 35).

However, the eschatological perspective is not merely a practical matter, allowing one greater opportunity to serve God. That practical conclusion flows out of a much broader set of priorities, given the certainty of the parousia, which necessarily shapes one's perception of ordinary matters and concerns in life. While Paul advocates a radical manner of life and posture toward the world, it is not the result of an ethical fanaticism or world-denying asceticism; for Paul, refraining from marriage is a preference, not a demand. Nor is Paul's view driven by an interim ethic that is designed only for a short term. To be sure, Paul asserts that the

---

51. Hays, *Moral Vision*, 22.

time is limited or "shortened" (v. 29 NASB), and "this world in its current form is passing away" (v. 31). Yet it is not the amount of time that grounds Paul's ethical conclusions, but rather the belief that in Christ the decisive "event" in human history has taken place. His perspective "does not stand or fall with the expectation of an imminent end," but rather with "the specific expectation of the ultimate victory of God and of his Christ."[52] Whether the remaining time is short or relatively long, in light of Christ, "from now on" his followers will live differently.

Further, the ethical implication of Paul's eschatological perspective does not entail a rejection of the things of this world. God's creation is good and not to be disparaged, and Paul assumes and accepts that many will marry, weep, rejoice, buy, and use the things of the world. Rather, the certainty of the future and knowledge of the kingdom necessarily give believers a different perspective, so that they will not engage in those things as others do. That is, in light of that certainty and that knowledge, Paul urges believers always to live with the end in view, and thus to live with a certain sense of detachment from the things of the world. Those things may be good, but "the perspective of the ultimate makes all else penultimate at best."[53]

Conclusion

The eschatological perspective provides an appropriate conclusion to this chapter. It draws our attention back to the "now" and the "not yet" of life between Christ's resurrection and return. It is a time marked by the uncertainties of the present age, in which Christians are called not to be conformed to a world that largely rejects the rule of Christ. At the same time, it is marked by the certainty of the future, which liberates Christians to live in obedience to the will of God, to practice works of love, to endure hardships, and to encourage one another. If we only hope in Christ for this life, we are to be pitied (1 Cor. 15:19); but because the future is certain, we can stand firm, being "steadfast, immovable, always excelling in the Lord's work, because you know that your labor in the Lord is not in vain" (1 Cor. 15:58). This also provides an appropriate point from which to move to a discussion of contemporary issues, which constitutes part 2 of this book.

---

52. Schrage, *Ethics of the New Testament*, 183.
53. Schrage, *Ethics of the New Testament*, 182.

Select Resources

Bonhoeffer, Dietrich. *The Cost of Discipleship*. London: SCM, 1959.

Cameron, Andrew J. B. *Joined-Up Life: A Christian Account of How Ethics Works*. Nottingham, UK: Inter-Varsity Press, 2011.

Carson, D. A. *The Sermon on the Mount: An Exposition of Matthew 5–7*. Grand Rapids: Baker, 1978.

Hays, Richard B. *The Moral Vision of the New Testament: Community, Cross, New Creation; A Contemporary Introduction to New Testament Ethics*. San Francisco: HarperSanFrancisco, 1996.

Lunde, Jonathan. *Following Jesus, the Servant King: A Biblical Theology of Covenantal Discipleship*. Grand Rapids: Zondervan, 2010.

Rosner, Brian S. *Paul, Scripture, & Ethics: A Study of 1 Corinthians 5–7*. Grand Rapids: Baker, 1994.

Rosner, Brian S., ed., *Understanding Paul's Ethics: Twentieth-Century Approaches*. Grand Rapids: Eerdmans, 1995.

Schrage, Wolfgang. *The Ethics of the New Testament*. Translated by David E. Green. Philadelphia: Fortress, 1988.

Stassen, Glen H., and David P. Gushee. *Kingdom Ethics: Following Jesus in Contemporary Context*. Downers Grove, IL: InterVarsity Press, 2003.

PART 3

MARRIAGE AND HUMAN SEXUALITY

CHAPTER 6

SEXUAL ETHICS

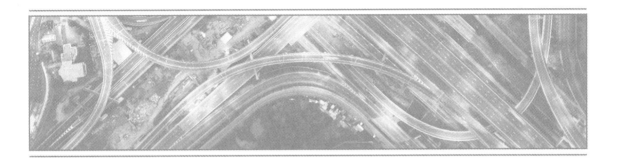

Run from sexual immorality! "Every sin a person can commit is outside the body." On the contrary, the person who is sexually immoral sins against his own body. Don't you know that your body is a sanctuary of the Holy Spirit who is in you, whom you have from God? You are not your own, for you were bought at a price. Therefore glorify God in your body.

1 Corinthians 6:18–20 HCSB

For this is God's will, your sanctification: that you keep away from sexual immorality, that each of you knows how to control his own body in holiness and honor, not with lustful passions, like the Gentiles, who don't know God.

1 Thessalonians 4:3–5

Introduction

> Before human beings can paint and sculpt, before they can trade or manufacture, before they can even eke a living from the soil, they must know how to live sexually. Sex is too urgent to leave to guesswork.[1]
>
> —Tim Stafford

In the 2008 United States presidential election, Sarah Palin, then governor of Alaska, was the Republican vice-presidential candidate for John McCain. Palin had a teenage daughter, Bristol, who was pregnant and not married. She was kept out of the media spotlight during the campaign, but after the election, Bristol Palin opened up to the media and spoke frankly to teenagers about sex. Her message appeared to be confused. On the one hand, she urged teenagers to avoid sex before marriage. On the other hand, she asserted that sexual abstinence is "not realistic at all."[2]

What appears to be a confused and self-contradictory message to teenagers is perhaps to be expected in an age of "sexual chaos," as Tim Stafford characterizes it. It may be a reflection of contradictory sexual desires. We want intimacy and satisfaction that comes with commitment and lasting love. On the other hand, we are tempted by intimacy and satisfaction through immediate pleasure. The pursuit of the first cautions us to avoid sex before marriage, as Bristol Palin urged. The pursuit of the second causes us to throw off caution and to believe that abstinence before marriage is not realistic at all.

There was once a widely held view that it was good and right and necessary to reserve sex for marriage, for the sake of individuals and society. What is more, it was thought possible to do so! The sexual revolution changed all that.[3] After the revolution, chaos and confusion reigns. Marriage hasn't disappeared, but it has been undermined and redefined. The old consensus has been ridiculed and its rationale forgotten in the demand for new (or no) sexual boundaries. "True," Stafford writes, "old forms like marriage still remain. But they have grown weak, hollowed out from the inside. They are like European royalty: ceremony and costumes intact, but real power gone."[4]

After the sexual revolution, Bristol Palin's confused and contradictory statement may not produce a coherent or rational argument, but it articulates common experience. In an age when experience trumps rational

---

1. Tim Stafford, *Sexual Chaos: Charting a Course through Turbulent Times* (Downers Grove, IL: InterVarsity Press, 1993), 12.
2. "Bristol Palin: Abstinence for All Teens 'Not Realistic,'" CNN, February 17, 2009, http://www.cnn.com/2009/POLITICS/02/17/bristol.palin.interview/#cnnSTCVideo.
3. Sometimes it seems that the reference to the "sexual revolution" is overused. Yet, as Stafford asserts, *"Revolution* appropriately summarizes what happened. The Old Consensus didn't get an overhaul. It got overthrown" (Stafford, *Sexual Chaos*, 39).
4. Stafford, *Sexual Chaos*, 11.

arguments or wisdom, it is important to try to understand the reality behind such a statement. It is important to understand the longing for lasting love, and the sense that such love demands reserving sexual intimacy for marriage. Further, it is important to understand why such a demand seems unrealistic or implausible, and to present an alternative that will make abstinence before marriage realistic.

This chapter will examine contrasting worldviews and the very different forms of sexual ethics that each produces. The emphasis will be on outlining a biblical perspective on sexuality and sex, and a "plausibility structure" that makes abstinence before marriage—and faithfulness in marriage—realistic. First, though, we ought to put sex in its place.

Is Sex All That Important?

It is not uncommon to hear a criticism that Christians, at least some of them, are too obsessed with the topic of sex, treating it as the most important moral issue (alongside abortion, perhaps). We should get over our fixation with sex and turn to things that really matter, especially social justice. In response, it should be said that this is a false dichotomy: it is not necessary to choose to address either sexual morality or social justice; we ought to speak to both of these and many others. Moreover, this contrast suggests that sexual morality is unrelated to social justice. In some cases it indicates biblical sexual morality is incompatible with the kind of "social justice" that is sought in contemporary culture. "Social justice" is used to refer to concerns about a broad range of issues, including poverty, human trafficking, racial justice, LGBT issues, environmental issues, and others. These issues are important to examine, as is sexual morality.

There is another point to be made in response to those who charge that some (especially conservative) Christians are obsessed with sexual morality. As Yuval Levin writes in his book *The Fractured Republic*, "That impression is, of course, terribly unfair." The reason "religious conservatives," as he says, frequently address issues of sex and sexuality is that they are regularly challenged on these issues. Levin adds, "They are not the ones who made sexuality the center of the culture wars. Social liberals have for the most part picked these fights because orthodox views about sexual morality (which insist on fundamental limits to the scope of personal choice) strike them as uniquely oppressive and backward, and they cannot abide their persistence."[5] In other words, Christians live in a culture that is obsessed with sex, and which insists on a new orthodoxy on sex in law and culture. Many Christians feel compelled to respond to the new orthodoxy, for "it matters a great deal to their understanding of virtue, flourishing,

---

5. Yuval Levin, *The Fractured Republic: Renewing America's Social Contract in the Age of Individualism* (New York: Basic Books, 2016), 171.

and moral order and their sense of their religious obligations."[6]

Sexual morality is not the only, or perhaps even the most, important issue for ethics, but it is important. First, Scripture addresses sex and sexual morality frequently from cover to cover, including a depiction of the beauty of sex in God's design and the ugliness of sexual sin that subverts God's design.[7] Second, sex is a gift from God, to be used for his glory and human flourishing. Human beings are sexual beings, which is a central aspect of theological anthropology, or what it means to be human. We cannot ignore that basic reality, and we dare not let its significance be declared without challenge by those whose worldview is opposed to God. Sexuality is a wonderful gift, but it is a curse when it is misused.

Third, sexual desire is powerful and easily corrupted. Sexual sin is an offense against God and against other persons, which threatens both our relationship with God and the very fabric of a community. Paul exhorts those in Corinth who would minimize the significance of sexual boundaries, "Flee sexual immorality!" (1 Cor. 6:18). Even the Thessalonians, who are affirmed

as an example for others (1 Thess. 1:2–10), Paul exhorts to abstain from sexual immorality, declaring that "this is God's will, your sanctification" (4:3). God's will and our sanctification are surely broader than abstaining from sexual immorality. Yet perhaps this particular temptation is sufficiently powerful and widespread and devastating to a community that Paul singles it out as something especially to be avoided. Jesus's teaching gets right to the heart of the matter, condemning not only sexually immoral acts, but desires as well, and exhorting his readers to do whatever it takes to avoid sexual immorality (Matt. 5:27–30).

Fourth, to narrow the previous point, sexual desire, when corrupted, damages and destroys lives. The powerful, especially men, prey on and exploit the vulnerable, especially women and minors, for their sexual pleasure. With power and influence, they attempt to cover up their abuse and silence their victims. In recent years many such abuses have been exposed by victims and their advocates, but much more needs to be done. Included among the victims are those who have been used, hurt (even if not physically abused), and deeply disappointed by casual, commitment-free sex.[8]

---

6. Levin, *Fractured Republic*, 171.
7. The references are far too many to list. This chapter will examine some of them. As a starting point, some key texts include Gen. 1:27; 2:18–25; Exod. 20:14; Lev. 18–20; Deut. 22:13–30; Prov. 5:15–23; Song; Matt. 5:27–32; 19:3–12; Acts 15:28–29; Rom. 1:18–27; 1 Cor. 5–7; Eph. 5 (esp. 1–5, 22–33); 1 Thess. 4:3–8.
8. Perhaps the most well-known recent campaign on behalf of victims of sexual abuse is the #MeToo movement, https://metoomvmt.org/; there are also advocates on behalf of adult survivors of child sexual abuse, such as RAINN, "Adult Survivors of Child Sexual Abuse," https://www.rainn.org/articles/adult-survivors-child-sexual-abuse; there is growing awareness of sex trafficking in the United States and worldwide—e.g., End Slavery Now, "Sex Trafficking," http://www.endslaverynow.org/learn/slavery-today/sex-trafficking; one group that receives less attention, perhaps in part because they are seen as willing participants rather than victims, and they are the majority group, is "survivors of the sexual revolution"—those who have been hurt, used,

Sexual morality is indeed important, as it deals with how people relate to and treat one another. In a very powerful way it teaches us what faithfulness means, and how unfaithfulness tears at the fabric of relationships and community. Thus, against those who would minimize it in favor of focusing on social justice, it is important to note that sexual morality is a matter of justice! Andrew Cameron makes this connection when he writes, "It often surprises people that the New Testament's sexual ethic pivots on treating others justly (1 Cor. 6:8–10; 1 Thess. 4:6). Chaste singleness and faithful marriages are, in the logic of the New Testament, the way to a new and *just* Jesus-shaped community."[9] Sex is a good gift from God. Yet it is easily corrupted, and because sexuality is central to who we are, sexual immorality has devastating results, leaving in its wake shattered lives, broken homes, damaged reputations, ruined ministries, and a culture in chaos. For these and other reasons, it is misleading at best to assert that the Bible is "relatively uninterested in the morality of sex per se."[10] Our culture, and some Christians, may exaggerate its importance, but the Bible is very much interested in the morality of sex.

Contrasting Worldviews

Contemporary Secular Western Perspective on Sexuality and Sex

Presuppositions and influential factors

There really is no "secular Western perspective" on sex, but rather numerous perspectives.[11] Nevertheless, those perspectives have many things in common, which we may outline at the risk of some overgeneralization. There are, for instance, certain broad presuppositions and influential factors at work:

- a post-Enlightenment perspective that is grounded in philosophical naturalism and secular humanism
- a rejection or severe qualification of the Judeo-Christian tradition that has long governed sexual ethics in the West
- an embrace of moral relativism, at least in terms of a rejection of universal moral norms
- a radical sense of autonomy and emphasis on individual liberty, rights, and privacy
- a rejection of traditional views of marriage, family, and sex
- a loss of an understanding of the public good of marriage and sex

---

and left feeling empty as a result of casual sexual encounters, Ruth Institute, "For Survivors," http://www.ruthinstitute.org/for-survivors.

9. Andrew J. B. Cameron, *Joined-Up Life: A Christian Account of How Ethics Works* (Nottingham, UK: Inter-Varsity Press, 2011), 290.

10. Erin Dufault-Hunter, "Sex and Sexuality," in *Dictionary of Scripture and Ethics*, eds. Joel B. Green et al. (Grand Rapids: Baker Academic, 2011), 719.

11. Daniel R. Heimbach outlines several perspectives in his book *True Sexual Morality: Recovering Biblical Standards for a Culture in Crisis* (Wheaton, IL: Crossway, 2004).

- a loss of influence on the part of churches, and churches that are complicit in accepting and adopting dominant cultural trends

General Western perspective on sex and sexual morality

Francis Watson describes (though does not endorse) the perspective on sex and sexual morality now familiar to modern people in the West: "Sex is natural. Sex is good. Sex is enjoyable. There is no need to be ashamed of it. Indeed, we inflict serious psychological damage on ourselves if we attempt to repress our sexuality. Repression stems from a negative view of the body, for which Christianity is largely responsible."[12]

This is told as a story of liberation. What is natural and good and enjoyable ought to be experienced in order to flourish fully as a human being. Hence, any external restraint, whether from religion or government, is a form of suppression, and self-imposed restraint must be a form of repression. This account, or something like it, is assumed and repeated so often that it hardly needs a defense, it would seem. Again, Watson writes, "The story of our sexual liberation is told and retold in many different versions; it is constantly updated, so as to incorporate new emphases overlooked by earlier renderings; and various qualifications and nuances may be added or subtracted. But in all these variations it is recognizably the same story that is told and retold, so compelling that it imposes itself as self-evidently true."[13]

The meaning of the story, however, is not clear. In one sense, there is no meaning; sex is merely an act. In a worldview grounded in philosophical naturalism, relativism, and the rejection of religious meaning, how could it be more than that? For some, not least on college campuses, "casual sex" is the order of the day.[14] If it is indeed casual, there can be no essential or intrinsic meaning. Meaning is whatever the people involved attribute to the act and relationship.

Yet, in another sense, this "liberation" takes the form of a pseudo-religious structure and experience. Sex is understood to be much more than an act and, it would seem, ultimate meaning is attributed to it. The very language of liberation indicates as much. It is the pursuit of pleasure, to be sure, but it is more than that. It is, in effect, the pursuit of a form of salvation through sex. Not, of course, in the biblical understanding of salvation—rather, "salvation" in the sense of a rescue from meaninglessness, the pursuit of some kind of wholeness,

---

12. Francis Watson, *Agape, Eros, Gender: Towards a Pauline Sexual Ethic* (Cambridge: Cambridge University Press, 2000), 93.
13. Watson, *Agape, Eros, Gender*, 93.
14. See accounts such as Nathan Harden, *Sex and God at Yale: Porn, Political Correctness, and a Good Education Gone Bad* (New York: Thomas Dunne, 2012); Leland Elliott and Cynthia Brantley, *Sex on Campus: The Naked Truth about the Real Sex Lives of College Students* (New York: Random House, 1997). See also surveys such as Robert T. Michael et al., *Sex in America: A Definitive Survey* (New York: Little, Brown, 1994); and Mark Regnerus and Jeremy Uecker, *Premarital Sex in America: How Young Americans Meet, Mate, and Think about Marrying* (Oxford: Oxford University Press, 2011).

and the throwing off of the shackles of religion and tradition.

Watson's description of contemporary views of sex captures this aspect. "To be embodied is to be innocent not guilty, and the sexual conjunction of bodies celebrates this innocence in the play of paradise. . . . Eros, demonized for so long, is again found to be a god who bestows on his devotees the bliss of participation in his own divinity."[15] The words of some of the leading figures in the sexual revolution speak frankly on this point. For instance, Margaret Sanger asserts that "through sex, mankind may attain the great spiritual illumination which will transform the world, which will light up the only path to an earthly paradise."[16] A book about the philosophy of Wilhelm Reich, a psychoanalyst whose radical work gained something of a following among sexual revolutionaries, is even called *Salvation through Sex*.[17] This stems in part from the view that sexuality has come to be thought of as the essence of who we are. Indeed, as Philip Turner notes, philosopher Michel Foucault asserted that "sexuality" has come to serve "the same purpose as did the word 'soul' in the Middle Ages." Turner adds, "At that time, 'soul' provided its users with a way to unite the various aspects of human identity and, in so doing, gave it significance. It is now the function of the word 'sexuality' to do the same thing."[18]

This is something like what Cameron refers to as "sexual essentialism." Sex has become an essential part of human experience and identity. Without sex, we are incomplete, less than fully human. If we have sexual desires that haven't been fulfilled, then something essential is missing. "We think we're like a machine that 'needs' sex, just as a car 'needs' fuel, and so we speak of our sexual 'needs.' In this 'sexual essentialism,' erotic intimacy or sexual ecstasy is the pinnacle and goal of human existence, and sexual acts complete our humanity."[19]

All of this represents the confusion and chaos regarding sex and sexual morality at present. Far too little weight is placed on sex, in order to be freed from a sense of moral responsibility, and yet far too much weight is placed on sex, in the hope of finding ourselves. In between the view that sex has no meaning and the view that sex carries ultimate meaning, there have been attempts to articulate views in which sex is not thought to have essential or intrinsic meaning, but rather meaning is attributed to sex by those engaged with one another in the act. Stafford characterizes the general view as the "Ethic of Intimacy," which exhibits seven features:[20]

---

15. Watson, *Agape, Eros, Gender*, 93.
16. Margaret Sanger, *The Pivot of Civilization* (New York: Brentano's, 1922), 271.
17. Eustace Chesser, *Salvation through Sex: The Life and Work of Wilhelm Reich* (New York: W. Morrow, 1973).
18. Philip Turner, "Sex and the Single Life," *First Things*, May 1993, 17. Turner refers to Foucault's first volume of *The History of Sexuality*, vol. 1, *An Introduction*, trans. Robert Hurley (New York: Random House, 1978).
19. Cameron, *Joined-Up Life*, 291.
20. The following seven features are from Stafford, *Sexual Chaos*, chap. 4, pp. 43–45.

1. *An invariably positive view of sex*—Sex is good as long as there is intimacy (and not terribly problematic in other contexts).
2. *The independent individual*—While sex is intimate, it is the joining of individuals in which each remains independent.
3. *Compatibility*—Intimacy is created by a sense of compatibility, in which the two just "click."
4. *Sex is a private matter*—Each individual must decide what is best, and how to navigate sexual relationships.
5. *Sex has no necessary personal consequences*—Like many things in life, there are ups and downs, each with an opportunity to learn something about yourself and move on to bigger and better things.
6. *No double standard*—Men and women have the same standard, where sex before (or perhaps outside of) marriage is acceptable for both.
7. *Sex requires maturity*—Since the meaning or significance of sex is situational, dependent on a number of variables, it requires a degree of wisdom or maturity to know when it is right (though this requirement is undermined by number 4, sex being a private matter and up to each individual).

While there is no consensus on the meaning of sex, Stafford's description does capture fairly well contemporary attitudes and expressions.[21]

Contemporary culture and an ethics of sex

What is the result of the general perspective on sexual morality just described, in terms of sexual ethics? What are the rules or boundaries governing sexual expression? In a sense, there are no rules. At least, there are no rules that are grounded in the nature of sex, no universal moral norms recognized within a naturalistic worldview. Yet there is a stubborn sense that sex requires rules, even that there is a moral order that governs sex. Indeed, it seems that most people recognize that society must enforce some rules in order to maintain some order.

Two rules governing sexual expression. There are two rules that are recognized as virtually universal, which are compatible with the general perspective described: *act only by consent* and *do no harm*. These fit with the emphasis on personal autonomy and the subjective meaning of sex determined by the individual. Of the two, the primary rule is the requirement of consent. This is, first, because "do no harm" is derived from the demand for consent (assuming that no one would consent to harm). Second, it is because "harm" is more subjective than consent. The old orthodoxy held that harm could occur even if it was not perceived by

---

21. Heimbach, in *True Sexual Morality*, describes various views as "Romantic Sexual Morality" (Sex as Affection); "Playboy Sexual Morality" (Sex as Pleasure); "Therapeutic Sexual Morality" (Sex as Wholeness); and "Pagan Sexual Morality" (Sex as Spiritual Life). Turner, "Sex and the Single Life," also gives an overview of the perspective of the "New Reformers" on sex. Among those reformers, James B. Nelson has been influential in proposing not simply a theology of sex, but a sexual theology. See James Nelson, *Embodiment: An Approach to Sexuality and Christian Theology* (Minneapolis: Augsburg, 1978). For Nelson, sex requires "love," but not necessarily marriage or heterosexual complementarity.

the individual. For example, parents might perceive their child to be harmed by sex before marriage even if the child didn't perceive it, and society held (and still holds) that a minor is harmed by sex with an adult even if the minor does not perceive it. In revisionist orthodoxy, within limits, the individual determines what is harmful (and the individual can conceivably consent to what others consider harmful).

Recently questions have been raised about how consent ought to be determined. In the old orthodoxy, consent to marriage was the objective, public statement of consent to sex. In the new orthodoxy, where sex and marriage have been separated, it is not obvious how consent should be understood. It seems simple enough: *No means no*—if an individual indicates that they don't want to have a sexual relationship, that must be respected. Yet, where there is coercion, or where drugs or alcohol have reduced or eliminated inhibitions and decision-making capacity, it is not always clear where genuine consent has been given.

As a result, some have proposed—and adopted—a new standard: *Yes means yes.* This standard is mandated on college campuses in New York and California, and on other university campuses around the country. As one article explains, "The idea is simple: In matters of sex, silence or indifference aren't consent. Only a freely given 'yes' counts. And if you can't tell, you have to ask."[22] "Yes means yes" may be well-intended, and it may also resolve some problems. Yet it doesn't resolve the problem of consent or eliminate confusion altogether, especially where decision-making capacity is compromised. One issue has to do with what is included in "matters of sex." Are holding hands and hugging or any touching "matters of sex" that require positive consent, where failure to obtain consent could result in a charge of sexual assault? Silly, perhaps, but who determines what acts are "matters of sex"? Is subjectivity eliminated when we read that "if you can't tell, you have to ask"? Wouldn't a charge of inappropriate sexual contact simply be met with, "I could tell—I was sure—that it was what we both wanted." A *New York Times* article reveals, perhaps inadvertently, some of the problems with "yes means yes."[23]

What this illustrates is that when biblical truth is rejected, and the objective standard of marriage for sexual intimacy is replaced with any subjective standard, it leads to sexual chaos.

What conduct is generated or permitted by our culture's general perspective and it's rules? If sex is private matter, and its meaning and boundaries are determined by autonomous individuals, governed by

---

22. Jaclyn Friedman, "Adults Hate 'Yes Means Yes' Laws. The College Students I Meet Love Them," *Washington Post*, October 13, 2015, https://www.washingtonpost.com/posteverything/wp/2015/10/14/adults-hate-affirmative-consent-laws-the-college-students-i-meet-love-them/.

23. Teens discussing the issue raised issues of awkwardness, confusion about how to ask, whether each advance requires a pause to ask about the next level, etc. Jennifer Medina, "Sex Ed Lesson: 'Yes Means Yes,' but It's Tricky," *New York Times*, October 14, 2015, http://www.nytimes.com/2015/10/15/us/california-high-schools-sexual-consent-classes.html?_r=0.

the requirement of consent, then what sexual behaviors are allowed? Essentially, anything is allowed that the persons involved understand to be loving, or intimate, or at least desirable in some sense and therefore something to which they give their consent. If it is perceived to be personally fulfilling, it is good, or at least acceptable. This perspective is a radical change from the old orthodoxy, with few boundaries. Sex before marriage is expected and accepted, for abstinence is understood to be unrealistic or even harmful. For many, "casual sex" is accepted as well, as long as the persons involved desire it. Homosexuality cannot be condemned in such a view, nor merely tolerated or accepted, but must be affirmed as of equal value with any heterosexual relationship. There is nothing in this perspective that can finally reject polygamy, so long as there is consent.[24] For some, this sexual liberty must even allow for incest.[25]

Not everyone accepts all of the implications of the new orthodoxy. Some remnants of the old orthodoxy are difficult to dispatch, whether incest or polygamy or other behaviors, even if the rationale for rejecting them has been lost. Perhaps the rationale for the Christian view on sexuality and sex needs to be recovered, grounded as it is in the truth of the Bible.

A Christian Perspective on Sexuality and Sex

Presuppositions

The basic framework and presuppositions for Christian ethics in general, and thus for Christian sexual ethics, has been outlined in earlier chapters. Here it is worth simply highlighting some key features. First, ethics is grounded in the character, will, and purposes of God. Scripture reveals a personal God who created all things with purpose as part of a grand design. Human beings play a central role in the purposes of God. His will for human beings corresponds to his design and purposes for us within a created order. Second, God reveals his character, will, and purposes for human beings in the Bible. The Bible is authoritative because it is inspired and given by God and it is true. Truth carries authority. Like an accurate map that serves as an authoritative guide for traveling, the Bible reveals God's design and purposes in the world, and his will for how we are to live in accordance with his design and purpose. That is, it reveals who we truly are, and how we are meant to live in order to flourish in the world God has created. Third, then, the Bible is the primary source for moral norms for human life and conduct, including our understanding of sexuality and sexual conduct. The commands of God

24. As Justice Scalia recognized in his dissent in the 2002 Supreme Court decision in Lawrence v. Texas 539 U.S. 558 (2003), https://caselaw.findlaw.com/us-supreme-court/539/558.html, which struck down the Texas sodomy law. Based on the court's reasoning, Scalia argued that laws against bigamy, same-sex marriage, adult incest, prostitution, bestiality, and other acts would not be sustainable.
25. Justin Huggler, "Incest a 'Fundamental Right,' German Committee Says" Telegraph, September 24, 2014, http://www.telegraph.co.uk/news/worldnews/europe/germany/11119062/Incest-a-fundamental-right-German-committee-says.html.

in Scripture fit human nature and design. Our understanding of sexuality and our sexual behavior should conform to the the explicit commands of God in his Word, for the good of the individual and society and for the glory of God. Sex is a gift from God, and should be received and lived as a gift.

A biblical perspective on sexual morality: the pattern of creation, fall, and redemption

Against the pattern of chaos and confusion about sexuality and sex that we find in our culture, the Bible reveals purpose and order. To be sure, it is a purpose and an order that has been confounded to a significant degree. Yet the Bible reveals the way things ought to be, according to God's plan. It also reveals what went wrong, and why there is chaos and confusion in our understanding and experience of sex. Finally, it reveals how God has not left us in chaos and confusion, to our own ruin, but has sought to redeem and renew all things, and to point us to our future in Christ and his kingdom. This pattern of creation, fall, and redemption helps us to understand the way that things were meant to be, the way that things actually are, and how God seeks to redeem us as we await a true future.

The ordering of sex in creation. The creation accounts in Genesis 1–2 reveal essential elements of God's design for human beings. These are brief accounts, packed with purpose and significance. Genesis 1 declares that God created human beings in his image, male and female (v. 27), and blessed them with the command to be fruitful, multiply, fill the earth, and subdue it, and have dominion over his creation (v. 28). The creation of male and female is not accidental or incidental, but is central to God's design and purpose for human beings as sexual beings—distinct and complementary.[26]

The account in Genesis 2 offers a more detailed picture of the creation of human beings, which helps us to understand something of the significance of male and female. There the man is created first, and he is given the task to work and keep the garden that God created (vv. 8, 15). God has not yet created the woman, and he declares that it is not good for the man to be alone, and that he will make "a helper corresponding to him" (v. 18). The "not good" of the man's aloneness stands in sharp contrast to the pronouncements in Genesis 1 that God saw that what he made was good (vv. 4, 10, 12, 18, 25, 31), highlighting in 2:18 that before the woman is created, God's work of creation is not yet complete. After God creates the woman, the man delights in her as his complement, saying,

This one, at last, is bone of my bone
and flesh of my flesh. (v. 23)

Then Genesis 2:24 explains, "This is why a man leaves his father and mother and bonds with his wife, and they become one flesh."

---

26. This is not an explanation of what it means to be made in the image of God, but rather a demonstration of our creatureliness. Being created in the image of God serves to underscore the uniqueness of human beings in God's design and purposes. As God's image bearers, human beings have not only unique value but also a unique role as stewards of God's creation.

These accounts provide the foundation for a Christian perspective on sexuality, sex, and marriage, describing God's design and purpose. The teaching on sex and marriage in the rest of the Bible is grounded in these texts and unpacks what is implicit here. The law and its commands support God's design and purpose and reveal aspects of it. Jesus and Paul both appeal to these accounts to establish or clarify what they hold to be true about marriage and sex (cf. Matt. 19:3–9; 1 Cor. 6:16; Eph. 5:23–33). The details of a Christian sexual ethics unfold in a study of the whole Bible, but here we can trace certain contours that are found in these accounts in Genesis 1–2.

As noted already, human beings are created male and female—sexual beings. God's design, purpose, and command is to create male and female, who will together be fruitful, multiply, fill the earth, subdue it, and rule over it as God's representatives. Without both man and woman, God's work of creation was incomplete. In male or female alone, there is a fundamental sense of incompleteness, for God has created male and female to be distinct and complementary, each with roles to play in his purposes. We need one another.

What is human sexuality? Sexuality is a term that is used frequently, and often without clear definition, or with a wide range of meaning. Lewis Smedes writes that "sexuality is the human drive toward intimate communion."[27] Similarly, James Nelson suggests that "the mystery of our sexuality is the mystery of our need to reach out to embrace others both physically and spiritually."[28] Both of these may touch on some aspect of what is true about sexuality, but they are both vague and each requires clarification. The indefinite notion of sexuality allows Nelson to claim that it "involves our affectional orientation toward those of the opposite and/or the same sex."[29] It appears that Nelson draws his account not so much from the teaching of the Bible as from human experience.

Stanley Grenz is a bit more precise. He understands sexuality as "a basic datum of our existence as individuals. Simply stated, it refers to our way of being in the world and relating to the world as male and female."[30] In addition, he says that "sexuality comprises all aspects of the human person that are related to existence as male and female. Our sexuality, therefore, is a powerful, deep, and mysterious aspect of our being."[31] Human beings are embodied persons, existing as either male or female, symbolizing our fundamental incompleteness. This basic understanding indicates the purpose of sexuality. For Grenz, sexuality is that which "calls us to move toward completeness. It forms the

---

27. Lewis B. Smedes, *Sex for Christians* (Grand Rapids: Eerdmans, 1976), 32.
28. Nelson, *Embodiment*, 18.
29. Nelson, *Embodiment*, 18.
30. Stanley J. Grenz, *Sexual Ethics: An Evangelical Perspective* (Louisville: Westminster John Knox, 1997), 20.
31. Grenz, *Sexual Ethics*, 21. In this perspective, sexuality is comprehensive, for it is difficult to identify aspects of our personhood that are unrelated to being male or female.

foundation for the drive which moves male and female to come together to form a unity of persons in marriage."[32]

So far, so good. Grenz's account deserves attention, for he attempts to understand both what sexuality is and what it is for. He does so in the course of a robust account of sexual ethics. He rightly recognizes sexuality—being male and female—as central to an understanding of the nature of human beings. However, it seems to me that when he relates sexuality to various aspects of human existence, he veers off course. For instance, he says, "Sexuality, then, is an expression of our nature as social beings. We are not isolated entities existing to ourselves; nor are we the source of our fulfillment. On the contrary, we derive fulfillment beyond ourselves. This need to find fulfillment beyond ourselves is the dynamic that leads to the desire to develop relationships with others and with God."[33]

In the end, Grenz's account of sexuality is too broad and all-encompassing, as the desire for all relationships—including all human relationships and our relationship with God—is driven by sexuality. Perhaps one of the problems is that Bible does not provide an explicit account of sexuality. It depicts human beings as embodied creatures who are male and female, and it speaks clearly about sexual desire and sex,

but it does not explicitly treat the concept of sexuality. As a result, it may be that our understanding is strongly influenced by accounts derived from social science and even popular culture.

Nevertheless, while we do well to exercise caution, due to the implicit nature of the Bible's treatment of sexuality, it is worth developing an account if for no other reason than to provide an alternative to the dominant cultural narrative. In essence, the dominant cultural narrative is that sexuality is an essential aspect of who we are as human beings, which produces sexual desire, which draws us to sexual union with the object of our desire.[34] By contrast, the biblical account suggests that human sexuality is a central aspect of who we are as human beings, which produces sexual desire, drawing us toward the (one-flesh) union of one man and one woman in marriage. It may seem like only a slight distinction, but it is a distinction with a significant difference. This account requires a brief elaboration.[35]

Sexuality and the desire for union. Human sexuality is grounded in God's design of human beings as male and female. In male or female alone there is some sense of incompleteness. Sexuality is a way of describing the dynamic of maleness and femaleness, which produces a desire that moves male and female to be completed

---

32. Grenz, *Sexual Ethics*, 20.
33. Grenz, *Sexual Ethics*, 193.
34. This seems to me the implication of separating sexual union from procreation, marriage, and heterosexual complementarity, as in Nelson's view. Also, to a greater or lesser degree in other revisionist writers. This is the result of reducing sex to pleasure, communion, mutuality, relational fulfillment, or other similar suggestions.
35. In this account, I draw broad outlines significantly from the work of Grenz, *Sexual Ethics*, and Dennis P. Hollinger, *The Meaning of Sex: Christian Ethics and the Moral Life* (Grand Rapids: Baker Academic, 2009).

through an intimate bond that Genesis describes as a one-flesh union (Gen. 2:24). Physical sexual union is included, but it is more than that, involving a desire for deeper intimacy—to know and to be known—in the union of two lives. Taken together, Genesis presents this union as the lifelong marriage covenant of one man and one woman designed for the purposes of physical union, fruitful labor, procreation, and fellowship.

Therefore, sexuality, sexual desire, and sex are designed by God and are good—they are to be celebrated—within the context of marriage and its purposes. For this reason Christian sexual ethics has been governed by the marriage relationship and its purposes. Sexual intimacy is designed to be exclusive and celebrated in marriage alone, and it is guarded by boundaries outside of the marriage relationship.

Sexual desire is intended to draw us to marriage, not merely to sex. Prior to marriage, sexual desire has sometimes been characterized as a bad or dangerous thing. This is not quite right. To be sure, sex before marriage is a bad and dangerous thing, for it does not fit with the very design of sex. However, prior to marriage, sexual desire should be understood as natural, God-given, and therefore good. The issue is how it is directed and channeled. As indicated earlier, the new orthodoxy understands sexual desire to be directed to sex quite apart from marriage. To repress or suppress the desire and to deny its fulfillment in sex is understood to be harmful. However, such a view

is contrary to the very design and purpose of sexual desire and sex as revealed in the Bible. Prior to marriage, sexual desire and the desire for physical intimacy is drawing us not merely toward sex but toward the one-flesh union of marriage. It must therefore be directed toward marriage and controlled prior to marriage.

This is not repressive. Rather, it recognizes the beauty of sexual intimacy, which creates and sustains a one-flesh union that is designed to be exclusive and permanent. It preserves that beauty and channels energy and desire to its proper outlet. It also denies that we are slaves to our sexual desire, recognizing that it is possible to live—as Jesus did—in chaste singleness before (or perhaps even instead of) entering into a faithful lifelong marriage.[36]

The disordering of sex in the fall

Sex is not what it is meant to be. Rather than realizing the design and purpose of sex, we experience confusion, chaos, and corruption brought about by sin. God's design and purpose—the *telos* of sex—is rejected and subverted. Having rejected God's design, and God himself, everyone does what is right in their own eyes. Objective moral standards are rejected, and the meaning of sex is thought to be whatever individuals make of it by their own intentions and purposes. Without a sense of an objective *telos* for sex, the biblical commands appear arbitrary or outdated and are rejected and replaced with minimal rules that fit a broad range of subjective intentions.

---

36. See Cameron, *Joined-Up Life*, 291.

Once the objective design and purpose of sex was precluded—and with it, the commands that sustained and reinforced it—it was only a matter of time before the rest of the structure would be rejected.

- The idea that marriage is designed by God to be a one-flesh union, lifelong covenant between one man and one woman, and that sex belongs to marriage, is rejected.
- The idea that marriage and sex are ordered to procreation, to the well-being of children rather than simply the pleasure of adults, is rejected.
- The idea that male and female represent two distinct and complementary genders is rejected.
- The idea that human beings exist as male or female, a concrete and fixed reality, is rejected.
- Objective, physical realities are replaced with subjective feeling and perception.
- Sex before marriage is accepted and expected.
- Sex outside of marriage is perhaps still frowned on (it is still commonly referred to as "cheating"), but understood ("it happens" and almost seems inevitable given certain circumstances and "chemistry").
- Homosexuality must not merely be tolerated or even accepted, but embraced.
- The new sexual "orthodoxy" is promoted zealously in the media and cultural structures (e.g., universities). Resistance is vigorously attacked.
- Pornography is widespread, and is a multibillion-dollar industry in the US.
- Cohabitation is now commonplace.

Reordering of sex in redemption

In spite of sin, and these challenges to the design and purpose of sex, all is not lost. The biblical message is one of hope, including the hope that sex can be redeemed in this fallen world, for God's glory and our good. The gospel, through the power of the Spirit, is transformational. The transformation with regard to sex and sexuality is cited frequently in the New Testament. We have seen already how Paul calls the Thessalonians to abstain from sexual immorality as part of their sanctification, which is God's will, rather than to pursue lustful desires as do those who don't know God (1 Thess. 4:3–5).

The transformation of sexual desires and acts is seen in 1 Corinthians as well. Among those whom Paul says will not inherit God's kingdom are the sexually immoral, adulterers, and homosexuals. Paul recognizes that some of the Corinthians were among them (6:11a, "some of you used to be like this"), but he declares that they have been transformed by the power of the gospel: "But you were washed, you were sanctified, you were justified in the name of the Lord Jesus Christ and by the Spirit of our God" (v. 11b).

Likewise, in Ephesians Paul shows the transformational change brought by the gospel. The first three chapters describe the outworking of God's eternal plan to reconcile people to him and to one another through faith in Jesus Christ and his work on the cross. At the end of chapter 3, Paul praises God, "who is able to do above and beyond all that we ask or think according to the power that works in us" (v. 20). Then he transitions to describe how that transforming power is to be worked out in the Christian life. Paul first urges Christians to "walk worthy of the calling you have received" (4:1). That is, the gospel demands and enables us to live according to the will of God.

The "worthy" life is contrasted with the way the Gentiles live (and the way that those transformed by the gospel used to live). Their thoughts are futile, their understanding is darkened, and they are excluded from the life of God because of their (willful) ignorance and hardness of heart (4:17–18). Because of their lack of understanding and hard hearts, Paul says, "They became callous and gave themselves over to promiscuity for the practice of every kind of impurity with a desire for more and more" (4:19). Due to sin, this is our "natural" state, for we are separated from the truth and power of God.

The gospel changes all that, transforming and renewing our minds and actions. Those who follow Christ are to "take off your former way of life, the old self that is corrupted by deceitful desires, to be renewed in the spirit of your minds, and to put on the new self, the one created according to God's likeness in righteousness and purity of the truth" (4:22–24). The change is brought to every aspect of our life, including our sexual life. Thus Paul says, "But sexual immorality and any impurity or greed should not even be heard of among you, as is proper for saints. Obscene and foolish talking or crude joking are not suitable, but rather giving thanks.

For know and recognize this: Every sexually immoral or impure or greedy person, who is an idolater, does not have an inheritance in the kingdom of Christ and of God" (5:3–5).

These examples suffice to show the outworking of the gospel to transform lives and redeem sex from the chaos and confusion caused by sin. It is possible to live lives of chaste singleness and faithful marriage. Abstinence outside of marriage is realistic, for not only is there hope through the power of God and the work of the Spirit, but there is a plausibility structure: the truth of God's Word with a coherent worldview; the resources of the Spirit to understand and live out God's will; and the body of Christ, the church, as the redeemed community called to embody God's will.[37] Ephesians does not address Christians merely as individuals, but as the people of God who are called to encourage and exhort one another.

In a sex-saturated culture, it may seem like we are beholden to our sexual desires. Yet God's people are called to display a counterculture where, as Cameron writes, "we find men and women forging contented marriages, and single people learning the art of a network of intimate, non-sexualized friendships."[38] Sexual purity becomes realistic and can be sustained because it is part of a plausibility structure where it is modeled (albeit imperfectly). Chaste singleness can be sustained, and even understood as a calling for some. Faithful marriages can

---

37. The further working out of these things, making chaste singleness and faithful marriage plausible, includes wisdom not to put ourselves in compromising positions, to guard our hearts and actions, and so on.
38. Cameron, *Joined-Up Life*, 291.

be formed and sustained, demonstrating the love, patience, and forgiveness of God. Sexuality and sexual desire can be directed to their proper end in marriage. Biblical commands can be understood not as oppressive or repressive but as preserving the good of sexuality, singleness, and marriage, for God's glory and our good.

The body of Christ is not only to be a redemptive community for the sake of the redeemed. As salt and light, Christians are to have a redemptive effect on the surrounding culture, as a model of goodness, righteousness, and truth (cf. Eph. 5:8–10), for the glory of God (Matt. 5:13–16).

The logic of biblical prohibitions against sex outside of marriage

In a culture where sex is at once no big deal and a very big deal, much like food is no big deal yet a very big deal, abstinence outside of marriage no longer makes sense. Moreover, it no longer seems possible. Further, the commands prohibiting sex outside of marriage seem unacceptably burdensome if not arbitrary. The truth is, in the fallen world, biblical commands cut across our desires. They interrogate our sexual desires and reveal false gods.[39] Yet, if we consider the logic of these biblical prohibitions, we can see that they reveal and sustain a vision of sexual wholeness and beauty that is worth pursuing.

One of the false assumptions or conclusions about biblical prohibitions of sex outside of marriage is that it treats sex itself as something negative. Thus, to the extent that the Christian tradition follows biblical teaching, it is charged with treating sex itself as shameful or dirty. One example of this mindset comes from an annual meeting of the Society of Christian Ethics, where it was reported that "many at the conference were determined to move away from traditional beliefs that Judeo-Christianity preaches, such as sex is shameful, sex should be restricted to procreation, masturbation is wrong, sex outside marriage is always bad and homosexuality is evil."[40] This wide-ranging statement is misleading at best, and does not adequately represent the Christian tradition (or the Bible) on sex. Even Augustine, who is often treated as the worst of offenders when it comes to creating a repressive tradition on sex, does not fit such a profile. Suffice it to say here that a more adequate rendering of both the Bible and the Christian tradition is that *shameful* sex is shameful. That is, sex that is taken out of its proper context, removed from the design and purposes of its Creator, in the pursuit of satisfying sexual desire for its own sake, is considered sinful and thus shameful.

The biblical view of sexuality does not view sex negatively, and it does not deny the goodness of sexual desire and pleasure. Rather, it celebrates pure sex and advocates satisfaction and delight in the sexual embrace of marriage (e.g., Gen. 2:23–25; Prov. 5:15–19; Song of Songs). Indeed, it is protective of human well-being. Sex by design forms and

---

39. Cameron, *Joined-Up Life*, 290–91.
40. Douglas Todd, Religion News Service, "Christian Ethicists: Sex Is Fun," *Amarillo Globe News*, February 7, 2002.

sustains an exclusive and permanent union of one flesh. It promotes well-being by establishing faithful, stable relationships for the sake of marriage partners, and any children who may be received in marriage. It establishes and maintains stability and trust in society. It effectively eliminates the fear and problem of sexually transmitted diseases and infections, unwelcomed pregnancies, distrust, and many scars.

Abstinence outside of marriage does not deny the goodness of sexual desire and pleasure, but it does deny short-term satisfaction of desire in favor of long-term satisfaction and pleasure. Contrary to a common narrative, which suggests that marital sex is boring, married people consistently report the highest frequency and satisfaction in their sex lives.[41] Abstinence outside of marriage protects the goodness and enjoyment to be found in marriage and sex, and the strength and integrity of marriage and sexual union. Only marriage provides true responsibility for sex, with the context and commitment that corresponds to sexual intimacy and the potential for procreation.

In 1 Thessalonians 4, Paul treats sex outside of marriage as both a personal and a corporate problem. Personally, it is a matter of sanctification and self-control; to pursue sex outside of marriage is to act like those who don't know God (v. 5). Corporately, sex outside of marriage defrauds others (v. 6). While Paul is not specific about who is betrayed, it is not difficult to see that it is a multifaceted offense that betrays many relationships and disrupts a community:

- As an extreme example, rape is first an offense against the victim, but also an offense against the victim's family and the community.
- Adultery is an offense against one's spouse and/or another person's spouse, and also against families and others who have an interest not only in the victim(s), including children involved, but also in the marriage that has been violated.
- Fornication is an offense against the other person's parents and family, who have an interest in their well-being; against that person's future spouse, who is meant to be the exclusive sexual partner; and even against that person and oneself (1 Cor. 6:18), both of whom should reserve sexual intimacy for marriage.

Finally, the prohibition of sex outside of marriage testifies to the fact that there is no such thing as "casual sex." It might be protested that such a statement is nonsense, and has been proved false every day by the fact that strangers meet in bars or clubs, leave together, and have one-night stands. As further evidence, hookups occur on college campuses every day between people who are not in a committed relationship. The notion of having "friends with benefits" also

---

41. Linda J. Waite and Maggie Gallagher, *The Case for Marriage: Why Married People Are Happier, Healthier, and Better Off Financially* (New York: Broadway, 2000). One survey concluded that "the group that has the most sex is not the young and the footloose but the married." Michael et al., *Sex in America*, 112.

testifies to the casual way in which people approach sex. Perhaps nothing testifies more clearly to the existence of casual sex than prostitution, for sex is treated like a commodity to be bought and sold.

Yet these examples miss the point of the argument that there is no such thing as casual sex. To treat sex in a casual way does not demonstrate that sex actually is casual any more than using a masterpiece from Rembrandt as a scratch pad demonstrates that it is, in fact, a scratch pad. The apostle Paul engages something like this point with some men in Corinth who visited prostitutes. They appear to have justified their acts by arguing that the body is meant for sex just as food is meant for the stomach (1 Cor. 6:13), that our bodies will be destroyed anyway (v. 13), and that what we do with our bodies does not affect us spiritually, perhaps because sin is a matter of the heart (v. 18).[42]

Paul counters such a view by maintaining that sex has intrinsic or essential meaning. That is, sex is not merely an act, but a union of two persons. He grounds his argument in the nature and design of sex in the creation accounts. He says, "Don't you know that anyone joined to a prostitute is one body with her? For Scripture says, The two will become one flesh" (1 Cor. 6:16). In other words, so-called casual sex violates the very nature of the act. To engage in "casual sex" is, at best, to practice self-deceit. It is not merely an act, for it enacts the one-flesh union of two persons in marriage. It is no wonder that often a person who has sex with someone who simply "moves on" feels used and betrayed. When it happens repeatedly, a person may become scarred and numb to the feeling of betrayal, but that doesn't change the reality.

In his book *Sex for Christians*, Smedes captures the principle that flows from Paul's statement and the Genesis account. Smedes argues that all sex outside of marriage is wrong because "it violates the inner reality of the act," for it involves "a life-uniting act without a life-uniting intent."[43] One need not think or know that they are violating the act for it to be true. That is, it is not a matter of subjective intent or meaning, but the objective meaning of the act, and the objective intent represented by marriage vows. Derrick Baily captures something of this—though he may say too much—when he writes, "Sexual intercourse is an act of the whole self which affects the whole self; it is a personal encounter between a man and a woman in which each does something to the other, for good or for ill, which can never be obliterated. This remains true even when

---

42. The HCSB captures the Corinthian slogan in verse 18: "Every sin a person can commit is outside the body," rather than adding "other," as many translations do, but which is not in the Greek (so to say, "every *other* sin a person can commit is outside the body"). On the Corinthian slogans in 1 Corinthians 6:12–20, see Denny Burk, *What Is the Meaning of Sex?* (Wheaton, IL: Crossway, 2013), 43–59. See also Richard B. Hays, *First Corinthians*, Interpretation: A Bible Commentary for Teaching and Preaching (Louisville: Westminster John Knox, 1997), 101–7; and Jay E. Smith, "The Roots of a 'Libertine' Slogan in 1 Corinthians 6:18," *Journal of Theological Studies* 59, no. 1 (2008): 63–95.

43. Smedes, *Sex for Christians*, 130.

they are ignorant of the radical character of their act."[44]

Sex has intrinsic purpose and meaning, designed by God to unite a man and a woman in the one-flesh relationship of marriage. Sexuality is other-seeking, producing a desire that draws us into the relationship of one flesh. However, in a fallen world, it is easily bent toward self-gratification. Biblical commands regarding sex guard against self-seeking acts and desires and call us to use sex according to the purposes for which God designed it.

Sexuality and singleness

If sexuality and sexual desire are ordered to marriage, what are we to think about singleness? What does it mean to say that God created male and female, so that in male or female alone there is a fundamental sense of incompleteness? Is singleness an option, or should we marry? For those who remain single, does it require repressing their sexuality? What do we even mean when we refer to "singleness"? For everyone is born single and grows up single; some adults are single though they desire marriage; some adults are single by choice, some for good reasons, some not so good; and some are single after marriage, by divorce or the death of a spouse. These and other questions pertaining to singleness deserve reflection.

What follows will briefly treat the matter of singleness in general.[45]

The most extended discussion of singleness in the Bible is found in 1 Corinthians 7. There Paul addresses sex and marriage, singleness, and divorce and remarriage. He states and develops the assertion that "I wish that all people were as I am. But each has his own gift from God, one person has this gift, another has that" (v. 7). And again, "I say to the unmarried and to widows: It is good for them if they remain as I am" (v. 8). Here Paul is talking about his singleness.[46] This creates an obvious tension, for if we are sexual beings, and sexuality is ordered to marriage, how can Paul say that he prefers singleness, not only for himself but in general? It seems that he is going against the created order and the will of God! He is also going against the norms of both Roman society and, even more, his Jewish roots. Though this issue is nuanced and deserves detailed treatment, space here permits some brief observations.

First, does Paul mean to urge singleness on *everyone* (or on all Christians)? Not exactly. While Paul does prefer and urges singleness for specific purposes, as we shall see, at least two qualifications keep him from insisting that all remain single. One is that he says, immediately after expressing his preference for singleness, "but if they do not have self-control, they should marry, for it is better

---

44. Derrick Sherwin Bailey, *The Mystery of Love and Marriage: A Study in the Theology of Sexual Relation* (New York: Harper, 1952), 53.

45. For fuller treatments, see Grenz, *Sexual Ethics*, chaps. 9–10; Albert Hsu, *Singles at the Crossroads* (Downers Grove, IL: InterVarsity Press, 1997); Barry Danylak, *Redeeming Singleness: How the Storyline of Scripture Affirms the Single Life* (Wheaton, IL: Crossway, 2010). My treatment of singleness draws broadly from these sources.

46. Though it is not certain, it is possible that Paul was a widower, since it would be unlikely that he could have risen to prominence as a Jewish leader (before his conversion) if he didn't marry.

to marry than to burn with desire" (v. 9). Paul recognizes that some are not well suited to remaining single, and if it opens the door to sexual immorality (including lust), singleness is not the better option! A second qualification is that, as Paul continues to discuss and urge celibate singleness later in the chapter, he says that the choice to marry is not a sin (vv. 28, 36, 38, 39).

Second, if Paul prefers and urges singleness, even if he doesn't insist on it, isn't he going against the created order and the will of God? Again, not exactly. Instead, he is declaring something of a new order, in light of the gospel. In creation, it is God's general will that human beings enter marriage and bear and nurture children. It was therefore unthinkable for the people of Israel to forgo marriage and procreation, unless enlisted in special service to God, as in the case of Jeremiah and his prophetic ministry. In the kingdom inaugurated by Jesus, marriage and procreation are relativized, and celibate singleness serves as a sign of the in-breaking of the kingdom.

This new, eschatological reality is the ground of Paul's preference for singleness. "The time is limited," and "this world in its current form is passing away" (vv. 29, 31). This qualifies everything, including marriage. Thus, "from now on," Paul says, "those who have wives should be as though they had none, those who weep as though they did not weep, those who rejoice as though they did not rejoice, those who buy as though they didn't own anything, and those who use the world as though they did not make full use of it" (vv. 29–31). Each of

these things is qualified, not precluded entirely. Christians can still marry, weep, rejoice, buy, and use the things of the world, but all these things must be understood in light of the gospel and the dawning of the kingdom. We are called to live with the end in view, and with a sense of detachment from the world, not making "full use of it."

This leads to a third observation, highlighting the reasons for Paul's preference for singleness. One reason is that it witnesses to the kingdom and a new future. Marriage and sex are good. They continue to be a blessing from God and a witness to his goodness. But they are not ultimate goods nor are they necessary for human flourishing. Indeed, Jesus declares that "in the resurrection they neither marry nor are given in marriage but are like angels in heaven" (Matt. 22:30). Marriage will pass away, good as it may be. Celibate singleness serves as a witness to the kingdom.

A second reason Paul urges singleness for some is that it provides a unique opportunity for serving God in wholehearted devotion. In light of the gospel, this is understood not as a burden but as a privilege and a joyous calling. We have already seen that Paul does not forbid marriage—he does not wish to burden with singleness those who are not well suited for it. Indeed, in a different way, those who marry have "trouble in this life," which Paul seeks to spare them (1 Cor. 7:28). Marriage and family require hard work, providing for physical and emotional needs, dealing with conflict, caring for one another when illness or other troubles come. All these and others are proper concerns that must not be neglected, and thus Paul says of those who are married that their interests are divided between the concerns of the Lord and the concerns of their family (vv. 32–34). It is not that the concerns of the family are in conflict with service to the Lord, for we are called by God to attend to the needs of those in our care (see 1 Tim. 5:8). Rather, it is that the unmarried person is freed from such concerns, and so may be "devoted to the Lord without distraction" (1 Cor. 7:35).

A third reason Paul urges singleness, which we can draw from his treatment, is related to the previous points. It is that celibate singleness provides an opportunity to draw close to God in a unique way, to testify that sex is not necessary for a full and flourishing life. Here Paul develops a nuanced position. First Corinthians 7 begins with Paul addressing specific issues about which the church had written. They have said that "it is good for a man not to have relations with a woman" (v. 1 HCSB, literally, "to touch a woman"). Paul's response does not entirely reject their slogan, but it does qualify and challenge it. Indeed, it launches him into a discussion of sex in marriage, singleness, and divorce and remarriage. Among the points Paul makes that are relevant for the current discussion are the following:

- Sex is not the problem. Paul is not an ascetic who would deny the body and its needs and desires, including sex. Indeed, he warns the Corinthians that those who are married should give themselves freely to one another (v. 3, it is a marital duty!), or they will become vulnerable to

temptation (vv. 2–5). Sex is good in the context of marriage.

- Sex is not a necessity. This underlies Paul's whole argument for singleness. Indeed, it is not merely singleness, but chaste singleness, since he urges those who do not have self-control to marry (v. 9). By obvious contrast, there are those who have self-control, and Paul urges them to consider chaste singleness. While singleness demands certain sacrifices, Paul indicates not only that it is *possible* but that it is *good*. As we have seen, singleness allows a person to avoid certain troubles in life (vv. 28, 32–34). Beyond that, or because of that, Paul asserts that singleness is, for some, the better option (v. 38) not only for service (v. 35) but also for happiness (v. 40).

- Singleness involves sacrifice. Paul does not draw a contrast between those who desire sexual intimacy (and thus should marry) and those who don't desire sexual intimacy (and thus should remain single). That is, it is not that some people have no sexual desire and they should serve the Lord in wholehearted devotion as single persons. Rather, he draws a contrast between those who do not have self-control and who burn with passion (v. 9), and thus should marry, and the rest, who should consider singleness. This is important, for though they may not burn with passion beyond what they can control, they still experience sexual desire. Some who don't burn with passion may nevertheless marry because they desire marriage for unnamed reasons (vv. 28, 36, 38, 39). Paul says they haven't sinned, even though they could presumably manage being single. Others remain single, by choice or circumstance. Even though there are benefits, which Paul highlights, there are also sacrifices. They may, by God's grace, be able to practice self-control, but they may be vulnerable to temptation in unique ways. They may feel called to serve God in and through their singleness, but not without moments when they desire the blessings of a lifelong intimate companion, children, and a ready-made network of relationships that often go with marriage and family. Forgoing these things involves some sacrifice, and provides opportunity and the necessity to draw close to God and trust him to provide for them in a unique way.[47]

The call to celibacy for those who remain single does not deny the existence of sexual desire. Sex may not be necessary, but it is good, and it may be desired even by those who are not consumed with that desire. Self-control is possible, but it is not always easy! It is a real possibility by God's grace through the power of the Spirit. In spite of a culture that is obsessed with sex and considers it a necessity for a full and flourishing life, sex is not a necessity. Contrary to the spirit of the age, sexual promiscuity is not liberating; it leads to bondage. Faithfulness to God is liberating.

Those who follow the path of chaste singleness still have a need for intimate relationships, free from sex. God created human beings as sexual beings, and as social beings. The two are related but not identical. Human beings are made in the image of God, who is a being-in-relationship but not a sexual being. Since human sexuality and sociality overlap and share some common features, the desire for sex—and its pursuit—may in some cases be driven by a search for intimacy and relationship. Where the need for intimacy is satisfied in healthy ways, sexual temptations and the desire for intimacy in inappropriate ways may be less intense. The church, as a fellowship of believers, can and must be a place where intimate companionship and fellowship are found, where we bear one another's burdens, including the burdens that accompany singleness.

Conclusion

In the midst of a revolution, with confusion concerning a basic understanding of human identity, it is critical for Christians to articulate a clear vision of the Creator's gift of sex, for his glory and for human good. A biblical worldview affirms that sexuality is for more than mere sex, and sex is for more than mere pleasure. This chapter has explored the basic meaning and purpose of sexuality and sex, including implications for singleness. The following chapters will explore the meaning and purpose of sexuality and sex further, with implications for marriage, contraception, divorce and remarriage, homosexuality, and gender.

---

47. The appendix in Albert Hsu's book *Singles at the Crossroads* provides an insightful interview with John Stott that touches on some of these points.

Select Resources

Burk, Denny. *What Is the Meaning of Sex?* Wheaton, IL: Crossway, 2013.

Danylak, Barry. *Redeeming Singleness: How the Storyline of Scripture Affirms the Single Life.* Wheaton: Crossway, 2010.

Grenz, Stanley J. *Sexual Ethics: An Evangelical Perspective.* Louisville: Westminster John Knox, 1997.

Heimbach, Daniel R. *True Sexual Morality: Recovering Biblical Standards for a Culture in Crisis.* Wheaton, IL: Crossway, 2004.

Hollinger, Dennis P. *The Meaning of Sex: Christian Ethics and the Moral Life.* Grand Rapids: Baker Academic, 2009.

Hsu, Albert. *Singles at the Crossroads.* Downers Grove, IL: InterVarsity Press, 1997.

Watson, Francis. *Agape, Eros, Gender: Towards a Pauline Sexual Ethic.* Cambridge: Cambridge University Press, 2000.

CHAPTER 7

MARRIAGE AND SEXUALITY

Let your fountain be blessed,
and take pleasure in the wife of your youth.
—Proverbs 5:18

For this reason a man will leave his father
and mother and be joined to his wife, and
the two will become one flesh. This mystery
is profound, but I am talking about Christ
and the church.
—Ephesians 5:31–32

Marriage is to be honored by all and the mar-
riage bed kept undefiled, because God will
judge the sexually immoral and adulterers.
—Hebrews 13:4

Introduction

> Marriage is a magnificent thing because it is modeled on something magnificent and points to something magnificent. . . . The greatness of marriage is not in itself. The greatness of marriage is that it displays something unspeakably great, namely, Christ and the church.[1]
>
> —John Piper

Marriage is glorious. Marriage is difficult. Both of these assertions are reflected in Scripture and in human experience. The beauty and glory of marriage is presented in the first two chapters of Genesis as a central feature of God's plan for human beings and the world, and ultimately in Paul's letter to the Ephesians. Yet, after the fall, the Bible describes both the beauty of marriage and many of the difficulties, such as conflict, betrayal, and divorce.

The beauty and glory of marriage, as well as the difficulties, are also often revealed in contemporary experiences. Its beauty is on display in the public exchange of wedding vows, and in the demonstration of those vows in the peaks and valleys of life together, in health and in sickness, in plenty and in want, in the gift of children and in the sorrow of infertility. Though the glory of marriage can often be glimpsed—even magnified—through the difficulties, sometimes the challenges in marriage, and to marriage as such, seem overwhelming. Deep differences, disagreements, anger, and conflict sometimes appear to be insurmountable obstacles to marital happiness. Fornication, cohabitation, infidelity, abuse, divorce, and same-sex civil marriage strike at the very foundation of marriage.

All is not lost. In spite of the difficulties couples face, the majority of those who get married stay together. Many more could, but lack the resources—spiritual, social, emotional, and moral—that would enable them to carry on. Yet some who stay together are barely hanging on. In the face of such challenges, we do well to reflect on what marriage is and what it is for. As Geoffrey Bromiley put it, "A theology of marriage can give a new direction. Far too many people, Christians not excluded, are self-centeredly preoccupied with their own marital problems and their attempt to engineer solutions to them. A theology of marriage can help them to achieve a God-centered look at the larger situation of which their marriages constitute a small, if by no means unimportant, part. In the long run a new look means a new understanding, and a new understanding means a new practice."[2]

This chapter will build on the key points from the previous chapter on sexuality and sex. Of particular significance for present purposes are the following propositions:

- Sexuality refers to features of human beings as male and female, designed by

---

1. John Piper, *This Momentary Marriage: A Parable of Permanence* (Wheaton, IL: Crossway, 2009), 138.
2. Geoffrey W. Bromiley, *God and Marriage* (Grand Rapids: Eerdmans, 1980), xii–xiii.

God as embodied beings who are distinct and complementary (not merely biologically, but distinct and complementary as whole persons).

- Sexuality is the basis of the desire for male and female to be united in a relationship of one flesh.
- The one-flesh union includes both physical union and a broader union of a man and a woman in an exclusive and permanent relationship.

That one-flesh relationship is marriage, which will be the focus of this chapter. Specifically, this chapter will provide biblical and theological reflection on the nature of marriage (what is marriage?) and the purposes of marriage (what is marriage for?). Sexuality and sex are ordered to marriage. That is, sexuality and sexual desire are designed to be fulfilled not merely in sex but also in marriage. In addition, the purposes of marriage and the nature of marriage are interconnected. In short, marriage is the comprehensive union of one man and one woman in an exclusive, permanent, fruitful relationship. Its purposes include fidelity in sexual expression, fellowship, and fruitfulness—through bearing and nurturing children, and through fruitful labor. It thus serves a public good as the foundation for society. Finally, marriage reveals a mystery, as it reflects and points to the relationship of God and his people, and particularly the union of Christ and the church.

Our view of sexuality and marriage has significant implications for our lives, because deliberation about how we ought to live flows out of reflection on the way things are (or ought to be). Worldview determines ethics. The view of sexuality and marriage put forth here thus raises certain questions, with implications for many issues: If we are sexual beings, designed for a one-flesh union in marriage, then how should we view singleness? (That question was addressed in the previous chapter.) If sexuality and marriage are designed for the union of male and female, how should we view homosexuality? If marriage is designed to be permanent, how should we view divorce and remarriage? If marriage is designed to be fruitful, then how should we view contraception, infertility, and assisted reproductive technologies?

It is therefore critical that we reflect on the nature and purposes of marriage. After doing so, this chapter will consider contraception as a matter for moral reflection and deliberation. Subsequent chapters will examine divorce and remarriage, homosexuality, and infertility and assisted reproductive technologies. Because of the intimate, personal, and yet public nature of sexuality and marriage, these issues are loaded with emotion. Much is at stake, and each of these matters requires pastoral sensitivity toward those whose experience has been shaped by distortions brought about by the fall and sinful human actions, as well as unflinching commitment to the truth revealed in God's Word concerning the design and purpose of sex, for God's glory and our good.

The Nature and Purposes of Marriage

Oliver O'Donovan describes the classical Christian understanding of marriage in

relation to Jesus's own statement on marriage and divorce (Matt. 19:4–5), itself a reflection on the creation accounts:

> In the ordinance of marriage there was
> given an end for human relationships, a
> teleological structure which was a fact of
> creation and therefore not negotiable. The
> dimorphic organization of human sexu-
> ality, the particular attraction of two adults
> of the opposite sex and of different parents,
> the setting up of a home distinct from the
> parental home and the uniting of their lives
> in a shared life (from which Jesus concluded
> the unnaturalness of divorce): these form a
> pattern of human fulfilment which serves
> the wider end of enabling procreation to
> occur in a context of affection and loyalty.
> Whatever happens in history . . . this is what
> marriage really is. Particular cultures may
> have distorted it; individuals may fall short
> of it. It is to their cost in either case; for it re-
> asserts itself as God's creative intention for
> human relationships on earth; and it will be
> with us, in one form or another, as our nat-
> ural good until (but not after) the kingdom
> of God shall appear.[3]

Against the idea that marriage is the result of historical development or merely a
cultural construct, O'Donovan asserts that
marriage has a definite and particular shape
and structure. It is part of God's good design
for human flourishing. Those wishing to

enter marriage do well to consider its given
nature and purposes, and to align their
understanding and intentions in marriage
with what marriage is (its given teleological
structure). When we marry, that is, we enter
into a covenant relationship that has a particular form; we do not create something of
our own design. Society does well to consider the true nature and purposes of marriage, and to support and reinforce it, for
stable marriages are vital as the context for
procreation and child-rearing, and thus for
a stable society and for human flourishing.
It is possible to distort marriage, individually and culturally, but only at great cost.

The central features of marriage are presented in the first two chapters of Genesis.
The key texts are as follows:

> So God created man
> in his own image;
> he created him in the image of God;
> he created them male and female.
>
> God blessed them, and God said to them,
> "Be fruitful, multiply, fill the earth, and
> subdue it. Rule the fish of the sea, the birds
> of the sky, and every creature that crawls on
> the earth." (Gen. 1:27–28)
>
> No shrub of the field had yet grown on
> the land, and no plant of the field had yet
> sprouted, for the Lord God had not made
> it rain on the land, and *there was no man*

---

3. Oliver O'Donovan, *Resurrection and Moral Order: An Outline for Evangelical Ethics*, 2nd ed. (Grand Rapids: Eerdmans, 1994), 69. See the helpful discussion of marriage in the created order, with reference to O'Donovan in
particular, in Christopher Ash, *Marriage: Sex in the Service of God* (Vancouver, BC: Regent College Publishing,
2005), chap. 4.

to work the ground. . . . Then the Lord God formed the man out of the dust from the ground and breathed the breath of life into his nostrils, and the man became a living being.

The Lord God planted a garden in Eden, in the east, and *there he placed the man he had formed. . . .*

The Lord God took the man and *placed him in the garden of Eden to work it and watch over it. . . .* Then the Lord God said, "It is not good for the man to be alone. I will make a helper corresponding to him. . . ." So the Lord God caused a deep sleep to come over the man, and he slept. God took one of his ribs and closed the flesh at that place. Then the Lord God made the rib he had taken from the man into a woman and brought her to the man. And the man said:

> This one, at last, is bone of my bone
> and flesh of my flesh;
> this one will be called "woman,"
> for she was taken from man.

This is why a man leaves his father and mother and bonds with his wife, and they become one flesh. (Gen. 2:5, 7–8, 15, 18, 21–24, emphases added)[4]

The Nature of Marriage

The first chapter of Genesis offers a rapid and breathtaking view of God's creative work, one that gives significant attention to its design, order, and goodness. Central to this account is the creation of male and female, who bear the image of God and are given the task of serving God, one another, and the rest of creation as God's representatives. The second chapter of Genesis narrows the scope considerably, while again giving attention to God's design, order, and goodness, sharpened by resolving what is described as "not good" in verse 18. Human beings again are central to the account, which describes the creation of the man and woman and their task in the garden. Taken together, these texts form the foundation for a biblical theology of marriage, including Jesus's own teaching on marriage.

What is marriage, then, and how may we describe its teleological structure (its design and purpose)? As stated above, in short, marriage is the comprehensive union of one man and one woman in a fruitful, exclusive, permanent relationship. It is a provision from God, given as a blessing for human well-being and for the fulfillment of God's creation purposes.

Marriage is a provision from God

Marriage is instituted and ordained by God as the most basic of human relationships, to fulfill creation purposes for God's glory and our good. This provision is the answer to the problem declared in Genesis 2:18, that the man is alone. So God declares his intention to create a helper for the man, and he creates the woman and brings her to the man and they are joined in the one-flesh union

---

4. This lengthy citation from Genesis 2 is necessary to show a significant feature of the text, as we will see—one that is often missed if we focus attention primarily on verses 18 and 23–24.

of marriage. The man's response is a glad reception of the blessing of marriage as God's provision. This is a reflection of Genesis 1, where God determines to create human beings in his image, and blesses them, followed by a charge to fulfill the purposes for which he has created them. Human flourishing and well-being are closely connected to fulfilling God's purposes for human beings, and the relationship between male and female in marriage is a central provision for fulfilling those purposes.

Marriage is permanent

Marriage is designed and given by God as a lifelong relationship. The man leaves his family and bonds with his wife (the KJV elegantly says "leave" and "cleave"); they become bonded as if they are flesh and blood or, in the Hebrew idiom, flesh and bone— "bone of my bones and flesh of my flesh."[5] God has designed marriage as a union of the man and the woman who may, uniquely, become one flesh. Thus, those who enter into marriage are joined together by God in a permanent bond. This was neglected in Jesus's day, and after citing Genesis 2 Jesus declares, "so they are no longer two, but one flesh. Therefore, what God has joined together, let no one separate" (Matt. 19:6). This saying has obvious implications for divorce, which will be addressed in the next chapter. It also has implications for sexual

relations outside of marriage, for sexual union is designed to form and sustain an enduring relationship. Marriage is provided as a permanent, secure relationship that guards against relational instability and insecurities, providing the stable relationship necessary for the well-being and flourishing of children. Finally, the permanence of marriage is modeled on and provides a picture of the faithfulness and covenant loyalty of God with his people.

In short, marriage is designed to be a permanent relationship, which is well suited to the purposes for which marriage is given.[6]

Marriage is exclusive

The relationship of one flesh entails not only permanence but also exclusiveness. Sexual union outside of marriage violates the nature of the act, involving a deeply personal marital act outside of the bond of marriage (see 1 Cor. 6:16). So Allen Verhey characterizes marriage as "the joining of two lives in a 'one-flesh' union to be characterized by fidelity. A 'one-flesh' union is both a mutual and exclusive sexual union and a sharing of the whole of life."[7] A unique and intimate bond of union is formed, which requires exclusive devotion to the marriage partner and is thus violated by union with another. Thus the seventh commandment demands simply, "Do not commit adultery" (Exod. 20:14; Deut. 5:18). Even lust is seen as a violation of the exclusive devotion

---

5. R. Laird Harris et al., *Theological Wordbook of the Old Testament* (Chicago: Moody Press, 1980), 2:690.
6. The language here and in similar statements reflects statements used by Sherif Girgis, Ryan T. Anderson, and Robert P. George, *What Is Marriage? Man and Woman: A Defense* (New York: Encounter, 2012).
7. Allen Verhey, "Marriage and Divorce," in *Dictionary of Scripture and Ethics*, eds. Joel B. Green et al. (Grand Rapids: Baker Academic, 2011), 508.

and faithfulness that properly belongs to marriage (Matt. 5:28), for it fixes sexual desire on someone other than one's spouse. Exclusivity and permanence are closely related, for Jesus declares that divorce and remarriage, at least in many cases, is a form of adultery (Luke 16:18; Matt. 5:32, 19:9; Mark 10:12).

One potential challenge to this characterization of marriage as the exclusive union of a man and a woman is polygamous marriages in the Old Testament, which are not explicitly condemned. Several brief points may be made. First, though polygamy is not explicitly condemned, neither is it endorsed. Rather, it seems to be tolerated or accommodated, perhaps much like divorce, which Jesus said was tolerated because of the hardness of hearts (Matt. 19:8). Second, polygamy was apparently not a widespread phenomenon in Israel, but was largely confined to rulers, and for political alliances. Third, while polygamy isn't explicitly condemned, it first arises in the case of the vicious Lamech (Gen. 4:19), which indicates a gross distortion of God's provision. It also creates a great amount of strife for the families of Abraham (Gen. 16, 21),[8] Jacob (Gen. 29–30), Elkanah (1 Sam. 1), and David (e.g., 2 Sam. 13–15). Most problematic is the case of Solomon, whose seven hundred wives and three hundred concubines led him into idolatry (1 Kings 11:4), which resulted in the sundering of the kingdom (1 Kings 11:11–13). Fourth, and perhaps most important, the creation account affirms monogamy as

God's design. John Murray comments on the one-flesh union in Genesis 2:24 that "the indissolubility of the bond of marriage and the principle of monogamy are inherent in the verse," and that "polygamy was a departure from the original institution and therefore, though suffered or tolerated under the Old Testament, was, nevertheless, a violation of God's instituted order."[9]

In short, marriage is designed to be an exclusive relationship, which is well suited to the purposes for which marriage is given.

Marriage is to be fruitful

Fruitfulness is a mark of the creation accounts. The first imperative given to humankind in Genesis 1:28 is to be fruitful, which we will see has broad significance. Indeed, the five imperatives (be fruitful, multiply, fill the earth, subdue, and rule or have dominion) each point to an aspect of fruitfulness—in offspring, expansion, labor, and governance. Male and female are created by God for the purpose of coming together in fruitful service to God and his creation. The theme of fruitfulness appears in Genesis 2 as well, most prominently in God's command to the man to work and keep the garden in which he was placed by God (v. 15), and in the responsibility to name the creatures (vv. 19–20). So work and governance appear as part of God's blessings again. Procreation doesn't appear in Genesis 2, yet as a complement to the account of creation in Genesis 1, procreation cannot be far off in chapter 2.

8. The case of Abram is not precisely polygamy, since Hagar is Sarai's servant, but the dynamic is similar, as is the strife.
9. John Murray, *Principles of Conduct: Aspects of Biblical Ethics* (Grand Rapids: Eerdmans, 1957), 30, 45.

The help needed in verse 18, and provided by the creation of the woman in verse 22, is certainly not focused on procreation, but neither is procreation excluded. It is, in general, help in fulfilling the purposes for which God created male and female. This point is discussed more closely in the examination of the purposes of marriage.

In short, marriage is designed to be a fruitful relationship, which is well suited to the purposes for which marriage is given.

Marriage is between one man and one woman

This aspect of marriage, in a sense, is already implied by the previous aspects. As a permanent and exclusive relationship, described as one flesh, marriage involves *one* man and *one* woman. As a relationship that is to be fruitful, including the fruit of offspring, marriage involves one *man* and one *woman*. God might have designed and decreed otherwise, providing for offspring and other purposes of marriage in some other manner. But God created human beings as male and female, two distinct and complementary beings, to be drawn into the one-flesh union of marriage in order to fulfill the purposes for which he created them. Thus the union of one man and one woman is not incidental or accidental, but an essential aspect of marriage.

Procreation is the most obvious reason for which marriage is the union of one man and one woman. Of course, it may be argued that to focus on procreation is to exclude from marriage those who are infertile or beyond childbearing age or, for that matter, those who marry and are voluntarily childless. Each case is problematic in some sense, in that the marriage does not realize a central purpose, but for different reasons. This will be discussed under the purposes of marriage. Suffice it to say here that marriage (and sexual union, for that matter) are ordered to procreation, so that there ought to be an openness to procreation and a readiness to receive children in sexual union. If that possibility is removed or made unlikely by age or infertility, it does not change the basic structure of the relationship. A couple may be open to and desire a child as a result of their union. It is not possible to say the same in any meaningful way about two persons of the same sex—they cannot anticipate or hope for a child as a fruit of their union. The structure of the relationship between a man and a woman justifies sexual union even when procreation is not possible.[10]

Beyond procreation, marriage is the union of one man and one woman because the two distinct and complementary beings become one. "Distinct and complementary" does not refer simply to two individuals who are different—which could obviously be used of any two people—but to the two ways of existing as human beings, male and female, each with basic distinct and complementary features. The union of male and female is a union of two who are alike yet different. As

---

10. See Ash, *Marriage*, 246–48.

Verhey puts it, "God made of the one, two, so that the two might become one."[11] Two who are not distinct and complementary may form a friendship, but they cannot form a one-flesh union—that is, marriage.

In short, marriage is designed to be the union of one man and one woman, which is well suited to the purposes for which marriage is given.

Marriage is a comprehensive union

In their treatise on marriage, Sherif Girgis, Ryan Anderson, and Robert George describe marriage as a comprehensive union, which they define as "a union of the will (by consent) and body (by sexual union); inherently ordered to procreation and thus the broad sharing of family life; and calling for permanent and exclusive commitment."[12] Their view of the comprehensiveness of marriage fits closely with the present description of the nature and design of marriage.

In particular, this description draws attention to the range of things signified by marriage as a one-flesh union. Put simply, a one-flesh union is comprehensive in uniting a man and a woman in a fruitful, exclusive, lifelong relationship. It is a commitment of body, mind, and heart in a complete and wide-ranging relationship that unites the trajectory of two lives into one whole. This does not mean that the two lose individual identity. Indeed, "it is impossible for two people to be one, or united, in *every* sense

without ceasing to be two people. So unity of that sort is not even desirable." Rather, as Girgis, Anderson, and George put it, comprehensive means that "first, it unites two people in their most basic dimensions, in their minds *and* bodies; second, it unites them with respect to procreation, family life, and its broad domestic sharing; and third, it unites them permanently and exclusively."[13]

Various types of relationships have important features that distinguish them. In the midst of confusion, it is worth emphasizing the things that make marriage unique among the many relationships that people enter into. As Girgis, Anderson, and George put it, not only does marriage unite spouses in body, mind, and heart, but it is "especially apt for, and enriched by, procreation and family life." That is why marriage requires permanence and exclusivity, why "spouses vow their *whole* selves for their *whole* lives."[14] Because of the importance of procreation and family for society, there is good reason for the state to recognize and protect marriage as the exclusive union of one man and one woman.

In short, marriage is designed to be a comprehensive union, which is well suited to the purposes for which marriage is given.

The Purposes of Marriage

The purposes of marriage are closely related to the design and nature of marriage. Yet it is important to give particular attention

---

11.   Verhey, "Marriage and Divorce," 508.
12.   Girgis, Anderson, and George, *What Is Marriage?*, 6.
13.   Girgis, Anderson, and George, *What Is Marriage?*, 23.
14.   Girgis, Anderson, and George, *What Is Marriage?*, 37.

to the purposes of marriage, for at least two reasons. One reason concerns our understanding of marriage. It is important to comprehend the purposes of marriage in order to understand better what marriage is. Indeed, as Christopher Ash argues, perceiving the purposes for which God instituted marriage helps to prevent us from offering an arbitrary definition of marriage, which lacks an inner logic, for "the definition of marriage follows theologically and logically from the purposes of marriage."[15]

A second reason for reflection on the purposes of marriage has to do with our motives, will, and actions concerning marriage. When two people enter into marriage, they are not entering into a relationship of their own design. Rather, they are entering into a relationship that has a structure designed by God, with particular purposes that God has willed, which fit its design, for God's glory and human well-being. Within the design and purposes given by God there is much freedom for spouses to express their unique interests, gifts, and love for one another. Yet when spouses impose their own design on their relationship, or choose their own purposes quite apart from God's will for marriage, they go against the grain of marriage. There are therefore practical reasons to consider the purposes of marriage. Those entering into marriage do well to consider whether they identify with the purposes for which God has instituted marriage, and whether they desire to pursue those good ends and align their purposes

with God's purposes. Likewise, those who are already married will do well to consider God's purposes for marriage, and to realign their purposes with God's purposes as necessary. Finally, those who do premarital and marriage counseling, and those who join couples in marriage, will do well to consider what marriage is and what it is for, to seek to understand whether a particular couple affirms the design and purposes of marriage, and whether the public ceremony reflects and communicates the truth about marriage to those present.

There are good reasons for using traditional marriage vows in a wedding ceremony. For one thing, they remind us what marriage is, and that this bride and groom are entering into a relationship that our forebears entered into. As such, they remind us that in spite of differing customs at points, they, too, held high hopes for marriage; they, too, discovered great joy and great challenges in marriage; and in order to sustain marriage, they, too, needed vows by which they would commit to something not merely of their own making. The use of traditional marriage vows also guards against the danger of spouses defining marriage in their own terms, which may be the case when the bride and groom write their own vows. If a couple write their own vows, they may do so as a way of expressing in their own words their commitment to the God-given design and purposes of marriage.

This section, then, will explore what marriage is for. Namely, marriage is

---

15. Ash, *Marriage*, 104.

provided for fidelity, fellowship, and fruitfulness, and it serves a public good as the foundation for society.[16] Marriage serves another purpose—namely, to reflect and point to the relationship of God and his people, as revealed in the relationship of Christ and the church. The order offered here does not suggest an order of priority or significance, a point that can be debated. It is simply, in one sense, a representation of the unfolding of the purposes in marriage.

Fidelity

Fidelity refers to a number of aspects of the relationship between husband and wife. Augustine, who shaped much Christian reflection on the "goods" or purposes of marriage, especially through his treatise *On the Good of Marriage*, refers to marriage as the "guarantee of chastity," "faith," "faithfulness," and "fidelity."[17] His discussion leans toward marriage as a bulwark against sexual temptation, by providing the proper context for the expression of sexual intimacy. This certainly is a purpose of marriage, and an aspect of fidelity (cf. 1 Cor. 7:2–5; Prov. 5:15–23). Yet fidelity indicates much more of the relational aspect of marriage than simply a bulwark against temptation. This can be grasped in two ways. First, to serve even this narrow purpose, marriage must be more than simply the context in which sex occurs. It is certainly true that physical intimacy is important in marriage, and that

it helps to guard against sexual temptation, so Paul indicates that we have a duty to one another, that we should give ourselves freely and not deprive one another (1 Cor. 7:3–5). Yet to sustain a relationship requires more than physical intimacy. It requires a purpose beyond the relationship itself (which shall be examined below), and a fidelity that goes beyond resisting sexual infidelity to a deeper sense of sharing life together, and delighting in one another, as Proverbs 5 instructs. Second, the assertion that fidelity signifies more than a bulwark against temptation may be grasped by considering marriage as part of the order of creation. What would be this purpose of marriage if no threat of infidelity were experienced? If this purpose of marriage does not belong only to marriage after the fall, we do well to reflect on the wider meaning of this purpose.

Considered in the created order, we can see that marriage, as the closest of human relationships, is given as a showcase of uncommon love and faithfulness. Fidelity underscores many traits that belong to, and are necessary for sustaining, the deep intimacy of marriage. It includes commitment, loyalty, devotion, trustworthiness, and faithfulness. Such a relationship prompts delight not only on the part of the lovers— "I am my love's and my love is mine" (Song 6:3)—but also on the part of those who observe their love—"we will rejoice and be glad in you; we will celebrate your caresses

---

16. Ash discusses the procreational good, the relational good, and the public good in *Marriage*, 106–11.
17. Augustine, *On the Good of Marriage*, trans. C. L. Cornish, in *A Select Library of the Nicene and Post-Nicene Fathers of the Christian Church*, eds. Philip Schaff and Henry Wace, series 1 (1886–1889; repr., Grand Rapids: Eerdmans, 1988), 3:399–413.

more than wine" (Song 1:4). Fidelity, then, is a great good of marriage, which blesses the couple and those who observe their love and fidelity. It entails deep intimacy that creates and sustains this one-flesh relationship, a life-sharing bond. Marriage, as a one-flesh bond between one man and one woman, is the most intimate relationship that human beings can form. It is a relationship that exemplifies and requires fidelity, which excludes all others from its inner bond.

Fellowship

Augustine, perhaps surprisingly to some, captures this aspect of marriage. His view of marriage is known largely for its emphasis on procreation as the end that justifies sexual union (not merely objectively, but subjectively, as the motivation for coming together). Yet Augustine marvels at the beauty of marriage as it justifies and serves ends other than procreation, saying, "So strong is that bond of fellowship in married persons, that, although it be tied for the sake of begetting children, not even for the sake of begetting children is it loosed. For it is in a man's power to put away a wife that is barren, and marry one of whom to have children. And yet it is not allowed."[18] That is, there is a bond of integrity in the marriage relationship so that some other goal, such as seeking children, is not prioritized over the marriage itself.

One of the great joys that married couples experience is a companionship that is deepened by fidelity and the bond of fellowship. Some see companionship as the primary purpose or essence of marriage, the remedy to the problem of loneliness, based on their interpretation of Genesis 2:18: "Then the LORD God said, 'It is not good for the man to be alone. I will make a helper corresponding to him.'" Commenting on this text, one author asserts, "The reason for marriage is *to solve the problem of loneliness. . . . Companionship*, therefore, is the essence of marriage."[19] Surely companionship is a great blessing of marriage. There may be reason to question, however, whether it is the *essence* of marriage, and also whether marriage is the essential answer to the need for companionship, at least in the relatively narrow sense as a remedy for loneliness. The immediate text declares not that the man was lonely (he may or may not have been), but that he was alone. There is a difference. In addition, the fuller context of Genesis 2 suggests that the woman is provided as a helper for more than companionship, as we will see shortly.

Fruitfulness

Fidelity highlights the exclusiveness of the one-flesh bond of marriage and its inward focus. But marriage is not intended to remain inward. Rather, on the strength of fidelity, marriage turns outward, highlighting

---

18. Augustine, *On the Good of Marriage*, 7.
19. Jay E. Adams, *Marriage, Divorce, and Remarriage in the Bible: A Fresh Look at What Scripture Teaches* (Grand Rapids: Zondervan, 1980), 8.

the inclusive nature of marital love. This begins with the outward, other-seeking nature of sexuality, in which desire is not directed to self-gratification but rather to a delight in one's spouse. Its outward, inclusive nature continues in the welcoming of children, where out of the one-flesh intimacy of husband and wife issues forth the one flesh of a child; not *his* child or *her* child, but *their* child. Marriage is designed not merely for receiving, but for giving; not merely for consuming, but for producing. In addition to the inclusiveness of marriage toward one's spouse and children, marriage is directed outward through hospitality and fruitful labor. Indeed, one of the purposes of marriage is fruitfulness. It is a partnership, where two are better than one, not only for the companionship they experience but also because they are better able to accomplish what either could not do on their own (see Eccles. 4:7–12).

Fruitfulness in procreation. The most obvious way in which marriage is to be fruitful is as a relationship that is ordered to and especially apt for procreation and the nurture of children.[20] Genesis 1:28 proclaims that procreation is a blessing from God, which is repeated in the hopeful promise of the Noahic covenant after the deluge (Gen. 9:1, 7). Indeed, the blessing of procreative fruitfulness is a theme in Genesis.[21] It is a blessing that is invoked by individuals on behalf of others, with the hope that God will carry out the blessing (see Gen. 24:60, 28:3, 48:15–20, 49:25). So Psalm 127 affirms that children are a blessing from the Lord in which to delight. In addition, marriage is ordered not merely to procreation, but to the nurture of children; spouses are not just to have children, but to "bring them up in the training and instruction of the Lord" (Eph. 6:4; cf. Deut. 6:6–7). Children require years of patient nurture, training, and instruction, and they thrive best in the care of their own parents in an exclusive and permanent relationship.[22] The demands of having and raising children lead some couples to avoid having them. Against such a view, Christians ought to affirm children as a gift and blessing from God, and to resist the temptation for their relationship to be turned

---

20. Girgis, Anderson, and George, *What Is Marriage?*, 3, 6, et passim.
21. In addition to Gen. 1:28 and 9:1, 7; cf. 17:20 (blessing to Ishmael); 28:3 (Isaac's blessing to Jacob); 35:11 (God's blessing of Jacob); 47:27 (fulfillment of the blessing in Israel).
22. Girgis, Anderson, and George, *What Is Marriage?*, summarize the research that concludes that children do best on virtually every measure when raised by their own parents in a stable marriage. See, e.g., Elizabeth Marquardt, *Family Structure and Children's Educational Outcomes* (New York: Institute for American Values, 2005); Paul R. Amato, "The Impact of Family Formation Change on Cognitive, Social, and Emotional Well-Being of the Next Generation," *The Future of Children* 15 (2005): 75–96; David Popenoe, *Life without Father: Compelling New Evidence That Fatherhood and Marriage Are Indispensable for the Good of Children and Society* (New York: Free Press, 1996); Kristin Anderson Moore, Susan M. Jekielek, and Carol Emig, "Marriage from a Child's Perspective: How Does Family Structure Affect Children, and What Can We Do about It?" *Child Trends Research Brief*, June 2002, 1–2, 6, https://www.childtrends.org/wp-content/uploads/2002/06/MarriageRB602.pdf; Wendy D. Manning and Kathleen A. Lamb, "Adolescent Well-Being in Cohabiting, Married, and Single-Parent Families," *Journal of Marriage and Family* 65, no. 4 (November 2003): 876, 890; W. Bradford Wilcox et al., *Why Marriage Matters: Twenty-Six Conclusions from the Social Sciences*, 2nd ed. (New York: Institute for American Values, 2005).

inward and centered primarily on their own needs and wants.

A number of factors have contributed to the marginalization of the importance of procreation for many people, including the sexual revolution, advanced birth-control technology, and a focus on autonomy and personal fulfillment. Yet procreation remains a central purpose of marriage. Indeed, an openness to procreation is an essential characteristic of marriage—even if procreation itself is not essential to marriage. This tension, and its implications for the use of contraception and infertility, will be explored later in this chapter (in the section on contraception) and in the chapter on infertility and assisted reproductive technologies.

Fruitfulness in hospitality and ministering to others. Procreation is central, but not essential, to marriage, for marriages of those who are infertile or beyond child-bearing years do not for those reasons lack integrity. Further, they may be fruitful even without children of their own, through hospitality and reaching out to those in need (Rom. 12:13), adoption, or simply investing in children who are not their own but who need a father or mother figure in their lives. No marriage need be truly barren, for every marriage may be blessed by God with spiritual fruit, just as God promises the barren woman (Isa. 54:1–3) and the eunuch (Isa. 64:4–5). Procreation remains a significant blessing and a central purpose of marriage, but those without children may bear fruit in every good work (Col. 1:10).

Fruitfulness in labor. Marriage is meant to be fruitful. This includes (most obviously and directly) procreation, and also hospitality broadly understood in terms of reaching out to those in need. There is another sense in which marriage is to be fruitful, which is perhaps not as obvious, and that is fruitful labor. That is, God intends marriage to be productive. This is evident in both Genesis 1 and 2. It is important enough, and central enough to marriage, that it requires a bit more space.

Returning to Genesis 2:18, the text reads, "Then the LORD God said, 'It is not good for the man to be alone. I will make a helper corresponding to him.'" What is the help for? As indicated earlier, some see it as a remedy to the problem of loneliness experienced by the man as a solitary human. This view anticipates Genesis 2:23, which first presents the man's response upon seeing the woman that God created:

> This one, at last, is bone of my bone,
> and flesh of my flesh;
> this one will be called "woman,"
> for she was taken from man.

This is followed by the comment in Genesis 2:24 that "this is why a man leaves his father and mother and bonds with his wife, and they become one flesh." There is in these verses a depiction of the delight of companionship that is found in marriage, which can be related back to Genesis 2:18.

Yet there is something more to the problem of the man alone identified by God, and the provision by God of the woman as a helper. This can be seen in the narrative of Genesis 2 leading up to verse 18, in which the purpose for the help given is seen. The following briefly summarizes the narrative leading up to verse 18.

Early in Genesis 2 the narrative declares that there are no shrubs or plants on the ground, because there is no rain yet, and there is no man yet to work the ground (v. 5). It is important to observe that even before God is finished creating, Genesis teaches that one of the reasons that God will create human beings is to work the ground, which is related to the command given to human beings in Genesis 1:28 to subdue the earth. As the narrative continues, God creates the man (v. 7), and then the garden of Eden (v. 8), where he places the man. After giving additional details, this is repeated in verse 15, which reads, "The Lord God took the man and placed him in the garden of Eden to work it and watch over it." This repetition indicates that work is a key feature of the narrative, of the purpose for which God created human beings, and thus a central part of human flourishing.

After providing some additional details, in which God commands the man (vv. 16–17), God declares that it is not good for the man to be alone, and that he will make a helper for the man (v. 18). Rather than solving the problem of the man's loneliness, in this context the help is for the work that God has given man to do in the garden.[23] Thus, while companionship is a wonderful feature of marriage, the explicit reason that God creates the woman is to help the man fulfill the work that God has given human beings to do. That is to say, fruitful labor is a central purpose of marriage; the focus on work in the context of the marriage relationship "contains an important pointer to the purpose for which marriage was ordained."[24] Practically speaking, a married couple is able to accomplish together what neither could accomplish as effectively on their own. Through encouragement, mutual support, a common vision, a division of labor, and so on, spouses are able to be more fruitful. This purpose of marriage is not in tension with the purpose of companionship. Indeed, working together toward the tasks that God has given them, married couples become closer companions, and their companionship enables them to be more effective in the work that God has given them to do.

The response of the man upon seeing the woman that God made is a wonderful expression of desire and delight. Yet, as Christopher Ash argues,

> We must not conclude that the final *goal* of this delightful and intimate companionship is to be found in the delight, the intimacy or the companionship. This is delight with a shared purpose, intimacy with a common goal, and companionship in a task beyond the boundaries of the couple themselves. As we rejoice with the lovers in the garden,

---

23. See Ash, *Marriage*, 120.
24. Ash, *Marriage*, 120n6.

we must not forget that there is work to be done. The garden still needs tilling and watching. The purpose of the man-woman match is not their mutual delight, wonderful thought that is. It is that the woman should be just the helper the man needs, so that together they may serve and watch.[25]

Such a vision for fruitful work may be lost on many couples today, and it may influence how marriage is understood. In the past, when couples were involved in agriculture or in a small enterprise, the necessity of working together in a common task was not difficult to understand. By contrast, the main thing that many couples now share together is their personal leisure time, so the primary mark of a successful relationship is whether they enjoy the same things (and whether they enjoy each other). As a result, perhaps, the main purpose of marriage has come to be understood as companionship in the rather narrow sense of being best friends and lovers. That is, marriage remains inward-oriented, focused on the personal needs, wants, and fulfillment of the couple (or, from each person's perspective, even self-fulfillment). If needs and wants are not met adequately, there is marital breakdown or failure.

Ash warns against the introverted relational primacy that is a feature of so many contemporary marriages. He affirms Karl Barth's assertion that "marriage is not permission to establish an egoistic partnership of two persons,"[26] and argues that a relationship is not loving "unless its charity extends beyond the bounds of reciprocity."[27] Like self-centeredness, couple-centeredness is destructive. Even the appearance that it is other-centered tends to give way to the self. "There is only a short step between marriage as coupledom and marriage as self-actualization. And once the relationship is self-actualization, all extrinsic motivation for faithfulness 'for better or worse' has evaporated."[28] This helps to explain why the unprecedented focus on marital relationships and compatibility over external goods of marriage has coincided with higher rates of marital breakdown. Ash cites Proverbs 30:15, "The leech has two daughters: 'Give, Give'" and comments: "Couple-centered marriage dissolves into self-centered marriage, and self-centered marriage is like a leech. Or, to put it another way, it is like a pair of parasites trying to feed off one another."[29]

Marriage simply cannot bear the weight of personal fulfillment, and it isn't intended to.[30] Indeed, the emphasis on personal autonomy

---

25. Ash, *Marriage*, 121.
26. Karl Barth, *Church Dogmatics*, trans. G. W. Bromiley (Edinburgh: T & T Clark, 1957–88), III/4, 225.
27. Ash, *Marriage*, 123.
28. Ash, *Marriage*, 124.
29. Ash, *Marriage*, 125.
30. Both Ash and Rodney Clapp note that the inward focus of marriage and family has led to a proliferation of books and sermons in which church attendance, Bible study, and prayer are promoted *as a means to strengthen marriage and family*. But, as Clapp notes, "this gets it all backwards." Rodney Clapp, *Families at the Crossroads: Beyond Traditional and Modern Options* (Downers Grove, IL: InterVarsity Press, 1993), 162; Ash, *Marriage*, 128.

stands in tension with the very nature and purposes of marriage. God's purposes for man and woman are outward: be fruitful, multiply, fill the earth, subdue the earth, have dominion; work and watch over the garden. Marriage is given to serve these purposes, not to be self-serving. "In the Bible's perspective the way forward is neither via individual autonomy nor in introspective companionship, but in the joyful shared service of God."[31]

When entering into marriage, perhaps we would do well to consider how our lives will come together to fulfill the tasks that God has called us to do. Raising children is a common task for most couples, and working together to build a home is a task for all. While we may not work together in farming or a small business, the support and encouragement that we offer one another is important, and it implies respect for what each spouse does. Beyond that, married couples will do well to turn outward and consider how they may best serve others in love (see 1 Pet. 4:10; Gal. 5:13). These and other tasks are ways in which a couple may work and watch over the garden that God has given them, enabling them to subdue their corner of the earth together and love their neighbors.

Foundation for society

Genesis 2:24 indicates that marriage serves as a foundation for society, and thus as a public good, in several ways: "This is why a man leaves his father and mother and bonds with his wife, and they become one flesh." In marriage, a new household is formed, distinct from that of either the man or the woman. It is in the context of this new and distinct relationship that children will be welcomed and nourished, and that the noble task of working and keeping the garden will take place.

The family and its structure and authority aren't created or authorized by the state, for the family is the most basic unit of society. Instead, as the family grows and reproduces and spreads, society is formed, and relationships and needs grow and become more complex. To regulate certain aspects of these relationships, families form governing bodies and grant them authority to rule. This understanding and relationship between the family and the state is delicate, as the state tends to claim more power for itself than is warranted, undermining the autonomy, structure, and authority of the family.[32]

Marriage provides for the right ordering of sex, and prevents the breakdown of relationships and order caused by promiscuity. Further, marriage provides for the right ordering of procreation. A stable society depends on a strong birthrate, and on a healthy environment in which children are born and nurtured. That environment is marriage,

---

31. Ash, *Marriage*, 126.
32. As a case in point, the Supreme Court in *Planned Parenthood of Central Missouri v. Danforth* considered, among other things, parental and spousal consent laws, which were overturned. In the majority opinion, the court declared that the state cannot delegate to parents or to a spouse veto power that the state itself does not possess. Planned Parenthood of Central Missouri v. Danforth 428 U.S. 52, 69 (1976). Rather than understanding marriage and the family to possess inherent authority, the court suggests that its authority is granted by the state.

ideally when children are raised by their biological father and mother.[33] Thus, not only should the state respect, defend, and protect marriage, but married couples should recognize the public responsibility they bear. Here, too, we recognize that marriage is not a private relationship. As Dietrich Bonhoeffer asserted in a wedding sermon written from his prison cell in Berlin,

> God is the founder of your marriage. Marriage is more than your love for each other. . . . In your love you see only the heaven of your own happiness; in marriage you are placed and given responsibility with the world and the human community. Your love belongs only to you personally; marriage is something beyond the personal, an estate [ein Stand], an office. Just as it takes a crown to make a king and not just his will to reign, so it takes marriage and not just your love for each other to make you a married couple both in human and in God's eyes.[34]

Christopher Ash summarizes the public good of marriage this way:

> It encompasses the benefits of ordered and regulated sexual relationships in human society. Undisciplined and disordered sexual behavior must be restrained, for it carries

with it a high social and personal cost in family breakdown, destructive jealousies, resentments, bitterness and hurt. Ordered behaviour is to be encouraged because this has benefits that extend beyond the couple to children, neighbours and the wider networks of relational society.[35]

Because marriage serves a public good, virtually all cultures have regulated marriage. As Girgis, Anderson, and George note, "There are no civil ceremonies for forming friendships or legal obstacles to ending them. Why is marriage different? The answer is that friendship does not affect the common good in structured ways that warrant legal recognition and regulation; marriage does." They continue, "This is the only way to account for the remarkable fact that almost all cultures have regulated male-female sexual relationships. These relationships alone produce new human beings."[36]

Historically the law and courts in the United States have recognized the public good of marriage as the foundation for a healthy society. Consider these statements in court decisions:[37]

- Marriage "is the foundation of the family and of society, without which there would be neither civilization nor progress."[38]

---

33. Cf. Girgis, Anderson, and George, *What Is Marriage?*, 43, and many sources they cite.
34. Dietrich Bonhoeffer, *Letters and Papers from Prison*, Dietrich Bonhoeffer Works 8, trans. Isabel Best et al., ed. John W. de Gruchy (Minneapolis: Fortress, 2010), 83–84.
35. Ash, *Marriage*, 110.
36. Girgis, Anderson, and George, *What Is Marriage?*, 38.
37. These and other statements are summarized by Girgis, Anderson, and George, in *What Is Marriage?*, 44, 116nn13–18.
38. Maynard v. Hill, 125 U.S. 190, 211 (1888).

- "Marriage exists as a protected legal institution primarily because of society values associated with the propagation of the human race."[39]
- "The family is the basic unit of our society, the center of the personal affections that ennoble and enrich human life. It channels biological drives that might otherwise become socially destructive; it ensures the care and education of children in a stable environment; it establishes continuity from one generation to another; it nurtures and develops the individual initiative that distinguishes a free people. Since the family is the core of our society, the law seeks to foster and preserve marriage."[40]
- "Virtually every Supreme court case recognizing as fundamental the right to marry indicates as the basis for the conclusion the institution's inextricable link to procreation."[41]

God instituted marriage not merely for pleasure or personal fulfillment, though it certainly is a blessing to individuals. Marriage is for God's glory and for human good, both personal and public. The public good of marriage can be ascertained apart from particular biblical or theological convictions and arguments, even if those convictions and arguments provide the rationale for why marriage is a public good. The state thus has an interest in protecting and defending marriage as the exclusive and permanent union of one man and one woman, to provide the context within which children are born and cared for.

The figurative purpose of marriage

At the end of Paul's discussion of the marriage union of husband and wife in Ephesians 5, he quotes Genesis 2:24: "For this reason a man will leave his father and mother and be joined to his wife, and the two will become one flesh" (Eph. 5:31). Then he declares, "This mystery is profound, but I am talking about Christ and the church" (v. 32). This declaration itself is profound and surprising! What does the statement about marriage in Genesis 2 have to do with Christ and the church?

The analogy of the Christ-church relationship to the husband-wife relationship is a significant part of Paul's treatment of marriage in Ephesians 5, yet to this point the comparison has been employed to instruct and exhort husbands and wives how to relate to one another: the husband is head of the wife like Christ is head of the church (v. 23); as the church submits to Christ, so wives should submit to their husbands (v. 24); husbands should love their wives as Christ loved the church (vv. 25–31). It would seem that emphasis is given to the exhortation for husbands to love their wives to guard against the potential abuse of his headship and her submission. So he is to love his wife

---

39. Singer v. Hara, 522P.2d 1187, 1195 (Wash. App. 1974).
40. De Burgh v. De Burgh, 39 Cal. 2d 858, 863–864 (1952).
41. Conaway v. Deane, 903 A.2d 416, 620 (Md. 2007).

as his own body, caring for her as he would for his own body, for this is what Christ does for the church (v. 29), "since we are members of his body" (v. 30). Thus, when Paul quotes Genesis 2:24, it might be natural to read it as the basis for his exhortation to husbands—that is, they should love their wives as their own body because, by God's design, in marriage they have become one flesh.[42]

It is thus surprising to read in Ephesians 5:32, "This mystery is profound, but I am talking about Christ and the church"! Paul shifts emphasis, employing the institution of marriage in Genesis 2:24 to reveal something about the relationship between Christ and the church. Ash cautions that the mystery revealed in 5:32 "does not mean Paul's whole purpose is to teach us about Christ and the church. The main thrust of the passage is to persuade husbands and wives in marriages to behave rightly towards one another."[43] This caution is substantiated by Paul's statement in the next verse, summarizing the whole passage: "To sum up, each one of you is to love his wife as himself, and the wife is to respect her husband" (v. 33). The "mystery"—a revealed truth—is the union of Christ and the church, and Paul sees the one-flesh union of human marriage (as it is meant to be) as a picture of that union: Christ is joined to the church, he gave himself sacrificially for the church, and he provides and cares for the church as his body.

So the comparison goes both ways: the union between Christ and the church teaches us something of what marriage should look like, and the one-flesh union of marriage as instituted in creation teaches us something about the union of Christ and the church. Paul's citation of Genesis 2:24 suggests at least two things about this latter comparison. First, it is marriage as God designed it, not as we see it, that serves as a model for understanding something of the union of Christ and the church. And yet, second, it is a reminder of what marriage is meant to look like, and that, to the degree that our marriages reflect what marriage is meant to be, they provide a picture (however shadowy) of the union of Christ and the church. In some way, marriages that honor God and pursue his will can do what marriage is, in part, intended to do—namely, "to put the covenant relationship of Christ and his church on display," or simply to "display God."[44]

Summary and Implications

God created male and female as sexual beings, with sexual desire, so that they will be drawn into the one-flesh union of marriage. Marriage is the comprehensive union of one man and one woman in an exclusive, permanent, and fruitful relationship. Earlier I noted that the view of sexuality and marriage affirmed here raises certain questions and carries certain implications (as does every view of sexuality and marriage). If male and

---

42. See John R. W. Stott, *The Message of Ephesians* (Downers Grove, IL: InterVarsity Press, 1979), 230.

43. Ash, *Marriage*, 326.

44. So Piper puts it in *This Momentary Marriage*, 25.

female are created by God to be joined in the one-flesh union of marriage, then how should we view singleness? That question was addressed in the previous chapter. If marriage is designed for one man and one woman, how should we understand polygamy? That question was addressed briefly in this chapter. Other questions remain. If sexuality, sexual desire, and marriage are designed for the union of male and female, how should we understand homosexuality? If marriage is designed to be permanent, how should we view divorce and remarriage? If marriage is designed to be fruitful, then how should we view contraception, or infertility and assisted reproductive technologies? Subsequent chapters will examine divorce and remarriage, homosexuality, and infertility and assisted reproductive technologies. What remains in this chapter is to consider how our reflection on procreation as a purpose of marriage informs our moral deliberation concerning the possible use of contraception within marriage.

Moral Deliberation on Birth Control and Contraception

Distinction between birth control and contraception

One point of deliberation concerns the distinction between birth control in general and contraception in particular, though there is some disagreement with regard to where the distinction lies. As Darlene Fozard Weaver notes, "Birth control encompasses a range of practices . . . for the purpose of avoiding or terminating pregnancy. Birth control methods that prevent fertilization or implantation of fertilized ova are commonly known as 'contraception.'"[45] Weaver understands contraception to apply to methods that prevent fertilization or implantation, while birth control would include abortion and abortifacient drugs. For present purposes, contraception is used only for those methods that prevent fertilization (or conception), while methods that prevent implantation of an embryo are abortive forms of birth control. It might be added that reference to "fertilized ova," though not uncommon, is confusing. Once fertilization occurs—that is, when the sperm penetrates the egg and chromosomes align—what exist are not "fertilized ova," but a new entity, an embryo (or a pre-embryo zygote). The present deliberation will not examine the distinct methods of birth control, but will focus on general patterns of thought that ought to inform our understanding and use (or nonuse) of contraception.[46]

Basic moral considerations

Contraception is more than a pragmatic matter. The first moral consideration is simply the recognition that the use of

---

45. Darlene Fozard Weaver, "Birth Control," in *Dictionary of Scripture and Ethics*, eds. Joel B. Green et al. (Grand Rapids: Baker Academic, 2011), 101.

46. For information on various types of birth control and how they function, which includes an ethical examination, see William Cutrer and Sandra Glahn, *The Contraception Guidebook: Options, Risks and Answers for Christian Couples* (Grand Rapids: Zondervan, 2005).

contraception is a moral issue, and not merely a pragmatic one. Often couples enter into marriage with the understanding that contraception is merely a pragmatic issue, to be used (or not) based primarily on whether children are desired. Indeed, the default position for many couples is that contraception should be used initially, in order to allow time to grow closer together, or to finish their education, or to obtain financial stability, and so on. These may be factors to consider in having children, but the point here is that they tend to be the only or primary factors for many couples. Contraception has become commonplace and accepted or even expected in society, and couples often conform to the cultural norm rather than being thoughtful and prayerful about the use of contraception and how it fits (or doesn't fit) with the purposes of marriage. Concerning Protestant Christians, for example, one author wrote, "It is not simply that the overwhelming majority of them come down on the same side of the issue, but that for most of them there is no real issue here at all. . . . This is not a matter that engages them."[47]

As a pragmatic matter, influenced heavily by cultural norms, the assumptions about marriage, procreation, and contraception are informed by the concept of autonomy and privacy, translated into procreative liberty, rather than by biblical and moral reflection. By contrast, consider the statement by the Conference of Anglican Bishops in 1930, the first major Protestant denomination to accept (cautiously and against significant dissent) a limited use of birth control. After offering "Christian principles" that may justify its use, the bishops noted, "The Conference records its strong condemnation of the use of any methods of conception control from motives of selfishness, luxury, or mere convenience."[48]

Marriage, procreation, and contraception in biblical perspective. Perhaps one of the reasons that many Christians don't think of contraception as a moral issue is that there is no explicit biblical prohibition of contraception.[49] Nevertheless, moral reasoning goes beyond the consideration of prohibitions, as we have seen. With respect to contraception, consideration has to be given to the purposes of marriage in God's design. Procreation is a central purpose, and children are a blessing from the Lord (Ps. 127). Under normal circumstances, marriage should be fruitful through procreation. For some couples, who think of marriage primarily in terms of meeting personal needs and achieving personal fulfillment, this may require some recalibration. Children are not to be pursued merely as the fulfillment of a moral obligation either, but as a

---

47. James Nuechterlein, "Catholics, Protestants, and Contraception," *First Things*, April 1999, 10.
48. Lambeth Conference 1930, Resolution 15. In John T. Noonan Jr., *Contraception: A History of Its Treatment by the Catholic Theologians and Canonists*, rev. ed. (Cambridge, MA: Belknap Press of Harvard University Press, 1986), 409.
49. Sometimes appeal is made to God's judgment against Onan for spilling his seed on the ground, instead of raising up a child with his brother's widow (Gen. 38:8–10). The offense is certainly to be taken seriously, as God puts Onan to death. However, the focus is not on practicing birth control, but on Onan's refusal to fulfill his duty—as he agreed to do—to his dead brother (and to his family and, for that matter, to the nation).

blessing from God and the fruit of the one-flesh union, to be received gladly. Further, the blessing of children isn't merely given to enhance parents' lives, though children very often are a delight, but also as a means of participating in God's promised blessing to fill the earth with his image bearers, and to subdue the earth and have dominion.

Thus, as part of moral deliberation concerning contraception, we ought to take certain questions seriously, such as: Why do we want, or not want, children? What is God's will for marriage, and in particular our marriage, and how may we glorify him? Is our attitude in line with the understanding of children as a gift from God? Are we open to God's gifts, and to the sacrifice of our pleasures, comforts, and personal desires in order to pursue a central purpose for which God has brought us together in marriage? Again, we ought to be careful not to embrace the cultural norm of procreative liberty that results in a birth-control mentality and prizes being "child free." We ought not to see children simply as a matter of our choice. Rather, the nature and design of sex and marriage implies or demands an openness to procreation.

Open to procreation in general or in each act of sex in marriage? What does it mean to say that marriage and sex ought to be open to procreation? The Roman Catholic Church (with growing dissent from many Catholic theologians) teaches that each act of sexual intercourse must take place only in marriage and must be open to the possibility of procreation.[50] Based largely on a natural-law perspective, it is argued not only that sex is ordered to procreation (i.e., that a primary purpose of sex is procreation) but also—and because of that—that it is morally wrong to prevent the possibility of procreation. Since "natural family planning" or the "rhythm method" do not prevent the possibility of procreation in a given act, they are permissible; but forms that obstruct procreation (such as condoms or other barrier methods) or break the connection between sex and procreation (such as oral contraception or sterilization) are condemned.[51] Sometimes the Roman Catholic position is associated with Augustine's view, but Augustine argued that licit

---

50. Weaver, "Birth Control," 102–3.
51. Paul VI, *Humanae Vitae*, Encyclical Letter, July 25, 1968, 2.16, affirms some use of the rhythm method: "If, then, there are serious motives to space out births, which derive from the physical or psychological conditions of husband and wife, or from external conditions, the Church teaches that it is then licit to take into account the natural rhythms immanent in the generative functions, for the use of marriage in the infecund periods only, and in this way to regulate birth without offending the moral principles which have been recalled earlier." The rejection of other means is articulated in 2.14: "In conformity with these landmarks in the human and Christian vision of marriage, we must once again declare that the direct interruption of the generative process already begun, and, above all, directly willed and procured abortion, even if for therapeutic reasons, are to be absolutely excluded as licit means of regulating birth. Equally to be excluded, as the teaching authority of the Church has frequently declared, is direct sterilization, whether perpetual or temporary, whether of the man or of the woman. Similarly excluded is every action which, either in anticipation of the conjugal act, or in its accomplishment, or in the development of its natural consequences, propose, whether as an end or as a means, to render procreation impossible."

sex requires a procreative intent, and thus he would reject the Catholic acceptance of natural family planning.[52]

In response, it may be argued that it is possible to be open to procreation in marriage without embracing the act-oriented Roman Catholic view. Further, the Roman Catholic view suggests too sharp a division between "artificial" means of birth control that prevent procreation and "natural" means that do not sever the connection between sex and procreation. Augustine would certainly condemn the view that a couple would organize sex around avoiding procreation—with the church's blessing.[53] In contrast to the view that each act of sex must be open to procreation, it is marriage in general that ought to be fruitful and open to the gift of procreation. That marriage is open to procreation does not require having as many children as possible. The gift of procreation may be responsibly stewarded with prayerful reflection, and if some forms of birth control are morally permissible, the primary consideration (but not the only consideration) is not whether it is artificial or natural (any form of birth control is artificial in some sense), but whether it is contraceptive or abortive.

Evaluating particular methods. The reason for drawing the distinction between birth control in general and contraception in particular is that it provides a clear moral point of deliberation. That is, methods that are not contraceptive, but rather function after fertilization has taken place, destroy a unique human life and thus are morally wrong.[54] These would include not only methods that act after implantation has occurred, such as surgical abortion, but also methods that act to prevent implantation. On the other hand, methods that are contraceptive—for example, barrier methods such as condoms and diaphragms, or natural family planning that uses periodic abstinence during a woman's fertile period each month—may be acceptable. Permanent sterilization is more problematic, since it is a permanent measure, and thus greater caution should be used in comparison to temporary measures.

Further, as this chapter on marriage concludes, it should be said that even a method of contraception that is permissible may be problematic if it creates conflict in the marriage relationship. Couples may be experience one form or another as burdensome on either the husband or wife. It will not be the same for every couple—for example, some may find natural family planning to be burdensome while others do not. Couples should come to prayerful agreement not only on whether to use contraception but also on what method is best to use.

---

52. Augustine, *On the Good of Marriage*, 407. For more on the difference between Augustine and the Roman Catholic Church see Kenneth Magnuson, "What Does Contraception Have to Do with Abortion? Evangelicals v. Augustine and Roe v. Wade," *The Southern Baptist Journal of Theology* 7, no. 2 (Summer 2003): 54–67.
53. The point here is not to affirm Augustine's view, but simply to note the sharp difference between his view and the Roman Catholic acceptance of natural family planning.
54. Chapter 10, "Bioethics and Human Personhood: The Case of the Human Embryo," will develop this point.

Select Resources

Ash, Christopher. *Marriage: Sex in the Service of God*. Vancouver, BC: Regent College Publishing, 2003.

Bromiley, Geoffrey W. *God and Marriage*. Grand Rapids: Eerdmans, 1980.

Cutrer, William, and Sandra Glahn. *The Contraception Guidebook: Options, Risks and Answers for Christian Couples*. Grand Rapids: Zondervan, 2005.

Girgis, Sherif, Ryan T. Anderson, and Robert P. George, *What Is Marriage? Man and Woman: A Defense*. New York: Encounter, 2012.

Köstenberger, Andreas J., with David W. Jones. *God, Marriage and Family: Rebuilding the Biblical Foundation*. 2nd ed. Wheaton, IL: Crossway, 2010.

Noonan, John T, Jr. *Contraception: A History of Its Treatment by the Catholic Theologians and Canonists*. Rev. ed. Cambridge, MA: Belknap Press of Harvard University Press, 1986.

Piper, John. *This Momentary Marriage: A Parable of Permanence*. Wheaton, IL: Crossway, 2009.

Waite, Linda J., and Maggie Gallagher. *The Case for Marriage: Why Married People Are Happier, Healthier, and Better Off Financially*. New York: Broadway, 2000.

CHAPTER 8

DIVORCE AND REMARRIAGE

For the man who does not love his wife but divorces her, says the LORD, the God of Israel, covers his garment with violence, says the LORD of hosts. So guard yourselves in your spirit, and do not be faithless.

—Malachi 2:16 ESV

"Haven't you read," [Jesus] replied, "that he who created them in the beginning made them male and female, and he also said, 'For this reason a man will leave his father and mother and be joined to his wife, and the two will become one flesh'? So they are no longer two, but one flesh. Therefore, what God has joined together, let no one separate."

—Matthew 19:4–6

Introduction

"In 1969, Governor Ronald Reagan of California made what he later admitted was one of the biggest mistakes of his political life," writes W. Bradford Wilcox, an expert on marriage and family. The mistake was signing into law the nation's first no-fault divorce bill. Then Governor Reagan's aim was not to make divorce more common, but rather he sought "to eliminate the strife and deception often associated with the legal regime of fault-based divorce."[1]

—W. Brandford Wilcox

Marriage is a covenant, the one-flesh union of a man and a woman that is intended to last "as long as they both shall live." Yet it is now easier to break the marriage covenant legally than to break a whole host of agreements that we enter into. The chief reason for this is the introduction of no-fault divorce in the United States.

With no-fault divorce, there is no longer a need to accuse the spouse of serious wrongdoing in order to obtain a divorce; thus it spares everyone involved the pain of an ugly divorce proceeding. But divorce is ugly and painful, and "no-fault divorce also gutted marriage of its legal power to bind husband and wife, allowing one spouse to dissolve a marriage for any reason—or no reason at all."[2] This, as we shall see, is just the situation that Jesus is asked to address when some Pharisees approach him to "test him," says Matthew. They asked, "Is it lawful for a man to divorce his wife on any grounds?" (Matt. 19:3). Like today, divorce could be obtained in Jesus's day, at least by men, for any reason. Jesus's answer to the Pharisees is as needed in our day as it was in his. Before examining that and other biblical texts, consider the divorce situation in our day, and its consequences.

The Evolution of Divorce: No-Fault Divorce and Its Consequences

During the 1960s seismic cultural shifts were taking place in the United States and elsewhere. One of the obvious changes was the momentum that the sexual revolution had gained, loosening the knot between sex and marriage and weakening the marriage bond. Underlying other changes was an increased sense of radical autonomy and individualism and, frankly, self-centeredness. The effect on marriage and divorce is not difficult to detect. Wilcox notes that "prior to the late 1960s Americans were more likely to look at marriage and family through the prisms of duty, obligation, and sacrifice." Intimacy was an important aspect of marital life, but marriage advanced other goods beyond the married couple. The shift to a focus on "individual fulfillment and personal

---

1. W. Bradford Wilcox, "The Evolution of Divorce," *National Affairs*, Fall 2009, https://nationalaffairs.com/publications/detail/the-evolution-of-divorce.
2. Wilcox, "The Evolution of Divorce."

growth changed all that. Increasingly, marriage was seen as a vehicle for a self-oriented ethic of romance, intimacy, and fulfillment," where "one's primary obligation was not to one's family but to one's self." As a result, "marital success was defined not by successfully meeting obligations to one's spouse and children but by a strong sense of subjective happiness in marriage—usually to be found in and through an intense, emotional relationship with one's spouse."[3]

With the shift from duty to personal fulfillment as a basis for marriage, it became difficult to sustain a marriage that failed to meet perceived needs. The demand for an easier divorce was met with new divorce laws, and marital breakdown increased dramatically. Indeed, no-fault divorce "helped to open the floodgates, especially because these laws facilitated unilateral divorce and lent moral legitimacy to the dissolution of marriages." Even religious groups got on board: "Many mainline Protestant, Catholic, and Jewish leaders were caught up in the zeitgeist, and lent explicit or implicit support to the divorce revolution sweeping across American society."[4]

Divorce became an expression of individualism and personal growth, thought to be a positive move forward, for the benefit of all involved. Many challenged the view that spouses should stay together for the sake of children. Indeed, "under the new soul-mate model of marriage, divorce could be an opportunity for growth not only for adults but also for their offspring. The view was that divorce could protect the emotional welfare of children by allowing their parents to leave marriages in which they felt unhappy."[5] The evidence—and there is plenty of it—proves otherwise. Perhaps the theory was not implausible, but the experiment has proved costly to children, and to society as a whole. The following demonstrates the tragic impact of divorce on children:[6]

- **Greater risk of health problems.** A researcher at the University of California at Berkeley studied six thousand children's health stories and concluded that children of divorce are at greater risk of illness, observing that children of divorce "are likely to have experienced very significant stress" and they "probably also lost many of the resources that contribute to good health."[7]
- **Higher use of Ritalin.** A study by a sociologist from the University of Alberta

---

3. Wilcox, "The Evolution of Divorce."
4. Wilcox, "The Evolution of Divorce."
5. Wilcox, "The Evolution of Divorce." Wilcox notes that such views were advocated in places like the journal titled *The Journal of Divorce*; also *The Courage to Divorce*, written by Susan Gettleman and Janet Markowitz (New York: Ballantine, 1975). See Barbara Dafoe Whitehead's work analyzing attitudes towards divorce, e.g., *The Divorce Culture: Rethinking Our Commitments to Marriage and Family* (New York: Vintage, 1996).
6. These and others are summarized in Lauren Hansen, "9 Negative Effects Divorce Reportedly has on Children," *The Week*, March 28, 2013, http://theweek.com/articles/466107/9-negative-effects-divorce-reportedly-children.
7. The Associated Press, "Links Seen in Divorce, Child Illness," *The Register-Guard*, Eugene, Oregon, Monday, August 13, 1990, 3A.

indicates that children of divorce are twice as likely to take medicine for ADHD.[8]

- **Lower rate of high school graduation.** One study found that children of divorce are less likely to complete high school.[9]
- **Higher rates of divorce, cohabitation.** A study by Nicholas H. Wolfinger from the University of Utah shows that children of divorce are more likely themselves to get a divorce—up to twice as likely—and if both spouses are children of divorce, they are up to three times as likely to divorce. They are also more likely to cohabitate.[10]
- **Reduced longevity of life.** The Longevity Project, started in 1921, tracked fifteen hundred children through their lives. The study found that "more than a third of the study participants experienced the death of a parent or parental divorce before the age of twenty-one. While the death of a parent had no measurable effect on life-span mortality risk, children

from divorced families died on average almost five years earlier than children whose parents did not divorce."[11]

- **Higher rates of child poverty.** According to Isabel Sawhill at the Brookings Institution, the breakdown of the family is responsible for virtually all of the increase in child poverty since the 1970s.[12]
- **What might have been?** Wilcox refers to the work of sociologist Paul Amato, who estimates that if the United States had the level of family stability today as it did in 1960, there would be 750,000 fewer children repeating grades; 1.2 million fewer school suspensions; 600,000 fewer kids receiving therapy; and 70,000 fewer suicide attempts per year.[13]

The obvious conclusion is that "the clear majority of divorces involving children in America are *not* in the best interests of the children."[14] Nor has it been positive for society as a whole. The cost of family

---

8. Lisa A. Strohschein, "Prevalence of Methylphenidate Use among Canadian Children Following Parental Divorce," *Canadian Medical Association Journal* 176, no. 12 (June 5 2007): 1711–14, https://www.ncbi.nlm.nih.gov/pmc/articles/PMC1877837.

9. Lisa Strohschein, Noralou Roos, and Marni Brownell, "Family Structure Histories and High School Completion: Evidence From a Population Based Registry," *Canadian Journal of Sociology* 34, no. 1 (2009): 83–103.

10. Nicholas H. Wolfinger, *Understanding the Divorce Cycle: The Children of Divorce in Their Own Marriages* (Cambridge: Cambridge University Press, 2005).

11. Mandy Walker, "What the Longevity Project Tells Us about Divorce and Children," *Huffington Post*, March 12, 2012, http://www.huffingtonpost.com/mandy-walker/what-the-longevity-projec_b_1319557.html. See Howard S. Friedman and Leslie R. Martin, *The Longevity Project: Surprising Discoveries for Health and Long Life from the Landmark Eight-Decade Study* (New York: Hudson Street Press, 2011).

12. Wilcox, "The Evolution of Divorce."

13. Wilcox, "The Evolution of Divorce." Amato notes that children in homes where there is no divorce but there is violence fare better if the parents split, but more than two-thirds of parental divorces do not involve high levels of conflict.

14. Wilcox, "The Evolution of Divorce." The effects of divorce on children is also discussed at length by Linda J. Waite and Maggie Gallagher in *The Case for Marriage: Why Married People Are Happier, Healthier, and Better Off Financially* (New York: Broadway, 2000).

breakdown is enormous, exceeding $100 billion each year.[15] Rather than improving the quality of marital life, marriage rates have declined, and it has become more difficult to achieve a happy marriage. Beyond that, cohabitation has increased dramatically, creating much less stable relationships.[16]

Evidence like this should make us wary of no-fault divorce, or, as the question was brought to Jesus, divorce "for any cause." The Bible, however, does not focus on the effects of divorce in order to reject it, for the most part, but on the reality of marriage. Biblical teaching on divorce and remarriage is the focus of the remainder of this chapter.

Biblical Teaching on Divorce and Remarriage

The following assertions represent a summary of the biblical teaching on divorce and remarriage that will be developed below:

1. *Divorce and remarriage* are not God's will or design for marriage and sexuality.
   - It is contrary to the nature of marriage as a one-flesh union.
   - It is contrary to the pledge of marriage as a covenant commitment.
   - It is adulterous.
   - Married couples are called to reconciliation.
2. *Divorce and remarriage* may be permitted in exceptional circumstances.
   - By the law of Moses as a concession to sin.
   - By Jesus on account of πορνεία.
   - By Paul as a concession to the demand an unbelieving spouse.

Summaries like this can be misleading, and one of the dangers is that we jump to the conclusions about the matter—focusing on deliberation and short-circuiting reflection—in order to make a decision without adequately hearing what the Bible has to say. Often I am asked, "What is your understanding of divorce and remarriage in the Bible?" My usual response is to say, "The Bible teaches that marriage is to be permanent and divorce is contrary to God's will." The follow-up is usually something like, "Oh, sure, but what I mean is, when does the Bible allow for divorce?" Of course, that is part of the problem. We want to get to the bottom line, in order to judge the acceptability of the case that is before us, but we may be asking (and answering) the wrong question. This is illustrated in a 2007 edition of *Christianity Today*, a flagship evangelical magazine, that gave attention to the debate about divorce. The cover heading says, "When to Separate What God Has Joined: A Closer Reading of the Bible on Divorce."[17] Whether intentional or not, the way that this is framed reflects the disposition toward marriage and divorce indicated by the question the Pharisees put to Jesus,

---

15. Wilcox, "The Evolution of Divorce." Waite and Gallagher, *The Case for Marriage.*
16. Wilcox, "The Evolution of Divorce."
17. David Instone-Brewer, "What God Has Joined," *Christianity Today*, October 2007, 26–29.

asking him whether it is lawful for a man to divorce his wife for any reason (Matt. 19:3). The questions we ask often strongly influence how we think about issues, and thus the conclusions we draw. Frequently we may need to refuse to answer the question as it is posed and instead reframe it in order to bring greater clarity to the issue. As we shall see, Jesus resisted directly answering the question that was put to him, and so should we. The fundamental question is not to ask *when* divorce is justified, but to ask what God's will is for marriage, and *whether* divorce is ever justified.

Related to this, we must seek to have our biblical interpretation and theological reflection determine how we approach practical problems, rather than letting our practical problems determine our interpretation and reflection. That is, we should begin with the text and move to the problems we need to solve rather than the other way around. This can be a difficult challenge, as illustrated by a personal anecdote offered by David Instone-Brewer in his article on divorce and remarriage in *Christianity Today* mentioned above.[18] As a new pastor, he was confronted with the issue of divorce, when divorced persons came asking if he would conduct their weddings, and he discovered that some deacons in his church had been divorced and remarried. He had to ask himself, "Should I throw them out of church leadership? If I did, I would lose people I

considered some of the most spiritual in the church, people with exemplary Christian homes and marriages."[19]

This highlights one of the many practical challenges that we face when we consider the Bible's teaching on divorce and remarriage, and its implications for people's lives and church order. Considering the common evangelical understanding of grounds of divorce, for adultery and abandonment, which we will examine shortly, Instone-Brewer says that "some pastors have found this teaching difficult to accept, *because it seems so impractical*—even cruel in certain situations."[20] We need to wrestle carefully with these matters, knowing that our conclusions and practices will have a profound effect on people. Practical questions like the ones that Instone-Brewer asks cannot be completely bracketed out, and they will often drive us back to the text to test whether we have understood rightly how to interpret and apply it. Yet if we begin with the practical questions—what will happen if I draw this conclusion?—instead of the textual questions—what does the Bible teach?—we may fail to consider difficult things that the Bible requires of us.

Divorce and Remarriage Are Against the Will of God

The biblical teaching on marriage and divorce is difficult, and it requires much of us! It must be said at the outset that divorce is

18. Instone-Brewer, "What God Has Joined."
19. Instone-Brewer, "What God Has Joined," 26.
20. Instone-Brewer, "What God Has Joined," 27 (emphasis added).

deeply problematic and it is not God's will. Any exception must take that fundamental truth seriously. We will first look at the rejection of divorce and remarriage in Scripture, and the reasons for it, and then we will consider whether Scripture allows for divorce, and seek to understand when and why.

The nature of marriage and the case against divorce "in the beginning": Genesis 1–2

The first two chapters of Genesis and its teaching on marriage are critically important for understanding the biblical teaching on divorce and remarriage. Since we have looked at marriage in a previous chapter, here I will only briefly note how Genesis 1–2 relates to the matter of divorce. In the first chapter of Genesis, we learn that God created humankind in his own image as male and female, equal in nature yet distinct and complementary, the same yet different (Gen. 1:26–28). In the second chapter of Genesis we see that the woman is created different from the man, to be his complement and helper in the task God has assigned to him (Gen. 2:15, 18), and so that they will be joined in a relationship of one flesh (Gen. 2:21–24). This is the design of marriage: "a man leaves his father and mother and bonds with his wife, and they become one flesh" (v. 24). God is the one who creates the woman as a unique counterpart for the man—their relationship is God's design. God is the one who brings her to the man—their one-flesh union is God's will and is pleasing to him. God authorizes, blesses, and seals their union. The language used indicates the permanence of their union, for the man is said to "bond" (CSB), or "hold fast" (ESV), or be "united" (NIV) or "be joined" (NASB) or "cleave" (KJV) to his wife, and they become one flesh. By God's will and design, marriage is permanent; divorce is against the will and design of God.

One might try to argue that this is reading too much into the text of Genesis 1–2. Sin has not entered into the world, so divorce would not be considered here, so the creation accounts may present the ideal of marriage, but they do not speak to the possibility of divorce in a sinful world. Yet, as we shall see, in his response to the Pharisees' question about divorce, Jesus turns first to these texts, and concludes that "they are no longer two, but one flesh. Therefore, what God has joined together, let no one separate" (Matt. 19:6). What looks to be the man's doing in Genesis 2:24 (*he* leaves his father and mother and is joined to his wife) is, according to Jesus, God's doing (Matt. 19:6: "what *God* has joined together"). And the conclusion is clear, that we ought not to seek divorce.

Treachery and injustice: divorce as a breach of the marriage covenant: Malachi 2:14–16

Malachi 2:14 begins with asking why the Lord "no longer respects your offerings or receives them gladly from your hands" (v. 13). The answer: "Because even though the Lord has been a witness between you and the wife of your youth, you have acted treacherously against her. She was your marriage partner and your wife by covenant" (v. 14). Verse 15 reminds the reader that God has made marriage for the sake of godly offspring and then warns, "so watch yourselves carefully, so that no one acts treacherously against the wife of his youth." Verse 16 continues the invective against those who seek divorce: "'If he hates and divorces his wife,' says the Lord God of Israel, 'he covers his garment with injustice,' says the Lord of Armies. Therefore, watch yourselves carefully, and do not act treacherously."

Though this passage is difficult to translate,[21] the basic meaning is clear: divorce is treacherous and unjust. It is a rejection of God's will for marriage, and it is an abandonment of one's spouse and children and of the promise made to them, with God as a witness. Though the context may shed some light on the specific nature of the charge against the men of Judah,[22] the condemnation is a general one. William Heth's view, that only wrongful divorces are in view here (those who hate and divorce, not everyone who divorces), is plausible but not convincing.[23] The text reads more like a sweeping prophetic denunciation. It does not mean that divorce is precluded for any and every reason, but Malachi does not consider what might be "valid" reasons for divorce. He simply condemns divorce as an act of treachery and injustice.

Jesus rejects divorce and remarriage as adultery: Mark 10:2–12 and Luke 16:18

In the midst of cultures—first and twenty first—that accept divorce and remarriage as normal and necessary, and in many cases even embrace divorce and remarriage as a positive or righteous way forward, Jesus makes startling claims:

> He said to [his disciples], "Whoever divorces his wife and marries another commits adultery against her. Also, if she divorces her husband and marries another, she commits adultery." (Mark 10:11–12)

> Everyone who divorces his wife and marries another woman commits adultery, and everyone who marries a woman divorced from her husband commits adultery. (Luke 16:18)

In these two passages, Jesus offers no exception: divorce and remarriage is adultery. The broader context in Mark, going back to God's purposes in creation, tells us why. In marriage, the man and woman

---

21. As a survey of various translations demonstrates. Cf. Gordon J. Wenham, "A Response to William A. Heth," in *Remarriage after Divorce in Today's Church: Three Views*, eds. Paul E. Engle and Mark L. Strauss (Grand Rapids: Zondervan, 2006), 86.

22. The return from exile led some men to leave their wives and/or intermarry with pagan women, a threat to their faith and community, and to the raising of godly offspring. It is not difficult to see how Malachi's denunciation represents a principle that goes well beyond the particular context.

23. William A. Heth, "Remarriage for Adultery or Desertion," in Engle and Strauss, *Remarriage after Divorce*, 65. Concerning the ESV translation, which could be taken that way, Gordon Wenham (who was on the translation committee) states, "I can assure readers that there was no idea in the translators' minds that this meant Malachi approved of some divorces." Wenham, "A Response to William A. Heth," 86. Of course, the text could mean something that the translators didn't recognize, but their understanding of the translation ought at least to be considered carefully.

become one flesh and they are joined together by God; therefore, Jesus says, "what God has joined together, let no one separate" (Mark 10:6–9). Jesus's declaration amounts to saying that the human decision to divorce and to declare the freedom to remarry "has no legal effect in God's eyes."[24] In other words, instead of justifying divorce and remarriage, human law simply creates legalized adultery.

We may make several additional brief observations about these texts. First, note that it is not divorce alone, but remarriage after divorce that constitutes adultery. Second, this is because a civil (i.e., legal) divorce does not actually break the bond created in marriage. Therefore, when a divorced person remarries, it is adultery; and when someone marries a divorced person, it is adultery. Matthew 5:32 says that the one who divorces his wife "causes her to commit adultery." It is not the divorce that constitutes adultery. Rather, the statement reflects the assumption that the divorced wife will remarry, and that is what constitutes adultery. Third, in the Markan saying, implied in Luke, the man who divorces his wife and marries another commits adultery against his wife. The common view, grounded in the Old Testament law, was that adultery is committed against another man by taking his wife.[25] Remarriage after divorce is committing adultery against one's spouse, as well as against the new partner's spouse.

"Until death do us part": death (not divorce) ends marriage: Romans 7:2 and 1 Corinthians 7:39

In these two texts, Paul asserts that marriage is binding "as long as we both shall live," or "until death do us part," as traditional wedding vows state. The two texts read as follows:

> A married woman is legally bound to her husband while he lives. But if her husband dies, she is released from the law regarding the husband. (Rom. 7:2)

> A wife is bound as long as her husband is living. But if her husband dies, she is free to be married to anyone she wants—only in the Lord. (1 Cor. 7:39)

It can be noted that neither one of these passages is dealing with divorce directly. In Romans 7:2, Paul is using marriage as an illustration of the believer's relationship to the law: having been put to death through the death of Christ (v. 4), the believer is no longer bound to the law. In 1 Corinthians 7, Paul discusses singleness at some length. He shows a preference for singleness, but is quick to say that the one who marries has not sinned. At the end of the chapter he makes the point that a widow is free to remarry (v. 39) but that he thinks she will be happy if she remains single (v. 40). Since the primary focus of these texts is not a treatment of divorce as such, it is important to be cautious

---

24. Gordon J. Wenham, "No Remarriage after Divorce," in Engle and Strauss, *Remarriage after Divorce*, 27.
25. Wenham, "No Remarriage after Divorce," 25.

in drawing conclusions. Here it may simply be noted that both texts support the case that marriage is a lifelong bond, and thus that divorce does not (necessarily at least) end the marriage, so that remarriage after divorce constitutes adultery (cf. Rom. 7:3).

Paul rejects divorce and remarriage and commends reconciliation: 1 Corinthians 7:10–16

To the married I give this command—not I, but the Lord—a wife is not to leave her husband. But if she does leave, she must remain unmarried or be reconciled to her husband—and a husband is not to divorce his wife. But I (not the Lord) say to the rest: If any brother has an unbelieving wife and she is willing to live with him, he must not divorce her. Also, if any woman has an unbelieving husband and he is willing to live with her, she must not divorce her husband. For the unbelieving husband is made holy by the wife, and the unbelieving wife is made holy by the husband. Otherwise your children would be unclean, but as it is they are holy. But if the unbeliever leaves, let him leave. A brother or a sister is not bound in such cases. God has called you to live in peace. Wife, for all you know, you might save your husband. Husband, for all you know, you might save your wife. (1 Cor. 7:10–16)

In this text, Paul declares that a wife is not to leave her husband (v. 10), and a husband is not to leave his wife (v. 11). If one of them does leave, they are not to remarry; the options are to remain unmarried or to be reconciled (v. 11). While Paul only explicitly tells the wife that she must not remarry, given the parallel, it surely applies to the husband whom he instructs not to leave his wife. Although Paul commands believers not to separate from their spouses, there may be situations in which some do. Yet, rather than simply accept such a situation, he instructs them to remain unmarried or else be reconciled. This reflects one of the points of Jesus's teaching, that it is not divorce as such, but remarriage that constitutes adultery.

Paul's emphasis on reconciliation flows from the gospel: if all believers have been reconciled to God and to one another through Jesus's death and resurrection, then surely reconciliation in marriage is possible and necessary for two believers. Marriage is to be a reflection of the relationship between Christ and the church (Eph. 5:21–33), and a witness to the power of the gospel is compromised when spouses fail to offer forgiveness and seek reconciliation. Put another way, "if the Christian husband and wife cannot be reconciled to one another, then how can they expect to become models of reconciliation before a fractured and broken world?"[26] Further, believers who are married to unbelievers are asked to extend forgiveness and reconciliation to them as well—if the unbelieving spouse is willing to live with the

---

26. Gordon D. Fee, *The First Epistle to the Corinthians*, New International Commentary on the New Testament, rev. ed. (Grand Rapids: Eerdmans, 2014), 328.

believing spouse, the believer is not to leave (vv. 12–13). By the commitment, patience, and forgiveness of the believer—by the power of the gospel—the unbelieving spouse and children may be saved (vv. 14–16).

The Mosaic Law Tolerates and Regulates Divorce and Remarriage: Deuteronomy 24:1–4

This text is important for a biblical understanding of divorce and remarriage. As John Murray notes, it "occupies a unique place in the Old Testament because it contains, as no other passage in the Old Testament, specific legislation bearing upon the question of divorce."[27] In addition, it serves as the backdrop for the Pharisees' question to Jesus on divorce. Matthew writes that some Pharisees came to Jesus to test him, asking, "is it lawful for a man to divorce his wife on any grounds?" (Matt. 19:3; cf. Mark 10:2). They are testing Jesus concerning his understanding of the Mosaic law on divorce, and in particular his understanding of Deuteronomy 24:1–4. We will consider Jesus's discussion with the Pharisees below, but first we will examine the Mosaic legislation in question. The text of Deuteronomy 24:1–4 reads as follows:

> When a man takes a wife and marries her, if then she finds no favor in his eyes because he has found some indecency in her, and he writes her a certificate of divorce and puts it in her hand and sends her out of his house, and she departs out of his house, and if she goes and becomes another man's wife, and the latter man hates her and writes her a certificate of divorce and puts it in her hand and sends her out of his house, or if the latter man dies, who took her to be his wife, then her former husband, who sent her away, may not take her again to be his wife, after she has been defiled, for that is an abomination before the Lord. And you shall not bring sin upon the land that the LORD your God is giving you for an inheritance. (Deut. 24:1–4 ESV)[28]

What did Moses command?

This is an example of case law, centering on a pattern of behavior that required a ruling. We may make several observations. First, note that it is not clear that divorce is justified in either of the cases. Indeed, in the case of the second husband, the indication is that the divorce is not justified, for it says that he "hates her and writes her a certificate of divorce" (v. 3). In the case of the first husband, he *may* be justified in divorcing his wife by something she has done, but there is no command or even explicit permission; his decision to give her a certificate of divorce is simply stated as a matter of fact (v. 1: "he has found some indecency in her, and he writes her a certificate of divorce"). The KJV makes it a command: "then let him write her a bill of divorcement."[29] The HCSB make

27. John Murray, *Divorce* (Phillipsburg, NJ: Presbyterian and Reformed, 1961), 3.
28. The reason for using the ESV translation here will be clear in the commentary that follows. All further biblical quotations in this chapter are from the ESV unless otherwise noted.
29. So too the Revised Version and American Standard Version.

it a permission: "he may write her a divorce certificate." To indicate a command, or even permission, in verse 1 is misleading. The only command in this text is found in verse 4.[30] The Pharisees, we will see, assume that the first case involves a command or at least a permission for divorce, but the ambiguity is important, and it should be left open. In some cases, perhaps the husband accusing his wife is justified, but in other cases perhaps he is not. The question at hand is, What happens when she has subsequently married another man and is divorced or widowed— can her first husband marry her again?

What is the abomination?

Second, the answer to the question just asked is that the first husband may not marry the wife that he divorced if she subsequently married another man, whether that man divorces her or dies. The prohibition is emphatic: she has been defiled, and to take her again to be his wife is said to be an abomination (v. 4). It is evident that if she had not married after he divorced her, he could have taken her again to be his wife. Further, there appears to be no prohibition to keep her from marrying a third husband. Why then is her first husband prohibited from marrying her again? Here questions arise concerning why she has been defiled. Murray asserts that "the defilement is not

regarded as inhering in the second marriage *per se*," and that the second marriage is not itself considered adultery (at least not in terms of Mosaic legislation).[31] He notes that "the one insurmountable obstacle to the marriage of this particular woman with this particular man is not that the woman had been married to another man but simply that the particular man concerned is the man from whom she had been divorced."[32]

Heth offers a plausible explanation for why her first husband cannot marry her again. In Jewish law, if the husband divorces his wife without cause, she retains her dowry when she leaves, which is often a considerable sum. If, on the other hand, the woman is divorced for cause ("anything indecent") the husband keeps her dowry. Some unscrupulous husbands would no doubt trump up charges of indecency in order to keep the dowry. Now she marries another man, and he either dies or divorces her without cause (he "hates her"). Either way, she retains her dowry. The first husband is not allowed to marry her again because, first, he had publicly shamed her by charging her with an indecency as the reason for the divorce. Second, by remarrying her, he would gain financially, which is to denigrate marriage and treat the woman like a prostitute.[33]

---

30. Murray states that "the understanding of the import of this passage has been perplexed, if not distorted" by the KJV and other translations that indicate that the divorce in the first case is mandatory. Murray, *Divorce*, 3. The Hebrew uses the *waw* consecutive, which the ESV captures with the repeated use of "and" (if *x*, and *y*, and *z* . . . then), indicating that everything up to verse 4 is a description rather than a prescription.
31. Murray, *Divorce*, 15.
32. Murray, *Divorce*, 15.
33. William A. Heth, "Remarriage for Adultery or Desertion," in Engle and Strauss, *Remarriage after Divorce*, 65–66.

What is עֶרְוַת דָּבָר*?*

Third, much of the discussion of this text centers on the meaning of the phrase "some indecency"[34] (עֶרְוַת דָּבָר) as a cause for divorce. As noted above, the text does not make it clear that the reason for divorce is justified. The language used is descriptive, leaving a certain ambiguity—perhaps this is because each case must be considered by judges on its own merit. It simply says that the wife "finds no favor" in her husband's eyes because he has found "some indecency," and so he writes her a certificate of divorce and sends her away. The Pharisees who come to Jesus assume that the man is justified by the wife's indecency, and they focus on how broadly to interpret that. May a man divorce his wife for "any cause" (Matt. 19:3)? Jesus's response to the Pharisees, that "Moses permitted you to divorce your wives because of the hardness of your hearts" (Matt. 19:8), should caution us not to take "some indecency" in Deuteronomy 24:1 as an automatic justification for divorce.

That said, getting some sense of the meaning of עֶרְוַת דָּבָר is important for understanding the Pharisees' debate with Jesus, since the phrase seems to be at the center of the question they put to him, and important for understanding Jesus's answer as

well. Unfortunately, the meaning of עֶרְוַת דָּבָר is not entirely clear. The occurrence of the same phrase in Deuteronomy 23:14 helps only a little. There we see that the people of Israel are to go outside the camp to relieve themselves, and to dig a hole and cover up their excrement. The reason is that God is in their camp, and "therefore your camp must be holy, so that he may not see *anything indecent* among you and turn away from you." Thus עֶרְוַת דָּבָר, "anything indecent," may refer to something that is uncovered that should be covered up. It raises a number of possibilities, but few certainties, related to sexual immodesty or shameful conduct.[35] Elsewhere the term עֶרְוַת refers to illicit sexual intercourse (Lev. 20:19–20) and to nakedness (Exod. 28:42; 1 Sam. 20:30; Isa. 47:3; Lam. 1:8, 4:21; Ezek. 16:8). So, in Deuteronomy 24:1, it is probable that the husband declares his wife to be shameful, immodest, or unclean.[36]

Many scholars have argued that the phrase cannot mean adultery, in part because the penalty for adultery was not divorce but death.[37] Yet, as Old Testament scholar Gordon Wenham asserts, the death penalty for adultery "was not mandatory (cf. Pr. 6:29–35), so 'something indecent' may cover adultery as well as other sexual acts."[38] The death

---

34. Elsewhere translated "something improper" (HCSB); "something indecent" (NIV); "some indecency" (NASB); "some uncleanness" (KJV).
35. Murray, *Divorce*, 12.
36. D. Freeman, "Divorce in the OT," in *The International Standard Bible Encyclopedia*, ed. Geoffrey W. Bromiley (Grand Rapids: Eerdmans, 1979–1988), 1:975.
37. Murray, *Divorce*, 10–11, offers several reasons why it cannot be adultery, describing the various ways that the law deals with adultery or suspected adultery.
38. Gordon J. Wenham, "Divorce," in *New Dictionary of Christian Ethics and Pastoral Theology*, eds. David J. Atkinson et al. (Downers Grove, IL: InterVarsity Press, 1995), 316.

penalty may have served as a maximum punishment, and if it was not carried out, surely divorce would have been considered justified. Instone-Brewer, having read rabbinic sources carefully, states that "most Jews recognized that this unusual phrase was talking about adultery."[39] Other scholars suggest that "anything indecent" may refer to some sort of sexual misconduct short of adultery;[40] menstrual irregularity, which would obstruct sexual relations;[41] or possibly barrenness, since it made it impossible to fulfill the command to "be fruitful"[42] (and since the barren woman was often suspected of unknown sin for which God was punishing her).

What is the certificate of divorce for?

In short, the certificate of divorce "afforded protection for the woman's reputation and guaranteed her freedom to remarry."[43] Without the possibility of remarriage, the woman may be left destitute, especially if she was unable to return to her father's household. And without the certificate of divorce, she was unable to remarry, for she would legally still be married to her former husband. The certificate of divorce included with it the right to remarry. Although the "wording on the divorce certificate is not stated in the Pentateuch," it is reasonable to conclude that "it was similar to the wording of standard rabbinic divorce certificates." They read, "You are allowed to marry any man you wish."[44] Whether this right is implied or understood by Jesus and Paul is a significant point of debate in the attempt to understand the New Testament teaching on divorce and remarriage.

Jesus Allows Divorce and Remarriage for Πορνεία: Matthew 5:31–32 and 19:3–9

Matthew's account of Jesus's teaching on divorce and remarriage is the only one that contains an exception to the rule that divorce and remarriage is adultery. He includes two distinct accounts of Jesus's teaching:

> It was also said, "Whoever divorces his wife, let him give her a certificate of divorce." But I say to you that everyone who divorces his wife, except on the ground of sexual immorality, makes her commit adultery, and whoever marries a divorced woman commits adultery." (Matt. 5:31–32)

> And Pharisees came up to him and tested him by asking, "Is it lawful to divorce one's wife for any cause?" He answered, "Have you not read that he who created them from the

---

39. Instone-Brewer, "What God Has Joined," 28. Cf. his scholarly treatment in *Divorce and Remarriage in the Church: The Social and Literary Context* (Grand Rapids: Eerdmans, 2002), 94–99.
40. D. A. Carson, *Matthew*, Expositor's Bible Commentary 8 (Grand Rapids: Zondervan, 1984), 413.
41. Daniel I. Block, "Marriage and Family in Ancient Israel," in *Marriage and Family in the Biblical World*, ed. Ken M. Campbell (Downers Grove, IL: InterVarsity Press, 2003), 49–50, citing Lev. 15:14.
42. Cf. Instone-Brewer, *Divorce and Remarriage in the Church*, 182.
43. Freeman, "Divorce in the OT," 975.
44. Instone-Brewer, *Divorce and Remarriage in the Church*, 29. The rabbinic teaching often cited from the Mishnah is Gittin 9:3.

beginning made them male and female, and said, 'Therefore a man shall leave his father and his mother and hold fast to his wife, and the two shall become one flesh'? So they are no longer two but one flesh. What therefore God has joined together, let not man separate." They said to him, "Why then did Moses command one to give a certificate of divorce and to send her away?" He said to them, "Because of your hardness of heart Moses allowed you to divorce your wives, but from the beginning it was not so. And I say to you: whoever divorces his wife, except for sexual immorality, and marries another, commits adultery." (Matt. 19:3–9)

Divorce and righteousness in Matthew 5

The account in Matthew 5 is similar to Matthew 19, which we will focus on, since it is a more detailed statement. However, before turning there it is worth noting two features of the statement in Matthew 5. First, it occurs in the context of Jesus's teaching in the Sermon on the Mount on righteousness. In verse 20, Jesus says, "For I tell you, unless your righteousness exceeds that of the scribes and Pharisees, you will never enter the kingdom of heaven." Following that, in 5:21–48, Jesus illustrates the deeper righteousness in six sayings, with the pattern, "You have heard . . . but I say to you."[45] On divorce, the scribes and Pharisees sought to be "righteous" in terms of compliance with the law by giving their wives a certificate of divorce when they sent them away. In so doing, they reasoned, they upheld the law, and some might even have believed that they were treating their wives with dignity. In reality, they used the law to justify their own sinful desires. Jesus reveals that their practice of divorce is not righteousness but adultery; a certificate of divorce does not effectively put asunder what God has joined. Thus, righteousness is not found in pursuing divorce, but in seeking to preserve and protect faithfulness in marriage.

Second, here Jesus says, "everyone who divorces his wife, except on the ground of sexual immorality, *makes her commit adultery*" (Matt. 5:32, emphasis added). How does divorce cause the wife to commit adultery? Adultery takes place when remarriage, not divorce, occurs. The assumption is that she will (even must) remarry, likely out of economic need, and so by divorcing her, in effect he causes her to commit adultery.[46] The exception is that if he has divorced her on the ground of sexual immorality (πορνεία), he has not caused her to commit adultery, for she has already done so. The exception clause appears in both of Matthew's accounts of Jesus's teaching on divorce, and will be discussed below in its context in Matthew 19:9.

Jesus challenges the Pharisees on marriage, divorce, and remarriage in Matthew 19

Matthew tells us that some Pharisees came to Jesus and tested him. Their test of Jesus

---

45. This is treated briefly in chap. 5. The six sayings deal with murder/hatred (5:21–26), adultery/lust (5:27–30), divorce (5:31–32), oaths (5:33–37), response to injury (5:38–41), and attitude toward enemies (5:42–48).
46. Cf. Wenham, "No Remarriage after Divorce," 28.

concerns his interpretation of the Mosaic law on divorce. Specifically, they ask him, "Is it lawful to divorce one's wife for any cause?" (19:3). The question about "any cause" concerns Jesus's interpretation of עֶרְוַת דָּבָר in Deuteronomy 24:1. There were two main rabbinic interpretations of עֶרְוַת דָּבָר in Jesus's day, the school of Hillel and the school of Shammai.[47] The more liberal Hillelites argued that a man could divorce his wife for any reason at all—she simply found no favor in his eyes (Deut. 24:1). This "any cause" divorce, according to Instone-Brewer, had become commonplace in Jesus's day.[48] The more conservative school of Shammai argued that Moses permitted divorce only for sexual immorality. As summarized in the Mishnah,

> The School of Shammai say: A man may not divorce his wife unless he has found unchastity in her, for it is written, Because he hath found in her *indecency* in anything [Deut. 24:1]. And the School of Hillel say: [He may divorce her] even if she spoiled a dish for him, as it is written, Because he hath found in her indecency in *anything*.[49]

The Pharisees want to know where Jesus stands, perhaps hoping that his answer will open him up to their attack and alienate the crowd. Indeed, his own disciples find his answer to be very difficult (Matt. 19:10).

Jesus refuses to answer the question as posed, at least initially (he will do so eventually, Matt. 19:9). Instead he redirects the Pharisees to God's will from the beginning. They came to question him, but he turns and questions them. They should not be asking whether divorce could be pursued for any reason, but rather, What is God's purpose and will for male and female in marriage? He grounds his answer in the objective authority of Scripture and creation norms. He asks, "Have you not read that he who created them from the beginning made them male and female, and said 'Therefore a man shall leave his father and his mother and hold fast to his wife, and the two shall become one flesh'?" (Matt. 19:4–5; cf. Gen. 1:27, 2:24). That they would ask him whether divorce is acceptable for any cause demonstrates that they fail to recognize what should be plain to them ("have you not read?"). And Jesus concludes, "so they are no longer two but one flesh. What therefore God has joined together, let not man separate" (Matt. 19:6).

The Pharisees respond by asking, "Why then did Moses command one to give a certificate of divorce and to send her away?" (Matt. 19:7). They have interpreted Deuteronomy 24:1 to mean that not only has Moses commanded them to give their wives a certificate of divorce when they send them away, but also that Moses has commanded

---

47. Instone-Brewer, who has studied the rabbinic sources carefully, summarizes the two schools briefly in "What God Has Joined," 26–29. For a fuller development, see Instone-Brewer, *Divorce and Remarriage in the Bible.*

48. Instone-Brewer, "What God Has Joined," 28; cf. Craig S. Keener, *And Marries Another: Divorce and Remarriage in the Teaching of the New Testament* (Peabody, MA: Hendrickson, 1991), chap. 4; and Craig S. Keener, "Remarriage for Adultery, Desertion, or Abuse," in Engle and Strauss, *Remarriage after Divorce*, 108.

49. Mishnah Gittin 9:10, cited in many sources. This form from Keener, *And Marries Another*, 39.

them to divorce their wives. Jesus corrects and rebukes them, for whereas they asked why Moses *commanded* them to divorce their wives, Jesus says that Moses only *permitted* divorce, and that was because of the hardness of their heart (Matt. 19:8). It is only after Jesus points them to God's purposes for marriage, and emphasizes that divorce is not God's will, that he answers their initial question about divorce directly: "And I say to you: whoever divorces his wife, except for sexual immorality, and marries another, commits adultery" (Matt. 19:9).

In summary, Jesus affirms that marriage is designed by God to be a lifelong bond. God created male and female with this purpose in mind, that a man and woman would join together in a one-flesh union. When they join together in marriage, it is God who has joined them, and if God has joined them together, no human being (including the spouses themselves) should separate them. Because of sin, or "hardness of heart," Moses permitted divorce, but that is not God's desire. As in Mark and Luke, here Jesus says that divorce and remarriage is adultery, except that in Matthew, there is an exception: if divorce is the result of sexual immorality, then remarriage is not adultery. Several further observations on this text are in order.

Let not man separate. Here Jesus is not declaring that marriage is indissoluble, in the sense that the marriage bond is ontologically unbreakable. He commands us not to separate what God has joined together;

he does not say it is impossible to do so (i.e., "let not man separate," not "man cannot separate"). What God commands should be enough! He commands: "You shall not murder," and "You shall not commit adultery." This does not mean that it is impossible to murder and commit adultery, but we are not to do so. And it is possible to separate what God has joined together, but we are not to do so. Dietrich Bonhoeffer takes "let not man separate" as a promise and a hope. He writes, "God makes your marriage indissoluble and protects it from any internal or external danger. God wills to be the guarantor of its permanence. To know that no power in the world, no temptation, no human weakness can separate what God has joined together is an abiding source of joy; indeed, those who know it may say with confidence: what God has joined together, no one can separate."[50]

Hardness of heart. When Jesus declares to the Pharisees that Moses permitted them to divorce their wives because of the hardness of their hearts (Matt. 19:8), we should take it as a sober warning. This fits with Malachi's portrayal of the men who divorced their wives as an act of treachery and injustice, for they "hate and divorce." To be hardhearted is to resist the Lord and his law (Zech. 7:12). It may have been possible, before Jesus, to belong to Israel and yet not be a faithful follower of God and child of Abraham. But can a person who is characterized as hardhearted be a follower of

50. Dietrich Bonhoeffer, *Letters and Papers from Prison*, Dietrich Bonhoeffer Works 8, trans. Isabel Best et al., ed. John W. de Gruchy (Minneapolis: Fortress, 2010), 84. This is from "Wedding Sermon from the Prison Cell, May, 1943."

Jesus? If the pursuit of divorce issues from a hard heart, is there any reason for which a follower of Jesus can seek a divorce? Jesus's answer is that anyone who divorces and re-marries commits adultery, except in the case of πορνεία—that is, sexual immorality.

What does πορνεία mean? In Matthew 19:9, Jesus says, "And I say to you: whoever divorces his wife, except for sexual immo-rality [πορνεία], and marries another, com-mits adultery." Here, πορνεία is commonly understood to mean adultery, yet some as-sert that it must mean something other than adultery, since πορνεία is a more general term for sexual immorality, and the spe-cific term for adultery (μοιχεία), which we might expect to see, is not used.[51] Because πορνεία is used, Piper believes it refers to the betrothal period.[52] In Jewish practice, divorce was required once a couple was be-trothed. If a betrothed person had sex with someone else during the betrothal, it would be considered fornication (πορνεία) rather than adultery (μοιχεία), since the marriage had not been consummated. This is the issue that Joseph faced when he learned that Mary was pregnant, so he sought to divorce her quietly, until it was revealed to him that Mary conceived by the Holy Spirit (Matt. 1:18–21). In this view, Matthew provides the

exception in order to make clear that Jo-seph was righteous, for divorce for πορνεία during the betrothal period is justified. Thus Matthew's exception does not contradict Mark or Luke, and once marriage has been consummated, all remarriage after divorce is adultery.[53]

This is a plausible view, and it offers an explanation for why Matthew provides the exception and Mark and Luke do not. It also reasonably explains why Matthew uses πορνεία rather than μοιχεία in his excep-tion. However, it does not seem finally to be convincing. Briefly, it may be noted that πορνεία—"sexual immorality"—is a general term for sexually immoral acts, including incest (1 Cor. 5:1), prostitution (Matt. 21:31–32; Luke 15:30; 1 Cor. 6:13–18), homosexu-ality (Lev. 18:22), bestiality (Lev. 18:23), adultery, and "any other sexual conduct condemned in the OT."[54] Gordon Wenham, who has long argued that remarriage after divorce constitutes adultery and is not per-mitted, even by Matthew, concludes that it is possible but unlikely that Matthew refers to the betrothal period, since there are no clear contextual indicators that signal the re-stricted nuance for πορνεία.[55] He writes that its normal meaning and the context of Mat-thew 19:9 "demand that it is understood in

---

51. See, e.g., John Piper, *What Jesus Demands from the World* (Wheaton, IL: Crossway, 2006), 313.
52. For a scholarly defense of the betrothal view, see Abel Isaksson, *Marriage and Ministry in the New Temple: A Study with Special Reference to Matt. 19:13 [sic]–12 and 1 Cor. 11:3–16*, trans. Neil Tomkinson and Jean Gray, Acta Seminarii Neotestamentici Upsaliensis 24 (Lund: Gleerup, 1965). See also the summary in Gordon J. Wenham and William E. Heth, *Jesus and Divorce*, updated ed. (Eugene, OR: Wipf & Stock, 2010), chap. 8.
53. See Piper, *What Jesus Demands of the World*, 314–16.
54. Robert H. Stein, "Divorce," in *Dictionary of Jesus and the Gospels*, eds. Joel B. Green, Scot McKnight, and I. Howard Marshall (Downers Grove, IL: InterVarsity Press, 1992), 195.
55. Wenham and Heth, *Jesus and Divorce*, 178.

a broad way of any sexual offences that are prohibited in the OT law: adultery, incest, homosexuality, etc.; anything that Deut. 24:1 might term 'something indecent.'"[56]

Adultery (μοιχεία) could be understood by some narrowly as an offense against another man by taking his wife, and not as an offense against one's own wife. Technically, then, a married man who went to a prostitute would not have committed adultery.[57] This could explain why Matthew uses the more general term, closing that loophole, for all the condemned sexual acts would constitute a serious offense against one's spouse and a violation of the marriage covenant. In short, πορνεία refers to "sexual immorality" in general, and acts of πορνεία committed by a married person constitute adultery. Thus one who divorces and remarries because of πορνεία does not commit adultery, for the marriage bond has already been broken. It does not mean that divorce is required, or that reconciliation is impossible. It is probably best to understand the exception as persistent and unrepentant adultery.

The disciples' reaction. Upon hearing Jesus's teaching, his disciples declare, "If such is the case of a man with his wife, it is better not to marry" (Matt. 19:10). What causes such a strong reaction? Some argue that it supports the view that Jesus does not permit remarriage after divorce.[58] Why would they respond so strongly if Jesus simply agreed with Shammai that divorce and remarriage is permitted only for adultery? Yet, given the widespread acceptance of divorce in Jesus's day, the restrictive view could make it seem better not to marry. By rejecting Hillel's view, divorce is rarely an option, so they might have thought about having to endure a difficult marriage. Even more so because Jesus goes further than Shammai in calling remarriage after invalid divorce adultery— a serious breaking of the law. In addition, Jesus does not require divorce even for sexual immorality, but merely permits it, indicating that the offended spouse should forgive and reconcile if possible.[59] Given that adultery was punishable by death in the law, it would have seemed scandalous to his disciples to forgive and remain married after adultery had occurred.

Harmonizing Luke/Mark and Matthew. It is noteworthy that whatever position one takes, there are difficulties in harmonizing the different accounts.[60] The "betrothal" view explains that Matthew's exception, which is not in Luke or Mark, is accounted

56. Wenham, "Divorce," 316.
57. See Allen Verhey, "Marriage and Divorce," in *Dictionary of Scripture and Ethics*, eds. Joel B. Green et al. (Grand Rapids: Baker Academic, 2011); also Craig S. Keener, "Adultery, Divorce," in *Dictionary of New Testament Background*, eds. Craig A. Evans and Stanley E. Porter (Downers Grove, IL: InterVarsity Press, 2000), 9–15.
58. Wenham, "No Remarriage after Divorce," 32
59. Andreas J. Köstenberger with David W. Jones, *God, Marriage and Family: Rebuilding the Biblical Foundation*, 2nd ed. (Wheaton, IL: Crossway, 2010), 227.
60. For a survey of attempts to explain the differences, see Wenham and Heth, *Jesus and Divorce.* Also, Wenham, Heth, and Keener each seek to explain the differences as they espouse their positions in Engle and Strauss, *Remarriage after Divorce.*

for because he seeks to make clear that in a situation like Joseph's, marrying after divorce is not adultery (because the marriage had not been consummated). The difficulties with this view are that, as Wenham noted, there are no clear textual indicators that Matthew is using πορνεία in such a limited way. In addition, the question put by the Pharisees has to do with the question of divorce in general, which is what the entire discussion is about, and Jesus appears to answer their question.

The majority view holds that Jesus permits remarriage after divorce for πορνεία. The main difficulty with this view is that in Luke and Mark, Jesus issues a blanket statement with no indication that there are any exceptions. How does the majority view account for this? In short, it is that the statements in Luke and Mark hyperbolic, taking aim at the adulterous divorce culture. A culture that permits divorce and remarriage for any cause—or a wide variety of causes—has simply legalized adultery. For those who would seek to justify divorce—with the authority of the law—Jesus expresses the general truth, that divorce and remarriage as commonly practiced is adultery, and he does so in a striking way to cause his hearers to consider the matter carefully.[61] It seems that the difficulty is resolved more simply by concluding that Matthew, for his own purposes (perhaps for the sake of his Jewish audience and a concern for the law), includes what he knows to be a valid exception, based on Jesus's own teaching.[62]

The use of "whoever" or "everyone who" does not mean that there are no possible exceptions. Examples elsewhere help us to see that there may be implied exceptions or qualifications. For instance, in Matthew 5:22, Jesus says, "Everyone who is angry with his brother will be liable to judgment." Yet there must be an implied exception such as "angry without cause," or Jesus himself would be guilty.[63] Similarly, the use of "everyone" rather than "virtually everyone" may be accounted for as "typical Jewish hyperbole—like Mark saying that 'everyone' in Jerusalem came to be baptized by John" (Mark 1:5).[64] Jesus also offers categorical statements, such as when he commands his followers to gouge out their eye or cut off their hand if it causes them to sin (Matt. 5:29–30), which are understood as hyperbole.[65] In the teaching on divorce, the parallel text in Matthew that offers an exception encourages us not to take the statements in Mark and Luke as exceptionless.

---

61. Stein, "Divorce," 197.
62. As John Jefferson Davis asserts, "It is likely that Jesus, like most preachers and teachers, repeated the same material in slightly different forms on various occasions. The differences would reflect not a fundamental change in content, but an adaptation of the message to different contexts and audiences." John Jefferson Davis, *Evangelical Ethics: Issues Facing the Church Today*, 4th ed. (Phillipsburg, NJ: P&R, 2015), 96.
63. Instone-Brewer, *Divorce and Remarriage in the Bible*, 153.
64. Instone-Brewer, "What God Has Joined," 28.
65. Other examples of hyperbole in Jesus's teaching include Matt. 5:23–24, 29–30, 34–36, 40; Mark 7:15. Stein, "Divorce," 197.

It does not take the bite out of Jesus's message to consider the exceptionless rule hyperbolic. The very use of exaggeration draws attention to the seriousness of the matter and to God's hatred of divorce.[66] The exception in Matthew should not lessen the problem of divorce. Jesus calls us to be faithful, and not to pursue divorce, and he warns us that if we divorce our spouse and remarry, it is adultery. No legal maneuvering changes that fact. Yet, Matthew notes, if our spouse commits adultery, and particularly if they are unrepentant, it is such a serious breach of the marriage covenant that divorce and remarriage is permissible.

Paul Allows Divorce as a Concession to an Unbelieving Spouse Who Leaves: 1 Corinthians 7:15

This text will be treated briefly. It has already been observed above that in 1 Corinthians 7:10–16, Paul's main point is to reject divorce and remarriage and commend reconciliation. Neither the wife nor the husband should leave the other, and if they do, they must either remain unmarried or be reconciled. If married to an unbeliever, Christians should not seek a divorce. But, Paul says, "If the unbeliever leaves, let him leave. A brother or a sister is not bound in such cases. God has called you to live in peace" (1 Cor. 7:15 CSB). Paul's concession here is not that a believer can pursue divorce, but that

he or she is not obligated to try to maintain the marriage at any cost. If an unbeliever seeks divorce, the believer may wish to reconcile and should be encouraged to try to do so, but in the end, it may be futile. If the unbelieving spouse is determined to get a divorce, the believer can accept it, for he or she "is not bound"—"God has called you to live in peace."

What does Paul mean when he says that the believer "is not bound" (οὐ δεδούλωται, from δουλόω)? The meaning is disputed, but it likely means that the believer is no longer bound to the marriage but is free to remarry.[67] There is a parallel later in chapter 7, where Paul says, "A wife is bound as long as her husband is living. But if her husband dies, she is free to be married to anyone she wants—only in the Lord" (1 Cor. 7:39 CSB). Just as the widow is no longer bound to the marriage but is free to remarry, so the believer who is abandoned is no longer bound but is free to remarry. The terms for "bound" (δουλόω and δέω) are different, but are related and can be used interchangeably.[68]

Note that Paul does not contradict Jesus, who allows for remarriage after divorce only for sexual immorality, for Jesus's exception concerns the possibility of remarriage for the one who has initiated divorce, whereas Paul's exception concerns the possibility of remarriage for the one who has been abandoned. Paul even distinguishes between his direct

---

66. Stein, "Divorce," 198.
67. See Stein, "Divorce," 197; and Gerald F. Hawthorne, "Marriage and Divorce, Adultery and Incest," in *Dictionary of Paul and His Letters*, eds. Gerald F. Hawthorne, Ralph P. Martin, and Daniel G. Reid (Downers Grove, IL: InterVarsity Press, 1993), 599.
68. Köstenberger and Jones, *God, Marriage and Family*, 286; Stein, "Divorce," 194.

application of Jesus's teaching ("not I, but the Lord," v. 10), and the unique situation of a believer married to an unbeliever ("I, not the Lord," v. 12). His teaching remains authoritative, but it is not a situation about which Jesus taught, and there is no conflict.[69]

Summary

The majority view argues that the Bible allows for divorce and remarriage for two reasons, most commonly expressed as adultery and desertion.[70] Those terms adequately reflect the position, but each needs to be nuanced. As we have seen, the first term (πορνεία) is, more precisely, "sexual immorality" or "unchastity." Adultery captures the essence, since the various forms of sexual immorality committed by a married person are adultery. The second term, "desertion," needs slight clarification. Paul says, "If the unbeliever leaves, let him leave." In essence, it is not that Paul considers desertion a cause for divorce, so that the believer is justified in divorcing the unbeliever if the unbeliever separates. Paul's emphasis on a readiness for reconciliation and commitment to marriage suggests otherwise. Rather, he is saying that if the unbeliever seeks a divorce, the believer can accept that.[71] So "desertion" means

something like "a concession to an unbeliever who seeks a divorce." As long as reconciliation is possible, Christians ought to seek it and remain open to it. We should not close the door, but if the door is closed to you, Paul says, you are not bound.

The biblical teaching on marriage, divorce, and remarriage is not concerned first with when divorce and remarriage are permissible, and that should not be our focus either. We ought to hold marriage in the highest regard. Understanding it to be a reflection and a signpost of God's love and faithfulness, we ought to be faithful to one another in marriage, to preserve our marriages and magnify God through them. As far as it is possible with us, we ought not to separate what God has joined together. The question is, What is someone to do when his or her spouse has broken the marriage covenant, either by sexual immorality or by demanding a divorce? The exceptions given by Jesus and Paul, then, do not offer permission to abandon one's spouse, but teach us what we can do if we are abandoned.

Questions and Pastoral Issues

Before drawing some conclusions, we will consider some difficult questions and pastoral issues that often arise.

---

69. For further discussion of the resolution of any possible conflict between Jesus and Paul, see Murray, *Divorce*, 70–72.

70. This is the view defended by William Heth, who formerly held to the "no remarriage" view, in Engle and Strauss, *Remarriage after Divorce*. It is also defended by Thomas Edgar, "Divorce and Remarriage for Adultery or Desertion," in *Divorce and Remarriage: Four Christian Views*, ed. H. Wayne House (Downers Grove, IL: InterVarsity Press, 1990), 151–96. Each of these examples uses the terms most often used by the majority view, adultery and desertion.

71. That is, the concession isn't so much that the believer can dissolve the marriage bond as that he or she can regard it as dissolved if the unbeliever has dissolved it. Cf. Murray, *Divorce*, 97.

Should Divorce Be Pursued if the Spouse Who Committed Adultery Repents?

This question has two dimensions. First, is divorce commanded for adultery? In Jewish and Roman law, a husband was required to divorce his wife immediately if he learned that she had committed adultery; indeed, in Roman law, the man could be prosecuted if he did not divorce her, for it could be taken as a form of pimping or prostitution.[72] Neither Jesus nor Paul requires divorce for adultery, and the example of God's forbearance toward an unfaithful people, demonstrated vividly in the story of Hosea and in the model of Christ's relationship with the church. The central emphasis on forgiveness, grace, and reconciliation in the gospel message seems to make clear that divorce is not mandatory in the case of adultery.[73] This would seem to make divorce a last resort, in cases of unrepentant, persistent adultery. As John Stott comments, "Jesus' purpose was emphatically not to encourage divorce for this reason, but rather to forbid it for all other reasons."[74]

Second, is divorce permissible if the guilty spouse repents? Jesus's permission for sexual immorality must be understood in the larger context of the gospel, and the offended spouse ought to be encouraged to forgive and make every effort to reconcile. Yet we must recognize that reconciliation may be extremely difficult in some cases, especially if the offender is unrepentant. Moreover, Jesus's permission does not specify only persistent and unrepentant adultery. So while pastors, counselors, and friends ought to encourage—and seek to facilitate—forgiveness and reconciliation where there is repentance, it does not seem that there is warrant to tell the offended spouse that they are absolutely not permitted to divorce.

Are Divorce and Remarriage Permitted in Cases of Abuse, or Only for "Adultery and Desertion"?

This is a common question, and a difficult one in many ways. On the one hand, it seems that if there is any reason that divorce (and remarriage) should be allowed, it would be physical abuse and the threat to one's life. On the other hand, Jesus only gives one possibility for divorce and remarriage, likely because adultery "violates the 'one flesh' principle which is foundational to marriage as divinely ordained and biblically defined."[75] Paul's additional exception, we have seen, is not a permission to divorce so much as permission to accept divorce that one cannot prevent. New Testament scholar Craig Keener suggests that what the exceptions of Jesus and Paul have in common is that "they are acts committed by a partner against an unbeliever," so that "the believer is not free to break up the marriage but only to accept

---

72. Keener, "Adultery, Divorce," 9. Cf. Stein, "Divorce," 197.
73. Stein, "Divorce," 197.
74. John Stott, *Issues Facing Christians Today*, 4th ed. (Grand Rapids: Zondervan, 2006), 373.
75. Stott, *Issues Facing Christians Today*, 372.

that the unrepentant partner has irreparably broken it."[76]

Is it possible that abuse, though not specified by Jesus, Paul, or any other biblical writer, is another exception that fits the pattern established by Jesus and followed by Paul? Keener notes that Paul's exception is given in light of a new situation that arose, when an unbeliever leaves a believer. He comments, "If this issue hadn't come up, we would not have an explicit exception for abandonment. What, then, of issues that did not come up? What if physical abuse had come up?"[77] This approach, it seems to me, is dangerously speculative. Scripture is sufficient, and God in his sovereignty has revealed what we need to know. The situation addressed by Paul is not random, as if it just happened to come up, but what we need for understanding God's will. It is one thing to discern a clear principle in Scripture and apply it to new situations. It is another to imagine that what we have in Scripture came by chance and might have been different.

Nonetheless, there are several ways to respond to the question of abuse that avoid this problem. One is to understand abuse as a form of abandonment, and thus justification for divorce. But we must be cautious about this, for the "abandonment" that Paul addresses is the refusal of the unbeliever to remain with the believer. The believer does not on that account divorce the unbeliever, but accepts a divorce. A second possibility is that

abuse is a justification for divorce and remarriage because it fits the principle established by Jesus and followed by Paul. In this view, sexual immorality and abandonment are severe violations of the marriage covenant, which justify divorce, and abuse is justification for divorce for the same reason. Again, we must be cautious here, in part because the two explicit exceptions, "sexual immorality" and "abandonment," do not necessarily issue from the same principle. "Sexual immorality," we might say, is the single ground for divorce and remarriage that Jesus gives because it uniquely violates the marriage bond.[78] Paul's exception is different, in a sense, because he does not give permission to divorce because one's spouse has violated the marriage bond; he frees the believer from being bound to marriage to an unbeliever who refuses to remain with the believer.

In these two views, the permission to remarry is assumed with the permission to divorce. Both of these first two views are possible, but it is difficult to establish them with certainty. Another possibility, given only two exceptions in Scripture, is that divorce and remarriage are not allowed in the case of abuse, but advocacy and assistance should be provided to the victim.[79] Concern for those who are abused should be paramount. The abused spouse and children should be removed from the abusive situation and protected. The hope is that reconciliation is possible, that the abuser will repent, and that there can be

---

76. Keener, "Remarriage for Adultery, Desertion, or Abuse," 110, 112.
77. Keener, "A Response to William A. Heth," in Engle and Strauss, *Remarriage after Divorce*, 94.
78. Cf. Stott, *Issues Facing Christians Today*, 372.
79. See, e.g., Heth, "Remarriage for Adultery or Desertion," 77.

confidence that there will be no more abuse. This is very difficult to assess, given the frequent pattern of abuse, apologies, and more abuse. Someone with experience counseling abusers and victims should assess the situation before recommending that the spouses come together again.

In addition to the safety of the victim, there is a different sort of problem that may arise with this view. Marriage and divorce are recognized by both the church and the government, but they are not necessarily recognized as the same thing. It is clear that the government accepts divorce "for any cause." If divorce is not pursued, then there may be legal issues with regard to child custody, financial holdings, separation, and so on. This raises a question for those who believe that divorce and remarriage are not permitted for abuse in Scripture: Is it possible for the person to pursue a divorce that is recognized by the state, in order to protect the abused spouse, to establish child custody, and so on, while not recognizing the divorce from a biblical perspective? The implication of this is simply that, even though the offended spouse has obtained a divorce recognized by the government, they should not remarry, but remain open to reconciliation in the event that the offender repents. Remarriage, in this case, would be allowed if the offender refuses to reconcile and marries another.

Abuse is a very difficult case. Priority, in terms of immediate action, should be given to the safety of the abused spouse and the couple's children. Yet priority also should be given to the pursuit of reconciliation, if at all possible. Each of the views mentioned have some grounding in Scripture. Pastors, counselors, and friends involved in such situations should seek diligently to discern and apply the will of God by seeking to understand how the Scriptures may be applied in the particular situation they are overseeing.

Can a Person Who Is Divorced and Remarried Serve in Church Leadership?

This question arises from the qualifications for overseers and deacons. Specifically, among the list of qualifications is "the husband of one wife" (1 Tim. 3:2, 12; Tit. 1:6). What does this require?[80] Does it mean that the man must not be single, or that he cannot have more than one wife, or cannot have remarried if he is a widower? Does it mean that he cannot have been divorced or remarried? It is unlikely that a single person or remarried widower is disqualified, as Paul himself was single and expressed some preference for singleness, for wholehearted devotion to the Lord (1 Cor. 7:35). It is possible that polygamy is included, but it was not common in the first century, and it is not likely that it is the primary aim. Because there is some ambiguity in the term, many different views have been held.

It seems that the focus of the qualifications is on the character rather than the status of the leader, though these two things are certainly related. As such, the phrase that is used, μιᾶς

---

80. For the various possibilities and a discussion of whether a divorced man can serve as overseer or deacon, see Köstenberger and Jones, *God, Marriage and Family*, 239–45.

γυναικὸς ἄνδρα, translated "husband of one wife," likely refers to a "faithful" or "devoted" husband, a "one-woman man." A man who is not faithful to his wife is obviously excluded. A man who divorces his wife on grounds not permitted by Scripture is excluded, but not necessarily every divorced man. For instance, a man who was divorced and remarried prior to his conversion, but now is an exemplary husband, could serve as an overseer or deacon. In addition, a man whose wife divorced him, or who divorced his wife for persistent and unrepentant adultery, may be eligible to serve in these offices. It seems that such decisions have to rest with those in the church who can assess the situation and determine if the man indeed is now (and has been for some time) above reproach, and is in his current marriage a faithful husband.

There have been significant disagreements on issues such as this one, from interpreters who hold a high view of Scripture and seek to be obedient to biblical teaching. We ought to exercise grace toward one another if we differ on these points. Denominations and churches will need to set guidelines for how they will handle such cases. This can be difficult in cases of disagreement. In all cases, we must seek to preserve marriage, and not merely to maintain marriages but to see them flourish.

Conclusion

In his discussion of divorce, Heth indicates that only the person who has been offended can decide whether divorce is appropriate, and we ought to respect them.[81] In cases that may allow for divorce, that seems to be unavoidable in some ways. Yet that must be qualified. First, in cases where divorce is pursued without biblical warrant, it is not enough to say that the person must decide, and thus yield to our culture's personal, private, autonomous decision-making view. Scripture teaches God's will on this issue, and there are cases that are clear enough that the church (pastors or other leaders) must "weigh in" on the situation, even to the point of church discipline. Second, to simply leave it to the person points to the failure of members of the church to be fully engaged with one another, bearing one another's burdens, exhorting and teaching one another, and holding one another accountable. Pastors and others in the church should be involved in counseling and guiding people through such difficulties, for people need counsel from godly shepherds, and the church needs to practice discipline where members act in ways that are clearly disobedient to God.

We ought to note, with John Stott, that marriages don't break down by themselves.[82] It is easy to let ourselves think that this marriage just broke down. It is more accurate to say that one or both spouses gave up on the marriage (often in the midst of very difficult struggles, to be sure). It happens over time, until it simply feels as if it is irreparable. But by God's grace, it is seldom irreparable. The church can help by

---

81. Heth, "Remarriage for Adultery or Desertion," 80.
82. Stott, *Issues Facing Christians Today*, 379.

stepping in the gap and encouraging, exhorting, and providing resources for married couples—not merely a book or even a marriage seminar, but spiritual resources, and human resources in the form of people significantly investing in one another. Before difficult times come, the church needs to teach clearly on marriage, divorce and remarriage, forgiveness and reconciliation. A culture needs to be established where help is sought before a crisis is at hand.

The church needs to stand firm on biblical truth, to confront, exhort, and ultimately discipline those who would seek divorce, and to refuse to join in marriage those who have broken their covenant without cause (but seek to counsel and encourage). The church also needs to minister to those whose marriages have been broken by divorce. Even in a culture where divorce is common, the reality is that something has been put asunder that God had joined. Not surprisingly, divorce doesn't make everything better. There is brokenness and hurt and often a sense of shame. There may be a need for genuine repentance. There is also a need for genuine forgiveness, grace, love, and restoration for those who have repented.

Select Resources

Engle, Paul E., and Mark L. Strauss, eds. *Remarriage after Divorce in Today's Church: Three Views*. Grand Rapids: Zondervan, 2006.

Instone-Brewer, David. *Divorce and Remarriage in the Bible: The Social and Literary Context*. Grand Rapids: Eerdmans, 2002.

Keener, Craig S. *And Marries Another: Divorce and Remarriage in the Teaching of the New Testament*. Peabody, MA: Hendrickson, 1991.

Murray, John. *Divorce*. Philadelphia, PA: Presbyterian and Reformed, 1961.

Piper, John. *This Momentary Marriage: A Parable of Permanence*. Wheaton: Crossway, 2009.

Wenham, Gordon J., and William E. Heth. *Jesus and Divorce*. Updated ed. Eugene, OR: Wipf & Stock, 2010.

Whitehead, Barbara Dafoe. *The Divorce Culture: Rethinking Our Commitments to Marriage and Family*. New York: Vintage, 1998.

CHAPTER 9

HOMOSEXUALITY, SEXUAL IDENTITY, AND GENDER

Come to me, all of you who are weary and burdened, and I will give you rest. Take up my yoke and learn from me, because I am lowly and humble in heart, and you will find rest for your souls. For my yoke is easy and my burden is light.

—Matthew 11:28–30

Do not be deceived; neither fornicators, nor idolaters, nor adulterers, nor effeminate, nor homosexuals, nor thieves, nor the covetous, nor drunkards, nor revilers, nor swindlers, will inherit the kingdom of God. Such were some of you; but you were washed, but you were sanctified, but you were justified in the name of the Lord Jesus Christ and in the Spirit of our God.

—1 Corinthians 6:9–11 NASB

Therefore, if anyone is in Christ, he is a new creation; the old has passed away, and see, the new has come!

—2 Corinthians 5:17

Introduction

Matters related to homosexuality and LGBT issues fuel many debates.[1] The debates are often heated because they involve foundational issues that intersect with morality, politics, and law, and are both personal and public, involving foundational issues about the meaning of sex and marriage, rights and freedoms, the interpretation and application of Scripture, and an understanding of gender and identity, among other things. Underlying these and other aspects of the debate are very different worldviews and different understandings of human beings.

In terms of Christian ethics, much of the recent debate has centered on an interpretation of Scripture and its implications for human sexuality and sexual behavior. Some, in light of changes in how homosexuality is understood, along with cultural pressure for LGBT equality (including equal recognition of same-sex relationships), have reconsidered what the Bible has to say about homosexuality, marriage, and other issues. In particular, they have reinterpreted the key texts concerning homosexuality, arguing that they do not deal with or apply to a current understanding of sexual orientation or to consensual, committed same-sex relationships. They further argue that love and justice require full inclusion of homosexuals

for church membership and consideration of ordination. Others consider the Bible to be clear in its condemnation of homosexual acts, and have rejected a "revisionist" interpretation of the Bible regarding homosexuality. Further, they have argued that faithfulness to God, as well as love and justice, demand that they do not affirm what the Bible condemns, and that those who are engaged in homosexual practices without repentance cannot be accepted into church membership, much less presented for ordination and leadership in the church.

Clearly, much is at stake here, for it involves the very understanding of the gospel and entrance into the kingdom of heaven (not "merely" church membership). Unfortunately, those who have stood with Christian tradition on this matter, seeking to defend the truth of Scripture, have sometimes only been heard to condemn and marginalize homosexuals. Evangelicals are often portrayed as homophobic and hateful. This should not be the case. In response, some have sought to soften the message, to be clear that the church welcomes those with same-sex orientation, but does not affirm homosexual acts. However, for those seeking full recognition of same-sex relationships, a welcome without affirmation is insufficient. As such, it is not surprising that

---

1. The initials LGBT (for lesbian, gay, bisexual, and transgender) are used in this chapter to refer to the broad coalition that engages issues related to sexual orientation and gender. Other initials that are often used include LGBTQ (adding Q for queer or questioning, or sometimes LGBTQQ for both), LGBTQI (adding I for intersex), and sometimes LGBTQIA (including A for asexual or allied). While the different acronyms are sometimes used, LGBT seems to be most common.

   Although there is much overlap in the concerns of LGBT advocates, there are also significant differences. This chapter will focus on issues particularly pertaining to a biblical view of homosexuality, with some attention to transgender issues.

there is not a lot of room for compromise; or, as one revisionist scholar put it, the middle ground is disappearing.[2]

As we examine the issue of homosexuality, we do well to remember that it is not an abstract issue. Behind the debate and the headlines, those who experience same-sex attraction are real people with faces and names, hopes and fears. They are our neighbors and friends, customers, employees, and employers. An important recent development with respect to LGBT issues is that many Christians have come to know something of the struggles and pain experienced by those who identify as LGBT, and some churches are learning how to understand, reach out, and minister to them without compromising the gospel or the truth of Scripture. In short, many Christians who love Jesus and stand uncompromisingly on the truth of the Bible are realizing that homosexuality represents not merely a moral issue, but a *people to be loved*.[3]

How should we understand biblical teaching on homosexuality? How should we respond to our LGBT neighbors and friends? What counsel should we give those who identify as gay Christians? Is it possible to hold to what was once the consensus of the church concerning the biblical prohibition of all homosexual acts, and yet love and reach out to those who identify as LGBT? In this chapter, we will survey the biblical material that relates directly to homosexuality, as well as the biblical framework within which those texts appear, and we will consider some of the key challenges put to the traditional interpretation of those texts. In addition, we will consider some of the frequently discussed and hotly debated issues pertaining to homosexuality, such as sexual orientation and gender identity, what causes homosexuality, whether it is possible to change sexual orientation, and questions of pastoral ministry. First we will briefly consider the context of the recent debate about homosexuality and LGBT issues.

Context

In one sense, the debate about homosexuality is like other moral debates we are discussing, and it should not be given disproportionate weight. Yet, in another sense, this issue is different. With some hotly debated issues (capital punishment and war, for instance), there is some movement in public opinion from time to time, but the debate is somewhat static. With other issues (such as physician-assisted suicide), there seems to be a significant moral shift taking place. But with homosexuality and LGBT issues, while there are ongoing and intractable debates, the moral shift can be described as part of a cultural and sexual revolution.[4]

2. David Gushee, "On LGBT Equality, Middle Ground is Disappearing," *Religion News Service*, August 22, 2016, http://religionnews.com/2016/08/22/on-lgbt-equality-middle-ground-is-disappearing.

3. This point is central to Preston Sprinkle's book *People to Be Loved: Why Homosexuality Is Not Just an Issue* (Grand Rapids: Zondervan, 2015).

4. Michael Hill briefly describes this change in *The How and Why of Love: An Introduction to Evangelical Ethics* (Kingsford, Australia: Matthias Media, 2002), 177–79. For a sustained treatment of the cultural and sexual revolution, homosexuality, same-sex marriage, and gender issues, see R. Albert Mohler Jr., *We Cannot Be*

Seismic Changes

One clear signpost of the sexual, moral, and cultural revolution is the redefinition of marriage, culminating in the US Supreme Court's Obergefell decision on June 26, 2015. In a five-four decision, the court ruled that same-sex couples are guaranteed a fundamental right to marry by the United States Constitution.[5] On the one hand, the decision seemed to be an example of judicial overreach, receiving harsh words from critics.[6] On the other hand, the court reflected the massive shift in public opinion that had already taken place, in which a majority of Americans had come to affirm what only a decade earlier a vast majority had rejected.[7] This was not the beginning or end of the revolution, but it was a significant signpost along the way.

Another example of the rapid change can be seen in the position of the American Psychiatric Association (APA).[8] Prior to 1973, the APA listed homosexuality as a mental disorder. Under pressure from activists who threatened to disrupt APA meetings, in 1973 homosexuality was categorized as a "sexual orientation disturbance." By 2015, the APA considered it to be "a normal expression of human sexuality," and applauded the Supreme Court's legalization of same-sex marriage.[9] What is notable is that the changes

---

Silent: Speaking Truth to a Culture Redefining Sex, Marriage, & the Very Meaning of Right and Wrong (Nashville: Nelson Books, 2015).

Many would trace the birth of the gay-rights movement to the Stonewall riots in Greenwich Village in June, 1969, when a police raid of the Stonewall Inn was resisted. But the resistance turned to revolution two decades later or so. A book that set out the strategy for the cultural revolution concerning homosexuality, with startling success, is Marshall Kirk and Hunter Madsen, *After the Ball: How America Will Conquer Its Fear & Hatred of Gays in the 90's* (New York: Doubleday, 1989). A book that documents and reflects on the success of the revolution is Linda Hirshman, *Victory: The Triumphant Gay Revolution; How a Despised Minority Pushed Back, Beat Death, Found Love, and Changed America for Everyone* (New York: HarperCollins, 2012); also David Eisenbach, *Gay Power: An American Revolution* (New York: Carroll & Graf, 2006).

5. Obergefell v. Hodges, 576 U.S. 644 (2015), https://www.supremecourt.gov/opinions/14pdf/14–556_3204.pdf. This decision represents a major cultural and legal shift, and a major victory for LGBT advocates.

6. Among the many examples, see "Judicial Watch Statement on Supreme Court's Ruling in Obergefell v. Hodges," *Judicial Watch*, June 26, 2015, http://www.judicialwatch.org/press-room/press-releases/judicial-watch-statement-on-supreme-courts-ruling-in-obergefell-v-hodges. The criticism hasn't ebbed with time, as evidenced in this reflection by Howard Slugh, "Obergefell's Toxic Judicial Legacy," *National Review*, April 10, 2017, http://www.nationalreview.com/article/446574/obergefell-judges-invent-rights-its-encouragement.

7. As noted by Mohler, *We Cannot Be Silent*, xv. For example, between 1993 and 2012, more than forty states had banned same-sex marriage, either by statute or by putting in place constitutional amendments that recognized marriage only between a man and a woman, and banned same-sex marriage. For a state-by-state graphic, see Haeyoun Park, "Gay Marriage State by State: From a Few States to the Whole Nation," *New York Times*, March 4, 2015, updated after Obergefell, https://www.nytimes.com/interactive/2015/03/04/us/gay-marriage-state-by-state.html.

8. See Hirshman, *Victory*, chap. 5. Also Ronald Bayer, *Homosexuality and American Psychiatry: The Politics of Diagnosis* (Princeton, NJ: Princeton University Press, 1987).

9. See the APA news release after the Supreme Court's Obergefell decision: "APA Applauds Supreme Court Decision Supporting Same-Sex Marriage," June 26, 2015, https://www.psychiatry.org/newsroom/news-releases/apa-applauds-supreme-court-decision-supporting-same-sex-marriage. On declassifying homosexuality from a "mental disorder" to "sexual orientation disturbance," and later removing any sort of label of disorder, see Neel Burton, "When Homosexuality Stopped Being a Mental Disorder," *Psychology Today*, September 18, 2015, https://www.psychologytoday.com/blog/hide-and-seek/201509/when-homosexuality-stopped-being-mental-disorder.

in the APA's position were not the result of scientific breakthrough, but rather social pressure. The success in getting the APA to change its position on homosexuality, which had obvious implications for therapy and other practices, was a precursor of the dramatic changes that would take place in American culture more generally in the following decades.

Revising the Bible and Morality: Scholarship and the Church

The cultural revolution has had significant impact on biblical scholarship and the church. Scholars began to challenge the long-standing consensus that all homosexual practices are condemned as sinful in Scripture, arguing that biblical writers never address committed, monogamous same-sex relationships.[10] Intense pressure has been put on denominations and churches, from within and without, to affirm same-sex relationships. Matthew Vines has gone so far as to assert that "it isn't gay Christians who are sinning against God by entering into monogamous, loving relationships. It is the church that is sinning against them by rejecting their intimate relationships."[11] In some cases, the pressure is barely veiled

coercion. After noting how waves of acceptance and affirmation of homosexuality have occurred in virtually every sector of society (education, medicine, corporate America, media and entertainment, the sports world, even the Boy Scouts), David Gushee issued what could be considered an ominous call to religious conservatives "to reconsider their position *voluntarily*."[12] Some mainstream denominations and many churches, including some evangelical churches, have indeed reconsidered and revised their views, affirming same-sex relations.[13]

Many evangelicals and other conservatives have been overwhelmed and perhaps shell-shocked by the dramatic and rapid changes that have taken place. They fear that more churches will capitulate to the sexual revolution, that marriage and the family will be further threatened, and that the authority of Scripture will continue to be undermined. Yet, in the midst of such challenges, there is opportunity to examine Scripture carefully, and to proclaim biblical truth with clarity and boldness, which does not end with a message of judgment and God's wrath against human sin and rebellion. It offers the life-giving message of grace and love lavishly poured out on

---

10. This will be discussed below. See early revisionist scholars, such as Derrick Sherwin Bailey, *Homosexuality and the Western Christian Tradition* (London: Longmans, Green, 1955); John Boswell, *Christianity, Social Tolerance and Homosexuality: Gay People in Western Europe from the Beginning of the Christian Era to the Fourteenth Century* (Chicago: University of Chicago Press, 1980). More recently, see James V. Brownson, *Bible, Gender, Sexuality: Reframing the Church's Debate on Same-Sex Relationships* (Grand Rapids: Eerdmans, 2013). A popular presentation of the revisionist perspective is Matthew Vines, *God and the Gay Christian: The Biblical Case in Support of Same-Sex Relationships* (New York: Convergent, 2014).
11. Vines, *God and the Gay Christian*, 162.
12. Gushee, "On LGBT" (emphasis added).
13. The website https://www.gaychurch.org offers a directory of over eight thousand churches worldwide.

undeserving sinners who repent and place their trust in Jesus, the perfect Son of God, who took on himself our sin in order to restore our broken relationship with God and to redeem our broken lives for his glory.

The Bible and Homosexuality

For Christians, the Bible is the decisive authority for faith and practice. In the past, that has been adequate reason to hold the view that God condemns homosexual acts, for the teaching of Scripture has long been understood to be clear and consistent on the matter. For the most part, those who affirmed homosexual practices rejected the Bible. More recently, however, some have made the case, as Vines states it, that "Christians who affirm the full authority of Scripture can also affirm committed, monogamous same-sex relationships."[14] Thus, in the following pages we will examine what the Bible teaches about homosexuality. In so doing, we will consider some of the key revisionist arguments and respond to them. Much of the focus will be on the contested texts that address homosexuality directly in some form. These are treated in four groupings: Genesis 19:1–11 (cf. Judg. 19); Leviticus 18:22 and 20:13; Romans 1:24–27 (or more broadly, verses 18–32); 1 Corinthians 6:9–11; and 1 Timothy 1:8–11.

Some will argue that the Bible is not much concerned with homosexuality, since it is rarely addressed, or at least that it is far more concerned about other things. As one author put it, the few proscriptive texts "are slim pickings among the Bible's 31,103 verses."[15] Even people who don't know exactly how many verses are in the Bible can recognize that this is an inadequate hermeneutical principle. As we will see, when the Bible does address homosexuality, it is clear and consistent, and never affirming of homosexual acts. But the relevance of biblical teaching isn't limited to the texts that directly address homosexuality, and we will begin at the beginning, where God's design and purposes for sex are revealed.

The Creation Pattern of Male and Female in Genesis 1–2

In previous chapters we examined certain aspects of the creation accounts as they relate to human sexuality and marriage. Here we will look at key features with specific attention to their relevance for homosexuality. In particular, we need to consider the significance of the creation of human beings as male and female, and the tasks given to them (Gen. 1:26–28); the creation of the woman as a "helper corresponding to" the man (Gen. 2:18); and the union of the man and the woman as "one flesh" in marriage (Gen. 2:23–24). These accounts resound with God's planning and intention, with order and purposefulness. Nothing is arbitrary, accidental, or incidental. They are obviously foundational for our understanding of God's

---

14. Vines, *God and the Gay Christian*, 3.
15. David G. Myers, who argues for gay marriage, in "Bridging the Gay-Evangelical Divide," *Wall Street Journal*, August 28, 2009, W11.

purposes in creation, especially with respect to the nature and role of human beings.

He created them male and female

In Genesis 1:26–28, God creates human beings in his own image, he creates them male and female, and he gives his human creatures five imperatives: to be fruitful, multiply, fill the earth, subdue the earth, and rule over the creatures of the earth. Genesis 2 will focus more closely on the relationship between the man and the woman. In Genesis 1 we see the bigger picture, that they are together given the task of filling the earth and ruling over it. The two accounts serve complementary purposes and must be read in relation to one another or we can easily distort the meaning of both.

Revisionist commentators downplay the normative significance of the creation narratives, or at least of the significance of male and female within the creation narratives. For Vines, for instance, same-sex orientation is not a "distortion caused by the fall" but rather a "created characteristic" that is "a good part of God's creation."[16] In addition, Vines argues, none of the purposes of God in creating image bearers—such as the value of each individual, the capacity for relationships and covenantal love, and having dominion over the earth—require heterosexuality.[17]

Below we'll look more closely at Genesis 2 and marriage. Here some general comments are worth noting. To begin with, God's design of human beings as male and female, in relation to one another, and his purposes for them feature prominently in these accounts and are not accidental or incidental. First, the creation of human beings as male and female is closely related to the imperatives given to them, not only to multiply and fill the earth, but also to subdue and have dominion. Second, every human being is an image bearer, and it is not necessary to be in a one-flesh union of male and female in order to bear the divine image.[18] Yet the roles given to God's image bearers are closely connected to their creation as male and female, so we ought not treat that reality as incidental. Together, male and female multiply and fill the earth, and together male and female exercise dominion. All humans bear God's image. Yet the roles given to God's image bearers flow out of the relationship of man and woman. Third, the revisionist claim that same-sex attraction is part of God's creative purposes, providing a

---

16. Vines, *God and the Gay Christian*, 161. Vines is important because he has read revisionist scholars, and summarized and popularized their views very well. For a significant recent scholarly defense of same-sex relationships, and treatment of the creation accounts, see Brownson, *Bible, Gender, Sexuality*.

17. See Vines, *God and the Gay Christian*, chap. 9, "What the Image of God Teaches Us about Gay Christians," 149–62.

18. Brownson notes that the creation of both male and female in God's image "is intended to convey the value, dominion, and relationality shared by both men and women." The question is whether it is right to assert, as he does, that the creation of male and female in God's image does not convey "the idea that the complementarity of the genders is somehow necessary to fully express or embody the divine image." See Brownson, *Bible, Gender, Sexuality*, 31. I agree that it is not necessary on an individual level, but Genesis 1 connects the role of God's image bearers to their being created male and female.

good variation of sexuality, is not indicated in the biblical creation account or anywhere else in Scripture. The revisionist arguments to this end are based on subjective experience and arguments from silence, and are contrary to the unified witness of the Bible where it does speak about homosexuality, including (in Romans 1) where it speaks of it as being contrary to the creation purposes of God.

A helper fit for him

Genesis 2:18 reads, "Then the LORD God said, 'It is not good that the man should be alone; I will make him a helper fit for him'" (ESV). In the chapter on marriage and sexuality, we have seen that God provides the woman for the man as a helper to accomplish the tasks that God has given them. Here the focus is shifted slightly to the question of the kind of helper that God provides. The text says that God provides a helper that is "fit for him" (ESV) or "suitable for him" (NIV). What does "fit" or "suitable" mean? Vines and James Brownson and others suggest that the woman is fit or suitable not because she is a woman but because she is human.[19] Of course, God did first bring all the animals before the man, and he recognized that they were not the help he needed, preparing him to recognize the helper that is suitable. In contrast to the animals, he recognizes that he needs a human. The focus, revisionists say, is on similarity rather than difference or complementarity of male and female.[20] Vines concedes that for the first man, a woman was indeed necessary for procreative purposes, but that is not as important now. Thus any human could provide the help needed, including companionship and sexual fulfillment.

However, this view is inadequate. First, the emphasis here is not primarily on companionship (though that is not absent), but on providing help to fulfill the purposes for which God has created the man. This is evident in the need for help to tend the garden (Gen. 2:5, 8, 15). Beyond that, if Genesis 1–2 are read together, the help includes the imperatives given to the male and female in Genesis 1:28. The absence of any reference to procreation in Genesis 2 leads some (not just revisionist commentators) to suggest that in this account at least, the emphasis is on companionship and not procreation, minimizing the significance of procreation for marriage.[21] Yet procreation is a central feature of the help provided, and it cannot be excluded from the purposes for which the woman is given as a help.

Second, the term "suitable" itself at least suggests complementarity (so the HCSB: "I will make a helper as his complement"), contrary to Brownson's claim. In verse 18 God determines to create for the man a helper (עֵזֶר) who is suitable (כְּנֶגְדּוֹ). Both terms are important, but the focus here is on the meaning of כְּנֶגְדּוֹ.[22] Is the woman suitable

19. Vines, *God and the Gay Christian*, 45–47; Brownson, *Bible, Gender, Sexuality*, 29–30.
20. Brownson, *Bible, Gender, Sexuality*, 29.
21. Cf. Vines, *God and the Gay Christian*, 45.
22. See the helpful study on כְּנֶגְדּוֹ by Preston Sprinkle in *People to Be Loved*, 32–34.

for the man because she is human, or is the fact that she is a woman significant? כְּנֶגְדּוֹ is a compound word from כְּ ("as" or "like") and נֶגֶד ("opposite" or "against" or "in front of"). If the focus was on similarity, as Brownson claims, it seems that כְּ would have been sufficient. So the compound word indicates something else. Preston Sprinkle asserts that "this word potentially conveys both similarity (*ke*) and dissimilarity (*neged*). Eve is a human and not an animal, which is why she is *ke* ('like') Adam. But she's also a female and not a male, which is why she is different from Adam, or *neged* ('opposite him')."[23] Compound words are not always easy to translate, and כְּנֶגְדּוֹ only appears in Genesis 2:18 and 2:20, so we must be careful not to make too much of this one term. Yet it is suggestive, fitting very well with the complementarity that we find with male and female, in a general and not merely biological sense.

Marriage as a one-flesh union

When God brings the woman to the man as his suitable helper, he exclaims,

> This one, at last, is bone of my bone
> and flesh of my flesh;
> this one will be called "woman,"
> for she was taken from man. (Gen. 2:23)

And then we read, "This is why a man leaves his father and mother and bonds with his wife, and they become one flesh" (v. 24). "One flesh" is related to "bone of my bone and flesh of my flesh." But what does that mean?

Though it includes sexual union, "one flesh" is broader, signifying that marriage forms a bond as strong as kinship.[24] Indeed, the Hebrew idiom "flesh and bone" is like the English "flesh and blood." In Genesis 29:14, Laban says to his nephew Jacob, "You are my bone and my flesh" (ESV; CSB says, "you are my own flesh and blood"). The use of "flesh" or "flesh and bone" or "flesh and blood" for kinship is common (see, e.g., Gen. 37:27; Judg. 9:2; 2 Sam. 5:1, 19:12–13; 1 Chron. 11:1). So, for instance, in his comments on Genesis 2:24, Gordon Wenham says that one flesh "does not denote merely the sexual union that follows marriage. . . . Rather it affirms that just as blood relations are one's flesh and bone, so marriage creates a similar kinship relationship between man and wife."[25] Sexual union is included, but it also signifies the close bond and permanence of the marriage union.

Does Genesis 2:24 leave open the possibility that this could also apply to a same-sex union? In his study on the significance of one flesh in the context of gender and sexuality, Brownson draws this conclusion: "It is clear

---

23. Sprinkle, *People to Be Loved*, 32. Danna Nolan Fewell and David M. Gunn agree. They say, "the 'helper corresponding to [like-opposite] the human/man is a sexual 'opposite.' According to this claim, human sexuality is clearly monogamous exogamous heterosexuality: one partner, outside of the family, of the opposite sex. Partnership, according to this agenda, demands sexual and familial difference." Fewell and Gunn, *Gender, Power, & Promise: The Subject of the Bible's First Story* (Nashville: Abingdon, 1993), 29.
24. See Brownson, *Bible, Gender, Sexuality*, chap. 5, "One Flesh," 85–109.
25. Gordon J. Wenham, *Genesis 1–15*, Word Biblical Commentary 1 (1987; repr., Grand Rapids: Zondervan, 2017), 71.

that Scripture *assumes* that this one-flesh bond only takes place between a man and a woman. Yet there is nothing inherent in the biblical usage that would necessarily exclude committed gay or lesbian unions from consideration as one-flesh unions, when the essential characteristics of one-flesh unions as kinship bonds are held clearly in view."[26]

This is a giant leap, for several reasons. First, the creation accounts in Genesis establish normative patterns. For example, the narrative in Genesis 2:24 turns from the description of this man and this woman to a description of marriage itself, explaining, "This is why a man leaves his father and mother and bonds with his wife, and they become one flesh." Second, the normative significance of the one-flesh union as a marital sexual union of a man and a woman seems to be central to Paul's point to the Corinthians when he appeals to Genesis 2:24 to rebuke them for visiting prostitutes. He asks, "Don't you know that anyone joined to a prostitute is one body with her? For Scripture says, the two will become one flesh" (1 Cor. 6:16). The sexual union is central to the notion of becoming one flesh. There is no evidence that this would apply to other sexual encounters, like a married man kissing another woman, or a same-sex relationship. Those acts are prohibited, but not on the basis of forming a one-flesh union.[27]

Third, if (as Brownson acknowledges) Scripture assumes that the one-flesh bond *only* takes place between a man and a woman, there must be significant evidence to support the assertion that it could also apply to committed gay or lesbian unions. The emphasis on "one flesh" as kinship simply doesn't support the case. In Genesis 2 it is clear that it is establishing the significance of the union of a man and a woman, with its sexual union and lifelong bonding, where the one-flesh union of the man and woman generates the one flesh of a child. While the emphasis on kinship is important, it is specifically stated in the context of the sexual union of a man and woman, and not just any type of union. There is a sexual and familial unity in view. A man leaves his father and mother and is joined to his wife, and the two become one flesh. The kinship between father, mother, and child is replaced by a new kinship between husband and wife. The child of their one-flesh relationship completes the pattern. A same-sex relationship simply cannot encompass the essential characteristics packed into the understanding of one flesh as sexual union and kinship. It *assumes* and *requires* the union of a man and a woman.

Other Biblical Texts Dealing with Homosexuality

Genesis 19

The story of Sodom in Genesis has become so closely associated with the condemnation

---

26. Brownson, *Bible, Gender, Sexuality*, 109.
27. Sprinkle, *People to Be Loved*, doesn't think that "one-flesh" necessitates sexual difference. For instance, if Paul had confronted men visiting male prostitutes, Sprinkle asks, "wouldn't they have still violated Genesis 2:24 by having a sexual encounter with another person? I think they would have" (30). This is doubtful. Paul treats homosexual acts differently, and he doesn't appeal to the one-flesh union.

of homosexuality that the term *sodomy* commonly refers to male homosexual acts. This is often understood to be the root sin of Sodom, for which it is destroyed by God. Thus Robert Gagnon comments, "Traditionally, Gen 19:4–11 has been regarded as the classic Bible story about homosexuality."[28] By contrast, revisionist interpreters have argued that the sin of Sodom has nothing to do with homosexuality, at least not committed, monogamous same-sex relationships.[29] Revisionist interpreters are not alone in challenging the view that homosexuality is the reason for Sodom's destruction. Sprinkle, a nonaffirming New Testament scholar, says, "I don't think the story of Sodom contributes to the discussion about homosexuality."[30] Richard Hays asserts that the story of Sodom "is actually irrelevant to the topic."[31] Gagnon, who provides perhaps the most sustained challenge to the revisionist arguments, is measured. He argues that the story of Sodom "does not deal directly with consensual homosexual relationships," and thus is not an "ideal" guide for Christian ethics. Nevertheless, he challenges the view that "the story has little or nothing to do with homosexual practice."[32] What, then, is the reason for which Sodom (and Gomorrah) is destroyed?

As Genesis 19 opens, two angels have come to Sodom to investigate the outcry against the city (Gen. 18:20). Lot finds them in the town square and invites them to his house to spend the night. They first decline his offer, but after Lot's urging they accept his invitation. Lot provides dinner for his visitors, and all seems well, but the reader is soon alerted to the fact that something is terribly wrong. "Before they went to bed, the men of the city of Sodom, both young and old, the whole population, surrounded the house" (v. 4). They call out to Lot, "Where are the men who came to you tonight? Bring them out to us, that we may know them" (v. 5 ESV). The dramatic intensity should be felt here, like when the music changes in a movie scene to indicate that something bad is going to happen. Why does everyone come? Why do they surround the house?

On the surface, the fact that the men of Sodom want to know who is staying with Lot doesn't seem to have anything to do with homosexual acts. Why, then, do many English versions read something like "bring the men out so that we can have sex with them" (e.g., HCSB, NIV)? It turns on the meaning of the Hebrew term יָדַע, which means "to know," and is used sometimes to mean sexual intercourse. However, Derrick Sherwin Bailey argues that in Genesis 19 we should take יָדַע to mean something like "get acquainted with," since the word appears 943 times in the Old Testament, and it only

---

28. Robert A. J. Gagnon, *The Bible and Homosexual Practice: Texts and Hermeneutics* (Nashville: Abingdon, 2001), 71.

29. For example, Bailey, *Homosexuality and the Western Christian Tradition*, chap. 1; Boswell, *Christianity, Social Tolerance, and Homosexuality*, 92–99; and Vines, *God and the Gay Christian*, chap. 4, "The Real Sin of Sodom," 59–75.

30. Sprinkle, *People to Be Loved*, 42.

31. Richard B. Hays, *The Moral Vision of the New Testament: Community, Cross, New Creation; A Contemporary Introduction to New Testament Ethics* (San Francisco: HarperSanFrancisco, 1996), 381.

32. Gagnon, *The Bible and Homosexual Practice*, 71.

refers to sex without qualification 10 times (if we don't count Genesis 19 and its parallel in Judges 19:22), plus an additional five occurrences when used with שָׁכַב, "lying."[33] Therefore, he asserts, we ought to accept the most common usage, and conclude that the men of Sodom simply wanted to know who Lot's visitors were.

Bailey's point is not convincing. The meaning of a word is determined by its usage in a given context, not merely by statistics. Admittedly, the meaning of יָדַע in verse 5 is ambiguous. Indeed, one might even assume, reading the text to this point, that the men do simply want to know whom Lot is hosting. Translating יָדַע as "know," as the ESV does, retains the ambiguity. However, the meaning quickly becomes clear. Lot immediately steps out of the house, shuts the door behind him, and pleads, "Don't do this evil, my brothers" (v. 7). What would be evil about their desire to "get acquainted with" the visitors? Lot understands their intention, saying, "I have two daughters *who have not known any man.* Let me bring them out to you, and do to them as you please. Only do nothing to these men, for they have come under the shelter of my roof" (v. 8 ESV, emphasis added). The horrible nature of Lot's offer notwithstanding, the same word for "know" is used here, clearly with reference to sex (which the CSB, NIV, and others

make clear). The use of יָדַע for sex in verse 8 indicates that it means the same thing in verse 5.[34] This is supported by the fact that יָדַע is used twelve times in Genesis, and in ten of those instances (including twice in Genesis 19), it refers to sexual intercourse.[35]

As the text continues, the men threaten Lot himself, but the angels pulled Lot to safety. They tell Lot to leave and take his family with him, because they are going to destroy Sodom—their investigation had found that it was indeed a wicked place—which they proceed to do. So, if the men of Sodom demanded that Lot send the angels (whom they thought were men) out so that they could have sex with them, is Sodom destroyed because of homosexuality? Not exactly, but that doesn't mean that it doesn't contribute to the discussion of homosexuality, or that it is irrelevant. What shall we conclude?

First, the story of Sodom doesn't present consensual, committed same-sex relationships. The men of Sodom sought to rape Lot's visitors. If the visitors had been female, or if Lot's offer of his daughters had been taken, the act would still have been heinous. Sexual violence is evil, whether same-sex or opposite-sex. If this were the only text in Scripture on homosexual acts, it would be difficult to draw definite conclusions. We need to consider other texts carefully. We have seen that the creation accounts give us

---

33. Bailey, *Homosexuality and the Western Christian Tradition*, 2, who for usage of the term cites Francis Brown, S. R. Driver, and Charles A. Briggs, *A Hebrew and English Lexicon of the Old Testament* (Oxford: Clarendon, 1952).
34. So Sprinkle, *People to Be Loved*, 43; Gagnon, *The Bible and Homosexual Practice*, 73–74; Vines, *God and the Gay Christian*, 62–63, accepts that it refers to sex, though he sees that as a minor part of the story, having nothing to do with consensual, committed same-sex partnerships.
35. P. Michael Ukleja, "Homosexuality and the Old Testament," *Bibliotheca Sacra* 140 (1983): 261.

a paradigm, and we will examine texts that deal directly with homosexual acts below.

Second, Scripture itself elsewhere declares the sin of Sodom and, perhaps surprisingly, doesn't focus on homosexual acts. For instance, Ezekiel says, "This was the iniquity of your sister Sodom: she and her daughters had pride, plenty of food, and comfortable security, but didn't support the poor and needy" (Ezek. 16:49). According to Ezekiel, the sin of Sodom is something like gross corruption and greed.[36] Some revisionists, in addition to the focus on sexual violence, thus argue that Sodom's sin is inhospitality.[37] Lot sought to offer the visitors food, shelter, and safety under his roof, away from the town square, but the men of Sodom sought to violate them. They even turn on Lot, calling him a stranger (Gen. 19:9).

However, the homosexual acts threatened in Genesis 19 are likely not absent from Ezekiel's account. He continues, "They were haughty and did detestable acts before me, so I removed them when I saw this" (v. 50). The term translated "detestable" (elsewhere "abominations") is תּוֹעֵבָה, which is used elsewhere in Ezekiel to refer to "a wide array of vices, including sins of social injustice," so

it could refer specifically to Sodom's failure to help the poor and needy. On the other hand, תּוֹעֵבָה is used in Leviticus to refer to homosexual acts, so that is certainly a possible allusion in Ezekiel, especially if there is a progression of sins (pride, abundance, selfishness and greed, and abominable acts).[38] The particular sin of homosexual rape may not have needed mentioning, since the story was well known.

Jude also mentions Sodom (and Gomorrah), and attributes their destruction to sexual sin, saying that they "indulged in sexual immorality and pursued unnatural desire" (Jude 7 ESV; cf. 2 Pet. 2:6–10, which also focuses on sexual sin). "Unnatural desire" is translated in the NASB as "strange flesh." The phrase is σαρκὸς ἑτέρας, literally "different flesh." Is it possible that Jude is referring to the men demanding sex with angels, who are indeed different flesh? Vines says, "Far from arguing that the men of Sodom pursued flesh too similar to their own," as in same-sex relationships, "Jude indicts them for pursuing flesh that was too different."[39] Yet for their part, the men of Sodom thought the visitors were men, and their intention was homosexual rape.[40] Why

---

36. Other references to Sodom also list sins other than homosexuality (Isa. 1:7–17; Jer. 23:14). Yet too much is made of some texts that refer to Sodom without any reference to homosexuality (Vines, *God and the Gay Christian*, 62–75; also Sprinkle, *People to Be Loved*, 44). Some of these texts simply use Sodom as a paradigmatic example of evil. So, e.g., Jesus says that towns that reject his messengers will be worse off than Sodom (e.g., Matt. 10; Luke 10). He doesn't say what Sodom's sin was. That can hardly be evidence that homosexuality is not in the picture.

37. Bailey, *Homosexuality and the Western Christian Tradition*, 4; Boswell, *Christianity, Social Tolerance, and Homosexuality*, 93–96; Vines, *God and the Gay Christian*, 63, 66–68.

38. Gagnon, *The Bible and Homosexual Practice*, 81.

39. Vines, *God and the Gay Christian*, 69.

40. Thomas R. Schreiner, *1, 2 Peter, Jude*, New American Commentary (Nashville: B&H, 2003), 452–53. Gagnon sees the connection to angels as plausible, though for the men it was inadvertent. Gagnon, *The Bible and Homosexual Practice*, 88.

would Jude say "different flesh" rather than "same" or "similar" flesh? In God's purposes, men were created to pursue sexual relations with women, and women with men. To pursue same-sex relations is, ironically, to pursue different (or strange) flesh: "The term more naturally refers to a desire for those of the same sex; they desired flesh other than that of women."[41]

Therefore, it says too much to assert that "no biblical writers suggested that the sin of Sodom was primarily or even partly engaging in same-sex behavior."[42] If homosexual acts are not the primary reason for which Sodom is indicted, they are not far from view. Gross corruption and greed, and ultimately idolatry, may be their root sin. Yet the fact that the men of Sodom would demand to have sex with other men is a feature of the text that demonstrates how far Sodom has fallen. Gagnon comments that social injustice may be the broad problem in Sodom. Yet, he says, "what makes this instance of inhospitality so dastardly, what makes the name 'Sodom' a byword for inhumanity to visiting outsiders in later Jewish and Christian circles, is the specific form in which the inhospitality manifests itself: *homosexual* rape."[43]

If the issue in Genesis 19 is homosexual rape, we might ask, "Does Genesis 19 condemn loving, consensual, monogamous gay sex?"[44] Perhaps not, but that is a misleading question. If the text does not have such relations in view, then we can only say that it doesn't condemn them because it doesn't address them. Yet, if homosexual rape is highlighted because Scripture casts a negative judgment on all homosexual practice, then it surely has negative implications for consensual acts as well. Further, if all homosexual acts are condemned because they are against God's will, then it is dubious to ask whether they can be loving. Nevertheless, we'll have to look elsewhere in Scripture to draw conclusions about homosexual acts in general.

Leviticus 18:22 and 20:13

These two texts from Leviticus pronounce a clear judgment on sex between two males. They read as follows:

> You shall not lie with a male as with a woman; it is an abomination. (Lev. 18:22 ESV)

> If a man lies with a male as with a woman, both of them have committed an abomination; they shall surely be put to death; their blood is upon them. (Lev. 20:13 ESV)

These two verses seem to condemn all homosexual acts, at least between men. But revisionist interpreters suggest that these texts are not applicable for us, and they do not speak to consensual, committed homosexual relations. For instance, Vines casts doubts on the relevance of these commands, since Christians believe that many laws in

---

41. Schreiner, *1, 2 Peter, Jude*, 453.
42. Vines, *God and the Gay Christian*, 69.
43. Gagnon, *The Bible and Homosexual Practice*, 76.
44. Sprinkle, *People to Be Loved*, 43.

Leviticus do not apply directly, such as restrictions on food and clothing.[45] In addition, he ultimately ascribes the negative judgment on male homosexual acts to be grounded in a patriarchal perspective that we do not share.[46] In this view, the penetrated man is treated like a woman, which is degrading.[47] Accordingly, to embrace the commands in Leviticus is to embrace the misogyny on which they are based. Further, some scholars have argued that these texts likely refer to exploitative homosexual acts or temple prostitution.[48]

In response, several points are relevant. First, it is dubious to attribute the prohibition of homosexual acts to a patriarchal, misogynistic perspective. This is at odds with the fundamental equality that is displayed in the Genesis creation accounts. Interpreters, ancient and modern, with a high view of Scripture would surely not accept such an internal contradiction between

Leviticus and the paradigmatic a‹ Genesis. The text gives no indica "women are inferior to men" or that the prohibition of homosexual sex is grounded in such a view.[49] There are assumed gender distinctions, but the reason men are to act like men (and women to act like women) is "not because they are superior, but because they were created differently."[50]

Second, there is no indication that the prohibition has to do with temple prostitution. The command in Leviticus is straightforward, simply prohibiting men from having sex with men, with no indication that it involves prostitution.[51]

Third, those who seek to relativize the prohibition of homosexual acts in Leviticus often compare it to food and clothing laws. Such arguments are simplistic and misleading, and fail to note the much more relevant comparison with other laws on sexual morality, including the prohibition of

---

45. Vines, *God and the Gay Christian*, 78–86.
46. Vines, *God and the Gay Christian*, 86–93.
47. This argument is made by Martti Nissinen, *Homoeroticism in the Biblical World: A Historical Perspective* (Minneapolis: Fortress, 1998), 42–44, and developed by Vines, *God and the Gay Christian*, 79–96.
48. Justin Lee, *Torn: Rescuing the Gospel from the Gays-vs.-Christians Debate* (Minneapolis: Fortress, 2012), 174–78. David F. Greenberg, *The Construction of Homosexuality* (Chicago: University of Chicago Press, 1988), 94, claims that "male homosexual prostitution having religious significance was an institutionalized feature of the archaic civilizations of the Mediterranean," and that "most authorities think it was practiced in the Temple of Solomon in Jerusalem," though he acknowledges that "a few scholars have expressed skepticism." Nissinen, *Homoeroticism in the Biblical World*, 39–41, considers it possible. Gagnon, *The Bible and Homosexual Practice*, 100–110, cites these latter two scholars and proceeds on the assumption that there is homosexual cult prostitution in Israel.
49. Sprinkle, *People to Be Loved*, 47.
50. Sprinkle, *People to Be Loved*, 48.
51. Sprinkle goes as far as to assert that although many "assume that the ancient world was filled with cultic prostitution," recent scholarship has concluded that "cultic prostitution probably didn't exist in the world at this time, let alone in Israel." Sprinkle, *People to Be Loved*, 46, citing Stephanie Budin, *The Myth of Sacred Prostitution in Antiquity* (Cambridge: Cambridge University Press, 2010). In his study, Sprinkle notes that the view that prostitution is involved rests on the assumption that קָדֵשׁ (e.g., 1 Kings 14:24), "holy ones," should be translated something like "male cult prostitutes." Based on recent scholarship, Sprinkle argues that while קְדֵשִׁים "probably refers to some sort of service at pagan shrines, there's no evidence that such service was sexual."

adultery, incest, and bestiality. As Hays notes, the early church consistently adopts "the Old Testament's teaching on matters of sexual morality, including homosexual acts."[52] Interpreting and applying Leviticus and its laws in the Christian life requires some hermeneutical nuance. Many revisionists, defending the goodness of homosexuality, simply do not offer adequate reflection on why the Bible uniformly characterizes homosexual acts as sinful, beyond (as above) citing misogynistic motives or idolatrous practices.

Some may even be tempted to dismiss a law as morally irrelevant to us simply because it is part of Leviticus in general, or the purity law in particular. However, as Sprinkle puts it, "We shouldn't dismiss Leviticus 18 and 20 just because they are in, well, Leviticus."[53] Of course, it would also be a mistake to hold that we must obey every law in Leviticus simply because they are in the Bible, for there are some laws, such as sacrificial laws or food laws, that we are not bound to keep. What is needed is a biblical rationale that helps us to know which laws we should follow today and which laws we should not. Sprinkle offers some reasonable and helpful guidelines here.[54]

- The commands about homosexuality are found in a section of Leviticus, chapters 18–20, that constitutes a literary unit, and in this section, most of the laws given are still relevant for Christians. They include prohibitions against incest (18:6–18; 20:11–14, 17, 19–21), adultery (18:20; 20:10), child sacrifice (18:21; 20:1–5), bestiality (18:23; 20:15–16), theft (19:11), lying (19:11), taking God's name in vain (19:20), oppressing your neighbor (19:13), cursing the deaf (19:14), showing partiality in the court of law (19:15), slander (19:16), hating your brother (19:17), making your daughter a prostitute (19:29), and turning to witches or necromancers (19:31). Also in this section is the second great commandment, to love your neighbor as yourself (19:18)! Surely Christians are to obey these Levitical laws, even if it is not because we are bound by the Mosaic law.

- All or most of the laws that deal specifically with sex are still binding today (e.g., laws against incest, adultery, bestiality).[55] Thus it is most natural to conclude that the prohibition of homosexual sex is still binding as well, for there is no rationale in the text that indicates otherwise. If one of the laws in Leviticus is not in force for people today, there should be a clear indication within Scripture as to why not. This brings us to the next point.

---

52. Hays, *Moral Vision*, 382.
53. Sprinkle, *People to Be Loved*, 49.
54. The following integrates much of Sprinkle's treatment in *People to Be Loved*, 50–52.
55. Old Testament scholar Barry Webb contests those who suggest that the censure of homosexuality is obsolete because it is part of the purity code, arguing that the prohibition of homosexual acts occurs in a block of laws focused on sexual morality, not in a block focused on ceremonial purity. Barry Webb, "Homosexuality in Scripture," in *Theological and Pastoral Responses to Homosexuality*, ed. Barry Webb (Adelaide, Australia: Openbook, 1994), 80, cited in Hill, *How and Why of Love*, 187.

- The clearest way to judge whether a Levitical law is in force today is whether it is repeated or repealed in the New Testament. Some laws are repealed in the New Testament, like dietary restrictions (Mark 7:19; Acts 10:10–15) and sacrifices (e.g., Heb. 10:11–14). Many laws are repeated in the New Testament, like prohibitions of murder, adultery, stealing, bearing false witness, and the commands to honor father and mother and love your neighbor (e.g., Matt. 19:18–19). Others require a more nuanced response, like the ban on tattoos or keeping the Sabbath, because they may not clearly be repealed or repeated. The question concerns where homosexual acts fit in this classification. As we will see, the prohibition of homosexual acts is repeated in the New Testament.

To summarize, in Leviticus 18:22 and 20:13 sex between two males is prohibited without qualification. There is no suggestion that rape or temple prostitution is in view, no one forcing another to have sex, "and if two men do sleep with each other, they are both condemned." That is, "the commands appear to include same-sex acts that are mutual and consensual; both partners are deemed guilty." Indeed, "the commands in these two verses don't come with any qualifications, comments, or specifications that could limit the commands to a particular type of same-sex behavior."[56]

1 Corinthians 6:9–11 (cf. 1 Timothy 1:8–11)

We will consider 1 Corinthians 6:9–11 next, because there is a connection with the passages in Leviticus. The text reads,

> Or do you not know that the unrighteous will not inherit the kingdom of God? Do not be deceived; neither fornicators, nor idolaters, nor adulterers, nor effeminate, nor homosexuals, nor thieves, nor the covetous, nor drunkards, nor revilers, nor swindlers, will inherit the kingdom of God. Such were some of you; but you were washed, but you were sanctified, but you were justified in the name of the Lord Jesus Christ and in the Spirit of our God.[57]

This is a critically important text for our discussion of homosexuality, for several reasons. First, it addresses Christians in Corinth, and is part of the New Testament witness. Second, it affirms the condemnation of homosexual acts and validates the Levitical prohibition as a moral norm. Third, it does not isolate homosexuality or treat it in a category apart from other temptations or sins. And fourth, while it condemns all of the sins described, it also holds out the hope of the gospel for the repentant sinner.

The meaning of μαλακοί *and* ἀρσενοκοίτης. The difficulty of interpreting this text in relation to homosexuality is understandable in some sense, but

---

56. Sprinkle, *People to Be Loved*, 45.
57. I use the NASB here because it translates the two relevant terms, μαλακοί (effeminate) and ἀρσενοκοίτης (homosexuals) distinctly. The meaning of the two terms is discussed below.

it is somewhat superficial. The challenge is understanding what is meant by the two terms that are associated with homosexual acts. Revisionist interpreters claim that it is impossible to know just what Paul means by these terms.[58] The difficulty can be seen in the way the two relevant Greek terms, μαλακοί and ἀρσενοκοίτης, are translated in various versions.

- NASB (above): "effeminate" (μαλακοί) and "homosexuals" (ἀρσενοκοίτης)
- ESV: "men who practice homosexuality" (taking the two together)
- CSB: "males who have sex with males"
- NIV: "men who have sex with men"

One of the reasons for the difficulty, and the various translations, is that the two terms are not common, and on the surface there seems to be some ambiguity. For instance, μαλακοί has a range of possible meanings, including "effeminate" or "soft." On its own, it would be difficult to tell just what Paul means by this. Vines studies various uses, and concludes that "if a man did anything that was typically associated with women, he opened himself to the charge of being a *malakos*."[59] One characteristic often attributed to women by ancient writers was a lack of self-control, so men who lacked

self-control might be in view, according to Vines.[60] It is true that μαλακοί referred in general terms to men who acted like women, which could mean many things, and has led some commentators to argue either that its meaning is not clear, or it is misogynistic (condemning anything feminine), or at least that it does not refer to homosexuality.[61] Dale Martin, considering the translation "effeminate," asks what we are to teach our congregations about its meaning. He notes, "In the ancient world a man could be condemned as effeminate for, among many other things, eating or drinking too much, enjoying gourmet cooking, wearing nice underwear or shoes, wearing much of anything on his head, having long hair, shaving, caring for his skin, wearing cologne or aftershave, dancing too much, laughing too much, or gesticulating too much."[62]

However, even if there is a range of possible meanings, Paul's use appears to be accessible, and it appears that some revisionists are creating unwarranted confusion. Surely Paul is not considering men to be excluded from the kingdom of God for "enjoying gourmet cooking," or "caring for his skin," or "laughing too much," to note several of the meanings cited by Martin. To include such possible meanings in the discussion of μαλακοί in the context in which it appears

---

58. Daniel Helminiak, *What the Bible Really Says about Homosexuality* (Tajique, NM: Alamo Square Press, 2000), 107.
59. Vines, *God and the Gay Christian*, 120.
60. Vines, *God and the Gay Christian*, 122.
61. Vines, *God and the Gay Christian*, 119–22; Dale B. Martin, "Arsenokoitēs and Malakos: Meanings and Consequences," in *Biblical Ethics and Homosexuality: Listening to Scripture*, ed. Robert L. Brawley (Louisville: Westminster John Knox, 1996), 124–28; also Martin, *Sex and the Single Savior: Gender and Sexuality in Biblical Interpretation* (Louisville: Westminster John Knox, 2006), 43–47.
62. Martin, "Arsenokoitēs and Malakos," 128.

is to obfuscate. Hays notes that μαλακοί "appears often in Hellenistic Greek as pejorative slang to describe the 'passive' partners—often young boys—in homosexual activity."[63] Philo, a first-century Jew, used the term in this sense.[64] This would likely be closer to Paul, a first-century Jew, than many other instances. This is particularly the case when considering the context in which it appears. While the term has many possible uses, often it is associated with a man who played the passive role in sex with another man. As Sprinkle puts it, "Not every person accused of being a *malakos* necessarily engaged in sex with other men, but every man who played the passive role in homosexual sex could be called *malakos*."[65] It is reasonable, therefore, that many translations associate μαλακοί with homosexual relations. However, it isn't absolutely certain, and some translations prefer to leave it somewhat ambiguous, as the NASB does with the use of "effeminate." Those that make it explicit do so because of its association with the next term, ἀρσενοκοίτης.

As with μαλακοί, some interpreters argue that we cannot know what Paul means by ἀρσενοκοίτης.[66] It is a compound word, from ἄρσεν (male) and κοίτη ("bed" or "lying"). While not entirely clear, at face

value it is suggestive of male homosexual sex. There is no precise term in Greek (or Hebrew) for "homosexuals," and this is the first extant use of ἀρσενοκοίτης in Greek,[67] so perhaps Paul coined the term for homosexual sex. Of course, we must be cautious about compound words, for they are often not the sum of their parts. Revisionist interpreters thus challenge those who say that Paul simply coined a term for homosexuals. Martin, for instance, says, "It is highly precarious to try to ascertain the meaning of a word by taking it apart, getting the meaning of its component parts, and then assuming, with no supporting evidence, that the meaning of the longer word is a simple combination of its component parts."[68]

However, it is dubious for Martin to claim that there is *no supporting evidence* that ἀρσενοκοίτης refers to male homosexual acts. Actually, the evidence is very strong. Indeed, Robin Scroggs argues that it is a literal translation of the Hebrew phrase *mishkav zakur*, "lying with a male," which is "most often used to describe male homosexuality."[69] This is derived directly from the prohibitions in Leviticus 18:22 and 20:13, which can be seen clearly in the Septuagint (LXX), the Greek translation of the Old Testament that was widely used in Paul's day. There Leviticus

---

63. Hays, *Moral Vision*, 382.
64. For examples and a discussion of Philo's usage, see Gagnon, *The Bible and Homosexual Practice*, 308–9.
65. Sprinkle, *People to Be Loved*, 107.
66. For instance, Martin concludes, "I am not claiming to know what *arsenokoitês* meant, I am claiming that *no one* knows what it meant." Martin, "Arsenokoitês and Malakos," 123. Cf. Martin, *Sex and the Single Savior*, 43.
67. Noted by Hays in *Moral Vision*, 382. Cf. Robin Scroggs, *The New Testament and Homosexuality* (Philadelphia: Fortress, 1983), 107.
68. Martin, "Arsenokoitês and Malakos," 119.
69. Scroggs, *New Testament and Homosexuality*, 108.

20:13 reads, "whoever lies with a man as with a woman [μετὰ ἄρσενος κοίτην γυναικός], they have both done an abomination."[70] There is thus *very strong evidence* that ἀρσενοκοίτης is derived from ἄρσενος κοίτην in this text, and that it refers to males having sex with males.

In light of this, we may affirm that Paul's use of ἀρσενοκοίτης in 1 Corinthians 6:9 unambiguously "presupposes and reaffirms the holiness code's condemnation of homosexual acts."[71] Interestingly, this indicates that Paul deems the prohibition in Leviticus to be relevant for Christian reflection. Further, this meaning of ἀρσενοκοίτης suggests strongly that μαλακοί refers to sexual immorality (specifically the passive partner in homosexual acts), sandwiched as it is between adulterers and men who have sex with other men.[72] As with Leviticus, so here, the condemnation of homosexuality is not limited to exploitation, prostitution, or promiscuity. Rather, homosexual acts as such are in view, and Paul issues a warning to both partners involved in such acts.

Though these two terms are somewhat strange at face value, the meaning of each and the two together point convincingly to homosexual acts. It may be noted that it appears, at least in some cases, that the debate isn't really about the meaning of the words. For instance, in his conclusion to the discussion of these terms, Martin asserts that "all appeals to 'what the Bible says' are ideological and problematic," and that "in the end, all appeals, whether to the Bible or anything else, must submit to the test of love."[73] We might simply respond that the "test of love," apart from "what the Bible says," is highly subjective and speculative.

Getting perspective on homosexuality in the context of 1 Corinthians 6:9–11. Although the focus of the above discussion—in the context of a discussion of homosexuality—has been to show that Paul indeed affirms the Old Testament prohibition of homosexual sex, we should not leave this text before observing some central points. First, it should be noted that homosexuality is not the focus of the larger text. To be sure, those who engage in homosexual acts are considered sinful, but they are not singled out. Rather, they are included in a much larger list of "the unrighteous," with idolaters, thieves, greedy people, drunkards, verbally abusive people, and swindlers. Thus we do not do justice to the text if we single out homosexuality and fail to warn others who are in view. Homosexual acts ought to be discussed in the context of the more general indictment of sinners.

Second, it is best to understand those who are unrighteous and excluded from God's kingdom in terms of habitual, unrepented practice and identity. The one who has committed these sins in the past who repents and is forgiven is not in view here. Neither is the one who continues to experience

---

70. Hays, *Moral Vision*, 382.
71. So Hays, *Moral Vision*, 382.
72. Gagnon, *The Bible and Homosexual Practice*, 308.
73. Martin, "Arsenokoitês and Malakos," 131.

temptation in various ways, or who lapses into sin and repents of it. Instead, the warning Paul issue is for those who reject the call to repent and to walk in newness of life, and instead embrace what God declares to be sinful patterns of behavior, essentially identifying with those acts and desires instead of finding their identity in Christ.

Third, the condemnation of unrighteousness is followed by a reminder of the gospel and one's identity in Christ. Some of the Corinthian Christians once practiced these things—"such were some of you"—and were under God's judgment. But they had come to know the grace of God through Jesus Christ, by the power of the Holy Spirit. They were forgiven and justified. It is as Paul says to the Colossians, "He has rescued us from the domain of darkness and transferred us into the kingdom of the Son he loves" (Col. 1:13). A radical change has taken place—"but you were washed, you were sanctified, you were justified" (1 Cor. 6:11). No one is beyond God's reach to save or to produce a radical transformation of both acts and desires.

Romans 1:18–32

Before considering what this text has to say about homosexual relations, it is important to note that Paul's primary concern here is not with homosexuality. That is, even this text, which is one of the most important biblical texts in the debate about homosexuality,[74] is about something much bigger. Homosexual relations are illustrative of the larger concern that Paul addresses. That larger concern is to explicate the gospel (Rom. 1:15–16), wherein the righteousness of God is revealed in his wrath against unrighteousness (v. 18), and in the salvation of sinners by faith (v. 17). First, Paul demonstrates the unrighteousness of the Gentiles (1:18–32), then he exposes the unrighteousness of the Jews (2:1–3:8) and all people (3:9–20).[75] Paul's Jewish readers may have eagerly agreed with Paul's assessment of God's judgment of the Gentiles in Romans 1, but then he asserts that the Jews too will be judged (Rom. 2). So before examining what Paul says about homosexuality in this text, it is critical to emphasize his larger argument, which is designed "to entice his readers first to feel revulsion and indignation against 'those sinful pagans' and then to recognize themselves as standing before God under the same judgment."[76] We ought to take heed, for we miss the point if we read Romans 1 and condemn homosexual relations, and fail to recognize God's condemnation of human sin more broadly, including our own sin.

Within the context of Romans 1:18–32, the reference to homosexual relations is found in verses 25–27:

---

74. Hays, *Moral Vision*, 383; Sprinkle, *People to Be Loved*, 87.
75. See Thomas R. Schreiner, *Romans,* Baker Exegetical Commentary on the New Testament, Second Edition (Grand Rapids: Baker Academic, 2018 [1998]), 87–183.
76. Richard B. Hays, "Relations Natural and Unnatural: A Response to John Boswell's Exegesis of Romans 1," *Journal of Religious Ethics* 14, no. 1 (Spring 1986): 184–15, 195.

They exchanged the truth of God for a lie, and worshiped and served what has been created instead of the Creator, who is praised forever. Amen.

For this reason God delivered them over to disgraceful passions. Their women exchanged natural sexual relations for unnatural ones. The men in the same way also left natural relations with women and were inflamed in their lust for one another. Men committed shameless acts with men and received in their own persons the appropriate penalty of their error.

Is the problem simply excessive lust? Some authors who affirm consensual same-sex relationships argue that in Romans 1 Paul condemns homosexual relationships that are driven by excessive lust, not those that reflect commitment to the other person.[77] Paul says that God "delivered them over to *disgraceful passions*" (v. 26), and that men "were *inflamed in their lust* for one another" (v. 27). Moreover, some Greco-Roman writers condemned male homosexual relations because they believed they were the result of an overflow of lust.[78]

Is that Paul's focus? It is highly unlikely. Sprinkle offers four reasons why.[79] First, for ancient writers, excessive lust is but one reason that they reject same-sex relationships. Second, Paul rejects female same-sex relationships alongside of male, and female homosexuality was not associated with excessive lust.[80] It is worth adding here that when Paul pairs female homosexual acts with male homosexual acts and condemns both equally, this is a major clue that he is not thinking merely of pederastic sex, or rape, or any other exploitative sex when he speaks of male homosexual acts. He doesn't focus on the active or dominating partner. Rather, "the language is all-inclusive and suggests mutuality." Third, the "excessive lust" view does not adequately account for Paul's critique of homosexual relations as "against nature" (see below). Fourth, Paul's use of the language of desire is focused on what it leads to—namely, the degrading of their bodies (v. 24) and unnatural sexual intercourse (vs. 26–27).

Further, in biblical terms, sinful lust does not merely refer to a desire that is excessive, for it includes pursuing a wrongful desire. When Jesus condemns lust in Matthew 5:28 and calls it adultery, the problem is not excessive desire, but simply sexual desire for another man's wife.

What does "against nature" (παρὰ φύσιν) mean? In Romans 1:26, Paul says that women exchanged "natural sexual relations for unnatural ones" (or "against nature," τὴν φυσικὴν χρῆσιν εἰς τὴν παρὰ φύσιν). The parallel in verse 27, where males left the "natural use" or "natural relations" with females for other males, "makes it

---

77. For example, Matthew Vines says that Paul "was condemning *excess* as opposed to *moderation*." *God and the Gay Christian*, 105.
78. See Sprinkle, *People to Be Loved*, 98; also Vines, *God and the Gay Christian*, 103–107.
79. Sprinkle, *People to Be Loved*, 98–102.
80. Sprinkle, *People to Be Loved*, 91.

unmistakably clear that the phrase refers to heterosexual intercourse as opposed to homosexual intercourse, which is categorized as 'contrary to nature.'"[81] John Boswell has made an influential argument that "against nature" refers to homosexual acts committed by heterosexual persons.[82] More recently, revisionist interpreters argue that it is a phrase used to reject any nonprocreative sex, whether heterosexual or homosexual, or it refers to acts that are against cultural expectations, such as treating a man like a woman.[83] In other words, in this latter sense, παρὰ φύσιν reflects a misogynistic culture. But these suggestions are highly unlikely, and there is no indication in Romans 1 that points to either of these.[84] Elsewhere Paul speaks of marriage, and even sex within marriage (e.g., 1 Cor. 7) without a mention of procreation, and he does not hint at misogyny.[85]

Ancient writers spoke out against a variety of sexual behaviors that they believed to be immoral, including nonprocreative sex, masturbation, seeking only pleasure, and homosexual sex. But the technical term παρὰ φύσιν, "against nature," is "reserved for same-sex erotic behavior."[86] Not all ancient writers condemned homosexual sex by any means, but those who did, when they used the phrase παρὰ φύσιν, were claiming that it goes against the design of nature. It is sometimes applied to things that are against custom, but when Paul uses the phrase in Romans 1, given that fact that the text is steeped in references to creation, he indicates that sexual relations between members of the same sex are against the design and purposes of the Creator. Thus Hays rightly concludes,

> The understanding of "nature" in this conventional language does not rest on empirical observation of what actually exists; instead, it appeals to a conception of what ought to be, of the world as designed by God and revealed through the stories and laws of Scripture. Those who indulge in sexual practices *para physin* are defying the Creator and demonstrating their own alienation from him.[87]

Nature, creation, and Creator in Romans 1. Paul's argument in Romans 1 is set in the context of several allusions to Creation in Genesis 1, meaning that Paul intends his depiction of sin to be in the context of God's good purposes in creation, against which

---

81. Hays, "Relations Natural and Unnatural," 192.
82. Boswell, *Christianity, Social Tolerance, and Homosexuality*, 109.
83. Brownson, *Bible, Gender, Sexuality*, 267, 245.
84. Sprinkle, *People to Be Loved*, 95–96.
85. As Sprinkle points out (*People to Be Loved*, 210n14), Vines does not charge Paul with misogyny, yet he believes that παρὰ φύσιν was loaded with misogynistic meaning, which is how Paul uses it, even though he doesn't share his culture's negative view of women (*God and the Gay Christian*, 110). This is a stretch.
86. This is the conclusion reached by Sprinkle, *People to Be Loved*, 97, in his study of ancient writers; Hays, "Relations Natural and Unnatural," 192–94, agrees.
87. Hays, *Moral Vision*, 387.

human beings have rebelled. In verse 20, Paul says, "Since the creation of the world" God has revealed his power and nature through creation. In verse 25, he asserts that people have worshiped and served the creation instead of the Creator.

The terms that Paul uses also draws attention to the creation account in Genesis.[88] For instance, in Romans 1:26–27, Paul uses the terms ἄρσενες (males) and θήλειαι (females), which are the same terms found in Genesis 1:27 in the Greek translation of the Old Testament (the Septuagint), which was used by many Jews in Paul's day. Genesis 1:27 says, "So God created man in his own image; he created him in the image of God; he created them male [ἄρσεν] and female [θῆλυ]." So, when reading Romans 1:26–27, attention is drawn to God's original design and purpose in creation, which has been upended.

One other allusion that can easily be overlooked relates to the terms used in Romans 1:23. It reads that human beings "exchanged the glory of the immortal God for images [εἰκόνος] resembling [ὁμοιώματι] mortal man [ἀνθρώπου], birds [πετεινῶν], four-footed animals, and reptiles [ἑρπετῶν]." The five Greek terms that are used here are also used in the Greek translation of Genesis 1:26:[89] "Then God said, 'Let us make man [ἄνθρωπον] in our image [εἰκόνα], according to our likeness [ὁμοίωσιν]. They will rule the fish of the sea, the birds [πετεινῶν] of the sky, the livestock,

all the earth, and the creatures [or reptiles, ἑρπετῶν] that crawl on the earth." Greek readers would not miss this reference to the original creation. The point is clear, that human beings were made distinct and complementary as male and female, to rule over the earth as God's representative, but they have rebelled against God and his purposes. This is seen in the language of exchange: human beings have exchanged the glory of God for creatures (v. 23), the truth of God for a lie (v. 25), and females exchanged "natural sexual intercourse for what is natural" (sex with males for sex with females, v. 26), and "in the same way," men have exchanged sex with females for sex with males (v. 27).[90]

The conclusion is difficult to miss, that sexual relations between members of the same sex is a departure from (and rejection of) God's purposes in creation. Paul doesn't merely reject a form of homosexual relations found in his culture. Rather, he indicates that "what is wrong with same-sex relations transcends culture. Violating God-given gender boundaries is universal and absolute. They go against the way God created males and females and intended them to relate to each other sexually."[91]

Conclusions on Paul's view of homosexuality in Romans 1. It is clear that Paul considers homosexual relations to be sinful, stemming from rebellion against God and his design and purposes in creation. Yet we are reminded that all sin bears the same

88. See Sprinkle, *People to Be Loved*, 92.
89. Sprinkle, *People to Be Loved*, 92.
90. Hays, "Relations Natural and Unnatural," 192; Sprinkle, *People to Be Loved*, 93.
91. Sprinkle, *People to Be Loved*, 93; cf. Hays, "Relations Natural and Unnatural," 200–202.

pattern (Rom. 1:28–32), that all are guilty and deserve God's wrath, as Paul makes clear to the Jews beginning in Romans 2. No one can boast, for justification is by grace through faith in Jesus (Rom. 3:24–25). Instead of drumming up special condemnation for homosexuals, Paul in Romans describes the situation that all people are in apart from repentance and faith in Jesus. In a world that is in rebellion against God, there are many casualties. Sin has distorted human understanding (vv. 21–22) and desire (vv. 24–28) yet we are responsible and accountable to a righteous God.

What does Jesus say about homosexuality?

Jesus does not address homosexuality directly. But that doesn't mean he has nothing to say about it. Indeed, to defend homosexual relations on the basis that Jesus did not condemn or even speak about homosexuality is unconvincing, for Jesus says nothing about rape or incest or polyamory. An appeal from silence is weak at best. Even though Jesus says nothing directly about homosexuality, there are good reasons to assert that he would not affirm same-sex relations. There are also good reasons to assert that he would love homosexuals and invite them to follow him.

First, Jesus would not affirm homosexual acts because, if anything, when it comes to sexual behavior, Jesus takes "a very strict stance compared to other rabbis of the day."[92] It seems likely, given his teaching on divorce and adultery, for instance, that he would have upheld the law and taken a strict stance on homosexual acts, not a lenient one. Other rabbis of Jesus's day condemned homosexual acts. In fact, every Jewish writer who mentions homosexual acts of any kind, from at least five hundred years before Jesus to at least five hundred years after Jesus, condemns such acts. If Jesus affirmed homosexual acts of any kind, he would be "the only Jewish person in more than a thousand years to do so. It's not impossible, just highly unlikely."[93]

Second, Jesus would not affirm homosexual acts because he affirms the Old Testament, his only Scriptures. Where he "adjusts" any teaching, as perhaps he does when he limits legitimate divorce to sexual immorality, it is clear in the text. Thus we might expect some hint that he overturned or did not endorse what the Old Testament—Jesus's Scripture—says about homosexual acts. Yet, "when it comes to same-sex relations, there is nothing explicit nor implicit suggesting that Jesus corrected, improved upon, or did away with the sexual commands in Leviticus 18:22 and 20:13. Nothing. There is no evidence."[94]

Further, Jesus affirms the creation pattern for marriage. When Jesus is approached by Pharisees who seek to test him on the question of divorce—and to justify their view of divorce—Jesus cites the creation

---

92. Sprinkle, *People to Be Loved*, 71.
93. Sprinkle, *People to Be Loved*, 71.
94. Sprinkle, *People to Be Loved*, 71.

accounts in Genesis 1–2. He begins by citing Genesis 1:27, "from the beginning of creation God made them male and female" (Mark 10:6). Immediately he follows this by citing Genesis 2:24, saying, "for this reason a man will leave his father and mother and the two will become one flesh. So they are no longer two, but one flesh. Therefore what God has joined together, let no one separate" (Mark 10:7–9). I examined the question of divorce in the previous chapter. What is instructive here is what Jesus teaches about marriage and sexual relations, which are restricted to marriage. To teach that married couples should not divorce, because marriage is a one-flesh relationship joined by God, Jesus would only need to cite Genesis 2:24. But he first cites Genesis 1:27, that "from the beginning of creation *God made them male and female.*" Here Jesus highlights not only the one-flesh relationship of marriage but the sexual differentiation of male and female as well. If sexual difference, in terms of marriage and sexual relations, was unimportant to Jesus, there was no need for him to cite Genesis 1:27. "Such difference is, in itself, irrelevant to the question of divorce."[95] One thing must be added before leaving this point. It would be hypocritical for Christians who have divorced their spouse for a reason other than adultery, or who have condoned such divorces, to use this text to condemn homosexual relationships. As

Sprinkle states, "How pretentious would that be—using a passage that's directed at you to sling at someone else?"[96]

Third, while Jesus would not affirm homosexual relations, he would reach out in love to homosexuals and invite them to follow him, with all that entails for anyone who will follow him, including repentance and obedience. But, as Sprinkle asserts, "Jesus pulls repentance and obedience out of our souls," not by condemning and rejecting sinners but by love and its demands.[97] All too often people who condemn homosexual acts show no love for people experiencing same-sex attraction. Jesus loved sinners such as Matthew and Zacchaeus, tax collectors. Again, Sprinkle observes, "Jesus' love comes without a background check." Jesus desires and demands obedience, but "to get that obedience he fronts love."[98] People were drawn to Jesus not because Jesus affirmed their behavior, but because he loved them and affirmed their humanity.[99]

Conclusions on the Bible and homosexuality

The aim of the preceding survey has been to understand what Scripture teaches about homosexual practice. The conclusion is that, where Scripture speaks about homosexual acts, it clearly and consistently condemns them. Further, where Scripture speaks of sexuality and marriage, it clearly and

95. Sprinkle, *People to Be Loved*, 35.
96. Sprinkle, *People to Be Loved*, 35.
97. Sprinkle, *People to Be Loved*, 74.
98. Sprinkle, *People to Be Loved*, 76.
99. Sprinkle, *People to Be Loved*, 79, 84.

consistently affirms God's design and purpose in creating male and female for the one-flesh relationship of marriage. Revisionists argue that God has created and delights in a variety of sexual identities and expressions. This is in spite of the fact that there is no evidence for it found in the creation accounts or the rest of Scripture, forcing the conclusion that God keeps hidden that which he delights in. Perhaps we are to believe that the biblical authors had no idea of this form of sexuality that God delights in, or perhaps there are simply cultural factors that obscure Scripture. But it is hard to understand why there is no celebration in Scripture itself, but only condemnation, if God delights in homosexuality. This tension is why it is difficult to take seriously the claim of some who affirm homosexual practice and say they hold to a high view of Scripture.

If Scripture is clear in rejecting homosexual practice, however, it is not a central emphasis. Rather, it is one example of human sin that stems from idolatry and rebellion against God, alongside fornication, adultery, lust, greed, and a catalog of other sins. Same-sex desire, like lust and greed, is a mark of living in a fallen world, where our very thoughts and desires are confused. Christians ought to know this better than anyone, and thus ought to offer to all a message of grace, forgiveness, love, and a call to repent and trust in Jesus and find deep fellowship and love in the church. Without this message of forgiveness of sins through faith in Jesus and his work of reconciliation on the cross, there is no gospel. And yet sometimes LGBT people hear only condemnation, causing them to avoid the church and seek community with those who proclaim a message of acceptance. Sprinkle relays the common testimony of those with same-sex attraction in relation to the church:

> I grew up in the church. I tried to follow Jesus. When I hit puberty, I experienced unwanted same-sex attraction that caused me unbearable pain and confusion. When I tried to talk about it, I was shunned, confronted, and made to feel like a monster. I become depressed, which led to isolation, which led to more depression, which led to fleeing the church in search of love.[100]

This should not be the case. If the church is formed by the truth of Scripture and the reality of redemption and reconciliation in Christ, and Christians are known by their love, there should be a different testimony. The church should be a place where the gospel is preached, where sinners, broken by the fall and the curse of sin, are told of the love of God who sent his son to die on the cross to redeem sinners and restore a relationship with the redeemed. It is where people are called to repent and believe in the one who broke the curse, and find refuge in him and among his people; where their

---

100. Sprinkle, *People to Be Loved*, 81. Cf. the description of the "gay script," by which so many with same-sex desire make sense of their experience in Mark A. Yarhouse, *Homosexuality and the Christian: A Guide for Parents, Pastors, and Friends* (Bloomington, MN: Bethany House, 2010), 48–50.

burden is lightened; where they can share their struggles and be met with grace and encouragement and love; where they find people who will listen and pray, and who will help others to find their identity in Christ and to follow him faithfully.[101] The biblical message concerning those who are attracted to members of the same sex is the same as its message for everyone else.

Common Questions in the Debate about Homosexuality

Homosexuality is one of the most contested issues of the late twentieth and early twenty-first centuries. The most important issue for Christians to sort out is what the Bible has to say about homosexuality. That has been the focus of the above survey of Scripture. Other significant questions are hotly contested, and thus important to discuss, even if they are not of first importance. I will address them briefly now.

What Causes Homosexuality?

This has been one of the central questions in the debate about homosexuality. It is often argued that if a person is "born that way," then homosexuality is like a person's sex or racial identity, and a homosexual person's rights ought to be protected in the same way. Further, some Christians who affirm that people are homosexual from

birth assert that homosexuality is part of God's design for sexuality, and should be celebrated as such, and homosexuals should not be excluded from church membership or leadership simply on the basis of their homosexuality. Thus much is at stake.

What causes homosexuality? There is no easy answer to that question. Or, to put it another way, as one psychologist who has studied the matter extensively says, "We don't know."[102] Though some claim that it is primarily "nature" or biology, and others claim that it is "nurture" or environment, studies show that it is more complex than that. After carefully reviewing studies of causation, Mark Yarhouse concludes, "When we look at the causes of homosexuality, we simply do not know why some people experience same-sex attractions or have a homosexual orientation. There are probably many factors that contribute in one way or another, with these factors varying from person to person."[103] Instead of finding a single cause, studies point to various contributing factors, including biology (in some way), childhood experiences, environmental influences, and adult experiences.

Claims that people are homosexual from birth tend to focus on biology or genetics by way of prenatal hormones and brain structure, genes and chromosomal markers, studies of twins, and so on.[104] Yarhouse

---

101. Cf. a description of a script for Christians in Yarhouse, *Homosexuality and the Christian*, 50–53.
102. Yarhouse, *Homosexuality and the Christian*, 59.
103. Yarhouse, *Homosexuality and the Christian*, 30.
104. See Yarhouse, *Homosexuality and the Christian*, 63–70, for a review of pertinent studies. Also the review of studies by Stanton L. Jones and Mark A. Yarhouse in *Homosexuality: The Use of Scientific Research in the Church's Moral Debate* (Downers Grove, IL: InterVarsity Press, 2000), 60–83.

shows that there is no conclusive evidence in these studies that biology or genetics causes homosexuality.[105] Yet he believes that biology may be a contributing factor: "Biology plays an important role in so much of human experience, so it would be strange to act as though homosexuality was the one area that biology played no role whatsoever."[106] In any case, it seems clear that "the recent movement toward biological theories may be as much due to political forces as any real or empirical or scientific dissatisfaction with the psychosocial theories."[107] This has been acknowledged by some behind the "gay rights movement"; it was understood that to make gains politically it was necessary to argue that people were born gay.[108] Yet, with victory in hand, some defenders of homosexuality now reject the narrative that they are "born this way," and argue that it is an insufficient account of fifty years of research and of their experience.[109]

Claims that homosexuality is caused by nurture or environment tend to focus on things such as parent-child relationships, including a father who was absent, distant, or critical, or a mother was overbearing or enmeshed; childhood sexual experiences, including sexual abuse; and other environmental factors such as same-sex parents.[110] Added to these are "other environmental influences (such as peer group influences, same-sex experimentation and early sexual debut) and adult experiences (for example, willful or purposeful experimentation with same-sex behavior and sub-culture disinhibition)."[111] As with evidence from nature, however, the evidence from nurture is not conclusive. While some of these factors contribute in some cases, they are not sufficient explanations. Not everyone who has had such experiences is homosexual, and not every homosexual has had such experiences. In cases where experiences are a factor, it may be helpful for the person with same-sex attraction to understand that, as a way of coming to terms with their experience and attractions.

The conclusion reached by Stanton Jones and Mark Yarhouse seems reasonable. They say that "the scientific evidence about causation is simply inconclusive at this time." Rather than attributing homosexuality to one theory or another, they assert that it is

---

105. To offer one example, in the study of twins, there was biased sampling (drawing participants from ads placed in pro-gay magazines), so that when unbiased sampling was used, the correlation fell by half. Further, if homosexuality was genetic, we would expect close to 100 percent correlation (if one identical twin is gay, the other will be). In reality, in almost two-thirds of the cases (twenty-seven out of forty-one), when one twin was gay, the other was not. And, given that twins share not only genetics but also environment, it is difficult to draw significant conclusions. See Yarhouse, *Homosexuality and the Christian*, 65–66.
106. Yarhouse, *Homosexuality and the Christian*, 70.
107. So Jones and Yarhouse, *Homosexuality*, 83.
108. As noted earlier, a book that set out the strategy for the cultural revolution concerning homosexuality, with startling success, is Kirk and Madsen, *After the Ball*.
109. Alia E. Dastagir, "'Born This Way'? It's Way More Complicated Than That," *USA TODAY*, June 15, 2017, https://www.usatoday.com/story/news/2017/06/16/born-way-many-lgbt-community-its-way-more-complex/395035001.
110. See Yarhouse, *Homosexuality and the Christian*, 70–77; Jones and Yarhouse, *Homosexuality*, 54–60.
111. Jones and Yarhouse, *Homosexuality*, 86.

more accurate to suppose that "various psy-chological, environmental and biological factors, together with human choice, con-tribute to different degrees that vary from person to person."[112] Whatever the cause, the reality is that many people experience same-sex attraction without having made a conscious choice. We shouldn't expect, then, that it is possible simply to decide not to ex-perience same-sex attraction. But is some kind of change possible?

Can Homosexual Desire Be Changed?

The research on this question is not clearly yes or no, so we ought not be simplistic in answering the question. Is change pos-sible? It is common now to deny or at least seriously downplay the possibility of change. Vines says, on the one hand, that sexual orientation "is highly resistant to change," which might at least leave open the possibility of change. However, he then says that same-sex attraction is "not some-thing I chose or something I can change." He also notes that "professional health organizations have rejected attempts to change people's sexual orientation." And perhaps most powerfully, he says that "even the president of Exodus Interna-tional, a former ex-gay ministry, acknowl-edged in 2012 that '99.9%' of the people he had worked with 'have not experienced a change in their orientation.'"[113]

It is important to recognize that same-sex desire is resistant to change. However, it seems that the case against change is over-stated, according to research and the prac-tice of those who help people pursue change. The example of Exodus International to sup-port the claim that change is impossible is not as conclusive as it may at first appear. For example, when Vines cites Alan Chambers's comment that 99.9 percent did not experi-ence change, he leaves out that Chambers included those who say "they could never be tempted" or who experience "some level of same-sex attraction."[114] Consider, by com-parison, persons who seek change because they experience lust for persons of the oppo-site sex, or they are addicted to pornography. If a survey said the 99.9 percent of those who sought change said they still experienced lust, or they would not say that they could never be tempted, it would not invalidate attempts to change. Rather, it would point to the need for ongoing support. Further, many counselors at Exodus International did not have adequate training, and many who sought change had unrealistic expecta-tions or did not truly desire the change.[115]

It is important to consider what we mean by change. If the idea is that someone with same-sex attraction can choose to ex-perience opposite-sex attraction if they re-ally want to, then it must be acknowledged that such change is unlikely. But when a

---

112. Jones and Yarhouse, *Homosexuality*, 84.
113. Vines, *God and the Gay Christian*, 28–29. The reference to Exodus International was a citation by Warren Throck-morton, "Alan Chambers: 99.9% Have Not Experienced a Change in Their Orientation," *Patheos*, January 9, 2012.
114. Throckmorton, "Alan Chambers"; Sprinkle, *People to Be Loved*, 220n2.
115. Sprinkle, *People to Be Loved*, 160–61.

broader sense of change is considered, many people who seek change experience a significant degree of success. Change might include a reduction in same-sex attraction or its intensity, including the ability to practice celibacy. In some cases, change includes an increased attraction to the opposite sex, either in general, or toward a specific individual in particular.[116] A significant longitudinal study of ex-gays by Jones and Yarhouse, which tracks people over a total of six to seven years, demonstrates that while change is not always complete or categorical, there are positive results. Forty-five percent reported positive change, while 40 percent reported no change, and others reported negative change or uncertain change. Some experienced increased heterosexual attraction (23 percent over the long term), while others simply experienced decreased homosexual attraction (30 percent long term), allowing them the "freedom to live chaste" more easily.[117]

Those who do not experience same-sex attraction must be sympathetic to people who experience difficulty in seeking change. Indeed, many heterosexuals know from experience that sexual desire, such as lust, is resistant to change. In our own will, change does seem impossible. But sexual desire, and even sexual orientation, is not absolutely fixed, and Christians through the centuries bear witness to the fundamental

transformation that occurs by the power of the Spirit through faith in Jesus Christ and a steadfast commitment to follow him. As Paul reminds the Corinthians, speaking of (among other things) fornication, adultery, and homosexual relations, "and some of you used to be like this. But you were washed, you were sanctified, you were justified in the name of the Lord Jesus Christ and by the Spirit of our God" (1 Cor. 6:11). For those who have undergone the radical transformation from alienation from God to union with God, the change in sexual desires cannot be considered impossible; the most significant change that someone can experience has already occurred.

How Prevalent Is Homosexuality?

Determining the percentage of the population that is homosexual is not central to a moral analysis of homosexual practice. Consider how many desires and practices are widespread and deeply ingrained yet are matters for correction rather than approval (envy, greed, lust, pornography). Yet understanding the prevalence of homosexuality is significant for perspective, and for correcting misperception, and because a high and inaccurate number is often used to promote and defend various viewpoints and policies. Consider the following examples of conclusions drawn from an understanding of the percentage of gay and lesbian people:[118]

---

116. Yarhouse, *Homosexuality and the Christian*, 90.
117. See the summary in Yarhouse, *Homosexuality and the Christian*, 87–89. For complete information from the study, see Stanton L. Jones and Mark A. Yarhouse, *Ex-Gays? A Longitudinal Study of Religiously Mediated Change in Sexual Orientation* (Downers Grove, IL: IVP Academic, 2007).
118. Cited in Jones and Yarhouse, *Homosexuality*, 32–33.

Given that lesbians and gay men comprise 10 to 15 percent of the general population, today's psychotherapist cannot afford to be ignorant of the mental health needs specific to these groups.[119]

If the best scientific data . . . seems to put the figures of gay and lesbian people in the world at about 10% of the population . . . then you and I need to realize that 10% is such a larger percentage that it could hardly be accidental.[120]

The most widely cited number for the prevalence of homosexuality in the United States seems to be around 10 percent. It is derived from influential studies on human sexuality conducted by Alfred Kinsey in the 1940s and 1950s (which have been recognized as deeply flawed because of oversampling and other problems).[121] The actual percentage is much lower, with studies finding numbers ranging from 2 to 4 percent, including studies by gay researchers.[122]

There is thus a significant gap between perception and reality. That gap was shown to be extremely wide in a 2015 Gallup poll. That poll found that Americans estimate that 23 percent of the population is gay or lesbian, compared with Gallup's finding that only 3.8 percent of adults identified themselves as lesbian, gay, bisexual, or transgender.[123] The Gallup findings attributed the inaccuracy at least in part to "American's general unfamiliarity with numbers and demography." That may be part of it, but a likely explanation is the prevalence of homosexual characters in television and other media, as well as the frequency with which LGBT issues are vocalized in politics and media.

As indicated, the prevalence of homosexuality is not decisive for either a positive or negative moral judgment, or for policy matters. However, it does matter that we have an accurate understanding, and to the extent that inflated numbers are used to shape public opinion and policies, they ought to be corrected.

Sexual Desire and Identity

The question of identity has become foundational in recent years. It is often said by revisionist interpreters of Scripture that the ancients—including the biblical authors—knew nothing of a homosexual orientation or identity. It is true that the discussion of

119. Kris S. Morgan and Rebecca M. Nerison, "Homosexuality and Psychopolitics: An Historical Overview," *Psychotherapy* 30 (1993): 133.
120. This citation made by Jones and Yarhouse is from Bishop John Spong in a debate at Virginia Protestant Episcopal Seminary, February 1992 (Truro Tape Ministries, Fairfax, VA). As Jones and Yarhouse point out (*Homosexuality*, 33), Bishop Spong here indicates that the prevalence of homosexuality is a key issue in the moral debate.
121. Dastagir, "Born This Way?"; Jones and Yarhouse, *Homosexuality*, 34–37.
122. Jones and Yarhouse, *Homosexuality*, 38–44, summarize numerous studies. As one would expect, the number can rise significantly if the survey question is broad enough. For instance, in one study cited by Jones and Yarhouse, the finding was closer to 20 percent when respondents were asked if they had ever been attracted to a member of the same-sex (*Homosexuality*, 40).
123. Frank Newport, "Americans Greatly Overestimate Percent Gay, Lesbians in U.S.," *Gallup News Social Issues*, May 21, 2015, http://news.gallup.com/poll/183383/americans-greatly-overestimate-percent-gay-lesbian.aspx.

homosexual orientation is relatively new. That does not mean that the ancients knew nothing of a fixed erotic attraction to persons of the same sex. Paul indicates something much like that in Romans 1. But it is true that it was not understood as part of a person's identity as it is today.

One of the problems in the whole discussion is the weight placed on sexual identity—that is, placing such a weight on sexual desires and subjective experience that they define who we are. This is true not only of those with same-sex desires but of those with heterosexual desires as well. As one author put it, sexuality has replaced the soul in modern minds as the essence of our identity.[124] It is true that sexuality is central to who we are, in the sense that human beings are sexual beings, so we ought not minimize it. Yet neither should we maximize sexuality as that which defines us.

It is not difficult to understand why something as central as sexuality can become the singular focus of our existence, especially for those with same-sex desire, since there is so much attention (positively and negatively) drawn to homosexuality and homosexual experience. Yet sexuality and sexual desire are not the essence of who we are, and while a person who experiences same-sex attraction is encouraged to make that their identity, attraction and identity are not the same thing. It may be helpful to distinguish between attraction, orientation, and identity.[125]

- *Same-sex attraction* is a description of a person's feelings or desires.
- *Homosexual orientation* is a way of describing same-sex attraction "that is strong enough, durable enough, and persistent enough for them to feel that they are *oriented* toward the same sex."[126]
- *Gay identity* goes beyond one's experience of sexual attraction, and is a way of labeling oneself (or someone else) according to one's sexual attraction. It moves beyond a description of attraction to an adoption of the attraction as part of one's core identity.

Can a Christian Identify as Gay?

Some of those who affirm homosexual relations and some who don't will find this question itself to be wrongheaded, and offer very different answers. Those who affirm consensual, committed homosexual relations will argue that one can certainly be a Christian and identify as gay. By contrast, some who believe that the Bible condemns all homosexual sex will argue that one cannot be gay and Christian. How might we answer the question?

To begin with, it is important to know what someone means when they say that they are a "gay Christian." Some may mean to affirm that being gay and being Christian are both a part of their fundamental identity. If this is what someone means by identifying as a "gay Christian," then we must say that it

---

124. See Phillip Turner, "Sex and the Single Life," *First Things*, May 1993, 15–21.
125. This distinction is used by Mark Yarhouse, based on extensive counseling with people who experience same-sex attraction. See Yarhouse, *Homosexuality and the Christian*, 41–43.
126. Yarhouse, *Homosexuality and the Christian*, 41.

is a contradiction. Others may simply mean to underscore the fact that they experience same-sex attraction. They reject homosexual sex, and do not understand their same-sex attraction to be part of their core identity, but they wish to acknowledge a significant aspect of the experience with which they struggle. That is understandable, in a sense. As Sprinkle points out, we have various identities, even if our primary identity is in Christ. You might talk about being an athlete, a scholar, a baseball-card collector, a traveler, a computer geek, or a teacher, in order to identify a passion that you have. These are all secondary identities, which are subordinate to your primary identity in Christ.[127] Or think of perhaps a closer analogy, since it is not something that the person affirms, when people say that they are an alcoholic. They don't mean to say that they affirm alcoholism, but simply that it is a part of their experience. In that sense, many would affirm that they are an alcoholic and Christian.

While such a view is understandable, it is also problematic. First, it can be confusing to others, communicating something that is not intended, since many people would take it to mean that being gay is part of the person's core identity, or that the person affirms homosexual relations. Second, it may confuse one's own sense of identity. For example, even if it is considered a secondary identity, it is not quite like identifying with a hobby or other passion that denotes not just how you feel, or what you are interested in, but what you do. Identifying as an alcoholic may get closer to

a person's identity, but that is not without its problems either. There is a similarity, in that someone may self-describe as an alcoholic in order to be open and honest about a central struggle in their life, and to identify it as something in their nature against which they need to fight. Yet, whether or not one thinks it is appropriate to identify as an alcoholic, it seems unhelpful to me to identify as a Christian alcoholic (or an alcoholic Christian).

Perhaps some mean something different, analogous to a person who has committed adultery continuing to self-identify as an adulterer in order to underscore their sin and God's grace (or similarly acknowledging themselves as a greedy or lustful person). There may be some merit to that, but none of these things ought to be put forward as such a central part of one's identity that someone is known fundamentally as such. We ought to remember Paul's encouraging words of exhortation, "Such were some of you. But you were washed, you were sanctified, you were justified in the name of the Lord Jesus Christ and by the Spirit of our God" (1 Cor. 6:11 ESV). In Christ our identity is so fundamentally changed that not only are all other identities secondary, but our sinful past and our sinful inclinations are swallowed up in our new identity, even if such inclinations do not immediately and totally disappear.

A New Narrative

Those who are in Christ have a new identity and a new narrative. They become part of

---

127. See his discussion in *People to Be Loved*, 141–44.

Christ's body, the church, where they are welcomed into a new fellowship, a new family, called to love one another and bear one another's burdens. The book of Acts shows a church that is marked by such love and grace, through the experience of the gospel and the power of the Spirit, that it draws others who are seeking God and a community to which to belong (Acts 2:44–47; cf. Eph. 4:1–16; Col. 1:4). Unfortunately, many who experience same-sex attraction—including those who identify with Christ—are not drawn to the Church but are repelled by it. That has to do, in part, with the sense that they feel rejected and condemned by the church while they feel welcomed and affirmed by the gay community and broader culture.

Whether these are accurate or not, Yarhouse notes that these two perceived alternatives function as "scripts," which is a way of talking about how "we come to understand ourselves and our lives."[128] A major script that influences young people is the culture that they are surrounded by, including their peers and school, music and media. The majority culture has embraced what Yarhouse calls the "gay script," which has a profound impact on young people who experience same-sex attraction. In this script, same-sex attraction is the same as identifying as gay. Same-sex attraction is understood to be natural, even as the way "God made me." It is integral to identity in order to how you discover who you really are. Same-sex behavior is the natural extension of gay identity, and "self-actualization (behavior that matches who you 'really are') of your sexual identity is crucial for your fulfillment."[129] The "gay script" is appealing to many people, in part because of the message that same-sex attractions are natural and good, and to embrace them is to be who you "really are." It is also the loudest script, the only culturally approved script, and sometimes the only script that young people hear. That is, many who experience same-sex attraction do not hear what they perceive to be a viable script from the church, but instead hear only condemnation, while they feel welcomed and affirmed by the "gay community" and broader culture.

The gay script isn't the only possibility, however, and some have found that there is a different way to be "authentic." Instead of seeing same-sex attraction as natural or God's intention, it can be understood as an experience, like many others, that is not chosen but is a consequence of the fall, and it need not be the defining part of one's identity. Rather than forming same-sex attraction into a gay identity, it is possible to center one's identity on Christ, where every human experience, including same-sex attraction, is to be understood in light of our identity in Christ. In this script, same-sex attraction is acknowledged, and yet it is understood that there are still "choices to make about both behavior and identity."[130] As part of a larger narrative, those who adopt a Christ-centered

---

128. Yarhouse, *Homosexuality and the Christian*, 48.
129. Yarhouse, *Homosexuality and the Christian*, 49.
130. Yarhouse, *Homosexuality and the Christian*, 51–52.

script rather than a gay script need (like everyone) the encouragement and support of church members as true brothers and sisters in Christ. They may have been rejected by their family and others, and they need to experience the reality that Jesus promises when he says, "I assure you . . . there is no one who has left house, brothers or sisters, mother or father, children, or fields because of me and the gospel, who will not receive 100 times more, now at this time—houses, brothers and sisters, mothers and children, and fields, with persecutions—and eternal life in the age to come" (Mark 10:28–30 HCSB). Part of the encouragement that they need is to hear from others—and there are many—who have experienced same-sex attraction and yet find their identity in Christ, and seek to live in faithfulness to him.[131]

Transgender: Sex, Gender, and Identity

While the cultural discussion about sexuality brings together a range of issues under LGBT (along with Q and others), this chapter has focused on homosexuality, because it addresses the central questions, and much of what has been discussed applies more broadly. However, before concluding, it is necessary to address issues pertaining to transgender, since

it has become a significant matter of cultural debate and confusion in its own right, and since it encompasses a number of distinct issues. What follows will only scratch the surface, but hopefully it will at least provide an overview of some of the key issues and challenges, and a biblical response to them. It is important to remember at the outset that, as with homosexuality, this is not simply about a debate—as significant as that is—but it is about real people who experience real pain and hurt and confusion and misunderstanding and who, like everyone else, need to be cared about and loved.

Although "LGBT" has been in use for some time, most of the public discussion has been focused on same-sex attraction and orientation and same-sex civil marriage, until recently. Many people took little notice of transgender issues prior to the very public transition of two celebrity figures. The first was the transition of Chastity Bono (the daughter of Sonny and Cher Bono) to Chaz, depicted in the documentary *Becoming Chaz* at the Sundance Film Festival and on the Oprah Winfrey Network in 2011.[132] The second featured the transition of Bruce Jenner to Caitlyn Jenner, with a cover story in *Vanity Fair* magazine in June 2015, and the very public debates over transgender

---

131. For example, see the website Living Out, http://www.livingout.org, which provides many stories of same-sex-attracted people who are following Christ and are part of the church. While I do not endorse everything taught or communicated on Living Out, the stories often communicate well the difficulties and challenges that accompany same-sex attraction in the lives of believers attempting to live faithfully in the body of Christ.

132. Hank Stuever, "TV Review: 'Becoming Chaz' on OWN—Chastity Bono's Emotional Transformation," *Washington Post*, May 9, 2011, https://www.washingtonpost.com/lifestyle/style/tv-review-becoming-chaz-on-own--chastity-bonos-emotional-transformation/2011/05/04/AF4u8RcG_story.html?utm_term=.91840291f82e.

bathroom access and other issues.[133] Yet, in a very short time transgender activists have had a massive influence on culture and politics, with the help of mass media that is trying to keep up with a revolution that is even more radical than the sexual revolution that it is built on.[134] In this revolution, a person's "true" gender may or may not be congruent with their biological sex, for what matters most—and what determines whether a person is male or female—is not their sex "assigned at birth," but the inner perception of their true self.[135] The Obama administration went so far as to redefine "sex" from a biological identity as male or female to a person's gender identity—that is, their self-perception of their gender. This is all part of what has been called the "transgender moment."[136]

The reference to "sex assigned at birth" is particularly revealing. It is part of the insistence that human beings are not male or female according to a fixed biological reality (at least not in terms of chromosomes or anatomical features) from conception or birth. In this view, one's "sex assigned at birth" refers to what was put on their birth certificate according to their bodily, anatomical features. That may or may not be the person's gender identity, which can only be known by the individual at some later time. This highlights one of the crucial aspects of the debate on LGBT issues—that is, both the meaning of terms and our understanding of reality (metaphysics or ontology).[137] This is illustrated by the insistence and repetition by transgender activists that "a transgender woman *is* a woman" and "a transgender man *is* a man."[138]

Language in the Transgender Discussion

One of the major problems in the transgender debate is that different people use the same terminology to signify vastly different things. One side understands "male" and "female" to signify biological sex to which gender corresponds. The other has completely rejected such a view and defines sex and gender according to psychological

---

133. On the Jenner story, see Buzz Bissinger, "Caitlyn Jenner: The Full Story," *Vanity Fair*, June 25, 2015, https://www.vanityfair.com/hollywood/2015/06/caitlyn-jenner-bruce-cover-annie-leibovitz. On the story about the ongoing battle over transgender access to public restrooms in North Carolina, see Jonathan Drew, "North Carolina's Transgender Rights Battle Isn't Over," *USA Today*, June 25, 2018, https://www.usatoday.com/story/news/nation/2018/06/25/north-carolina-bathroom-bill-transgender/729791002.

134. For the radical nature of the transgender revolution, see Mohler, *We Cannot Be Silent*, chap. 5.

135. The use of "sex assigned at birth" is just one indication of the speed in which the transgender revolution is moving, for until recently transgender-activist organizations used terms like "birth sex" or "physical sex." See Ryan T. Anderson, *When Harry Became Sally: Responding to the Transgender Moment* (New York: Encounter, 2018), 29.

136. See Anderson's first chapter in *When Harry Became Sally*, "Our Transgender Moment," 9–26.

137. On metaphysics or ontology in the debate, see Anderson, *When Harry Became Sally*, 29–33.

138. This can be seen, for instance, in the Wikipedia article "Trans Woman," which states (as of January 31, 2020), "A trans woman (sometimes trans-woman or transwoman) is a woman who was assigned male at birth"; https://en.wikipedia.org/wiki/Trans_woman.

perception.[139] Before discussing a few key points on how to respond to transgenderism, it is worth outlining some key terms.[140]

Gender: Gender has commonly been used to refer both to a person's biological sex and to cultural understandings and expressions of biological sex as masculine and feminine.

Gender dysphoria: The experience of persons whose perception of their gender does not match their biological sex, causing distress. This is sometimes expressed by saying that a man feels trapped in a woman's body, or a woman feels trapped in a man's body.

Gender identity: a person's self-perception of their gender (which may or may not be congruent with their biological sex)

Intersex: a term that refers to a variety of conditions in which a person is born with ambiguous sex characteristics or anatomy that are not clearly identifiable as male or female. Causes may be chromosomal, gonadal, or genital.

Sex: This term is used for identity and activity; in terms of identity, it refers to a person's biological or genetic structure (males have XY chromosomes, females have XX chromosomes), with corresponding sex characteristics (physical or anatomical). More recently, transgender activists and allies have defined sex in terms of a person's self-perception of their gender.

Transgender: While this is a broad term used for a variety of understandings of gender experience, expression, and identity, for present purposes *transgender* refers to persons who in some way express a gender identity that is not congruent with their biological sex. This expression may include dressing or otherwise assuming the gender opposite of their biological sex and/or pursuing hormone treatment or gender-reassignment surgery.

Transgenderism: an ideology with a political agenda advocated by those who believe that gender is different from biological sex, that gender identity is more fundamental than biological sex, and so on. Many who adopt transgenderism are not transgender, and many who are transgender do not adopt transgenderism.

---

139. Some transgender activists argue that some people who experience gender dysphoria have a brain structure that doesn't match their biological sex. However, there are no conclusive studies to demonstrate such a claim, and even if some disparity is shown, it doesn't tell us whether the difference in brain structure or activity is the cause or the result of identifying with the sex that is not congruent with their biological sex. For a discussion of brain studies, see Anderson, *When Harry Became Sally*, 33, 106–8.
140. For these and other terms related to transgenderism, see Mark A. Yarhouse, *Understanding Gender Dysphoria: Navigating Transgender Issues in a Changing Culture* (Downers Grove, IL: IVP Academic, 2015), 20–21; Andrew T. Walker, *God and the Transgender Debate: What Does the Bible Actually Say about Gender Identity?* (Epsom, UK: Good Book Company, 2017), 29–35; also Joe Carter, "From Agender to Ze: A Glossary for the Gender Identity Revolution," The Gospel Coalition, May 13, 2016, https://www.thegospelcoalition.org/article/from-agender-to-ze-a-glossary-for-the-gender-identity-revolution.

Understanding Gender Dysphoria and Transgender

Gender dysphoria is complex and serious. For reasons that are not well understood, some persons (of any age) perceive that their gender does not match their biological sex. The experience is often expressed as the feeling of being "a man trapped in a woman's body" or "a woman trapped in a man's body." It causes significant distress, mental health problems, anxiety, and depression.[141] People who experience gender dysphoria or who are transgender are much more likely to attempt suicide. Even though people who experience gender dysphoria represent a small percentage of the population (about one-half of 1 percent or less), it is a matter that deserves care and attention, especially given the distress it causes.

Unfortunately, relatively little is known about the causes of gender dysphoria, which makes it difficult to know exactly how to treat it. In the process of development, some children will sense that they are different from their peers of the same sex. This may be due to their preferences or self-perception relative to what they believe is expected of girls or boys. As a result they may identify more closely with the opposite sex, and in extreme cases they may believe that inside they are a member of the sex different from their physical sex. In most cases this sense is resolved naturally over time. In their testimony before the US Supreme Court, Paul McHugh, Paul Hruz, and Lawrence Mayer state that the best studies "agree that between 80 and 95 percent of children who say that they are transgender naturally come to accept their sex and to enjoy emotional health by late adolescence."[142]

Sadly, in spite of a lack of knowledge of the causes, and the fact that the vast majority of children who identify as transgender will naturally come to resolution and accept their biological sex, transgender activists advocate that even young children with gender dysphoria should transition to express and live as the gender that they perceive themselves to be, particularly if the dysphoria is consistent, persistent, and insistent.[143] Increasingly they are seeking to have policies and legislation in place to force compliance (even on the part of parents of children with gender dysphoria). Transition involves several stages:[144]

- Initially gender transition for a child involves a social transition: the child should be treated as a member of the gender with which they identify—that is, they should be given clothes appropriate to their gender identity, referred

---

141. For a discussion of gender dysphoria, transgender identity, and mental health, with a survey of studies, see Anderson, *When Harry Became Sally*, chap. 5.

142. Citing the American College of Pediatricians and the American Psychological Association's Diagnostic and Statistical Manual of Mental Disorders (DSM-5). See Paul R. McHugh, Paul Hruz, and Lawrence S. Mayer, Brief of *Amici Curiae* in *Gloucester County School Board*, Petitioner, v. *G.G.*, Respondent, Supreme Court of the United States, No. 16–273 (January 10, 2017), 12. Also Anderson, *When Harry Became Sally*, 119.

143. Anderson, *When Harry Became Sally*, 120.

144. See *When Harry Became Sally*, 120–21.

to with pronouns matching their gender identity, and even given a new legal name if appropriate.

- Next, when a child is approaching puberty, they may be given puberty-blocking drugs to suppress their biological sex development and/or reverse development that has already taken place.
- Around age sixteen, the child may be prescribed cross-sex hormones (e.g., estrogen for biological boys and testosterone for biological girls) to mimic the natural development of the gender with which they identify. Girls will develop a lower voice, facial hair, and a more masculine body shape, while boys will experience some breast development and a more feminine body shape. They will remain on cross-sex hormones for the rest of their lives (unless they decide to detransition).
- Last, a transgender person may undergo sex-reassignment surgery after they turn eighteen, which involves "amputation of primary and secondary sex characteristics, and plastic surgery to create new sex characteristics."[145]

Responding to the Transgender Debate

First, it is crucial to remember that behind these terms and debates, and the politics of transgenderism, are people, many of whom are confused and experience high levels of anxiety and distress.[146] Our response to them should not be ridicule or scorn. Followers of Jesus must seek to emulate our Lord by having compassion, expressing love, and seeking to understand those who are hurting. We live in a fallen world that is marked by brokenness and alienation in many ways, even a sense of alienation from one's own body. Christians know that healing and peace come only through reconciliation with God and others, and we are called to be agents of reconciliation.

Second, God created male and female, distinct and complementary, as a central feature of his good creation, for his glory and for human flourishing. Male and female denote two biological sexes from which gender identity and expression are derived. In the fallen world, these distinctions are confused, distorted, and even rejected, but they remain good. There are certainly cultural differences in how gender is expressed, and we should be careful not to stereotype or draw rigid lines with regard to gender expression where the Bible does not draw them (e.g., women are supposed to cook and play with dolls; men are supposed to build things and play with trucks; nursing is a woman's job; engineering is a man's job). Yet the Bible does make clear that human beings are created male and female, and that our biological sex should govern our gender identity and expression. That is, God created male and female as distinct and complementary,

---

145. Anderson, *When Harry Became Sally*, 121. As Anderson notes, this treatment plan is the current standard promoted by transgender activists, though the commencement of treatment for each stage is getting younger.
146. See Yarhouse, *Understanding Gender Dysphoria*.

and he delights in the differences, which are to be recognized and honored. To dishonor either male or female is to reject and rebel against God's good creation.[147]

Third, we may distinguish between the experience of gender dysphoria and transgender expression. The experience of gender dysphoria is an aspect of the brokenness that all people experience in various ways in a fallen world. The causes of gender dysphoria are surely complex, and ultimately unknown.[148] Great sensitivity and pastoral care ought to be extended to someone who experiences gender dysphoria. Transgender expression goes beyond the experience of gender dysphoria, to where someone seeks to identify and live as the sex that is different from their birth sex. Again, we must recognize the pain, confusion, and anxiety that has led someone to adopt a transgender identity, and we ought to seek to understand and extend compassion.

Fourth, we do well to point out the inherent contradictions with transgenderism, which refers to the ideology promoted by activists, rather than the experience of gender dysphoria or the identification of transgender. Ryan Anderson summarizes this point well:

> Activists promote a highly subjective and incoherent worldview. On the one hand, they claim that the real self is something other than the physical body, in a new form of Gnostic dualism, yet at the same time they embrace a materialist philosophy in which only the material world exists. They say that gender is purely a social construct, while asserting that a person can be "trapped" in the wrong body. They say there are no meaningful differences between man and woman, yet they rely on rigid sex stereotypes to argue that "gender identity" is real while human embodiment is not. They claim that truth is whatever a person says it is, yet they believe there's a *real* self to be discovered inside that person.[149]

Fifth, we should realize just how radical are the proposals made by transgender activists. It is, in part, a radical extension of human autonomy and freedom, which is ultimately expressed in defiance of God. A person with gender dysphoria, or identifying as transgender, is experiencing a disassociation or alienation from their body or between their mind and body. A person who undergoes transition to seek to conform their body to their gender identity remains alienated, for a person remains in the biological sex that they were born with, regardless of the gender that they choose to express or cosmetic changes in appearance. With hormone treatment and sex-reassignment surgery, a male may

---

147. One way that we recognize and honor the difference between male and female is the way we present ourselves, such as in the way we dress. On Deut. 22:5, which addresses this, see Jason DeRouchie, "Confronting the Transgender Storm: New Covenant Reflections from Deuteronomy 22:5," *Journal for Biblical Manhood and Womanhood* 21, no. 1 (May 25, 2016): https://cbmw.org/topics/transgenderism/jbmw-21–1-confronting-the-transgender-storm-new-covenant-reflections-from-deuteronomy-225.
148. Yarhouse, *Understanding Gender Dysphoria*, chap. 3.
149. Anderson, *When Harry Became Sally*, 45–46.

be feminized and a female masculinized, but sex-reassignment surgery does not and cannot "reassign" sex, turning a biological male into a biological female or a biological female into a biological male. The only way that it makes sense to assert that "a transgender man is a man" or "a transgender woman is a woman," as activists do, is to redefine what it meant by "male" and "female." However, to do so is simply to change definitions, not reality. Unfortunately, while transition may have some positive results in some cases, many do not resolve the trauma of gender dysphoria. What is more, the treatments can cause harm in many ways, including infertility and incontinence.

A much better way forward is to try to understand the causes of gender dysphoria, and to help those affected resolve the sense of alienation by coming to terms with their biological sex.[150] Among other things, those who have gone through transition, remained in distress, and therefore detransitioned and came to terms with their bodies, should have their voices heard.[151] Many of them realize that transitioning didn't solve their problems, that their body wasn't the problem, and that they were running away from themselves. One of the sobering things

that we ought to learn from them is that many feel like outcasts from society, commonly experiencing hostility because they didn't "fit" or conform to gender norms. It is a reminder that when we encounter people who are different from us, or who don't conform to cultural norms, we ought to show love and kindness, not hatred, rejection, and alienation. We need to hold out the hope of the gospel.

Finally, the transgendered person who seeks to follow Christ ought to be encouraged, in whatever way is appropriate, to embrace and live out their gender identity in congruence with their biological sex. These issues ought to be engaged with great humility before God and others, as we recognize signs of human brokenness that all of us experience. We ought to be reminded of our need for God's grace and the good news of the gospel, and the great hope that those who repent and trust in him will one day experience the fullness of human flourishing that God has promised. As Paul declares to the Corinthian believers, "Some of you used to be like this. But you were washed, you were sanctified, you were justified in the name of the Lord Jesus Christ and by the Spirit of our God" (1 Cor. 6:11).

---

150. For a thorough discussion of gender dysphoria and transgender, with extensive review of the relevant literature, see Anderson, *When Harry Became Sally*. See also the work of Paul McHugh, Lawrence Mayer, Paul Hruz, and others. For example, Paul R. HcHugh, "Surgical Sex: Why We Stopped Doing Sex Change Operations," *First Things*, November, 2004, https://www.firstthings.com/article/2004/11/surgical-sex; Lawrence S. Mayer and Paul R. McHugh, "Sexuality and Gender: Findings from the Biological, Psychological, and Social Sciences," *The New Atlantis*, Fall 2016, https://www.thenewatlantis.com/publications/introduction-sexuality-and-gender; Jesse Singal, "What's Missing from the Conversation about Transgender Kids," *The Cut*, July 25, 2016, https://www.thecut.com/2016/07/whats-missing-from-the-conversation-about-transgender-kids.html?mid=full-rss-scienceofus.

151. They are often denounced by transgender activists. For several of their stories, see Anderson, *When Harry Became Sally*, 49–76.

Select Resources

Anderson, Ryan T. *When Harry Became Sally: Responding to the Transgender Moment*. New York: Encounter, 2018.

Beilby, James K., and Paul Rhodes Eddy. *Understanding Transgender Identities: Four Views*. Grand Rapids: Baker, 2019.

Gagnon, Robert A. J. *The Bible and Homosexual Practice: Texts and Hermeneutics*. Nashville: Abingdon, 2001.

Hays, Richard B. "Relations Natural and Unnatural: A Response to John Boswell's Exegesis of Romans 1." *Journal of Religious Ethics* 14, no. 1 (Spring 1986): 184–215.

Jones, Stanton L., and Mark A. Yarhouse. *Homosexuality: The Use of Scientific Research in the Church's Moral Debate*. Downers Grove, IL: InterVarsity Press, 2000.

Pearcey, Nancy. *Love Thy Body: Answering Hard Questions about Life and Sexuality*. Grand Rapids: Baker Books, 2018.

Roberts, Vaughan. *Transgender*. Epsom, UK: The Good Book Company, 2016.

Sprinkle, Preston. *People to Be Loved: Why Homosexuality Is Not Just an Issue*. Grand Rapids: Zondervan, 2015.

Walker, Andrew T. *God and the Transgender Debate: What Does the Bible Actually Say about Gender Identity?* Epsom, UK: The Good Book Company, 2017.

Yarhouse, Mark A. *Understanding Gender Dysphoria: Navigating Transgender Issues in a Changing Culture*. Downers Grove, IL: IVP Academic, 2015.

PART 4

THE SANCTITY OF HUMAN LIFE

CHAPTER 10

BIOETHICS AND HUMAN PERSONHOOD: THE CASE OF THE HUMAN EMBRYO

Your eyes saw me when I was formless;
all my days were written in your book and planned
before a single one of them began.

—Psalm 139:16

Introduction

The dignity of human life is a basic presupposition that grounds the protection and proper treatment of all human beings. It is the basis in society for the prohibition of murder, reckless indifference to human life, and the mistreatment of human beings. It is the basis for limits set on experimentation on human subjects. Human dignity is the basis for treating human beings differently from animals. Justice depends on the presumption that the dignity of every human being is affirmed. Yet the basic presumption that every human being possesses a dignity that is deserving of equal regard, care, and protection is qualified by some, often by the claim that not all human beings ought to be considered persons.

Who Is a Person?

This chapter will consider the question of personhood and, in particular, whether the human embryo is a person. This is an important starting point, since the personhood of the human embryo is frequently challenged, both by arguments and by actions. If willful disregard and destruction of the human embryo is considered permissible, then it is clearly not viewed as a person, nor as a human being with inherent dignity.[1] The discussion of the human embryo will have obvious implications for the broader question having to do with the dignity and personhood of all human life prior to birth, and for our view of human cloning, embryonic stem-cell research, assisted reproductive technologies, birth control, abortion, and other moral issues. Thus the question about whether the human embryo, and by extension all human beings prior to birth, possesses the dignity shared by all persons, is worth exploring before we examine a variety of issues in bioethics.

Before examining the question, we may recognize that even to ask whether the human embryo is fully human, or is a person, is troubling because it puts the burden of proof on those who affirm the dignity of every human being, and who defend and seek to protect human life from its earliest stages. That is, the question itself suggests, or perhaps even demands, that we cannot assume that every human being possesses dignity and deserves protection. By analogy, to ask expectant parents whether their unborn child has a right to life would be offensive, for it suggests that they must defend an affirmative answer. Nonetheless, it is necessary to examine the question of the embryo, and defend one's position, precisely because there is a lack of consensus, and because the consequences are so great.

Test Case: The Warnock Report

In 1984, a noteworthy and influential statement was published in the United Kingdom, with significant implications for human embryos. The report represents the findings of a committee appointed by the British government in 1982, chaired by philosopher (later Baroness) Mary Warnock, to examine and offer recommendations on *in vitro* fertilization (IVF) and embryology. Rapid developments in technology had led to the birth in 1978 in England of the first child conceived by means of IVF. The achievement of human fertilization in a laboratory petri dish raised concerns about "test-tube" babies and experimentation on human embryos. The Warnock Report, as it became known, offers the committee's findings and proposals.[2] Included in the report are recommendations

---

1. Some would assert that the human embryo is fully human but remain agnostic on the question of personhood, or possibly see the embryo as fully human (and therefore to be protected), but a potential person. It would be possible to make the basic arguments in this chapter simply by defending the full humanity of the embryo. However, for reasons that will become evident, I will defend the personhood of the embryo.

2. The official name is the *Report of the Committee of Inquiry into Human Fertilisation and Embryology*, presided over by Mary Warnock under the auspices of the British government's Department of Health and Social Security, July 1984, https://www.hfea.gov.uk/media/2608/warnock-report-of-the-committee-of-inquiry-into-human-fertilisation-and-embryology-1984.pdf. Hereafter referred to as the Warnock Report.

for the regulation of IVF and research on human embryos. The committee concludes, in short, "that the human embryo should be protected, but that research on embryos and IVF would be permissible, given appropriate safeguards."[3] This statement reveals a sharp tension in the report. On the one hand, it calls for the human embryo to be protected, for it is human. On the other hand, it allows for the embryo to be the subject of destructive experimentation, which indicates the belief that the human embryo is not *fully* human, for the "appropriate safeguards" do not include full protection from lethal harm.

The particular findings of the Warnock Report will not be examined in detail here.[4] The reason that the report is significant for this chapter is that it is one of the first to make recommendations on IVF and the treatment of embryos, and to offer a framework for the discussion. Thus it established a baseline for continued discussion, with ongoing relevance for many issues in bioethics, influencing deliberation in bioethics around the world.[5] Moreover, the Warnock Report is significant for the fact that it fails in perhaps its most important task, by leaving unanswered the most critical question it faced. That is, it makes recommendations concerning the

treatment of the embryo, but not its *status* (or identity). The problem with this is obvious, for surely its status determines its treatment! Consider an analogy. If an archaeologist is presented with what appears to be an artifact from an ancient ruin, it is critically important to determine what the artifact is before determining what should be done with it—whether to discard it or treat it carefully and display it. The question of identity of the artifact cannot be neglected, for the question of treatment depends on it. Moreover, if there is any doubt about its identity, it should be protected until the question of identity is answered. If this is true of an object of unknown origin, should it not be true of a subject of known, human origin?

The question of the status of the embryo is the most fundamental issue the committee faced, and yet it fails to address that critical issue until the eleventh chapter of the report, having spent the first ten chapters discussing infertility and its treatments. When it gets to what the report calls "the starting point for discussion," it sidesteps the question of status in favor of the question of treatment. The report states, "Although the questions of when life or personhood begins appear to be questions of fact susceptible of straightforward

---

3. This summary comes from the website of the British Human Fertilisation and Embryology Authority, which was formed in response to a proposal in the Warnock Report.

4. For an early response to the Warnock Report that is theologically informed, by a variety of authors, see Nigel M. de S. Cameron, ed., *Embryos and Ethics: The Warnock Report in Debate* (Edinburgh: Rutherford House, 1987). For a significant discussion of broad issues involved with assisted reproductive technologies and the Warnock Report, see Oliver O'Donovan, *Begotten or Made?* (Oxford: Clarendon, 1984).

5. For instance, Michael Sandel, a professor from Harvard University, while serving on the President's Council on Bioethics under President George W. Bush, suggested that the regulations in the United Kingdom, based on the Warnock recommendations, would be appropriate to adopt in the United States. See Michael J. Sandel, "Embryo Ethics—The Moral Logic of Stem-Cell Research," *New England Journal of Medicine* 351, no. 3 (July 15, 2004): 209.

answers, we hold that the answers to such questions in fact are complex amalgams of factual and moral judgments. Instead of trying to answer these questions directly we have therefore gone straight to the question of *how it is right to treat the human embryo.*"[6]

In fact, the committee does make a judgment on the status of the embryo, even if it is only implicit. On the one hand, the committee asserts that the human embryo should be protected, since it is an "embryo of the human species" and as such has "special status."[7] On the other hand, by a narrow majority the committee recommends that research be allowed on embryos, including experimentation that allows for the destruction of embryos up to fourteen days.[8] In so doing it makes clear that it does not consider the human embryo up to that point to be a human being deserving of protection from lethal harm. The tension in the report is evident by the dissent of the minority as well as by the awkward—and seemingly arbitrary—reasoning of the majority.

If the Warnock Report does not clearly articulate the philosophical and scientific reasons for not considering the human embryo to be fully human, the practical reason is quite evident. Medical guidelines prohibit treatment and experimentation that does harm to human subjects without the consent of the subject. For example, at the time of the Warnock Report, the Declaration of Helsinki stated, "Every biomedical research project involving human subjects should be preceded by careful assessment of predictable risks in comparison with foreseeable benefits to the subject or to others. *Concern for the interests of the subject must always prevail over the interest of science and society.*"[9] It is thus clear why the question of the status of the embryo is supremely important, and why the Warnock Report failed to answer it. If the embryo is considered a human subject, then no destructive research is permitted.

The Status of Human Embryos

The discussion that follows will offer an answer to the question concerning the status or identity of human embryos, and whether they are fully human and to be considered persons. There are two broad views concerning human personhood before birth (though there are many possible nuances, especially with regard to the first view). One is that a human being is not fully human or at least is not a person (and thus not deserving of full moral respect) until birth. The other is that a human being is fully human and therefore a person (and thus deserving of full moral respect) from the

---

6. Warnock Report, 60 (emphasis original). Again, the discussion of how to treat the embryo cannot properly take place until an answer is given to the prior fundamental question on which it depends, concerning the status or identity of the embryo.
7. Warnock Report, 63.
8. Warnock Report, 69. See two expressions of dissent by the minority, 90–94.
9. Declaration of Helsinki (1975), principle 5 (emphasis added). Adopted by the eighteenth World Medical Assembly, Helsinki, Finland, 1964, and as revised by the twenty-ninth World Medical Assembly, Tokyo, Japan, 1975. Additional revisions or emendations have occurred in 1983, 1989, 1996, 2000, 2002, 2004, 2008, http://www.ncbi.nlm.nih.gov/pmc/articles/PMC1884510/#app2.

moment of fertilization. For simplicity, I will defend the argument that a human embryo is a person.[10] Of course, some argue that an unborn human being becomes a person, or its potentiality as a person increases, later in development. In that case, it would be possible to argue that later in gestation, a human being deserves a degree of protection that the embryo does not. Such is the logic of the Warnock Report and *Roe v. Wade*. However, if the embryo is fully human and is therefore a person deserving of full protection, then all human beings in subsequent stages of development should be considered persons and treated as such. As indicated already, the implications are obvious for bioethical issues.

Two Broad Arguments on the Status of Human Life before Birth

Argument 1: Human embryos are not persons and therefore are not worthy of full moral respect

There are many nuances to the general argument that human beings are not worthy of full moral respect before birth. Some do not affirm personhood or the respect due to human persons, and thus protection from willful destruction, at any point prior to birth. Others argue for such respect at a certain point in development. Some of the arguments are substance arguments, based on what constitutes a human being or a human person, with the conclusion that the embryo

is not fully human or is not a person. Other arguments are consequentialist: regardless of the *human* status of the embryo or fetus, there are weighty reasons not to accord it full *moral* status, which allows for destructive experimentation and treatment. The reasons may include the quest for knowledge about fertilization and embryology, the alleviation of suffering and disease among those already born, the interests of the pregnant mother, or some other reason. What the various arguments have in common is the belief that human beings are not fully human—not persons—at the moment of fertilization. Consequentialist arguments, which may not focus on the status of the embryo or fetus, are nonetheless dependent to some degree on substance arguments, for the reason that the interests of society or the mother outweighs those of the unborn is that the status of the unborn is not considered to be equal to others. A brief outline of several substance arguments will be offered before moving to the main argument of this chapter, that human beings are fully human, and thus persons, from the moment of fertilization, from which time they are therefore deserving of full protection.

Substance arguments maintaining that the embryo is not a person

The embryo is not like us. A variety of substance arguments have been used to support the view that the embryo or fetus

---

10. I will not make a distinction between the embryo and earlier stages of development that are sometimes used, with terms like *pre-embryo* or *zygote*. Such distinctions may be useful for designating particular stages of development, but they do not affect the argument I am making.

is not fully human, or at least not a person. For instance, it was common in the early debates about abortion to refer to the developing life as a "clump of cells" or "blob of tissue." This type of argument, or rather assertion, made its way into the Warnock Report, in support of allowing research that would involve the destruction of human embryos. The report said that some people believe that "a human embryo cannot be thought of as a person, or even as a potential person. It is simply a collection of cells which, unless it implants in a human uterine environment, has no potential for development."[11] Given the appearance of human life during the early stages of cell division, it is not difficult to understand why this assertion is persuasive for some. Yet it ignores the substance of the embryo. The bottom line, it seems, is that the embryo is excluded as a person because it simply *does not look like us*. That is, "psychologically speaking, we are more likely mentally to associate paradigmatic persons with individuals who *look like* the paradigm than we are to associate them with individuals who do not look like the paradigm."[12] It should be clear, however, that appearance is an accidental, not an essential, feature of what it is to be human. A newborn baby, or a severely deformed person, looks significantly different from a "paradigmatic" adult, but they are not for that reason less human.

The embryo, even in its earliest stages, is not simply a blob of tissues or collection of cells. It is a human being that, from the moment of fertilization, is highly complex and well organized, though very early in its development. It therefore seems disingenuous for a prominent scientist to claim that "this thing, often called early embryo, is far less complex in any biological sense than the average potato."[13] Such statements are thinly veiled attempts to distance the embryo (or in other cases the fetus) from the circle of human compassion and care. The fact that it is possible to cause fertilization to occur in a petri dish, and observe it with a microscope, reinforces that distance. R. G. Edwards, the physiologist who, with obstetrician and gynecologist Patrick Steptoe, were the British pioneers of IVF treatment and the first to succeed with a live birth via IVF, offers an example of this distancing when he says, "Cleaving embryos are not sentient and are minute, so why should they be defended? . . . There does not seem to be much intrinsically valuable in an embryo human being. . . . An embryo is an embryo, not a fetus or a child."[14] This view ignores or deliberately cloaks the fact that the embryo is a nascent human being. "The embryo, from the time it is created, is a unified, unique,

---

11. Warnock Report, 62.
12. Carson Strong, *Ethics in Reproductive and Perinatal Medicine: A New Framework* (New Haven, CT: Yale University Press, 1997), 57.
13. Lord May of Oxford (then president of the Royal Society, a British organization of eminent scientists), quoted in Tim Radford, "Scientists Call for International Ban on Human Cloning," *The Guardian*, September 23, 2003, https://www.theguardian.com/uk/2003/sep/23/science.highereducation.
14. R. G. Edwards, "The Current Clinical and Ethical Situation of Human Conception *In Vitro*," *Proceedings of the Annual Symposium of the Eugenics Society* 19 (1983): 103.

dynamic, self-directed whole, not just a collection of cells."[15]

The embryo is a potential but not actual person. Some who argue against the personhood of the embryo do not deny that it is fully human, but accept that it is "like" us in this crucial way. Yet, even if its full humanity is acknowledged—and it is in fact quite difficult to deny—they will argue that an embryo should not be considered a person. It may be admitted that an embryo is fully human and a potential person in a way that eggs and sperm are not, but it is not yet an actual person. While it may deserve a certain amount of respect, as the Warnock Report admits, it does not deserve the full respect of an actual person, by which is meant a human being who has been born or has certain active functions required for personhood. For some, as it grows, its rights may become stronger, so that it is deserving of more and more respect and protection. Such is the logic, if not the result, of *Roe v. Wade*.[16] Yet its rights are not equal to actual persons, such as the mother, or perhaps those in society who could be healed by use of embryonic cells, or infertile couples who may benefit from experimentation on embryos.

In this view, to be a person is to possess some quality of personhood that the embryo or fetus lacks. The necessary quality or function may be brain activity, heartbeat, sentience, viability, self-consciousness, or some other function that allows for personal existence. It is understandable that there is a search for some common thread that is present in all humans, some aspect of identity that unites us as persons. The question concerns what it is that unites us. At a minimum, Peter Singer argues that consciousness is necessary to ascribe value to human life, for "life without consciousness is of no worth at all."[17] Joseph Fletcher offers a similar standard: "Humans without some minimum of intelligence or mental capacity are not persons, no matter how many of these organs are active, no matter how spontaneous their living processes are."[18] This focus on consciousness or mental capacity is common and appealing to many, for it seems that a person must be conscious of self and others. John Locke argues, for instance, that a person is a "thinking intelligent being, that has reason and reflection, and can consider itself as itself, the same thinking thing in different times and places."[19] Similarly, Michael Tooley claims,

---

15. Helen Pearson, "Your Destiny, from Day One," *Nature* 418, no. 6893 (July 4, 2002): 14–15, https://www.nature.com/articles/418014a. Cited in Megan Best, *Fearfully and Wonderfully Made: Ethics and the Beginning of Human Life* (Kingsford, Australia: Matthias Media, 2012), 30.

16. *Roe v. Wade* allows for restrictions on abortion after the first trimester, and even the possibility of prohibition of abortion late in pregnancy, so long as there is an exception provided for the health of the mother. Yet, because "health" is broadly defined to include not only physical health but also emotional or psychological health, etc., this exception proves to be virtually limitless, allowing for abortion on demand throughout pregnancy.

17. Peter Singer, *Rethinking Life and Death: The Collapse of Our Traditional Ethics* (New York: St. Martin's Griffin, 1994), 190.

18. Joseph Fletcher, *The Ethics of Genetic Control: Ending Reproductive Roulette* (Garden City, NY: Anchor, 1974), 137.

19. John Locke, *An Essay Concerning Human Understanding* (London: Thomas Tegg, 1841), 217.

"An organism possesses a serious right to life only if it possesses the concept of a self as a continuing subject of experiences and other mental states, and believes that it is itself such a continuing entity."[20]

What these philosophers are saying reflects significant aspects of human ontology, for they are expressing something that is unique about human beings. Among that which distinguishes human beings from other creatures is the capacity for reason and will, to think and to reflect and to choose and to interact on a personal level with one another, unlike other creatures. However, these requirements for personhood may be more exclusive than they seem at first glance, reaching further than a challenge to the personhood, or right to life, of the human embryo or fetus. It is difficult to see, for instance, how the newborn meets such standards for reason and self-reflection, yet few wish to make the case that a newborn is not a person. The personhood of other humans may be called into question as well. That is to say, the problem with such criteria is that while they are properties that are part of what it means to be human, they are considered only "as they exist at the height of their development," as Robert George and Christopher Tollefsen note. Yet, they ask, "where could such properties have come from if they were not already rooted in the nature of the being that possessed them?"[21] If a particular function or active capacity is necessary as a criterion for personhood,

it seems difficult to find the proper one, especially since humans possess different functioning levels of given capacities, and each human has capacities that function in different degrees at various stages in life. It appears that there is a search for a function that an embryo (or fetus) does not have, in order to omit it from the category of persons.

It seems that there must be a different and better way to understand human beings and personhood. It is not the active expression of a certain capacity that makes human beings persons, but rather it is that human beings possess a nature that has such personal capacities. The view that is affirmed below is that from the moment of fertilization human beings are fully human and are therefore persons with human dignity, worthy of full moral status. Human embryos are thus persons by virtue of the fact that they are human beings, and ought to be treated with the dignity that is accorded all human beings.

Argument 2: Human embryos are persons and therefore worthy of full moral respect

The argument for the personhood of human embryos is simply stated like this:

Premise 1: A human embryo is a human being.
Premise 2: All human beings are persons.
Conclusion: Therefore, a human embryo is a person.

20. Michael Tooley, "Abortion and Infanticide," *Philosophy and Public Affairs* 2 (1972): 59.
21. Robert P. George and Christopher Tollefsen, *Embryo: A Defense of Human Life* (New York: Doubleday, 2008), 6.

If these two premises are true, then the conclusion follows.[22] However, a problem with this argument can be readily admitted. If one of the two premises is false, then the conclusion will not follow, and since some will reject one of the premises, they may also reject the conclusion. Yet it is not always clear which premise will be rejected.[23] As we have seen, some reject the first premise, suggesting that the embryo becomes a human being at a later point. It should become clear that such an argument is unconvincing. The more difficult challenge concerns the second premise, for it is the question at hand, so it may appear to be a circular argument. For that reason, the second premise will be the primary focus of what follows, though the first premise will be addressed briefly as well. If the two premises are accepted, then the conclusion should be accepted.

Premise 1: A human embryo is a human being. At one level, this premise is obvious. As John T. Noonan puts it, "If you are conceived by human parents, you are human."[24] A human embryo is clearly human, not a dog or a fish or a tree or a pebble. It is human and it is a being—it is alive and growing steadily and rapidly into a more mature human form. Thus it is a human

being. One might argue that a sperm or egg or some cell that is part of a mature human being is also living and human, but it is not a human being. There is a major difference, because a sperm or egg or other cell cannot develop into a mature human individual without undergoing radical transformation through fertilization or somatic cell nuclear transfer (cloning). The human embryo is fully human from the moment of fertilization, with the intrinsic capacity to develop into a mature human individual. Indeed, as one author and medical doctor plainly says, "In public debate, no educated person questions the humanity of the human embryo anymore."[25]

The moment of fertilization is significant because it is the beginning of a distinct human being. Many who argue this basic point will refer to conception rather than fertilization. However, there can be confusion about what is meant by the term *conception*, for it is used in different ways, with important implications. Some define *conception* as the point when the embryo implants in the womb. Others define *conception* as the point of fertilization—that is, when the sperm penetrates the egg and chromosomes align. The two definitions have significant consequences

---

22. A third premise could be added, to say that all human beings, as persons, ought to be protected from harm. In that case, an additional conclusion could be added, that human embryos therefore ought to be protected from harm. For the sake of simplicity, the third premise will be assumed, since it is fairly uncontroversial. For present purposes, it will be assumed that if it is accepted that a human embryo is a person, it should be protected from harm the same as other persons.
23. In my own survey of students, when asked which premise is less certain, students are divided on the answer. Of course, this could mean that both premises are problematic, but I do not think that is the case. Rather, there is some confusion because they have not thought about the statements thoroughly.
24. John T. Noonan, "An Almost Absolute Value in Human History," in *The Morality of Abortion: Legal and Historical Perspectives*, ed. John T. Noonan (Cambridge, MA: Harvard University Press, 1970), 51.
25. Best, *Fearfully and Wonderfully Made*, 19.

for what is meant by protecting human life from the moment of conception.

The second definition of *conception* is preferable and more commonly used in everyday language. However, in order to avoid any confusion over the use of the term, I will use the term *fertilization* instead of *conception*. Fertilization is the decisive moment, when a new and distinct life comes into being, and there is continuity from that time through birth and/or until death. R. G. Edwards, cited earlier, disagrees, claiming that life does not begin at fertilization because "life is continuous and patently begun biochemically in the oocyte long before this."[26] Yet this ignores or denies the substantial difference between the embryo and the gametes from which it came. Edwards surely knows better. As noted above, neither the egg nor the sperm alone has the intrinsic capacity to grow into a mature human being. Fertilization is the decisive point, for "this highly specialized, totipotent cell marked the beginning of each of us as a unique individual."[27] The fact that there is much development after that point does not diminish the significance of this point, for "although life is a continuous process, fertilization is a critical landmark because, under ordinary circumstances, a new, genetically distinct human organism is thereby formed."[28]

Megan Best, a physician and bioethicist, agrees: "The first 'significant moment' is when a particular sperm penetrates the egg so that the sperm and the egg individually no longer exist. At this time the structure of the egg wall changes so that no other sperm can enter. This is the moment when the unique combination of genetic material of the new individual is first together within one cell, and all other genetic combinations (had a different sperm won the race) are no longer possible. The gender of the embryo is decided. To choose any later 'significant' point is arbitrary."[29] Arguments against the personhood of the embryo typically assert that personhood requires some milestone or function that comes later in development, such as the primitive streak, implantation, heartbeat, brain activity, sentience, or viability. Yet, as Best observes, "Each one of these points is a significant milestone in the life of the human involved. But there will be many more significant moments that come afterwards. Once you go beyond fertilization, that's all it is: the next stage of development, then the next, one after another."[30]

Premise 2: All human beings are persons. A human embryo is a human being, for a new human life begins at fertilization. However, is each and every human being a person? If not, they may be due some respect, but they may not be considered to possess full moral respect, including the same right to live and be

26. Edwards, "Current Clinical and Ethical Situation," 103.
27. Keith L. Moore and T. V. N. Persaud, *The Developing Human: Clinically Oriented Embryology*, 6th ed. (Philadelphia: Saunders, 1998), 18.
28. Ronan O'Rahilly and Fabiola Muller, *Human Embryology and Teratology*, 2nd ed. (New York: Wiley-Liss, 1996), 8.
29. Best, *Fearfully and Wonderfully Made*, 23.
30. Best, *Fearfully and Wonderfully Made*, 35.

protected from harm that is due to all human persons. But if each human being is a person, then human embryos should be accorded the moral respect and dignity that is attributed to all persons. They should not only have a right to live and be protected from harm but should also not be treated as a commodity to be bought or sold or given away, or produced for research. But *is* each and every human being a person?

Acknowledging a difficulty. A key problem in this argument, and in the larger debate about the status of human beings before birth, is that "personhood" is an attribute that cannot fully be demonstrated, at least not by scientific proofs. It is an anthropological statement— that is, a social, philosophical, theological, or biblical description of human beings. But this difficulty cuts both ways. When the definition of a person is based on some scientific claim, it may be misleading, for it is actually based on an unacknowledged worldview commitment. The science of biology or genetics may tell us when human life begins, but they cannot tell us what constitutes a person. That is derived from certain worldview commitments that undergird our understanding of human beings. No "qualitative" or "functional" definition of personhood is adequate. As indicated, some of the very requirements given for a human being to be recognized as a person, excluding the personhood of embryos and fetuses, could also exclude infants, those who are severely retarded, some who are comatose (even temporarily), some who have advanced dementia, and so on. It is not simply those who defend human life from its beginning who argue this point. Helga Kuhse and Peter Singer, for instance, assert, "It is the beginning of the life of the person, rather than of the physical organism, that is crucial so far as the right to life is concerned." They add, "When I think of myself as the person I am now, I realize that I did not come into existence until sometime after my birth." Following this reasoning to its logical conclusion, they boldly declare that "when we kill a newborn, there is no person whose life has begun."[31]

If demonstrating that the embryo is a person is difficult, denying that the embryo is a person has its own difficulties. Once the identification between *human being* and *person* is broken, it is not clear how and when personhood is to be established. In other words, if it is difficult to prove that an embryo is a person, it is because it is difficult to prove the concept of personhood, period. How do you go about testing to prove that your child or spouse or friend is a person, or that your neighbor's dog or cat or pet monkey is not a person? This is one reason some philosophers find common definitions of personhood, which *exclude certain human beings*, to *include certain nonhuman beings*.[32] As the title of an article in *The New York Times* put it, "Dogs Are People, Too."[33]

31. Helga Kuhse and Peter Singer, *Should the Baby Live? The Problem of Handicapped Infants* (New York: Oxford University Press, 1985), 133.

32. Singer, *Rethinking Life and Death*; Tooley, *Abortion and Infanticide*.

33. This was not a spoof, nor was it intended as a figure of speech. Indeed, the author is a neuroscientist doing experiments on dogs, including MRI scans. This is particularly pertinent for our purposes, given research protocols

Pressing the point that all human beings are persons

Human nonpersons? One of the reasons for affirming that all human beings are persons is that there seems to be no good reason not to. In fact, the distinction between *human being* and *person* appears to be subjective, arbitrary, and grounded in a dangerous utilitarian framework. Consider the logic of the distinction, which produces two subcategories of human beings: "human persons" and "human nonpersons." It appears to be a circular argument, in which *person* is simply defined by some quality—a certain active capacity or function—that some human beings do not (yet) possess. Human dignity is ascribed only to human beings that are considered persons. The reason for the distinction is pragmatic: to exclude a particular group of human beings from the protective care given to persons. That is, they are identified as nonpersons not so that they become objects of special care, but so that their destruction may be justified. Peter Kreeft contends that the category of "human nonperson" is dangerously utilitarian: "I think no one ever conceived of this category before the abortion controversy.

It looks very suspiciously like the category was invented to justify the killing, for its only members are the humans we happen to be now killing and want to keep killing and want to justify killing."[34] In fact, some such category was conceived before and beyond the issue of abortion, for, as Kreeft notes, historically something like this is the way many have "justified their genocide, lynching, slavery, jihad, or gulag."[35]

Similarly, as George and Tollefsen state, "It is perhaps somewhat suspicious" that the claim that the embryo is a "potential human life" is rather recent and "has more or less coincided with the rise in interest in experimentation on early human embryos."[36] As an example, they cite Ronald Green, an ethicist who served on a panel for the National Institutes of Health in 1994 at the request of President Clinton to examine the ethics of experimentation on embryos.[37] The panel faced similar questions about the embryo and research that the Warnock committee had faced a decade earlier. Green writes that they had to ask, "How much were we prepared to limit researchers' activities? How much were we willing to put the health of children and adults at risk?"[38] The implication is clear: if

---

for personal subjects. The author writes, "From the beginning, we treated the dogs as persons. We had a consent form, which was modeled after a child's consent form but signed by the dog's owner. We emphasized that participation was voluntary, and that the dog had the right to quit the study. We used only positive training methods. No sedation. No restraints. If the dogs didn't want to be in the M.R.I. scanner, they could leave. Same as any human volunteer." Gregory Berns, "Dogs Are People, Too," *The New York Times*, October 5, 2013, SR5. http://www.nytimes.com/2013/10/06/opinion/sunday/dogs-are-people-too.html.

34. Peter Kreeft, "Human Personhood," *Religious and Theological Studies Fellowship Bulletin* 11 (March/April 1996): 4.
35. Kreeft, "Human Personhood," 4.
36. George and Tollefsen, *Embryo*, 174.
37. George and Tollefsen, *Embryo*, 125.
38. Ronald Green, *The Human Embryo Research Debates: Bioethics in the Vortex of Controversy* (Oxford: Oxford University Press, 2001), 32. Cited in George and Tollefsen, *Embryo*, 128.

research and possible health treatments that require embryo destruction are to proceed, it must be concluded that the human embryo is not a person.

It is not obvious, at least, how we are to decide which human beings belong to the category of "person" and which belong to the category of "nonperson." Where, for instance, do we place the following, and by what criteria: an unborn human being (further "divided" into blastocyst, embryo, fetus, and so on); a newborn; one who is comatose; one who is severely brain damaged; one with severe dementia; one who is severely retarded; one with activity only in the brain stem?

Human beings are personal *beings*. To divide human beings into categories of persons and nonpersons fails to recognize what the concept of personhood signifies. It is not an active capacity or functional ability. The attribute of personhood denotes the type of being that humans are. All human beings are persons because human beings are by nature personal beings. This points to the nature of human beings rather than any particular active expression of that nature. For instance, human beings are rational beings, possessing the capacity to reason and will and so on; beings of this sort are persons, by their very nature, marked off "from the rest of the (subpersonal) world of nonhuman animals and nonliving things."[39] It is not the active expression of that capacity that makes a human being a person, but the capacity itself, which is part of human nature. That nature, that capacity, is not acquired some time along the way, but is there from the very beginning. These observations are independent of theological or biblical claims, though they are consistent with a biblical perspective.

In biblical terms, human beings are created in special relationship to God, in his image (Gen. 1:26–28). It is human beings as such, and not merely human beings who possess a particular quality or function, who are created in special relationship to God. As God is a personal Being, so humans are personal beings. In this view, the categories are reversed. The category of person is the broader category, which is understood first in terms of God, who is personal God. Human beings are a subset of persons. It might be said that angels are also a subset of the category of person, as personal beings in relation to God.[40]

Biblical and Theological Perspective on Human Life before Birth

A biblical perspective not only supports the assertion that human beings are by nature personal beings, made in the image of God and in special relation with God. It also supports the assertion that personal human life begins in the womb when a new human being is conceived. The following paragraphs will survey some of the relevant biblical passages.

References to conception

Genesis 4:1 describes the first instance of procreation in the Bible. "The man was intimate with his wife Eve, and she conceived

---

39.   George and Tollefsen, *Embryo*, 107.
40.   Kreeft, "Human Personhood," 6.

and gave birth to Cain. She said, 'I have had a male child with the Lord's help'." This verse describes not only the involvement of God in procreation but also stages in the process, where the couple "had relations," Eve "conceived," and she "gave birth." That is, it does not simply offer a birth announcement, as verse 2 does for Abel. While Abel's case shows that the Bible does not always draw attention to conception, the example of Cain is not unique. There are more than forty references to conception in the Bible. In general, its mention draws attention to God's sovereignty over even the womb. Several of the uses involve the drama of barrenness and the delight of fertility: as in the cases of Hagar (Gen. 16:4–5); Sarah (Gen. 21:2; cf. Heb. 11:11); Rebekah (Gen. 25:21; cf. Rom. 9:10); Leah (Gen. 29:32, 33, 34, 35; 30:17, 19); Bilhah, Rachel's servant who bore Jacob two children on Rachel's behalf (Gen. 30:5, 7); Rachel (Gen. 30:23); Manoah and his wife (Judg. 13:3, 5, 7); Hannah (1 Sam. 1:20; 2:21); the Shunammite woman, who was promised a son by Elisha (2 Kings 4:17); and Elizabeth (Luke 1:24; 2:21).[41] Others involve the drama of pregnancy and birth, in the story of Judah and Tamar (Gen. 38:18; cf. vv.3–4); Moses (Exod. 2:2); David and Bathsheba (2 Sam. 11:5); Job (Job 3:3); Hosea and Gomer (Hosea 1:3, 6, 8; 2:5); and Mary's virginal conception of Jesus by the Holy Spirit (Matt. 1:20, 23; Luke 1:31; 2:21; cf. Isa. 7:14). These references are significant. For one thing, they draw attention to conception as

the beginning of life, and to the period of time between conception and birth. Further, they highlight God's work in procreation and his care for the life in the womb from its very beginning, a point that is made by other references to unborn children as well.

Prenatal personal identity and relationship to God

Several biblical texts draw attention to God's personal knowledge of and relationship to children in the womb. For instance, when God calls Jeremiah, he declares to him,

> Before *I formed you in the womb* I knew you, and before you were born I consecrated you; I have appointed you a prophet to the nations. (Jer. 1:5 NASB, emphasis added)

Allowing for poetic language, there is nevertheless an inescapable message not only that God is sovereign but also that God is intimately involved in creating and sustaining life in the womb, and that God's knowledge of and purpose for individual human beings precedes their birth (cf. Judg. 13:5; Isa. 49:1; Luke 1:15; Gal. 1:15).

Nowhere does the Bible emphasize this point more strongly than in the eloquent confession of David in Psalm 139, in which David reflects on God's total, personal, intimate knowledge of him. He begins by declaring that God knows everything about him, including his actions, thoughts, and words (vv. 1–4). He marvels

---

41. Dimensions of these stories of barrenness will be explored in the chapter on infertility and assisted reproductive technologies.

at how incomprehensible and comprehensive is God's knowledge (v. 6). Further, just as there is *nothing* beyond God's knowledge, David proclaims that there is no *place* beyond God's presence, from the heights of the heavens to the depths of Sheol and the most faraway place (vv. 7–9). In addition, there is no place out of God's sight or awareness, for the darkness is as light to God (v. 12). In this context, David declares (vv. 13–16),

> For it was you who created my inward parts;
> you knit me together in my mother's womb.
> I will praise you
> because I have been remarkably and wondrously made.
> Your works are wondrous,
> and I know this very well.
> My bones were not hidden from you
> when I was made in secret,
> When I was formed in the depths of the earth.
> Your eyes saw me when I was formless;
> All my days were written in your book and planned
> before a single one of them began.

It may be objected that David's declaration, like Jeremiah's, doesn't state, let alone prove, when human life or personhood begin. We might even agree, for that is not the purpose of these texts, which are offered as confessions of faith, not proofs of personhood. Indeed, if they are used as proofs of when personal human life begins, they may prove too much, for God's personal knowledge and calling extends to a time even before conception. Nevertheless, these texts remain significant for biblical reflection on prenatal human life. God's knowledge of human beings prior to their existence does nothing to lessen the reality of his care for us from our very beginning (and thus the moral duty for us to care for others from the very beginning). We know from scientific observation when life begins, and references to conception in the Bible are consistent with that knowledge. Jeremiah and David are not concerned with demonstrating when life begins. They do affirm the continuity of life from the very beginning in the womb onward, and they affirm God's knowledge of them and care for them even in the womb.

David's reflection on his prenatal life is in the context of God's knowledge, presence, and awareness of him at all times. This includes a reference to when he was "formless," by which David points to the earliest time that he can imagine. One of the reasons for his reflection is that it offers reassurance (vv. 5, 10, 11; 17–24), for he knows that God has always known and cared for him, from the time that he was in his mother's womb. Interestingly, it also evokes a certain kind of fear and reverence regarding God's inescapable knowledge and presence. This fear and reverence should guide our understanding and treatment of life from its earliest stages.

The incarnation

The significance of the incarnation of Jesus for our understanding of human life from its very beginning should not be overlooked. This is a central "event" for Christian faith, as Jesus rescues sinners by fully identifying with our humanity. It is marked by humility, risk, suffering, and death (Phil. 2:5–11). Jesus does not appear in human form as an adult, nor even as a newborn baby, but rather at the very beginning. While Mary's virginal conception by the Holy Spirit (Matt. 1:18–25) is a mystery, the language of conception and the usual length of pregnancy indicate that Jesus takes on human flesh from the earliest stage in the womb (Matt. 1:18; Luke 2:5). Jesus fully identifies with human beings from the very beginning of human development, so it is reasonable to conclude that human beings are fully human from the moment of fertilization. Gilbert Meilaender notes the significance of the incarnation, that "in Jesus of Nazareth God has lived and redeemed the entirety of human life, from its very beginnings to the death toward which we all go. . . . We have, therefore, good theological reason to affirm the continuity of life from its earliest beginnings to its last breath."[42]

Terminology for the child in the womb

In biblical perspective, it is also instructive that the Greek term βρέφος is applied to both the newborn baby and to the child in the womb. Luke uses βρέφος to refer to the baby Jesus, announced to the shepherds by the angels (Luke 2:12), and then seen by the shepherds in the manger (v. 16). He uses the same term to describe the baby in Elizabeth's womb (Luke 1:41, 44). This is consistent with the recognition that the preborn and newborn share a common identity. That identity is clouded in debates about embryonic research or abortion, where terms like *zygote*, *pre-embryo*, *embryo*, or *fetus* are

sometimes used to differentiate as sharply as possible the newborn baby from the human being that may be targeted for destruction (though they are also used simply to distinguish various stages of development). Words may be effective in shaping perceptions, or causing confusion, but they don't change reality. It is curious, for instance, that someone in favor of abortion rights may insist on avoiding emotional manipulation by using the term *fetus* rather than *baby*, for *fetus* is Latin for "young," or "offspring," or "progeny." While it may be practical to use *fetus* in medical terminology to refer to a particular stage of development, it hardly changes the fact that the fetus is the child of its parents. No child of an expectant mother refers to "the fetus in mommy's tummy." Neither do adults, when the offspring in the womb is not targeted for destruction. It is a baby, and everyone knows that. Recognizing the personal relationship makes all the difference for acknowledging the reality.

The good Samaritan and "fellow fetuses"

Much can be drawn from the Bible that carries implications for our understanding and treatment of human life before birth. One of its teachings that we have seen is central to ethics is that we are called to love our neighbor as ourselves (Matt. 22:39 and parallels; cf. Lev. 19:18; Matt. 5:43; 19:19; Rom. 13:9; Gal. 5:14; James 2:8). We may ask, as the expert in the law asked Jesus, wanting to justify himself (Luke 10:29), "Who is my neighbor?" Is the embryo, or fetus? Jesus's answer was to

---

42. Gilbert Meilaender, *Bioethics: A Primer for Christians* (Grand Rapids: Eerdmans, 1996), 29–30.

tell the story of a good Samaritan, who goes out of his way to care for a man who had been beaten, robbed, and left for dead, even though the man is his enemy. No one else would stop to help, not even the man's own countrymen who were supposed to be spiritual guides. But the despised Samaritan does, for he sees not an enemy but a helpless human being for whom he has compassion, which compels him to care for the hurting man. Jesus then asks the lawyer, "Which of these three do you think proved to be a neighbor to the man who fell into the hands of the robbers?" (Luke 10:36) The expert answers, "The one who showed mercy to him," to which Jesus responds, "Go and do the same." (v. 37)

Oliver O'Donovan asserts that the question, Who is a person? is not unlike the question, Who is my neighbor? They can both be asked in order to offer an answer that justifies our disregard for a class of human beings. Jesus pushes us toward a different way of thinking. "To discern my neighbor I have first to 'prove' neighbor to him," as O'Donovan says.[43] The question concerning embryos is whether we will treat them as objects that may be discarded or as fellow human beings to care for. Reflecting on the solidarity that comes from our common human origin and development, Paul Ramsey asks, "What is this but to say that we are all fellow fetuses?"[44] O'Donovan's conclusion is worth our reflection:

To know one another as persons we must adopt a different mode of knowledge which is based on brotherly love. This implies a commitment in advance to treat all human beings as persons, even when their personal qualities have not yet become manifest to us; because there is no road which leads us from observation first to fellowship second, only a road which leads us from fellowship first to discernment second. . . . Unless we approach new human beings, including those whose humanity is ambiguous and uncertain to us, with the expectancy and hope that we shall discern how God has called them out of nothing into personal being, then I do not see how we shall ever learn to love another human being at all.[45]

Who Is a Person? (revisited)

Early Christian reflection

When Christian thinkers first gave significant attention to the question of personhood, it was not with the concern to determine whether some human beings are, and some are not, persons.[46] Indeed, it was not first concerned with a description of *human* personhood, but with a description of the personal Triune God, and in particular a confession of Jesus Christ, "both God and man and yet one person."[47] In order to describe something of this mystery, early Christians described the

---

43. O'Donovan, *Begotten or Made?*, 60.

44. Paul Ramsey, "Reference Points in Deciding about Abortion," in Noonan, *Morality of Abortion*, 67.

45. O'Donovan, *Begotten or Made?*, 66. Cf. Ramsey, who asserts that we are all "fellow fetuses . . . bound together" from our beginnings, in "Reference Points," 67.

46. These paragraphs are indebted to the insightful work of O'Donovan on this subject in his chapter "And Who Is a Person?" in *Begotten or Made?*, 49–66.

47. O'Donovan, *Begotten or Made?*, 50.

concept of person through nuances found in the relevant terms used in Greek (ὑπόστασις) and Latin (*persona*). The Greek term ὑπόστασις means "substance" or "essence," and it indicates that which "*underlies or supports* all the characteristics and qualities, all the variable appearances which one and the same person might present."[48]

The Latin *persona* adds nuance to the Greek. O'Donovan draws insight from its use in ancient theater, where a *persona* is a mask representing a character. In such dramas, an actor may play more than one role, or the same role may be shared by several actors. In order to follow the story, the mask is critical, for it allows the audience to recognize a particular character through the various appearances in the drama. It is crucial to recognize the *persona* because it represents "not simply the reappearance of the actor but the reappearance of the character. A *persona* is an individual appearance that has continuity through a story."[49] The implication for our understanding of "person" is significant, for there is a historical dimension. A person is someone with a history, and with whom we may have a relationship through time. "Person" refers to an "'identity,' that which constitutes sameness between one appearance and another, and so makes us beings with histories and names."[50] This sense of "appearance" and history is not a matter of "quality" or "function" as such, but a character that exists in relation to others and is identifiable through time.

The two terms complement one another. O'Donovan observes, "When one spoke of a 'person' one spoke of these different, successive, and changing appearances as one connected appearance; when one spoke of 'hypostasis' one spoke of something that underlay them all and so made them one, the hidden thread of individual existence on which, so to speak, they were all hung like clothes on a line."[51]

Continuity from fertilization

Particular qualities do not define what it means to be a person. That is, a person does not emerge with particular qualities; rather, certain qualities emerge over time in a particular person. The argument made above is that every human being is a person, so that a person's history begins with his or her first appearance as a human being, at fertilization. Development alters our appearance to a greater or lesser degree, but not our essence. To illustrate this point, consider an elderly man, John, who entertains a visitor by showing his autobiography in his book of photographs:

- The tall, yet worn, grey haired, seventy-five-year-old, at his retirement dinner;
- The slightly overweight, clean-shaven, brown-haired, forty-five-year-old salesman with a receding hairline;
- The sturdy, athletic, bearded twenty-one-year-old, at college graduation;

48. O'Donovan, *Begotten or Made?*, 52.
49. O'Donovan, *Begotten or Made?*, 50.
50. O'Donovan, *Begotten or Made?*, 51.
51. O'Donovan, *Begotten or Made?*, 52–53.

- The thin, long blond-haired, fifteen-year-old high school student;
- The awkward eleven-year-old middle school kid, with braces and a buzz cut;
- The little six-year-old, just starting school with missing teeth;
- The preschool child at home, playing with toys;
- The toddler, first learning to walk;
- The baby on his father's lap;
- The newborn, being held for the first time by his mother.

Through all the changes, it is the same person, John, tracing his life back from near the finish to birth. There is undeniable continuity, going back through the years. But does it make sense to go back further? Certainly, and with the help of ultrasound and, in some cases even fiber-optic technology, it is possible to add photos to the album from before birth:

- The one in a 3D ultrasound at thirty-six weeks, when the doctor needed to check on an irregular heartbeat;
- The one in an early ultrasound, when his parents couldn't tell whether he was a boy or a girl;
- The one before that, seen by the wonder of technology, just days old, somehow navigating his way to his mother's womb;
- And there, the first picture seen of John, just after fertilization, when he was going through rapid cell division.

The point is that even these earliest "photos" depict the same person. It makes sense to say that it is John in a way that does not apply to the egg or sperm before fertilization occurs. It is at that earliest appearance—fertilization—that a life story begins, the story of a person.

It is true that an embryonic human being does not look much like us, though, in the words of Meilaender, the embryo "looks very much as we did when we were that age."[52] Such a statement is obviously not a scientific proof. It is more an affirmation and a recognition that the embryo is one of us, that we share a common identity as "fellow embryos." Moreover, science provides information that fits best with this perspective rather than challenging it. That may seem an odd claim to some, for it runs contrary to how science is often actually used in this debate, emphasizing the discontinuity rather than the continuity between the embryo and the adult human being. It is not science itself but the interpretation of science that leads to differing conclusions.

Further Challenges to the Personhood of the Human Embryo

This defense of the personhood of the embryo is not intended to be exhaustive, and it has not examined a number of arguments that challenge the assertion that embryos (and fetuses) are persons.[53] In the remainder of this chapter, we will briefly consider several of those challenges that are commonly

---

52. Meilaender, *Bioethics*, 32.
53. For a much more complete defense, see George and Tollefsen, *Embryo*.

made, and offer brief responses. While these debates could be given much fuller treatment, the following should provide the main lines of these arguments.

Brain function is a minimal requirement for personhood at the end and beginning of life

One argument against the personhood of the embryo is that there is no brain activity. Since it is widely accepted that a person is considered to have died when brain activity has ceased, it is reasonable to conclude that personal human life does not begin until there is brain activity. Further, it is possible to keep the body functioning mechanically after brain activity has ceased, yet it is recognized that the person no longer lives. So too it is asserted that, even if the embryo is a living organism, it should not be considered a human person since it has not manifested brain activity.

This argument is not convincing, however, and it rests on a faulty perception of brain death. When a person is said to be dead because their brain activity has ceased, it is not merely because there is no brain activity that they are considered dead. We do not think of that human being as a living human being—a living body—who happens no longer to be a person. Brain death does not merely signify that a person's brain no longer functions, but that, as a result of the irreversible cessation of

brain activity, that person has no capacity or possibility of "self-directed integral organic functioning."[54] By contrast, in spite of the fact that brain activity has not yet developed, an embryo is "a complete, unified, self-integrating" human being.[55]

Implications from the natural loss of embryos

Another objection is that the large loss of embryonic life in natural circumstances—where fertilization has occurred in the human body but the embryo does not survive—suggests that the embryo is not a person. Put differently, one of the implications of considering the embryo to be a person is that a massive number of persons die before birth. One embryology textbook cites a study that estimates the number at about 45 percent.[56] Some estimates are even higher.

In response, first, it appears that a significant percentage of natural embryonic loss is caused by chromosomal abnormalities.[57] In some cases, abnormalities in the process of fertilization may produce what must be considered something other than a human embryo, such as when an egg that lacks a nucleus is penetrated by more than one sperm.[58] Still, even considering such examples, there may be significant loss of embryonic life. That leads to a second response, that the number of embryos that perish naturally does not say anything definitive about their nature or the

---

54. George and Tollefsen, *Embryo*, 133.
55. George and Tollefsen, *Embryo*, 134.
56. Moore and Persaud, *The Developing Human*, 42.
57. Moore and Persaud, *The Developing Human*, 42–43.
58. George and Tollefsen, *Embryo*, 134.

moral respect that is owed them. If moral respect is determined by the mortality rate, are human beings of less value where there is a higher rate of miscarriage or infant mortality? For that matter, where there is a high death rate due to disease or natural disaster—both of which are analogous to natural loss of embryonic life—should we think of those who died as nonpersons, or seek to justify killing others of the same age (which in that case would represent every point in the human life cycle)?

The problem of monozygotic twinning

In essence, this challenge to the personhood of the human embryo is that monozygotic twinning may occur in the first two weeks after fertilization.[59] Monozygotic twinning (identical twins) occurs when a single egg is fertilized by a single sperm, and subsequently two embryos—or zygotes—develop from the division of one. (Dizygotic twinning—fraternal twins—occurs when two different eggs are fertilized by two different sperm to form two zygotes.) If personhood is based on an understanding that a human being is a unified whole, then twinning presents a problem, it is said, for if the early embryo is potentially two, then it cannot be understood as one. Until the point is reached when twinning

cannot occur, there is no individual human life, and therefore no person. It is simply a collection of undifferentiated cells.[60]

Several points can be made in response. First, it is not clearly understood what causes twinning, whether there is a genetic cause, or if some external disruption causes the division (something that can be simulated in the laboratory). In any case, it is difficult to see how the possibility of twinning demonstrates that personhood begins only later, or how it challenges the human dignity of the early embryo. If twinning occurs, we have not one but two individual human beings, both of whom, from the moment of fertilization, clearly existed in some form and share a genetic code. The early embryo is not simply a collection of undifferentiated cells. Why should destructive research be allowed on embryos prior to fourteen days, following the recommendations of the Warnock Report, which was based on the relatively rare occurrence of twinning and on embryology that was not well understood? "We now know that this science is out of date. Subsequent research has shown that the human embryo is organized from its very first day."[61] As we have seen, it is undoubtedly the destruction of a human life (and possibly two).

59. Moore and Persaud, *The Developing Human*, 159–61.
60. Some distinguish between individual human life and person. See Norman M. Ford, *When Did I Begin? Conception of the Human Individual in History, Philosophy, and Science* (Cambridge: Cambridge University Press, 1988), 139–49; cf. 119–22. While monozygotic twinning calls into question personhood at the earliest stages, Ford states that "fertilization is the most biologically significant stage in the whole process of the transmission of human life. There does not appear to be any other comparable discontinuity in the process of reproduction to warrant settling on any other stage to mark the beginning of the life of an individual human being. The mitotic cleavages and multiplication of cells from fertilization onwards continue without any apparent prejudice to the unity and continuity of existence of the same ontological individual in the zygote, the multicellular embryo, the fetus, the infant, the child and the adult person" (110). Ford distinguishes the ontological individual from a person, however.
61. Best, *Fearfully and Wonderfully Made*, 36.

The argument from twinning is a form of the argument that the embryo is not an individual human being but a clump of cells. However, George and Tollefsen point out that this is patently false. The reality is that the embryo, even if it twinning will later occur, is a "unitary, self-integrating, actively developing human organism."[62] As an analogy, when a flatworm is divided, each part may become a whole flatworm. Yet it would be wrong to suggest that "prior to the division of a flatworm to produce two whole flatworms, the original flatworm was not a unitary individual."[63] The embryo is functioning as a unified, coordinated human being, which is actively carrying out important tasks for its survival and growth. George and Tollefsen describe this in terms of three goals that the embryo has in the first week. It will try to make its way to the uterus for implantation; it will undergo change in order to develop structures that make implantation possible; and it will seek to "preserve its structural unity against various threats."[64] This is not accomplished by a clump of cells that just happen to work together consistently to achieve what is necessary for survival. The complementary tasks of the various cells to accomplish what is necessary for survival and growth indicates not simply a clump of cells but an integrated, unitary, whole human being (which, by some unknown mechanism, in rare cases produces twins). George and Tollefsen summarize things this way:

> The position that the embryo up until day four or even up to day fourteen is only a mass of cells posits a unification or coordination of perhaps over hundreds of cells, occurring with predictable regularity, but without any cause. Between day one and day four, or day fourteen, nothing is added to the embryonic system that could explain the appearance of unity. That is, if the organization or integration is *manifested* at day four, but nothing occurs between day one and day four to account for its production, then that integration was present from day one.[65]

Acorns and oak trees

In the debate over federal funding for embryonic stem cell research (ESCR), a brief article was published in the *New England Journal of Medicine* by Michael Sandel, a professor of government from Harvard University and at the time a member of George W. Bush's President's Council on Bioethics.[66] In the article, Sandel defends ESCR, in part by challenging the objection that ESCR is wrong because it involves the destruction of human embryos. Just because all human beings began as embryos, he argues, doesn't mean that embryos are persons, or have the same value as mature human beings.

---

62. George and Tollefsen, *Embryo*, 150.
63. George and Tollefsen, *Embryo*, 150.
64. George and Tollefsen, *Embryo*, 151–52. Examples include the prevention of penetration of the egg by more than one sperm, which is accomplished when fertilization occurs by immediately undergoing changes; also the prevention of premature implantation.
65. George and Tollefsen, *Embryo*, 158.
66. Sandel, "Embryo Ethics," 207–9.

To make his point, he uses the analogy of acorns and oak trees, as follows: "Although every oak tree was once an acorn, it does not follow that acorns are oak trees, or that I should treat the loss of an acorn eaten by a squirrel in my front yard as the same kind of loss as the death of an oak tree felled by a storm. Despite their developmental continuity, acorns and oak trees are different kinds of things. So are human embryos and human beings."[67]

This is, at a glance, a potent analogy. Indeed, it seems that it summarizes very well the most common basis on which arguments for the personhood of the human embryo—and against destructive embryo research—are made. However, upon further reflection, it is less potent than it appears initially. Several responses are in order.[68]

First, in one obvious sense, Sandel is correct in asserting that acorns are not oak trees. It is easy to tell the difference, in size, shape, and portability. Sandel's claim holds if he means that an acorn is not an oak tree in the sense of a mature example of the oak species. On the other hand, if "oak tree" means simply the oak species or "oaky" substance, then an acorn is an oak tree. As an intermediate example, we might also consider whether an oak sapling is an oak tree. In Sandel's sense, we might argue that an oak sapling is not an oak tree, but in the sense of an oak species, surely the sapling is an oak (not a maple or elm). The acorn, the sapling, and the mature oak "are, after all, identical substances, differing only in maturity or stage of natural development."[69] So, then, he is wrong to say that acorns and oak trees are different *kinds* of things. Interestingly, Genesis has something to say on this: "Then God said, 'Let the earth produce vegetation: seed-bearing plants and fruit trees on the earth bearing fruit with seed in it *according to their kinds.*' And it was so. The earth produced vegetation: seed-bearing plants *according to their kinds* and trees bearing fruit with seed in it *according to their kinds*" (Gen. 1:11–12).

Second, consider the fact that we experience the loss of an acorn as insignificant, while the loss of a mature oak tree is very sad. Sandel asserts that it is because the acorn is not an oak—that is, because they are essentially two different things, which possess different value. However, while he is right to say that we attribute different value to these two entities, it is not because they are essentially two different things. Indeed, if the mature oak was destroyed in a storm, and there was only one remaining acorn, it would then possess inestimable value, and if a squirrel ran off with the last acorn, it would be very sad indeed. Why? It is because the different valuation of the acorn and oak is not due to their essence but to their instrumental value. An acorn is not terribly valuable to us, unless it is the last one, in which case we would want to plant and

---

67. Sandel, "Embryo Ethics," 208.
68. The following response to Sandel's acorns and oaks analogy is heavily indebted to Robert P. George and Patrick Lee, "Acorns and Embryos," *The New Atlantis*, Fall 2004/Winter 2005, 90–100; and to George and Tollefsen, *Embryo*, 176–84.
69. George and Tollefsen, *Embryo*, 180.

nurture it. The mature oak, on the other hand, has great instrumental value: its majestic size (and the time it takes to grow), its beauty, the provision of shade in the summer, its change of color in the autumn, its quality for building things—all contribute to its overall value.

Third, then, Sandel sidesteps the most significant issue with respect to the human embryo, that it is of full moral value because it is a member of the human species. Of course, an embryo is not an *adult* human being, so in that sense they are different. But it is, essentially—that is, in its nature—a human being. Thus Sandel is simply wrong when he asserts that human embryos and human beings are different kinds of things. Consider the implications of his argument from his analogy, beyond the acorn. Is the oak sapling an oak tree, whose value is worth protecting? Not if compared to a mature oak. Perhaps, though, Sandel would answer that it is, for it has a form like the mature oak. Yet, if we follow his reasoning, we do not value the sapling like we do the oak, for we will pull them up by the root if they have grown where they are not wanted. Yet in his analogy the sapling most closely corresponds to an infant or young child, and surely Sandel is not asserting that infanticide is morally justified.

To press this point further, consider another argument that Sandel makes. To allow for the destruction of embryos is not to say that they have no value, he claims. A human embryo need not be considered a human person to be given significant respect. That

is, we should not destroy embryos for just any reason at all, such as "developing a new line of cosmetics."[70] Yet, why would such a purpose be illegitimate? If the embryo is not valued as a human being, and it feels no more pain than the acorn, why protect it at all? His rationale is justified by a further analogy. We value a giant sequoia tree, and demand that it be treated with respect, not because it is a person, but "because we regard it as a natural wonder worthy of appreciation and awe." That is, we accord it a high degree of instrumental value, so it is not to be defaced or cut down without good reason. He concludes, "to respect the old-growth forest does not mean that no tree may ever be felled or harvested for human purposes. Respecting the forest may be consistent with using it. But the purposes should be weighty and appropriate to the wondrous nature of the thing."[71]

In the first analogy, Sandel compares the human embryo to the insignificant acorn, hardly worthy of our care, compared to the magnificent oak, arguing that the human embryo is not a human being. Yet, in the second analogy, the embryo is considered to be of great value, like a giant sequoia. As such, it should be accorded significant respect—which we surely do not owe the acorn—though it is a respect that may not protect it from harm if it may be harvested for significant human purposes. What is missing, again, is the failure to ground respect for a human embryo, or oak or sequoia, in the kind of thing it is and the kind of value (intrinsic

70. Sandel, "Embryo Ethics," 208.
71. Sandel, "Embryo Ethics," 208.

or instrumental) that should be accorded it according to its nature. If the two analogies are brought together, it would suggest that an adult human being, though of wondrous nature, could be harvested for purposes that are weighty enough! The embryos-and-acorns analogy fails because it does not recognize that human embryos are deserving of full moral respect as human beings.

Conclusion

One of the basic objections to the view that the human embryo is a person is that the implications of such a view are unacceptable. If the human embryo is a human person, then it is deserving of full moral respect, and it should not be subject to destructive treatment. For many, the conclusion is undesirable, for to prevent destructive treatment would shut down promising research, limit the success of infertility treatments, and threaten abortion rights. As we have seen, these implications shaped the findings of committees that were responsible for determining the status of the embryo and the ethical framework for its treatment. The National Institutes of Health panel asked, "How much were we prepared to limit researchers' activities? How much were we willing to put the health of children and adults at risk?"[72] Earlier, the British Warnock Committee stated, "Although the questions of when life or personhood begins appear to be questions of fact susceptible of straightforward answers, we hold that the answers to such questions in fact are complex amalgams of factual and moral judgments. Instead of trying to answer these questions directly we have therefore gone straight to the question of *how it is right to treat the human embryo*."[73] These statements are revealing, and the implication is clear: if research and possible health treatments that require embryo destruction are to proceed, it must be concluded that the human embryo is not a person. This is merely *consequentialist* reasoning.

Instead, proper moral reasoning will move from a determination of the status of the embryo to conclusions about how the embryo ought to be treated. If the human embryo is a human being, and human beings are persons, and persons deserve full moral respect, then the human embryo deserves full moral respect. As such, human embryos should not be subject to destructive experimentation, in spite of the potential benefits for more mature human beings. Rather, as Best argues, "We are to treat all human beings with respect for the whole of their lives, regardless of their particular characteristics. It is not our respect that gives them dignity; rather, it is because they have dignity that we owe them respect."[74] The implications are significant not only for embryonic stem cell research but also for human cloning research, abortion and some forms of birth control, and certain types of assisted reproductive technologies. These and other issues of bioethics are addressed in the next several chapters.

---

72. Green, *Human Embryo Research Debates*, 32. Cited in George and Tollefsen, *Embryo*, 128.
73. Warnock Report, 60.
74. Best, *Fearfully and Wonderfully Made*, 42.

Select Resources

Best, Megan. *Fearfully and Wonderfully Made: Ethics and the Beginning of Human Life.* Kingsford, Australia: Matthias Media, 2012.

George, Robert P., and Christopher Tollefsen. *Embryo: A Defense of Human Life.* New York: Doubleday, 2008.

Gushee, David P. *The Sacredness of Human Life: Why an Ancient Biblical Vision Is the Key to the World's Future.* Grand Rapids: Eerdmans, 2013.

Hui, Edwin C. *At the Beginning of Life: Dilemmas in Theological Bioethics.* Downers Grove, IL: InterVarsity Press, 2002.

Meilaender, Gilbert. *Bioethics: A Primer for Christians.* Grand Rapids: Eerdmans, 1996.

Mitchell, C. Ben, and D. Joy Riley. *Christian Bioethics: A Guide for Pastors, Health Care Professionals, and Families.* B&H Studies in Christian Ethics. Nashville: B&H Academic, 2014.

O'Donovan, Oliver. *Begotten or Made?* Oxford: Clarendon, 1984.

CHAPTER 11

INFERTILITY AND ASSISTED REPRODUCTIVE TECHNOLOGIES

Three things are never satisfied,
four never say, "Enough!":
Sheol; a childless womb;
earth, which is never satisfied with water;
and fire, which never says, "Enough!"
                                    —Proverbs 30:15–16

"Rejoice, childless one, who did not give birth;
burst into song and shout,
you who have not been in labor!
For the children of the desolate one will be more
than the children of the married woman,"
says the LORD.

                                    —Isaiah 54:1

Introduction

"On 25 July 1978, in Kershaw's Cottage Hospital in Oldham, Lancashire, Louise Brown was born. With her was born a new era in making babies."[1] As the title of their book indicates, Peter Singer and Deane Wells see the birth of baby Louise as a *Reproduction Revolution*, for she is the first human being to be born after having been conceived outside of the human body, via *in vitro* fertilization (IVF). Today's high-tech treatments are a far cry from the mandrakes that Rachel bartered from Leah in the hope of overcoming infertility (Gen. 30:14–16).[2] The problem of infertility may be similar to what it was in ancient times, but the possible treatments for it are radically different. Indeed, advances in reproductive medicine have been nothing short of spectacular. From modest beginnings, using technology learned in animal husbandry, such as intrauterine insemination (IUI) and donor insemination (DI), infertility treatment has gone high-tech. The problem of infertility is now met by an impressive array of assisted reproductive technologies (ARTs), led by the success of IVF.[3]

The advances in technology have translated into rapid growth in the number of births from ARTs, in the number of clinics offering treatments, and in revenues, creating a "baby business" around the world.[4] In the United States in 2012, just thirty-four years after the first child was born via IVF, the number of IVF treatment cycles was around 165,000, and over 60,000 babies were born after conception by IVF. At an average cost of around $12,400 per cycle, that represents about $2 billion spent on IVF in one year in the United States.[5] That is double the amount spent on IVF in 2002, just ten years earlier.[6] In 2004, over $1.3 billion was spent on fertility drugs, over $74 million on donor sperm, and over $37 million on donor eggs.[7]

Our Children, Technically

While such procedures make it possible for some infertile couples to have children of

---

1. Peter Singer and Deane Wells, *The Reproduction Revolution: New Ways of Making Babies* (Oxford: Oxford University Press, 1984), v.
2. The use of mandrakes for infertility among Jews is noted by Christian Feller, Lydie Chapuis-Lardy, and Fiorenzo Ugolini, "The Representation of Soil in the Western Art: From Genesis to Pedogenesis," in *Soil and Culture*, eds. Edward R. Landa and Christian Feller (New York: Springer, 2010), 13.
3. For a description of these technological remedies, and of the causes of infertility that they are used to overcome, see Sandra L. Glahn and William R. Cutrer, *The Infertility Companion: Hope and Help for Couples Facing Infertility* (Grand Rapids: Zondervan, 2004). See also the Society for Assisted Reproductive Technology at www.sart.org, and the American Society for Reproductive Medicine, www.reproductivefacts.org.
4. The "commerce of conception" in the United States is discussed by Debra L. Spar in her book *The Baby Business: How Money, Science, and Politics Drive the Commerce of Conception* (Boston: Harvard Business School Publishing Corporation, 2006).
5. Michaeleen Doucleff, "IVF Baby Boom: Births from Fertility Procedures Hit New High," NPR, February 18, 2014, http://www.npr.org/blogs/health/2014/02/18/279035110/ivf-baby-boom-births-from-fertility-procedure-hit-new-high. See also the Society for Assisted Reproductive Technology and the American Society for Reproductive Medicine.
6. Debra Spar reports the 2002 revenue for IVF treatment at $1,038,528,000. Spar, *Baby Business*, 3 (table 1.1).
7. Spar, *Baby Business*, 3 (table 1.1).

their own, technology must be held in check by moral limits, which are at points difficult to define and concerning which there is little consensus. For some clinics and patients, there seem to be *no* limits. The following cases are the stuff of headlines, what we might call "extreme ARTs":

- Junior and Mary Sue Davis had seven embryos in frozen storage from IVF when they divorced. Mary Sue sought custody of the embryos, in order to donate them to a couple seeking a child. Junior did not want their children to be born after their marriage ended. The court decided in his favor and the embryos were destroyed.[8]

- Christa Uchytil was unable to carry a child, though her ovaries functioned normally. After IVF, using her eggs and her husband Kevin's sperm, Christa's mother Arlette served as a surrogate and gave birth to her own twin grandchildren.[9]

- After Keivin Cohen, an Israeli soldier, was killed, his parents had his sperm extracted posthumously. After a four-year legal battle, they won the right to impregnate a twenty-five-year-old woman, chosen from over two hundred women who volunteered to help. Their lawyer declared it a "boost for family rights."[10]

- In 2005, a sixty-six-year-old Romanian woman, Adriana Iliescu, made headlines at the time as the oldest woman to give birth using donor insemination, following nine years of fertility treatment.[11] This dubious record was eclipsed in the same year, when Maria del Carmen Bousada gave birth to twins at age sixty-six, 130 days Iliescu's senior. Bousada died three years later at age sixty-nine.[12] Meanwhile, in 2010, at age seventy-two, Iliescu was contemplating having another child.[13]

- In the attempt to have a child, Melanie Thernstrom and Michael Callahan went through six cycles of IVF without success. Undeterred, they used Michael's sperm and eggs from an anonymous donor to conceive embryos that were then placed for implantation into two different surrogate mothers. The babies, dubbed "Twiblings," were born five days apart. Melanie said she "can't

---

8. *Time*, "Conflicted Custody," March 8, 1993, http://content.time.com/time/magazine/article/0,9171,977890,00.html.

9. New York Times News Service, "Woman Is Pregnant with Grandchildren," *Chicago Tribune*, August 6, 1991, https://www.chicagotribune.com/news/ct-xpm-1991-08-06-9103260265-story.html. At the time, this was headline news. Now there have been multiple cases of mothers serving as surrogates for their daughters, giving birth to their grandchildren.

10. BBC, "Mother Wins Dead Son Sperm Case," January 19, 2007, http://news.bbc.co.uk/2/hi/middle_east/6279061.stm.

11. BBC, "Romanian Woman Gives Birth at 66," January 16, 2005, http://news.bbc.co.uk/2/hi/europe/4179057.stm.

12. Associated Press, "World's Oldest New Mom Dies, Leaves 2 Toddlers," NBC News, July 15, 2009, http://www.nbcnews.com/id/31921390/ns/health-womens_health/t/worlds-oldest-new-mom-dies-leaves-toddlers.

13. Helen Weathers, "Broody Again at 72," *Daily Mail*, November 14, 2010, http://www.dailymail.co.uk/femail/article-1329255/Worlds-oldest-mother-Adriana-Iliescu-broody-72.html.

imagine having children any other way."[14]

- James Alan Mack Jr. is the son of James and Linda. His paternal line is simple: James is his biological and social father. His maternal line is more complex. Linda was unable to provide an egg or carry the child, so James's sister Kathy agreed to be a surrogate. She could not contribute the egg, however, since she is the father's sister. So Linda's sister Ann agreed to be the egg donor. Thus little Jimmy's gestational mother is his aunt Kathy, his genetic mother is his aunt Ann, and his social mother—Linda, his father's wife—is his genetic aunt.[15]

Cases such as these led ethicist Michael Banner to state, "We have in recent times multiplied significantly the occasions on which the question 'who are my mother and my brothers?,' taken quite literally, could have a use."[16] These cases raise acute moral questions, for technology demonstrates what *can* be done, but it doesn't tell us what *should* or *should not* be done to overcome infertility.

The questions raised about ARTs, and our understanding of infertility, reveal several things about Christian ethics. First, it illustrates the breadth of Christian ethics, which, grounded in the Bible and theology, intersects with philosophy, science, medicine, politics, and other fields, and is at the center of many challenges in pastoral ministry. Second, it raises questions about the authority and relevance of the Bible in a technological age, and about how we are to discern what to do when the Bible doesn't speak explicitly about a particular issue. Does the Bible have something to say about infertility, and even about the use of reproductive technology? How should we think about such procedures, and how should we evaluate them morally? Third, then, it indicates the importance of moral reasoning, and the relation between reflection and deliberation, for one's judgment about ARTs will be shaped by one's worldview and understanding of marriage, procreation, parenting, and other issues.

The Moral Debate about ARTs

There has been a wide spectrum of views concerning ARTs, even among Christians. Some argue that they ought to be rejected altogether, while others embrace them as good news for infertile couples. A case in point is found in the first edition of the book *On Moral Medicine*, edited by Stephen Lammers and Allen Verhey, a significant text on theology and medical ethics, where two opposing perspectives are presented in consecutive essays. Janet Dickey McDowell argues that "conceptions via IVF ought not simply

---

14. "Meet the 'Twiblings': The Baby Brother and Sister Born from Two Different Wombs," *Daily Mail*, January 5, 2011, http://www.dailymail.co.uk/health/article-1344116/Meet-twiblings-The-baby-brother-sister-born-different-wombs.html. See also Melanie Thernstrom, "Meet the Twiblings," *New York Times Magazine*, December 29, 2010, http://www.nytimes.com/2011/01/02/magazine/02babymaking-t.html.
15. William Plummer and Lynn Emmerman, "And Baby Makes Five," *People*, March 15, 1993, 73–74.
16. Michael Banner, *Christian Ethics and Contemporary Moral Problems* (Cambridge: Cambridge University Press, 1999), 225.

to be tolerated; they should be celebrated, for they enable otherwise infertile couples to join in passing along the gift of life."[17] By contrast, Paul Ramsey insists that "*in vitro* fertilization and embryo transfer should not be allowed by medical policy or public policy in the United States—not now, not ever."[18] These early responses to IVF represent strong opposing opinions expressed concerning ARTs.

With such strong opinions, grounded in theological and biblical principles, among other things, it might be suggested that the debate is interminable, and that we are unable to answer with confidence questions like, What is the path of discipleship for infertile couples, and how should pastors and friends counsel them? In my view, it is not necessary to adopt Ramsey's complete rejection of IVF or other ARTs, but neither should we accept their use without qualification. Instead, by reflection on marriage, procreation, and infertility, it is possible to offer criteria by which to reject the use of some forms, to accept others as a possible means for infertile couples to have children, and to urge caution with regard to others. In all cases, it is critical to exercise careful reflection and deliberation.

Before discussing relevant criteria, it is important to offer some moral reflection. If we are to deliberate about the use of reproductive technologies, we need to understand something of the context for their use. If

ARTs are the solution to the problem of infertility, how should we best understand infertility? The problem of infertility is not simply that someone wants a child and cannot have one. It goes deeper than that. Infertility is a problem, and is experienced as a deep hurt, because God's intent in creation is for human beings—and all living things—to be fruitful. We are wired with a God-given desire for children. Of course, good desires and goals must be constrained by good acts, which is why infertile couples need to be guided by wisdom in the pursuit of the good desire for children. In what follows, I will survey the Bible for reflection on the promise of procreation and the problem of infertility, and then suggest criteria to shape our deliberation concerning the possible use of assisted reproductive technologies.

Biblical Reflection on Fruitfulness and Barrenness

The Promise of Procreation

The problem of barrenness in Scripture is set against the background of the blessing of fertility. The account of creation in Genesis 1 emphasizes the goodness and bounty of all that God has created. The mandate of procreation is presented not primarily as a command with a corresponding duty but as a blessing with a corresponding promise that God's purpose will be fulfilled. It is something that human beings would naturally

---

17. Janet Dickey McDowell, "Ethical Implications of In Vitro Fertilization," in *On Moral Medicine: Theological Perspectives in Medical Ethics*, eds. Stephen E. Lammers and Allen Verhey (Grand Rapids: Eerdmans, 1987), 337.
18. Paul Ramsey, "On In Vitro Fertilization," in Lammers and Verhey, *On Moral Medicine*, 339.

pursue and receive gladly, and it is tied to the other mandates given to those who are created in God's image: "God blessed them, and God said to them, 'Be fruitful, multiply, fill the earth, and subdue it. Rule the fish of the sea, the birds of the sky, and every creature that crawls on the earth'" (Gen. 1:28). The desire for children is good, and springs from God's purposes in creation.

However, those purposes are threatened by human rebellion in the fall. I will return shortly to the problem of barrenness as a consequence of sin and a dramatic contrast to God's creation purposes. First, note that fruitfulness continues to be part of God's blessings after the fall, and is taken up in his covenantal purposes. After the flood that destroys nearly all living creatures, including humankind, God gives a word of hope and blessing in his covenant with Noah, repeating the words of blessing in creation, "Be fruitful and multiply and fill the earth" (Gen. 9:1, 7). How reassuring that God repeats his blessing of fruitfulness in the face of uncertainty after such devastation.

While all of humanity is blessed by fruitfulness after the flood, the primary biblical storyline shifts from humankind in general to a particular person, Abraham, and a particular nation, Israel, called by God to live out his purposes in the world. God's purpose in calling Abraham is to bless all nations through him, and that purpose is closely connected to the blessing of procreation, by which God promises to make Abraham into a great nation (Gen. 12:1–3; 15:5–6; 17:1–8). God's promise to Abraham is repeated to the patriarchs Isaac (Gen. 26:4–5)

and Jacob (Gen. 28:14). Exodus 1:7 calls attention to God's faithfulness to his promise to make Abraham's descendants numerous, even when they live as sojourners in Egypt: "The Israelites were fruitful, increased rapidly, multiplied, and became extremely numerous so that the land was filled with them." The significance of procreation as a promise from God is further seen in God's covenant with Israel, as it is a blessing for Israel's obedience to God (Lev. 26:9; Deut. 7:13; 28:11; cf. Exod. 23:26; Deut. 7:14).

The Bible thus underscores that procreation is a blessing from God in creation and in his covenant with Noah, and with Abraham, Isaac, and Jacob, and the entire nation of Israel. As such, Israel's understanding of procreation as a blessing from God to be desired is well summarized in Psalm 127:3–5:

> Sons are indeed a heritage from the LORD,
> offspring, a reward.
> Like arrows in the hand of a warrior
> are the sons born in one's youth.
> Happy is the man who has filled his quiver
> with them.
> They will never be put to shame
> when they speak with their enemies at the
> city gate.

The Problem of Barrenness

Set against the background of fruitfulness as a desirable blessing from God is the problem of barrenness. The perspective on barrenness in the Bible is multifaceted. It is clearly contrary to God's creation purposes, and it is a result—at least in a general sense—of human sin. It is in sharp contrast to the blessing of procreation in Israel's relationship with God, where fruitfulness is promised for Israel's obedience and barrenness is threatened for disobedience (Deut. 28:63; Jer. 15:7; Ezek. 5:17; Hosea 9:10–18; cf. Gen. 20:17–18; Lev. 20:20–21; 2 Sam. 6:23; Jer. 22:30; Job 18:19). In Hosea, the threat is progressive: no birth, no pregnancy, not even conception, and even if children are born they will die (Hosea 9:11–12). This serves as a warning that the nation may be removed entirely because of persistent and unrepentant rebellion against God and the abandonment of the covenant, in spite of repeated warnings.

However, even though barrenness is threatened against Israel for disobedience, there is good reason not to draw the conclusion that barrenness in particular cases is the direct result of an individual's sin. The primary emphasis of the threat of barrenness is corporate punishment for Israel if the nation abandons God, and not necessarily as a punishment for the sin of an individual.[19] Indeed, the Bible cautions us not to draw a tight correspondence between sin and hardship or between obedience and prosperity. For instance, various psalms lament that God's enemies seem to prevail and succeed, and Jesus affirms that God's blessings do not always discriminate between the just and the unjust (cf. Ps. 13:2; 38:19; 73:12, 82:2; Matt. 5:45). In addition, Jesus makes clear that calamity is not necessarily the result of an individual's sin (Luke 13:1–5), a lesson that is a central feature of the book of Job. Indeed, this point is also a feature of the stories of barren women in the Bible, whose barrenness is not attributed to their sin. Rather, it is presented as a matter of fact and faith, and it is taken up into the redemptive purposes of God.

Stories of barrenness and hope: a matter of fact and faith

The stories of barren women in the Bible stretch from Genesis to Luke. These stories illustrate God's mercy and compassion toward those who are suffering, and how a tragedy of human existence can be taken up into the purposes of God in redemptive history. As such, they provide an understanding of the ultimate significance of procreation and barrenness. A perspective emerges in these stories, within the broader story arc of Scripture, in which barrenness is not understood as a punishment for sin but as a matter of fact and faith, wherein God acts to fulfill his promises and purposes in the face of seemingly insurmountable difficulties. Consider some of the following features of these stories.[20]

---

19. Even when it appears that punishment is connected to an individual sin, there is some ambiguity. For instance, in response to sexual sin, it is possible that the cause of childlessness is that the sinful person is punished with death before having children (e.g., Lev. 20:20–21). In the case of David's wife Michal (2 Sam. 6:23), it may be that her conjugal rights are denied, leaving her childless; it may, in fact, be related to the complete rejection of the house of Saul, since Michal is Saul's daughter. See Robert Gordon *1 & 2 Samuel: A Commentary* (Exeter, UK: Paternoster, 1986), 235.

20. For an analysis of the stories of barren women, particularly as discussed in Jewish midrash, see Mary Callaway, *Sing O Barren One: A Study in Comparative Midrash*, SBL Dissertation Series 91 (Atlanta: Scholars Press, 1986);

Barrenness is a matter of fact. In these stories, barrenness is not attributed to sin. Indeed, no reason is given; it is simply stated as a matter of fact in each of the following cases: Sarai/Sarah (Gen. 11:30), Rebekah (Gen. 25:21), Rachel (Gen. 29:31), Leah (secondary infertility, after having children; Gen. 29:35), the unnamed wife of Manoah (Judg. 13:2), Hannah (1 Sam. 1:2,5), the Shunammite woman (2 Kings 4:14), and Elizabeth (Luke 1:7).

Barrenness is a painful experience. In ancient Israel, barrenness is depicted as a particularly devastating and painful experience. This tragedy is expressed by those who suffer, and is even offered as a proverbial example of desperation and angst:

- Abraham (then Abram) expresses to God his anxiety about his infertility, saying, "Lord God, what can you give me, since I am childless and the heir of my house is Eliezer of Damascus?" (Gen. 15:2).
- Sarah's pain is compounded by the fact that her servant Hagar becomes pregnant when Sarah gives her to Abram. She exclaims to Abram, "You are responsible for my suffering! I put my slave in your arms, and when she saw that she was pregnant, I became contemptible to her" (Gen. 16:5).
- Rachel similarly expresses to Jacob her agony, in words that are understood by many who are infertile, exclaiming, "Give me sons, or I will die!" (Gen. 30:1).

- Hannah's distress, like Sarah's, is made worse by the derision she receives from Peninnah, her husband's fertile second wife: "Her rival would taunt her severely just to provoke her, because the LORD had kept Hannah from conceiving. Year after year, when she went up to the LORD's house, her rival taunted her in this way. Hannah would weep and would not eat" (1 Sam. 1:6–7).
- Elizabeth's pain is revealed only after she conceives, when she says, "The Lord has done this for me. He has looked with favor in these days to take away my disgrace among the people" (Luke 1:25).
- Nowhere is the pain of barrenness put more poignantly than in Proverbs 30:15–16: "Three things are never satisfied; four never say, 'Enough!': Sheol; a childless womb; earth, which is never satisfied with water; and fire, which never says, 'Enough'!" The longing for children is powerful, for children are a blessing from God and he has given men and women a strong desire to bear and nurture children. Proverbs reminds us that childlessness creates a deep void and should not be minimized.

God opens and closes the womb. Barrenness in these stories not attributed to sin, but it is explicitly attributed to God in some cases—and no doubt assumed in others—for it is God who opens and closes the womb.

for a study of the theme of special children who are eventually born to the barren women, see Susan Ackerman, "Child Sacrifice: Returning God's Gift," *Bible Review* 9, no. 3 (June 1993): 20–28, 56.

- Abraham and Sarah attempt to overcome childlessness on their own with Hagar, which creates strife (Gen. 16:4–6; 21:8–16), but it is God who opens Sarah's womb and gives the promised child Isaac (Gen. 21:1–5).
- Isaac and Rebekah were married twenty years without a child (Gen. 25:20, 26), and Genesis says simply, "Isaac prayed to the LORD on behalf of his wife because she was childless. The Lord was receptive to his prayer, and his wife Rebekah conceived" (Gen. 25:21).
- The story of Jacob and his wives, Rachel and Leah, also attributes the opening and closing of the womb to God (e.g., Gen. 29:31, 35; 30:17, 22). When Rachel demands children from Jacob, his response, though perhaps short-tempered, expresses a sense of God's sovereignty: "Jacob became angry with Rachel and said, 'Am I in God's place, who has withheld offspring from you?'" (Gen. 30:2).
- That God opens the womb of Manoah's wife is made clear by the appearance of an angel who announces to her that she will have a child (Judg. 13:3).
- First Samuel affirms that God kept Hannah from conceiving (1 Sam. 1:5–6), and later answered her prayer and she conceived (1:19–20).
- Elisha learns that the Shunammite woman who has cared for him has no child, and he promises that she will have a son in the next year, which happens as he promised (2 Kings 4:16–17).
- An angel appears to Zechariah to announce that his wife Elizabeth will bear a son, and she conceives and gives birth (Luke 1:13, 24, 57).

God's providence and purposes. Barrenness is thus within the providence of God, and it is taken up in the purposes of God. Those who are barren are not scorned but shown compassion by God, who hears their cries. He opens their wombs and grants them children, and they are taken up in his redemptive purposes. What is more, all of the children born to barren women are prominent figures in Israel who are used by God in significant ways in Israel's history: Isaac (born to Abraham and Sarah), Jacob and also Esau (born to Isaac and Rebekah), Joseph and his brothers (born to Jacob through Rachel, Leah, and their servants), Samuel (born to Elkanah and Hannah), Samson (born to Manoah and his wife), and John the Baptist (born to Zechariah and Elizabeth). The exception is the nameless child born to the Shunammite woman.[21] This striking reality suggests that in these stories the primary issue isn't barrenness, but God's providence and purposes at work in the midst of seemingly impossible obstacles. The children granted are not merely to appease the angst of barrenness, but to fulfill the purposes of God. That serves as a reminder that barrenness and procreation

---

21. The exception may be significant, but that significance will not be explored here. Perhaps it is connected to the fact that Elisha does not consult God before promising the Shunammite woman a son.

are not merely personal matters but are to be understood in relation to God's purposes and for God's glory.

Barrenness is a matter of faith. That leads to a final observation, which is a thread through each of these stories: barrenness—like everything in our lives—is a matter of faith. This is prominent in the story of Abraham, who is held up as the paradigm of faith. From the beginning his faith in God is tested. When Abraham and Sarah (then Abram and Sarai) are first introduced, the text mentions incidentally (or so it may seem) that Sarai is barren and has no child (Gen. 11:30). The significance of her barrenness—beyond personal tragedy—is highlighted very shortly, when God calls Abram and tells him to go to a new land where God will make him a great nation (Gen. 12:2). How God will bring forth a great nation from a barren couple is a dramatic test of faith that plays out over several chapters. After a period of waiting, Abram becomes anxious, thinking that what God has promised will come through his servant Eliezer because God has given him no offspring of his own (Gen. 15:2–3). But God tells Abram that his heir will be his own son, and that his offspring will be as numerous as the stars in the sky (Gen. 15:5). Then the paradigmatic statement of faith is made: "Abram believed the Lord, and he credited it to him as righteousness" (Gen. 15:6).

However, Sarai remains barren, and Abram and Sarai struggle to understand how God will fulfill his promise, so they pursue their own plan. Sarai brings her maidservant Hagar to Abram in order that she might have a child for Sarai (Gen. 16:2). Abram is eighty-six years old when Hagar bears his child Ishmael (v. 16). Thirteen years later, the Lord appears to Abram, whom he now names Abraham, and reaffirms his promise to give him countless descendants, saying that it is through Sarai, now Sarah, that the great nation will come (Gen. 17). A year later, when Abraham is one hundred years old, Sarah gives birth to Isaac (Gen. 21:1–7). The focus of this account is not so much barrenness itself as it is God's promise to Abraham and Abraham's faith in God in the midst of barrenness. So Paul cites the story at length as an example for others to follow, and barrenness is taken up into the redemptive purposes of God:

> He believed, hoping against hope, so that he became the father of many nations according to what had been spoken: So will your descendants be. He did not weaken in faith when he considered his own body to be already dead (since he was about a hundred years old) and also the deadness of Sarah's womb. He did not waver in unbelief at God's promise but was strengthened in his faith and gave glory to God, because he was fully convinced that what God had promised, he was also able to do. Therefore, it was credited to him for righteousness. Now it was credited to him was not written for Abraham alone, but also for us. It will be credited to us who believe in him who raised Jesus our Lord from the dead. (Rom. 4:18–24)

The other stories of barrenness also raise the matter of faith, each of which could be developed. However, just one other text dealing with barrenness will be noted as it relates to faith, one that anticipates Paul's connection between Abraham's faith and Jesus who is the object of our faith. Isaiah 54:1 exclaims,

> Rejoice, childless one, who did not give birth;
> burst into song and shout,
> you who have not been in labor!

Given the desperation associated with barrenness in Israel, how can the barren one rejoice and burst into song? Isaiah gives us two reasons. First, because the one who is barren and forsaken will become fruitful, even more fruitful than the woman who now has children, to the point where she needs to expand her tents to make room (Isa. 54:1–3). Second, because her shame will be taken away by God himself, for "your husband is your Maker" and "the Holy One of Israel is your Redeemer" (v. 5), and he will show great compassion and love (vv. 7–8).

J. A. Motyer interprets this as a promise of spiritual fruitfulness for Israel. He claims that "the *barren woman* sings, not because she has ceased to be barren," like the other barren women, "but because the Lord has acted in his Servant with the effect that his 'seed' (53:11) become her *children*/'sons.'" This, he says, is a prophecy attributable to Christ and the church: "The gathering family cannot be explained naturally as a fact (she is *barren*, she *never bore* a child, was *never in labour* and is *desolate*) and is more than can be explained naturally in extent (her children are *more than of her who has a husband*). The church, the Lord's people, are created by supernatural birth."[22]

A similar promise is made to the eunuch in Isaiah 56. The eunuch is also childless, and is cut off from the people of God. Isaiah 56 begins with God declaring that his righteousness will be revealed (v. 1) and realized by those who obey God and join themselves to him (vv. 2–3). And then the Lord declares,

> For the eunuchs who keep my Sabbaths,
> and choose what pleases me,
> and hold firmly to my covenant,
> I will give them, in my house and within my walls,
> a memorial and a name
> better than sons and daughters.
> I will give each of them an everlasting name
> that will never be cut off. (vv. 4–5)

The problem of barrenness is thus seen in a new light. What is enduring is not a physical legacy, as some in Israel believed, but a spiritual legacy. The promise to the barren one in Isaiah 54 and to the eunuch in Isaiah 56 is fulfilled in Jesus Christ. As Paul indicates in Romans 4, Abraham's legacy is one of faith, not of procreation, and his children are those who have faith in Christ (Rom. 4:13, 16). Those who obey God and are faithful to him, who live by faith, will have something that cannot be attained through childbearing—that is, "an everlasting name that will never be cut off."

---

22. J. A. Motyer, *The Prophecy of Isaiah* (Leicester, UK: Inter-Varsity Press, 1993), 445.

Summary of Biblical Reflections on Barrenness

The following statements represent a summary of a biblical perspective on marriage, procreation, and infertility, as reflected the preceding discussion:

- A central purpose *of marriage is procreation*. God's intention in creation is to bless human beings with procreative fruitfulness through the union of man and woman in marriage. It may be tempting to play down this reality, from a desire to forgo children or in the face of infertility, perhaps in order to ease the burden and pain of childlessness. This may be a reason why some prefer to speak of being "child*free*" rather than "child*less*." However, the significance of procreation in marriage should not be minimized, for several reasons. First, it *is* a central purpose, as the Bible reveals. Second, the problem and painfulness of infertility will not be fully understood without understanding first the centrality of procreation. Third, the sting of infertility is not relieved by attempts to minimize the significance of procreation. A term like *childfree* not only doesn't change the reality but also, by adopting a term that is used by those who consider children to be a burden rather than a blessing and who deliberately avoid procreation, seems to minimize *children* rather than *childlessness*.
- *Procreation is not the only purpose, or even the primary purpose, of marriage.* Procreation is not an absolute duty, and

marriage does not lack what is essential to it merely because it is childless. This is worked out more fully in the chapter on marriage, with reflection on procreation and contraception. It will suffice to say here that the integrity of marriage itself should be given priority over procreation. Even apart from procreation, marriage can reflect God's glory and demonstrate God's love, as evidenced by many married couples who are beyond childbearing years or who suffer from infertility.

- *Infertility is the result of sin in general but often not in particular.* That is, barrenness is a result of the fall, and therefore of sin in general, but it does not correspond directly in each case to an individual's sin (Job 1:8–22; Luke 13:1–5).
- *Infertility is a painful reality.* The cry of the barren woman in Scripture, and today, isn't merely the murmur of one who is discontent. It is, rather, the cry of one whose proper desire for God's blessing is frustrated by the curse of sin. It is the cry of the barren womb that is never satisfied, as Proverbs 30 states. It is good to desire children, and appropriate to grieve over childlessness, though grief gives way to hope in God. Infertility should be met with compassion and understanding on the part of God's people.
- *In spite of infertility, marriage can still be fruitful.* Isaiah 54 reminds us of this even as it affirms that our hope is found in God and his promises in Jesus, and not in procreation or any other earthly thing. An infertile marriage can be fruitful in many ways, not least by displaying the

faithful, forgiving love of God, and its outward expression through friendship, hospitality, adoption, productive work, and various forms of ministry to others.

All of this is part of a reflection that is meant to give some perspective on infertility. What remains is deliberation over appropriate ways to respond to infertility. What, if anything, should an infertile couple do if they desire children, and how should a friend or pastor counsel them?

The (Modern) Problem of Infertility and the Possibility of Assisted Reproductive Technologies

The Problem of Infertility

In addition to the reflection on the problem of barrenness in the Bible, before discussing moral considerations with ARTs, it is important to have something of an understanding of infertility in our contemporary context. Here is some basic information on infertility:

- *The definition of infertility.* Infertility is understood as the inability to become pregnant after one year of trying—that is, regular intercourse without the use of contraception, or the inability to carry a pregnancy to live birth, affecting 10–15 percent of couples.[23]

- *Causes of infertility.* According to the Mayo Clinic, infertility is attributed to men in roughly one-third of cases, to women in roughly another one-third, and in another one-third infertility may involve both male and female or a cause is not identified. Male factors include abnormal sperm production or function, problems with sperm delivery, as well as such things as overexposure to certain chemicals, radiation, or drugs like anabolic steroids or marijuana, excessive exposure to heat (including saunas or hot tubs), and cancer treatments like radiation and chemotherapy. Female factors include ovulation disorders, uterine and cervical abnormalities, damaged or blocked fallopian tubes, thyroid problems, cancer treatments, endometriosis, as well as things like excessive exercise, eating disorders, and early menopause.[24]

- *Infertility increases with age.* Infertility and "impaired fecundity"[25] increase with age, disproportionately affecting women. Infertility among married women rises from 9 percent for ages

---

23. See the American Society for Reproductive Medicine, "Defining Infertility," https://www.reproductivefacts. org/news-and-publications/patient-fact-sheets-and-booklets/documents/fact-sheets-and-info-booklets/ defining-infertility.

24. Mayo Clinic, "Infertility," http://www.mayoclinic.org/diseases-conditions/infertility/basics/causes/con-20034770. See also American Society for Reproductive Medicine, "Infertility: An Overview," 2012, 6–14, https://www.repro- ductivefacts.org/globalassets/rf/news-and-publications/bookletsfact-sheets/english-fact-sheets-and-info-book- lets/infertility-an_overview_booklet2.pdf.

25. "Impaired fecundity" refers to "physical difficulties getting pregnant or carrying a pregnancy to live birth." See Anjani Chandra, Casey E. Copen, and Elizabeth Hervey Stephen, "Infertility and Impaired Fecundity in the United States, 1982–2010: Data from the National Survey of Family Growth," *National Health Statistics Reports Number* 67 (August 14, 2013): 7, http://www.cdc.gov/nchs/data/nhsr/nhsr067.pdf.

twenty-five to thirty-four to 25 percent for ages thirty-five to thirty-nine to 30 percent for ages forty to forty-four, while impaired fecundity increases from 11 percent for ages twenty-five to twenty-nine to 14 percent for ages thirty to thirty-four to 39 percent for ages thirty-five to thirty-nine and 47 percent for ages forty to forty-four.[26] A guide book on infertility published by the American Society for Reproductive Medicine states the decline in fertility this way: "Each month that she tries, a healthy, fertile 30-year-old woman has a 20% chance of getting pregnant. . . . By age 40, a woman's chance is less than 5% per cycle."[27]

Statistics tell us something about the frequency of infertility and the use of ARTs. Yet, as we have already seen in the biblical reflection above, infertility goes beyond statistics, to particular cases of human suffering. Contemporary experience confirms what the Bible teaches, that infertility is among the most painful of human experiences. A study from Harvard Medical School discovered that "women with infertility had levels of emotional distress equal to patients with cancer or heart disease."[28] The responses are varied: "Distress, anxiety, loneliness, sleep problems, grief and marital stress occur in many women with infertility who are trying to conceive with or without medical assistance. Men tend to have these problems to a lesser degree." Dr. Nada Stotland, professor of psychiatry at Rush Medical College in Chicago, confirms this, stating that "the literature has tended to show that women regard infertility as the most disastrous thing that's ever happened to them."[29] Kimberly Monroe writes of her experience of the pain of infertility: "Grief. No funeral. No burial. No flowers. No cards. Yet there is a death: the death of hopes of the wonder of a child emerging from your love."[30] She notes, "In one study, 63% of women who experienced both infertility and divorce rated their infertility as more painful than their divorce."[31]

Rachel's cry to Jacob, "Give me children or I will die!" (Gen. 30:1), it turns out, reflects a common experience. It is a cry substantiated not only by the proverbial statement that the barren womb is never satisfied (Prov. 30:15–16), but by vast numbers who suffer from infertility, ancient and modern. In light of the deep-seated, God-given desire to experience the blessing and promise of children, what is a faithful response to

26. Chandra, Copen, and Hervey Stephen, "Infertility and Impaired Fecundity," 7.
27. American Society for Reproductive Medicine, "Age and Fertility," revised 2012, 4, https://www.reproductivefacts. org/globalassets/rf/news-and-publications/bookletsfact-sheets/english-fact-sheets-and-info-booklets/Age_and_ Fertility.pdf.
28. Laurie Tarkan, "Fertility Clinics Begin to Address Mental Health," *The New York Times*, October 8, 2002, http:// www.nytimes.com/2002/10/08/health/psychology/08FERT.html.
29. Tarkan, "Fertility Clinics."
30. Kimberly Monroe and Philip Monroe, "The Bible and the Pain of Infertility," *Journal of Biblical Counseling* (Winter 2005): 53.
31. Monroe and Monroe, "The Bible and the Pain of Infertility," 50.

the problem of infertility? Specifically, how should infertile couples think about the possibility of making use of ARTs?

What can be done?

First, it is worth offering a brief glossary of a few of the things that can be done in the world of high-tech, reproductive medicine:[32]

- **AI or IUI (artificial insemination or intrauterine insemination)**: using a syringe, sperm is deposited at the cervix or into the uterus.
- **Cryopreservation**: the process of freezing embryos, which can maintain viability so that they can later be thawed and transferred to a woman's uterus.
- **DI (donor insemination)**: AI/IUI using sperm collected from a donor rather than a spouse or partner.
- **GIFT (gamete intrafallopian transfer)**: egg(s) and sperm are mixed together and transferred to the fallopian tubes, to allow fertilization to take place in its natural environment.
- **ICSI (intracytoplasmic sperm injection)**: a micromanipulation process where a single sperm is injected into an egg for fertilization, which can be used in cases of low sperm count or low sperm motility.
- **IVF (*in vitro* fertilization)**: drugs are given to a woman to stimulate ovulation and produce multiple eggs, which are surgically removed from the woman

and mixed with sperm in a laboratory petri dish (*in vitro* means "in glass"); embryos are then transferred to the woman's uterus.
- **PGD (preimplantation genetic diagnosis)**: after IVF, a procedure in which an embryo is tested for abnormalities before being transferred to the uterus (with the purpose of being discarded if a genetic disorder is discovered).
- **Superovulation (or hyperstimulation)**: the use of drugs to cause the production of a large number of eggs in order to allow for the creation of multiple embryos in one treatment cycle.
- **Surrogacy**: the use of IUI, DI, or IVF and transfer of embryos to the uterus of a surrogate or gestational carrier.
- **ZIFT (zygote intrafallopian transfer)**: similar to IVF, but zygote(s) or early embryo(s) are transferred to the fallopian tube, to allow for natural migration to the uterus.

What should be done?

These things represent a dazzling array of technical possibilities for treating or bypassing infertility in order to have a child. Yet we are not interested only in what *can* be done, but especially in what *should* be done in response to infertility. Technology provides possibilities for overcoming sickness and disease, and yet it also opens up possibilities for doing great harm. Technology is in some sense neutral in itself, and yet it

32. For more detail and discussion, see Glahn and Cutrer, *The Infertility Companion*. See also the Society for Assisted Reproductive Technology and the American Society for Reproductive Medicine.

can easily shape the way we think and act, as though there are few, if any, limits to the pursuit of our desires. Further, as it is developed and made available for dubious uses, it is an empty statement to claim that it is itself neutral. Rather than succumb to a technological imperative that allows—or tempts—us to do everything possible in such pursuits, it is necessary to establish moral limits that will keep technology in check, lest we be mastered by it.

Moral Framework for Evaluating ARTs: Problematic Procedures and Perspectives with ARTs

The following discussion will consider various ARTs and the perspectives on marriage and family, human beings, and the world that are relevant to the discussion. I will draw certain boundary lines for suggesting whether various uses of ARTs are morally problematic. Readers may draw different boundaries, either broader or narrower, but the hope here is to cultivate biblical wisdom and thoughtful moral action. Attention will be focused especially on *in vitro* fertilization, since it is the most common ART. Much of the focus in the following pages will urge caution concerning certain uses of ARTs, because it seems proper to focus on those procedures that are most questionable. Yet it is worth saying at the outset that

some forms of fertility treatment may be welcomed as a gift from God, as part of the wisdom that God has given human beings to exercise stewardship over his creation and mitigate the effects of the fall.

Before offering boundary lines for the use of ARTs, it is important to note that many couples remain infertile even after pursuing fertility treatment. According to the ART Fertility Clinic Success Rates Report from the CDC, ART cycles that resulted in live births in 2012 was just over 29 percent.[33] Even with multiple attempts, some couples will remain infertile. Before pursuing any treatment, it seems wise for a couple to consider prayerfully the possibility that they may not have children of their own, and may be called to serve God and others in and through the experience of infertility.

On the other hand, infertility treatment need not be ruled out as a proper course of action for some infertile couples. They are well advised to make decisions in advance concerning what treatments they may or may not pursue, and not to pursue any treatment without prayer, counsel, and adequate reflection. In a sense, these things go without saying, for it ought to be the way that Christians approach every significant decision. Yet we often proceed without pausing for prayer and reflection. This is easy to do with

---

33. Centers for Disease Control and Prevention, "2011 Assisted Reproductive Technology Fertility Clinic Success Rates Report," http://www.cdc.gov/art/ART2011/PDFs/ART_2011_Clinic_Report-Full.pdf. This is from 451 clinics reporting in the United States. For a chart showing the 2011 National Summary of ART cycles success rates, see "Success Rates Report," 24. The chart shows that the percentage of cycles resulting in live births, followed by the percentage of embryo transfers resulting in live births, varies greatly by age, as follows: under age 35 (40% of cycles / 46% of transfers); age 35–37 (31.9% / 38.4%); age 38–40 (21.5% / 27.3%); age 41–42 (12.1% / 16.5%); age 43–44 (5.3% / 7.6%); over age 44 (1.1% / 2.1%).

infertility, for it is understood as a medical problem and, like a broken bone, once the diagnosis is made the treatment is obvious—we need not pray and reflect on whether to fix a broken leg! However, in the case of infertility and ARTs, there may be significant moral reasons to forgo treatment. It is to that deliberation that we now turn.

If ARTs represent a possible good, which allow some couples to have children of their own, it is important to assert (if necessary, again and again) that they are not an unqualified good. There are, indeed, some strong reasons for rejecting some ART procedures and the perspectives that ground them.

The willful destruction of human embryos

Perhaps the most straightforward reason for rejecting some uses of IVF and other ART processes is the disregard for and destruction of human embryos. One of the troubling realities is the willingness to take risks, not with our own health and life in the hope of resolving a medical problem, but with the health and life of millions of embryos. The creation of "excess" embryos is a case in point. Consider the typical way that the process of IVF is done (though there can be variation):[34]

- Medication-induced ovarian stimulation ("superovulation") by means of injectables over about a ten-day period is done with the goal of producing large numbers of oocytes (eggs), which are then retrieved (or "harvested") using needle aspiration.

- Eggs are separated, and each egg may be exposed to healthy sperm within a few hours of retrieval (in some cases, ICSI is used in order to inject a single healthy sperm into an egg). Within a day they are observed to see whether fertilization has been successful.

- Resulting embryos (called zygotes in the one-cell stage of development) are evaluated. Infertility specialist William Cutrer writes, "An embryologist identifies and rates, or 'grades,' the embryos from A to D or 1 to 4 based on appearance and evidence of trauma to the surrounding, supporting structures. Grade A (or 1) embryos are perfect; grade D (or 4) embryos have retarded development. B and C (or 2 and 3) embryos fall in the middle."[35]

- Abnormal embryos are destroyed, sometimes after being analyzed for various genetic conditions through preimplantation genetic diagnosis (PGD).

- Of the remaining healthy embryos, one or two (in some cases more) will be placed for implantation.

- "Excess" healthy embryos can be frozen (cryopreserved) with the possibility of being thawed for future attempts at implantation.

In this typical process, a consequentialist perspective is at work, prioritizing advances

---

34. See a description of the process in Glahn and Cutrer, *Infertility Companion*, 151–55.
35. Glahn and Cutrer, *Infertility Companion*, 152.

in technology and scientific "knowledge," the fulfillment of the desire to have a child of one's own, and clinical efficiency over the well-being of the embryo. In the sometimes desperate quest for a child, "excess" human beings are created and those who are deemed unhealthy or unwanted are destroyed. This is a clear case of doing harm to a human subject, something that is prohibited in most medical codes. In the most egregious cases, where embryo transfer results in a multiple pregnancy (successful implantation of two or more embryos), a patient may undergo "fetal reduction" in order to "reduce the risk inherent in a multiple pregnancy."[36]

Beyond direct destruction, the cryopreservation of embryos is itself dubious. As indicated, typically more eggs are exposed to sperm than the number of embryos that can safely be transferred to the uterus. The reason for this is to increase the chance for one or more viable and healthy embryos, and because the use of cryopreservation makes it possible to access embryos for future attempts at implantation without having to go through another full cycle of IVF treatment. In one sense, the mere fact that human beings are frozen in suspended animation should trouble us. It is, unfortunately, a common practice, as there are well over 500,000 embryos in frozen storage at clinics in the United States. And the problem with cryopreservation of human embryos goes beyond the judgment that it is "troubling." The reality is that once embryos are frozen, 30–50 percent will not survive the process of thawing.[37] The percentage of successful live births is lower than with fresh, nonfrozen embryos.[38] Further, it is not known how long embryos can remain frozen without suffering damage. So, for example, in the United Kingdom, there has been a policy that excess frozen embryos must be destroyed if they are not used within ten years. The result is that, according to a British Department of Health report in 2007, over *one million* embryos that were created for fertility treatment in British clinics were destroyed over a fourteen-year period.[39] This mixing of death in the quest for life is profoundly disturbing, signaling that the pursuit of personal (and scientific) desires matters above all else. In addition, the creation of excess embryos is sometimes done without careful consideration of other consequences, and many couples are torn over what to do with "embryos that they no longer need."[40] The fact that the fate of these frozen nascent human beings is considered a private matter—or even a property

36. See Liza Mundy, *Everything Conceivable: How Assisted Reproduction Is Changing Our World* (New York: Anchor, 2008), 253.

37. Glahn and Cutrer, *Infertility Companion*, 176.

38. See the Centers for Disease Control and Prevention, "Success Rates Report," 24. The live birth rate per transfer when using donor eggs is much higher with fresh embryos versus using frozen embryos.

39. Marie Woolf, "IVF Clinics Destroy 1M 'Waste' Embryos," *Sunday Times*, December 30, 2007, http://www.thesundaytimes.co.uk/sto/style/living/Health/article77744.ece.

40. Denise Grady, "Parents Torn Over Fate of Frozen Embryos," *New York Times*, December 4, 2008, A26, http://www.nytimes.com/2008/12/04/us/04embryo.html?pagewanted=all&_r=0.

matter—is another indication of the disregard for human life at its beginning.

Procreation outside of a one-flesh union

A second problem with some uses of ARTs
is that they undermine the one-flesh principle in marriage (Gen. 2:24). In what is
sometimes called "collaborative reproduction," procreation involves not only husband
and wife but a "third party" who contributes sperm or egg or womb. Consider the
possibilities:

1. Husband provides sperm + wife provides egg + surrogate provides womb
2. Husband provides sperm + donor provides egg + wife provides womb
3. Husband provides sperm + donor provides egg + surrogate provides womb
4. Donor provides sperm + wife provides
   egg + wife provides womb
5. Donor provides sperm + wife provides
   egg + surrogate provides womb
6. Donor provides sperm + donor provides egg + wife provides womb
7. Donor provides sperm + donor provides egg + surrogate provides womb

Not everyone considers these possibilities, or at least some of them, to be a problem.
For instance, Stanley Grenz, an evangelical
theologian and ethicist, argues that collaborative reproduction is not morally wrong,
and indeed there may even be a compelling

reason to use it, arising from the gospel and
explicitly Christian convictions.

In defense of the possibility of collaborative reproduction, Grenz contends that it
does not constitute an act of adultery, since
"neither the intent to be unfaithful to one's
marital vows nor the act of intercourse is
present." [41] He argues that such techniques
do not introduce a third party "directly
into the marriage bond itself (as in adultery), but into the procreative process." [42]
As such, he asserts, collaborative procreation could be considered adulterous only
if adultery is understood as "the violation
of the assumed right of each spouse to become [a] parent only through the other." [43]
Such is not the case, Grenz argues. Indeed,
he claims, the New Testament emphasizes
not the claiming of rights, but "the willingness to give up one's rights for the sake
of another." He appeals to the example of
Jesus's sacrifice, and asserts that "a case
can be made for practices involving donor
sperm or egg within the context of marriage." His case is this: "Modern technological capabilities allow a married person,
motivated by the desire to facilitate the
wish of one's spouse to give birth to biological offspring, to choose willingly to
set aside his or her 'right' to be the sole
means whereby the spouse is able to become a parent." [44] The infertile spouse may
consent to such a procedure, since there
is no "intended or physical act of marital

41.   Stanley J. Grenz, *Sexual Ethics: An Evangelical Perspective* (Louisville: Westminster John Knox, 1997), 172.
42.   Grenz, *Sexual Ethics*, 172.
43.   Grenz, *Sexual Ethics*, 173.
44.   Grenz, *Sexual Ethics*, 173.

unfaithfulness," so that the fertile spouse is able to become the biological parent of their child.[45]

Evaluation of collaborative reproduction

This is a significant issue, for thousands of children are born every year as a result of sperm or egg donation, and the number continues to grow.[46] Grenz's argument, in particular, requires a response, because he makes a biblical and theological case that explicit Christian convictions may lead an infertile spouse to embrace the use of donor eggs or sperm for the sake of the fertile spouse. In contrast, I will assert that biblical and theological reflection about the nature of marriage as one flesh implies that couples ought to avoid collaborative reproduction, and that Grenz presents an inadequate understanding of adultery, marital rights, and sacrifice.[47]

First, is collaborative reproduction adultery? Grenz is not the only theologian who argues that it is not. John and Paul Feinberg, for instance, suggest that while DI may be ruled out on other grounds, it should not be considered adultery, since it does not involve a sexual act, or lust, or intimate contact with the donor. The woman does not forsake her husband for him. The procedure is not unitive, "it is purely procreative."[48] Likewise, Norm Geisler calls the charge of adultery "far-fetched" since there is no sexual act with another man, and no lust.[49] This is crucial for his assessment, and he concludes that, from a biblical perspective, there is no moral reason to reject the use of a third party.[50]

Indeed, collaborative reproduction is not adultery in the sense of a sexual act or desire involving another person. However, it is at least possible that an act is adulterous

---

45. Grenz, *Sexual Ethics*, 173. Though Grenz does not think collaborative practices are intrinsically unethical, he recognizes potential difficulties, such as a strain on the marriage, legal complications, trauma for the child, and the possibility of bringing a third parent into the child's life. Yet he does not think these problems are insurmountable.
46. Mundy, *Everything Conceivable*, 94.
47. The following are representative of those who argue against collaborative techniques for procreation, for a variety of reasons. Allen Verhey, *Reading the Bible in the Strange World of Medicine* (Grand Rapids: Eerdmans, 2003), chap. 7, 253–303; Brent Waters, *Reproductive Technology: Towards a Theology of Procreative Stewardship* (Cleveland: Pilgrim, 2001); Gilbert Meilaender, "A Child of One's Own: At What Price?," in *The Reproduction Revolution: A Christian Appraisal of Sexuality, Reproductive Technologies, and the Family*, eds. John F. Kilner, Paige C. Cunningham, and W. David Hager (Grand Rapids: Eerdmans, 2000), 36–45; Roman Catholic Church, Sacred Congregation for the Doctrine of the Faith, *Donum Vitae: Instruction on Respect for Human Life in its Origin and on the Dignity of Procreation*, ed. Charles Connolly (Belfast: Four Courts, 1987); Stanley Hauerwas, "Theological Reflection on *In Vitro* Fertilization," in *Suffering Presence: Theological Reflections on Medicine, the Mentally Handicapped, and the Church* (Notre Dame: University of Notre Dame Press, 1986), 142–56; Paul Ramsey, *Fabricated Man: The Ethics of Genetic Control* (New Haven, CT: Yale University Press, 1970); Oliver O'Donovan, *Begotten or Made?* (Oxford: Clarendon, 1984). Norman L. Geisler, *Christian Ethics: Options and Issues* (Grand Rapids: Baker, 1989), 187.
48. John S. Feinberg and Paul D. Feinberg, *Ethics for a Brave New World* (Wheaton, IL: Crossway, 1993), 218. Cutrer and Glahn agree, saying that since there is "no physical contact between the donor and the recipient" and no lust, then "adultery is not involved in the process of DI." Glahn and Cutrer, *Infertility Companion*, 191.
49. Geisler, *Christian Ethics*, 187. Geisler goes a bit further in an earlier book, saying that "it could in some cases be a great good." Geisler, *EthicsAlternatives and Issues* (Grand Rapids: Zondervan, 1971), 229–30.
50. Geisler, *Christian Ethics*, 187.

even without these characteristics. For example, if the purpose (*telos*) of the seventh commandment is not merely to prohibit the act of adultery but also to protect and promote the integrity of marriage, then various attacks on the integrity of marriage could be considered "adulterous." Jesus declares that wrongful divorce and remarriage is adultery (Matt. 5:32, 19:3–9; Mark 10:2–12; Luke 16:18), and that lust is adultery of the heart (Matt. 5:28). The teachers of the law might have argued that there is no explicit act or even intent to be unfaithful in such cases, but that would miss the point of Jesus's teaching about the nature of marriage and faithfulness. Certain acts and desires violate marital faithfulness simply by their nature, with or without the explicit intent to do so. If the use of a third party entails no conscious intent to be unfaithful, it may still strike at the "mysterium of marital fellowship," as Helmut Thielicke puts it.[51]

Further, we may distinguish at least two aspects of intent. One relates to the aim (or end) of an act, which in this case is to have a child, not to be unfaithful. Yet another aspect of intent relates to means, which in this case certainly includes bringing a third party into the procreative act of marriage. By analogy, consider Sarai's offer of Hagar to Abram in Genesis 16. The intent is to procure a child for Abram and Sarai, yet it can also be said that they intended to do so by means of the sexual union between Abram and Hagar. The explicit or conscious intent is not adultery, but that does not mean that the act is not adultery. While the act is different from collaborative reproduction, it illustrates the point that both aspects of intent—ends and means—are relevant to the overall moral evaluation.

It does not necessarily follow that the use of third parties is adulterous. However, the charge may not be "far-fetched," as Geisler claims. Our judgment turns on whether collaborative reproduction is, as such, an attack on the integrity of marriage. Grenz doesn't think so, for the third party is only brought into the "procreative process" and not "directly into the marriage bond itself." Similarly, the Feinbergs argue that DI is not unitive, but "purely procreative." However, these claims—not to mention the act itself—represent a radical and fundamental disconnection of procreation from the one-flesh union of marriage.[52] The personal presence of the donor is denied, and his contribution is considered *merely* reproductive material. As Oliver O'Donovan claims, "The only basis for a successful defence of gamete-donation is the outright denial that the donor is in any way personally present through his genetic contribution. We must regard the sperm and ovum rather in the same light as we would regard a donated kidney, as human material but not as

51. Helmut Thielicke, *The Ethics of Sex*, trans. John W. Doberstein (London: James Clarke, 1964), 262.
52. See Verhey, *Reading the Bible*, where he argues that "procreative acts—including procreative acts utilizing ART—belong within the context of the commitments of marriage" (290), and that they must involve a commitment to parenting (303).

personally human."[53] Ironically, this denial undermines the very thing that drives such procedures in the first place—namely, the biological connection between parent and child.

It is difficult to avoid the "personal presence" of the donor, for the child that results is not from the husband and wife, but from one spouse and a donor, who is forever personally present in the life of the child. If it is not adultery, it is the intrusion of a third party in the one flesh of the couple's marriage. In any case, if DI is not technically adultery, it is worth noting that some have perceived it that way. One study revealed that for men whose wives were impregnated with donor sperm, "that sperm was emotionally equivalent to infidelity. Intellectually they know that the sperm came in a test tube and was administered in an impersonal, technical way. However, their gut feelings . . . were strong and disturbing."[54]

Second, how should we weigh marital "rights" when it comes to procreation? Grenz argues that there is no assumed right to become a parent only through one's spouse, that the New Testament emphasizes

a willingness to give up one's rights for the sake of another rather than to claim rights, and that an infertile spouse may set aside the supposed "right" to be "the sole means whereby the spouse is able to become a parent" so that the fertile spouse can have a biological child. Such an account of rights in this case is dubious. Why, we may ask, should we *not* assume that marriage implies having a child only with and through one's spouse? That seems to be a reasonable implication of the nature of marriage as one flesh.[55] Adoption is not an exception to this position, for in adoption couples become parents together—neither spouse has a child apart from the other—and they are in the same relationship to the child.

In addition, while Grenz appropriately says that a marriage relationship should not be based on competing rights, his conclusion that the infertile spouse can "set aside" the "right" to have a child only together is far from certain. Whether it is only a supposed "right," or "merely" a desire, it is reasonable to affirm that it is something that belongs to marriage, which cannot simply be "set aside" by consent to the use of a third

---

53. O'Donovan, *Begotten or Made?*, 43.
54. Lynda Beck Fenwick, *Private Choices, Public Consequences: Reproductive Technology and the New Ethics of Conception, Pregnancy, and Family* (New York: Dutton, 1998), 285. See also Ted Peters, *For the Love of Children: Genetic Technology and the Future of the Human Family* (Louisville: Westminster John Knox, 1996), 42.
55. Biblical examples of surrogacy (with Abraham, Sarah, and Hagar), polygamy, and Levirate marriage are sometimes raised as counterexamples that do not fit this picture of marriage. Yet it can be argued that surrogacy and polygamy are not affirmed and indeed are inconsistent with the creation model of one-flesh monogamy. Moreover, in the case of Abraham and Sarah, of course, the child Ishmael was not treated as theirs, and was sent away (Gen. 21). In the case of polygamy, while it cannot be said that both spouses have children only through each other, the children they do have are through each other, not involving a third party. As for Levirate marriage, the whole point is different, to have a child on behalf of someone else (i.e., the dead brother/husband). Yet even there, the father assumes responsibility for the child and the child's mother (as is the case with polygamy), which sets it apart from the anonymous donor who takes no responsibility for the child.

party. Furthermore, the issue of rights has not been eliminated, for Grenz implies that the fertile spouse has a right to have a biologically related child with or without his or her spouse. In response, the fertile spouse should not assert such a right. Indeed, there is no such right, and the infertile spouse should not be asked to "step aside" in order for the fertile spouse to have a child—a child that, in any case, is not *their* own, but *his* or *her* own, with the help of a third party.

Finally, to justify collaborative reproduction by appealing to Jesus's sacrifice, as Grenz does, is also troubling. The example of Jesus encourages the strong to sacrifice on behalf of the weak (e.g., 2 Cor. 8:9). In the case of infertility, it is the infertile spouse who is more vulnerable or "weak," and that vulnerability sometimes leads to an uneasy consent to use a third party. In some cases, husbands "feel they have no right to deny their wives the experience of having a baby, even though they are opposed to [DI]."[56] Rather than expecting the infertile spouse to sacrifice so that the fertile spouse may have a child of his or her own, the model of sacrifice in the New Testament is better exemplified by the reverse. The fertile spouse ought to set aside the supposed "right" to have a child of his or her own for the sake of the infertile spouse.

The biblical picture of marriage as one flesh involves not only sexual union, and through it procreation, but also a life union of one man and one woman, for better or for worse, in sickness and in health, as traditional vows rightly declare. This suggests, as indicated above, that husband and wife should have children only through one another, that they commit to share together the possibility not only of the joy of procreation, but also the burden of infertility.[57] By refusing to bear children through some means other than his or her spouse, the one who is fertile can express the reality of marriage as one flesh, so that together they share the burden of not having a child of their one flesh. Indeed, to distinguish the fertile from the infertile spouse is itself problematic, for we ought not to speak of an infertile spouse, but rather an infertile couple.

The one-flesh principle does not rule out the use of ARTs as such, but it determines that the use of collaborative reproduction is dubious. It remains to examine the perspectives that drive or shape an understanding of ARTs. If we are not to be conformed to this world, but to be transformed by the renewing of our minds (Rom. 12:2), we ought to resist the perspective of *reproductive liberty* within which much of the discussion takes place.

---

56. Fenwick, *Private Choices*, 260, citing Annett Baran and Reuben Pannor, *Lethal Secrets: The Shocking Consequences and Unsolved Problems of Artificial Insemination* (New York: Warner, 1989), 37.

57. Though Augustine held that procreation was the primary purpose of marriage and the only completely licit aim of intercourse within marriage, he marveled at the bond of even a childless marriage, which "although it be tied for the sake of begetting children, not even for the sake of begetting children is it loosed." Turning to a third party to procure a child may be considered one form of "loosing" the bond of marriage. Augustine, *On the Good of Marriage*, trans. C. L. Cornish, in *A Select Library of the Nicene and Post-Nicene Fathers of the Christian Church*, eds. Philip Schaff and Henry Wace, series 1 (1886–1889; repr., Grand Rapids: Eerdmans, 1988), 7 (cf. 3).

The perspective of reproductive liberty

John Robertson articulates a perspective by which he defends virtually all forms of ARTs.[58] For Robertson, a professor of law, the primary framework for evaluating such technology is procreative liberty, which he defines as "the freedom either to have children or to avoid having them." While it is "often expressed or realized in the context of a couple," he claims that it is *first and foremost* an *individual* interest."[59] Though an individual may choose not to have children, Robertson argues that "being deprived of the ability to reproduce prevents one from an experience that is central to individual identity and meaning in life."[60] This "identity and meaning" is derived mainly from the ability to choose, rather than from procreation itself, which is treated as a subjective value that is secondary to individual goals and choices.[61] Procreative liberty is so strong that Robertson believes the use of ARTs "should be accorded the same high protection granted to coital reproduction."[62] It may be limited where harm can be demonstrated; however, objections grounded in "deontological" principles or based on subjective moral convictions, such as the destruction of embryos or collaborative techniques, "seldom meet the high standard necessary to limit procreative liberty."[63] As a result, a couple, or an individual, should be free to pursue virtually any means available.

Evaluation of reproductive liberty

Robertson's argument is relevant to any assessment of ARTs, for, according to Brent Waters, he "provides a representative account of how procreation is now pursued, marking the cultural background against which Christian moral deliberation is conducted."[64] Accordingly, this is a debate about more than the use of ARTs. It is about competing accounts of morality. As Waters indicates, "Displacing a normative framework of marital and familial relationships in favour of one emphasizing individual interests and rights entails a collision of contending principles shaping subsequent moral deliberation."[65]

Robertson's case for procreative liberty represents an impoverished vision—or perhaps none at all—of marriage, procreation, and the family. It is with remarkable ease that he asserts that procreation is primarily an individual interest, undaunted by the fact that natural necessity alone (for now) requires the involvement of two people (at least). It is equally remarkable that he is able to dismiss moral concerns—and nature

---

58. John A. Robertson, *Children of Choice: Freedom and the New Reproductive Technologies* (Princeton, NJ: Princeton University Press, 1994).
59. Robertson, *Children of Choice*, 22 (emphasis added).
60. Robertson, *Children of Choice*, 24.
61. This is made clear by the defense of not just ARTs, but birth control and abortion.
62. Robertson, *Children of Choice*, 35.
63. Robertson, *Children of Choice*, 35, 102.
64. Waters, *Reproductive Technology*, 29.
65. Waters, *Reproductive Technology*, 19.

itself—as of little account in comparison to civil liberties, declaring that ARTs are to be "accorded the same high protection granted to coital reproduction."[66] Against such a view, it must be asserted that procreative liberty cannot override significant moral concerns, and it cannot serve as a sufficient basis for the use of ARTs. Rather, Christians ought to affirm what Waters calls "procreative stewardship," and challenge the understanding of procreation fundamentally as an individual interest, as though the good of children is primarily about satisfying one's personal desires. Procreation should be understood as an outward manifestation of the one-flesh union of marriage in the one flesh of a child, a gift to be received and loved, not first or primarily a right to be pursued and chosen.

This does not entail a rejection of ARTs as such, but a rejection of the framework of his argument. Driven by procreative liberty, it is difficult to know any limits at all to ARTs, as Robertson himself demonstrates. The case studies presented earlier indicate that where procreative liberty is understood as a basic right, "everything conceivable" becomes reality, even if not ordinary, for there are few legal or moral regulations in place to prevent any use of ARTs.[67] The only limitation, other than current technology, is the willingness of those involved. That tells us much about how marriage and procreation are conceived. This raises a final concern.

More perfect offspring: ARTs, the making of children, and the problem of eugenics

In addition to resisting the notion of procreative liberty, it is important to recognize the danger that the pursuit of ARTs can subtly shape and be shaped by an understanding of procreation in which children become a project of our making.[68] It was perhaps inevitable that fertilization successfully accomplished outside of the human body would be described as assisted *reproduction*, using the language of manufacturing. Instead of an unseen mystery that springs from the intimacy of a loving embrace, IVF allowed, and perhaps even encouraged, a different understanding of procreation, one that is more distant and sterile, that can be observed, and over which we may gain control and mastery. The temptation of eugenics, one that has been pursued historically by many gruesome means, is almost irresistible when the sterile environment of the laboratory meets the demand for more perfect offspring and the corresponding rejection of those who are "defective."

Indeed, R. G. Edwards, who was part of the first team to achieve IVF, remarks, "I wanted to find out exactly who was in charge, whether it was God Himself or whether it was scientists in the laboratory,"

---

66. Robertson, *Children of Choice*, 35.
67. Debra Evans, *Without Moral Limits: Women, Reproduction, and Medical Technology*, updated ed. (Wheaton, IL: Crossway, 2000); Mundy, *Everything Conceivable*; and Amy Laura Hall, *Conceiving Parenthood: American Protestantism and the Spirit of Reproduction* (Grand Rapids: Eerdmans, 2008).
68. Ramsey, *Fabricated Man*; O'Donovan, *Begotten or Made?*

and declares with brazen hubris: "it was us."[69] Once in control, we are prone to think we can even offer a better, healthier product of our choice, and do it more efficiently, just as we learned to manufacture everything else more efficiently. Perhaps it is even part of dominion, and thus eminently human. So Joseph Fletcher claims, "Laboratory reproduction is radically human compared to conception by ordinary heterosexual intercourse. It is willed, chosen, purposed, and controlled, and surely these are the traits that distinguish *Homo Sapiens*."[70] Fletcher demonstrates that technology is not merely a tool to help us pursue natural human goods, for it can transform the way we think about "nature"—even human nature—as raw material for us to mold in any way that we choose, creating the illusion that human beings are nearly omnipotent, an illusion accompanied by a sense of omniscience.

Against such a view, we ought to affirm that children are begotten, not made, as O'Donovan has forcefully argued.[71] To the extent that ARTs cause us to forget that, they pose a threat, and such a mindset, if not the technology itself, ought to be resisted. Rather than being radically human, as Fletcher argues, such mastery over procreation may produce what Michael Banner calls a "radical dissociation and alienation" between parent and child.[72] Even the control

is deceptive, for it trades dependence on nature for dependence on technology, and the technician. If we make use of such technologies, we will need to remind ourselves and our contemporaries that children are not products of our making, but gifts of love to be received.

It may be that few hold such radical views, or at least state the case so boldly, as do Edwards and Fletcher. Nevertheless, the language and methods of assisted reproduction ought to give us pause. We should not refuse all technology with the charge that it is "playing God." Yet, especially given the hubris communicated by Edwards, we may heed the words of Paul Ramsey, who asks, "What does it mean, if indeed it means anything, to say that men should not play God before they have learned to be men, and that when they learn to be men, they will not play God?"[73] Technology can be used for great good, but it can also be destructive, and it is often difficult to discern one "end" from the other. Wisdom demands that we place certain limits on our making, and this is especially pertinent with regard to ARTs. But it is difficult to legislate moral wisdom.

Not all procedures should be rejected
Due to some of the questionable uses to which ARTs may be put, it may be tempting to reject infertility treatment outright, as

---

69. Anjana Ahuja, "God Is Not in Charge, We Are," *The Times of London*, July 24, 2003, http://www.thetimes.co.uk/tto/life/article1716703.ece.
70. Joseph Fletcher, "Ethical Aspects of Genetic Controls," *New England Journal of Medicine* 285 (1971): 781.
71. O'Donovan, *Begotten or Made?*
72. Banner, *Christian Ethics*, 225.
73. Ramsey, *Fabricated Man*, 143.

the beginning of a slippery slope that we ought not to risk entering. However, that response seems to be too reactionary. It is easy to lose perspective and think that all treatments of infertility involve high-tech ARTs. That is not the case. Indeed, according to the American Society for Reproductive Medicine, 85–90 percent of infertility cases are treated with "conventional therapies, such as drug treatment or surgical repair of reproductive organs."[74] Treatments that allow a husband and wife to have a child together may be embraced with thanksgiving to God. This is the case where surgical repair is possible. This may also be true of certain ARTs, such as IUI and perhaps IVF, when they avoid the moral problems discussed already. There may still be significant reasons for couples to avoid such procedures, such as the financial cost, or because the husband or wife considers the procedure to be burdensome or invasive, or for some other reason. There should be no sense of a procreative duty to pursue ARTs, even those procedures that are morally unproblematic. These are matters for the couple to consider prayerfully together and with appropriate counsel.

Conclusion

I have suggested that we should reject ARTs that involve the destruction of embryonic life, and that involve collaborative reproduction. In addition, we should reject perspectives driven by procreative liberty or technological mastery, which understand procreation to be primarily a matter of our making rather than a gift of love in marriage.

We do well, in conclusion, to return to the theme of discipleship, to consider further implications of the gospel for our understanding of marriage, infertility, and ARTs as followers of Christ. In doing so, we may recognize not only certain limits but also opportunities that are a matter of moral wisdom. These are offered as words of encouragement, not only for infertile couples, but also for friends and pastors who may minister to and alongside them, and for the church.

First, we should again be reminded that infertility is a painful experience. Instead of quickly offering simple, perhaps well-intentioned, words about God's love and sovereignty, we ought first to try to understand the hurt, and care about, pray for, and encourage those among us who long for the blessing of procreation that has not been realized.

Second, we ought not to minimize the significance of a biological relationship between parent and child. It is a natural bond and a good desire. Indeed, it is part of the divine order of creation, and some techniques that allow a married couple to have a child that is a manifestation of their one flesh should be welcomed, not rejected out of hand. The biological relationship may be

---

74. The American Society for Reproductive Medicine, "Frequently Asked Questions about Infertility: How Is Infertility Treated?," https://www.reproductivefacts.org/faqs/frequently-asked-questions-about-infertility/q04-how-is-infertility-treated.

relativized, but it is not eradicated by the gospel,[75] or by an embrace of adoption, the significance of which is founded in part on the natural parent-child relationship.

Third, at the same time, as Stanley Hauerwas asserts, Christians understand parenthood in more than biological terms, for we are guided by "a moral portrayal of parenting that cannot be biologically derived."[76] An understanding of parenting may begin with the biological. Yet it is expanded through adoption, and through parental roles, including teaching and many other ways of caring for children, that can be assumed by those with or without children.[77] Gilbert Meilaender underscores the desperate measures that some will pursue to have a child "of their own."[78] The tragic irony is that for some couples, the quest is deceptive, for with collaborative parenting, the child is biologically related to only one, or neither, of the parents.

Finally, infertile couples may be a powerful witness that ultimate hope is not founded on having children. Isaiah 54:1 declares, "Sing, O barren one, who did not bear; break forth into singing and cry aloud, you who have not been in labor!" (ESV). These are arresting words. How can the barren one sing? Isaiah does not minimize the distress of barrenness, and this should not understood as a trite word from a counselor. It is, rather, a profound implication of the gospel, precisely because it is

set against the suffering of barrenness. The barren woman (Israel) is exhorted to shout for joy, despite the fact that she has borne no child, because something greater than procreation is coming (and now has come). Her fruit will be greater than the fertile woman, and her shame will be forgotten for she is redeemed by God and belongs to the people of God (Isa. 54:1–8). We can conclude with two implications.

One implication is that a childless marriage can still be fruitful. This is important to recognize since a significant number of infertile couples will not have biological children even after pursuing ARTs. We may distinguish what is central to marriage from what is essential to it. Procreation is a central purpose of marriage, and yet an infertile couple lacks nothing *essential* simply because they have no children. Childlessness can even be taken up into the redemptive purposes of God, and open up possibilities that a couple would not have initially sought or embraced. By being detached from the usual patterns of life, a childless couple, like a single person, may testify to the fact that "the present form of this world is passing away" (1 Cor. 7:31 ESV; see also v. 9), and they may come to see their situation as an opportunity to serve the Lord in a unique way (1 Cor. 7:35; cf. Matt. 19:12).

A second implication is that infertile couples have a place among the people of God. There is in this a call to the church to

---

75. See the discussion of the family in Christian perspective in *Studies in Christian Ethics* 9, no. 1 (1996).
76. Hauerwas, "Theological Reflection," 145, 152.
77. Cf. Karl Barth, *Church Dogmatics*, trans. G. W. Bromiley (Edinburgh: T & T Clark, 1957–88), IV/4, 267–68.
78. Meilaender, "A Child of One's Own," 36–45.

be a place of consolation and encouragement, so that infertility may turn out to be
not meaningless suffering, but an opportunity to receive and to be an agent of God's
grace (2 Cor. 1:3–7). Dietrich Bonhoeffer
wrote that "the physical presence of other
Christians is a source of incomparable joy
and strength to the believer."[79] We are challenged to realize that no one in the church is
without family, for the church *is* family. The
promise of Isaiah is echoed in Jesus's words
that "there is no one who has left house or
brothers or sisters or mother or father or
children or lands, for My sake and for the
gospel, who will not receive a hundredfold
now in this time, houses and brothers and
sisters and mothers and children and lands,
with persecutions, and in the age to come
eternal life" (Mark 10:29–30 ESV). May infertile couples be able to experience and testify to that reality.

---

79. Dietrich Bonhoeffer, *Life Together*, trans. John W. Doberstein (New York: Harper & Row, 1954), 19.

Select Resources

Arbo, Matthew. *Walking through Infertility: Biblical, Theological, and Moral Counsel for Those Who Are Struggling.* Wheaton, IL: Crossway, 2018.

Glahn, Sandra L., and William R. Cutrer. *The Infertility Companion: Hope and Help for Couples Facing Infertility.* Grand Rapids: Zondervan, 2004.

Hauerwas, Stanley. "Theological Reflection on *In Vitro* Fertilization." In *Suffering Presence: Theological Reflections on Medicine, the Mentally Handicapped, and the Church*, 142–56. Notre Dame, IN: University of Notre Dame Press, 1986.

Kilner, John F., Paige C. Cunningham, and W. David Hager, eds. *The Reproduction Revolution: A Christian Appraisal of Sexuality, Reproductive Technologies, and the Family.* Grand Rapids: Eerdmans, 2000.

Mundy, Liza. *Everything Conceivable: How Assisted Reproduction Is Changing Our World.* New York: Anchor, 2008.

O'Donovan, Oliver. *Begotten or Made*? Oxford: Clarendon, 1984.

Rae, Scott B., and D. Joy Riley. *Outside the Womb: Moral Guidance for Assisted Reproduction.* Chicago: Moody Press, 2011.

Roman Catholic Church, Sacred Congregation for the Doctrine of the Faith. *Donum Vitae: Instruction on Respect for Human Life in Its Origin and on the Dignity of Procreation.* Edited by Charles Connolly. Belfast: Four Courts, 1987.

Spar, Debra L. *The Baby Business: How Money, Science, and Politics Drive the Commerce of Conception.* Boston: Harvard Business School Publishing Corporation, 2006.

Waters, Brent. *Reproductive Technology: Towards a Theology of Procreative Stewardship.* Cleveland: Pilgrim, 2001.

CHAPTER 12

ABORTION

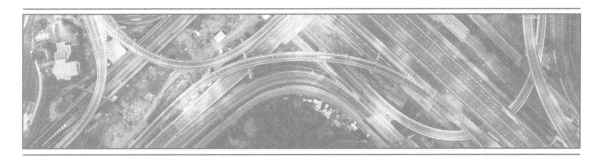

For it was you who created my inward parts;
you knit me together in my mother's womb.
I will praise you
because I have been remarkably and wondrously made.
Your works are wondrous,
and I know this very well.

— **Psalms 139:13–14**

Rescue those being taken off to death,
and save those stumbling toward slaughter.

— **Proverbs 24:11**

Woe to those who call evil good
and good evil,
who substitute darkness for light
and light for darkness,
who substitute bitter for sweet
and sweet for bitter.

— **Isaiah 5:20**

Introduction

Abortion is one of the most divisive and intractable moral and political debates of our time. On the one side are those who believe that the decisive factor is a woman's autonomy and control over her body and future, including the right to choose whether she will continue her pregnancy and bear her child, or end the life of the human being in her womb. This is frequently defended as reproductive health, but that obscures the specific question at hand about abortion. On the other side are those who believe that the decisive factor is the sanctity of human life, and the responsibility to protect innocent human life, especially the lives of the most vulnerable. With so much at stake, it is difficult to have a reasoned debate or to find a compromise. This is especially true because abortion is a perennial election and political issue, about which polls reveal that the public is deeply divided. While a majority believe that abortion should not be criminalized, a majority also believe that it should be permitted for only very serious reasons such as rape, severe fetal deformity, and serious threats to a woman's health and life.

The Irrationality of the Practice of Abortion

It would seem that the deep divide over abortion, together with strong arguments for understanding the unborn child as a human being (conceded even by many defenders of abortion), would lead to a robust skepticism toward the acceptance of abortion, and would include at least significant limitations with regard to its practice.[1] Yet the law of the land in the United States has adopted the extreme view that permits abortion on demand throughout a woman's pregnancy. That is, the practice of abortion, in the United States and elsewhere, simply does not reflect the serious moral, social, political, philosophical, and theological concerns raised in the debate. Opponents of abortion have good reason to claim that abortion is immoral and unjust, even irrational. For it is not that no arguments against abortion are convincing, or that there could be such arguments, but that no arguments are even seriously considered that might challenge the sacred rite.

This chapter will examine some of the key issues and arguments discussed in the abortion debate. While there is a deep political and moral division on this issue, making it a complex political and legal matter in some respects, the radical defense of abortion on demand cannot be justified. The moral issue is the primary concern of this chapter. While it must serve as the basis for political and legal solutions, it is not exactly the same. As I argued in the chapter introducing bioethics, from the moment of fertilization there exists a human being that deserves and demands our care and protection. Abortion is thus not justified except in extreme cases that threaten the mother's life.

To condemn abortion is not to deny that there are complexities to be solved concerning

---

1. This point is made by Michael Banner concerning abortion in the United Kingdom in *The Practice of Abortion: A Critique* (London: Darton, Longman & Todd, 1999), 44.

issues that lead women to seek an abortion. Lives are often dramatically affected by unplanned pregnancies, complicated by a broken relationship or lack of financial support, or overwhelming circumstances with other children to care for, or the disruption of plans for the future, or in rare cases even by pregnancy following sexual assault. It is important to consider and find solutions to these situations. But it is critical first to consider the issue in its most basic or general form, for if we begin with the most difficult challenges, solving moral problems from the view of "emergency and expediency,"[2] we will most certainly take wrong turns and reach dubious conclusions. At its most basic, the morality of abortion is simple.

Bonhoeffer's "Simple View"

With the fierce contemporary debate on abortion, it may surprise some today that when the noted German theologian Dietrich Bonhoeffer addresses the issue, he doesn't even acknowledge a debate. Rather, he takes a straightforward and "simple view," as Michael Banner describes it.[3] Bonhoeffer asserts,

> To kill the fruit in the mother's womb is to injure the right to life that God has bestowed on the developing life. Discussion of the question whether a human being is already present confuses the simple fact that, in any case, God wills to create a human being and that the life of this developing human being has been deliberately taken. And this is nothing but murder. Various motives may lead to such an act. It may be a deed of despair from the depths of human desolation or financial need, in which case guilt falls often more on the community than on the individual. It may be that on this very point money can cover over a great deal of careless behavior, whereas among the poor even the deed done with great reluctance comes more easily to light. Without doubt, all this decisively affects one's personal, pastoral attitude toward the person concerned; but it cannot change the fact of murder. The mother, for whom this decision would be desperately hard because it goes against her own nature, would certainly be the last to deny the weight of guilt.[4]

The simple declaration that abortion is "nothing but murder" is surprising partly because for Bonhoeffer the matter is simple. As Banner writes, "This critical attitude is so very obviously the right and proper one as to stand in need of no extended defence."[5] Indeed, the above citation is essentially all that Bonhoeffer has to say directly on the matter. Such a perspective can barely be comprehended or even tolerated by many in our day—including many Christians—let

---

2. So Oliver O'Donovan, *The Christian and the Unborn Child*, 2nd ed., Grove Booklet on Ethics 1 (Nottingham: Grove, 1975), 3.
3. Banner, *Practice of Abortion*, 3.
4. Dietrich Bonhoeffer, *Ethics*, ed. Clifford J. Green, trans. Reinhard Krauss, Charles C. West, and Douglas W. Stott, Dietrich Bonhoeffer Works 6 (Minneapolis: Fortress, 2005), 206–7.
5. Banner, *Practice of Abortion*, 1.

alone appreciated by "enlightened" thinkers. Comments by the editors of the critical edition of Bonhoeffer's work tell us much. They note that while abortion was illegal in Bonhoeffer's day, the Nazis had made abortion compulsory up to six months for "genetically unfit" fetuses, and they conclude that "such Nazi 'genetic engineering' is clearly in Bonhoeffer's sights: 'this is nothing but murder.'"[6]

Perhaps the simple view is unintelligible to the editors, or perhaps they find it necessary to "rescue" this greatly admired theologian for contemporary audiences. In any case, they seem to ignore Bonhoeffer's own words. While the Nazis' actions are important for understanding the mistreatment and devaluation of human lives under their regime, Bonhoeffer does not refer to their eugenic program or to the Nazis at all. Rather, he cites the personal motivations and choices that lead to abortion, such as "despair from the depths of human desolation or financial need." Decisions made out of such despair, he continues, may affect our response to abortion, but they do not change its nature. Whatever the particular reasons, he speaks of the woman's decision as a difficult one that brings a weight of guilt. In this particular context, it is not the Nazis' program of forced abortion but rather individual choices that he calls murder.

What makes Bonhoeffer's simple view incomprehensible to so many today is essentially a matter of worldview. Rather than

reasoning from a point of view that extols personal bodily autonomy and freedom of choice, Bonhoeffer reasons from a biblical worldview, in particular the call to obedience to God and what it means to be a follower of Jesus. As society distances itself from a Judeo-Christian worldview, a simple condemnation of abortion makes no sense. Banner thus argues, "The simple view will only gain understanding and acceptance as the Christian gospel is itself understood and accepted."[7] This point is made not only by those who condemn abortion but also by those who defend it. For instance, Peter Singer defends abortion, and argues that opposition to both abortion and infanticide may be attributed to Christian teaching on the sanctity of human life. Yet, he argues, "perhaps it is now possible to think about these issues without assuming the Christian moral framework which has, for so long, prevented any fundamental reassessment."[8] Worldview matters!

Abortion in Biblical Perspective
One of the challenges that Christians face when confronting the practice of abortion has to do with the nature of the debate itself. The default position is not that human life in the womb ought to be protected against harm unless there is some reason that justifies abortion, such as saving the mother's life. Some such argument is normally required to overcome the presumption against taking a life. Rather, the contemporary practice of

6. Clifford J. Green, introduction to *Ethics*, 24–25.
7. Banner, *Practice of Abortion*, 42.
8. Peter Singer, *Practical Ethics,* 3rd ed. (Cambridge: Cambridge University Press, 2011), 154.

abortion has so shaped the debate that access to abortion must be protected against any infringement unless there is some very strong reason that justifies denying abortion. In other words, in the current debate, the very existence of the unborn must be justified against any reason given to end its life. Even those who are opposed to abortion illustrate this point when their arguments against abortion focus on justifying the existence of the unborn child. Against that framework of the debate, the simple view comes from the good news that "human life needs no further justification than the justification it has from God."[9]

It is often stated, by those that defend abortion and those that challenge its practice, that the Bible is silent on the issue of abortion, or at least that the Bible does not address it directly.[10] This apparent silence of Scripture on the issue may lead to "certain erroneous or misguided claims: that abortion was unknown in antiquity; that Scripture should have no role in the abortion debate; that Jews and Christians cannot formulate a robust position on the issue; or that Scripture's silence necessarily implies divine neutrality or approval, and that the faith community should follow suit."[11] If the Bible says nothing directly concerning abortion, it would be a mistake to say that it is silent on the matter or to accept the "false impression that the Bible says nothing much to the point."[12] Both in its general perspective, or what Richard Hays refers to as its symbolic world,[13] and in particular texts, the Bible has much to say to shape an understanding of abortion. What follows is a brief survey of a general biblical perspective as well as particular texts that inform our understanding of abortion.

General Perspective

The Bible clearly declares that life is a gift from God, that God creates and sustains life and all things (e.g., Gen. 1–2; John 1:3–4; Acts 17:25, 28; Col. 1:16–17). Not only is human life a gift from God, but human beings are created by God in his own image (Gen. 1:26–28). That human beings are made in God's image is the ground for the prohibition of shedding human life, and for the punishment for doing so (Gen. 9:6). The sixth commandment (Exod. 20:13; Deut. 5:17) prohibits murder explicitly, and serves as the basis for requiring the protection of innocent life (e.g., Exod. 21:22–25; Deut. 22:8). Life is a gift of God: we come to be from him and through him and for him (Col. 1:16–17; 1 Cor. 8:6). Hays thus concludes, "To understand ourselves and God in terms of the

---

9. Banner, *Practice of Abortion*, 42.
10. For instance, Richard B. Hays, *The Moral Vision of the New Testament: Community, Cross, New Creation; A Contemporary Introduction to New Testament Ethics* (San Francisco: HarperSanFrancisco, 1996), 448; Glen H. Stassen and David P. Gushee, *Kingdom Ethics: Following Jesus in Contemporary Context* (Downers Grove, IL: InterVarsity Press, 2003), 216.
11. Michael Gorman, "Abortion," in *Dictionary of Scripture and Ethics*, eds. Joel B. Green et al. (Grand Rapids: Baker Academic, 2011), 35.
12. O'Donovan, *The Christian and the Unborn Child*, 4.
13. Hays, *Moral Vision*, 450.

Bible's story is to know that we are God's creatures. We neither create ourselves nor belong to ourselves. Within this worldview, abortion—whether it be 'murder' or not—is wrong for the same reason that murder and suicide are wrong: it presumptuously assumes authority to dispose of life that does not belong to us."[14]

As life is a gift of God, children are to be desired and received as a blessing from the Lord (Ps. 127:3–5). As such, barrenness is understood to be among the worst of calamities (Prov. 30:15–16; cf. Gen. 30:1), and overcoming barrenness is received with great joy (Gen. 21:6; 1 Sam. 2; Luke 21:25). As a reminder that life is a gift from God and that only he can claim it, Israel is warned in strict terms against the sacrifice of children to Molech, which was one of the idolatrous practices of the inhabitants of Canaan and elsewhere (Lev. 18:21; 20:1–5). It is not difficult to see a connection between child sacrifice and abortion. One of the reasons that the Bible does not prohibit abortion explicitly is not that it is permissible, but that the Bible "portrays a world in which abortion" is "unthinkable or unintelligible."[15] For Hays, the symbolic world of the Bible provides strong evidence against abortion. Since God is the giver of life, "we are stewards who bear life in trust. To terminate a pregnancy is not only to commit an act of violence but also to assume responsibility for destroying a work of God."[16]

A Survey of Relevant Texts

While Hays sees the symbolic world of the Bible in terms that caution strongly against abortion, he argues that no particular texts speak to the issue. He asserts that there are "no *rules* pertinent to the topic" in the New Testament, "nor will an appeal to biblical *principles* resolve the impasses in the current debate." [17] He is right that no text directly or explicitly addresses abortion, but that is not the same as saying that no text speaks to abortion. There may well be rules and principles in Scripture that speak to abortion, depending on how we understand the life in the womb. While Hays's chapter on abortion is insightful and reflective of a faithful biblical perspective on God as the giver and Lord of life, he may be too quick to bypass certain texts as irrelevant.

Luke 1:39–44

Here Mary goes to visit the pregnant Elizabeth, and when Elizabeth hears Mary's voice, the text says that "the baby leaped inside her" (Luke 1:41, 44). Hays comments that "to extrapolate from this text—whose theological import is entirely christological—a general doctrine of the full personhood of the unborn is ridiculous and tendentious exegesis; indeed, it should not be dignified with the label 'exegesis.'"[18] He is right to caution against developing a "general doctrine of the full personhood of the unborn," but

---

14. Hays, *Moral Vision*, 450.
15. Hays, *Moral Vision*, 449.
16. Hays, *Moral Vision*, 450.
17. Hays, *Moral Vision*, 449.
18. Hays, *Moral Vision*, 448.

it is surprising to see how strongly he states the point. This is not least because such a general doctrine is not usually attempted from this text. Yet it does seem reasonable to say that it tells us something about personal life in the womb. Hays acknowledges that "the phrase 'the *child* in my womb' implies an attitude toward the unborn that is very different from speaking clinically of 'the fetus.'"[19] In this comment alone the text is saying a lot. Hays continues, "but the text cannot be used to prove any particular claim about prenatal personhood, nor does it have the issue of abortion in any way in view."[20] To make a modest claim that this text speaks to the abortion issue is different from claiming that it has the issue of abortion in view, and surely if the text implies a particular attitude toward the unborn, then it has *something* to say about abortion. Further, if it describes the child in the womb in personal terms, then it also presents something that informs our understanding of prenatal personhood.

The appeal to Luke 1:41, 44, along with Jeremiah 1:5 to defend a Christian opposition to abortion was first articulated by Tertullian (ca. 160–ca. 240).[21] These texts are relevant to the discussion for several reasons. First, Luke (the physician) uses the Greek term βρέφος (child or baby) to refer both to the unborn child, John the Baptist, in the womb (Luke 1:41, 44) and to the newborn baby Jesus (Luke 2:12, 16).

This fits not only with the continuity between the unborn and newborn but also with how we naturally use the term *baby* to refer to newborn and unborn children—that is, unless they are not wanted. Second, the references in Luke 1:41 and 44 emphasize the activity of the child in the womb, and not just its movement, but its response to the presence of Mary and the baby Jesus in her womb. The point is not that Luke included these references to demonstrate that a human being is a person from the moment of fertilization. Rather, it is that the unborn are included as human characters in the unfolding drama of redemption history. Further, there is complete continuity between the baby in the womb and John's later appearances as an adult. Luke does not seek to prove that the unborn are human persons; he assumes that is the case! This is important for a third reason—namely, that in his incarnation Jesus took on human flesh at its earliest stage. If in the incarnation Jesus identifies with humanity in order to redeem us, it is significant that Jesus identifies with the humanity of the helpless, dependent unborn child.

Psalm 139:13–16; Isaiah 44:1–2; 49:1; Jeremiah 1:5

These texts highlight several significant points with respect to the child in the womb. First, they call attention to God's personal work of creation in the womb:

---

19. Hays, *Moral Vision*, 448.
20. Hays, *Moral Vision*, 448.
21. Michael J. Gorman, *Abortion and the Early Church: Christian, Jewish and Pagan Attitudes in the Greco-Roman World* (Downers Grove, IL: InterVarsity Press, 1982), 57. See Tertullian, *De anima* 26.4–5.

- "For it was you who created my inward parts; you knit me together in my mother's womb" (Ps. 139:13).
- "This is the word of the LORD your Maker, the one who formed you from the womb" (Isa. 44:2).
- "I chose you before I formed you in the womb" (Jer. 1:5).

Second, each author calls attention to God's personal knowledge of and relationship to them, and his sovereign plan and calling for each of them while they were yet in the womb:

- "Your eyes saw me when I was formless; all my days were written in your book and planned before a single one of them began" (Ps. 139:16).
- "The LORD called me before I was born. He named me while I was in my mother's womb" (Isa. 49:1).
- "I chose you before I formed you in the womb; I set you apart before you were born" (Jer. 1:5).

In Psalm 139, the language of "I" and "you" is found repeatedly. Third, then, these texts assume and affirm personal identity in the womb and continuity from the earliest time in the womb through to adulthood. The recognition of the poetic language used in these texts should not be employed to obscure the implications they make concerning the

continuity in the unfolding of human life from conception through birth and into adulthood, God's activity in the womb, and God's knowledge of and relation to human beings before birth. Hays offers a reasonable approach, saying that we ought not to "read too much into this text [Ps. 139]," but that it can "inform the discussion of abortion," for "it portrays a symbolic world in which God is active in the formation of the unborn life in the womb, and God knows the individual even before birth."[22]

Exodus 21:22–25

This passage is an example of case law, and it deals with the application of the *lex talionis* as it applies to a situation in which a pregnant woman and her child (or children) are endangered by men who fight near her.[23] It says, "When men get in a fight and hit a pregnant woman so that her children are born prematurely but there is no injury, the one who hit her must be fined as the woman's husband demands from him, and he must pay according to judicial assessment. If there is an injury, then you must give life for life, eye for eye, tooth for tooth, hand for hand, foot for foot, burn for burn, bruise for bruise, wound for wound."

This law covers two scenarios when the fight between the men causes the woman to give birth prematurely. In the first, the premature delivery does not result in injury, while in the second scenario the fight

---

22. Hays, *Moral Vision*, 447.
23. For a discussion of this passage, see John M. Frame, *The Doctrine of the Christian Life* (Phillipsburg, NJ: P&R, 2008), 718–21; Scott B. Rae, *Moral Choices: An Introduction to Ethics*, 3rd ed. (Grand Rapids: Zondervan, 2009), 130–31.

causes injury. Those who appeal to this text in defense of abortion rights argue that both situations deal with a miscarriage—that is, a premature birth that results in the death of the child or children—so that the reference to injury pertains only to the mother. According to this view, in the first scenario the men who caused the miscarriage are only fined because there is no injury to the mother. However, if the mother is injured, as in the second scenario, then the *lex talionis* applies, so the penalty for the men is according to the degree of injury caused to the mother. Thus some who take this view argue that since only a fine is applied when the unborn child is killed, then the law doesn't treat the unborn as a human being under the protection of the law.

Several points need to be made in response to this view. First, the text does not refer clearly to a miscarriage, though some English versions translate it that way.[24] The terminology is somewhat ambiguous, meaning "her children come out" (וְיָצְאוּ יְלָדֶיהָ), which is captured by the somewhat ambiguous translation, "her children are born prematurely." As such, it does not clearly signify whether they survive, suffer injury, or die.[25] The use of the plural "children" is somewhat strange, but according to Douglas Stuart, it is "a standard grammatical device in Hb. to convey the abstract, i.e., 'any child or children she might have.'"[26] In any case, depending on the stage of pregnancy the mother is in, the result could be a stillbirth or a premature delivery in which the child or children live.[27] The ambiguity may be due to the varied possibilities that this case covers, for the survival of the child or children in a premature birth would depend on the stage of the pregnancy. Though, admittedly, in the ancient world a child would only survive premature birth if it was late in the pregnancy, this is a possibility. The fact that a late-term pregnancy is more obvious means that the men who fight nearby bear greater responsibility.

Second, a very natural reading of the text, where it does not necessarily involve a miscarriage, suggests a different perspective on the two scenarios, where injury may refer

---

24. See the discussion of alternative interpretations in Russell Fuller, "Exodus 21:22–23: The Miscarriage Interpretation and the Personhood of the Fetus," *Journal of the Evangelical Theological Society* 37, no. 2 (June 1994): 180–84. Fuller favors the miscarriage interpretation, while maintaining emphatically that it does not support arguments for abortion.

25. In his commentary on Exodus, John Durham asserts that "premature labor and birth as a result of accidental blow are clearly the point here; the question of the survival of the child or children is ambiguous, though the context . . . must surely imply penalty also for the loss of, or injury to, the child or children being carried by the woman." John I. Durham, *Exodus*, Word Biblical Commentary 3 (Nashville: Thomas Nelson, 1987), 312n22a; see also 323–24. Cassuto also sees this as "premature birth." U. Cassuto, *A Commentary on the Book of Exodus* (Jerusalem: Magnes, 1967).

26. Douglas K. Stuart, *Exodus*, New American Commentary 2 (Nashville: B&H, 2006), 490n135.

27. As Frame points out, the term translated "children" (יֶלֶד) is the same one used for children that are already born and alive. If the case was primarily about what happens when there is a miscarriage, other terms could be used, such as נֵפֶל or שָׁכֹל. See Frame, *Doctrine of the Christian Life*, 719n3. See also a discussion of terminology in Fuller, "Exodus 21:22–23," 179.

to either the mother or the children in the womb. In the one case, if there is premature birth but no injury to the mother or child, the penalty is a fine because of the carelessness of the men fighting near a pregnant woman, and the risk brought about by their reckless behavior. In the other case, if there is injury to either the mother or the child, then the penalty imposed on the men is proportional to the injury to either the mother or child. In effect, then, this is a strong case for the defense of the unborn.

Third, even if we interpret the text to refer only to miscarriage, it does not lead to the conclusion that the unborn child is not fully human. In the Mosaic law, the penalty of a fine instead of exact proportion for the injury does not imply that the injured one is not a person or is less than fully human. For instance, based on parallel texts in other ancient laws, Russell Fuller points out that different punishments, including a fine versus execution, has to do with legal status, not personhood.[28] Later in the same chapter, for example, in Exodus 21:32, a fine is imposed as a penalty if an ox kills a slave, whereas death can be imposed if it kills a neighbor or a son or daughter. This does not mean that the slave is not a person or is less than fully human.

Fourth, then, even if it is asserted that the text refers only to miscarriage, it does

not support an argument for abortion, but rather it supports the defense of unborn human beings. This is because, on the one hand, a penalty is imposed for the reckless act of fighting near a pregnant woman, leading to the death of the child. It is a defense of the unborn because it warns people to be careful not to cause their death, even if unintentionally.

Finally, this leads to another reason that this text does not support arguments for abortion. The act in question is careless, but *unintentional*, and a fine is due nonetheless. Abortion, on the other hand, is the *intentional* killing of the unborn child, which not only is not in view in this text but is unthinkable in Jewish perspective. If there is any direct application to the abortion issue, it is that there would be—at the very least—a fine for procuring abortion, if not proportional punishment. Thus, whether this text is interpreted in a straightforward way as referring to a premature birth, or as a miscarriage or stillbirth, the conclusion is that it is a crime punishable in the Mosaic law to cause the death of an unborn child.

Early Jewish and Christian Attitudes toward Abortion

Michael Gorman contrasts early Jewish and Christian views on abortion with

---

28. Fuller shows that both the Code of Hammurabi and the Middle Assyrian Laws, which deal with fetal deaths and the death of slaves, imposed penalties ranging from fines to death, depending on the circumstances. Fuller, "Exodus 21:22–23," 169–84. After surveying relevant laws, for instance, Fuller concludes, "The argument that differences in punishments imply differences in personhood, if carried to its conclusion, would suggest that some fetuses were human and that others were not since the Middle Assyrian laws punished the loss of the fetus sometimes by fines and at other times by execution" (173).

their ancient contemporaries. While abortion was prevalent and approved by many pagan thinkers in the Greco-Roman world, it was not so among early Jews and Christians. As they reflected on the blessing of procreation, the sanctity of human life, and the teaching of Scriptures, they concluded that deliberate abortion was unthinkable. For instance, of the Jewish perspective, Gorman writes, "Despite the absence of a specific condemnation or prohibition of abortion in their Scriptures, extensive research has discovered no mention of a nontherapeutic Jewish abortion in any texts of the Hebrew Bible or of other Jewish literature through A.D. 500."[29] Indeed, the lack of abortion among the ancient Jews may be both an indication of the universal belief that children are a blessing and an understanding that abortion is unthinkable and prohibited by laws against the taking of innocent human life. Though there were different schools of thought concerning penalties for accidental and therapeutic abortions, Jewish teachers were "united on the subject of deliberate abortion. Alexandrians and Palestinians of both the majority and the minority legal opinions condemned deliberate abortion as disrespect for life and as bloodshed."[30]

Christian thinkers from the beginning have also opposed abortion, which was well-known and widespread in the ancient world, and early Christian apologists often included their opposition to abortion as part of their defense of their faith and morality.[31] Some pagan philosophers opposed abortion, and for some of the same reasons—for example, "Pagans and Christians alike criticized the use of abortion to conceal sexual immorality or as a means of birth control."[32] Yet the main reason for Christian opposition is different from that of pagans, whose statements against abortion are "consistently mindful of the welfare and rights of the state, the father, the family and even occasionally the woman, but never those of the fetus." Such reasons may be valid and count against abortion, and some Christians may agree that they call abortion into question. However, "when compared to pagan opinion, the most distinctive feature of early Christian rejection of abortion is its placing the well-being of the fetus at the center of the issue."[33]

That the unborn child is understood to be a human being deserving of protection is established by Christians in the earliest teaching manuals on the Christian life, the Didache and the Epistle of

29. Gorman, *Abortion and the Early Church*, 33.
30. Gorman, *Abortion and the Early Church*, 45. The case for a defense of abortion in Judaism, made by Daniel C. Maguire, is weak, and fails to account for the case against abortion in Jewish tradition. Daniel C. Maguire, *Sacred Choices: The Right to Contraception and Abortion in Ten World Religions* (Minneapolis: Fortress, 2001), 95–105.
31. Gorman, *Abortion and the Early Church*, 53–59.
32. Gorman, *Abortion and the Early Church*, 76.
33. Gorman, *Abortion and the Early Church*, 77.

Barnabas. Describing the "Way of Life," reminiscent of Deuteronomy, the Didache offers a list of prohibitions, including the following: "Thou shalt not murder a child by abortion/destruction."[34] Similarly, describing the "Way of Light," the Epistle of Barnabas commands, "Thou shalt not procure abortion, thou shalt not commit infanticide," immediately after commanding, "Thou shalt love thy neighbor more than thy own life."[35] In these teachings, killing a child in the womb is considered murder and a violation of love for one's neighbor, both of which underscore the full humanity of the unborn child. Throughout its history, Christianity has opposed abortion, and while there have been numerous reasons given for its opposition, it has consistently returned to the belief that the child in the womb is fully human and a gift from God.

Abortion in Contemporary Perspective

A Brief Review of Abortion Law in the United States

Background to Roe v. Wade

Beginning in the middle of the nineteenth century, states began to pass laws prohibiting abortion throughout pregnancy, with some providing exceptions for a woman's life.[36] These laws replaced British common law, which allowed for abortion prior to "quickening," when the mother can feel the fetus move.[37] In the 1960s, some states adopted laws to allow for abortion in cases of rape, fetal deformity, and the health of the mother.[38] A few states (Alaska, Hawaii, New York, and Washington) permitted abortion for broad reasons. Some states, including

---

34. Didache 2.2, cited in Gorman, *Abortion and the Early Church*, 49.
35. Epistle of Barnabas 19.5, cited in Gorman, *Abortion and the Early Church*, 49.
36. See Pew Research Center, "A History of Key Abortion Rulings." For the texts of Supreme Court decisions up to the early 1990s, see *Abortion: The Supreme Court Decisions*, ed. Ian Shapiro (Indianapolis: Hackett, 1995). See also Francis J. Beckwith, *Defending Life: A Moral and Legal Case against Abortion Choice* (New York: Cambridge University Press, 2007), chap. 2, "The Supreme Court, Roe v. Wade, and Abortion Law," 18–41; and Pew Research Center, "A History of Key Abortion Rulings of the U.S. Supreme Court," January 16, 2013, https://www.pewforum. org/2013/01/16/a-history-of-key-abortion-rulings-of-the-us-supreme-court.
37. This was based on the embryology and biology of the time, which held that the life of the unborn began or the soul was infused at quickening. Abortion laws changed in the nineteenth century with greater knowledge of embryology and biology. See Beckwith, *Defending Life*, 24–25.
38. The trend to expand reasons for abortion can be seen in a 1971 resolution of the Southern Baptist Convention. At the SBC meeting in St. Louis, Missouri, that year, after affirming "a high view of the sanctity of human life, including fetal life," the Resolution on Abortion resolved that Southern Baptists should "work for legislation that will allow the possibility of abortion under such conditions as rape, incest, clear evidence of fetal deformity, and carefully ascertained evidence of the likelihood of damage to the emotional, mental, and physical health of the mother." Southern Baptist Convention, "Resolution on Abortion," 1971, http://www. sbc.net/resolutions/13/resolution-on-abortion. After seeing the results of *Roe v. Wade*, the SBC began to adopt resolutions rejecting abortion each year in the late 1970s, and by 1980, meeting in St. Louis, Missouri, again, the SBC called for legislation or a constitutional amendment "prohibiting abortion except to save the life of the mother." Southern Baptist Convention, "Resolution on Abortion," 1980, http://www.sbc.net/resolutions/19/ resolution-on-abortion.

Texas, permitted abortion only to save the life of the mother.

Roe v. Wade *(January 22, 1973)* and Doe v. Bolton *(January 22, 1973)*

In 1970, "Jane Roe" filed a class-action suit, claiming that she was pregnant as a result of rape, and that her rights were infringed because she could not procure an abortion in Texas.[39] A federal district court in Dallas ruled that the Texas abortion law was unconstitutional. The federal court decision was appealed before the US Supreme Court, which ruled in the *Roe v. Wade* decision on January 22, 1973, that the Texas law was unconstitutional. Justice Blackmun wrote the opinion, which effectively legalized abortion on demand in all states. The court divided pregnancy into trimesters, ruling that a state could not regulate abortion in the first trimester. A state may regulate abortion in the second trimester, but only "to the extent that the regulation reasonably relates to the preservation and protection of maternal health."[40] In other words, there was no protection offered for the unborn child during the first two trimesters—it has no interest in the unborn child until viability—but the state may have an interest in regulating abortion in the second trimester to make sure that proper medical standards are practiced to safeguard the mother's health (qualifications of the person performing the abortion, licensure of the facility, etc.). In the third trimester, at viability, the state has a "legitimate interest in potential life," and *Roe* allowed states to regulate or even prohibit abortion, with the exception that abortion must be permitted throughout the course of pregnancy if there is risk to the mother's health.

The "health exception" effectively allowed for abortion on demand throughout pregnancy. This is because the Supreme Court in *Doe v. Bolton*, the companion decision to *Roe v. Wade*, defined "health" as broadly as possible, "in light of all factors—physical, emotional, psychological, familial, and the woman's age—relevant to the well being of the patient. All these factors relate to health."[41] Whatever restrictions might be put in place in the interest of the unborn child, these "factors" (emotional, psychological, familial health, and the woman's age) eliminate meaningful enforcement of any restrictions. As Francis Beckwith summarized the ruling, "It is safe to say that in the first six months of pregnancy a woman can have an abortion for no reason, but in the last three months she can have it for any reason."[42]

---

39. In fact, *Roe v. Wade* was based on a false claim, because "Jane Roe" (whose real name is Norma McCorvey) was not actually raped. She later became a pro-life advocate. Norma McCorvey shared her story in *Won by Love* (Nashville: Thomas Nelson, 1997).
40. Roe v. Wade, 410 U.S. 113 (1973).
41. Doe v. Bolton, 410 U.S. 179, 192 (1973). See Beckwith, *Defending Life*, 20–21.
42. Francis J. Beckwith, *Politically Correct Death: Answering Arguments for Abortion Rights* (Grand Rapids: Baker, 1993), 34.

Webster v. Reproductive Health Services *(1989)*

In this five-four ruling,[43] the Supreme Court upheld a Missouri statute (overturning a lower court decision) that included three significant provisions. First, it stated that human life begins at conception. In part because the statute stated that it was contingent on prior Supreme Court decisions, the court did not believe this statement posed a threat to abortion rights. Second, the statute barred the use of government facilities, funds, or employees from abortion services unless the mother's life was at risk. Third, the statute required that physicians conduct a fetal-viability test before performing an abortion on a woman who was twenty weeks pregnant or more. This ruling was understood to be a threat to *Roe v. Wade*, which can be seen in the vigorous dissent expressed by Justice Blackmun.

Casey v. Planned Parenthood *(1992)*

In this case,[44] the Supreme Court considered a Pennsylvania law that included the following five requirements:

- A woman seeking an abortion would be required to undergo a twenty-four-hour waiting period and to be given information on abortion.
- A minor seeking abortion was required to obtain parental consent, though this

requirement could be waived in extenuating circumstances.

- A woman was to notify her husband of her intent to seek an abortion, a requirement that also could be waived in extenuating circumstances.
- It defined medical emergencies providing exceptions to restrictions on abortion, to save the woman's life or avoid "serious risk of substantial and irreversible impairment of a major bodily function."
- It included reporting requirements for abortion facilities.

The Supreme Court was deeply splintered in this decision. Three of the justices (Kennedy, O'Connor, and Souter) authored a joint opinion. They were joined by Justices Blackmun and Stevens (five-four) in reaffirming *Roe*'s basic principle that states could not restrict abortion prior to viability, and by Justices Rehnquist, Scalia, White, and Thomas (seven-two) in upholding all requirements of the Pennsylvania law except for spousal notification.[45] *Casey* replaced the "strict scrutiny" standard of *Roe* with an "undue burden" standard, where laws restricting abortion "may not withstand strict scrutiny but nevertheless do not result in an undue burden for the pregnant woman."[46] Thus, for example, the waiting period was not considered an undue burden, but the

---

43. Webster v. Reproductive Health Services, 492 U.S. 490 (1989). See Beckwith, *Defending Life*, 32–33, and Pew Research Center, "A History of Key Abortion Rulings."
44. Casey v. Planned Parenthood, 505 U.S. 833 (1992).
45. Pew Research Center, "A History of Key Abortion Rulings."
46. Beckwith, *Defending Life*, 33.

spousal-notification requirement was struck down because it was considered an undue burden on married women.

Casey gave reasons for both sides on the abortion debate to be concerned and consoled. On the one hand, *Roe* was upheld and in some ways strengthened as legal precedent by an appeal to *stare decisis* (stand by things decided). On the other hand, *Roe* was weakened in principle by providing states with greater freedom to regulate abortion. One of the most disturbing aspects of the decision, related to precedent, was that a significant reason for upholding *Roe* was simply that for twenty years women had come to rely on the right to abortion and organize their lives with abortion as a right.

Stenberg v. Carhart *(2000) and* Gonzales v. Carhart *(2007)*

One other significant milestone that should be considered in the Supreme Court decisions on abortion has to do with what is referred to as partial-birth abortion, or D & X (dilation and extraction).[47] In this late-term procedure, the abortionist uses a forceps to grab the legs of the fetus and pull it through the birth canal so that all but its head is delivered. At that point an incision is made in the skull of the fetus, a catheter is inserted, and the brain of the fetus is vacuumed out. The dead fetus is then removed from the birth canal.[48]

In the 1990s, the US Congress passed several bills prohibiting partial-birth abortion, which were vetoed by President Clinton. Meanwhile, thirty states passed laws banning the procedure. The rationale for the ban included the fact that the baby was nearly born, and that there was no significant increase in risk to the mother to complete the live birth rather than killing the unborn child. In *Stenberg v. Carhart*, however, the US Supreme Court struck down Nebraska's partial-birth abortion ban in a five-four decision, because it did not have an exception for the mother's health, and because in the opinion of the court it also put at risk women's access to other abortion procedures. The decision struck down the ban in other states as well.[49]

In November 2003, President George W. Bush signed into law the Partial-Birth Abortion Ban Act of 2003.[50] The ban included an exception for the life of the mother. It was challenged in federal court and struck down, citing *Stenberg*. However, in the 2007 *Gonzales v. Carhart* decision, by a five-four vote the Supreme Court overruled the lower court and upheld the ban on partial-birth abortion.[51]

In addition to the partial-birth abortion ban, in recent years some states have sought to ban virtually all abortions after twenty weeks. These laws face significant opposition in the courts.

---

47. Stenberg v. Carhart, 530 U.S. 914 (2000); Gonzales v. Carhart, 550 U.S. 124 (2007).
48. See Beckwith, *Defending Life*, 39.
49. Beckwith, *Defending Life*, 39; Pew Research Center, "A History of Key Abortion Rulings."
50. 18 U.S.C. § 1531 (2003).
51. Beckwith, *Defending Life*, 40–41; Pew Research Center, "A History of Key Abortion Rulings."

Abortion Statistics

Statistics bear out the point that the practice of abortion shows very little evidence of its moral difficulty. Consider the following:[52]

- Eighteen percent of pregnancies in 2017, not including miscarriages, ended in abortion (AGI).
- According to survey reports, 862,320 abortions were performed in the United States in 2017 (AGI).
- In 2016, 86 percent of women who obtained abortions were unmarried (CDC).
- The most common reasons that women gave for obtaining an abortion:
    - Three-fourths cited responsibilities to other people.
    - Three-fourths cited the inability to afford raising a child.
    - Three-fourths said that having a baby would interfere with work, school, or the ability to care for dependents.
    - One-half said that they did not want to be a single parent or were having relationship difficulties.
- One percent claimed to be a victim of rape, less than 0.5 percent became pregnant as a result of incest, and statistics did not register anyone who claimed to have an abortion to save their life.[53]
- After *Roe v. Wade* legalized abortion on demand in all fifty states, the number of abortions increased each year. In 1975, the number of abortions in the United States rose above 1 million; by 1980 abortions reached over 1.5 million; abortions peaked at over 1.6 million in 1990, and have been on a gradual decline since then. In 2011, the number of abortions had dropped to 1.06 million, by 2014 it was 926,200, and by 2017 it was 862,320.[54]

Engaging the Arguments on Abortion

In the introductory chapter on bioethics I argued that human life begins at fertilization, at which time the being that exists is fully human. It is on that basis, though not on that basis alone, that abortion is judged to be morally wrong and it should

52. The following statistics come from the Guttmacher Institute, a pro-choice research organization, "Induced Abortion in the United States," September 2019, https://www.guttmacher.org/fact-sheet/induced-abortion-united-states (AGI) and The Centers for Disease Control, "Abortion Surveillance—United States, 2016," https://www.cdc.gov/mmwr/volumes/68/ss/ss6811a1.htm (CDC).
53. Lawrence B. Finer et al., "Reasons U.S. Women Have Abortions: Quantitative and Qualitative Perspectives," *Perspectives on Sexual and Reproductive Health* 37, no. 3 (September 2005): 110–18, https://www.guttmacher.org/journals/psrh/2005/reasons-us-women-have-abortions-quantitative-and-qualitative-perspectives. See table 2, "Percentage of women reporting that specified reasons contributed to their decision to have an abortion, 2004 and 1987" (https://www.guttmacher.org/sites/default/files/pdfs/tables/370305/3711005t2.pdf).
54. See the Guttmacher Institute, "Induced Abortion in the United States." See also the National Right to Life Committee, "Abortion Statistics: United States Data and Trends," http://www.nrlc.org/uploads/factsheets/FS01AbortionintheUS.pdf. The numbers from the Guttmacher Institute are consistently higher than the Centers for Disease Control, most likely because the CDC uses numbers reported by health agencies, and some abortionists do not report. In addition, since 1998, the CDC doesn't include abortions from California and New Hampshire, as well as some other states. The Guttmacher Institute gets their numbers from surveys of abortion providers.

be prohibited. Yet the reality in the United States is that abortion is permitted virtually on demand throughout pregnancy, and those who defend access to abortion do so vigorously. Is this because arguments in defense of abortion are persuasive to most people? Ongoing, strong opposition to abortion suggests otherwise, as do polls that consistently reveal a nation divided on this issue. Regardless, we do well to consider the arguments in defense of abortion, for there are many people who assert and affirm them, and it is important to engage them. The following section will briefly consider some of the key pro-choice arguments, along with a response to them. This is not an attempt to offer a comprehensive list of arguments or responses. Other arguments could be examined, and each argument could be developed more fully, but this will suffice to outline significant arguments on both sides.[55]

Virtually every argument on abortion boils down to one central question—namely, is the life in the womb—at every state—fully human? If so, then nearly every argument in favor of abortion collapses. My conclusion, developed in the chapter on the human embryo, is as follows. Since the unborn human being is fully human, whether fully developed or not, then taking deliberate action to end its life is never morally justified, except to save the mother's life. The responses to arguments below will assume this position, while making additional points.

In the Early Stages of Pregnancy, There Is Merely a Blob of Tissue or a Clump of Cells

This issue is addressed in the chapter on the embryo, but I include it here because it reflects assertions or assumptions that many hold in defense of abortion. The actual arguments may be more sophisticated, but the basic point is the same: the life in the womb is not fully human. This assertion was made frequently by pro-choice advocates in the early days of the abortion debate, and by workers at abortion clinics in counseling women considering abortion.[56] It continues to be made in debates, though not often by sophisticated abortion-rights proponents.[57] It simply is not convincing when confronted by the science of biology and embryology, and advanced ultrasound technology.[58]

---

55. For more in-depth analysis, see Louis P. Pojman and Francis J. Beckwith, *The Abortion Controversy: 25 Years after Roe v. Wade, a Reader*, 2nd ed. (New York: Wadsworth, 1998). My summaries in this chapter owe much to Beckwith, *Politically Correct Death*; and Beckwith, *Defending Life*. See also John S. Feinberg and Paul D. Feinberg, *Ethics for a Brave New World*, 2nd ed. (Wheaton, IL: Crossway, 2010).

56. See some powerful firsthand accounts in the documentary-style DVD, *After the Choice* (Washington, DC: Concerned Women for America), http://concernedwomen.org.

57. Beckwith engages with arguments defending abortion by those who acknowledge that the life in the womb is fully human. See, e.g., *Defending Life*, 172–99.

58. See, e.g., Jon A. Shields and David Daleiden, "Mugged by Ultrasound: Why So Many Abortion Workers Have Turned Pro-life," *Weekly Standard*, January 25, 2010, http://www.weeklystandard.com/article/413203 (article discontinued); also William Saletan, "Window to the Womb," *Washington Post*, April 29, 2007, http://www.washingtonpost.com/wp-dyn/content/article/2007/04/27/AR2007042702040.html.

A Woman Has the Right to Privacy and Control over Her Own Body

This argument is a key part of the basis for the legal defense of abortion in the relevant US Supreme Court rulings, beginning with *Roe v. Wade*. In that landmark case, the majority stated, "This right of privacy, whether it be founded in the Fourteenth Amendment's concept of personal liberty and restrictions upon state action, as we feel it is, or . . . in the Ninth Amendment's reservation of rights to the people, is broad enough to encompass a woman's decision whether or not to terminate her pregnancy."[59] In short, since every person has a right to privacy, and a woman has the right to control her own body, and since the unborn child is dependent on her body, neither the state nor any person can prevent her from having an abortion.

In response, individuals do have a significant right to privacy and to be free from interference in the course of their lives. However, these rights are not absolute. This argument for abortion collapses if the unborn child is fully human, for the right to privacy does not justify killing innocent human beings. Autonomy has limits. While we ought to defend freedom and a significant degree of autonomy, we also ought to (and we do) require that we take responsibility for our choices. This includes responsibility for our children, born and unborn, even from an unplanned pregnancy. In addition, such responsibility extends not just to women but to men also.

Further, concerning privacy and autonomy, the unborn child is not part of the woman's body. Rather, the child is a unique individual, distinct from his or her mother. The fact that the child is dependent on the mother does not mean that the mother has a right to kill the child. Consider the life of a ten-month-old baby who is also dependent on his or her mother. Why doesn't she, or the father, have the right to end the life of a ten-month-old baby if they are not ready for the child, or they find that the child has become too great a burden, or they cannot adequately care for their other children? Why should the government, whether the police or Child Protective Services, interfere with their privacy and the affairs of their home? If we see that it is because their privacy does not outweigh the protection of human life, then we have gained insight into the problem of abortion.

Abortion Rights Are Necessary as a Component of a Woman's Reproductive Freedom

This argument is related to the previous argument about a woman's control over her body. It asserts that abortion is necessary as a form of birth control if all else fails (or if nothing else is used). This freedom is thought to be necessary if women are to be on a level playing field with men, who are not subject to unintentional pregnancy. Abortion-rights advocate Laurence Tribe articulates this type of argument. He writes, "Laws restricting abortion so dramatically

---

59. The text of the *Roe v. Wade* decision is reprinted in Pojman and Beckwith, *Abortion Controversy*, quotation from 27.

shape the lives of women, and only of women, that their denial of equality hardly needs detailed elaboration. While men retain the right to sexual and reproductive autonomy, restrictions on abortion deny that autonomy to women. Laws restricting access to abortion thereby place a real and substantial burden on women's ability to participate in society as equals."[60]

It seems difficult to believe that a civil society could accept that abortion could be justified as a form of birth control, and this was not a prominent argument before or soon after the *Roe v. Wade* decision, at least not overtly. Yet is has been a significant aspect of the legal justification of abortion. To begin with, the right to privacy was invoked in *Roe*, against state interference. The Supreme Court had found that right just a few years earlier, in a ruling on the sale and use of contraceptive devices, in *Griswold v. Connecticut* (1965). That is, the right to privacy, which was used as the basis for the Supreme Court to prevent interference with the use of contraception within the intimacy of marriage in 1965, was applied just eight years later in *Roe* to prevent the state from interfering in a woman's choice to terminate her pregnancy and kill her unborn child.[61]

The connection between birth control and abortion is made clear in other significant cases on abortion. In *Planned*

Parenthood v. Casey (1992). Several aspects of that Supreme Court ruling are important, but one statement in the majority opinion especially relates to the matter of abortion as birth control. The majority stated that "the Roe rule's limitation on state power could not be repudiated without serious inequity to people who, for two decades of economic and social developments, have organized intimate relationships and made choices that define their views of themselves and their places in society, in reliance on the availability of abortion in the event that contraception should fail."[62]

Similarly, in his dissenting comments in the Supreme Court decision in *Webster v. Reproductive Health Services* (1989), Justice Blackmun asserts,

Thus, "not with a bang, but a whimper," the plurality discards a landmark case of the last generation and casts into darkness the hopes and visions of every woman in this country who had come to believe that the Constitution guaranteed her the right to exercise some control over her unique ability to bear children. The plurality does so either oblivious or insensitive to the fact that millions of women, and their families, have ordered their lives around the right to reproductive choice, and this right has become vital to the full participation of

60. Laurence Tribe, *Abortion: The Clash of Absolutes* (New York: Norton, 1990), 105.
61. Griswold v. Connecticut, 381 U.S. 479 (1965). See Beckwith, *Defending Life*, 219, on the Griswold decision. For a discussion of the connection between contraception and birth control, see Kenneth Magnuson, "What Does Contraception Have to Do with Abortion? Evangelicals v. Augustine and *Roe v. Wade*," *Southern Baptist Journal of Theology* 7, no. 2 (Summer 2003): 54–67.
62. Planned Parenthood of Southeastern PA. v. Casey (1992), No. 91–744 (e).

women in the economic and political walks of American life.[63]

This is a striking argument, essentially stating that any threat to overturn *Roe* is a threat to cause great upheaval for women who have organized their lives around abortion rights, specifically as a failsafe method of birth control. That is a startling argument for abortion. It is analogous to arguments in the nineteenth century that slavery should not be prohibited because thousands of landowners, and indeed an entire economy, had been organized around the availability of slave labor. Such an argument is outrageous and appalling. Once again, if the unborn are fully human, abortion cannot be justified as a means of birth control, no matter how many people have organized their lives around it. There are solutions to that problem that do not involve the taking of innocent human lives.

Interestingly, in 1970, prior to the *Roe v. Wade* decision, a federal court recognized that arguments for procreative liberty ended once conception has taken place. While defending the *Griswold* decision and affirming people's right to determine whether to get pregnant, the federal court in *Steinberg v. Brown* argued, "The legal conclusion in *Griswold* as to the rights of individuals to determine without governmental interference whether or not to enter into the process of procreation cannot be extended to cover those situations wherein, voluntarily or involuntarily, the preliminaries have ended, and a new life has begun. Once human life has commenced, the constitutional protections found in the Fifth and Fourteenth Amendments impose upon the state the duty of safeguarding it."[64] In short, the life in the womb is deserving of protection, and procreative liberty does not include the right to abortion.

I Personally Think That Abortion Is Wrong, but Women Should Have the Right to Choose Abortion

This "argument" reflects moral relativism and emotivism, and is flawed and evasive from a moral point of view. It's bumper-sticker (and more provocative) version is "If you don't like abortion, don't have one." It confuses moral claims with preference claims, such as, "I don't like asparagus, but I believe people should have the right to eat asparagus."[65] But having an abortion is not like eating asparagus or other preferences, for the argument against abortion is a moral argument, not merely a preference argument. That is, if someone thinks abortion is *wrong*, that is a *moral* claim, grounded in the assertion that the unborn are fully human. Yet if an unborn child is fully human, one can hardly concede that it is permissible to take its life.

Consider the following example. When Abraham Lincoln and Stephen A. Douglas

---

63. *Webster v. Reproductive Health Services*, 492 U.S., I,D.
64. *Steinberg v. Brown*, 321 F. Supp. 741 (ND Ohio 1970), cited in Beckwith, *Defending Life*, 28.
65. On this distinction, see Beckwith, *Defending Life*, 4–5.

were opponents for the US Senate seat from Illinois, they engaged in a now famous series of debates. One of the issues of debate was whether the federal government in US territories should permit slavery. Douglas argued that he personally believed that slavery is wrong but that the federal government should not prohibit slavery, for to do so would be to violate the right of individuals and territories to decide for themselves, free of federally imposed law. Lincoln responded by arguing that Judge Douglas could not on the one hand say that slavery is wrong and yet on the other hand say that it doesn't matter whether it is voted up or down. "He cannot say that he would as soon see a wrong voted up as voted down. When Judge Douglas says that whoever, or whatever community wants slaves, they have a right to have them, he is perfectly logical if there is nothing wrong in the institution; but if you admit that it is wrong, he cannot logically say that anybody has a right to do a wrong."[66]

Safe, Legal, and Rare: We Should Never Return to the Dangerous Days of Back-Alley Abortions

This argument emphasizes that women should have access to safe abortions, and therefore abortion should be legal. If abortion is illegal, women will have to resort to back-alley abortions, which are unregulated and dangerous. Further, there is an implication here is that abortion is not a good thing, so it should be rare.

In response, this argument, too, collapses if the unborn child is fully human. There is no right to have a safe means to kill an innocent human being, nor should it be legal. Further, clinical abortions may be safe, for the most part, in physical terms, but abortion-rights advocates generally fail to acknowledge the emotional and psychological harm caused by abortion.[67]

In addition, references to a return to dangerous, back-alley abortions—where the image of a coat hanger is used graphically to illustrate the danger—are greatly misleading. In fact, Beckwith surveys information on abortion prior to *Roe*, including those who support abortion rights, indicating that prior to 1973, the vast majority of illegal abortions—not to mention legal abortions—were actually performed by licensed doctors in good standing.[68]

What is more, claims about the number of women who died as a result of illegal abortion have been greatly exaggerated. Some claimed that there were between five thousand and ten thousand deaths per year, numbers that one former abortion provider and advocate, Bernard Nathanson, later admitted repeating even though he knew they were false.[69] The actual number was much smaller. Though the exact number is difficult to determine, as

---

66. *The Collected Works of Abraham Lincoln*, ed. Roy P. Basler (New Brunswick, NJ: Rutgers University Press, 1953), 3:256–57, cited in Hadley Arkes, *First Things: An Inquiry into the First Principles of Morals and Justice* (Princeton, NJ: Princeton University Press, 1986), 24; also in Beckwith, *Defending Life*, 16.
67. See Concerned Women for America, *After the Choice* (DVD).
68. Beckwith, *Politically Correct Death*, 58.
69. Beckwith, *Politically Correct Death*, 57. Beckwith cites Bernard Nathanson, *Aborting America* (New York: Doubleday, 1979), 193.

expected with an illegal procedure, one abortion-rights scholar estimated it closer to five hundred per year on average, and other assessments are much lower than that. For instance, John and Barbara Willke cite the US Bureau of Vital Statistics to demonstrate that the high number of deaths reported by pro-choice advocates are simply false. Based on those statistics, they argue that "you must go back to the pre-Penicillin era to find more than 1,000 maternal deaths per year from illegal and legal abortions combined" (in the 1940s). There was a significant drop in maternal deaths in the 1950s and 1960s, when abortion was still illegal. They conclude that by 1972, the year before *Roe v. Wade*, the number of maternal deaths by legal and illegal abortions in the United States was thirty-nine.[70] Any loss of life is tragic, but these are vastly different numbers from those offered by proponents of legalized abortion, showing that the frequently used numbers were deceptive and manipulative. Further, the way to deal with this tragedy is to find ways to prevent abortions, not to make killing unborn children safer.

Besides advocating safe and legal abortion, this argument asserts that abortion should be rare. This seems to be an acknowledgment that abortion is not a good thing. Or it may simply be used to appease those opposed to abortion. The reality is that, though abortion is legal and may be relatively safe, it is not rare. Indeed, rather than becoming

rare, abortion numbers increased dramatically after it was legalized. Again, Beckwith examines claims of the number of abortions prior to *Roe*, along with the best actual estimates. Some claim that there were one to two million abortions annually prior to *Roe*, but there is no evidence for such claims. Although it is difficult to arrive at a precise estimate, Beckwith examines relevant statistics that indicate dramatically lower numbers. One sophisticated study concluded that "a reasonable estimate for the actual number of criminal abortions per year in the pre-legalization era [prior to 1967] would be from a low of 39,000 (1950) to a high of 210,000 (1961) and a mean of 98,000 per year."[71] Compare these numbers to the range of 1 to 1.6 million abortions per year since *Roe*, and it is clear that making abortion legal does not make it rare, but instead causes the number to increase significantly. This is not a surprise, for one of the purposes of law is to serve as a teacher, and thus if something is made legal, many will conclude that it must be morally permissible.

Abortion Rights Are Necessary for Some Women to Avoid or Escape Economic Hardship

This argument claims that abortion must be an option because the birth of a child or additional children will sometimes create a financial burden that places or keeps

---

70. John C. Willke and Barbara Willke, *Abortion: Questions and Answers*, rev. ed. (Cincinnati: Hayes, 1990), 105.
71. Beckwith, *Politically Correct Death*, 57, citing Barbara J. Syska, Thomas W. Hilgers, and Dennis O'Hare, "An Objective Model for Estimating Criminal Abortions and Its Implications for Public Policy," in *New Perspectives on Human Abortion*, eds. Thomas Hilgers, Dennis J. Horan, and David Mall (Frederick, MD: University Publications of America, 1981), 78.

some women and their families in poverty, making life difficult for the mother and her existing children.

Again, this argument fails if the unborn child is fully human. We would not accept an argument that parents can kill their one-year-old child because he or she is a financial burden, nor would we accept that society can eliminate any human beings or class of human beings who are economic burdens. There are better solutions to poverty and financial hardship than to kill our unborn children.

Sometimes this argument is presented as part of a compassionate response to those in poverty. This argument, however, amounts to a form of institutionalized racism and discrimination against the poor and minorities. Early on, abortion-rights advocates showed clear racial prejudice and discrimination. Yet even if such bias is no longer explicit, there is a disturbing reality, for a high proportion of abortions are procured by African American and poor women, while the argument for abortion as a solution to poverty is often expressed by elite, well-educated, wealthy, and middle-class proponents. Killing is not caring, and it is not compassion.

The abortion rate and ratio show that black women are more than three times as likely to have an abortion than white women. This is likely in part because abortion clinics are located in urban areas, where there is a greater percentage of poor and minority women, and also because abortion is promoted as a solution for poverty-stricken women. Abortion is not a solution to poverty, and it amounts to an assault on poor and minority communities.

Women Should Not Have to Give Birth to Children They Do Not Want

This argument begins with the assertion that every child should be wanted. If a woman doesn't want a child and gets pregnant unexpectedly, or finds out that her child is handicapped, she should be able to have an abortion. In such cases, abortion allows women to avoid emotional and social hardships, and may help to reduce child abuse.

Consider the following statistics reported by the CDC:[72]

	The number of abortions in 2013, by race	The abortion rate by race (i.e., the number of abortions per 100 women in each group)	The abortion ratio by race (i.e., the number of abortions obtained per 1,000 live births for each group)
White women	134,814 (37.3%)	7.2	121
Black women	128,682 (35.6%)	27.0	420
Hispanic women	68,761 (19%)	13.8	178

---

72. Centers for Disease Control and Prevention, "Abortion Surveillance—United States, 2013," November 25, 2016, https://www.cdc.gov/mmwr/volumes/65/ss/ss6512a1.htm.

In response, this argument collapses if the unborn child is fully human, for it would be a morally vacuous argument to claim that we can kill children if we do not want them, or that killing a child is a way to reduce child abuse. It is true that every child should be wanted. If a child is not wanted, the problem does not lie with the child. Even in dire circumstances, there are better options than to kill the child who is not wanted by its mother, such as adoption, or parental training, as some pregnancy centers offer. Further, most women who have children that they did not want or plan do not abuse them, and as Scott Rae points out, legal abortion has not led to the reduction of child abuse. Instead, noting an increase in child abuse since 1973, he asserts, "If anything, it could be that the callousness toward the fetus engendered by liberal abortion laws has carried over into a greater societal tendency toward child abuse."[73]

Handicapped children are special targets of abortion. For example, studies have shown that over 85 percent of unborn children diagnosed with Down syndrome are aborted.[74] Several points may be made about the case for aborting handicapped children who are not wanted. First, this is completely unjustified, for we would not justify the killing of a two-year-old child because he or she is handicapped. Second, it is tragic that a society would approve of killing its unborn children with special needs instead of caring for them. Besides the wrong of sacrificing the children, society sacrifices the opportunity to learn to be virtuous. Third, though some might rationalize that aborting a severely handicapped child spares the child of a burdensome life, it is clearly not for the child's benefit, for death is not a benefit and being handicapped is not correlated with having an unhappy life.[75] Finally, in terms of justification for legalized abortion, the actual percentage of abortions for this reason is very small, and it is a smoke screen used to justify abortion on demand.

A Woman Who Becomes Pregnant from Rape or Incest Should Not Be Forced to Have the Baby

This argument asserts that when a woman is a victim of rape or incest, she did not consent to sex and therefore did not accept

---

73. Scott B. Rae, *Moral Choices: An Introduction to Ethics*, 3rd ed. (Grand Rapids: Zondervan, 2009), 135.
74. See, e.g., R. L. Kramer et al., "Determinants of Parental Decisions after the Prenatal Diagnosis of Down Syndrome," *American Journal of Medical Genetics* 79, no. 3 (September 23, 1998): 172–74, https://www.ncbi.nlm.nih.gov/pubmed/9788556; M. B. Forrester and R. D. Merz, "Prenatal Diagnosis and Elective Termination of Down Syndrome in a Racially Mixed Population in Hawaii, 1987–1996," *Prenatal Diagnosis* 19, no. 2 (February 1999): 136–41, https://www.ncbi.nlm.nih.gov/pubmed/10215071.
75. A story to this effect was carried in the *London Daily Telegraph* years ago, when Elane Duckett, Glynn Verdon, and Caryl Hodges wrote to say that they were thankful not to have been aborted because they were disabled. They wrote that they were glad that they were allowed to live, "and we want to say with strong conviction how thankful we are that none took it upon themselves to destroy us as helpless cripples. . . . We have found worthwhile and happy lives and we face our future with confidence." Cited by C. Everett Koop, *The Right to Live, The Right to Die* (Wheaton, IL: Tyndale, 1976), 51–52; and in John Jefferson Davis, *Evangelical Ethics: Issues Facing the Church Today*, 4th ed. (Phillipsburg, NJ: P&R, 2015), 158–59.

responsibility for parenthood. To force her to bear the child of a rapist would be to victimize her a second time. She should not have to bear a living reminder of her victimization.

This is a special case in the abortion debate in many ways, because most cases in which abortion is considered is in the context of consensual sex, in which it can be argued that responsibility is taken for procreation whether it is intended or not. But is this the case for the victim of rape? Should she be required to bear a child when she did not consent to an action that implies responsibility for a child?

First, we ought to have great compassion and care for a woman who is a victim of rape or incest, and part of that care will be to consider how best to help her deal with the impact of being a victim of a heinous assault on her bodily integrity and personhood. Second, consideration must be given to the child who has come into being, for the circumstances of the child's origin do not change the reality that he or she is a living, innocent human being. To kill the child is to create another victim. Compassion and care ought to be extended both to the victim of rape and to the child. Third, the situation should not be construed as a conflict of rights between the mother and child, or even as a choice between caring for the mother and caring for the child. In fact, the interests of the mother and child come together. One study followed women who became pregnant after

rape or incest. Some of the women decided to have an abortion, while others decided to have their babies. When asked whether they had made the right decision, only 1 of 50 rape victims who became pregnant and chose abortion reported no regrets about the decision, and none of the 133 women who carried their children to term said that they wished they had chosen abortion.[76] Rather than making her a victim again, bearing the child may serve to heal some of the wounds caused by rape or incest. At least it cannot be assumed that the best interests of a woman who becomes pregnant through rape or incest are served by abortion.

Fourth, the argument for permitting abortion in cases of rape and incest does not support abortion on demand, and should be rejected as part of the more general argument for legalized abortion. Finally, one response to the problem of rape and incest is a compromise position. Some who believe that abortion is *morally* wrong even in the case of rape and incest nevertheless could allow that it should not be criminalized in those cases. One obvious reason for such a compromise is the recognition that a woman who has become pregnant through rape has been victimized, and her case is far different from the vast majority. Another reason is that such a compromise would significantly reduce the number of abortions, saving many lives of unborn children. In addition, it is almost certain that any proposal to prohibit abortion that did not allow

---

76. David C. Reardon, Julie Makimaa, and Amy Sobie, eds., *Victims and Victors: Speaking Out about Their Pregnancies, Abortions, and Children Resulting from Sexual Assault* (Springfield, IL: Acorn, 2000), 19, 22.

exceptions in the case of rape and incest would have no chance of being enacted into law. Finally, if this type of compromise were reached, pro-life groups would be able to focus their attention on caring for victims of rape and incest, and seeking to help them carry and care for their babies.

The State Has No Grounds to Protect Unborn Life before Viability

Central to the court's reasoning in *Roe v. Wade*, *Planned Parenthood v. Casey*, and other decisions is that there may be state interests in protecting the unborn child once it is viable—that is, once it is able to survive independently outside of the womb. Prior to that, the woman should not be prohibited from having an abortion for any reason.

There are many problems with the viability criteria. First, viability changes with technology. In 1900, an unborn child may not have been viable before thirty weeks, but in 2000, an unborn child could survive outside the mother's womb at twenty-four weeks or even earlier. According to the court's criteria, the unborn child at twenty-six weeks was not a human deserving of protection in 1900, but it is in 2000. Technological advancements do not change the status of human life. Second, we ought to protect the most vulnerable among us, not permit killing them. Beckwith asserts that "a human being's dependence and vulnerability is a call for her parents, family, and the wider human community to care and

nurture her, rather than a justification to kill her."[77] Third, consider the implications of the court's reasoning, if it is applied consistently. A normative premise that would seek to justify the right to kill the unborn when it is dependent on its mother might be stated like this: "Whenever a human being cannot live on its own because it uniquely depends on another human being for its physical existence, it is permissible for the second human being to kill the first to rid the second of this burden."[78] Unborn children should not be exempt from protection simply because they are dependent on their mothers.

Conclusion on Abortion Arguments

Abortion is, to say the least, a contested issue. The arguments listed above are some of the many made for and against abortion. The conclusion reached is that the majority of arguments for abortion collapse because the unborn child is a living, innocent human being. In the rare case when the mother's life is threatened, it is right to take action to save her life, even at the expense of the unborn. This is not because the unborn is not fully human, but because a tragic choice has to be made between the two lives, and there are many considerations involved (including existing relationships and responsibilities that the mother has). The case of rape (and incest) is difficult, because the woman did not consent to sex or pregnancy, and she is the victim of a heinous assault. On the other hand, the

---

77. Beckwith, *Defending Life*, 36.
78. Beckwith, *Defending Life*, 37.

child that has come into existence as a result is still a living human being who does not deserve to be killed. Abortion even in the case of rape is thus not morally justifiable, though pro-life advocates may disagree on whether abortion should be legal in those cases.

Given the reasonable arguments made in defense of the unborn child as a living human being, acknowledged even by many abortion-rights advocates, we should expect the burden of proof to be on those who defend abortion, and we should expect abortion to be rare. Yet that is not the case. As Banner notes, the "practice" does not fit the reality:

> It would be only the most dogmatic of defenders of the status quo who could declare that the foetus is, without a shadow of doubt, unworthy of moral regard or consideration. But if that is so, were current practice to reflect the state of argument, we would expect it to be somewhat tentative and hesitant, whereas what we find is a rather confident, clear-cut and decisive practice, the routinisation of which effectively denies the existence of moral difficulties regarding abortion. The practice seems to presuppose, that is to say, that the case for the acceptability of abortion is beyond any reasonable debate, whereas a review of the arguments in their own terms hardly suggests the possibility of such absolute conviction.[79]

It seems that the practice of abortion is irrational, for it is not simply that no arguments could conceivably defeat abortion rights, but that no arguments are permitted that threaten the sacred rite of abortion on demand.

Beyond the Right to Privacy

Those who defend abortion see it as a matter of privacy, reproductive liberty, and the right for a woman to have control over her body. The reasons that women give for having abortions seem to fit with these values. In one sense, it is not difficult to see why abortion is framed this way by those who defend it, for pregnancy—and what we do with our bodies in general—is a very intimate, personal matter. What is more, having a child has a profound impact on one's life trajectory. These realities need to be considered by all who engage in the debate about abortion. Yet it is clear that pregnancy and abortion are not merely personal, private matters. As with many or most moral issues, there are many factors to be considered. In particular, among other things we need to consider the woman, who may be in a crisis; the child in the womb; the father and his responsibility; and society as a whole.

Women in crisis pregnancy

Often abortion is treated as a moral dilemma, by those who defend it and by many who oppose it. In reality, abortion statistics like those listed above demonstrate that in the vast majority of cases, the choice concerning abortion is not a moral dilemma, in which it is very difficult to determine which moral value or principle should determine the decision. In other words, it is not weighing

---

79. Banner, *Practice of Abortion*, 44.

one human life against another. Rather, it is weighing finances, work, school, or other conveniences against the life of the unborn. These are often very difficult situations—indeed crises—but they should not be resolved at the cost of the life of the unborn child. Instead of understanding abortion as a moral dilemma, then, we should understand it as a crisis situation. That is not to minimize its significance. In fact, to recognize it as a crisis is to recognize a need and seek to ways other than abortion to help.

This is precisely what crisis pregnancy centers have devoted themselves to doing. They provide assistance for women in crisis pregnancies in many ways, through education and counseling on abortion and prenatal development, dealing with crisis, as well as practical help with completing school, parenting classes, supplies to care for a baby, financial training and budgeting, job training, and so on. Against criticisms that pro-life groups are really just anti-abortion or pro-birth, crisis pregnancy centers and other groups have demonstrated holistic care for women in crisis.

This kind of care is not just good for babies whose lives are saved, but it is also good for women and for society as a whole. A significant aspect of the intimacy of pregnancy is the recognition of the bond that is forged between mother and child. It is one that we rightly recognize, preserve, and nurture, not destroy. Nor ought we to abandon an understanding of the relationship between mother and child as a beautiful bond in favor of one in which they have competing rights.

Unborn babies and abortion

Fetal development. As indicated above, abortion concerns more than a woman in a crisis pregnancy. It also concerns the unborn child, who has been at the center of the debate on abortion for decades. One of the central questions in the *Roe v. Wade* case had to do with the status of the unborn. Is the unborn child fully human? If so, is the human being in question a person? The decision made by the court effectively declared that the unborn child is not fully human, or at least is not a person with the rights and protections granted to those who are born. In the introductory chapter on bioethics I addressed the question of the embryo and personhood, and concluded that at every stage of development human offspring are fully human. Here I will simply highlight certain stages and aspects of embryonic and fetal development, indicating how unborn children are fearfully and wonderfully made:[80]

- Week 2: implantation occurs
- Week 3: the brain, spinal cord, heart, and other organs begin to form
- Week 4: rapid growth, the heart begins to beat, there is early development of the brain, and basic facial features begin to appear
- Week 5: the brain and face develop rapidly
- Week 8: eyes are visible, lungs start to form

---

80. See Megan Best, *Fearfully and Wonderfully Made: Ethics and the Beginning of Human Life* (Kingsford, Australia: Matthias Media, 2012), chap. 2. Best notes that there can be some variation in development.

- Week 10: spontaneous movement observable on ultrasound
- Weeks 11–14: nails appear on fingers and toes, genitalia are recognizable as male or female, the baby can make a fist, tooth buds appear
- Weeks 15–18: fine hair grows on the head, baby begins to move and make sucking motions
- Weeks 19–21: baby can hear, becomes more active, mother can feel first movements, baby can swallow by the end of this period
- Week 22: heartbeat can be heard with a stethoscope
- Week 26: baby may be startled by loud noises
- Weeks 27–30: brain grows rapidly, eyelids can open and close

When do abortions occur? According to statistics given by the Guttmacher Institute, 65.4 percent of abortions occur by week 8, 14.7 percent between weeks 9–10, 8.2 percent between weeks 11–12, 6.3 percent between weeks 13–15, 3.4.1 percent between weeks 16–20, and 1.3 percent after week 21.[81] While a large majority of abortions takes place by week 8, and almost 89 percent take place in the first trimester, based on the number of abortions annually, almost one hundred thousand abortions occur after the first trimester, and about ten thousand occur after twenty-one weeks.

Fathers and abortion

Abortion has largely been framed as an issue that weighs a woman's right to privacy against the baby's right to life. One of the issues that is often neglected concerns the father's responsibilities and rights. On the one hand, it is often the father who puts pressure on the mother to have an abortion. There may be many reasons for this, but ultimately it is a failure to take responsibility for the child. Legalized abortion, it is said, is necessary to empower women and allow them to have sexual liberty without being burdened by an unplanned pregnancy. Yet it has emboldened men to pursue sexual relationships without taking responsibility for fatherhood. Fathers should take responsibility for their children, planned or not. If more fathers will do so, more women will have the courage to bear their children.

On the other hand, fathers are not considered to have any rights with respect to their child until birth. Yet fatherhood begins at conception, not at birth, and men too can be hurt by abortion.[82] Attempts have been made to require spousal consent for abortion, but these provisions have been denied. Fathers should have a voice, particularly as advocates for their unborn children.

Society and abortion

The twentieth century witnessed horrific bloodshed through world wars, genocide, and ethnic cleansing. Yet one of the most

---

81. Numbers are by weeks after the last menstrual period. See Guttmacher Institute, "Induced Abortion in the United States," https://www.guttmacher.org/fact-sheet/induced-abortion-united-states.
82. See, e.g., BBC, "Fathers Rights," http://www.bbc.co.uk/ethics/abortion/legal/fathers.shtml; Priests for Life, "Men Hurt Too," http://www.priestsforlife.org/postabortion/fathersandabortion.htm.

horrific legacies of the twentieth century is that of abortion, with over sixty million legal abortions in the United States alone since *Roe v. Wade* in 1973. Instead of a safe haven for development, the womb has become the most dangerous place to live. Some of those who advocate care for the poor, the vulnerable, those in prison, and immigrants, and who expound what it implies to love one's enemy, are the same people who defend the killing of a child in the womb.

A professor told me of a state dinner for those who served on various committees, which brought together politicians, educators, medical professors, and others. At his table, the conversation turned to abortion. One person quipped, "I can't imagine anything worse than a society that forces women to bear children they do not want." The professor answered, "What about a society that kills the children it does not want?" Abortion is not merely a personal issue, and it is not only those who have abortions that are accountable to God. As Bonhoeffer asserted, there arc numerous motivations for abortion, and often guilt falls on the community as much as on the individual. No society that tolerates, let alone encourages, the killing of children in the womb can call itself civilized, for "reverence for human life is an indisputable characteristic of a humane and civilized society."[83]

Conclusion

Abortion is a contentious issue, politically and morally. It is a matter of life and death, in which we must separate out the moral issue from political rhetoric, and in which our legal and political judgments must follow our moral judgments. Arguments defending abortion, except to save the mother's life, are unconvincing. Every human life is precious and should be welcomed and received as a gift, not terminated. Special protection and assistance ought to be given to the most vulnerable. This includes both the child in the womb and women in crisis pregnancies.

Terminology is important, and euphemisms tells us much about what we try to conceal. To refer to the developing human being as the "product of conception," "cluster of cells," "blob of tissue," and the like is to conceal what we know to be true, and what virtually everyone acknowledges when we wait during pregnancy with expectancy: there is a baby in Mommy's tummy. To insist otherwise when the baby is unwanted is moral blindness. Abortion is, in short, a great moral evil. There may come a day when future generations look back at the late twentieth and early twenty-first century and wonder how abortion could have been tolerated, how it could even have been defended with philosophical and theological arguments. Perhaps it will be to some future generation what slavery is to ours, an unthinkable, unmistakable injustice.[84]

83. John Stott, *Issues Facing Christians Today*, 4th ed. (Grand Rapids: Zondervan, 2006), 392.
84. On this point, see Karen Swallow Prior, "Abortion Will be Considered Unthinkable 50 Years From Now: The Moral Case Against Abortion," *Vox*, April 3, 2019, https://www.vox.com/platform/amp/2019/3/27/18194710/abortion-will-be-considered-unthinkable-50-years-from-now.

Select Resources

Banner, Michael. *The Practice of Abortion: A Critique.* London: Darton, Longman & Todd, 1999.

Beckwith, Francis J. *Defending Life: A Moral and Legal Case against Abortion Choice.* Cambridge: Cambridge University Press, 2007.

———. *Politically Correct Death: Answering Arguments for Abortion Rights.* Grand Rapids: Baker, 1993.

Best, Megan. *Fearfully and Wonderfully Made: Ethics and the Beginning of Human Life.* Kingsford, Australia: Matthias Media, 2012.

George, Robert P., and Christopher Tollefsen. *Embryo: A Defense of Human Life.* New York: Doubleday, 2008.

Gorman, Michael J. *Abortion and the Early Church: Christian, Jewish and Pagan Attitudes in the Greco-Roman World.* Downers Grove, IL: InterVarsity Press, 1982.

Johnson, Abby. *Unplanned: The Dramatic True Story of a Former Planned Parenthood Leader's Eye-Opening Journey across the Life Line.* Carol Stream, IL: Tyndale House, 2010.

Kilner, John F., ed. *Why People Matter: A Christian Engagement with Rival Views of Human Significance.* Grand Rapids: Baker Academic, 2017.

Klusendorf, Scott. *The Case for Life: Equipping Christians to Engage the Culture.* Wheaton, IL: Crossway, 2009.

Pojman, Louis P., and Francis J. Beckwith, eds. *The Abortion Controversy: 25 Years after Roe v. Wade: A Reader.* 2nd ed. New York: Wadsworth, 1998.

CHAPTER 13

EUTHANASIA AND PHYSICIAN-ASSISTED SUICIDE

*The life of every living thing is in his hand,
as well as the breath of all mankind.*

—Job 12:10

*Blessed be the God and Father of our Lord
Jesus Christ, the Father of mercies and the
God of all comfort. He comforts us in all
our affliction, so that we may be able to
comfort those who are in any kind of affliction, through the comfort we ourselves
receive from God.*

—2 Corinthians 1:3–4

*Rejoice in hope; be patient in affliction; be
persistent in prayer.*

—Romans 12:12

Introduction

On September 11, 2015, the California State Legislature approved the End of Life Option Act. The bill, which would allow doctors to prescribe medicine to help terminally ill patients end their lives, was signed into law by California governor Jerry Brown on October 5, 2015. The addition of California represents a significant step toward broader acceptance of physician-assisted suicide and the right-to-die movement.[1] Five other states had previously approved some form of physician-assisted suicide, or "aid-in-dying," as supporters call it: Oregon (1997), Washington (2009), Montana (2009), Vermont (2013), and New Mexico (2014). By the spring of 2019, Colorado, the District of Columbia, and Hawaii had been added to the list.[2]

Several prominent cases over a forty-year period in the United States have drawn national attention to many of the issues that surface in the debate over euthanasia and physician-assisted suicide.

Karen Ann Quinlan (1976)

On April 15, 1975, at age twenty-one, Karen Ann Quinlan collapsed and stopped breathing after arriving home from a party where she had consumed alcohol and tranquilizers. She fell into a coma and was placed on a respirator and a feeding tube. After several months, her parents requested that doctors remove the respirator. When doctors refused, Quinlan's parents filed a lawsuit on September 12, 1975. A New Jersey superior court judge ruled against the parents, but that ruling was overturned by the New Jersey Supreme Court on March 31, 1976. The respirator was removed, but Quinlan continued to breathe on her own. She was given medically assisted nutrition and hydration, and lived almost ten more years, until she died on June 11, 1985, at age thirty-one.[3]

Nancy Cruzan (1990)

On January 11, 1983, at age twenty-five, Nancy Cruzan was in an accident and thrown from her car, landing face down in water. Paramedics arrived at the scene to find that she had no vital signs. After being resuscitated, Cruzan remained unconscious. She was kept alive with medically assisted nutrition and hydration, but there was no improvement in her condition. Eventually Cruzan's parents requested that the feeding tube be removed. A county judge granted permission, but that decision was overturned by the Missouri Supreme Court on November 16, 1988. The parents appealed to the United States Supreme Court, and on June 25, 1990, the court denied the request to remove the feeding tube on the basis that there was no clear evidence that

1. Ian Lovett, "California Legislature Approves Assisted Suicide," *New York Times*, September 11, 2015, http://www.nytimes.com/2015/09/12/us/california-legislature-approves-assisted-suicide.html?_r=0. For an overview of the states that permit physician-assisted suicide, see Emily Barone, "See Which States Allow Assisted Suicide," *Time*, November 3, 2014, http://time.com/3551560/brittany-maynard-right-to-die-laws. This article is ironically posted in the "Living" section of *Time* online.
2. See the list from "Death with Dignity" advocates: https://www.deathwithdignity.org/learn/death-with-dignity-acts.
3. Robert D. McFadden, "Karen Ann Quinlan, 31, Dies; Focus of '76 Right to Die Case," *The New York Times*, June 12, 1985, http://www.nytimes.com/1985/06/12/nyregion/karen-ann-quinlan-31-dies-focus-of-76-right-to-die-case.html.

Nancy Cruzan would have wanted that. On August 30, 1990, the Cruzans brought evidence to a Missouri judge, in the form of testimony from Nancy's friends and coworkers, that she would not want to be kept alive under such conditions. With the new evidence, the judge ruled on December 14, 1990, that the feeding tube could be removed, and Nancy died on December 26, 1990.[4]

Terri Schiavo (2005)

On February 25, 1990, twenty-six-year-old Terri Schiavo collapsed from heart failure and suffered severe brain damage due to a lack of oxygen to her brain. She required medically assisted nutrition and hydration to stay alive. Eventually her husband Michael claimed that Terri had indicated that she would not want to live like that, and sought to have the feeding tube removed. However, he had become involved with another woman with whom he had two children, and questions arose as to whether he had Terri's best interest in mind. In any case, Terri's parents strongly objected to having her nutrition and hydration removed, insisting that she would want to live and that they were willing to care for her. In 1998 the dispute gained national media attention and turned to a battle in the courts that lasted for years. Ultimately, a circuit judge in Florida ruled in Michael Schiavo's favor,

and the case became heavily politicized when legislators attempted to intervene to stop the removal of the feeding tube. The US Supreme Court refused more than once to hear an emergency appeal, and the feeding tube that had kept Terri Schiavo alive for over a decade was removed on March 18, 2005. Almost two weeks later, on March 31, 2005, she died at age forty-one.[5]

Brittany Maynard (2014)

In January 2014, Brittany Maynard was diagnosed with terminal brain cancer. Facing a painful illness and death, Maynard "quickly decided that death with dignity was the best option for me and my family." She and her husband soon moved from their home in California to Oregon in order to take advantage of Oregon's physician-assisted suicide law. Maynard's case received national attention. She had many who supported her choice, as well as many who exhorted her not to take her own life. In November 2014, at age twenty-nine, she died after taking a fatal dose of medicine prescribed for her by a doctor under Oregon's Death with Dignity Act.[6]

The case of Brittany Maynard is different from the other three cases described here, and it illustrates several important issues. First, unlike the other cases, she was conscious, she expressly requested to die, and (with help) she took her own life. Second,

---

4. Andrew H. Malcolm, "Nancy Cruzan: End to Long Goodbye," *The New York Times*, December 29, 1990, http://www.nytimes.com/1990/12/29/us/nancy-cruzan-end-to-long-goodbye.html.

5. Ninette Sosa et al., "Terri Schiavo Has Died," CNN, March 31, 2005, http://www.cnn.com/2005/LAW/03/31/schiavo/index.html.

6. Catherine E. Shoichet, "Brittany Maynard, Advocate for 'Death with Dignity,' Dies," CNN, November 3, 2014, http://www.cnn.com/2014/11/02/health/oregon-brittany-maynard/index.html.

her case illustrates legal—and moral—developments that have taken place concerning end-of-life decisions over a period of decades. Cases such as Cruzan, Quinlan, and Schiavo have been discussed for years, with moral debates about human dignity, autonomy, suffering, whether there is a right to die or to receive help in dying, and so on. As a legal matter, in 1997 the Supreme Court of the United States considered two cases related to the concept of a right to die (*Vacco v. Quill* and *Washington v. Glucksberg*). The Supreme Court denied that there was a right to die, but they left open the possibility that states could permit physician-assisted suicide. States that have made such provisions have justified it on the basis of arguments from patients and their families that there is a right to choose death in order to avoid prolonged suffering or existence in a permanent comatose state. Indeed, the Maynard case played a role in the adoption of the California law mentioned above, since she had to move from her home in California to Oregon in order legally to obtain a prescription for a lethal dose of drugs.

Proponents of physician-assisted suicide appeal to values or rights such as individual liberty and autonomy, which they understand to be essential to human dignity. Brittany Maynard expressed her view, saying, "The worst thing that could happen to me is that I wait too long because I'm trying to seize each day . . . but I somehow have my autonomy taken away from me by my disease."[7] She did not see her choice as suicide, for she said, "I'm not killing myself. Cancer is killing me. I am choosing to go in a way that is less suffering and less pain." To call that suicide, she argued, is "highly inflammatory and just incorrect, because I am already dying from cancer. I don't want to die. People who commit suicide are typically people who want to die."[8] This comparison is illuminating, and her assertion questionable, for many who commit suicide do not want to die so much as escape the pain they are experiencing, which is not unlike arguments for physician-assisted suicide.

The desire to allow physician-assisted suicide testifies to the desperation experienced by those facing suffering and death, who see no better option than to choose death before death chooses them. Supporters argue that suffering, extreme pain, and disease that rob patients of their autonomy represent an attack on human dignity, and compassion demands that we help to end the suffering of those who wish to die. It is certainly a terrible thing to suffer, and to have a disease take away our independence, little by little. Having learned to prize autonomy, and to be in control of our lives, it is a devastating thing to lose. It seems undignified to become once again like a child, dependent on others. This may explain why polls indicate that almost seven in ten Americans agree that doctors should be permitted to help a patient commit suicide

---

7. Shoichet, "Brittany Maynard."
8. Bill Briggs, "Death with Dignity Advocate Brittany Maynard Dies in Oregon," NBC, November 2, 2014. http://www.nbcnews.com/health/health-news/death-dignity-advocate-brittany-maynard-dies-oregon-n235091.

if the patient requests it.[9] Such numbers suggest that there will be more victories for the legalization of physician-assisted suicide. At least, in the midst of suffering, the patient is in control, and the choice represents to them "death with dignity." But is it?

This chapter will examine moral perspectives and questions about physician-assisted suicide and euthanasia. We will consider relevant matters such as autonomy, human dignity, suffering, despair, compassion, and hope. As with other moral issues, our understanding of euthanasia and physician-assisted suicide is a matter of worldview. We will begin with some arguments for euthanasia, along with some definitions and distinctions, followed by an evaluation of some of the key arguments and a Christian response.

Definitions and Distinctions

Euthanasia literally means "good death," from the Greek εὖ (good or well) and Θάνατος (death). For some, euthanasia is believed to be a good death, or at least a better death than what they perceive to be the alternatives. However, if euthanasia is accepted in principle as a good death, or better-than-alternatives death, is it possible to limit the reasons for which one might choose euthanasia over perceived alternatives? That is a concern shared by some supporters of euthanasia, who have sought to describe when euthanasia is morally acceptable and, at least

by implication, when it is not. Consider, for instance, the case made by James Rachels, a prominent defender of euthanasia.[10]

James Rachels's Case for Euthanasia

Paradigm case
Beginning with the case of a cancer patient who is near death, suffering extreme pain, and asks his doctor to end his life by a lethal injection, Rachels develops a paradigm case for his defense of euthanasia, with the following criteria:

- The person is *deliberately* killed.
- The person is going to die soon anyway.
- The person is suffering terrible pain.
- The person has asked to be killed.
- The killing is an act of mercy—that is, the *reason* for the killing is "to prevent further needless suffering and to provide the patient with a 'good death,' or at least as good as it could be under the circumstances."[11]

Argument from mercy
In developing his case for euthanasia, Rachels believes that the argument from mercy is the simplest and most powerful argument. Indeed, "mercy killing" is one of the common euphemisms for euthanasia. When a terminally ill patient is suffering beyond comprehension, "the argument from mercy says

9. Andrew Dugan, "In U.S., Support Up for Doctor-Assisted Suicide," Gallup, May 27, 2015, http://www.gallup.com/poll/183425/support-doctor-assisted-suicide.aspx.
10. James Rachels, "Euthanasia," in *Matters of Life and Death*, ed. Tom Regan, 2nd ed. (New York: Random House, 1986), 35–76.
11. Rachels, "Euthanasia," 36.

euthanasia is justified because it provides an end to *that*."[12] For Rachels, it is virtually self-evident that mercy or compassion will lead us to help others die when they are in extreme pain and request such help. Mark A. Duntley Jr., whose essay appears in an influential text on theology and medical ethics, agrees, asserting that mercy is the essence of what it means to care for one another, and that mercy within a caring, covenant relationship between doctor and patient may lead the doctor to help the patient die.[13] Below we will consider what mercy, along with related virtues of love and compassion, imply and require in our treatment of those who suffer.

Utilitarian arguments

Another argument for euthanasia is adopted from a utilitarian approach. It should be said that Rachels is cautious about a utilitarian defense of euthanasia, primarily out of a concern that the promotion of happiness or the avoidance of misery could be used to defend involuntary euthanasia. Nonetheless, he argues that the idea of promoting happiness and avoiding misery is sound if these things are not absolutized. Thus, if the principle behind utilitarianism is qualified, it can serve to justify euthanasia—for example, if it "promotes *the best interests of everyone concerned* and violates no one's rights."[14] Rachels argues that it may be in the patient's best interest

to die an easier death; it may be in the best interest of the patient's spouse who suffers alongside the patient; it may be in the best interest of hospital staff who can better help other patients, and in the interests of those patients who receive their care; and if the patient asks to die, it is not a violation of his or her rights. So, Rachels concludes, "how can active euthanasia in this case be wrong? How can it be wrong to do an action that is merciful, that benefits everyone concerned, and that violates no one's rights?"[15]

As a brief response, this account represents a highly dubious concept of interests, making it wholly subjective, and even then questionable. Further, it assumes a view of rights that should be scrutinized, and it reflects a strongly utilitarian conception of morality. A fuller response will be included below, flowing from a Christian worldview.

Argument from the Golden Rule

Rachels also argues that the Golden Rule supports euthanasia. That is, he supposes, many people in the situation of great pain near the end of life would prefer to die more quickly and painlessly. If we would want euthanasia in such a case, then we should grant it to others.[16] Indeed, this argument seems to strike a chord with many people, evidenced by poll numbers mentioned earlier, and comments such as, "I would never want to live like that."

---

12. Rachels, "Euthanasia," 49.
13. Mark A. Duntley Jr., "Covenantal Ethics and Care for the Dying," in *On Moral Medicine: Theological Perspectives in Medical Ethics*, eds. Stephen E. Lammers and Allen Verhey, 2nd ed. (Grand Rapids: Eerdmans, 1998), 663–66.
14. Rachels, "Euthanasia," 52 (emphasis added).
15. Rachels, "Euthanasia," 52.
16. Rachels, "Euthanasia," 53.

It is one of the reasons that euthanasia or physician-assisted suicide have either been decriminalized or legalized in some places.

Several initial comments may be made in response to this argument. First, it is difficult to predict in advance just what we would want to do in such a situation, which is so often complex and has many variable. Second, there are certain things that we ought not to want; we can neither demand that others grant us whatever we want, especially if the want is dubious, nor can we grant to others what we would want *on that basis alone*. Third, and related to the second, the Golden Rule assumes a worldview and morality that is undermined by utilitarianism and proponents of euthanasia, which makes the appeal to it rather questionable.

Argument from autonomy and the right to die

The above arguments are grounded in personal autonomy—that is, the right of individuals to choose the course of their lives. The case for euthanasia is based on the concept of the right to die. If autonomy includes the right to choose how to live, and have control over our lives, then it is reasoned that it also implies the right to choose death and, as far as possible, how to die. Karen Lebacqz defends euthanasia (or physician-assisted suicide), contending that "there are circumstances in which active euthanasia is *morally* justified," as when "patients are terminally ill and have requested that their lives be terminated, along with the further

qualification that they are in enduring and intractable pain." Indeed, in such circumstances, she finds it "absurd, if not obscene" to question whether euthanasia is permissible. She goes so far as to ask if it is "ever permissible *not* to use active euthanasia for one who suffers so, with no hope of recovery?"[17]

Such a strong statement appears to be based on the view that a patient's autonomy should prevent anyone from challenging their decision to die. Yet it is stated so emphatically that it is reasonable to wonder if the patient's consent is required in such cases. Further, it ignores the highly relevant question of whether it is ever permissible to assist in another person's death, which is required by those seeking euthanasia.

Distinctions in the Debate

Physician-assisted suicide and euthanasia
In simple terms, the person who triggers the lethal act is what distinguishes physician-assisted suicide, where the patient initiates the act, and euthanasia, where typically it is a physician who initiates the lethal act.

Active and passive euthanasia (and letting die)
Rachels describes active euthanasia and passive euthanasia as follows: active euthanasia refers to cases in which "the patient is killed"—for example, when given a lethal injection—whereas passive euthanasia refers to cases in which "the patient is not killed but merely allowed to die." In the traditional

---

17. Karen Lebacqz, "Reflection," in Lammers and Verhey, *On Moral Medicine*, 666–67.

view, he says, active euthanasia—killing patients—has been widely condemned, while passive euthanasia—letting patients die—is sometimes considered morally acceptable.[18] Rachels contends that such a distinction is not morally valid, and that just as passive euthanasia is sometimes permissible, so active euthanasia should sometimes be permitted, especially since it is often preferable and more humane, because it alleviates suffering.[19]

Several things should be said in response. To begin with, Rachels and others fail to note that there is a real distinction between passive euthanasia and "allowing a patient to die," and to blur the distinction is misleading and unhelpful.[20] Simply put, most people are "allowed to die" without their deaths involving elements associated with euthanasia. In such cases, while their death may be foreseeable, the decision not to begin or continue treatment is made without the intent to hasten death. Patients are "allowed to die" regularly, when intervention is deemed to be futile, and such decisions are not properly described as passive euthanasia. Rather, it may simply be a recognition that the person is actively dying, and we rightly distinguish between "saving life by prolonging the living of it and only prolonging a patient's dying."[21] There is no necessity to begin or continue futile treatment. Further,

in cases of suffering, it is misleading to suggest that we must choose between active euthanasia and simply allowing the patient to die in great pain and without dignity, a point that will be developed below.

A more helpful distinction between active and passive euthanasia is this: active euthanasia refers to cases in which a patient is killed by an act aimed at their death, such as intentionally giving the patient a lethal dose of a drug, whereas passive euthanasia refers to cases in which necessary and ordinary treatment is withheld with the intention to hasten death. Each case has to be considered carefully, but this could refer to a situation in which the patient requires medically assisted nutrition and hydration, at least for a time, or perhaps temporary use of a breathing tube. If the patient is not in the active dying process, and the patient's health could be sustained or improved by treatment, then to withhold the treatment is to intend death and could be considered passive euthanasia. By contrast, if the patient is dying and all potential treatments are futile, then allowing the patient to die is not the same as intending their death, and therefore should not be confused with euthanasia.

John Stott gets the distinction right when he says that "to withhold or withdraw useless treatment from a terminally ill patient is

---

18. Rachels, "Euthanasia," 38.
19. For details of his case, see James Rachels, "Active and Passive Euthanasia," *New England Journal of Medicine* 292 (January 9, 1975): 78–80.
20. For a different type of response and challenge to Rachels, see J. P. Moreland, "James Rachels and the Active Euthanasia Debate," *Journal of the Evangelical Theological Society* 31, no. 1 (March 1988): 81–90.
21. Paul Ramsey, *The Patient as Person* (New Haven, CT: Yale University Press, 1970), 118. Further, Ramsey makes a distinction between euthanasia and "merely allowing a patient to die by stopping or not starting life-sustaining procedures deemed not morally mandatory."

not euthanasia. Nor is the administration of painkillers to a dying patient which may incidentally accelerate death, but the primary intention of which is to relieve pain. In both these cases death is already irreversibly present." He adds that "although this distinction is not always amenable to precise definition, there is a fundamental difference between causing somebody to die (which is euthanasia) and allowing him or her to die (which is not)."[22]

Ordinary and extraordinary treatment

In the previous point, I referred to passive euthanasia in terms of withholding necessary and *ordinary* treatment in order to hasten death. The distinction between ordinary and extraordinary treatment is sometimes said to be unhelpful, in part because it may be difficult to define and it changes over time. What was once extraordinary may now be ordinary, such as kidney dialysis or quadruple bypass heart surgery. Nevertheless, the distinction can be useful. Ordinary treatment may be used to refer to treatment that is generally effective or promising, not excessively burdensome, is low risk for the patient, and so on. Extraordinary treatment, then, is excessively burdensome, presents a high risk verses benefit for the patient, may even be judged to be futile or at least is not proved to be effective, and so on.

The point of this distinction is that ordinary treatment to restore health or maintain life is generally expected, while extraordinary treatment is not considered morally necessary. As John Jefferson Davis points out, "There is no moral obligation to prolong artificially a truly terminal patient's irreversible and imminent process of dying. This is sometimes called employing 'useless means' of treatment." He continues, "The point of any form of medical treatment is to cure the patient, or if curing is not possible, at least to contribute to a reasonable expectation of life and level of comfort. A form of treatment with no reasonable expectation of accomplishing these ends is not therapy in any meaningful sense of the word, but may in fact represent an inappropriate imposition upon the dying patient."[23] Gilbert Meilaender suggests that the distinction between ordinary and extraordinary is not always clarifying, but he employs the concepts when arguing that patients need not receive treatment that is either useless or burdensome.[24]

Tom Beauchamp and James Childress, in their influential work on biomedical ethics, consider distinctions mentioned here and reject them, claiming that "the venerable position that these traditional distinctions occupy in professional codes, institutional policies, and writings in biomedical ethics provides no warrant whatever for retaining them."[25] With respect to the distinction between ordinary and extraordinary, they find it to be "unacceptably vague and morally

22. John Stott, *Issues Facing Christians Today*, 4th ed. (Grand Rapids: Zondervan, 2006), 410.
23. John Jefferson Davis, *Evangelical Ethics: Issues Facing the Church Today*, 3rd ed. (Phillipsburg, NJ: P&R, 2004), 191.
24. Gilbert Meilaender, *Bioethics: A Primer for Christians* (Grand Rapids: Eerdmans, 1996), 72–75.
25. Tom L. Beauchamp and James F. Childress, *Principles of Biomedical Ethics*, 5th ed. (Oxford: Oxford University Press, 2001), 120.

misleading," and as such they reject it. They acknowledge that "the customary or usual in medical practice can be relevant to a moral judgment," but they add that it "is not by itself sufficient or decisive."[26]

However, the distinction is not invalid simply because it is not in itself sufficient or decisive. It may, in fact, serve a helpful role in making decisions.[27] Of course, there are sometimes ambiguities in making these distinctions, which is one of the reasons that they are challenged, but they do offer patients and their families useful categories for considering their options. Treatments do change over time, and so it can be acknowledged that the analysis of a given treatment or a particular disease may change. However, that doesn't mean that the distinction between ordinary and extraordinary is useless, for they are used to help make a decision about a particular patient at a particular time, not about a patient in the future or the past.[28] The question is thus whether a given treatment is ordinary or extraordinary in the present situation. If it is extraordinary, it may still be pursued in some situations, but it need not be. If it is ordinary, and it is required to sustain life, then to forgo such treatment may cause us to wonder if it is a case of passive euthanasia.

There are always difficult cases—for example, a cancer patient deciding whether another round of chemotherapy or radiation should be pursued: though often it is fairly ordinary and there is a possibility of restored health, it may also be very painful and unpleasant, to the point of being considered excessively burdensome. The specifics of the case must be weighed, and in some cases it is reasonable to forgo treatment even if it is the best opportunity, humanly speaking, for healing. The point is that some way of thinking about ordinary and extraordinary treatment is useful in this and many other cases.

Withdrawing and withholding treatment

A brief mention can be made about the distinction between withdrawing treatment that has begun and withholding treatment. In one sense the distinction is obvious from the very description. However, it can be confused with active and passive euthanasia and letting a patient die. Several observations are in order. First, in many cases, there is no significant moral difference between withdrawing and withholding a particular treatment in the same case or type of case. That is, on the one hand, if a given treatment is deemed to be useless or burdensome, then when considering whether to withhold or later (or in a different but similar case) to withdraw, both withholding and withdrawing treatment may be justified. On the other hand, if a treatment is necessary and ordinary, both withholding and withdrawing could be considered unjustified. Second, in cases where there is some question about the usefulness of a given treatment,

26. Beauchamp and Childress, *Principles of Biomedical Ethics*, 123.
27. Ramsey, one of the pioneers in thinking through moral implications of advances in medical ethics, used this distinction in *The Patient as Person*, 118–24.
28. Cf. Moreland, "James Rachels and the Active Euthanasia Debate," 82.

there may be good reason to start treatment to see whether it might be effective, and withdraw treatment if it is not. Third, it may be noted that it is sometimes more difficult emotionally to withdraw treatment than to withhold it in the first place, since the act of withdrawing may feel like direct killing, even if it is the underlying disease rather than the act of removal that kills the patient. In some cases, to begin treatment creates an expectation on the part of patients and their families that it will be continued, so that they resist a physician's recommendation to discontinue treatment, which makes the decision about withholding treatment in the first place more complicated.[29]

Voluntary, nonvoluntary, and involuntary euthanasia

This distinction, or sometimes the distinction simply between voluntary and involuntary euthanasia, is often invoked in the debate. *Voluntary* euthanasia refers to a situation in which a patient who is suffering great pain near the end of life is killed after asking for help in dying. *Nonvoluntary* euthanasia refers to a situation in which a patient is killed without having been capable of expressing a wish to die, such as in the case of a newborn, a comatose patient, or a patient suffering from severe dementia. This does not fit with the paradigm case of euthanasia that Rachels and others wish to defend, for if the patient is unable to express their wishes, then they have

not asked to die, and further, it seems that it is difficult to know that they are suffering great pain. Instead, someone else decides that the patient's life is not worth living. *Involuntary* euthanasia takes it a step further, where a patient's life is deemed not to be worth living, or they are considered a burden on society, and they are killed in spite of the fact that the patient does not want to die and has expressed a desire to live. This is an appalling notion even to most advocates of euthanasia, such as Rachels, who says, "My view is that it is simply murder and that it is not justified."[30]

Result, aim, and motive

Another important moral distinction for the discussion of euthanasia is between result, aim, and motive. Result refers to what occurs (e.g., death); aim refers to the intended result (death, for instance, or care); and motive refers to the subjective reason for the act. For some, what matters is only the result, such as death or the end of suffering: If a person is suffering and wants to die, why does it matter whether death occurs sooner by intention or later by "natural" cause, by withdrawing "futile" or "effective" treatment, by giving medicine for pain relief that could also hasten death and giving enough pain medicine to certainly hasten death, and so on?

Aim and motive can be morally decisive.[31] For example, Christians have denounced suicide but honored martyrdom. The result is the same, yet the evaluation is different, because

---

29. Beauchamp and Childress address problems with the distinction between withholding and withdrawing treatment in *Principles of Biomedical Ethics*, 120–23.
30. Rachels, "Euthanasia," 39.
31. Meilaender's discussion of aim and result is helpful, in *Bioethics*, 69–71.

the aim and motive are different. Suicide despairs of life and aims at death. Martyrdom does not despair of life, but accepts death (caused by someone else) as the result of faithfulness. It is thus deceptive to think that a Christian can pursue martyrdom, for then it takes on the characteristics of suicide.[32]

In the treatment of a patient, a critical moral consideration is whether the aim is to care for or to kill the patient. Judgments sometimes may not be easy, but they are important nonetheless. Bioethicist Nigel Cameron points out that "in traditional Hippocratic medicine the priority in terminal care has always been the comfort of the patient, even if securing that comfort (by treating with pain-killing drugs) may also have the effect of shortening life."[33] Treatment with pain-killers may be justified even though a quicker death is foreseeable, in part because the act is not aimed at death but pain relief. On the other hand, if the patient is given a large enough dose of the drug to be lethal, with the intention of ending the patient's life quickly, it is not justified. In that case, the aim is not merely to care for the patient as well as possible, but to kill the patient.

Further Considerations

Futile treatment

The discussion of distinctions above raised the idea of "futile" treatment, and a bit more needs to be said about that. At times, a patient's loved ones will feel it is necessary to "do everything possible" to keep the patient alive, and they will pressure health-care providers to do just that. This is understandable for many reasons: the reality of disease and death as enemies to be resisted; the finality of death and separation from a loved one; the hope for a miracle of restoration of health; doubts about the prognosis; and so on. As such, some—including many Christians—feel that everything possible should be done to keep the patient alive.

However, Christians have reason not to insist on futile treatment. In part, this conclusion relates to the patient's immediate situation. A patient should not be forced to endure treatment that is excessively burdensome, with little or no hope of success, as when the treatment simply prolongs the dying process and the suffering that goes with it. If the patient desires treatment, it is a different matter, for that is often (though perhaps not always) itself a sign that it is not excessively burdensome and that death is not imminent.

There is another reason that Christians need not pursue futile treatment, based on a larger perspective. As Andrew Cameron puts it, at this point in redemption history, "death always wins (Heb. 9:27a). Death is only finally defeated when the new future comes (1 Cor.

---

32. For a discussion and comparison of suicide and martyrdom in antiquity and the early church, see Edward J. Larson and Darrel W. Amundsen, *A Different Death: Euthanasia and the Christian Tradition* (Downers Grove, IL: InterVarsity Press, 1998).

33. Nigel M. de S. Cameron, "Euthanasia," in *New Dictionary of Christian Ethics and Pastoral Theology*, eds. David J. Atkinson et al. (Downers Grove, IL: InterVarsity Press, 1995), 357.

15:24–26). Given this sad truth, there comes a time when death *has* won. Switching off life-support is often the recognition of this truth."[34] To accept that is not a lack of faith and hope, but it is part of a sure hope in the future. And it is not a sheer act of the will, in which death is chosen, but rather an acknowledgment that death is inevitable and it is imminent. Paul Ramsey, in *The Patient as Person*, recognizes the tension at the end of life. On the one hand, we should not act in such a way that we aim at death. On the other hand, we need not fight death with a full arsenal of technological weapons when it is futile to do so (a temptation that has become acute in our advanced technological age). Meilaender summarizes Ramsey, saying that life "is not a god, but a gift of God. Thus we should neither aim at death nor continue the struggle against it when its time has come. 'Allowing to die' is permitted; killing is not. Within these limits lies the sphere of our freedom."[35]

This sphere requires wisdom, with certain commitments. The wise course of action is not always easy to discern, and for that reason we rely on physicians with technical skill and knowledge to help us to understand when a treatment may be effective and when it is futile. Sadly, quality of life has become a significant factor in many physicians' assessment of whether treatment is worth pursuing.[36] In order to trust physicians to guide us in the complexity of such decisions, we need physicians who are committed to being healers and caregivers, and we need institutions that maintain and reinforce those commitments. Otherwise physicians will be merely purveyors of medicine and equipment to be used alternatively for life or death, not according to whether they advance life, but whether the life in question is deemed to be worth advancing.

Individual autonomy and the right to die

One of the arguments for euthanasia cited above is the argument from autonomy and the "right to die." Indeed, these have featured significantly in the case for euthanasia in the late twentieth and early twenty-first century. It is reasoned that if freedom for human beings includes the right to determine how we live, then it is also true that we have the right to determine how and when we die. This is death with dignity: rather than having our lives ravaged and taken from us by disease, we have (or ought to have) the right to take control of the manner and timing of our death. How ought we respond to such a claim?

First, it might be noted that the Supreme Court of the United States, having heard formal arguments to this effect in two cases in 1997 (*Vacco v. Quill* and *Washington v. Glucksberg*), concluded that there

---

34. Andrew J. B. Cameron, *Joined-Up Life: A Christian Account of How Ethics Works* (Nottingham, UK: Inter-Varsity Press, 2011), 302.
35. Meilaender, *Bioethics*, 69.
36. See, e.g., "Will Your Advance Directive Be Followed?" (report by the Robert Powell Center for Medical Ethics at the National Right to Life Committee, rev. ed., October 2013), http://www.nrlc.org/uploads/medethics/WillYourAdvanceDirectiveBeFollowed.pdf.

is no "right to die" to be found in the United States Constitution, though they left open the possibility that states could permit physician-assisted suicide. Unfortunately, situations that involve end-of-life decisions have been asserted in legal terms as a right to die. However, in the case of a person (like Nancy Cruzan) who is in a persistent vegetative state and is kept alive by medically assisted nutrition and hydration, the issue is not whether there is a right to die but whether life must be continued under all circumstances and whether there is a right to decline certain types of medical treatment.[37]

Second, consider how the notion of a right to die relates to suicide. The decriminalization of suicide is not based on a right to die, but rather on the conclusion that the complex circumstances surrounding suicide are not best solved by the threat of sanctions against the one who is in despair. If a person chooses to commit suicide, it may not always be possible to prevent it, but that does not mean that the state should condone the choice by attributing to it a right. Indeed, to the contrary, the state may have an interest in preventing suicide, which is one reason to deny claims of a right to die, even if it does not prosecute someone who fails in an attempted suicide.

Third, the right to die is rooted in a radical sense of autonomy, one that no society—by the very nature of society—can properly affirm. A radical sense of autonomy denies the social nature of human beings. We are dependent, first and last, on God, who is our creator and sustainer. We are also dependent on one another, which is ironically evident in the fact that an "autonomous" patient requires help in dying. That is, the "right to die" requires not merely individual liberty but also a demand that others in society— the medical community in particular—assist someone in their pursuit of death, and thus affirm their death. It is reasonable to consider it not an act of "assistance" but, tragically, one of abandonment by the community.

Fourth, the argument for a right to die is misguided at a most basic level, for the whole language of rights is grounded in the right to life, and presupposes self-interest, not self-destruction.[38] A biblical response to autonomy affirms freedom, but in the context of human finitude. It is a great irony that the case for euthanasia and physician-assisted suicide asserts that autonomy is exercised—for the last time—in choosing death. For, as Meilaender puts it, "try as we may to forget it, death *is* the starkest reminder of our limits. It is therefore a peculiar moment at which to attempt to seize ultimate control of our life and pretend that we are independent self-creators."[39]

Fifth, the logic of a right to die cannot be limited to a narrow set of circumstances, such as the paradigm case proposed by Rachels. If

---

37.   Cf. John S. Feinberg and Paul D. Feinberg, *Ethics for a Brave New World*, 2nd ed. (Wheaton, IL: Crossway, 2010), 206.

38.   Gary P. Stewart et al., *Basic Questions on Suicide and Euthanasia: Are They Ever Right?* (Grand Rapids: Kregel, 1998), 37–38; Leon R. Kass, "Is There a Right to Die?," *Hastings Center Report* 23, no. 1 (January–February 1993): 36. J. Daryl Charles, "The 'Right to Die' in the Light of Contemporary Rights Rhetoric," in *Bioethics and the Future of Medicine: A Christian Appraisal*, eds. John F. Kilner, Nigel M. de S. Cameron, and David L. Schiedermayer (Grand Rapids: Eerdmans, 1995), 263–79.

39.   Meilaender, *Bioethics*, 64.

it is granted, it applies not only to the person suffering great pain near the end of life but also to the person diagnosed with a disease who wishes to avoid pain altogether (as in the Brittany Maynard case). Indeed, how can it discriminate against the person who suffers from emotional anxiety? The right to die leads to death on demand, which, much like abortion on demand, may require a reason for justification, but any reason will do. Anyone despairing of life is a candidate. This argument is not a scare tactic or merely hypothetical. Rather, these are the logical, foreseeable consequences of accepting the concept of a right to die and with it euthanasia, and these things are actually happening where euthanasia and assisted suicide are permitted.[40]

Sixth, it is a dubious proposition that the right to die increases freedom. Indeed, what follows on the notion of a right to die is the notion of an obligation to die. For once a society determines that death may be preferable to life, it is difficult to defend sustaining some lives—which many consider to be not worth living—at great expense to society. Those who are vulnerable are not in a position to defend their claim to life. Meilaender traces this progression, starting with arguments based in autonomy. He argues, "If self-determination is truly so significant that we have a right to help in ending our life, then how can we insist that such help can rightly be offered only to those who are suffering greatly?" What of others who wish to end their lives, who find life to be unbearable? "They, too, are autonomous, and, if autonomy is as important as the argument claims it is, then their autonomous requests for euthanasia should also be honored, even if they are not suffering greatly." And then again, why should suffering not be sufficient to end life? For "if the suffering of others makes so powerful a claim upon us that we should kill them to bring it to an end, it is hard to believe that we ought to restrict such merciful relief only to those who are self-determining, who are competent to request it."[41] It is not reassuring to suggest that safeguards can be put in place to prevent such a development, for, to paraphrase C. S. Lewis, what first appears to be an individual's exercise of autonomy and power over nature turns out to be the exercise of power by the strong over the weak, appealing to autonomy and freedom from nature.[42]

Euthanasia and human dignity
Often the case for euthanasia is connected with human dignity, to such a degree that "death with dignity" is a common slogan or even a euphemism in the case for euthanasia.

---

40. Stewart et al., *Basic Questions on Suicide and Euthanasia*, 53. Cf. Richard Fenigsen, "The Report of the Dutch Governmental Committee on Euthanasia," *Issues in Law and Medicine* 7 (Winter 1991): 339–44; Winston Ross, "Dying Dutch: Euthanasia Spreads across Europe," *Newsweek*, February 12, 2015, https://www.newsweek.com/2015/02/20/choosing-die-netherlands-euthanasia-debate-306223.html; Wesley J. Smith, "Euthanasia Comes to Canada," *Weekly Standard*, February 23, 2015, https://www.washingtonexaminer.com/weekly-standard/euthanasia-comes-to-canada.
41. Meilaender, *Bioethics*, 63.
42. See chap. 3 in C. S. Lewis, *The Abolition of Man: Or, Reflections on Education with Special Reference to the Teaching of English in the Upper Forms of School* (New York: Macmillan, 1947).

We are to understand that dignity is threatened by dependence and the loss of autonomy, and we are to believe that taking control of the decision concerning the timing and manner of death will maintain human dignity.

However, rather than being grounded in human dignity, the case for euthanasia and the right to die undermines human dignity. Consider the argument often heard, that if we are willing to act humanely toward animals who suffer by euthanizing them, why do we not do the same for human beings?[43] One obvious response is that we draw distinctions between human beings and animals, which determines how we treat them. We should care for animals, but they do not possess human dignity. More specifically, if we decide to treat human beings in the same way as we treat animals, should we condone nonvoluntary and even involuntary euthanasia? In the case of animals, we do not ask their consent to euthanize them; rather, someone decides that it is more merciful to them that they die than continue to live.

The Physician's Covenant

The Hippocratic oath, long sworn by physicians, originated with Hippocrates of Cos (460–ca. 370 BC). It is a solemn oath, appealing to deities to underscore its binding character, and it includes promises of fidelity, including a lengthy pledge to patients. The one who swears the oath promises, among other things, neither to "give a deadly drug to anybody if asked for it," nor to "make a suggestion to this effect."[44] As such, it prohibits both euthanasia and abortion.

This oath and its promises remind the physician of the professional guild to which he or she belongs, and of the commitments required to serve patients well. These commitments require physicians to understand and respect the limits of their services, providing boundaries that are never to be crossed if they are to fulfill their calling and serve patients well. The most basic moral requirement of medical professionals is summed up with the words "Always to Care, Never to Kill."[45] This commitment, strengthened by an oath or code, not only focuses physicians on their true calling but also protects them against demands made by patients, families, and society.

In recent decades, however, the physician's covenant has been challenged, as reflected in this statement in a leading

43. Both Duntley and Lebacqz, cited earlier, who have articles in an influential text on theology and medicine, ask this question. Mark A. Duntley Jr., "Covenantal Ethics and Care for the Dying," in Lammers and Verhey, *On Moral Medicine*, 663–66; Lebacqz, "Reflection," 666–67.

44. "The Hippocratic Oath," in Lammers and Verhey, *On Moral Medicine*, 107. This translation is from Ludwig Edelstein, "The Hippocratic Oath: Text, Translation and Interpretation," in *Ancient Medicine*, eds. Oswei Temkin and C. Lillian Temkin (Baltimore, MD: Johns Hopkins University Press, 1967), 3–63. For perspectives of several authors on the Hippocratic oath in relation to Christian practices in medicine, see Lammers and Verhey, *On Moral Medicine*, 108–37. See also C. Ben Mitchell and D. Joy Riley, *Christian Bioethics: A Guide for Pastors, Health Care Professionals, and Families*, B&H Studies in Christian Ethics (Nashville: B&H, 2014), 11–17.

45. For a statement on this, see the declaration produced by the Ramsey Colloquium of the Institute on Religion and Public Life in New York City, "Always to Care, Never to Kill," *First Things*, February 1992, http://www.firstthings.com/article/1992/02/006-always-to-care-never-to-kill.

biomedical ethics text: "We maintain that physician assistance in hastening death is best viewed as part of a continuum of medical care."[46] Such a statement—*to consider a physician's role in hastening death to be part of medical care rather than its subversion*—ought to be understood as radical. Yet it reflects the view of a growing number of people in society, including physicians and ethicists. What is more, rather than being used as a bulwark against such changes, the Hippocratic oath has simply been ignored, or altered to accommodate a changing view of medical practice. For example, Ben Mitchell and Joy Riley note that in a survey of 157 medical schools in the mid-1990s,[47]

- one school used the original oath;
- sixty-eight schools used some version of the oath;
- 8 percent prohibited abortion;
- 14 percent prohibited euthanasia and assisted suicide;
- 43 percent included some notion of accountability; and
- 3 percent forbade sexual contact with patients.

It is an ominous sign that what stood for centuries as a statement of the duties of physicians, both negative and positive, can be so easily ignored or replaced. The changes in the Hippocratic oath have not driven, but have simply reflected, the change in perspective and practice in society and in medical practice. Though from the beginning it was not a Christian oath, its appeal to deity did serve to underscore its binding character as an oath with accountability beyond the immediate physician-patient relationship. For these and other reasons, it has easily been adapted and affirmed by various religious traditions. It is not difficult to understand that the rejection of the Hippocratic oath, or fundamental changes to it, have been generated by a growing secular perspective that now governs medical practices. That is, as with many other moral issues, it is worldview that determines ethics. Yet ethics shapes worldview as well, and the changes in the oath are sure to have an impact on the thinking and professional identity of future physicians.

The increasing marginalization of these core values and commitments in medicine has been reinforced by an increasing emphasis on patients' rights, which has been well-intentioned but with sometimes unfortunate results. Joy Riley, a physician, comments that there has been "a shift in the character of medicine away from professionalism toward a market-based medicine, complete with customers who are supposedly 'always right.'"[48] A move away from paternalism, though it may be justified, has

---

46. Beauchamp and Childress, *Principles of Biomedical Ethics*, 183–84. As attitudes and law have changed on euthanasia and physician-assisted suicide, Beauchamp and Childress have become more bold in their defense of physician assistance in hastening death, which is clear when comparing the above statement with earlier versions of their text.
47. See Mitchell and Riley, *Christian Bioethics*, 17.
48. Mitchell and Riley, *Christian Bioethics*, 19.

led to consumerism in medical practice. If the patient can demand assistance in dying, and the physician's treatment options are not governed in part by the duty "never to kill," then it is no surprise that euthanasia and physician-assisted suicide are able to gain momentum.

The result is a medical profession—though not all who practice medicine—that is in danger of losing its way, if it hasn't already. If it is not clear that the purpose of physicians is "always to care, never to kill," then it is an open question whether to seek to cure, to care, or to kill in circumstances that are said to justify euthanasia (an ever-widening set of circumstances at that). The medical profession then attracts not just those committed to healing and caring but also those who may advocate euthanasia. How else could a Dutch doctor complain that when a child under the age of twelve satisfies conditions for euthanasia (they are terminally ill, suffer unbearably, desire to die), "paediatricians are currently powerless."[49] They are not powerless to care for children; they are simply powerless to kill them.

The slippery slope and the dance with death

It is here that we do well to consider what happens when a society accepts that one of the options in medical treatment, to serve patients well, is to assist in their death. Are warnings about the slippery slope simply scare tactics? The "slippery slope" or "wedge"

argument in moral debates functions as a warning that if a particular act is permitted, it will lead to further acts that are undesirable or immoral. The initial act may or may not be morally dubious.

Several things ought to be noted briefly about the slippery-slope argument in moral debate. First, as with many moral debates, we may distinguish between things that are deemed by many to be morally wrong but should not be prohibited through legislation, and those things that are both wrong and should be prohibited, because of public harm or interests, for instance. Second, if there is nothing morally problematic about the initial act in question, then it is generally difficult to prohibit it based on subsequent illicit acts or harm that may follow. Third, nonetheless, even if the initial act is not morally wrong or publicly harmful in itself, the slippery-slope argument gains force if the subsequent illicit or harmful act is understood to be not only foreseeable but also highly likely or especially dangerous. Prudence may dictate that the initial act should be prohibited in such cases. One of the tasks of moral reasoning is to cultivate wisdom. Fourth, if the initial act is morally wrong and would cause public harm, then arguments for its prohibition stand on their own, though they may be strengthened by the possibility of even greater dangers if the initial act is permitted. Fifth, actual historic or current examples where the initial act leads to an illicit or harmful act do not

---

49. *The Guardian*, "Dutch Pediatricians: Give Children under 12 the Right to Die," June 22, 2015, http://www.the-guardian.com/society/2015/jun/19/terminally-ill-children-right-to-die-euthanasia-netherlands.

necessarily prove that the illicit or harmful act will always follow the initial act, for it is possible that safeguards can be put in place to avoid the illicit or harmful act. Nonetheless, the slippery-slope argument—and moral wisdom!—demands that such examples be taken seriously, to avoid illicit or harmful acts that are most likely to follow.

This brings us to the question of whether slippery-slope arguments related to euthanasia and physician-assisted suicide are well founded. Recall that the initial defense of euthanasia by those such as James Rachels focused on a narrow range of cases, where the patient is suffering extreme pain and is near the end of life, has asked for help in dying, and is assisted in death out of the motivation of mercy or compassion. In this case, the slippery-slope arguments actually point to several slopes, indicating the various consequences of accepting any form of euthanasia:

- To begin with, it is argued that even the paradigm case, which is limited to voluntary active euthanasia, is morally problematic, since it is never right to kill an innocent person if it is possible to avoid doing so.
- In addition, it is virtually impossible to restrict euthanasia to those who are suffering great physical pain and who are about to die soon anyway; the logic of euthanasia itself extends to those who know they will suffer and who wish to avoid suffering altogether—how can it be compassionate to force them to suffer first?
- It also extends to those who are not expected to suffer physical pain at all but

are suffering in other ways and prefer to die.
- Further, the logic of euthanasia extends in another direction: Voluntary euthanasia cannot be limited to adults, for there may be children who "qualify" as candidates for euthanasia—and why should they be denied, especially if parents consent on behalf of those who may be deemed too young to make a decision that carries such finality?
- Likewise, voluntary euthanasia opens the door to nonvoluntary euthanasia, for if someone fits the conditions for euthanasia and yet is unable to consent (as with a newborn, a comatose patient, one suffering severe dementia, or one who is otherwise incompetent to decide), someone else may make the decision for them, such as a doctor who is accustomed to walking down this path with patients.
- Finally, the acceptance of euthanasia may lead even to involuntary euthanasia, where a patient has expressed a desire to receive treatment, but that treatment is a significant burden on the family and society, and the patient meets the profile of one whose life is "not worth living."

In summary, it might be said first that the slippery-slope argument is unnecessary for prohibiting euthanasia and physician-assisted suicide, for they ought to be understood as both morally wrong and a cause of public (and private) harm. Yet, second, even for those who are not convinced that these are wrong or cause public harm, the slippery-slope argument is effective, for additional harmful consequences are both foreseeable and highly likely.

Some would doubt such a claim, and would reject, for instance, the possibility of *involuntary* euthanasia. That prospect conjures up images of the Nazi program begun before the Jewish Holocaust, where the frail and "unfit"—"lives unworthy of life"—were rounded up and put to death. It seems we are far removed from that. Yet it is not difficult to inch in that direction. One study of advanced directives indicates that doctors regularly disregard patient's (and their families') wishes to receive life-sustaining treatment not only for the reason that the treatment is futile but in some cases simply because of the doctor's determination of the patient's quality of life.[50] More telling, however, is an examination of places where physician-assisted suicide and/or euthanasia have been accepted, as we will see next.

Death by doctor in the Netherlands

Perhaps the clearest example of the trajectory that takes place when euthanasia and physician-assisted suicide are accepted is the Netherlands, which has for decades tolerated and finally decriminalized euthanasia under certain conditions. Patients are candidates for euthanasia if they are experiencing unbearable suffering and have persistently sought euthanasia, as long as they

are at least twelve years old. (Twelve- to sixteen-year-olds require parental consent.)[51]

The paradigm case may seem reasonable to many, yet the actual attitude toward and practice of euthanasia in the Netherlands is explored in a headline story in *Newsweek* magazine from February 2015.[52] Winston Ross reports that he sat down with a sixty-five-year-old woman in near perfect health, Jannie Willemsen, in a café in Amsterdam to discuss when she wants to die. He writes that "she showed me papers that laid out the circumstances under which she no longer wants to live: if she's severely and permanently lame; if she can no longer leave the house on her own; if she's dependent on others to eat, drink, shower and put on her clothes; if she goes blind or deaf or is suffering from dementia." Willemsen gives her rationale, saying, "I'm an autonomous person. . . . For me, it seems a disaster not to be able to go out and visit friends, to a concert, to the theatre."[53]

Of course, one anecdotal account of a particular person's wishes does not indicate a culture's trajectory on the issue. The question is whether this case is indicative of a broader trend, and how physicians would respond to such a request. The physician's oath has long provided a rigid boundary that would prevent doctors from assisting in the death of a patient, especially where

50. "Will Your Advance Directive Be Followed?"
51. See Henk Jochemsen, "Legalization of Euthanasia in the Netherlands," *Issues in Law & Medicine* 16, no. 3 (2001): 285–87. Also Bert Gordijn and Rien Janssens, "New Developments in Dutch Legislation Concerning Euthanasia and Physician-Assisted Suicide," *Journal of Medicine and Philosophy* 26, no. 3 (2001): 299–309.
52. Ross, "Dying Dutch."
53. Ross, "Dying Dutch."

the patient simply wants to die. When that boundary is removed it is difficult to establish a clear fire wall. Perhaps it is not a surprise, then, even if it is (or should be) shocking, when the *Guardian* reports, "Almost one in five Dutch doctors would consider helping someone die even if they had no physical problems but were 'tired of living,' according to one of the most comprehensive academic studies of such attitudes."[54] This is in spite of the fact that one of the conditions of the Dutch law that governs physician-assisted deaths is that the patient is "experiencing unbearable suffering without hope of improvement."[55] *The boundary between caring and killing is much clearer than the boundary between killing for one reason and killing for another.*

Euthanasia for unbearable pain—or if you are tired of living

Ross highlights the predictable, perhaps inevitable, expansion of physician-assisted killing once it is accepted that personal autonomy includes a "right to die." He writes that "doctor-assisted euthanasia . . . is booming in the Netherlands. In 2013, according to the latest data, 4,829 people across the country chose to have a doctor end their lives. That's one in every 28 deaths in the Netherlands, and triple the number of people who died this way in 2002," when the legal codification

of euthanasia was enacted. Whatever intentions, it is the presupposition that personal autonomy includes the right to choose the timing and manner of one's death, and to receive a physician's assistance, that makes it difficult to limit such choices once the fundamental principle is embraced. "The Dutch don't require proof of a terminal illness to allow doctors to 'help' patients die. Here, people can choose euthanasia if they can convince two physicians they endure 'unbearable' suffering, a definition that expands each year." Notice the reasons that are placed together: "Residents here can now choose euthanasia if they're tired of living with Lou Gehrig's disease, multiple sclerosis, depression or loneliness. The Dutch can now choose death if they're tired of living."[56]

Once accepted, euthanasia expands. It expands in those who "qualify" for it, in those who pursue it, and of course, in the number of people who actually die from it. Ominously, Ross writes that "last year, Right to Die–Netherlands used its funding surplus to open a mobile clinic. Twenty-three nurse-doctor teams now stand ready to be dispatched to people's homes—to dispatch those people."[57] Just as ominous is the expansion of euthanasia-qualified people downward in age. Ross writes, "Children ages 12 to 15 may ask to die if they can get parents' permission. After age 16, young

54. Peter Walker, "One in Five Dutch Doctors Would Help Physically Healthy Patients Die," *The Guardian*, February 17, 2015, http://www.theguardian.com/society/2015/feb/17/assisted-dying-dutch-doctors-patient-law-netherlands.
55. The conditions of the law that was approved in 2001 are discussed by Jochemsen, "Legalization of Euthanasia in the Netherlands."
56. Ross, "Dying Dutch."
57. Ross, "Dying Dutch."

people can make the decision with only 'parental involvement.'" Presumably at age sixteen, parental objection will be noted but the child can still choose death.

To give children age twelve and up the option of choosing death, at a time in life that many relatively short-lived experiences seem "unbearable," is morally reprehensible. Yet that is not enough for some. "Pediatrician Eduard Verhagen helped establish the Dutch euthanasia guidelines for infants," and he thinks the age threshold is not low enough. He argues, "If we say the cutoff line is age 12, there might be children of 11 years and nine months who are very well capable of determining their own fate and making their own decisions, but they're not allowed to ask for euthanasia."[58] As noted earlier, elsewhere the same pediatrician says, "If a child under 12 satisfies the same conditions, paediatricians are currently powerless. It's time to address this problem." His statement is chilling: here is a children's doctor complaining not that he is powerless to heal or care but that he is powerless to assist in the killing of his underage patients. It is difficult to imagine the moral blindness and plain evil that would lead a children's doctor to advocate the right for children to choose to die.

Is this a European problem, which could never happen in the United States? Ross comments, "It is hard to imagine an American pediatrician making that argument. But no one envisioned euthanasia in the Netherlands would expand the way it has in the past 13 years. Perhaps the U.S. isn't far behind."[59] For anything like that to happen, it seems that a significant percentage of the population has to be convinced that it is acceptable. That groundwork may already be laid, for according to a May 2014 Gallup poll, seven in ten Americans believe that "physicians should be able to 'legally end a patient's life by some painless means.'" When Gallup first asked that question, in 1947—in the wake of the atrocities of World War II—that number was 37 percent.[60]

The expansion of the numbers in the Netherlands isn't fully appreciated by official reports on euthanasia. A study of euthanasia from 1990 to 1995, when it was tolerated but not yet decriminalized, provides some alarming indicators.[61] In 1995, reporting indicates that death was attributed to euthanasia in 3,200 cases, or 2.4 percent of all deaths (up from 2,300 cases, or 1.8 percent in 1990). However, according to the study, the definition of euthanasia is rather narrow, and if cases are added in which doctor's actions intended to shorten life, the total rises significantly. "Adding the cases of assisted suicide (400); life-termination without explicit request (900) and the intensification of

58. Ross, "Dying Dutch."
59. Ross, "Dying Dutch."
60. Ross, "Dying Dutch." Justin McCarthy, "Seven in 10 Americans Back Euthanasia," Gallup, June 18, 2014, http://www.gallup.com/poll/171704/seven-americans-back-euthanasia.aspx.
61. See Henk Jochemsen and John Keown, "Voluntary Euthanasia under Control? The Latest Empirical Evidence on Euthanasia in the Netherlands," Journal of Medical Ethics 25, no. 1 (1999): 16–21, http://graphics.tudelft.nl/~rafa/pl/jochemsen.htm. The following information is taken from that report.

pain and symptom treatment with the explicit intent to shorten life (2,000), the total more than doubles from 3,200 to 6,500."[62] The report further states that there were an additional 18,000 cases where treatment was withheld or withdrawn "with the explicit intent to shorten life," bringing the total number of cases of treatment by doctors with the intent to shorten the patient's life to 24,500, or 18 percent of all deaths in 1995. These numbers raise serious questions, perhaps none more than the 900 deaths "without explicit request." Henk Jochemsen and John Keown explain what that means. "The main reason for not discussing the issue with the patient was stated to be the patient's incompetence (due, for example, to dementia)." That is troubling enough, for the decision to end life is not the patient's request (voluntary euthanasia), but the doctor's judgment that the patient's life is not worth living (nonvoluntary euthanasia). If possible, though, it gets worse: "Not all patients whose lives were terminated without an explicit request were incompetent. In 15 percent of the cases where no discussion took place but could have, the doctor did not discuss the termination of life because the doctor thought that the termination of the patient's life was clearly in the patient's best interest." Further, "in a third of the 900 cases, there had been a discussion with the patient about the possible termination of life, and some 50% of these patients were fully competent, yet their lives were terminated without an explicit request."[63]

Chilling as it is, it is perhaps inevitable that when it is thought that an individual can determine that there are certain conditions under which life is not worth living, it will be decided for other individuals in similar (or additional) cases that their lives are not worth living—no request is necessary. Such practices will certainly create an atmosphere of fear. As Riley reports, "already some elderly patients in Holland are fearful they will be euthanized without their consent," and six thousand members of the Dutch Patients' Association "carry cards stating that they do not want euthanasia if they are taken into hospital or a nursing home."[64] In a culture that rejects euthanasia altogether, it is not necessary to justify your existence at the end of life, or to provide papers declaring that you want to live.

The experiment with euthanasia in the Netherlands provides a cautionary tale about what happens when a culture permits or demands that physicians assist in the deaths of their patients. In the United States, Oregon legalized physician-assisted suicide in 1997, and the number of people making use of that provision has increased steadily. Between 1998 and 2010, there was

---

62. Jochemsen and Keown, "Voluntary Euthanasia under Control?" 19.
63. Jochemsen and Keown, "Voluntary Euthanasia under Control?" 18.
64. Mitchell and Riley, *Christian Bioethics*, 97. They cite Carlos F. Gomez, *Regulating Death: Euthanasia and the Case of the Netherlands* (New York: Free Press, 1991); and Martin Beckford, "Fearful Elderly People Carry 'Anti-euthanasia Cards,'" *Telegraph*, April 21, 2011, http://www.telegraph.co.uk/news/health/news/8466996/Fearful-elderly-people-carry-anti-euthanasia-cards.html.

significant growth in several telling areas: physician-assisted suicide prescriptions, up from twenty-four to ninety-six; the number of physicians prescribing lethal medications, up from fourteen to fifty-nine; and deaths from physician-assisted suicide, up from sixteen to sixty-five. One telling index that went down is the number of patients referred for counseling, down from four to one.[65] In one case, in 2008, Ross reports that "Oregon Medicaid officials sent a letter to Barbara Wagner and Randy Stroup after the couple sought treatment for her lung cancer and his prostate cancer. The state denied their (costly) treatment, but on a list of alternative options, it offered to pay for assisted suicide."[66] Though the state changed its mind under pressure, it is not difficult to see that when death is an option, subtle (and not so subtle) pressure may be exerted for the sick and vulnerable (and costly) among us to choose that option.

What happens when a physician who by profession is called "always to care, never to kill" is willing to assist in a patient's death? Ross writes that "most doctors find euthanasia counterintuitive to the Hippocratic oath and terrifying." It's not merely counterintuitive; it goes directly against the oath, with serious consequences. Is there a fear of doing the wrong thing, a thing that is irreversible? "For Bert Keizer," Ross notes, "that fear has subsided with time. He's a Dutch physician who has, in 33 years of practicing medicine, assisted the deaths of dozens of patients—*mostly without regret*. His first few cases were difficult . . . but over time, he says, *that angst subsided*."[67] This, too, is a chilling reminder that the human heart can be hardened and the conscience seared, making the unthinkable all too plausible. The lessons of human experience, including the case of Nazi doctors, are not easily learned and too easily unlearned, even by those who not long ago were victims of a regime that turned physicians into killers.[68]

Evaluation of Euthanasia and Physician-Assisted Suicide

The Driving Force behind Euthanasia

Sometimes opposition to euthanasia can lose sight of underlying issues. While there are important reasons to highlight the inconsistencies and dangers with various presuppositions and arguments that are employed, which have deadly consequences, it is possible to fail to recognize what really drives the demand to have the right to die. At one level, it is straightforward: we do not want to endure a long, drawn-out, painful death. Instead, many people wish to live long and healthy, but then to die quickly and painlessly when the time comes. Advancements in technology and medical treatment that can restore

---

65. Mitchell and Riley, *Christian Bioethics*, 94.
66. Ross, "Dying Dutch."
67. Ross, "Dying Dutch" (emphasis added).
68. The Netherlands is not alone. For example, as Ross, "Dying Dutch," points out, assisted suicide has been permitted in Switzerland since 1942, in the midst of the Nazi atrocities.

health and remedy disease can also sometimes extend life indefinitely, sometimes in a debilitating condition, without restoring health. The argument for euthanasia based on autonomy need not be of a radical form, for it is sometimes a combination of a desire for a certain quality of life—not wanting to lose all that one finds meaningful in life—and not wanting to become a burden to others. These concerns are understandable, and yet there is something deeper driving euthanasia than these concerns.

John Wyatt, a London physician and professor of ethics and perinatology, contends that much of the case for euthanasia and physician-assisted suicide is driven "not by *compassion* but by *fear*."[69] Indeed, the focus on compassion is not a focus on the patient's motivation, for patients who wish to die are not driven by compassion toward themselves; compassion is a virtue exercised toward another who is suffering, a point that will be discussed below. Rather, patients who wish to die, whatever other reasons are present, are so often driven by fear. As one defender of euthanasia said, "It's not so much that I'm afraid of death, but I am afraid of the process of dying."[70] Wyatt identifies three fears in particular.

The fear of pain

Physical pain can be tolerated when there is a purpose in view, as with an athlete in intense training, or when there is an end in sight, knowing that a broken bone will heal. But pain can seem intolerable when it has no apparent purpose and there is no end in sight, and simply must be endured. Moreover, the pain experienced by those with terminal or chronic diseases goes beyond physical pain, to what some specialists refer to as *total pain*. By its nature, it is difficult to define, for it is complex and involves not only physical pain but also emotional/psychological pain and relational and spiritual angst. Those who are suffering from debilitating disease have experienced great loss, such as jobs, mobility, independence, and daily comforts, to name a few things. Often they are uncertain about the future, the course of the disease, how long they have to live, how much physical pain and discomfort they will have to endure, whether they will have to leave their home, and so on. Frequently, relationships suffer or change as some friends or family withdraw, when they feel uncomfortable and don't know what to say or do, or they fail to come to terms with the patient's condition. In addition, as patients face suffering and death, their faith may be tested and they may struggle with what seems to be the pointlessness of their disease and even the meaning and purpose of their life. Finally, where there is a loss in society of the biblical meaning of faith and hope, and a drift toward a hedonistic worldview that seeks to maximize personal happiness—"let us eat and drink, for tomorrow

69. John Wyatt, *Matters of Life and Death: Human Dilemmas in the Light of the Christian Faith* (Nottingham, UK: Inter-Varsity Press, 2009), 197.
70. Wyatt, *Matters of Life and Death*, 197. Or, as Woody Allen humorously put it, "It's not that I'm afraid of death, it's just that I don't want to be there when it happens."

we die" (1 Cor. 15:32)—then pain and suffering are commonly seen as meaningless and terrifying.[71]

The fear of indignity

Proponents of euthanasia and physician-assisted suicide often employ the slogan "death with dignity." The obvious implication is that disease and dying rob people of their dignity, for many reasons, including the loss of control of their lives, the loss of bodily functions, and the need to receive help with basic things such as eating and getting dressed and toileting. Further, these things are compounded for many who are transferred to the sterile environment of a hospital where they are poked, prodded, and exposed, and often alone. When we observe or hear about patients who are unconscious and unlikely to recover, and who are hooked up to machines with tubes inserted into their bodies, it is easy to feel that there has been a loss of dignity, and that we would not want that to happen to us. As one defender of euthanasia said, "It is not death that people fear most, but undignified dying."[72]

The fear of dependence

A study published in 2009 reported, "By far the most common reasons" offered by fifty-six Oregonians who requested physician assistance in dying were "the desire to be in control, to remain autonomous and to die at home." Linda Ganzini, who published the study, concluded that for these people, "dying is less about physical symptoms than personal values."[73] Often people who are growing old or declining in health will feel, and say, that they "don't want to be a burden to others" or they "don't want to be dependent on others." It is not difficult to understand this sentiment, though it may mask a sense of autonomy and independence that simply fails to recognize human finiteness and inescapable dependence on others and ultimately on God. In the extreme, people will live their whole lives in defiance of the reality that they are dependent, emphasizing self-determination above almost all else. In the words of Ronald Dworkin, "Freedom is the cardinal, absolute requirement of self-respect: no one treats his life as having any intrinsic, objective importance unless he insists on leading that life himself, not being ushered along it by others, no matter how much he loves or respects or fears them."[74] Whether or not one holds to an extreme view of autonomy like Dworkin, it is difficult to become more and more dependent on others, and disease

---

71. Wyatt, *Matters of Life and Death*, 197–98.

72. Ludovic Kennedy, *Evening Standard* (UK), November 1992; cited by Wyatt, *Matters of Life and Death*, 198.

73. Katie Hafner, "In Ill Doctor, a Surprise Reflection of Who Picks Assisted Suicide," *New York Times*, August 11, 2012, http://www.nytimes.com/2012/08/12/health/policy/in-ill-doctor-a-surprise-reflection-of-who-picks-assisted-suicide.html?_r=0. Cf. Wyatt, *Matters of Life and Death*, 203–4, who discusses another study in which the most common reasons given were "controlling the time of death," "being ready to die," "wanting to die at home instead of in a hospital," "existence being pointless," "losing independence," and "poor quality of life."

74. Ronald Dworkin, *Life's Dominion: An Argument about Abortion, Euthanasia, and Individual Freedom* (New York: Vintage, 1993), 239.

often will take away independence before it takes a person's life.

Often a person suffering a debilitating disease will have to depend on a caregiver to be bathed, dressed, fed, walked, or pushed in a wheelchair, toileted and cleaned afterward, and the cycle is repeated over and over. The sense of being a burden may be magnified by the way the caregiver communicates with the patient. The fear of dependence may be the most deep-rooted fear of all.[75] Further, the patient's fear may be mirrored by the fear of those around them who face the prospect of watching their loved one decline, and the need to care for them.

The answer to these fears? In short, for a growing number of people, like Brittany Maynard, the answer to the fear of pain, indignity, and dependence is euthanasia or physician-assisted suicide. It is the way to take control of things and to avoid what is feared most. It is the way to get things over with quickly. In this view, given the alternatives, euthanasia is understood to be a "good death." However, reflection on euthanasia and the debate surrounding it points to something different. Rather than a good death, euthanasia is a sign of a despairing death. How should Christians respond?

A Christian Response

Is it possible for Christians to speak of a good death? Perhaps, yet we are reminded that death is not one of life's goods. Rather, it is part of the curse brought about because of human sin (Rom. 5:12). We mourn and weep at a funeral, not as those without hope, but we are right to mourn and weep, for death is an enemy (1 Thess. 4:13; 1 Cor. 7:30). If death is not a good, Christians nevertheless can know and teach something about dying well. To die in peace, reconciled to God and others; to understand that we are not finally in control of our life or our death; to accept our dependence and the help of caregivers; to face death with courage and steadfastness, neither seeking it nor refusing to acknowledge its arrival, knowing that death itself has been conquered and is swallowed up in victorious resurrection in Jesus (1 Cor. 15: 50–58). These are aspects of what it means to die well.[76]

Beyond speaking about what it means to die well, we may speak of the fears that drive the quest for euthanasia. The fear that is present in suffering and death testify to the truth that in illness and death there is something wrong. Yet Scripture teaches that the answer to these fears is found in the hope of the gospel. The apostle Paul moves from death and fear to life and hope in Romans 5: "Just as sin entered the world through one man, and death through sin, in this way death spread to all people, because all sinned" (v. 12). "How much more have the grace of God and the gift which comes through the grace of the one man Jesus Christ overflowed to the many" (v. 15). "So then, as through one trespass there is condemnation for everyone, so also through one

---

75. Wyatt, *Matters of Life and Death*, 198–200.
76. See also a discussion of dying well in Wyatt, *Matters of Life and Death*, 228–29.

righteous act there is justification leading to life for everyone" (v. 18). And "just as sin reigned in death, so also grace will reign through righteousness, resulting in eternal life through Jesus Christ our Lord" (v. 21). The promise of life through faith in Jesus is the ultimate answer to the fears that drive euthanasia. However, Christians can respond to the fears by offering not only hope and confidence in death but also care and comfort in life. John Wyatt provides some very helpful responses.[77]

The answer to the fear of pain is good palliative care

Palliative care focuses on managing physical pain and providing comfort for those who are dying. It is at the center of the hospice movement, which developed out of a refusal to accept that the only options physicians sometimes have is "to watch their patient die in agony or to kill them out of compassion."[78] Although euthanasia is driven, in part, by a fear of pain, pain is not the primary reason. In fact, in a study cited earlier, physical pain was not among the main reasons people seek physician assisted suicide: "Everybody thought that this was going to be about pain," Ganzini is quoted as saying. "It turns out that pain is kind of irrelevant."[79] Palliative care must account for that. As Wyatt says, "Modern

palliative care is a way of using specialized medical and nursing techniques, and a multidisciplinary team of carers, to treat the whole person in response to the 'total pain' of dying."[80] Physical pain can be controlled in a majority of cases, and improvements in pain management should be encouraged. What those who are dying desperately need is true care and comfort, human interaction and love.[81] This is a Christian calling as an overflow of the gospel: "Blessed be the God and Father of our Lord Jesus Christ, the Father of mercies and the God of all comfort. He comforts us in all our affliction, so that we may be able to comfort those who are in any kind of affliction, through the comfort we ourselves receive from God. For just as the sufferings of Christ overflow to us, so also through Christ our comfort overflows" (2 Cor. 1:3–5).

The answer to indignity is compassion and "invested dignity"[82]

Suffering and dying often create conditions that easily lead to a sense of indignity, which many people wish to escape. One of the great tragedies of the call for "death with dignity" is that many have become convinced that the compassionate response to one who is dying is to assist them in their death. This is reflected in both the arguments and the very names of pro-euthanasia organizations, such

---

77. The following paragraphs are adapted from Wyatt, *Matters of Life and Death,* 229–31.
78. Wyatt, *Matters of Life and Death,* 229.
79. Hafner, "Ill Doctor."
80. Wyatt, *Matters of Life and Death,* 230.
81. Wyatt, *Matters of Life and Death,* 230–31.
82. Wyatt says "compassion mingled with respect." *Matters of Life and Death,* 231.

as Compassion and Choices, Death with Dignity, and Dignity in Dying (UK).[83] Ultimately such a response undermines the deep conviction to care for those who suffer, sometimes in creative ways. Reflecting on the problem of caring for those experiencing pain and suffering, Wyatt states, "I have become convinced that, as Christian carers, perhaps the single most important attribute we need is creativity. . . . We seem to lack the creativity, the originality, the ability to innovate, the perception to see a new way forward."[84] We have great resources to do better, and technology should be used to help us care better, not simply to keep someone alive longer.

The person who is suffering may cry out for help, and may even ask to die, but to fulfill that request is not compassion. Compassion is a virtue that moves us to action, but it is a corruption of compassion that leads us to kill. The term itself teaches us better: "to suffer alongside." Compassion needs to be reinfused into our modern medical practice that is sterile and often strips patients of their dignity, but ultimately it is the people of God who need to demonstrate what true compassion looks like. To have compassion for those who suffer is to come alongside them, to respect them as those who have dignity, who bear the image of God, and to remind them of that dignity. It is to "invest dignity" in those who may feel like they have lost it: to hold the hand of the one who is suffering; to sit patiently with the one who cannot carry a conversation because disease has robbed them of speech, as in advanced Parkinson's; to love anew with each visit one who has lost their memory, as in Alzheimer's and other cases of dementia; to care for those who have lost consciousness; to remind those who are hurting of the God who loves them, who suffered and died for them; to remind them that we love them and that they matter to us, not because of what they could or can do, but because of who they are. These are ways of investing dignity in those who suffer.

The answer to the fear of dependence is the care and comfort that flows from the gospel

I recall listening to an interview of a woman whose husband was suffering in the late stages of Lou Gehrig's disease (also known as ALS). They were making an appeal for the right to die. She said, "I have to clothe him. I have to feed him. I have to bathe him. I have to toilet him and clean up after him. He doesn't want to go on living like this." He was completely dependent on her, and life was too great a burden, lacking anything meaningful for him now. It is understandable that hopelessness and despair would set in when one experiences such great loss, and that death may seem like the only escape. Yet that is not the whole story.

One of the things that stood out in that interview, and that stands out in other

---

83. Compassion and Choices, http://www.compassionandchoices.org; Death with Dignity, https://www.deathwith-dignity.org/; Dignity in Dying, http://www.dignityindying.org.uk.
84. Wyatt, *Matters of Life and Death*, 230.

situations like it, is that the spouse was expressing the burden that the patient was experiencing, since the patient was unable to speak. Further, the burden that was expressed seemed to be experienced equally, or perhaps to an even greater degree, by the caregiving spouse as by the patient. The difficulty of feeling like a burden to others is magnified when caregivers, often unintentionally, confirm that the patient is a burden to them. This is not to lay blame, for suffering so often overwhelms both the patient and the caregiver. Time seems to pass both painfully slowly and rapidly at the same time, stealing all of our thoughts and energy, leaving no time to reflect and regroup.

The previous point emphasized the compassion that flows from the gospel through the sufferings of Christ, with the result that we can invest dignity in those who are suffering. The extension of that compassion is the care and comfort that Christians are called to offer to those in need, especially those who we are charged to care for as members of God's family (Matt. 25:35–40). It is care made possible by the grace of God and the power of the Spirit. Two aspects of that care need to be recognized. First, it is care and comfort that communicates to the one who is suffering that they are not a burden to us but a joy. What we communicate both verbally and nonverbally, and not just through our acts, will have a significant impact on whether the one who is suffering feels like a burden to others. We need to lay bare the deception that we are autonomous and independent in the first place, and to recognize and communicate our mutual dependence. Second, care and comfort must be extended to caregivers and not only to suffering patients. The burden on caregivers can be enormous and overwhelming, and it is easy for them unintentionally to communicate anger and bitterness to the patient that is really a response to the disease. Caregivers need care and comfort as well, and refreshment that allows them to continue to care well for the patient.

When Muriel McQuilkin was diagnosed with Alzheimer's disease and her condition deteriorated, her husband displayed the kind of care and comfort that communicates: "I love you, and it is my joy to care for you. You are not a burden to me, but a blessing." Robertson McQuilkin stepped down from his position as president of Columbia Bible College and Seminary (now Columbia International University), in order to care for his wife full time. Some tried to talk him out of his decision, and encouraged him to let others care for his wife while he continued to do the work that God had called him to do. Yet he was convicted that caring for his wife *was* God's calling for him. His care for her flowed out of love, without resentment. It was not without difficulties and frustration, but he was sustained by their mutual love and commitment, by the nurture he had received from her for so many years, and ultimately by God's grace and faithfulness.[85]

---

85. See Robertson McQuilkin, "Living by Vows," *Christianity Today*, October 8, 1990, 38–40; and Robertson Mc-Quilkin, "Muriel's Blessing," *Christianity Today*, February 5, 1996, 32–34.

Conclusion

Euthanasia and physician-assisted suicide are driven by a number of factors. At one level, they are the secular answer to the loss of quality of life, related in part to a loss of autonomy. In part, they are driven by hopelessness and fear, and a sense that suffering is pointless. If Christians are going to have an influence on our culture, we need to address not merely the act but also the motives and emotions that drive the desire for a hastened death.[86]

Out of a biblical understanding of life and death, and of morality, we need to make a clear and compelling case for why we should not act in such a way that we intend death. We ought to affirm the life of human beings, made in the image of God, in all of its stages. This reality should prompt us not just to fight to keep someone alive but to offer care and comfort, to act in such a way toward those who are suffering that we communicate their worth to us. We ought to affirm God's sovereignty over life and death, as the gracious Creator and Lord of life. This reality should prompt us not only "always to care, never to kill" but also to realize when death's time has come so that we do not feel the need to "do everything possible" to keep a patient alive, if we are merely prolonging the dying process. We ought to affirm that it is possible to glorify God and find meaning even in suffering. This reality should prompt us to find courage and hope to replace fear and hopelessness, and to resist the idea that our only solution in the face of suffering is to end life. We should seek to establish care facilities that do not isolate patients, but that focus on quality care. We should seek to provide the best possible pain management and comfort care. We should give patients as much control of their lives as possible, including treatment decisions, not to emphasize their autonomy, but to emphasize their dignity and to underscore that they are not merely the object of our treatment protocols.

Christian care for the suffering and dying will emphasize these things and more. It will provide care, comfort, and hope, and will resist the despair that seeks death. In effect, those who accept euthanasia and physician-assisted suicide are saying to a suffering person who expresses a wish to die, "You are right, your life is not worth living; may we help you die?" Christians will challenge the idea that it is necessary to kill the patient to express compassion, and will encourage those in despair: "Not only will we help you to die in dignity, but we will help you to live before you die."[87]

---

86. For a provocative reflection on death and dying, see "Dying and 'Death before Death': On Hospices, Euthanasia, Alzheimer's, and on (Not) Knowing How to Dwindle," in Michael Banner, *The Ethics of Everyday Life* (Oxford: Oxford University Press, 2014), 107–34.
87. Wyatt, *Matters of Life and Death*, 230, citing one of the slogans of the hospice care movement.

Select Resources

Banner, Michael. *The Ethics of Everyday Life.* Oxford: Oxford University Press, 2014.

Gorsuch, Neil M. *The Future of Assisted Suicide and Euthanasia.* Princeton, NJ: Princeton University Press, 2006.

Lammers, Stephen E. and Allen Verhey, eds. *On Moral Medicine: Theological Perspectives in Medical Ethics,* Second Edition. Grand Rapids: Eerdmans, 1998.

Larson, Edward J., and Darrell W. Amundsen. *A Different Death: Euthanasia and the Christian Tradition.* Downers Grove, IL: InterVarsity Press, 1998.

Meilaender, Gilbert. *Bioethics: A Primer for Christians.* Grand Rapids: Eerdmans, 1996.

Mitchell, C. Ben, and D. Joy Riley. *Christian Bioethics: A Guide for Pastors, Health Care Professionals, and Families.* B&H Studies in Christian Ethics. Nashville: B&H, 2014.

President's Council on Bioethics. *Taking Care: Ethical Caregiving in Our Aging Society.* Washington, DC, 2005.

Smith, Wesley J. *Culture of Death: The Assault on Medical Ethics in America.* San Francisco: Encounter, 2000.

Wyatt, John. *Matters of Life and Death: Human Dilemmas in the Light of the Christian Faith.* Leicester, UK: Inter-Varsity Press, 2009.

PART 5

SOCIAL ORDER AND THE ENVIRONMENT

CHAPTER 14

CAPITAL PUNISHMENT

Whoever sheds human blood,
by humans his blood will be shed,
for God made humans in his image.

—Genesis 9:6

You are not to accept a ransom for the life of someone
who is guilty of murder; he must be put to death.

—Numbers 35:31

You must not deny justice to a poor person
among you in his lawsuit.

—Exodus 23:6

Friends, do not avenge yourselves; instead,
leave room for God's wrath, because it is
written, Vengeance belongs to me; I will
repay, says the Lord. . . .

If you do wrong, be afraid, because [govern-
ment] does not carry the sword for no reason.
For it is God's servant, an avenger that brings
wrath on the one who does wrong.

—Romans 12:19; 13:4

Introduction

In her book *Death Defying*, Pam McAllister offers a plea for abolishing the death penalty. She argues that the "sad and sordid" history of capital punishment includes terrible injustice and abuse of power, in which people have been put to death for minor offenses and religious or political views and practices. In recent history, many countries have put an end to capital punishment, and abolition is required for members of the European Union. Indeed, McAllister states, "An estimated ninety-eight percent of all executions are implemented under dictatorial regimes," and "the United States is one of the very few nations with a representative government which still uses the death penalty."[1]

McAllister argues that there are intrinsic problems with capital punishment, and she contends that support for the death penalty is rooted in revenge and in the perpetuation of certain "myths":

- that it will help families of victims to find closure;
- that it serves as a deterrence against violent crimes;
- that it is proportional—that is, only the worst offenders receive the ultimate punishment.

She asserts that these arguments are wrong and misguided, and for that reason, and because of its "sad and sordid history," capital punishment ought to be abolished.

To that end, she argues for a campaign for abolition that is peaceful, patient, and personal—not allowing it to remain abstract. McAllister represents many who deeply oppose capital punishment on practical and moral grounds, raising serious objections that should be carefully considered and answered by those who seek to justify capital punishment.

Capital punishment, it should go without saying, is a significant moral issue—a life-and-death issue—involving matters of basic justice in society, including equal protection, due process, and proportional punishment. Yet there is a certain level of ambivalence in the United States concerning the death penalty. On the one hand, opinions are strongly held and passionately argued. On the other hand, it does not seem to be a matter of priority in public moral and political debates. It is consistently supported by a majority, but vigorously opposed by a significant minority. Christians reflect something of this division in society, with biblical and theological arguments brought to bear on both sides of the issue.

In this chapter, I will offer a defense of capital punishment in principle, grounded not on revenge or "finding closure" or even deterrence, but on an account of justice. What is justified in principle, however, is difficult to carry out in practice. This is true of criminal justice in general, but the issue is more acute when it comes to the ultimate penalty. Thus, after justifying capital

---

1. Pam McAllister, *Death Defying: Dismantling the Execution Machinery in 21st Century U.S.A.* (New York: Continuum, 2003), 21.

punishment in principle, I will ask whether it is possible to administrate it justly. This is not an easy question to answer. Capital punishment, I will argue, is not sustainable as it is currently practiced, if for no other reason than that it is clear that many of those sentenced to death will not be executed. Yet there are other reasons for concern about how it is carried out, and it is necessary to address some of the injustices in the administration of capital punishment. It is not enough simply to argue that this calls for the reform, not the abolition of capital punishment; it is necessary to offer specific reforms that will address those injustices. To that end, I will consider the findings of a significant report that offers recommendations for reform in the administration of capital punishment. But first, I will consider the morality of capital punishment in principle, especially as it pertains to biblical justice.

Capital Punishment in Biblical Perspective

Capital Punishment in the Old Testament

The Mosaic law
In the Mosaic law, the death penalty is prescribed by God for numerous offenses. The exact count of the number of offenses varies, depending on whether some are counted uniquely or as repeated in different places.[2] A representative list includes the following:

1. Murder (Exod. 21:12,14; Num. 35:16–21, 31; Lev. 24:17, 21)
2. Striking parents (Exod. 21:15)
3. Kidnapping (Exod. 21:16; Deut. 24:7)
4. Cursing parents (Exod. 21:17; Lev. 20:9)
5. Fatally injuring a pregnant woman, and perhaps the fetus as well (Exod. 21:22–25)
6. For the death of someone by an animal that had killed before and was not subsequently restrained (Exod. 21:28–29)
7. Sorcery/witchcraft (Exod. 22:18)
8. Bestiality (Exod. 22:19; Lev. 20:15–16)
9. Offering sacrifice to false gods (Exod. 22:20)
10. Work on the Sabbath (Exod. 35:2)
11. Offering human sacrifice (Lev. 20:2)
12. Adultery (Lev. 20:10; Deut. 22:22)
13. Incest (Lev. 20:11–12)
14. Homosexual intercourse (Lev. 20:13)
15. Blasphemy/cursing God (Lev. 24:15–16)
16. Disobeying the court's decision (Deut. 17:12)
17. False testimony in a death-penalty case (Deut. 19:16–21)
18. An incorrigibly rebellious son (Deut. 21:18–21)

2. Walter Kaiser lists sixteen offenses in Walter C. Kaiser Jr., *Toward Old Testament Ethics* (Grand Rapids: Zondervan, 1983), 91–92; Michael L. Westmoreland-White and Glen H. Stassen list twenty-five offenses in "Biblical Perspectives on the Death Penalty," in *Religion and the Death Penalty: A Call for Reckoning*, eds. Erik C. Owens, John D. Carlson, and Eric P. Elshtain (Grand Rapids: Eerdmans, 2004), 124; Christopher Marshall says that the Mosaic law "stipulates the death sentence for up to three dozen offenses" in "Capital Punishment," *Dictionary of Scripture and Ethics*, eds. Joel B. Green et al. (Grand Rapids: Baker Academic, 2011), 118.

19. Premarital sex (Deut. 22:20–21)
20. Rape of an engaged virgin (Deut. 22:23–27)

Clearly the Mosaic law prescribes capital punishment for more than murder, which raises questions for contemporary application. Isn't this list repugnant to our moral sensibilities and evidence of the barbaric practices of ancient peoples? If the Mosaic law calls for the death penalty for all of these offenses, is it not inconsistent for Christians to appeal to it to support the death penalty only for murder today? Is the death penalty relevant in any way to a discussion of contemporary Christian ethics? Several brief points can be made.

To the point that the prescription of capital punishment for so many offenses is repugnant, two things should be noted. First, to reach such a conclusion is not merely to indict ancient Israel; it is to indict God who prescribed it. Second, the prescription of capital punishment calls attention to the seriousness of these sins, which we may too readily overlook. Finally, it indicates that capital punishment is not intrinsically immoral but is a just response to certain offenses (whether or not it is believed to be mandated in our day).

This raises the question of consistency, however, for it is argued that "few Christian retentionists advocate the death penalty for all of the crimes carrying that penalty in the Torah. Most single out premeditated murder as the one crime continuing to merit death. What is not clear is their rationale for citing Mosaic Law when making this argument."[3] However, the rationale is actually not difficult to ascertain. Even within the Mosaic law it is reasonable to argue that murder is a special case, for it is singled out within the law, when it says, "You are not to accept a ransom for the life of someone who is guilty of murder; he must be put to death" (Num. 35:31). The presumption is that a ransom or lesser penalty could be accepted for other offenses, but not for murder, suggesting that the death penalty functions as a maximum penalty for other offenses, but that judges could reduce the sentence in all but the case of premeditated homicide.[4] This distinction within the Mosaic law indicates that murder is a special case, and thus the support of capital punishment for murder alone does have a rationale in the Mosaic law. What is more, it is grounded in a command and a rationale that predates the law code, from the post-flood narrative of Genesis.

Genesis 9:5–6

A key Old Testament text relevant to the death penalty is Genesis 9:5–6. Not surprisingly, the interpretation of this text is

3. Westmoreland-White and Stassen, "Biblical Perspectives on the Death Penalty," 124. Cf. Glen H. Stassen and David P. Gushee, *Kingdom Ethics: Following Jesus in Contemporary Context* (Downers Grove, IL: InterVarsity Press, 2003), 200.
4. Christopher J. H. Wright, *Old Testament Ethics for the People of God* (Downers Grove, IL: IVP Academic, 2004), 407; Kaiser, *Toward Old Testament Ethics*, 73; Gordon J. Wenham, "Law and the Legal System," in *Law, Morality, and the Bible: A Symposium*, eds. Bruce N. Kaye and Gordon J. Wenham (Leicester, UK: Inter-Varsity Press, 1978), 35.

contested. Some abolitionists focus on verse 6a, which reads,

> Whoever sheds human blood,
> by humans his blood will be shed.

It is argued that this could be interpreted as a prescription, but it is better understood as a prediction or a proverb.[5] According to John Howard Yoder, for instance, "It is a simple description of the way things already are, an accurate prediction of what does happen, what will happen, as surely as summer is followed by winter, seedtime by harvest"—alluding to what he considers a similar type of statement in Genesis 8:22.[6] As such, it is given as a warning not to kill because violence begets violence, so the one who kills will eventually be killed. While this interpretation of these words is plausible, the broader context suggests a different reading. Genesis 9:5–6 states,

> And I will require a penalty for your life-blood; I will require it from any animal and from any human; if someone murders a fellow human, I will require that person's life.
> Whoever sheds human blood,
> by humans his blood will be shed,
> for God made humans in his image.

What is noteworthy is that three times God says "I will require" a reckoning for bloodshed. Verse 6a says that the reckoning God requires is the life of the killer. Further, verse 6b offers a rationale—namely, that the victim (and every human being) is made in the image of God. The fact that Genesis 9:5–6 includes a demand for a reckoning and a rationale for that reckoning indicates that it is not merely a proverb or prediction, but a command from God. To focus on verse 6a alone does not provide adequate context for interpreting the text, and as a result, it leads to an inadequate conclusion.

Two points should be noted about this text as it pertains to a Christian view of capital punishment. First, it predates the Mosaic law code. Thus, as Gilbert Meilaender observes, "The law of retribution articulated here is not the civil law of ancient Israel. It would be better called moral or natural law, specifying, as it does, fundamental truths about human life."[7] Second, it offers a basic rationale for understanding murder as an offense that justifies capital punishment, even while it addresses what seems to some to be an irreconcilable tension between a belief in the sanctity of human life and support for the death penalty.

The Catechism of the Catholic Church, for instance, which accepts the necessity of capital punishment "in cases of extreme gravity," nevertheless argues for other means of punishment if at all possible,

5. Westmoreland-White and Stassen, "Biblical Perspectives on the Death Penalty," 126–27. Cf. Stassen and Gushee, *Kingdom Ethics*, 199–203.
6. John Howard Yoder, "Against the Death Penalty," in *The Death Penalty Debate: Two Opposing Views of Capital Punishment*, by H. Wayne House and John Howard Yoder (Dallas: Word, 1991), 124.
7. Gilbert Meilaender, "The Death Penalty: A Protestant Perspective," in Owens, Carlson, and Elshtain, *Religion and the Death Penalty*, 50.

because they "are more in conformity to the dignity of the human person."[8] Yet it is precisely because the victim of murder bears God's image, and thus possesses human dignity, that the murderer is to be punished by death. The rationale in Genesis 9 is clear. Of course, as Meilaender rightly notes, there is still tension, for the murderer, too, bears God's image, and "it might seem that by punishing the murderer in order to honor the image in the victim, we simultaneously demean the image in the murderer."[9] The tension is resolved, however, by the fact that the victim is innocent and the murderer is guilty. Having committed an offense that is deserving of death, the murderer is not demeaned but is treated as a responsible moral agent who receives a just punishment for the crime committed.

Evaluating Capital Punishment in New Testament Perspective

John 8:3–11

Here is the story of the woman caught in adultery.[10] The scribes and Pharisees bring this woman to Jesus, claiming that she was "caught in the act of committing adultery" (8:4), and then pose a question for Jesus. "In the law Moses commanded us to stone such women. So what do You say?" (8:5). Jesus answers, "The one without sin among you should be the first to throw a stone at her" (8:7). Confounded, the accusers leave one by one. Jesus then asks the woman,

> "Where are they? Has no one condemned you?"
> "No one, Lord," she answered.
> "Neither do I condemn you," said Jesus. "Go, and from now on do not sin anymore." (8:10–11)

Christopher Marshall, who argues against the death penalty, draws conclusions on this pericope that are questionable. First, he states that "all the legal prerequisites for a 'just' execution of the adulterous woman were in place (otherwise, his opponents would scarcely have used the episode to test his fidelity to the law [John 8:6])." As a result, Jesus's refusal to condemn the woman must not be "on legal grounds but rather on moral and religious grounds." He adds that "it is only those without sin who are properly qualified to discharge" the death penalty, so that "ultimate jurisdiction over human life belongs only to Christ, the sinless one."[11]

---

8. *Catechism of the Catholic Church*, §§2266, 2267.

9. Meilaender, "Death Penalty," 50.

10. Many scholars have argued, based on early manuscripts and other evidence, that John 7:53–8:11 was not originally part of John's Gospel. See, e.g., Bruce Metzger, *A Textual Commentary on the Greek New Testament* (New York: United Bible Societies, 1971), 219–222; D. A. Carson, *The Gospel according to John*, Pillar New Testament Commentary (Grand Rapids: Eerdmans, 1991), 333; C. K. Barrett, *The Gospel according to St John: An Introduction with Commentary and Notes on the Greek Text* (London: SPCK, 1962), 490–493. However, it doesn't appear to be inconsistent with Jesus's teaching, and even if it was not originally part of John's Gospel, it could be part of an authentic oral tradition that made its way into the canon later (Carson, *John*, 333; Barrett, *John*, 491). In any case, it has been significant in the teaching of the church, and as it is part of church tradition, it is worth examining what it says.

11. Christopher Marshall, "Capital Punishment," in Green et al., *Dictionary of Scripture and Ethics*, 120.

This interpretation is inadequate for several reasons. First, it is doubtful that the accusers were following the requirements of the law, for if the woman was caught in adultery, then where is the man who, by law, must also be tried (Lev. 20:10; Deut. 22:22–24)? Second, it is not likely that Jesus here is saying that only sinless judges can enforce the death penalty. It is more likely that it is one "without fault" by the requirements of the law. Otherwise, this text would stand as a rejection of the possibility of justice in the Mosaic law. It would also stand in tension with Romans 13—including Marshall's own interpretation of that text, which understands that civil governments have authority to use capital punishment even if they are not required to do so.[12] Paul would not affirm what Jesus condemns—namely, sinful human beings condemning another person to death.

Further, it should be noted that these experts in the Mosaic law have a motive that has little to do with the woman: "They asked this to trap him, in order that they might have evidence to accuse him" (8:6). If Jesus says she should be set free, they can accuse him of breaking the law of Moses. Not only would they be able to challenge his credibility as a teacher of the law, but they could bring him before Jewish authorities. On the other hand, if Jesus condemns her to death, he could lose credibility with the crowds, for whom he has shown great compassion and mercy, and he could be brought before Roman authorities.[13] It may not be known exactly why the accusers left, but this alone indicates that it would have been difficult for them to make a case that Jesus did not follow the law. Without any accusers, Jesus tells the woman that he does not condemn her either, and she is free to go.

To the extent that this text speaks to the issue of capital punishment in contemporary society, it is inconclusive on whether it is ever justified. On the one hand, it does not offer strong support against capital punishment as such. On the other hand, it does serve as an indictment against the unjust administration of the death penalty, whether it be individual cases or systemic injustices.

The Sermon on the Mount

Some argue that Jesus's teaching in the Sermon on the Mount indicates a rejection of capital punishment, in principle at least. For example, Jesus says, "You have heard that it was said, An eye for an eye and a tooth for a tooth. But I tell you, don't resist an evildoer. On the contrary, if anyone slaps you on your right cheek, turn the other to him also" (Matt. 5:38–39). Glen Stassen and David Gushee assert that this teaching "is about preventing violent retaliation" and that "Jesus opposed taking a life as retribution for a life."[14]

Then Jesus teaches, "You have heard that it was said, Love your neighbor and

---

12. Marshall, "Capital Punishment," 120.
13. Carson, *John*, 335.
14. Stassen and Gushee, *Kingdom Ethics*, 198.

hate your enemy. But I tell you, love your enemies and pray for those who persecute you, so that you may be children of your Father in heaven. For he causes his sun to rise on the evil and the good, and sends rain on the righteous and the unrighteous" (Matt. 5:43–45). Opponents of capital punishment argue that it is wrong to think that Jesus is here addressing only personal relationships, and not the response of government to evil. Michael Westmoreland-White and Glen Stassen contend that those who advocate the death penalty resist Jesus's teaching by "suggesting it applies only to interpersonal encounters between Christians, thus making Jesus' teachings here irrelevant to the death penalty discussion." Further, "this marginalizes the lordship of Jesus to a very small part of life."[15] Similarly, Stassen and Gushee state that some interpreters (i.e., who support the death penalty) act as if Jesus's teaching isn't there.[16]

In response, these sweeping charges are not well supported. It is not easy to find an interpreter who limits Jesus's teaching here to "interpersonal encounters between Christians." As far as "interpersonal encounters" understood more broadly, Jesus does indeed teach us not to seek vengeance against those who wrong us, but to love our enemies. If we took Jesus's teaching here seriously, what a huge impact it would have, not only in our personal relationships but on

a whole society. This is not limited to "a very small part of life"!

It is reasonable to ask what implications Jesus's teaching about love for enemies and preventing violent retaliation have for the government's use of the death penalty. Does it clearly indicate that the government is wrong to execute a violent murderer? Opponents of capital punishment suggest that it does, but not always in clear terms. For instance, Westmoreland-White and Stassen state that "people who regularly emulate the merciful, compassionate character of God have moral characters that are highly suspicious of executing societal enemies."[17] That is not a blanket condemnation of the government's use of execution. In any case, defenders of the death penalty normally reserve its application to aggravated murder, and would not include the dubious category of "societal enemies"! Part of the problem is that Jesus's teaching in the Sermon on the Mount is addressed to his disciples and the crowd that is listening, and he does not there address government directly. That is why many turn elsewhere, and especially to Paul in Romans 13, to understand the matter further. It is not to diminish Jesus's teaching, but to seek the whole counsel of God in Scripture. Specifically, it is to see how Paul echoes, interprets, and applies the received teaching of Jesus.

15. Westmoreland-White and Stassen, "Biblical Perspectives on the Death Penalty," 133.
16. Stassen and Gushee, *Kingdom Ethics*, 199.
17. Westmoreland-White and Stassen, "Biblical Perspectives on the Death Penalty," 135.

Romans 13:1–7 (and 12:14–21)

In Romans 13, the apostle Paul lays out a brief but important understanding of government. He declares, "Let everyone submit to the governing authorities, since there is no authority except from God, and the authorities that exist are instituted by God" (v. 1). This includes flawed governments led by immoral people, as was the case with the Roman government in power as Paul wrote. In relation to punishment, Paul says that government "is God's servant for your good. But if you do wrong, be afraid, because it does not carry the sword for no reason. For it is God's servant, an avenger that brings wrath on the one who does wrong" (v. 4). The sword represents the authority and power of government to punish wrongdoers and, it must be noted, it is a lethal instrument.

Is Paul's teaching here in conflict with what Jesus taught? If we are to love our enemies and not seek violent retaliation, shouldn't we condemn a government that would use the sword against a wrongdoer? Otherwise, are we not compartmentalizing and marginalizing Jesus's teaching?

First, when considering what Paul says in Romans 13, it should be noted that in Romans 12 he reflects very closely what Jesus teaches in the Sermon on the Mount (as Stassen and Gushee note).[18] There Paul says,

> Bless those who persecute you; bless and do not curse. . . . Do not repay anyone evil for evil. . . . Friends, do not avenge yourselves; instead, leave room for God's wrath, because it is written, Vengeance belongs to me; I will repay, says the Lord. But
>> If your enemy is hungry, feed him.
>> If he is thirsty, give him something to drink.
>> For in so doing
>> you will be heaping fiery coals on his head.
> Do not be conquered by evil, but conquer evil with good. (Rom. 12:14, 17a, 19–21)

Is he compartmentalizing and marginalizing not only Jesus's teaching but his own as well when he asserts (in Rom. 13) that government is given authority by God to do what (here in Rom. 12) he urges everyone not to do?

First, Paul is not in conflict with Jesus, but develops what Jesus did not address in the Sermon on the Mount—that is, the role of governing authority. Second, he shows precisely that there is a distinction between how individuals ought to respond to a wrongdoer and how government is commissioned to respond. There is no conflict here. Consider what Paul says about vengeance:

> Friends, do not avenge yourselves; instead, leave room for God's wrath, because it is written, Vengeance belongs to me; I will repay, says the Lord. (Rom. 12:19)

> For [government] is God's servant, an avenger that brings wrath on the one who does wrong. (Rom. 13:4b)

---

18. Stassen and Gushee, *Kingdom Ethics*, 198.

Paul argues, on the one hand, that we are not to take vengeance into our own hands, because vengeance belongs to the Lord who will repay. But just six verses later he asserts that God's vengeance is carried out in this age by government, which is God's servant. It is precisely the case that, as Meilaender argues, "what none of us is permitted to do as a private citizen on his own authority the state may do—not because it is itself 'lord' of life and death, but because it is the authorized agent of the God who is that Lord."[19]

We may conclude that Christians can and should affirm government as a positive good, instituted by God. We can and should affirm our leaders and pray for them (see 1 Tim. 2:1–2). At the same time, this does not give the government absolute authority. *Government is given the responsibility to reward good and punish evil, but not the authority to determine what is good and evil.* Government is ordained by God and is responsible to God and will answer to God, and while Christians can affirm governing authority, it is necessary also to speak prophetically to governing authorities and to condemn the abuse and misuse of their power and authority.

Some have argued that Romans 13 has nothing to do with the death penalty, but is about paying taxes that government demands—"Pay taxes that are owed and don't rebel!" The sword, in this view, is carried by the Roman guards that accompanied tax collectors.[20] However, this interpretation is not convincing. Paul's reference to government as God's servant and avenger that bears the sword (Rom. 13:4) follows logically on the exhortation not to seek personal vengeance (Rom. 12:19), which has no apparent connection to taxes. Instead, Paul says, just as we are to submit to government because it is God's servant, so too we are to pay taxes, because governing authorities are God's servants (Rom. 13:6). Henlee Barnette makes this connection in his reflection on Romans 13: "[Paul] sees the state as a God-given institution, functioning to protect the good and to restrain the evildoers. It has the power of life and death over its citizens, acting as God's servant and the agent of God's wrath against the evildoer. And, since the state is God's instrument to promote order and well-being, it is the consequent duty of all men to support it by being good citizens, paying taxes, and honoring those in power."[21] Christopher Marshall, who makes a case against the death penalty, nevertheless recognizes that Romans 13 is consistent with a defense of the death penalty. He writes that the reference to the sword underscores not the state's power to kill but its responsibility to restrain evil and reward good, and then concludes, "This function may include, but certainly does not require, use of the death penalty."[22]

---

19. Meilaender, "Death Penalty," 50.
20. Stassen and Gushee briefly trace this view, though they do not make a strong case in its defense. *Kingdom Ethics*, 207.
21. Henlee H. Barnette, *Introducing Christian Ethics* (Nashville: Broadman, 1961), 162.
22. Marshall, "Capital Punishment," 120.

Other relevant texts

Stassen and Gushee consider a wide range of Scripture in their discussion of the death penalty, centered on the teaching of Jesus. They conclude that in the New Testament, Jesus's followers never advocate the death penalty. Further, they list instances when it is threatened or imposed, and argue that in each case "the death penalty is presented as an injustice":

- the beheading of John the Baptist (Matt. 14:1–12);
- the crucifixion of Jesus (John 18:38);
- the stoning of Stephen (Acts 7);
- the stoning of other Christians (Matt. 21:35; 23:37; John 10:31–32; Acts 14:5);
- Herod's killing of James (Acts 12:2);
- the threatened death penalty for Paul (Acts 25:11, 25; 26:31); and
- the persecution of Christians in the book of Revelation.[23]

In response, it is true that these are instances of terrible injustices, yet that is precisely because they are put to death even though they are innocent. None of these examples are focused on the justice of capital punishment as such, and it is difficult to see how they demonstrate that capital punishment is an unjust response to murder. The death penalty must be judged from a broader biblical perspective.

Concerning the argument that no followers of Jesus advocated the death penalty, several brief comments are in order.

First, the death penalty is not discussed perhaps because it is not immediately relevant in the Gospel narratives or the Epistles. Second, Paul is a follower of Jesus, and he defends the just use of the sword by government, which undermines Stassen and Gushee's claim. Third, one or two other texts may imply that government has the authority to use the death penalty in some circumstances.

When Paul is on trial and answers charges against him before Festus, he proclaims that he has been falsely accused. Then he says, "If then I did anything wrong and am deserving of death, I am not trying to escape death; but if there is nothing to what these men accuse me of, no one can give me up to them. I appeal to Caesar!" (Acts 25:11). Paul is not arguing for or against the death penalty here, but he does imply that there are things deserving of death, for which the magistrate has the authority to execute a person. Paul is pointing out the injustice not of the death penalty as such but of the trumped-up charges brought against him, because he is innocent.

Nowhere is there greater injustice displayed than in the crucifixion of Jesus. Pilate recognizes his innocence, yet he desires to placate the crowd, and he is disturbed by Jesus's silence when questioned. So Pilate says, "Don't you know that I have the authority to release you and the authority to crucify you?" (John 19:10). Jesus does not deny that Pilate has such authority, at least in principle. Instead, he declares that Pilate's

---

23. Stassen and Gushee, *Kingdom Ethics*, 205.

authority comes from God, while high-lighting his own innocence: "'You would have no authority over me at all,' Jesus answered him, 'if it hadn't been given you from above'" (John 19:11).

Summary of a Biblical Perspective on Capital Punishment

This survey of biblical teaching indicates that capital punishment is not intrinsically immoral, but is a just punishment for the murder of a human being made in God's image. God has established government to administer justice and punish those who do wrong, with the use of proportional punishment, including capital punishment for murder. *That severe punishment underscores the severity of murderous violence and of God's wrath against evil, which will ultimately be carried out in the final judgment by God directly, but which for now is administered by governing authorities as God's servants.* The understanding that government serves to carry out God's justice is a reminder that government is, and will be, accountable to God. Thus, if and when capital punishment is administered, it must be with justice. Christians may therefore affirm government's authority to use the death penalty in response to murder, but must also hold the government accountable to justice in its administration.

In the next section, some arguments against capital punishment will be considered, along with some of the troubling realities and injustices in its implementation in the United States. If the death penalty is just punishment for certain crimes in principle, can it be implemented justly in contemporary society, or must it be abolished due to injustices in the system? It is argued here that, in the face of injustices, we may call for reform rather than the abolition of the death penalty. However, it is not enough simply to call for reform, whether from a classroom or a pulpit or the pages of a book. What is needed is to urge specific, practical, and realizable reforms that will reduce unjust practices. As such, I will consider several recommendations for reform offered in a substantial report on the death penalty, in response to specific problems of injustice that are highlighted in that report.

Capital Punishment in Contemporary Society

Capital Punishment in the United States

Number of persons sentenced and executed by year (1997–2012)[24]			
Year	People Sentenced	People Executed	Difference
1997	265	74	191
1998	294	68	226

24. Statistics on death sentences taken from Death Penalty Information Center, "Facts about the Death Penalty," http://www.deathpenaltyinfo.org/documents/FactSheet.pdf. Statistics on executions taken from US Department of Justice, Bureau of Justice Statistics, "Prisoners Executed," See http://www.bjs.gov/index.cfm?ty=pbdetail&iid=2079.

Year	People Sentenced	People Executed	Difference
1999	277	98	179
2000	224	85	139
2001	155	66	89
2002	165	71	94
2003	152	65	87
2004	138	59	79
2005	140	60	80
2006	125	53	72
2007	120	42	78
2008	121	37	84
2009	118	52	66
2010	109	46	63
2011	80	43	37
2012	79	43	36

Number of persons sentenced and executed by year (1997–2012)[24]

Whether or not one is convinced that capital punishment is just, and should be used in some cases, the reality is that *capital punishment is not sustainable as it is currently implemented in the United States*. Consider the following data. According to the Bureau of Justice Statistics, the number of people under the sentence of death grew steadily over a thirty-year period, from under 500 in the mid-1970s to around 3,500 in the early 2000s.[25] At the end of 2012 there were over 3,033 prisoners in the United States under the sentence of death.[26] Seventy-nine people were sentenced to death in 2012, while 43 were executed, continuing a trend in which a much higher number of people have been sentenced to death than executed each year.

During the period from 1997 to 2012, there was a significant reduction in the number of death sentences, due in part to the option of a sentence of life without the possibility of parole. Still, the numbers show that there are more people sentenced to death than executed every year, and that many of those who are sentenced to death will never be executed. Between 1973 and 2012, the total number of people sentenced to death was 8,374. Of those, 1,320 were executed (15.8 percent); 478 died (5.7 percent); 3,118 had their sentence or conviction overturned (37.2 percent); 392 had their sentence commuted (4.7 percent); there were 33 "other removals" (0.4 percent); and 3,033 remained under sentence of death (36.2 percent).[27]

Even though in recent years both the number of people sentenced and the number of people executed have fallen, and the gap between the two has been reduced significantly, the current practice is unsustainable. The alternatives for dealing with this are limited to several possibilities: either abolish the death penalty, increase the number of executions, reduce the number of death sentences, commute a great number of death

---

25. US Department of Justice, Bureau of Justice Statistics, "Capital Punishment 2012—Statistical Tables," 2, http://www.bjs.gov/content/pub/pdf/cp12st.pdf.
26. US Department of Justice, "Capital Punishment 2012," 1.
27. US Department of Justice, "Capital Punishment 2012," 20.

sentences, or some combination of these, as part of the reform of capital punishment in the United States. The options need to be considered in light of other issues, which are considered below.

In the following pages, I will contend that government is justified in using capital punishment as a penalty for some cases of murder, and that therefore it should be retained and not abolished. However, if it is to be sustainable, states must consider changing guidelines for sentencing that will reduce the number of death sentences to correspond more realistically with the number of guilty persons who will actually be executed. Others who would have been sentenced to death should be considered for a life sentence without the possibility of parole.

I will survey several key arguments against the death penalty, and offer a response to the arguments in light of the biblical perspective outlined above, as well as other relevant factors. Many nuances could be added to the way the arguments are presented below. I will include some of them, but the purpose here is to describe and respond to arguments that are used to make a case that capital punishment should be abolished because it is unjust either in principle or in the way that it is administered.

Arguments against Capital Punishment (and Response)

Capital punishment is simply state-sanctioned vengeance

Argument. According to Amnesty International, "The death penalty is . . . the premeditated and cold-blooded killing of a human being by the state."[28] Or, as one author put it, "Behind the justice of capital punishment lies the human motive of vengeance."[29] Opponents of capital punishment consider it to be merely bloodthirsty revenge that is sanctioned by the state. Further, retribution of this nature, if not retribution as such, is understood to be inconsistent with the purposes of the criminal-justice system, or biblical justice, which are said to focus on rehabilitation and restitution.[30] Restitution may include punishment, or paying one's debt to society, but not *capital* punishment, either because there is then no possibility of rehabilitation or because no debt is considered so great that it demands one's life as payment.

Response. This line of argument, or something like it, has been very influential since at least the middle of the twentieth century. It is what C. S. Lewis called the humanitarian theory of punishment, which understands retribution in this way: "to punish a man because he deserves it, and as much as he deserves, is mere revenge, and,

28. Amnesty International, "The Death Penalty: Questions and Answers," https://www.amnesty.org/download/Documents/56000/act500102007en.pdf.
29. Victor Anderson, "Responsibility, Vengeance, and the Death Penalty," in Owens, Carlson, and Elshtain, *Religion and the Death Penalty*, 202.
30. Cf. Yoder, "Against the Death Penalty," 130.

therefore, barbarous and immoral."[31] By focusing instead on rehabilitation, Lewis adds, punishment serves primarily as therapy. This is the progress of an enlightened and therapeutic society, which appears at first to have moved "from the harsh and self-righteous notion of giving the wicked their deserts to the charitable and enlightened one of tending the psychologically sick."[32] However, Lewis contends, there are serious problems with this view. One is that by denying retributive justice, in which a person receives what is deserved, the concept of justice is emptied and the full humanity of the wrongdoer is denied, for a sentence can only be considered just or unjust if it is deserved or undeserved.[33] A second problem with the focus on rehabilitation or cure rather than retribution, Lewis asserts, is this: "If crime and disease are to be regarded as the same thing, it follows that any state of mind which our masters choose to call 'disease' can be treated as crime; and compulsorily cured."[34] Lewis urges "a return to the traditional or Retributive theory" not only for the sake of society but also for the sake of the criminal.[35]

More recently, J. Budziszewski has defended the concept of retributive justice. He argues that "retribution is the primary purpose of just punishment *as such*." There may be other goods that come from punishment, or secondary motivations for punishment, such as rehabilitation, protection of society, or deterrence, but these are not essential to just punishment, for at least three reasons: "In the first place, punishment might not achieve them. In the second place, they can sometimes be partly achieved apart from punishment. Third and most important, they cannot justify punishment by themselves. In other words, we *may not do more* to the criminal than he deserves—not even if more would be needed to rehabilitate him, make him harmless, or discourage others from imitation."[36]

Retribution is the principle outlined in the biblical concept of justice, not only as the rationale for capital punishment in Genesis 9:6, but of justice in general as governed by the *lex talionis*, or the law of retaliation (e.g., Exod. 21:23–25). Rather than being a harsh law that seeks to exact maximum vengeance on a wrongdoer, the *lex talionis* enacts the principle of justice that each person ought to receive what is due them. It is the principle of proportionality, which limits punishment to that which is proportional to the wrong that has been done. It is life for life, eye for eye, tooth for tooth, and so on, not life for tooth or tooth for life, both of which would be unjust, being either far more harsh or far more lenient that what is deserved. Further,

---

31. C. S. Lewis, "The Humanitarian Theory of Punishment," in *God in the Dock: Essays on Theology and Ethics*, ed. Walter Hooper (Grand Rapids: Eerdmans, 1970), 287.
32. Lewis, "Humanitarian Theory," 288.
33. Lewis, "Humanitarian Theory," 288.
34. Lewis, "Humanitarian Theory," 293.
35. Lewis, "Humanitarian Theory," 287.
36. J. Budziszewski, "Categorical Pardon: On the Argument for Abolishing Capital Punishment," in Owens, Carlson, and Elshtain, *Religion and the Death Penalty*, 110–11.

this principle of justice applies to all, rather than having one set of scales for citizens and another set for noncitizens, or for rich and poor (Lev. 24:19–22; Exod. 23:3, 6).

It may be asked—and often is—whether this is an Old Testament concept of justice that is replaced in the New Testament. Does Jesus abolish and forbid the *lex talionis* when he says, "You have heard that it was said, An eye for an eye and a tooth for a tooth. But I tell you, don't resist an evildoer. On the contrary, if anyone slaps you on your right cheek, turn the other to him also" (Matt. 5:38–39)? The answer requires a distinction. On the one hand, Jesus makes it clear that his followers are not to use the *lex talionis* to justify personal vengeance against those who wrong us. On the other hand, as indicated earlier, Paul repeats something very much like Jesus's teaching in Romans 12, that we ought not to repay evil for evil but leave vengeance to the Lord, yet he goes right on to affirm the power of the state to punish wrongdoers, for God has given the state the authority to enact justice. This is why Meilaender argues that "it is so essential that we understand civil and criminal punishment as public retribution, not private vengeance."[37] Capital punishment is therefore not a matter of the person

who is wronged finding closure, though that may happen. Indeed, Meilaender writes that when the state "executes a convicted murderer, it is essential that we not think of this as responding to the desires of family or friends of the murderer's victim or victims. . . . The criminal's punishment (even execution) satisfies not our need for therapeutic closure but our need for a just society."[38]

In short, the purposes of criminal justice may include rehabilitation, restitution,[39] and deterrence (discussed below), but its primary purpose is retribution, which is not bloodthirsty revenge but the punishment of wrongdoing that is proportionate to the wrong done. That is, the essential meaning of retribution is justice—to seek justice for the victim of murder and to maintain justice in society. The defense of capital punishment is grounded in the conviction that there is such a thing as an evil act that deserves death— namely, murder. It may not be necessary for the state to apply the death penalty to every murder, so long as the punishment that is applied signifies the seriousness of the act, such as life in prison without the possibility of parole. Yet the state should retain the possibility of capital punishment for the most heinous cases of murder, at least as a reminder that there are crimes worthy of death.[40]

---

37. Meilaender, "Death Penalty," 50.
38. Meilaender, "Death Penalty," 53.
39. Though the purposes and length of this chapter do not permit further discussion of this point, as an aside it may be said that restitution (and true rehabilitation) ought to be taken *more* seriously in our justice system. For instance, sentencing for nonviolent crimes, such as certain cases of theft and fraud, could consider ways in which the perpetrator would be required to make restitution to the victim(s), as an alternative to a prison sentence (which may not include restitution but which creates additional economic costs to society). Ephesians 4:28 has significant implications for some such policy.
40. Cf. Budziszewski, "Categorical Pardon," 116.

Capital punishment is not an effective deterrent for violent crime

Argument. Some opponents of capital punishment argue that it does not deter violent crime effectively. There are various reasons offered, including that murder is often a crime of passion or rage and is often not affected by the threat of execution in the future.[41] Similarly, it is argued that it is not effective as a deterrent to those who commit violent crime under the influence of drugs or alcohol, or who panic and kill someone during the commission of another crime, such as robbery.[42] Further, murder rates are lower in states that do not have the death penalty.[43] Though some opponents insist that capital punishment has no deterrent effect, others indicate that the research is inconclusive. One report, released in 2012 and based on three decades of research, simply states that studies claiming a deterrent effect are flawed, and its own conclusion is that research to date "is not informative about whether capital punishment decreases, increases, or has no effect on homicide rates."[44]

Response. Arguments about the deterrent effect of capital punishment are made on both sides, and involve some detailed analysis that is not possible here.[45] While we ought to be cautious about drawing certain conclusions about the deterrent effect of capital punishment, we may make several observations. First, it is not totally clear whether capital punishment is an effective deterrent. The comparison between states (or between countries) that have and those that do not have the death penalty are not conclusive because there are many factors to consider with respect to homicide rates. Second, as one expert claims, there is no conclusive research about "how potential murderers actually perceive their risk of punishment."[46] Third, the case for (or against) capital punishment does not depend on whether it acts as a deterrent. The primary purpose for the death penalty is retributive justice, not deterrence. Fourth, however, deterrence is—or should be—a secondary purpose of capital punishment and all criminal justice (Deut. 17:12–13, 19:20; 1 Tim. 5:20). The reasons it may not be an effective deterrence include the lack of certainty and

---

41. See Raymond Bonner and Ford Fessenden, "Absence of Executions: A Special Report; States with No Death Penalty Share Lower Homicide Rates," *The New York Times*, September 22, 2000, http://www.nytimes.com/2000/09/22/us/absence-executions-special-report-states-with-no-death-penalty-share-lower.html.

42. Amnesty International, "The Death Penalty and Deterrence," http://www.amnestyusa.org/our-work/issues/death-penalty/us-death-penalty-facts/the-death-penalty-and-deterrence.

43. Death Penalty Information Center, "Murder Rate of Death Penalty States Compared to Non-Death Penalty States," http://www.deathpenaltyinfo.org/deterrence-states-without-death-penalty-have-had-consistently-lower-murder-rates.

44. This and other reports are summarized online at the Death Penalty Information Center, "Discussion of Recent Deterrence Studies," https://archive.deathpenaltyinfo.org/discussion-recent-deterrence-studies.

45. Among the many resources on this issue, see arguments on both sides in Stephen E. Schonebaum, ed., *Does Capital Punishment Deter Crime?* (San Diego: Greenhaven, 1998).

46. Statement from criminologist Daniel Nagin of Carnegie Mellon, who chaired the panel of experts on the 2012 report by the National Research Council of the National Academies, which summarized three decades of research. Cited by the Death Penalty Information Center, "Discussion of Recent Deterrence Studies."

the length of time between sentence and execution, which on average has increased from 74 months (just over six years) in 1984 to 190 months (just under sixteen years) in 2012.[47] Ecclesiastes declares that where punishment is delayed, instead of deterring evil, the human heart determines to do evil (Eccles. 8:11).

Capital punishment is an attack on human dignity and violates human rights

Argument. Amnesty International is opposed to the death penalty "without exception regardless of the nature of the crime." The primary reason is that, in their view, "the death penalty is the ultimate denial of human rights," which violates the Universal Declaration of Human Rights against "cruel, inhuman or degrading treatment or punishment."[48] As such, it is also seen to violate the Eighth Amendment to the US Constitution, which prohibits cruel and unusual punishment. In relation to the basic point about human dignity, arguments are made from philosophical and theological perspectives. For instance, Jeffrey Reiman, who argues that capital punishment may be deserved, nevertheless maintains that a civilized society ought to refrain from using it.[49] From a theological perspective, Gushee,

who also concedes that capital punishment may be justifiable in principle, contends that opposition to it is "most in keeping with Christian respect for the sacredness of human life."[50] Many argue that a robust pro-life perspective requires opposition to the death penalty just as much as it requires opposition to abortion.

Response. Christians certainly ought to defend human dignity and, in terms of the language used in contemporary debates, embrace a "pro-life" perspective. The question is whether this entails opposition to the death penalty "without exception" as "cruel, inhuman, and degrading punishment." Several observations indicate otherwise, though these do not suggest unqualified support for capital punishment. First, it is difficult to make a strong constitutional case against the death penalty as cruel and unusual punishment, since the Eighth Amendment was not considered at the time to entail the abolition of capital punishment. One of the possibilities suggested in the Eighth Amendment itself is that "cruel and unusual" is excessive punishment, or, we might add, punishment that inflicts unnecessary pain.[51] Hence, some methods of capital punishment may be consistent with human dignity while other are

---

47. Death Penalty Information Center, "Time on Death Row," https://deathpenaltyinfo.org/death-row/death-row-time-on-death-row.
48. Amnesty International, "Questions and Answers."
49. Reiman makes this argument as part of his case against capital punishment in Louis P. Pojman and Jeffrey Reiman, *The Death Penalty: For and Against* (New York: Rowman and Littlefield, 1998), 108–12.
50. David P. Gushee, *The Sacredness of Human Life: Why an Ancient Biblical Vision Is Key to the World's Future* (Grand Rapids: Eerdmans, 2013), 372.
51. The Eighth Amendment says that "excessive bail shall not be required, nor excessive fines imposed, nor cruel and unusual punishments inflicted." See National Constitution Center, "Eighth Amendment: Excessive Fines, Cruel and Unusual Punishment," https://constitutioncenter.org/interactive-constitution/amendments/amendment-viii.

not. Second, a biblical view of human dignity is consistent with capital punishment, which recognizes both the dignity of the victim and the dignity of perpetrators as moral agents who are required to take moral responsibility for their crimes. To argue otherwise is to create artificial tensions within the Bible and to call into question the justice and righteousness of God, the very one who gives human beings dignity in the first place, and thus to fail to understand justice fully. Third, while it may be reasonable to oppose both abortion and capital punishment, the relevant features of these issues are very different, and it is perfectly reasonable and consistent to hold a pro-life perspective that recognizes the dignity of human life by opposing abortion and defending capital punishment. The obvious difference between the two is that the one who is justly sentenced to death is guilty of a heinous crime, while the unborn child is innocent. It is a terrible irony that many who oppose capital punishment, based on human rights and the inherent value of each human life, also support the "right" to virtually unqualified access to abortion.

Capital punishment cannot be administered justly

Argument. In January 2000, the governor of Illinois, George Ryan, declared a moratorium on executions in Illinois. In spite of his belief that the death penalty is justified for heinous crimes, Ryan made his decision because he did not have confidence that the system in Illinois would prevent an innocent person from execution. He stated,

> I cannot support a system, which, in its administration, has proven to be so fraught with error and has come so close to the ultimate nightmare, the state's taking of innocent life. Thirteen people have been found to have been wrongfully convicted. . . . Until I can be sure that everyone sentenced to death in Illinois is truly guilty, until I can be sure with moral certainty that no innocent man or woman is facing a lethal injection, no one will meet that fate. . . . We must ensure the public safety of our citizens but, in doing so, we must ensure that the ends of justice are served.[52]

One argument against the death penalty is not necessarily that it is *intrinsically* unjust, though many believe that it is, but that it is *irretrievably* unjust. That is to say, even if it is granted that certain crimes are deserving of death, so that the state is justified in executing certain criminals who are guilty of heinous acts, there are too many procedural injustices to tolerate capital punishment in practice. These include inadequate legal representation, coercive interrogations, coerced and mistaken eyewitness testimony, and social and political pressures, among other things, leading to wrongful convictions and a process that is discriminatory against the poor and minorities.

---

52. Illinois Government News Network, "Governor Ryan Declares Moratorium On Executions, Will Appoint Commission To Review Capital Punishment System," Governor's Office Press Release, January 31, 2000, http://www3.illinois.gov/PressReleases/ShowPressRelease.cfm?SubjectID=3&RecNum=359.

Response. This, in my mind, is the most potent argument against the use of capital punishment, and requires a more sustained treatment. Injustices in the administration of capital punishment cannot simply be ignored. Some who defend capital punishment may wish to argue that procedural injustices do not point to the injustice of capital punishment as such; that in cases where capital punishment is deserved, justice is served in executing that person whether or not another person who deserves capital punishment receives it; and that any inequities in the administration of capital punishment demonstrate a need for reform, not the abolition of the death penalty. Such arguments may be valid in principle, but they ring hollow while there exists widespread, systemic injustices in the administration of capital punishment. It is not enough to say that reform is needed: real reform, with concrete and realizable recommendations, must be offered. To that end, it is worth examining a substantial report on the death penalty submitted by the Constitution Project in 2014, "Irreversible Error: Recommended Reforms for Preventing and Correcting Errors in the Administration of Capital Punishment," which outlines procedural problems with capital punishment and offers recommendations to remedy those problems.[53] Several of the key points made in that report will be considered here, before drawing some conclusions on capital punishment.

Procedural problems with capital punishment

Safeguarding innocence and protecting against wrongful execution. One of the procedural problems with capital punishment is the difficulty of overturning a wrongful conviction, in spite of the appeals process. The proof of innocence required to overturn a conviction is a very difficult standard to achieve. It is reasonable to recognize a point of finality in the judicial process, and to refuse to hear every possible claim of innocence. However, legal procedures and precedents ought not to rule out considering legitimate claims, even after conviction.

In the case of Georgia death row inmate Troy Davis, who was eventually executed on September 21, 2011, the US Supreme Court ordered a federal district court to inquire "as to whether evidence that could not have been obtained at the time of trial clearly establishes petitioner's innocence."[54] In dissent, Justice Scalia claimed that the Supreme Court "has never held that the Constitution forbids the execution of a convicted defendant who has had a full and fair trial but is later able to convince a habeas court that he is 'actually' innocent."[55] It should be said that the defendant's claims had already been heard

---

53. The Constitution Project, "Irreversible Error: Recommended Reforms for Preventing and Correcting Errors in the Administration of Capital Punishment," 2014, http://www.constitutionproject.org/wp-content/uploads/2014/06/Irreversible-Error_FINAL.pdf.
54. *In re Davis*, 557 U.S. 952, 952 (2009). Cited in Constitution Project, "Irreversible Error," 3.
55. *In re Davis*, 557 U.S. 955 (2009). Cited in Constitution Project, "Irreversible Error," 3. A writ of *habeas corpus* (Latin for "that you have the body") is used to bring a prisoner or other detainee (e.g., institutionalized mental patient) before the court to determine whether the person's imprisonment or detention is lawful.

multiple times and, further, that the lower court ruled that Davis was unable to establish his "actual innocence" by "clear and convincing evidence." However, it is worrisome that a legitimate claim and evidence of innocence may not be considered because of procedural obstacles, or because the burden of proof is too difficult to meet. Or, concerning Scalia's statement, whatever the Constitution allows or forbids, it is a travesty that a person might be executed, and evidence of "actual innocence" might not be considered, on the grounds that there was a full and fair trial.

"Irreversible Error" recognizes the need for finality, but also recognizes possible errors, and argues for legislation that "sets standards to facilitate the review of credible post-conviction claims of innocence."[56] Whether the particular recommendations will accomplish the objective, or alternative recommendations ought to be offered, it seems right to seek to "strike the appropriate balance between the interests in preserving the finality of the verdict and in ensuring that convictions are accurate and just."[57]

It is thus a reasonable recommendation that "if a prosecutor becomes aware of new, credible, material evidence that it is reasonably likely that an innocent person has been convicted," they should disclose that evidence to defendants and/or their lawyers.

"Irreversible Error" notes that a "review of approximately 6,000 cases, which was in response to an inspector general's investigation of misconduct at the FBI crime lab in the 1990s, uncovered numerous crime lab errors and revealed certain forensic evidence to be unreliable."[58] Yet the results were only made available to the prosecutors in the relevant cases and, according to the *Washington Post*, some prosecutors did not disclose the results, or disclosed them incompletely or years later.[59] For its part, the Justice Department claimed that they were not required to inform defendants or their lawyers, and that it had met its legal and constitutional obligations by informing prosecutors. Dozens or even hundreds of defendants may have been affected. In one case, Donald Gates was exonerated by DNA evidence after spending twenty-eight years in prison, even though prosecutors had discovered *twelve years earlier* that "the forensic findings that contributed to his conviction were flawed."[60] There may be many reasons for lapses such as this, but it is difficult not to think that low priority is placed on such cases at least in part because those who are incarcerated are considered guilty and are of little concern, even if the evidence points to their innocence.

An additional recommendation seeks not merely to exonerate the innocent but

56. Constitution Project, "Irreversible Error," 4.
57. Constitution Project, "Irreversible Error," 4.
58. Constitution Project, "Irreversible Error," 6.
59. Constitution Project, "Irreversible Error," 6. See Spencer S. Hsu, "Convicted Defendants Left Uninformed of Forensic Flaws Found by Justice Department," *Washington Post*, April 16, 2012, http://www.washingtonpost.com/local/crime/convicted-defendants-left-uninformed-of-forensic-flaws-found-by-justice-dept/2012/04/16/gIQAWTcgMT_story.html.
60. Constitution Project, "Irreversible Error," 7.

also to identify and correct systemic problems. "Irreversible Error" asserts that "when the criminal justice system fails in its most critical function—*convicting the guilty and exonerating the innocent*—the government should step in to determine the causes of the failure and identify appropriate reforms."[61]

Isaiah 5:23 declares woe to those

> who acquit the guilty for a bribe
> and deprive the innocent of justice.

Proverbs 17:15 says,

> acquitting the guilty and condemning the just—
> both are detestable to the LORD. (cf. Exod. 23:1; Deut. 25:1; 27:25; Ps. 94:20–21)

We are guilty of something detestable to the Lord if we condemn the innocent, and surely this includes the failure to consider evidence of innocence after they are convicted.

At times those sentenced to death are later exonerated.[62] Some argue that this shows that the justice system works. Justice Thomas claims in his majority opinion in the 2006 case *Kansas v. Marsh*, "Reversal of an erroneous conviction on appeal or on habeas, or the pardoning of an innocent condemnee through executive clemency, demonstrates not the failure of the system but its success."[63] When the system has prevented the execution of an innocent person by such means, it is successful in one sense. However, if an innocent person spends years on death row for a false conviction, the "success" of the system is rather dubious. It is a long, tiresome, expensive, and uncertain process to overturn a wrongful conviction, which victimizes not only the innocent person but the person's family and friends as well. Justice Thomas's argument does not recognize the intermediate failure of the system, nor does it take into account the cases in which the innocent are not exonerated, but may be executed or spend their entire sentence in prison.

Ensuring reliable eyewitness testimony. Eyewitness testimony is often a critical part of identifying and convicting perpetrators, but it can be unreliable. For example, in 1986, Frank Lee Smith was convicted of the rape and murder of an eight-year-old girl in Broward County, Florida, on the testimony of three witnesses who "caught only brief glimpses of the killer at night. . . . No physical evidence linked him to the crime." More than a decade later, one of the witnesses recanted her testimony, after defense investigators showed her a picture of another possible suspect, whom she identified as the true perpetrator. She claimed to have been pressured by friends and police to identify Smith at the time, even though she was uncertain. DNA evidence then cleared

---

61. Constitution Project, "Irreversible Error," 8.
62. The report notes that, "since 1973, 144 people in twenty-six states have been released from death row based on evidence of their innocence." Constitution Project, "Irreversible Error," 52, citing the Death Penalty Information Center, "The Innocence List," http://www.deathpenaltyinfo.org/innocence-list-those-freed-death-row.
63. *Kansas v. Marsh*, 548 U.S. 163, 193 (2006). Cited in Constitution Project, "Irreversible Error," 2.

Smith and confirmed that the new suspect was guilty of the crime. Sadly, Smith died of pancreatic cancer before being exonerated, and almost a year after his death, in December 2000, he "became the first death row prisoner in history to be posthumously exonerated by DNA."[64]

False identification by eyewitnesses is one of the leading causes of wrongful convictions, according to the Innocence Project, "playing a factor in 72 percent of post-conviction DNA exoneration cases."[65] The problem with misidentification is underscored by field experiments, which have shown that "where the true perpetrator *was not in the lineup*, eyewitnesses identified as the suspect an innocent lineup participant more than one-third of the time."[66] This is a serious concern, because eyewitness identifications are persuasive to juries.

The accuracy of an eyewitness identification of a suspect in a lineup is affected by numerous factors, including such things as "a suggestively-formed lineup" (characteristics of "fillers" that are used), "suggestive instructions," "an administrator who is predisposed to a particular suspect," and "similarities or differences between the witness' and the suspect's age, race, or ethnicity."[67]

One of the problems that the report identifies is that "there is no uniform national standard for identification procedures," and in fact, "many police departments have no written procedures."[68] It seems reasonable to identify and recommend for adoption practices that will ensure much greater accuracy in police-lineup identifications.

In order to reduce mistakes, the report commends certain "best practices" when it comes to eyewitness identification, including the following:[69]

- Double-blind administration: someone who does not know the identity of the suspect should administer the lineup, to avoid giving the eyewitness nonverbal or inadvertent hints.
- Fillers with similar characteristics to the suspect should be added to the lineup, to avoid suggestive lineups, where the suspect stands out from others in the lineup. In one extreme case, a suspect was the only one shirtless, which fit the description of the perpetrator; in another, the suspect was the only one wearing an orange prison jumpsuit!
- The eyewitness should be instructed that the perpetrator may not be in the lineup.

---

64. Constitution Project, "Irreversible Error," 51.
65. Constitution Project, "Irreversible Error," 52, citing the Innocence Project. The current data from The Innocence Project cites 69 percent misidentification. "Exonerations in the United States," https://www.innocenceproject.org/dna-exonerations-in-the-united-states.
66. Carol Krafka and Stephen Penrod, "Reinstatement of Context in a Field Experiment on Eyewitness Identification," *Journal of Personality and Social Psychology* 58 (1985): 49, cited in Constitutions Project, "Irreversible Error," 52n6 (emphasis added).
67. Constitution Project, "Irreversible Error," 53. See Beth Schuster, "Police Lineups: Making Eyewitness Identification More Reliable," NIJJ. No. 258 (Oct 2007).
68. Constitution Project, "Irreversible Error," 54.
69. For the following recommendations, see Constitution Project, "Irreversible Error," 54–60.

- The eyewitness should be asked to state their level of confidence.
- No feedback should be given to the eyewitness that they have selected the suspect, since assurances that they "did well" has an impact on the witness.

Ensuring effective counsel. Among the greatest concerns with capital punishment is that *economic status is the most significant factor determining whether a person who is convicted of a heinous crime will receive the death penalty.* The problem with inadequate counsel for the poor is illustrated by the following case:

Jeffrey Leonard, a 20-year old African American, was tried and sentenced to death in Kentucky under the name James Slaughter. His real name was contained in the prosecution's file and in four different places in the trial court record. But the lawyer did not investigate and, as a result, never learned his client's name or that he was brain damaged and suffered through a horrific childhood. When challenged about his representation, the lawyer testified that he had tried six capital cases and headed an organized crime unit for a New York prosecutor's office. Neither statement was true. The lawyer was later indicted for perjury.

The charges were dismissed in exchange for him resigning from the bar. The Court of Appeals, still referring to Leonard by the inaccurate name, concluded that the lawyer's performance was deficient because his failure to investigate his client's background "resulted from inattention, not reasoned strategic judgment." Nevertheless, it upheld the death sentence based upon its conclusion that the outcome would not have been different even if the lawyer had known his client's name and presented the evidence of his brain damage, childhood abuse, and other mitigating factors.[70]

"Irreversible Error" asserts that "the quality of capital defense counsel seems to be the most important factor in predicting who is sentenced to die—far more important than the nature of the crime or the character of the accused."[71] Of course, the quality of defense counsel is closely correlated to the ability to afford experienced representation. The lack of quality counsel means not only that the accused is more likely to receive a death sentence but also that, because of an inadequate trial record—which does not contain the results of a full investigation and which fails to expunge errors—the appellate review process is greatly affected, making it difficult to correct errors later.[72] Two of the

70. Stephen B. Bright, "The Right to Counsel in Death Penalty and Other Criminal Cases: Neglect of the Most Fundamental Right," *Journal of Law in Society* 11, no. 1 (Fall 2009 / Winter 2010): 22–23. Cited in Constitution Project, "Irreversible Error," 85.
71. Constitution Project, "Irreversible Error," 86. The report cites Stephen B. Bright, "Turning Celebrated Principles into Reality," *The Champion* 6 (2003); also Southern Center for Human Rights, "'If You Cannot Afford a Lawyer . . .': A Report on Georgia's Failed Indigent Defense System," 2003, http://www.deathpenaltyinfo.org/jan.%202003.%20report.pdf.
72. Constitution Project, "Irreversible Error," 86.

most significant problems that lead to inadequate representation in capital trials are interrelated: the failure to provide counsel "with specialized training and experience in death penalty cases," and "funding for defense lawyers to engage necessary investigators and experts."[73] These are costly, and while they are secured by those with adequate resources, they are often not provided for the very poor, who depend on court-appointed attorneys.

This problem has not gone unnoticed. As "Irreversible Error" indicates, "The Innocence Protection Act, which encourages training and resources for capital defense lawyers and provides for increased DNA testing, became law in October 2004 as part of the Justice for All Act." The issue has even been taken up at the presidential level in the State of the Union address when, in 2005, George W. Bush stated that "capital cases must be handled more carefully and that more resources should be directed to correcting the problem of inadequate defense lawyers."[74]

"Irreversible Error" asserts that adequate defense in a capital case requires thousands of hours, including 500–1200 hours at the trial level, another 700–1000 hours in the direct appeal process, with hundreds of additional hours for successive stages, so that adequate funding for a typical capital case would be about $190,000.[75] A wealthy person could afford that amount and more if necessary. Even a typical middle-class person, with their life on the line, could manage that amount or something close to it by selling their house, raising money, and so on. But the poor have no access to adequate resources, and are typically dependent on court-appointed attorneys, who often lack experience and receive little payment for their work.

The problem of inadequate resources for defense is highlighted in "Irreversible Error" by comparing what is needed for sufficient defense to what is actually provided in some jurisdictions. The difference is jarring. Indeed, in many cases attorneys are given incentives to "keep their costs low and their hours on the case few."[76] Some jurisdictions have startlingly low caps on the amount available for defense. In some Ohio counties, "attorney compensation is capped at $5,000 or $6,000 despite the fact that attorneys can invest as many as 2,000 hours on a capital case."[77] Even if "Irreversible Error" overestimates the amount required for adequate representation, such caps are obviously far too low to provide a just defense.

Related to the lack of compensation available for defense attorneys, "many of them have little knowledge of capital litigation or even criminal law in general. Many of them have little experience or skill in

---

73. Constitution Project, "Irreversible Error," 87.

74. Constitution Project, "Irreversible Error," 86.

75. Constitution Project, "Irreversible Error," 91.

76. Constitution Project, "Irreversible Error," 90.

77. Constitution Project, "Irreversible Error," 91n22, citing Kimbal Perry, "Lawyer: More $ for Capital Cases; Judge: No Way," *Cincinnati Enquirer*, July 1, 2012. See also *Christianity Today*, "The Lesson of Karla Faye Tucker," April 6, 1998, 15.

the courtroom." Even worse, "a disproportionate number of them have records of dis-
ciplinary action or even disbarment."[78]

When evidence indicates this type of systemic bias against the poor, justice cries out.
This should not be tolerated in our justice
system. The report offers recommendations
that seek to address the problem of ineffective
counsel through more effective training and
compensation for capital-defense lawyers to
build their case, on the basis that "providing
qualified counsel is perhaps the most important safeguard against the wrongful conviction, sentencing and execution of capital
defendants."[79]

Response. One of the biblical arguments
used to justify capital punishment is based
on Numbers 35:31, which stipulates that
"you are not to accept a ransom for the life
of someone who is guilty of murder; he must
be put to death." This text is part of a biblical
defense of the death penalty for murder, and
rightly so, for it calls attention to murder as
a special case of wrongdoing that must be
punished. At the same time, it is also the
basis for a challenge to the actual administration of the death penalty, because the
wealthy do "pay a ransom" in order to avoid
the death penalty (in the form of adequate
counsel), while the poor are unable to do so.
This should not be; it is not enough to say
that the poor who commit murder and are
sentenced to death get what they deserve,
even if the wealthy do not get what they deserve. Of course, there will never be perfect

equity in our justice system. But we should
not tolerate systemic inequity, so that we feel
satisfied that justice is served, even if imperfectly, when the poor are condemned while
the wealthy are ransomed. A society that is
content with such inequity is unjust.

Exodus 23:6 says, "You must not deny
justice to a poor person among you in his
lawsuit." It is too often the case that the poor
cannot defend themselves adequately in a
system that favors expensive representation.
This is perverted justice. Perhaps this means
that it should be made more difficult for the
wealthy to avoid the death penalty for heinous crimes. Certainly greater representation should be available to the poor. That
may be difficult, and it may be very unpop-
ular to provide greater funds to defend those
charged with monstrous deeds. It would
likely result in fewer capital cases—which
is necessary for a number of reasons—but
it need not require the abolition of capital
punishment.

The concerns raised about the just administration of capital punishment are
serious. Even if capital punishment is warranted as just retribution for murder, it is
deeply problematic if there are entrenched
injustices in the way that it is carried out.
Some opponents of the death penalty call for
abolition, not because it is intrinsically immoral, but because they do not believe it can
be administered fairly. One response to this
type of objection is that, even if many who
are guilty are not given the death penalty, it is

---

78. Constitution Project, "Irreversible Error," 90.
79. Constitution Project, "Irreversible Error," 92.

nevertheless the case that justice is served in cases where those who are guilty of a capital offense are executed. However, the problem is not simply that some who deserve capital punishment do not receive it while others do. The problem is that the evidence indicates systemic socioeconomic inequity.

Another response to those who oppose capital punishment based on systemic injustices is that it should be reformed but not abolished. This may be true, but more must be said. On the one hand, there are good reasons not to abolish capital punishment, because it is sanctioned biblically and it is a just response of the government to the heinous act of murder. On the other hand, it is not enough just to say that the answer is to reform, rather than abolish, capital punishment. It is necessary to offer—and seek to enact—specific reforms aimed at eliminating systemic injustices so that safeguards are put in place to prevent wrongful convictions and executions, and to prevent socioeconomic discrimination. Following some of the recommendations in the report "Irreversible Error," or developing and adopting adequate alternative recommendations, would go a long way toward addressing errors.

A biblical perspective not only offers a justification of capital punishment but also outlines a pattern to prevent systemic injustices. In the first place, it denounces a prejudice against the poor. In the second place, it presents higher standards of proof. For instance, the Mosaic law demands diligent investigation and certainty of guilt, including more than one witness (Num. 35:30; Deut. 17:4–6; 19:15), and a false witness would receive the penalty that would have been given to the one charged (Deut. 19:16–19). As John and Paul Feinberg have argued, if contemporary standards were as high as Old Testament standards, we would have fewer capital convictions, and, they add, "better to have few convictions where the accused is conclusively shown guilty than to have many questionable convictions."[80]

Conclusion

In this chapter I have argued that in the case of murder, the death penalty is a just punishment. That is not the end of the matter, however, as is evident from the foregoing discussion. The administration of capital punishment in a contemporary, secular state is a complex issue that raises important questions for Christians. The following paragraphs raise some of those questions, while recognizing that these issues require a much fuller response.

If capital punishment is just, should it be mandated in the case of murder, and should Christians advocate capital punishment? In a biblical perspective, capital punishment for murder is justified and it underscores the need for government to respond proportionately to evil, which serves to communicate that there is a crime deserving of death, to warn and impede those who would perpetrate evil, and to protect innocent lives. It is proper, then, for Christians to oppose the abolition of capital punishment and to

---

80. John S. Feinberg and Paul D. Feinberg, *Ethics for a Brave New World*, 2nd ed. (Wheaton, IL: Crossway, 2010), 249.

support its use by the government for at least the most heinous cases of murder.

The question of whether capital punishment should be mandated is difficult for Christians to answer in a simple way. One response is to say that it should be mandated for certain heinous cases of murder. Yet Christians are not in a position to enact such a mandate. Nevertheless, it is necessary to speak prophetically and make a case for the government to act justly, and this includes defending the use of capital punishment for certain cases of murder, and influencing others to support its use. While Paul's teaching in Romans 13 supports the use of capital punishment, it does not necessarily mandate its use in every case of murder. The sword indicates that the government may use the death penalty for a heinous crime, but more generally it serves as a symbol of its authority to punish evil, and not only its power to kill. It must punish evil proportionately, which means that light offenses should receive a relatively light punishment, while more grievous offenses should receive a heavier punishment. As such, proportionality requires responding to murder with one of the heaviest punishments available, which could be the death penalty, but it could be life in prison.

Since God is slow to anger and desires that people repent (2 Peter 3:9), shouldn't Christians oppose capital punishment to allow the guilty person opportunity to repent and put their trust in Jesus? God's patience and desire that people repent, and therefore ours as well, is not incompatible with punishment of evil. Romans 12 and 13

make this clear, as discussed earlier. Indeed, the one who is sentenced to death has opportunity to repent, an opportunity that is brought into sharp focus in the face of death. It is not self-evident that a sentence of life in prison is more likely to produce repentance. Of course, Christians ought not to delight in any execution, for it is a sobering reality, but at the same time we may be satisfied that justice has been done.

If we cannot be assured that capital punishment is administered in a just manner, should it be abolished? This question, too, requires a nuanced answer. On the one hand, in the fallen world, we never have and we never will achieve perfect justice, yet capital punishment is justly prescribed for certain crimes. It is not unjust to give some people the punishment that is due them simply because others do not receive what they deserve. On the other hand, this fact does not justify tolerating systemic injustice with the application of capital punishment, such that the justice system discriminates against the poor. The Law and the Prophets spoke against such injustices, and so should we. Furthermore, it is not enough, in the face of injustices, simply to say that what is called for is reform, rather than abolition, of capital punishment. Rather, the call for reform must be accompanied by actual proposals that would reduce injustices. If we cannot achieve substantial reforms where needed, then capital punishment should be significantly restricted, and perhaps a moratorium on capital punishment should be imposed until such reforms are enacted.

Select Resources

Bedau, Hugo Adam. *The Death Penalty in America*. 3rd ed. New York: Oxford University Press, 1982.

The Constitution Project. "Irreversible Error: Recommended Reforms for Preventing and Correcting Errors in the Administration of Capital Punishment." 2014. http://www.constitutionproject.org/wp-content/uploads/2014/06/Irreversible-Error_FINAL.pdf.

House, H. Wayne, and John Howard Yoder. *The Death Penalty Debate*. Dallas: Word, 1991.

Lewis, C. S. "The Humanitarian Theory of Punishment." In *God in the Dock: Essays on Theology and Ethics*, 287–300. Edited by Walter Hooper. Grand Rapids: Eerdmans, 1970.

Megivern, James J. *The Death Penalty: An Historical and Theological Survey*. Mahwah, NJ: Paulist Press, 1997.

Owens, Erik C., John D. Carlson, and Eric P. Elshtain. *Religion and the Death Penalty: A Call for Reckoning*. Grand Rapids: Eerdmans, 2004.

Pojman, Louis P., and Jeffrey Reiman. *The Death Penalty: For and Against.* Lanham, MD: Rowman & Littlefield, 1998.

CHAPTER 15

Just War, Pacifism, and the Use of Lethal Force

Blessed are the peacemakers,
for they will be called sons of God.

—Matthew 5:9

What is the source of wars and fights among
you? Don't they come from your passions
that wage war within you? You desire and do
not have. You murder and covet and cannot
obtain. You fight and wage war.

—James 4:1–2

For [government] is God's servant for your
good. But if you do wrong, be afraid, because
it does not carry the sword for no reason. For
it is God's servant, an avenger that brings
wrath on the one who does wrong.

—Romans 13:4

Introduction

> The soldier above all other people prays for peace, for he must suffer and bear the deepest wounds and scars of war.[1]
> —General Douglas MacArthur

Human history is marked by violence, bloodshed, and war, and the history of war itself is marked by escalation, using advances in technology and strategy to kill more efficiently, with increasing capacity for devastation.[2] From infantry to cavalry to chariots, and on to ships, submarines, tanks, planes, and drones; from swords and spears to arrows, to the armor-penetrating English longbow, to guns, canons, and siege artillery, to hand grenades, biological weapons, bombs, and nuclear weapons, human beings have applied ingenuity and technology to kill more effectively so that nations and rulers can meet force with more force, in order to exercise power and dominance over others. Wars have been fought for territorial expansion, riches, revenge, vainglory, nation-building, as well as self-defense, revolt against tyrannical rule, and other reasons.

The horror of war is portrayed by evangelical philosopher Arthur Holmes when he writes,

> War is evil. Its causes are evil, whether they be deliberate aggression, unbridled greed, lust for power, fear and distrust, an exaggerated national pride, a perverted sense of honor or some form of social injustice. Its consequences are evil, for it produces ghastly loss of life and limb; it orphans and widows and horribly maims the innocent both physically and emotionally; it cheapens life and morality; it destroys the means people count on to sustain their existence, and it produces economic disaster. Modern weaponry could decimate and even destroy the human race. And wars that are intended to arrest violence and injustice seem only in the long run to breed further injustice and conflict. . . . To call war anything less than evil would be self-deception.[3]

This is how Holmes begins his essay *defending* just war doctrine! Holmes's case for the just war is based on a lesser-of-two-evils view. He argues that "not all evil can be avoided," and defends the view that "participation in war" is "a lesser evil than allowing aggression and terror to go unchecked and unpunished."[4] By contrast, some Christians

---

1. General Douglas MacArthur, farewell speech given to the Corps of Cadets at West Point, May 12, 1962. "General Douglas MacArthur's Farewell Speech," National Center for Public Policy Research, https://nationalcenter.org/MacArthurFarewell.html.
2. See the brief account in John Jefferson Davis, *Evangelical Ethics: Issues Facing the Church Today*, 4th ed. (Phillipsburg, NJ: P&R, 2015), 234–36.
3. Arthur F. Holmes, "The Just War," in *War: Four Christian Views*, ed. Robert G. Clouse (Downers Grove, IL: InterVarsity Press, 1981), 117.
4. Holmes, "The Just War," 118.

assert that those who follow Jesus must never resort to violence, even against an enemy.

Scripture is clear that the fundamental cause of conflict and war is our sinful human nature. James writes, "What is the source of wars and fights among you? Don't they come from your passions that wage war within you? You desire and do not have. You murder and covet and cannot obtain. You fight and wage war" (James 4:1–2).

This chapter examines the question of how followers of the Prince of Peace ought to think about violence and war. Does Jesus's command not to resist an evildoer but to turn the other cheek and to love our enemies (Matt. 5:39, 44) mean that every use of force is prohibited for Christians? Should Christians affirm that government is authorized to use force to uphold justice and punish evil (Rom. 13:4)? Should Christians ever enter into military service? Is war intrinsically evil, or is it sometimes just? Can it be both?

These are questions that Christians have wrestled with for two millennia, with varied responses. At one end of the spectrum is militarism, which depends on the use of whatever force is necessary to advance objectives. Against such a view, pacifists argue that the use of violence is never permissible to advance one's interests, even in self-defense or the defense of one's neighbor. A view that may be understood as a mediating position between these two views is just war doctrine, which serves both to limit the use of force and to establish criteria under which the use of force may be justified. There are many variations of each of these views. In this chapter I will outline prominent features of pacifism or nonviolence, which was the dominant view of the church in the first three centuries, and has had strong advocates as a minority position, especially since the Reformation. I will then defend a version of just war doctrine, which has been the majority view among Christians historically, at least since the fourth century. First I will briefly discuss militarism.

Views on War and the Use of Force

Militarism

In his case for nonviolence, Preston Sprinkle defines militarism as "the overarching 'belief or desire' of having a strong military to protect or advance national interests."[5] He is concerned that American evangelicals have become militaristic, asserting that in the late twentieth and early twenty-first centuries "the dominant view among evangelicals has been that militarism is the key to religious freedom and the hope for peace in the world."[6] He cites statements by Christian leaders and theologians who make a case for America's having a strong military and then states that "being an evangelical has become synonymous with being pro-family, anti-abortion, pro-Republican, and pro-war."[7]

---

5. Preston Sprinkle, *Fight: A Christian Case for Nonviolence* (Colorado Springs: David C. Cook, 2013), 26.
6. Sprinkle, *Fight*, 26. In support of this assertion, Sprinkle cites Andrew Bacevich, *The New American Militarism* (New York: Oxford University Press, 2005), 122–46.
7. Sprinkle, *Fight*, 27.

He also cites the conclusion by military historian Andrew Bacevich, who writes, "Were it not for the support offered by several tens of millions of evangelicals, militarism in this deeply and genuinely religious country becomes inconceivable."[8]

All of this reads as a strong indictment of American evangelicals. At points the case is overstated, or perhaps needs some nuance. Is it true that being an evangelical is synonymous with being "pro-war"? And if America is militaristic, is that owing to the support of evangelicals, to the extent that it is otherwise "inconceivable"?[9] It is possible, for instance, to argue for a strong defense—and thus a strong military—without being "militaristic," let alone believing that militarism is the key to religious freedom and hope for world peace. It is possible, even necessary, to defend a just war without being "pro-war." It is also possible to support and honor military personnel without being militaristic.

Yet, while we might make these nuances, we ought to heed the warning to be concerned about militaristic tendencies. Just war doctrine, for instance, recognizes the problem of unchecked and unjust use of military power and develops criteria to guard against it, as we will see. Yet if those who defend just war doctrine never reject their country's actual wars, or do so only

retrospectively decades later, then we might well be concerned about militarism. Likewise, if we immediately marginalize those who make a case against war and violence, or even against a particular war, then we might well be concerned about militarism.

It is helpful to indicate what we mean by militarism. If the defense of just war doctrine and even of a strong military for defense is not militarism, and yet we want to avoid militarism, then what is it we are talking about? Sprinkle cites part of the definition of *militarism* offered in the *Oxford English Dictionary* (*OED*), which reads, "the belief or policy that a country should maintain a strong military capability and be prepared to use it aggressively to defend or promote national interests."[10] Based on this definition, it is not difficult to see how many Americans, including many evangelicals, could be considered militaristic, insofar as many believe that it is proper to maintain a strong military capability.

However, there are features of this definition, and the dictionary's larger reference to militarism, that find far fewer proponents, and are distinguished from just war doctrine (which will be described below). First, it defines militarism as a belief or policy not only to maintain a strong military capability but also to use it "aggressively" for both

---

8. Sprinkle, *Fight,* 27, citing Bacevich, *New American Militarism,* 146.
9. One might question this last point, made by Bacevich, but cited approvingly by Sprinkle, on several grounds. Given the decline in regular church attendance, and the rise of the "nones" (those who claim no religious affiliation), it is dubious to call America a "deeply and genuinely religious" country. Further, there are plenty of examples of things in America that persist or have been brought about in spite of the resistance of tens of millions of evangelicals—such as abortion on demand and same-sex civil marriage.
10. *Oxford English Dictionary,* s.v., "militarism," www.oed.com. Sprinkle's citation reads "belief or desire." I could not find a reference to desire.

defense and to "promote national interests." Of course, it depends on how one interprets these terms, but these qualifiers likely go beyond just war doctrine.

Second, the *OED* provides a further definition, which says, "a political condition characterized by the predominance of the military in government or administration or a reliance on military force in political matters." Together, these suggest that militarism is something like a worldview, and the predominant way of solving conflicts or advancing interests. One may argue that at times the United States leans in this direction, but it is hardly the normative way of dealing with conflicts or advancing interests, and the military is not used to enforce an administration's domestic policy. One need only to consider various military regimes, both historically and in the present, to see the distinction between the belief in a strong defense and militarism.

Given these considerations, it seems to me that militarism should be understood as a belief or policy in which a government is dominated by the military and/or its interests are advanced by any means necessary, including military force. Such interests would include, and historically many nations have used military force for, the expansion of territory, riches, vengeance, ideological interests, and so on. Historically, militarism has not only characterized many nations but at times even the church and

other religious bodies, especially when the highest authorities in the church or other religious bodies have also held political power. The Crusades stand as a paradigmatic (even if complex) example.

If this is how we characterize militarism, then it is fair to say that most Christians are not rightly characterized as militaristic, though they hold views along a spectrum from pacifist to militarist. Nonetheless, as James reminds us, sinful human beings are prone to fighting and wars (Jas. 4:1–2). One of the first consequences of the fall that the Bible tells of is the murder of Abel by his brother Cain out of jealousy (Gen. 4:8). Christians know too well the tendency of sinful human beings to resort to force and bloodshed to take what they desire and to protect their interests, so we ought to be particularly alert to the temptation to rely on militarism, and to be ready to speak out against it. The Bible calls us to a different way. The two primary views that Christians have adopted as a critique of militarism and unbridled war are pacifism and just war doctrine.

Pacifism

There are many variations of pacifism.[11] For the sake of simplicity, we can consider two broad categories. One category includes those who advocate pacifism or nonviolence in principle, based on religious, philosophical, moral, or political values, beliefs, and commitments. A second type may be

---

11. John Howard Yoder, one of the most influential and prolific Christian pacifists of the latter part of the twentieth century, describes more than twenty different types of pacifism in his book *Nevertheless: The Varieties and Shortcomings of Religious Pacifism* (Scottdale, PA: Herald Press, 1992).

identified as pragmatic pacifists because, while they may not believe that all use of violent force, even war, is wrong in principle, they contend that it is impossible to engage in a just war, especially with the use of nuclear weapons. The intention here is to describe basic ideas, beliefs, and commitments of those who are Christian pacifists in principle, though some of the concerns of pragmatic pacifists will be considered as well. In particular, the focus will be on those arguments that are formed by the belief that a faithful understanding and application of Scripture, and especially the teachings of Jesus, leads to pacifist commitments. Indeed, many pacifists treat the commitment to nonviolence and to peacemaking as perhaps that which most clearly defines what Jesus's followers are called to be and to do.[12]

Before proceeding, a ground-clearing comment is necessary. In conversations with those who defend war, it is not uncommon to hear pacifists accused of being naïve or cowardly or both. In response, it needs to be said that this is an ad hominem argument, and a poor one at that. For one thing, those who defend war may also be naïve and cowardly. More importantly, a consideration of examples such as Gandhi or Martin Luther King Jr. demonstrates that many pacifists know the cost of nonviolent resistance, and face that reality with amazing courage.

Whether pacifism in principle is convincing or not, it is very often admirable, and pacifists serve an important witness to the commitment to peacemaking that followers of Christ ought to embrace.

Basic assertions and affirmations

A basic tenet of pacifism is that all violence or killing is evil, and therefore never morally justified. Deadly force should thus never be employed, not even to overcome a greater evil. Violence and war are opposed both in principle and on pragmatic grounds, for violence begets violence, and to resort to lethal force is to be corrupted by the very evil we wish to vanquish. Even if the concept of a just war sounds reasonable in principle, there is no such thing as a just war in practice. While lethal force is rejected, pacifism is not *passivism*—that is, forgoing war does not mean doing nothing to resist evil and to seek justice. Pacifists seek actively to confront evil and violence, but only by peaceful means, for war and violence can never establish a lasting peace. For Christian pacifists, it is more than a position on war; it is the way of discipleship. Indeed, it is common for Christian pacifists to assert that pacifism was the dominant view of the church through the first several centuries, until Constantine ended the persecution of Christians and affirmed the Christian

---

12. Perhaps the most prominent and widely read pacifist in recent decades is the moral theologian Stanley Hauerwas. For a broad sampling of his work, see *The Hauerwas Reader*, eds. John Berkman and Michael Cartwright (Durham, NC: Duke University Press, 2001). See, e.g., chap. 6, "Jesus and the Social Embodiment of the Peaceable Kingdom"; chap. 16, "Peacemaking: The Virtue of the Church"; chap. 20, "Should War Be Eliminated? A Thought Experiment"; chap. 21, "On Being a Church Capable of Addressing a World at War: A Pacifist Response to the United Methodist Bishops' Pastoral *In Defense of Creation*."

religion. Some Christian pacifists argue for a view of the separation of church and state wherein the government may be justified in using force to accomplish its objectives, but neither the church nor Christians are ever justified in using force, for they are to pattern their lives after Jesus's teaching in the Sermon on the Mount.

This brief summary is meant only to highlight key aspects of pacifism. Before developing some of these a bit more and responding to its claims, it is necessary to look at how Christian pacifists understand what Scripture has to say about violence and war. What about war in the Old Testament, or God establishing government and giving it the sword to punish evildoers and exact just vengeance on those who do wrong? These and other questions are frequently posed to pacifists, and we will offer a sketch of how they are answered.

Understanding violence in the Old Testament

One of the difficulties for anyone wrestling with the biblical teaching on violence, whether pacifists or just war advocates, is the violence that is authorized by God in the Old Testament. One solution proposed by pacifists is to emphasize significant discontinuity between the Old Testament and New Testament, with a progressive trajectory that leads to the rejection of violence altogether in the New Testament. In this view, "the biblical narrative tells the story of how God progressively weans his children away from the use of violence to the point that they can see in the model of Jesus one who shows what it means to overcome evil through suffering."[13] Thus the permission to use violence, as with capital punishment, the *lex talionis*, and war are not God's ideal, but he meets Israel where they are at, in a bloody and violent world, gives them instructions that are an improvement over the nations around them, and takes them incrementally toward the ideal.[14]

This interpretation may be commended for seeking to develop a biblical theology that grapples with Scripture as a whole, and for seeking to scrutinize how to understand violence in the Old Testament. Like polygamy, just because it is there does not mean that God approves of it. However, the argument that God weans Israel off violence, or that his commands that prescribe violence are only incremental steps toward the ideal of nonviolence, is not satisfactory. To put it bluntly, it incriminates God. That is, if all use of force, and particularly killing, is wrong, then God's own authorization of war and capital punishment must be unjust. Does God himself need to be weaned off violence? No, instead, God condemns unjust violence and evil emphatically, but not all use of force, not even every killing, is unjust.

Nevertheless, if capital punishment and war are justified for the people of God in

---

13. Charles E. Gutenson, "Pacifism," in *Dictionary of Scripture and Ethics*, eds. Joel B. Green et al. (Grand Rapids: Baker Academic, 2011), 574. Here Gutenson is summarizing, affirmingly, the work of Vernard Eller, *War and Peace: From Genesis to Revelation* (Scottdale, PA: Herald Press, 1981).
14. See Sprinkle, *Fight*, 46, 53.

the Old Testament, under some circumstances, that does not mean that they are justified for followers of Jesus today. There are unique features concerning the authorization of war for Israel that are not transferable to the church—or the United States of America! First, the land is given by God to Israel as his chosen people who are constituted as a nation: Israel is God's people in God's land.[15] The church as the people of God is not constituted as a nation, but is multinational, made up of a spiritual body through faith. Second, Israel's war to take the land given by God was directly sanctioned by God, for a unique purpose, which no nation today can claim. That is, if war is justified today, it cannot be for the same purpose that it was justified for Israel in the Old Testament. Third, Israel's wars are not fought or won by their great military power, but by God himself.[16] Indeed, Israel does not need to develop military power or a professional army like the other nations had, for God is their protector. Israel's desire to have a king is a rejection of God's kingship over them (1 Sam. 8:7), which in particular demonstrates a lack of faith in God's protection, since Israel wants a king who will "go out before us, and fight our battles" (v. 20).[17] Israel's warfare policy as authorized by God is limited and not dependent on Israel's military might. When various kings and other leaders go beyond that policy and engage in wars for their own purposes, with unrestrained violence and bloodshed, it is not merely a sign of their disobedience, but of their Canaanization.[18]

For instance, Gideon obeys God by trimming his army down to three hundred men, so that it is clear that God gains the victory in driving out the Midianites (Judg. 7); but after the victory, Gideon embarks on a mission of vengeance and bloodshed, even beating and killing fellow Israelites who would not help him (Judg. 8). Though the narrative does not explicitly condemn Gideon's violence, the story raises serious questions. He sounds godly and pious, rejecting the people's offer to install him as king, saying "the LORD will rule over you" (Judg. 8:23). Yet his faults are laid bare: he creates an idol by which "all Israel prostituted themselves" (v. 27); he takes many wives and through them has seventy sons (v. 30); and to a son born to him by a concubine, he gives the name Abimelech, which means, "my father is king" (v. 31). So much for rejecting kingship!

There are plenty of other examples in the book of Judges, as the people degenerate

---

15. For a study of the importance of the land for Israel, with implications for the church, see Christopher J. H. Wright, *God's People in God's Land: Family, Land, and Property in the Old Testament* (Grand Rapids: Eerdmans, 1990). Also Wright, *Old Testament Ethics for the People of God* (Downers Grove, IL: IVP Academic, 2004).
16. Consider, for instance, the victory over the great army of Egypt in Israel's exodus (Exod. 14), the defeat of Jericho (Josh. 6), and the defeat of the Midianites (Judg. 7).
17. For a nice discussion of "Israel's bizarre warfare policy," which in the beginning is nonmilitaristic and conducted by God, see Sprinkle, *Fight*, chap. 3.
18. Sprinkle highlights this feature well in *Fight*, 95–105.

into bloody chaos. Perhaps, though, the most intriguing example is David.[19] The humble king, a man after God's own heart, early on David clearly depends on the Lord for victory in war (1 Sam. 17:37, 45–47), and he inquires of the Lord before going to war (2 Sam. 5:19). But there seems to be a shift in the narrative: David builds up his own military (2 Sam. 8:4, 16); the text says that "David made a reputation for himself" (v. 13), even though the text says that the Lord gave David victory (v. 14); by 2 Samuel 10, it is not clear that David's wars are sanctioned by God, and in 2 Samuel 11, David attempts to use war to cover up his adultery. Then, in what might seem like an innocent act, David takes a census, for which he recognizes he is guilty (2 Sam. 24:10), and for which God punishes the people harshly (v. 13–17). Why? Because it was a military census, and David was putting his confidence in his own military might. If there is a doubt that God looked on much of David's military exploits unfavorably, when he wants to build a house for God, the word of the Lord came to him, saying, "You are not to build a house for my name because you have shed so much blood on the ground before me" (1 Chron. 22:8).

In short, advocates of nonviolence are right to remind us that we must examine the reality of war in the Old Testament carefully. We cannot simply say that God condoned war then, so it is justified today, even for limited reasons, for war in the Old Testament is engaged for unique reasons and fought in unique ways. On the other hand, it is not completely irrelevant to modern just war doctrine, for it at least indicates that engaging in war is not intrinsically evil. We must tread carefully here, for it is a matter of great (and grave) consequence to make a case that justice can best be achieved by engaging in war. Yet just war doctrine is intended for careful treading and to establish the case for justice in war.

The call to reject violence in the New Testament

Matthew 5. The most significant passage in Scripture for pacifists is in Matthew 5. Matthew presents Jesus's teaching in a striking way. Jesus has come from his wilderness temptation (4:1–11), called his disciples (4:18–22), and his teaching and healing ministry has begun to attract crowds (4:23–25). With the crowds near, the disciples come to Jesus, and he gives the Sermon on the Mount, "a definitive charter for the life of the new covenant community."[20] Jesus calls his followers to be a countercultural community, salt and light in the world, a city on a hill (Matt. 5:12–14). This community is composed of citizens who belong to the kingdom of heaven, who embody the

---

19. See Sprinkle, *Fight*, 100–103, for a detailed account.
20. Richard B. Hays, *The Moral Vision of the New Testament: Community, Cross, New Creation; A Contemporary Introduction to New Testament Ethics* (San Francisco: HarperSanFrancisco, 1996), 321. Hays notes that the delivery of the sermon from a mountain "probably echoes the Exodus story of Moses and suggests that Jesus' teaching is a new Torah" (321).

qualities of character taught by Jesus in the Beatitudes (Matt. 5:3–12).[21] Jesus describes that community further in Matthew 5:21–48, as he teaches what it means to fulfill the law in true righteousness. The most relevant part of Jesus's teaching that frames the pacifist commitment to nonviolence is Matthew 5:38–48.

Don't resist an evildoer. In verses 38–39, instead of following the legal procedure of "an eye for an eye and a tooth for a tooth," Jesus commands, "don't resist an evildoer." The "eye for an eye" is a reference to the *lex talionis*, found in the Old Testament (Exod. 21:22–25; Lev. 24:20; Deut. 19:21), which functioned to secure just retribution by establishing that punishment for an offense is to be proportionate to the offense. That is, you must not be too harsh, giving out a severe punishment for a minor offense (e.g., a life for a tooth), but neither should you be too lenient, giving out a very light punishment for a serious offense (e.g., a tooth for a life). In response to the legal standard of just retribution, Jesus commands, "Don't resist an evildoer."

Advocates of nonviolence are right to recognize that this is a difficult teaching (to say the least!), and that Jesus's followers are to obey it. Does it require that Christians literally offer no resistance to evil? Sprinkle argues that the term "resist" here (from the Greek ἀνθίστημι) is often used to refer to violent resistance, so, "put simply, when Jesus says, 'Do not resist the one who is evil,' He specifically prohibits using violence to resist evil."[22] This eases the difficulty of Jesus's teaching somewhat, for it doesn't require nonresistance entirely; it only prohibits the use of violence. Perhaps there is hope to resist evildoers through nonviolent means.

The problem with this is that when Jesus gives specific examples that show what he means when he commands his followers not to resist the evildoer, each of them involves no resistance at all:

- "If anyone slaps you on your right cheek, turn the other to him also" (v. 39).
- "As for the one who wants to sue you and take away your shirt, let him have your coat as well" (v. 40).
- "If anyone forces you to go one mile, go with him two" (v. 41).
- "Give to the one who asks you" (v. 42a).
- "Don't turn away from the one who wants to borrow from you" (v. 42b).

It is notable that these examples cover various spheres of life: "Jesus takes the 'do not resist evil' command and scatters it across *all of life*—and so should we."[23] Sprinkle describes these as, first, "a physical attack"; second, "a legal attack"; third, "political oppression by a foreign army" (Roman soldiers could require someone to carry their pack up to a mile); and the fourth and fifth examples have to do with "unpleasant

21. Hays, *Moral Vision*, 321.
22. Sprinkle, *Fight*, 134.
23. Sprinkle, *Fight*, 135.

financial scenarios" in which someone takes advantage of you (since Jesus is describing what it means not to resist an evildoer).[24] He concludes that Jesus's teaching here applies "to all citizens of God's kingdom, and it should saturate all areas of life."[25] This means, for advocates of nonviolence, that there can be no distinction between private and public spheres or one's role in personal relationships verses the role of the state. We will return to that below with respect to an understanding of Romans 13.

Love your enemy. The climax of Matthew 5:21–48 (the six sayings of Jesus) is the command, "Be perfect, therefore, as your heavenly Father is perfect" (τέλειος, v. 48). The way that this is most clearly seen is to "love your enemies and pray for those who persecute you" (v. 44). In so doing, "you may be children of your Father in heaven" (v. 45). To love your enemy is to reveal the profound and unexpected truth of what it means to love your neighbor (v. 43). Jesus reveals this in the story of the good Samaritan (Luke 10:30–37), when asked by an expert in the law who rightly understood that the greatest commands are to love God completely and to love one's neighbor as oneself (v. 27). Then, "wanting to justify himself," the man asks Jesus, "Who is my neighbor?" (v. 29). Jesus responds by revealing that obedience to the command to love our neighbor as ourselves is seen most profoundly in the expression of love to our enemy (v. 37). Sprinkle

asserts, "A person who chooses to love his or her enemies can have no enemies. That person is left only with neighbors."[26] Such love is disarming and transformational. It is peacemaking!

Jesus demonstrates love for enemies most radically on the cross. Paul highlights this when he says that someone might dare to die for a good person; "But God proves his own love for us in that while we were still sinners, Christ died for us" (Rom. 5:7–8). Lest we miss how radical this is, Paul declares that our sin separated us from God, putting us at enmity with him—enemies of God, deserving of death (Rom. 6:23)—but "while we were enemies, we were reconciled to God through the death of his Son" (Rom. 5:10). And while Jesus is on the cross, being persecuted and punished with a torturous death, even though he is innocent, he prays for those who are persecuting him: "Father, forgive them, because they do not know what they are doing" (Luke 23:34).

What Jesus demonstrates in his suffering and death on the cross he calls his followers to do. Each of the Synoptic Gospels repeat Jesus's words, saying, "If anyone wants to follow after me, let him deny himself, take up his cross, and follow me" (Mark 8:34; cf. Matt. 16:24). In Luke, Jesus says that his followers must "take up his cross daily" (Luke 9:23). And Jesus says, "Whoever does not bear his own cross and come after me cannot be my disciple" (Luke 14:27; cf. Matt.

---

24. See Sprinkle, *Fight*, 135–38.
25. Sprinkle, *Fight*, 140.
26. Sprinkle, *Fight*, 144.

10:38, "is not worthy of me"). The cross is central to the New Testament, not only because of what Jesus accomplished on the cross, but also as the paradigm for understanding what it means to follow Jesus.[27]

Peter writes to Christians who are facing trials (1 Pet. 1:6) and suffering (3:14), and who are slandered for not participating in immoral behavior (4:4), and he reminds them of Jesus's example of suffering (3:18). He exhorts them to follow his example: "For you were called to this, because Christ also suffered for you, leaving you an example, that you should follow in his steps. . . . When he was insulted, he did not insult in return; when he suffered, he did not threaten but entrusted himself to the one who judges justly" (1 Pet. 2:21, 23).

For advocates of nonviolence, the emphasis on taking up the cross of Jesus must lead believers to find concrete application in the renunciation of violence as a mark of faithful discipleship, whether it is *effective* in overcoming injustice or not. "We love our enemies, do good to those who hate us, bless those who curse us, extend kindness to the ungrateful, and flood evil people with mercy *not* because such behavior will always *work* at confronting injustice, but because such behavior showcases God's stubborn delight in un-delightful people."[28] In short, Christians ought to be known as peacemakers, as those who are willing to suffer and be wronged rather than to resort to violence.

By contrast, "when people around the globe think that American Christians are pro-war, enamored with violence, and fascinated with military might, something is terribly wrong."[29]

Romans 12:9–13:10

Pacifists and just war advocates alike appeal to this passage. Each argues that Paul's statements, about leaving vengeance to God and about how to treat our enemies, must be read together with his treatment of the role of government in punishing evil. Yet they draw very different conclusions. Paul's instructions to believers in Romans 12 include exhortations that closely reflect Jesus's teaching about love for enemies in the Sermon on the Mount. Jesus commands his followers to "love your enemies and pray for those who persecute you" (Matt. 5:43); Paul says, "Bless those who persecute you; bless and do not curse" (Rom. 12:14). Jesus commands, "Don't resist an evildoer" (Matt. 5:39); Paul says, "Do not repay anyone evil for evil. . . . Friends, do not avenge yourselves; instead, leave room for God's wrath, because it is written, Vengeance belongs to me; I will repay, says the Lord" (Rom. 12:17, 19). Jesus says to turn the other cheek; to the one who sues you, give them more than they ask for; go the extra mile; give to those who ask (Matt. 5:39–42). Paul says to feed your enemy and give him something to drink, and he sums things up by saying, "Do not

---

27. Hays sees it as one of three focal images, which finds a textual basis across all of the New Testament as a major emphasis and ethical concern. See Hays, *Moral Vision*, 195.
28. Sprinkle, *Fight*, 148.
29. Sprinkle, *Fight*, 148.

be conquered by evil, but conquer evil with good" (Rom. 12:20–21).

It is clear, then, that Paul closely reflects Jesus's call to love our enemies instead of retaliating against those who do wrong to us. As such, Richard Hays claims, "There is not a syllable in the Pauline letters that can be cited in support of Christians employing violence."[30] Hays acknowledges one point made by just war advocates, concerning the sword in Romans 13:4, that God has given government the use of the sword to punish evildoers. (This will be discussed below in relation to just war doctrine.) Yet he draws a sharp distinction between the role of believers and the role of government when it comes to the use of force: "Though the governing authority bears the sword to execute God's wrath (13:4), that is not the role of believers."[31] Another pacifist, Myron Augsburger, asserts that Christians "can only encourage the government to be the government and to let the church be the church." Strikingly, he adds, "As Christians we will respect the right of the government to declare war to protect its own territory," though Christians cannot take part in it.[32]

Can Christians serve as governing authorities who participate in the use of force? Augsburger argues that it may be possible for Christians to serve in government, but that "Christians should only serve at government levels where they can honestly carry out the functions of their office without compromising their fidelity to Jesus Christ as Lord."[33] Sprinkle agrees that if Christians are to serve in government, they cannot resort to the use of force, for they are bound by Jesus's teaching in their private and public lives. He argues that "it would make no sense to say that the Sermon on the Mount is fine for individual Christians—even better for the church—but that it doesn't apply to Christians in the government."[34]

Other emphases

Jesus's renunciation of violence. Jesus, on trial before Pilate, says, "My kingdom is not of this world. . . . If my kingdom were of this world, my servants would fight, so that I wouldn't be handed over to the Jews" (John 18:36). In his influential book *The Politics of Jesus*, John Howard Yoder argues that Jesus's teaching and example provides significant political implications for Jesus's followers. Chief among them is the renunciation of violence and coercive power. While Jesus rejects violence, Yoder understands the resort to violence to be a significant temptation for him. Reflecting on Jesus's request to "take this cup away from me" (Luke 22:42), Yoder writes that "the only imaginable real option," and "the only one with even a slim basis in the text," is that "Jesus was drawn,

---

30. Hays, *Moral Vision*, 331.
31. Hays, *Moral Vision*, 331. So, too, John Howard Yoder, *The Politics of Jesus* (Grand Rapids: Eerdmans, 1972), 199: "The function exercised by government is not the function to be exercised by Christians."
32. Myron S. Augsburger, "Christian Pacifism," in Clouse, *War: Four Christian Views*, 87–89.
33. Augsburger, "Christian Pacifism," 89.
34. Sprinkle, *Fight*, 140. For Sprinkle's understanding of Romans 13 with respect to the use of force, see *Fight*, 166–72.

at this very last moment of temptation, to think once again of the messianic violence with which he had been tempted since the beginning." He goes on to say, "The one temptation the man Jesus faced—and faced again and again—as a constitutive element of his public ministry, was the temptation to exercise social responsibility, in the interest of justified revolution, through the use of available violent methods."[35] Hays agrees, saying that "the temptation to refuse the cup is precisely the temptation to resort to armed resistance."[36]

A brief response will have to suffice. It is certainly true that Jesus renounced violence as a means to establish his kingdom. This is also true for his followers. Indeed, Jesus's kingdom *cannot* be established by force, for faith cannot be coerced. However, to argue that the resort to violence is a constant temptation in Jesus's public ministry, and further, that it is precisely the temptation to avoid the cup of suffering, is to read too much into the text, using nonviolence as a primary interpretive lens. Instead, Jesus's desire to avoid the cross is both the very human desire to avoid suffering and the knowledge that as he bears the weight of human sin on the cross, he will experience the excruciating pain of separation from God (Matt. 27:46).

Warfare language. Paul uses the language of war to indicate the spiritual battle that is raging. He writes that "although we live in the flesh, we do not wage war according to the flesh, since the weapons of our warfare are not of the flesh, but are powerful through God for the demolition of strongholds. We demolish arguments and every proud thing that is raised up against the knowledge of God, and we take every thought captive to obey Christ" (2 Cor. 10:3–5). Christians are thus to put on the "armor of God" (Eph. 6:11) in order to engage in the battle at hand, which is "not against flesh and blood, but against the rulers, against the authorities, against the cosmic powers of this darkness, against evil, spiritual forces in the heavens" (v. 12). The armor of God that is necessary to resist evil includes truth, righteousness, the gospel of peace, the shield of faith, the helmet of salvation, and the sword of the Spirit, which is God's word (vv. 14–17). Rather than resisting the evildoer through physical force, Christians are called to resist evil by means of spiritual weaponry (cf. Rom. 6:12–13).

The war of the Lamb in Revelation. Against interpretations of the book of Revelation that would condone violence, pacifists argue that it does just the opposite. For example, Hays argues that, like the rest of the New Testament, Revelation exhorts believers to "faithful endurance in suffering, trust in God's eschatological vindication of his people, and a response to adversity modeled on the paradigm of 'the lamb who was slaughtered.' The saints conquer the power of evil through 'the blood of the Lamb and

35. Yoder, *Politics of Jesus*, 55–57, 98.
36. Hays, *Moral Vision*, 322.

by the word of their testimony' (Rev. 12:11), not through recourse to violence."[37]

The early church, nonviolence, and military service

One of the significant challenges to the Christian just war tradition is the rejection of violence and killing by the early church fathers.[38] Several facets of the views of early Christians, over the first several centuries, are prominent. First, the earliest Christians who spoke to the issues were critical of bloodshed, war, and military service, though some allowed or at least recognized military service.[39] Two of the most outspoken on these issues were Origen (184–253) and Tertullian (160–220), both of whom asserted that Christians were not permitted to kill another human being. Perhaps most significant in this respect is Origen. He says first that Jews "were permitted to take up arms in defense of the members of their families, and to slay their enemies." Yet, he argues, "he nowhere teaches that it is right for His own disciples to offer violence to any one, however wicked. For He did not deem it in keeping with such laws as His, which were derived from a divine source, to allow the killing of any individual whatever."[40] Tertullian says that God forbids "every kind of man-slaying by one summary law: 'Thou shalt not kill,'" though he specifically refers to murder by various means.[41]

Second, there is no evidence of Christians serving in the military from the close of the New Testament period to AD 173, after which Christians begin to join the military in increasing numbers.[42] Indeed, this reality likely led some of the early church fathers to speak out against Christians in the military.[43] For instance, Tertullian notes that John the Baptist gave soldiers a rule for how they should be soldiers, and that a centurion had believed, yet he famously said, "still the Lord afterward, in disarming Peter, unbelted every soldier."[44]

Third, Constantine ended the persecution of the church in AD 313, and Christianity later became the official religion of the empire. The defense of just war and Christian service in the military comes after Christianity gains prominence and political power. For pacifists, this is the Constantinian compromise of the church. Yoder is

37. Hays, *Moral Vision*, 332; cf. an extensive discussion of Revelation in terms of its rejection of violence in Sprinkle, *Fight*, 173–93.
38. For a collection of statements by early church fathers on war and military service, see "War," in *A Dictionary of Early Christian Beliefs*, ed. David W. Bercot (Peabody, MA: Hendrickson, 1998), 676–82. For a discussion of the early church perspective on violence, from an advocate of nonviolence, see Sprinkle, *Fight*, 195–214.
39. For a survey of early Christian views from an advocate of nonviolence, see Sprinkle, *Fight*, 200–214. See also David G. Hunter, "A Decade of Research on Early Christians and Military Service," *Religious Studies Review* 18, no. 2 (April 1992): 87–94.
40. Origen, *Against Celsus* 3.7, in *The Ante-Nicene Fathers*, eds. Alexander Roberts and James Donaldson (1885–1887; repr., Grand Rapids: Eerdmans, 1994), 4:467.
41. Tertullian, *De spectaculis* 2, in Roberts and Donaldson, *Ante-Nicene Fathers*, 3:80.
42. Hunter, "Decade of Research," 90.
43. See Sprinkle's survey in *Fight*, 207–208
44. Tertullian, *On Idolatry* 19, in Roberts and Donaldson, *Ante-Nicene Fathers*, 3:73.

representative of those who view the pacifist teaching of the early church as the faithful response to the gospel, and the later acceptance and endorsement of military service and just war doctrine as a compromise with worldly power.[45]

The early church had a significant witness against violence and bloodshed, to be sure. While there is evidence of pacifist convictions, reasons included not only an aversion to violence but also an imminent eschatology that ordered priorities, as well as the idolatrous practices of Roman soldiers.[46] Yoder, who argues that early Christians were pacifist, cites as reasons that Christians were opposed to military service such things as polytheism, idolatry, swearing oaths, and the persecution of Christians.[47]

Nonviolent resistance

The commitment to nonviolence does not require a commitment to do nothing in the face of evil. Many pacifists, like Yoder, do not merely condemn war, but seek to effect change through *nonviolent direct action*.[48] His book titled *The War of the Lamb* underscores the point that peacemaking is not passive, for there are many strategies that can be pursued in order to overcome

evil and oppression through nonviolent means.[49] Further, he argues, nonviolent direct action is more effective than war at defeating evil, "because it goes with the grain of the universe, and that is why *in the long run* nothing else will work."[50]

As strongly as most any pacifist, Yoder argues that the cost of discipleship, the suffering love involved in taking up one's cross, requires nonviolence. Followers of Jesus must resist violence in the double sense of being willing to suffer rather than resorting to violence and of being actively opposed to violence. When harmed, our instinct is to respond with force, and to justify doing so. Yoder seeks to cultivate a different instinct, which resists violence when wronged. Against those who argue that nonviolence is ineffective in the face of evil, he responds that the problem is not that nonviolent action has failed, but that it has not been attempted with anything like effort and resources put into war. To be effective, it requires discipline, training, and fortitude, just as the use of force does. He points out that in war, loss of life is considered an unfortunate but expected cost, and yet in considering nonviolence, the predictable loss of life is seen as evidence of failure

---

45. John Howard Yoder, *The War of the Lamb: The Ethics of Nonviolence and Peacemaking*, eds. Glen Stassen, Mark Thiessen Nation, and Matt Hamsher (Grand Rapids: Brazos Press, 2009), 45; see also Yoder, "The Meaning of the Constantinian Shift," in *Christian Attitudes to War, Peace, and Revolution*, eds. Theodore J. Koontz and Andy Alexis-Baker (Grand Rapids: Brazos, 2009), 62–63.
46. See Edward A. Ryan, "The Rejection of Military Service by the Early Christians," *Theological Studies* 13 (1952): 1–32. See also the balanced perspective of Hunter, "Decade of Research," 87–94.
47. Yoder, *War of the Lamb*, 48–49.
48. For Yoder's understanding of pacifism, see *The Politics of Jesus*.
49. *The War of the Lamb* develops aspects of Yoder's work that he believed had not been taken seriously enough by his critics. Published posthumously, it was a book Yoder planned to publish before he died.
50. Yoder, *War of the Lamb*, 62.

and sufficient reason to reject the strategy from the outset.[51]

The Just War Tradition

Just war advocates ought to affirm much of what pacifists emphasize, as part of what is a critical witness to what it means to follow Jesus. Followers of Jesus are called to be peace-makers, to resist the temptation to return evil for evil. The impulse to use violence to serve our interests is driven by sinful desires (James 4:1–2). Those who defend just war should not be militaristic, as outlined above, for war is devastating, and we ought to resist military action as far as possible. Yet, sometimes war may be necessary in a fallen world, as a last re-sort, to restrain evil and tyranny and to seek to restore and maintain a just peace, for peace is not simply the absence of war but a justly ordered society. Just war criteria are thus advanced not to promote warfare but to specify the conditions under which a war may be justified and how it may be conducted.

In what follows, I will respond to some of the main arguments made by pacifists, and describe in some detail the case made for just war. I prefer to use the terms just war *doctrine* or just war *tradition* rather than just war *theory*, which is, as Oliver O'Donovan asserts, something of a misnomer. This is because "it is not, in the first place, a 'theory,' but a proposal of *practical* reason; and it is not, in the second place, about 'just wars,' but about how we may enact just judgment even in the theatre of war."[52]

Beginnings of the just war tradition

The just war tradition and its criteria have developed over more than two millennia, and while for most of the Christian era it has been the dominant view in Christian thought, it did not originate in Christian reflection.[53] Certain aspects of the just war tradition are rooted in Greco-Roman philosophical thought. Plato (427–347 BC) asserts that war requires many laws, including that only a governing authority can declare war.[54] Plato also affirms something akin to noncombatant immunity and proportionate objectives, where the enemy's property ought not to be ravaged or unnecessarily destroyed.[55] Aristotle (384–322 BC) asserts that many reasons for going to war are not justified, but war may be justified under certain circumstances, such as self-defense, the defense of a neighbor, to correct a previous injustice, when the goal is to achieve a lasting peace.[56] The Roman Stoic Cicero (106–43 BC) develops something of the idea of war as a "last resort," after exhausting all reasonable

---

51. Yoder, *War of the Lamb*, 162–63.

52. Oliver O'Donovan, *The Just War Revisited* (Cambridge: Cambridge University Press, 2003), 6–7.

53. For a brief summary of the just war tradition, see Gary M. Simpson, "Just War Theory," in Green et al., *Dictionary of Scripture and Ethics*, 445–49. For a more detailed account, see J. Daryl Charles, *Between Pacifism and Jihad: Just War and Christian Tradition* (Downers Grove, IL: InterVarsity Press, 2005).

54. Plato, *Laws* 12 (942a–b, 955 b–c), in *The Laws of Plato*, trans. Thomas L. Pangle (Chicago: University of Chicago Press, 1980).

55. Plato, *Republic* 4 (471 a–b). See Charles, *Between Pacifism and Jihad*, 32.

56. Aristotle, *Nicomachean Ethics* 10 (1177b) and *Politics* (1425 a–b). See Charles, *Between Pacifism and Jihad*, 32.

diplomatic efforts. He also asserts that there must be a just cause, such as self-preservation, and war must be declared by a proper authority.[57] These are all significant contributions to thinking about a just war, during an era when wars of aggression to obtain territory and wealth and power were common.

The just war tradition in Christian thought began to develop with Bishop Ambrose of Milan (339–397) and especially with his famous convert, Augustine, bishop of Hippo (354–430). Ambrose understands justice and its virtues—such as courage and prudence, and even love—to apply to a nation's self-defense in war and to the defense of the weak and powerless, provided restraint is used.[58] Indeed, Ambrose states that "he who does not keep harm off a friend, if he can, is as much in fault as he who causes it."[59]

Augustine may be "the most important figure in the historical development of the just-war tradition."[60] Augustine develops principles that govern both the decision whether to go to war and how to engage in war. As J. Daryl Charles writes, these include "just cause, proper authority, formal declaration, the aim of securing a just peace, retribution as distinct from revenge, and discrimination between innocence and guilt."[61] Augustine echoes Ambrose, arguing that the defense of the innocent is required by love (not, it is worth noting, by the "lesser evil").[62] Love for an aggressor may entail the use of force "to punish him 'with a sort of kind harshness,' doing him the service of constraining him from further wrongdoing and encouraging him to repent and embrace peace."[63] Love seeks to defend the innocent, restrain evil, and secure peace. In developing his view on war, Augustine works to navigate central themes in Scripture and Christian thought. He also seeks to show "how followers of Jesus, who had told his disciples to turn the other cheek, may participate in a just war."[64]

Just war doctrine

These represent the beginnings of the Christian just war tradition. It is a tradition that

57. Cicero, *De republica* 3.23, and *De officiis* 1.11. See Charles, *Between Pacifism and Jihad*, 33.
58. Ambrose, *On the Duties of the Clergy* 1.27.129, in *A Select Library of the Nicene and Post-Nicene Fathers of the Christian Church*, eds. Philip Schaff and Henry Wace, series 2 (1886–1889; repr., Grand Rapids: Eerdmans, 1997), 10:22; *Epistle* 51.6–12, To Theodosius, in Schaff and Wace, *Nicene and Post-Nicene Fathers*, 10:450–53. See Charles, *Between Pacifism and Jihad*, 38–39.
59. Ambrose, *On the Duties of the Clergy* 1.36.179.
60. Simpson, "Just-War Theory," 447.
61. Charles, *Between Pacifism and Jihad*, 44. Augustine's thought on war is scattered throughout his treatises and letters, much of it in the *City of God* (e.g., 14.6; 15.22; 18.13; 19.12–13, 15; 22.6), in Schaff and Wace, *Nicene and Post-Nicene Fathers*, vol. 2.
62. Augustine, *City of God* 15.22. The defense of just war as motivated by charity is developed in the twentieth century by Paul Ramsey, *The Just War: Force and Political Responsibility* (Savage, MD: Littlefield, Adams, 1983), e.g., 150–51. Also, on "love in war," see Nigel Biggar, *In Defence of War* (Oxford: Oxford University Press, 2013), 61–91.
63. Biggar, *In Defence of War*, 61, inner citation from Augustine, *Letter* 138 (to Marcellinus), in *Political Writings*, eds. E. M. Atkins and R. J. Dodaro, Cambridge Texts in the History of Political Thought (Cambridge: Cambridge University Press, 2001), 38.
64. Simpson, "Just-War Theory," 447.

has developed over time, seeking to apply certain basic tenets to new developments as they arise.[65] The tradition is often summarized by a number of principles that belong to two distinct categories, both of which were discussed by Augustine: principles that clarify whether a war is justified and, if it is, principles that govern how warfare is conducted. These are known by their Latin terms as *jus ad bellum* (justice to war) and *jus in bello* (justice in war). These criteria create a burden of proof, putting restraints on the pursuit of war and warfare itself. Some will argue that just war doctrine implies a presumption against war, while others maintain that the presumption is not against war itself, but against injustice.[66] While there are varying accounts with different lists of principles, they may be summarized as follows.

Jus ad bellum: *criteria under which entering a war may be justified*

Just cause. The reason for entering war must be in the cause of justice. This would preclude wars of aggression against an enemy, revenge, or the expansion of territory, wealth, or power. Rather, just cause includes such things as self-defense and preservation against an aggressor, the defense of innocents who cannot defend themselves, the protection of human rights, to remedy injustice, and to restore a rightly ordered peace. Although a just cause for war is primarily seen to be defensive—that is, in response to an injustice that cannot be remedied otherwise—this principle may include a preemptive strike in order to thwart an imminent attack.

Right intention. This principle underscores the previous one in that the proper intention for engaging in war must be to put an end to a grave injustice and to restore a rightly ordered peace. It repudiates the motives that are common causes of war, such as hatred for one's enemy and a desire to kill and destroy them. Of course, it is difficult to know the motives of those who make a case for war, but one of the purposes of just war doctrine is to examine and test intentions.

Legitimate authority. Aquinas discusses the justice of war in a time when wars were engaged by princes and nobles for private reasons. He distinguishes between "*duellum* (the private quarrel or duel) and *bellum*

65. Space does not allow a summary of each of the primary contributors to the Christian just war tradition, which is well done by Charles, *Between Pacifism and Jihad*, chaps. 2–4. The following are some key figures. Thomas Aquinas (1225–1274): see "On War," in *Summa Theologiae* II–II, q. 40; Martin Luther (1483–1546): see "Temporal Authority: To What Extent It Should Be Obeyed," in *Luther's Works*, eds. Jaroslav Pelikan and Helmut Lehmann (Philadelphia: Muhlenberg Press, 1962); John Calvin (1509–1564): see *Institutes of the Christian Religion* 4.20.10, ed. John T. McNeill, trans. Ford Lewis Battles, Library of Christian Classics (Philadelphia: Westminster Press, 1960), 2:1497–99; Francisco de Vitoria (ca. 1485–1546), the Spanish Roman Catholic Dominican natural law theologian who defended the American Indians against unjust treatment by Spanish (and other European) conquerors: see *Vitoria: Political Writings*, eds. Anthony Pagden and Jeremy Lawrence, Cambridge Texts in the History of Political Thought (Cambridge: Cambridge University Press, 1991); Francisco Suarez (1548–1617), a Spanish scholastic theologian who wrote on just war as an obligation of love in *The Three Theological Virtues* (1622): see *On Laws and God the Lawgiver* (1612); Hugo Grotius (1583–1645), the Dutch legal and moral philosopher who is widely considered the father of international law, who wrote on the rules for war in his *The Law of War and Peace* (1625).
66. Charles, *Between Pacifism and Jihad*, 17.

(war). Insofar as war is a *public* matter, *bellum* must be adjudicated by political-legal means and not private citizens."[67] Without legitimate, governing authority to adjudicate conflict, disputes over injustices may quickly devolve into a quest for vengeance, as exemplified by the infamous feud between the Hatfields of West Virginia and the McCoys of Kentucky in the late nineteenth century. Often just war doctrine is taken to mean a rejection of any form of revolution. Sprinkle argues, for instance, that when "the government sanctioned genocide in Rwanda was stopped when the rebel RPF (Rwandan Patriotic Front) intervened," the rebels "violated the just war criterion of legitimate authority" since they were not the government in power.[68] One of the problem with trying to establish criteria that justify a revolution is that, in Sprinkle's words, "determining whether a government is evil or legitimate is a matter of perspective."[69] These objections cloud the issue and border on treating two sides of every struggle with moral equivalence. It seems better to consider, in each case, the nature of the injustice inflicted by the government in power, and whether the rebels constitute a representative authority or simply a group of insurrectionists. Admittedly, it is not easy to tell the difference in some cases, but such difficulties do not negate the necessary inquiry.

Last resort. This principle requires that all reasonable attempts have first been made at a peaceful resolution. Just war advocates thus share with advocates of nonviolence the commitment to seek a peaceful resolution, the distinction being that just war advocates desire to avoid war if at all possible, while advocates of nonviolence seek to avoid war no matter the consequences. It is not a convincing argument against the principle of last resort to assert that you cannot know whether you have exhausted every possible diplomatic resolution.[70] For one thing, the principle pertains to every *reasonable* attempt, not every *conceivable* attempt. Moreover, when war is a defense against an aggressor, it is often forced on the defender, without recourse to another attempt at peace.

Proportionate objectives. Here the question is whether, all things considered, the cost of going to war (in human lives, as well as economic and other losses) outweighs the injustice that war seeks to remedy. If the cost of war is greater than the existing injustice, it weighs against going to war. That is, the cure must not be worse than the disease.

Reasonable chance of success. This principle is another way of counting the cost. If there is no reasonable chance of success in realizing the just cause, then war is not justified. This also applies, once a war has begun, to the point when it is clear that there is no reasonable chance of success. Interestingly, when teaching about the cost of following him, Jesus used this war analogy. He asks,

---

67. Charles, *Between Pacifism and Jihad*, 45. See Aquinas, "On War."
68. Sprinkle, *Fight*, 268–69.
69. Sprinkle, *Fight*, 269.
70. See Sprinkle, *Fight*, 271.

"What king, going to war against another king, will not first sit down and decide if he is able with ten thousand to oppose the one who comes against him with twenty thousand? If not, while the other is still far off, he sends a delegation and asks for terms of peace" (Luke 14:31–32). At times, such grave injustices have been inflicted or are threatened that great risk is justified. It may be difficult to assess, but it must be considered.

Jus in bello: *criteria by which a war may be justly waged*

Noncombatant immunity. This is also known as the principle of discrimination. A just war requires that the focus of engagement be on military targets and enemy combatants. It requires that intentional attacks against civilians be avoided, following the prohibition of killing innocent people. For Dietrich Bonhoeffer, the distinction has to do with arbitrary killing. He condemns all "arbitrary" killing, where "innocent life is deliberately killed." Yet he does not believe that killing in war is necessarily arbitrary, since the enemy who is killed, though perhaps not personally guilty, is identified with the guilty and bears the consequences. Self-defense or defense of a neighbor under attack is not arbitrary. Even the killing of civilians in war is not arbitrary if a genuine attempt to avoid doing so has been made. By contrast, "the killing of defenseless prisoners or the wounded, who are not capable of attacking my life, is arbitrary."[71] In the fog

of war, with its violence and bloodiness, realism tends toward a consequentialist perspective, which can find justification for all manner of evil. This principle represents an important restraint against militarism, or a win-at-all-costs perspective.

. *Proportionate force.* The use of force must be limited to what is necessary to secure just objectives. In many cases in war, merciless attacks are used to beat the enemy into submission, especially if the enemy is weaker and less powerful, yet refuses to quit fighting. This principle seeks to restrain the amount of force used to the necessary minimum.

• *Good faith.* Justice demands that the enemy is treated humanely, and this is important for the hope of achieving a lasting peace. Actions that are thus prohibited include the torture or abuse of prisoners, the use of human beings as shields, intentional destruction of sacred and significant places, the use of chemical or biological weapons, terrorism, and so on.

Summary

It is fair to ask whether a just war is possible in reality, even if it is theoretically possible. It might be added that it is difficult to find a just war historically speaking. The fog of war, the callousness caused by war, the "collateral damage" that is the inevitable result of war, all press the question of whether a just war is possible. These are real concerns, for war produces unimaginable evil. In response, it is important to say that if

---

71. Dietrich Bonhoeffer, *Ethics*, ed. Clifford Green, trans. Reinhard Krauss, Charles C. West, and Douglas W. Stott, Dietrich Bonhoeffer Works 6 (Minneapolis: Fortress, 2005), 189.

Christians are right to defend a just war, then we must speak prophetically to those in power, and hold them accountable to just war criteria. It can also be said that unimaginable evil is also produced in the absence of war, with the slaughter of innocents; the goal of a just war is to reduce, not increase, such evil. We are reminded that just war doctrine is a matter of practical reason, about how to enact just judgments in the theater of war, as O'Donovan put it.[72] Just war tradition does not produce zeal for war, but seeks to bring about justice and peace in a world at war.

The Bible, the Early Church, and Just War Doctrine

One argument made against the just war tradition is that "the Bible does not explicitly argue for just war, and most just war proponents don't say that it does."[73] While it is true enough to say that the Bible does not lay out what we know as just war doctrine—it does not explicitly argue for just war—that does not invalidate the tradition. Scripture does not argue explicitly for or develop in detail numerous doctrines that are nonetheless deduced from Scripture and developed in Christian theology.[74] As O'Donovan notes, it is "a longstanding tradition of thinking about war with deep roots in Christian theology."[75] The just war doctrine in Christian tradition

is biblical and theological reflection on justice and war.

The Significance of the Old Testament for Just War Doctrine

The Old Testament relates stories of warfare commanded by God. These are just wars, though they do not provide a template for modern just war doctrine. Israel's authorization to go to war had a unique claim to divine authority that no nation can rightly claim today. Israel was a theocracy with Yahweh as their king, uniting the people of God in both a national and spiritual kingdom. Now the people of God are constituted in the universal church, spread among the nations as a spiritual, not a national, entity. The purposes of the church, including making disciples, cannot be advanced through force or coercion.

That is not to say that the wars of the Old Testament have no significance for modern just war doctrine. First, they indicate that engagement in war is not intrinsically evil. Second, Israel was not to glorify violence as the nations around them did.[76] They had limited objectives—for example, they were given the land, but they were not to fight to expand their territory (cf. Amos 1:13). They were also to practice discrimination in their warfare—God even commands Israel not

---

72. O'Donovan, *Just War Revisited*, 6–7.
73. Sprinkle, *Fight*, 267.
74. Some doctrines are more explicit in Scripture than others, but the list is long, including the Trinity, Jesus's divine and human natures the atonement, the church, baptism, the Lord's Supper, and the last things, to name a few.
75. O'Donovan, *Just War Revisited*, vii.
76. For a helpful survey of Israel's warfare policy, from an advocate of nonviolence, see Sprinkle, *Fight*, chaps. 2–5, from which the substance of this paragraph and the next are derived.

to destroy trees when laying siege to a city (Deut. 20:19).

What about the command to "completely destroy" the inhabitants of the land (e.g., Deut. 20:16–17)? This deserves an extended discussion, but here space allows only a sketch of a few points. First, the Bible says that the sin of the inhabitants of the land had come to full measure, so that God is just in judging them and removing them (Lev. 18:25). Israel is warned that the same will happen to them if they become like the Canaanites (Lev. 18:28). Second, we do not know the whole story of God's dealing with the people of Canaan, but they had ample time—430 years—to repent and fear God (Gen. 15:16). Rahab did, and she was saved (Josh. 2). Third, the language of the conquest includes not just killing the people but driving them out of the land as well (Exod. 34:24; Num. 32:21; Deut. 4:38). Fourth, there may be some hyperbole at work, where the language of destroying the enemy refers to a complete victory (a common device in our own day). Indeed, even after we are told that everyone was destroyed, we learn that there remained some inhabitants. Fifth, some of the cities that were to be completely destroyed may have been primarily military outposts (e.g., Jericho and Ai).

It is notable that the Old Testament portrayal of Israel's wars is not all favorable. The book of Judges depicts a devolution from their God-ordained conquest to a bloody civil war. Israel later rejects God as their king, and demands a king like the other nations (1 Sam. 8:5), who will fight their wars for them. The story of David is perhaps a surprising case in point. From the beginning, God is with him, from his victory over Goliath to his battles against Israel's enemies. Why, if God has ordained his battles, does he not allow David to build the temple (1 Chron. 22:8)? Perhaps David took matters into his own hands and fought and killed beyond what God had authorized (e.g., 2 Sam. 8, 11–12), and he takes a military census, demonstrating a militarism and dependence on his own might rather than on God (2 Sam. 24:2, 4).

In summary, it seems we are justified in drawing some implications from the portrayal of war in the Old Testament for just war doctrine. First, engaging in war is not intrinsically evil, and some of the war in the Old Testament was justified. That does not mean that the New Testament approves of war, for much has changed, and that requires its own examination. Second, there are significant restraints on war in the Old Testament, and a strong case against violent militarism. Third, while it is dubious to claim a direct warrant from God, if a case for war is made, it is based on justice, such as the defense of the innocent, which is at least in Christian terms an indirect justification from God. Proverbs 24:10–12, for example, does not deal directly with war, but it does require that we "rescue those being taken off to death," and it is this principle of justice on which just war doctrine is formed.

The New Testament and Just War Doctrine

We have seen that advocates of pacifism and nonviolence base their view on the New

Testament teachings to be peacemakers, to love enemies, not to resist evildoers, to leave vengeance to God, and patiently to endure suffering. These are all marks of the kingdom of heaven, which followers of Jesus are to proclaim and embody. Further, entrance into the kingdom is by faith and cannot be coerced. Based on all these things, and more, it is not difficult to understand how the case for pacifism can be made. A question for advocates of just war doctrine is thus whether there is any indication in the New Testament that war is ever justified. The primary text that just war advocates appeal to is Romans 13.

Romans 13 and just war doctrine

Earlier we looked at how advocates of non-violence assert that Romans 13 does not authorize the use of violence by Christians, when understood in the context beginning in Romans 12. As we have seen, Sprinkle interprets these chapters to means that government may be authorized to use force, but Christians cannot do so: "Paul explicitly forbids the church in Romans 12 from doing what the government does in Romans 13. The church is only commanded to *submit to* (not partake in) the state's practice."[77] Similarly, Hays says, "Though the governing authority bears the sword to execute God's wrath (13:4), that is not the role of believers. Those who are members of the one body in Christ (12:5) are never to take vengeance (12:19)."[78] It is a significant concession, to say the least, to acknowledge that governing authorities may use force to execute God's wrath. To those who object that this seems to authorize government to do the "dirty work" while Christians refuse to participate in it, Sprinkle responds that he is "only trying to make sense of what Paul actually says in Romans 12 and 13."[79]

Just war advocates are also trying to make sense of what Paul says in Romans 12 and 13, but come to a very different conclusion. Several points may be made. First, followers of Jesus are not to resort to retribution, because we can trust that God will take care of it. We are not to repay anyone evil for evil (Rom. 12:17), or avenge ourselves, because God says, "Vengeance belongs to me; I will repay" (v. 19). As John Stott says, "The reason why wrath, revenge and retribution are forbidden us is not that they are in themselves wrong reactions to evil, but that they are God's prerogative, not ours."[80]

Second, while Paul makes clear that we are to leave vengeance to God, he also makes it clear that God uses human agents to enact just retribution. Indeed, God institutes government partly for this purpose. The language is striking, especially coming after Paul's instructions (echoing Jesus) not to take vengeance when we are wronged, for he then says that government "is God's servant,

---

77. Sprinkle, *Fight*, 171–72.
78. Hays, *Moral Vision*, 331. Herman Hoyt also draws this conclusion in "Nonresistance," in Clouse, *War: Four Christian Views*, 48.
79. Sprinkle, *Fight*, 172.
80. John Stott, *Issues Facing Christians Today*, 4th ed. (Grand Rapids: Zondervan, 2006), 109.

an avenger that brings wrath on the one who does wrong" (Rom. 13:4). In other words, when Paul says that we are not to avenge ourselves, but to leave vengeance to the Lord (Rom. 12:19), he does not mean merely that all things will be settled in the eschatological future (though that is surely true). God does not let evil go unchecked here and now, but appoints governing authorities as his ministers to punish evil. Believers are not to retaliate against evil, but government has been given authority and responsibility to do so. Indeed, it is God's "servant" or "minister" (διάκονος, Rom. 13:4), through which God will accomplish his just purposes.

Third, then, if God authorizes government to "carry the sword," then it must not be unjust for it to do so. Sprinkle argues that we ought to understand the government in Romans 13 as God's servant in the same sense that figures in the Old Testament, like Cyrus (king of Persia, Isa. 44–45), Nebuchadnezzar (king of Babylon, Jer. 27:6; 43:10), and the nation of Assyria (Isa. 10:5) are considered God's servants. Thus Romans 13 "doesn't refer to Rome's happy service to Israel's God, but to God's ability to use Rome as an instrument in His hands."[81] This is a reasonable point to make, as far as it goes, and certainly the rulers of the Roman Empire were not moral exemplars. God does use evil rulers to accomplish his purposes. Yet we ought not to miss that Paul is emphasizing not whether the ruler happens to

be good or bad but that God has *established* governing authorities for this purpose, to act on his behalf—as his servants—to punish wrongdoing. Stott notes that Paul repeats three times that "the state's 'authority' is God's authority and three times that the state's 'ministry' is God's ministry" (vv. 4a, 4b, 6). Thus he adds that "these are not grudging concessions that God has 'assigned a place' to the state, which when using force to punish evil is nevertheless 'sinning'; this is a genuine affirmation that God has 'established' the state with his authority and that when exercising its authority to punish evil it is doing God's will."[82]

Fourth—and this is the most contested point between advocates of just war doctrine and advocates of nonviolence—it seems reasonable to draw a distinction between a private and public response to evil. Sprinkle argues that Rome is permitted to do what the church is prohibited from doing, and if we miss this point, we've missed what Paul is saying to believers in Romans 12 and 13.[83] It is true that the church is not to use force to carry out what the church is called to do and, further, that believers are not to seek vengeance on those who harm them. However, that is a different distinction from the distinction between private and public response to evil. In Romans 12, Paul's emphasis is on the response of believers in their personal relations and response to injustice. Yet, if government is justified in using force

---

81. Sprinkle, *Fight*, 168.
82. Stott, *Issues Facing Christians Today*, 108.
83. Sprinkle, *Fight*, 170.

against evildoers, and has a responsibility to do so, then it seems that Christians can and should guide the government in how to do so justly. Further, individuals who serve in governing roles that involve retraining or punishing evil (such as police, prosecutors, judges) *must* distinguish their public role from their personal response to those who do wrong.

Is it possible for a Christian to serve in a governing capacity that involves the use of force against evildoers? In spite of what advocates of nonviolence argue, it seems fair to assert that there is no reason why Christians could not be obedient to the teaching of Scripture concerning nonretaliation in their personal response to someone who wrongs them, while serving in a government position that punishes wrongdoers. The New Testament doesn't address directly whether a believer could serve in such a role, but that is perhaps because Christians were a persecuted minority who were not serving in government positions. As Holmes argues, "If Christians may properly participate in governmental tasks, and if limited uses of force are legitimate for governments, then prima facie it is right for the Christian [in their governmental role] to participate in the uses of force."[84] Indeed, Christians above all should be able to understand how to serve as God's agents in seeking justice without falling prey to the tyranny that sometimes comes with the belief that we must take matters into our own hands. Christians can and must distinguish their response to personal injury and their participation—representing the state—in upholding justice and order. And Christians can and must distinguish between the means by which they participate in the advance of the kingdom of heaven, the mission of the church, and the means by which justice and order are upheld in society. Christians who are not in public offices can speak prophetically to government by reminding governing authorities of their roles and their limits.

It is fair to ask whether it is impossible for a believer, in any capacity, to use lethal force if we are called to love our enemy, to turn the other cheek, and not to repay evil for evil. Yet these things are not incompatible, for God is both a loving God who is the model of our love for our enemies (Matt. 5:38–48) and a God who exercises wrath toward injustice and avenges evil.[85] Further, love for one's neighbor who is under attack may well require that we use the minimum force necessary to protect them. In some cases that could require lethal force. In addition, the use of force against an attacker may well prevent them from bringing greater wrath on themselves for perpetrating gross evil.

Fifth, critics of just war doctrine argue that Romans 13 does not address war, but only speaks of Rome's domestic police and judicial roles.[86] In response, while the context may relate most directly to domestic

---

84. Holmes, "The Just War," 120.
85. Davis, *Evangelical Ethics*, 245.
86. Sprinkle, *Fight*, 167–68.

authority, Rome's "police force" was also its army, and it is not too great an extrapolation to extend the principle of punishing evildoers and protecting the innocent to international relations in support of just war doctrine. That is, if the perpetrator of evil is not an individual but one nation against another, or against its own people, then it may be proper for another government to avenge wrongs and restore order, for there is no other human authority to do so.[87]

Other relevant New Testament texts

While Romans 13 is the most relevant text for understanding the justification of the use of necessary force for upholding justice, there are other texts that are consistent with such a view.

Soldiers and centurions: Luke 3:14; Matthew 8:5–13; Luke 7:1–10; Acts 10:22. In Luke 3, John the Baptist calls the crowds to repent and to produce fruit consistent with repentance. The crowds ask what that means, specifically. John tells them to give clothes and food to those who are without (Luke 3:11). Then tax collectors ask John what they should do, and he tells them not to collect more taxes than they should (vv. 12–13). Finally, some soldiers ask John what they should do, and he says, "Don't take money from anyone by force or false accusation, and be satisfied with your wages" (v. 14). In other words, John tells them not to abuse their position and power, as many

soldiers would do. He did not say that they can no longer be soldiers, a profession that resembled both modern armed services and police force, both of which could involve the use of lethal force. We should be cautious about the conclusions we draw from this story. One of the main points may be that the gospel is received by the least likely of persons, including tax collectors and soldiers! Yet, if the fruit of repentance requires that they lay down their swords, it seems to be a significant omission that John doesn't say so, even when asked.

In addition to this account, there are accounts of Roman centurions. In one, Jesus heals a centurion's servant, and marvels at his faith (Matt. 8:5–13; Luke 7:1–10). There is no suggestion that his profession is incompatible with his faith. Another centurion, Cornelius, is said to be "an upright and God-fearing man" (Acts 10:22), and there seems to be no conflict with his profession as such. It may be that a primary purpose of these stories is to show that even soldiers are responding to the call to repent.[88] However, if the use of force is forbidden entirely, and it is a significant part of the soldier's profession, we might expect to see some indication that they are told to leave their profession or lay down their arms. Thus, Hays, who argues that the New Testament makes a strong case for nonviolence, concedes that "these narratives about soldiers provide the one possible legitimate basis for arguing that Christian

---

87. John S. Feinberg and Paul D. Feinberg, *Ethics for a Brave New World*, 2nd ed. (Wheaton, IL: Crossway, 2010), 656. Cf. Oliver O'Donovan, *In Pursuit of a Christian View of War*, Grove Booklet on Ethics 15 (Cambridge: Grove, 1977), 13–14.

88. E.g., Sprinkle, *Fight*, 208.

discipleship does not necessarily preclude the exercise of violence in defense of social order or justice" (though not in the spread of the kingdom of God).[89]

Hebrews 11:32–34. Hebrews 11 commends "a large cloud of witnesses" (Heb. 12:1), who serve in some way as an example of faith. After recounting the patriarchs, Moses, Rahab, and others, the writer refers to Gideon, Barak, Samson, Jephthah, David, Samuel, and the prophets (11:32). Though there are some deeply flawed characters here, it says that they "by faith conquered kingdoms, administered justice . . . became mighty in battle, and put foreign armies to flight" (vv. 33–34). This should not be taken as a direct endorsement of modern warfare, but it is a strange example for the author of Hebrews to use if Christians are to repudiate the use of force altogether.

The book of Revelation. The book of Revelation doesn't provide an endorsement of just war doctrine as such. Though there is warfare imagery, much greater emphasis is placed on encouraging persecuted Christians to endure suffering. Rather than seeking retribution or recourse to violence, believers are encouraged that the power of evil is conquered

> by the blood of the Lamb
> and by the word of their testimony;
> for they did not love their lives
> to the point of death. (Rev. 12:11)[90]

Even in Revelation 19, to which appeal may be made that Jesus will return with an army to vanquish evil, the "sharp sword" that came from his mouth, to "strike the nations," may best be understood as the Word of God (Rev. 19:15).[91] Yet, even if Revelation doesn't directly address just war doctrine, and it is focused on encouragement in the face of persecution, it is not completely irrelevant. First, the use of warfare language, even if much of it is metaphorical, suggests that all war is not evil. Scripture does not describe God's righteous activities by using evil metaphors and analogies. Second, even if Revelation 19 needs to be interpreted along the lines that advocates of nonviolence assert, it is difficult to escape here and elsewhere in the New Testament that God will oppose and defeat evil violently. The beast and the false prophet are thrown into the lake of fire (Rev. 19:20), and God's enemies are "killed with the sword that came from the mouth of the rider on the horse" (v. 21).

Conclusion on the Bible and warfare

From this survey, we may conclude, first, that warfare is not intrinsically evil, for it can be brought in line with the pursuit of justice. That doesn't mean that warfare is justified now, for it is possible that God no longer permits what he once did. Second, though, it seems that the New Testament does not condemn the just use of force, even lethal force, by government. Further, if the

---

89. Hays, *Moral Vision*, 335–36.
90. See Hays, *Moral Vision*, 332.
91. For a discussion of Revelation and its warfare language by an advocate of nonviolence, see Sprinkle, *Fight*, 173–93.

just use of force is permitted by governments, then it seems permissible for Christians serving in government to use such force. Rather than understanding there to be a fundamental distinction between what Christians can do and what a secular government can do, it is better to see the fundamental distinction as that which an individual is commanded (not to avenge wrongdoing) and what the government is responsible to do. A Christian serving in government may be faithful to both aspects of this distinction. How government may bring force in line with the proper pursuit of justice is not clearly spelled out in the New Testament. Christians must take great care in doing so, which is precisely what the just war tradition seeks to do. But before concluding our examination of just war, it is necessary to respond to the evidence of pacifism in the early church, and its implications for just war arguments.

The Early Church Fathers and the Just War Tradition

Earlier we saw that early Christians held that followers of Jesus do not resort to violence and killing. The justification of war comes only after Christianity receives recognition from the Roman emperor Constantine. Advocates of nonviolence thus conclude that the Christian just war

tradition amounts to a compromise with political power. This is an important argument that requires a response.

First, if war is ever justified, or rather, if Christians are ever permitted to participate in the use of force and killing, we ought nevertheless to take seriously the strong aversion to killing that early Christians express. These Christians testify to the horror of killing, to the willingness to suffer rather than to inflict harm, and to the seriousness with which they take the command to love our enemies, something that ought to mark followers of Jesus.

Second, we should not assume that the only reason that Christians came to affirm just war thinking, and Christian participation in military, is because the church gained political power through Constantine and was corrupted by it.[92] Clearly the change would prompt new thinking about a lot of things. Further, not only should we not simply assume that the change is due to corruption, but also the change might not be as dramatic as pacifists claim. Significantly, some of the early Christians who were strongly against any killing or military service nevertheless conceded that there was such a thing as a just war, or even a "necessary" war.[93] As we have seen, contemporary advocates of nonviolence accept the possibility of this position. Sprinkle summarizes

---

92. For a discussion of some of these issues, see Peter J. Leithart, *Defending Constantine: The Twilight of an Empire and the Dawn of Christendom* (Downers Grove, IL: IVP Academic, 2010).
93. As indicated earlier, in his argument for nonviolence, Sprinkle, *Fight*, 204–206, makes this point, citing Origen, Cyprian, and Irenaeus. Sprinkle himself adds, "Just because there may be such a thing as a 'just war' does not give Christians a license to participate" (*Fight*, 205).

it by saying, "The state can punish enemies; the church must love them."[94]

When Christians were no longer persecuted by the government, new questions naturally arose. Can Christians serve as governing officials? If so, in their governing role, can they authorize or participate in the use of force—not for the advance of the gospel, but for enacting justice? To come to a different view given a different situation does not necessarily imply compromise or corruption. Augustine, who was the first to develop a robust Christian just war position, did not accept pagan arguments uncritically, but rather tested them through careful biblical and theological reflection. Of course, he could be wrong, and he should be tested, but he should not be characterized as uncritical of pagan thought. Indeed, the Christian just war tradition attests that just war arguments have been examined and tested and have been found convincing.

Third, at least part of the reason that relatively few Christians participated in the Roman military before 313 is because of idolatrous practices of the military and its identification with Roman religion. Christians serving in the military would have faced unacceptable compromise, and would have faced persecution if they did not compromise. Another thing to note is that there were, in fact, Christians serving in the military, at least from the late second century, and they were not required to leave.[95] Some of the early Christian writers said that Christians in the military are not permitted to kill, and there were many responsibilities of soldiers that did not involve killing. At the same time, as noted already, some of those same writers seem to concede that there is such thing as a just war and a just killing. It is not clear why, if a killing is just, a Christian must not take part in it.

Special Case: The Threat of Nuclear War

The atomic bomb dropped on Hiroshima, Japan, on August 6, 1945 had an explosion with a force of more than fifteen thousand tons of TNT.[96] Three days later, on August 9, 1945, an atomic bomb was dropped on Nagasaki, Japan, with a force equal to twenty-one thousand tons of TNT.[97] As Michael Walzer writes, "Truman used the atomic bomb to end a war that seemed to him limitless in its horrors. And then, for a few minutes or hours in August 1945, the people of Hiroshima endured a war that actually was limitless in its horrors. . . . Though fewer people were killed than in the fire-bombing of Tokyo, they were killed with monstrous ease. . . . After Hiroshima, the first task of political leaders everywhere was to prevent its recurrence."[98] Modern nuclear bombs

---

94. Sprinkle, *Fight*, 206.
95. See the helpful discussion of Christians in the military in the first centuries in Sprinkle, *Fight*, 207–13.
96. For a discussion of nuclear war in the context of Christian ethics, see Feinberg and Feinberg, *Ethics for a Brave New World*, 678–93. See also Michael Walzer, *Just and Unjust Wars: A Moral Argument with Historical Illustrations* (New York: Basic Books, 1977), 269–83.
97. "Atomic Bomb," *Encyclopaedia Britannica*, https://www.britannica.com/technology/atomic-bomb.
98. Walzer, *Just and Unjust Wars*, 269.

have the capability of creating more than three thousand times the force of the first atom bombs, equivalent to as much as fifty million tons of TNT.[99]

The incomprehensible destructive force of nuclear weapons, cumulatively capable of destroying the entire population of the earth many times over, presents particular problems for just war advocates.[100] For instance, the use of nuclear weapons threatens massive civilian populations, not only with the initial damage, but also with the fallout and long-term effects. These are prohibited by the criterion of noncombatant immunity, going well beyond any level of "collateral damage" that is acceptable under *jus in bello* criteria. In addition, it is difficult to imagine a situation in which the use of such a destructive force could be justified as proportionate. Further, with the proliferation of nuclear weapons, any use of a nuclear weapon by one side involves the likelihood that the nation under attack will retaliate with nuclear weapons. Within hours, untold devastation would result for all nations, not only those engaged in the conflict, due to the fallout and impact on the environment.[101] How should we respond to the possibility of the use of nuclear weapons?

Nuclear Pacifism

In response to the nuclear threat, some advocate "nuclear pacifism," even if they otherwise defend just war doctrine. In short, nuclear pacifism is "the belief that a war involving nuclear weapons is not a winnable or 'just' war, and is unjustifiable because of its uniquely devastating consequences."[102] Just war criteria simply cannot be applied in a nuclear war. Due to such a serious threat, nuclear pacifists argue that the only reasonable policy is to pursue disarmament, something that the United Nations has sought through multilateral and bilateral (especially between the United States and the USSR/Russia) treaties since its establishment. Short of disarmament, which has proved very difficult, various United Nations treaties have called for a ban on nuclear proliferation and a reduction in the stockpile of nuclear weapons.[103] While the elimination of nuclear weapons altogether is arguably the surest way to prevent a global catastrophe caused by a nuclear war, the reality is that it is unlikely that nuclear

99. Jay Bennett, "Here's How Much Deadlier Today's Nuke Are Compared to WWII A-Bombs," *Popular Mechanics*, October 10, 2016, https://www.popularmechanics.com/military/a23306/nuclear-bombs-powerful-today.

100. For concerns about nuclear weapons and the nuclear arms race, see Ronald J. Sider, *Completely Pro-Life: Building a Consistent Stance* (Downers Grove, IL: InterVarsity Press, 1987), chaps. 8–9.

101. Alok Jha, "Climate Threat from Nuclear Bombs," *The Guardian*, December 12, 2006, https://www.theguardian.com/environment/2006/dec/12/nuclearindustry.climatechange; *Effects of Nuclear Earth-Penetrator and Other Weapons: Human and Environmental Effects* (Washington, DC: The National Academies Press, 2005), https://www.nap.edu/read/11282/chapter/8.

102. Oxford Reference, "Nuclear Pacifism," 2020, https://www.oxfordreference.com/view/10.1093/oi/authority.20110803100241331.

103. United Nations Office for Disarmament Affairs, "Nuclear Weapons," https://www.un.org/disarmament/wmd/nuclear.

weapons will be eliminated anytime soon, if ever. Indeed, there is a growing number of nations that possess them or the technology to build them. As such, many believe that nuclear pacifism is not a realistic position, and there are other proposals for dealing with the nuclear threat.

Deterrence and MAD

To prevent the recurrence of Hiroshima and Nagasaki, and to prevent a nuclear war, nations—particularly the United States and the Soviet Union—early on adopted a policy of deterrence. During the height of the arms race between the two superpowers, the nuclear deterrence strategy was known ominously as *mutual assured destruction* (MAD). The strategy is this: since nuclear weapons and the technology to make them are here to stay, the only way to prevent an aggressor from using them is to threaten a devastating retaliatory nuclear strike, including the targeting of major civilian populations. To be effective, the threat would have to be real—not just a bluff—which means maintaining the capability of decimating population centers. In effect, a nuclear war could lead to annihilation of the nations involved. No nation acting rationally would attack another nation with nuclear weapons because

it would mean their own destruction. As Walzer puts it, "Against the threat of an immoral attack, they have put the threat of an immoral response. This is the basic form of nuclear deterrence."[104]

While the USA eventually moved away from a policy of MAD,, the strategy of deterrence continues, for several reasons.[105] One is that it has proved successful in preventing the use of nuclear weapons and preserving peace between nuclear powers since World War II. Although there are significant moral questions about the use of deterrence, for advocates the bottom line is that it works. A second, related argument is that it seems to be the only viable policy, given the existence of nuclear weapons and technology. Anything that maintains a relative peace and prevents the use of nuclear weapons is considered a reasonable policy. Indeed, one might argue, given that deterrence is the only viable policy available, it is necessary as the means of protection of innocent people against unjust aggressors.[106]

Walzer concludes that "the reason for our acceptance of deterrent strategy . . . is that preparing to kill, even threatening to kill, is not at all the same thing as killing."[107] Further, it has worked with relatively little impact on people's lives. Walzer continues,

---

104. Walzer, *Just and Unjust Wars*, 269. The discussion here is specifically about nuclear deterrence. Deterrence has long been a strategy of defense to avoid war, by building armed forces strong enough to deter an aggressor. Nuclear deterrence is of a different quality, since it relies on the threat of retaliation that is capable of annihilation.

105. See Feinberg and Feinberg, *Ethics for a Brave New World*, 690–91; D. J. E. Attwood, "Deterrence, Nuclear," in *New Dictionary of Christian Ethics and Pastoral Theology*, eds. David J. Atkinson et al. (Downers Grove, IL: InterVarsity Press, 1995), 303–5; for a theological discussion of deterrence, see Oliver O'Donovan, *Peace and Certainty: A Theological Essay on Deterrence* (Grand Rapids: Eerdmans, 1989); also Ramsey, *Just War*, chaps. 13–15.

106. See Davis, *Evangelical Ethics*, 254–55.

107. Walzer, *Just and Unjust Wars*, 270.

"The strategy works because it is easy. . . . Not only don't we do anything to other people, we also don't believe that we will ever have to do anything."[108] On whether the threat of nuclear annihilation is morally acceptable, Walzer states, "We threaten evil in order not to do it, and the doing of it would be so terrible that the threat seems in comparison to be morally defensible."[109]

Many concerns and criticisms have been raised about the policy of nuclear deterrence. One is that, at least with respect to the policy of MAD, to carry out the policy by targeting civilian population centers would be immoral. It would violate the just war criteria of noncombatant immunity and proportionate means. Further, if carrying out the policy would be immoral, then threatening to carry it out is immoral.[110] Second, the strategy produces an arms race, so that each nation has a sufficient threat to deter aggressors. While the arms race between the United States and the former Soviet Union was eventually contained and talks led to reduced arms, there are now numerous countries that have or are pursuing nuclear technology, and there is danger or a new arms race. Third, nuclear deterrence is a strategy with very high risk. It does not provide a defense against attack, and it is not likely to work against an enemy that does not act rationally. If an aggressor believes it can win a nuclear war, or if it is willing to risk its own destruction if it can destroy its enemy in the process, deterrence is not likely to be effective.[111] The risk can be put in historical terms. Even though nuclear deterrence has been effective since World War II, and that is no small matter, it is a brief period of time in the span of history. Given that an increasing number of nations possess nuclear weapons or the technology to make them, it is not at all clear what might happen if at some point a conflict in the world escalates and several nations are drawn into war. The use of a nuclear weapon by one side could start a devastating nuclear war. It is not at all certain that the strategy of deterrence that has worked in the past is stable enough to prevent the use of nuclear weapons indefinitely.

Strategic Defense Initiative

The Strategic Defense Initiative, begun by President Ronald Reagan, is the attempt to develop technology that can intercept and destroy enemy missiles before they land. Reagan's critics derided his proposal as expensive and fanciful, calling it "Star Wars" because of the talk of space-based laser shields and such. However, the Clinton administration continued the work, with the name changed to the Ballistic Missile Defense Organization, and later the Missile Defense Agency. Instead of laser defense shields, focus shifted to "hitting an inbound

---

108. Walzer, *Just and Unjust Wars*, 271.
109. Walzer, *Just and Unjust Wars*, 274.
110. Walzer highlights this problem in *Just and Unjust Wars*, 269–74.
111. This is the concern about both rogue nations and terrorist groups, should they obtain nuclear weapons and a viable delivery system.

missile with a faster outbound missile."[112] Though the specific focus shifted, the bottom line is to provide defense against a nuclear attack. Indeed, the biggest argument in favor of missile defense is that it focuses on defense rather than the threat of deterrence. In support of his proposal, President Reagan asked, "Would it not be better to save lives than to avenge them?"[113]

The Missile Defense program seems, on the surface at least, to be a promising answer to the nuclear threat, focused as it is on self-defense. But it is not without its problems, and critics.[114] One concern is that developing a missile defense system is taken as a threat to those countries that do not have it. If it truly works, then the nation that possesses it has a significant advantage over nations that do not. That is, one nation could launch an attack and then prevent a counterattack by shooting down incoming missiles. After decades of operating under a policy of deterrence, this has a destabilizing effect. Missile defense thus has the effect of escalating tensions. Further, it encourages other nations to develop counterstrategies. One counterstrategy, by an enemy with a large arsenal, would be to launch enough missiles—including decoy missiles—to overwhelm the missile defense system. Another counter strategy would be to deliver the nuclear bomb by a means other than a missile, concealing it and smuggling it past security systems. Thus missile defense systems may provide some protection, but they may also provide a false sense of security: "The best one could hope for is reduced vulnerability, not invulnerability."[115] For these and other reasons, even though missile defense seems like a good strategy, the United States and the former Soviet Union engaged in talks in the 1960s and 1970s to limit the development of antiballistic missile technology and of the stockpile of weapons.[116]

Conclusion on Nuclear Weapons

Given the catastrophic destruction that nuclear weapons would cause, nuclear pacifism is, on the surface, the most attractive response to the possibility of a nuclear war. However, the problem is that disarmament is elusive and unlikely. It is not clear that unilateral disarmament is the answer, in a world of terrorism and unstable leaders who may have access to nuclear weapons, as it puts a nation's entire population at risk of annihilation or nuclear blackmail. Deterrence is a strategy that has worked,

---

112. Kevin D. Williamson, "A Satisfying 'Star Wars' Sequel," *National Review*, June 11, 2017, http://www.nationalreview.com/article/448473/ronald-reagan-missile-defense-star-wars-initiative-huge-success-despite-critics.

113. Cited in Williamson, "A Satisfying 'Star Wars' Sequel."

114. For concerns of critics and a response to them, see Williamson, "A Satisfying 'Star Wars' Sequel"; also Feinberg and Feinberg, *Ethics for a Brave New World*, 688–89.

115. Feinberg and Feinberg, *Ethics for a Brave New World*, 689.

116. These talks, called the Strategic Arms Limitations Treaty, SALT I and SALT II, spanned the administrations of Presidents Johnson, Nixon, Ford, and Carter. President Reagan was very critical of the SALT treaties, due to the lack of verification, ongoing vulnerability, and other reasons, and pressed forward with the Strategic Defense Initiative. Department of State, Office of the Historian, https://history.state.gov/milestones/1969–1976/salt.

it seems, but it is morally problematic. Walzer underscores the uneasiness about both nuclear war and nuclear deterrence when he asserts, "Nuclear war is and will remain morally unacceptable, and there is no case for its rehabilitation. Because it is unacceptable, we must seek out ways to prevent it, and because deterrence is a bad way, we must seek others." Unfortunately, other ways of avoiding nuclear war have proved elusive. Hence, Walzer concedes that "deterrence itself, for all its criminality, falls or may fall for the moment under the standard of necessity."[117]

In the meantime, the size and destructive impact of nuclear weapons has been greatly reduced with advanced technology that allows for much more precise targeting.[118] In addition, the deterrence strategy has moved away from targeting civilian populations, focusing on military targets.[119] While these changes represent attempts to limit the scope of a nuclear attack, and while they may be shaped in part by a commitment to just war doctrine, it is difficult to imagine the use of a nuclear weapon that conforms to just war criteria. Surely the present situation is neither morally satisfying nor sustainable in the long term.

Just Peacemaking

Before concluding, we do well to note a view that seeks to distinguish itself by focusing the discussion on "proactive practices that prevent war and create peace."[120] If pacifists are against war under any circumstances, and just war advocates see war as a last resort, then they both have good reason to work out strategies that are aimed at avoiding war. If alternatives to war are left unspecified, it is less likely that war will be avoided, so advocates of just peacemaking have developed ten specific practices that they believe will establish and maintain peace. Those who advocate the doctrine of just peacemaking include both just war advocates and pacifists, "who disagree on whether war is ever justified but agree that the ten practices of just peacemaking are effective in preventing many wars and are obligatory for people and governments to support."[121] The ten practices of just peacemaking are as follows:[122]

1. Support nonviolent direct action.
2. Take independent initiatives to reduce threat.
3. Use cooperative conflict resolution.
4. Acknowledge responsibility for conflict and injustice; seek repentance and forgiveness.

---

117. Walzer, *Just and Unjust Wars*, 283.
118. Davis, *Evangelical Ethics*, 250–52.
119. Davis, *Evangelical Ethics*, 252.
120. Glen H. Stassen, "Just-Peacemaking Theory," in Green et al., *Dictionary of Scripture and Ethics*, 442. For a fuller account, see Glen H. Stassen, *Just Peacemaking: Transforming Initiative for Justice and Peace* (Louisville: Westminster John Knox Press, 1992).
121. Stassen, "Just-Peacemaking Theory," 442.
122. For a summary of these initiatives see Stassen, "Just-Peacemaking Theory," 443. These initiatives are developed in detail by multiple authors in Glen H. Stassen, ed., *Just Peacemaking: The New Paradigm for the Ethics of Peace and War*, 2nd ed. (Cleveland: Pilgrim, 2008).

5. Advance democracy, human rights, and religious liberty.
6. Foster just and sustainable economic development.
7. Work with emerging cooperative forces in the international system.
8. Strengthen the United Nations and international efforts for cooperation and human rights.
9. Reduce offensive weapons and weapons trade.
10. Encourage grassroots peacemaking groups and voluntary associations.

Conclusion

Whether these initiatives are effective, or others should be developed, we should appreciate the desire to develop in specific terms what it means to be peacemakers. Christians who are advocates of pacifism and just war doctrine alike should be peacemakers, "for they shall be called sons of God" (Matt. 5:9). The statement on peace and war in the Baptist Faith and Message sums things up well:[123]

> It is the duty of Christians to seek peace with all men on principles of righteousness. In accordance with the spirit and teachings of Christ they should do all in their power to put an end to war.
>
> The true remedy for the war spirit is the gospel of our Lord. The supreme need of the world is the acceptance of His teachings in all the affairs of men and nations, and the practical application of His

law of love. Christian people throughout the world should pray for the reign of the Prince of Peace.

The apostle Paul exhorts Christians, "If possible, as far as it depends on you, live at peace with everyone" (Rom. 12:18). Those who follow the Prince of Peace will not merely seek to avoid violence, but will take the initiative to reconcile with others and avoid escalation (Matt. 5:21–26), and to "love your enemies and pray for those who persecute you, so that you may be children of your Father in heaven" (Matt. 5:44–45).

---

123. Southern Baptist Convention, "The 2000 Baptist Faith and Message," http://www.sbc.net/bfm2000/bfm2000.asp.

Select Resources

Charles, J. Daryl. *Between Pacifism and Jihad: Just War and Christian Tradition*. Downers Grove, IL: InterVarsity Press, 2005.

Clouse, Robert G., ed. *War: Four Christian Views*. Downers Grove, IL: InterVarsity Press, 1981.

O'Donovan, Oliver. *The Just War Revisited*. Cambridge: Cambridge University Press, 2003.

Ramsey, Paul. *The Just War: Force and Political Responsibility*. Savage, MD: Littlefield, Adams, 1983.

Sprinkle, Preston. *Fight: A Christian Case for Nonviolence*. Colorado Springs: David C. Cook, 2013.

Stassen, Glen H. *Just Peacemaking: Transforming Initiative for Justice and Peace*. Louisville: Westminster John Knox Press, 1992.

Walzer, Michael. *Just and Unjust Wars: A Moral Argument with Historical Illustrations*. New York: Basic Books, 1977.

Yoder, John Howard. *The Politics of Jesus*. Grand Rapids: Eerdmans, 1972.

CHAPTER 16

RACE RELATIONS

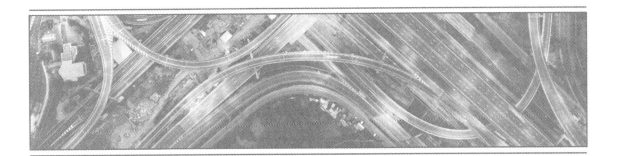

From one man he has made every nationality to live over the whole earth.

—Acts 17:26

You are being renewed in knowledge according to the image of your Creator. In Christ there is not Greek and Jew, circumcision and uncircumcision, barbarian, Scythian, slave and free; but Christ is all and in all.

—Colossians 3:10–11

Introduction

On November 4, 2008, Barack Obama was elected the forty-fourth president of the United States, marking a defining moment in American history. Many had hopes that the election of the first black president would bring about a time of healing in a nation torn by racial division throughout its history, while "sweeping away the last racial barrier in American politics," as the *New York Times* put it. In his acceptance speech, referring to a range of issues including race relations, Obama struck a hopeful tone, announcing that "change has come to America." He asserted, "If there is anyone out there who still doubts that America is a place where all things are possible, who still wonders if the dream of our founders is alive in our time, who still questions the power of our democracy, tonight is your answer."[1]

Indeed, a majority of voters (52 percent) expected that the election of President Obama would lead to better race relations. Among black voters, the optimism was much higher, with 75 percent believing there would be better race relations.[2] In the months following the election, the percentage of adults who said that race relations are "generally good" was at an all-time high.[3] Sadly, however, by the end of Obama's presidency, the hope of many black voters for progress in race relations was gone: In 2016, 61 percent of African Americans polled said that race relations "are generally bad" (compared with 45 percent of white people polled).[4] What caused the optimism and hope held by a majority of black people in 2009 to vanish in fear and anger?

Black Lives Matter

Though there are multiple factors, the shift from hope to fear and anger is symbolized by the movement that came to be known as Black Lives Matter. The movement began in 2013 after George Zimmerman was found not guilty of second-degree murder in the 2012 killing an unarmed seventeen-year-old black man named Trayvon Martin. In response, Alicia Garza posted on social media what so many other black people were thinking: "Black people are

---

1. Adam Nagourney, "Obama Elected President as Racial Barrier Falls," *The New York Times,* November 4, 2008, https://www.nytimes.com/2008/11/05/us/politics/05elect.html.
2. Pew Research Center, "High Marks for the Campaign, A High Bar for Obama: Section 2: The President-Elect's Image and Expectations," November 13, 2008, https://www.people-press.org/2008/11/13/section-2-the-president-elects-image-and-expectations.
3. Michael Dimock, "How America Changed during Barack Obama's Presidency," Pew Research Center, January 10, 2017, http://www.pewresearch.org/2017/01/10/how-america-changed-during-barack-obamas-presidency. The Pew Research Center polls since 1990 on whether adults say that race relations are "generally good" or "generally bad" reveal a negative attitude in the 1990s, bottoming out in 1992 after the Los Angeles riots. Attitudes were generally positive in the 2000s, peaking in April 2009.
4. Pew Research Center, "On Views of Race and Inequality, Blacks and Whites Are Worlds Apart," June 27, 2016, https://www.pewsocialtrends.org/2016/06/27/on-views-of-race-and-inequality-blacks-and-whites-are-worlds-apart/. Interestingly, in this same poll, in spite of strong hope at the beginning, and negative feelings at the end, 51 percent of African Americans polled said that President Obama made progress on race relations.

not safe in America."[5] Garza's friend Patrisse Cullors reposted with the hashtag #blacklivesmatter, and a movement was born, protesting police brutality against black people, as well as what many in the movement believe to be indifference to the killing of black people.

The story of Trayvon Martin is not an isolated incident. The names and events are etched in the psyche of so many people of color:[6] Jordan Davis (2012), Renisha McBride (2013), Eric Garner (2014), John Crawford (2014), Michael Brown (2014), Tamir Rice (2014), Walter Scott (2015), Freddie Gray (2015), Alton Sterling (2016), Jordan Edwards (2017) Stephon Clark (2018), Ahmaud Arbery (2020), Breonna Taylor (2020), and George Floyd (2020). All of these were black people killed, in most (but not all) cases, by police officers or while in police custody. They include a range of circumstances, and in some cases the death resulted in a conviction and prison sentence for persons responsible, while in others charges were dropped or the person charged for the death was acquitted. The reasons that these and other cases received national attention and galvanized a movement are numerous, but at the core was the sense that

the deaths were either criminal or unnecessary, and it seemed to many black people that many simply didn't care about those who were killed because they were black.

These cases highlight the racial tensions in America. Many in the Black Lives Matter movement cite such cases to underscore their view that black people in America are not safe and many live in fear. They argue that the civil rights movement made significant gains, but there is a long way to go. Critics have said that Black Lives Matter is different from the civil rights movement in the 1960s, in part because it is difficult to tell the activists from opportunists that burn and loot and visit demonstrations with hate speech and profanity. One civil rights activist complained that "even if the BLM activists aren't the ones participating in the boorish language and dress, neither are they condemning it."[7] Other critics have responded to the movement with slogans of their own, like "All Lives Matter," or "Blue Lives Matter" (a reference to police who are killed in the line of duty, or simply who put themselves in harm's way).

There may be reasonable debate about whether a particular killing was justified, and there may be problems with aspects of the Black Lives Matter movement, but

5. Elizabeth Day, "#BlackLivesMatter: The Birth of a New Civil Rights Movement," *The Guardian*, July 19, 2015, https://www.theguardian.com/world/2015/jul/19/blacklivesmatter-birth-civil-rights-movement.

6. For a description of most of these cases, see Holly Yan, "'Black Lives Matter' Cases: When Controversial Killings Lead to Change," CNN, May 4, 2017, https://www.cnn.com/2017/05/04/us/black-lives-matter-updates-may-2017/index.html; and Jonathan Capehart, "From Trayvon Martin to 'Black Lives Matter,'" *Washington Post*, February 27, 2015, https://www.washingtonpost.com/blogs/post-partisan/wp/2015/02/27/from-trayvon-martin-to-black-lives-matter.

7. Barbara Reynolds, "I Was a Civil Rights Activist in the 1960s. But It's Hard for Me to Get Behind Black Lives Matter," *Washington Post* online, August 24, 2015, https://www.washingtonpost.com/posteverything/wp/2015/08/24/i-was-a-civil-rights-activist-in-the-1960s-but-its-hard-for-me-to-get-behind-black-lives-matter.

the underlying point should not be missed. Many black people who have done no wrong live in fear in twenty-first-century America, or simply have grown used to being looked on with suspicion. That should not be the case. The feelings of many black people are summed up in remarks by President Obama after the not-guilty verdict was issued by the jury in the Trayvon Martin case:

> When you think about why, in the African American community at least, there's a lot of pain around what happened here, I think it's important to recognize that the African American community is looking at this issue through a set of experiences and a history that doesn't go away. . . . There are very few African American men in this country who haven't had the experience of being followed when they were shopping in a department store. . . . There are very few African American men who haven't had the experience of walking across the street and hearing the locks click on the doors of cars. . . . There are very few African Americans who haven't had the experience of getting on an elevator and a woman clutching her purse nervously and holding her breath until she had a chance to get off. . . . Those sets of experiences inform how the African American community interprets what happened one night in Florida. And it's inescapable for people to bring those experiences to bear.[8]

African Americans, and other people of color, can tell of countless similar experiences. The reality of daily life for many African Americans has led some to refer to a phenomenon of being pulled over for "driving while black." To respond to the Black Lives Matter movement by asserting that "all lives matter" is to remain tone-deaf to what our black neighbors and friends, our Christian brothers and sisters, are pleading for white people to understand. Perhaps, instead of responding in such a way, or seeking to defend and explain a particular case, we may start simply by grieving that our friends and neighbors, our brothers and sisters, have had to experience and endure such things.

Make America Great Again?

For many, it is as if we live in "two nations."[9] Consider the 2016 presidential campaign, in which Donald Trump ran with the slogan "Make America Great Again." It resonated especially with working-class white voters and many white evangelicals, especially those concerned with issues like the advance of the sexual revolution, threats to free speech and freedom of religious expression, reigning in a judiciary that legislates from the bench, illegal immigration, and sluggish economic progress.[10] For many, a vote for Trump was based on a hope that he would slow or reverse the trend on some of the

---

8. Capehart, "From Trayvon Martin to 'Black Lives Matter.'"
9. From the title of the book by Andrew Hacker, *Two Nations: Black and White, Separate, Hostile, Unequal*, rev. ed. (New York: Scribner, 2003).
10. A large majority white evangelicals—as high as 80 percent—voted for Trump, in spite of reservations about his significant moral flaws and bombastic style. For results from exit polls, see Sarah Pulliam Bailey, "What Evangelicals

issues that they were most concerned about, and it was a vote against Trump's opponent, Hillary Clinton, whom they feared would accelerate those trends. Whatever their reasons, many white evangelicals seemed to be unaware of, or insensitive to, the concerns of black voters (as well as Hispanic voters anxious about Trump's rhetoric on immigration). For many, the intention and appeal of the campaign slogan seemed to be to highlight a decline in various things that have made America great, like freedom and opportunity and democracy, which have (ironically) drawn countless immigrants to the United States. However, America has not been great for everyone, and the cry to "make America great again" did not resonate with many whose history has been marked by enslavement, exclusion, and fear. To understand this in some measure, we need to remind ourselves of the history and legacy of racism in America, which remains the backdrop to the experience of many black people today.

The History of Racism in America

Slavery

The institution of slavery has existed around the world, in various forms, from the beginning of recorded history. In some cases slaves have been treated well and given great responsibility. In other cases, they have been treated brutally. While certain practices have been condemned, the institution itself remained virtually unchallenged through much of its history, in part because of economic necessity for both slave owners and, in many cases, slaves themselves.

However, one of the things that stands out with slavery in America is that the dehumanizing practice of slavery existed in a country that proclaimed freedom for all, declaring that "we hold these truths to be self-evident, that all men are created equal, that they are endowed by their Creator with certain unalienable Rights, that among these are Life, Liberty and the Pursuit of Happiness."[11] The first slaves from Africa had been brought to America in the early seventeenth century, and at the time of the Declaration of Independence, slavery was legal in all thirteen colonies. Slaveholders included the majority of the founding fathers and eight of the first twelve presidents of the United States.[12] The words of the great declaration were not applied to all people. By the Civil War in 1861, the slave population was around four million—four million people who were denied the self-evident

---

Voted Overwhelmingly for Donald Trump, Exit Polls Show," *Washington Post*, November 9, 2016, https://www.washingtonpost.com/news/acts-of-faith/wp/2016/11/09/exit-polls-show-white-evangelicals-voted-overwhelmingly-for-donald-trump.

11. National Archives, "Declaration of Independence: A Transcription," https://www.archives.gov/founding-docs/declaration-transcript.

12. For a concise history and description of the African slave trade and slavery in the American colonies and the United States, see Peter Kolchin, "Slavery in the United States," in *Africana: The Encyclopedia of the African and African American Experience*, eds. Kwame Anthony Appiah and Henry Louis Gates Jr. (New York: Basic Civitas Books, 1999), 1728.

truth and unalienable right of liberty. One historian asserts, "What slaves hated most about slavery was not the hard work to which they were subjected (most people in the rural United States expected to engage in hard physical labor), but the lack of control over their lives—their lack of freedom. Masters may have prided themselves on the care they provided for their 'people'; the slaves, however, had a different idea of that care. They resented the constant interference in their lives and struggled to achieve whatever autonomy they could."[13]

The transatlantic slave trade involved the forced migration of approximately twelve million people from Africa, who were packed onto ships, at times stacked on top of one another, for the voyage to the Americas. Many died in transit in deplorable conditions. The largest number of slaves, more than three-quarters, went to Brazil and Caribbean colonies. About 600,000–650,000 (roughly 6 percent) were sent to the colonies in what is now the United States. Brazil and the Caribbean colonies continued to depend on the importation of slaves from Africa because slave mortality exceeded birth rates in those territories, and when the slave trade ended, the slave population declined. By contrast, in the United States, the mortality rate among slaves was much lower, and even after the slave trade was

outlawed in 1808, the slave population continued to grow rapidly through rising birth rates. As a result, many slaves in the United States were born into slavery. Further, while an early form of slavery in the colonies was indentured servanthood (largely consisting of Europeans seeking passage to America), whereby one could earn their freedom after several years of service, laws in the colonies were changed so that black slaves could be enslaved for life.[14]

Slavery in the United States included dehumanizing, inhumane treatment. Not only were slaves owned and treated as property, but they were also put in shackles, they were sold at auction blocks, they were branded and whipped. It is no surprise that black people in general saw white people as their oppressors. Since most black people in the antebellum South were slaves, and since even whites who did not hold slaves treated black people as inferior, it became clear that "the line separating black from white approximated the line separating slave from free, and the class exploitation of slave by master often appeared indistinguishable from the racial oppression of black by whites."[15] Slaves developed their own sense of identity, with their African origins, their own traditions, community, and various forms of culture, "forged in the crucible of slavery."[16] Given patterns of

---

13. Kolchin, "Slavery in the United States," 1732. It was not uncommon for slave owners to view themselves as "kindly patriarchs" who were firm but fair, and looked after the needs of their slaves. They did provide certain basics, such as food, clothing, and housing (all modest). However, as Kolchin writes, "few slaves saw their owners as the kindly guardians that they proclaimed themselves to be" (1730).
14. Kolchin, "Slavery in the United States," 1729–30.
15. Kolchin, "Slavery in the United States," 1732.
16. Kolchin, "Slavery in the United States," 1733.

oppression and segregation that continued well after the abolition of slavery, and a black community that even today largely remains segregated in urban areas that often continue to be (among other things) economically depressed, it is not surprising that racial tensions and a suspicion of the white majority remains.

Arguments defending slavery

As pernicious as slavery itself were the arguments defending the institution. By the middle of the nineteenth century, slavery existed in only a few territories in the Americas, including the Southern United States. As the Southern economy and way of life had become dependent on slave labor, slavery was defended not only as a necessity but also a "positive good." Thomas Sowell observes that historically slavery did not grow out of racism—that is, it was not primarily race-based or defended by racist ideology; indeed, it was so prevalent that it required little defense before the nineteenth century. However, he asserts, slavery could never gain universal acceptance in the United States, which was "founded upon a principle of freedom, with which slavery was in such obvious and irreconcilable contradiction." Yet slaveholders in the American South were determined "to hold on to their slaves and, for that, some defense was necessary against the ideology of freedom and the widespread criticisms of

slavery that were its corollary. Racism," he argues, "became that defense."[17]

Even though only about 25 percent of white families owned slaves by 1860, many whites who did not own slaves saw it in their interests to defend white superiority. "Scientific" evidence was purported to demonstrate that the differences between whites and blacks indicated that they were of different races, that black people were not suited for freedom but needed the "firm direction" of white people. As the Northern economy became more and more industrial, proslavery arguments in the South asserted that slaves were cared for better than wage laborers ("wage slavery") in the North who were exploited and treated inhumanely. Religious arguments were advanced as well, appealing to God's purposes and will, and the "curse of Ham" (or Canaan; Gen. 9), a perverse interpretation of the text, which was supposed to explain the divinely ordained subjugation of black people.[18]

Dred Scott and constitutional rights for black people

In 1857, the United States Supreme Court made several controversial rulings on slavery and black people in the infamous *Dred Scott v. Sanford* decision. Dred Scott was a slave who was born in Virginia and was later sold to John Emerson, an army surgeon who brought him to western territories where slavery was banned. Emerson

---

17. Thomas Sowell, *Economic Facts and Fallacies*, 2nd ed. (New York: Basic Books, 2011), 181.
18. These and other arguments can be found in Kolchin, "Slavery in the United States," 1733–34. For brief comments on the "curse of Ham" see Kenneth A. Matthews, "The Table of Nations: The 'Also Peoples,'" *Southern Baptist Journal of Theology* 5, no. 3 (Fall 2001): 42–43.

died and left his property, including Scott, to his wife. Because Scott had been brought to a territory where slavery was banned, he sued for his freedom. His case eventually made it to the Supreme Court. Under Chief Justice Roger Taney, the court ruled against Scott by a seven-two decision, and used the opportunity to rule on several aspects of slavery. The court ruled that slaves were not considered citizens by the Constitution, and had no standing to sue in federal courts. It also ruled that Congress could not ban slavery in the territories. Taney argued that blacks were inferior to whites, and had no rights that whites were bound to recognize. Significantly, Justices Benjamin Curtis and John McLean challenged the ruling in a dissenting opinion, citing the fact that many black people were citizens both before and after the ratification of the Constitution.[19]

The Dred Scott decision and the reaction to it may have played a role in the strengthening of the Republican Party's antislavery position and in the election of Abraham Lincoln to the Presidency in 1860. The Civil War, which first was focused on preserving the union, became a battle to end slavery. The Union's victory in 1865, along with the passing of the Thirteenth Amendment, ratified by the states in December of 1865, abolished slavery. That amendment read that "neither slavery nor involuntary servitude, except as a punishment for crime whereof the party shall have been duly convicted, shall exist within the United States, or any place subject to their jurisdiction." The Fourteenth Amendment (guaranteeing due process and equal protection under law to all citizens) and Fifteenth Amendment (protecting the right to vote for citizens or any race or color) were aimed in part at strengthening rights for freed slaves, and served as a refutation of the Dred Scott decision.[20]

Post-slavery racism: The Jim Crow Era, Plessy v. Ferguson, and Segregation

The Civil War victory by the Union army and amendments to the Constitution gave to black people rights that had long been denied them. However, these were short-lived. Soon Jim Crow laws and practices enforced racial segregation in public places, treating black people as second-class citizens.[21] In 1890, New Orleans passed a law that required separate railway cars for black and white passengers, claiming that it would protect people of both races. Soon other states in the South passed similar laws. In 1896, the Supreme Court of the United States ruled in the case of *Plessy v. Ferguson* that "separate but equal" accommodations were constitutional, for equality under the

---

19. See Library of Congress, Primary Documents in American History, *Dred Scott v. Sanford*, https://www.loc.gov/rr/program/bib/ourdocs/dredscott.html. See also "Dred Scott v. Sanford," in Appiah and Gates, *Africana*, 630–31.

20. See United States Senate, "Constitution of the United States," https://www.senate.gov/civics/constitution_item/constitution.htm.

21. "Jim Crow" is a term that came from a stereotype of black people played by white actors in blackface. The term came to be used pejoratively for black people, and eventually "Jim Crow laws" referred to racial segregation. See Kate Tuttle, "Jim Crow," in Appiah and Gates, *Africana*, 1050–51.

law could be maintained as long as each race had access to such accommodations.[22] In the majority opinion, Justice Henry Brown wrote, "We consider the underlying fallacy of the plaintiff's argument to consist in the assumption that the enforced separation of the two races stamps the colored race with a badge of inferiority. If this be so, it is not by reason of anything found in the act, but solely because the colored race chooses to put that construction upon it." Further, "Legislation is powerless to eradicate racial instincts or to abolish distinctions based upon physical differences, and the attempt to do so can only result in accentuating the difficulties of the present situation."[23] These are the types of arguments that are used to maintain the status quo, not by those interested in truth and justice.

In dissent, Justice John Harlan wrote that the law was clearly aimed in one direction, to prevent black people from using the same car as white people, and not the reverse, and he challenged the notion that legislation is neutral when it comes to racial instincts. He argued that that government "shall not permit the seeds of race hate to be planted under the sanction of law. What can more certainly arouse race hate, what more certainly create and perpetuate a feeling of distrust between these races, than state enactments which, in fact, proceed on the ground that colored citizens are so inferior and degraded that they cannot be allowed to sit in public coaches occupied by white citizens?"[24]

After *Plessy*, racial segregation became commonplace in public facilities, especially in the South, including transportation, hotels, theaters, schools, restrooms, and drinking fountains. In principle, there was supposed to be access to public facilities for all people, even if they were separate. In practice, facilities for black people were inferior, and "separate but equal" was a fiction. Jim Crow laws were only first seriously challenged more than a half century later, when the Supreme Court ruled in the 1954 case of *Brown v. Board of Education* that segregation of public schools was unconstitutional. Segregation in other areas was officially overturned with the civil rights movement in the 1960s. Given the long history of legal segregation and its enduring effects, it is not difficult to understand why many people continue to point to racial division as a major problem.

Lynching and the portrayal of black people as criminals

"Separate but equal" was not the only injustice perpetrated on black people after the abolition of slavery. The white majority, especially in the South, quickly found "legal" ways around the Constitution to oppress black people. The Thirteenth Amendment, for instance, stated, "Neither slavery nor involuntary servitude, *except as a punishment*

---

22. See Library of Congress, Primary Documents in American History, *Plessy v. Ferguson* (1896), https://www.loc.gov/rr/program/bib/ourdocs/plessy.html. See also Tuttle, "Jim Crow," 1050–51.

23. *Plessy v. Ferguson* (1896), 551, http://cdn.loc.gov/service/ll/usrep/usrep163/usrep163537/usrep163537.pdf.

24. *Plessy v. Ferguson* (1896), 560.

for crime whereof the party shall have been duly convicted, shall exist within the United States, or any place subject to their jurisdiction." It was not long before the exception was used as a loophole to create a form of re-enslavement by convicting black men of crimes at a high rate and submitting them to forced labor. Black men were depicted as dangerous criminals, leading to a horrific era of imprisonment, forced labor, lynching, and eventually to mass incarceration.[25]

On April 8, 2018, the CBS news program *60 Minutes* aired a segment titled "The Legacy of Lynching."[26] The episode featured the National Memorial for Peace and Justice, which draws attention to the period between the Civil War and World War II, when "millions of African Americans were terrorized and traumatized by the lynching of thousands of black men, women and children."[27] Opened by the Equal Justice Initiative, this national memorial is located

in Montgomery, Alabama, and is the first memorial in America to be dedicated to the legacy of slavery, Jim Crow, and lynching.[28] The director of the Equal Justice Initiative Bryan Stevenson explains, "Our nation's history of racial injustice casts a shadow across the American landscape." He adds, "This shadow cannot be lifted until we shine a light of truth on the destructive violence that shaped our nation, traumatized people of color, and compromised our commitment to the rule of law and to equal justice."[29] The memorial reflects similar memorials in the United States and other countries that draw attention to such historic injustices as genocide, the Holocaust, and apartheid.

The Equal Justice Initiative has documented over four thousand lynchings, and thousands more are undocumented. Many of the lynchings were public events, reported in newspapers, in which crowds dressed up to go and watch, and people took pictures

---

25. An example of this depiction is found in the 1915 film *Birth of a Nation*, produced by D. W. Griffith, adapted from Thomas Dixon's novel *The Clansman*. It glorifies the KKK as heroic, and portrays black persons as violent, rapists, and criminals. As Richard Corliss wrote for *Time* magazine on the significance of the film on its one hundredth anniversary, "This was not simply a racist film; it was one whose brilliant storytelling technique lent plausibility and poignancy to the nation of blacks as stupid, venal and brutal." Richard Corliss, "D. W. Griffith's *The Birth of a Nation* 100 Years Later: Still Great, Still Shameful," *Time*, March 3, 2015, http://time.com/3729807/d-w-griffiths-the-birth-of-a-nation-10.

26. CBS, "The Legacy of Lynching," *60 Minutes*, August 12, 2018, https://www.cbsnews.com/video/oprah-winfrey-inside-the-memorial-to-victims-of-lynching-60-minutes/.

27. The citation is from the Equal Justice Initiative, *Lynching in America: Confronting the Legacy of Racial Terror*, 3rd ed. (Montgomery, AL: Equal Justice Initiative, 2017), opening page.

28. See "The National Memorial for Peace and Justice," https://museumandmemorial.eji.org/memorial. Just a short walk away is a museum that vividly depicts the dark story of racism in America. Called the Legacy Museum: From Enslavement to Mass Incarceration, it is located "on a site in Montgomery where enslaved people were once warehoused. A block from one of the most prominent slave auction spaces in America, the Legacy Museum is steps away from an Alabama dock and rail station where tens of thousands of black people were trafficked during the 19th century." The purpose of the memorial and museum focused on slavery and lynching is, in part, to acknowledge and come to terms with part of America's history. Its aim is to remember what happened and recognize that the brutal treatment of black people in America did not end with slavery, and to promote the healing of racial divides.

29. "National Memorial for Peace and Justice."

and even sent postcards.[30] In some cases, newspapers did not merely report a lynching after it happened, but announced that it would take place. For example, a headline in the Jackson, Mississippi *Daily News* on Thursday, June 26, 1919 read "John Hartfield Will Be Lynched by Ellisville Mob at 5 O'Clock This Afternoon." Underneath the headline it read, "Thousands of People Are Flocking into Ellisville to Attend the Event—Sheriff and Authorities Are Powerless to Prevent It."[31]

The lynchings were not just done by the Ku Klux Klan or other overtly racist groups, but by community leaders and public officials, and mobs. A trial was not necessary, simply an accusation. Sometimes women and children were lynched, either because they were accused of an offense or because the accused man could not be found, so his wife or child was taken to be lynched. While many were lynched after being accused of rape or some other crime, often it was simply because a black man sought equal treatment under the law or in the workplace. In some cases the "offense" was even more trivial. At the National Memorial for Peace and Justice, one plaque reads, "Robert Morton was lynched in Rockfield, Kentucky, in 1897 for writing a note to a white woman." Another reads, "David Hunter was lynched in Laurens County, South Carolina, in 1898 for leaving the farm where he worked without permission."[32] One man is lynched for allegedly trying "to enter a room where three white women were sitting"; another for knocking on the door of a white woman's house; another for calling a white police officer by his name without referring to him as "mister"; still another for "accidentally bumping into a white girl as he ran to catch a train."[33]

These atrocities are part of the history of racism in the United States, and while the period of violent lynching eventually came to an end, it ought never to be forgotten. Among other things, it alerts us to the reality of hatred that exists in the human heart, and to the danger that violence can be perpetrated against other people for no other reason than the color of their skin.

Beyond Racism? Civil Rights and Ongoing Wrongs

Brown vs. Board of Education

In 1951, after more than a half century of the legal standard of "separate but equal," Oliver Brown tried to enroll his nine-year-old daughter Linda at Sumner Elementary

---

30. The *60 Minutes* segment, for example, describes a newspaper account in which a teenage black man named Jesse Washington was convicted of murder in Waco, Texas, after a one-hour trial. A mob dragged Washington from the courthouse to the public square to be lynched. The newspaper printed a picture of the crowd and the lynching, with the headline: "Burn Young Negro in Public Square as 15,000 Look On: His Clothing Oil-Soaked, He Is Strung to Tree, Fire Is Set Under Him, and He Is Dropped into Flames." CBS, "Legacy of Lynching."
31. A picture of the actual newspaper page is printed in the Equal Justice Initiative report, *Lynching in America*, 34.
32. These examples were featured in the *60 Minutes* episode "Legacy of Lynching." The Equal Justice Initiative report, *Lynching in America*, details many other trivial examples.
33. Equal Justice Initiative, *Lynching in America*, 30–31.

School in Topeka, Kansas. Sumner was an all-white school at the time, and when Linda was blocked from enrollment, her father sued the Topeka Board of Education. The court's landmark decision in the case of *Brown v. Board of Education* came on May 17, 1954, declaring that the doctrine of "separate but equal" in public education was unconstitutional, requiring the desegregation of public schools.[34] While the unanimous ruling was decisive, the implementation was slow. Because of white defiance of the decision, the court issued a separate decision a year later, allowing for gradual implementation that would take into account various difficulties in local municipalities. "While calling for compliance 'with all deliberate speed,' the Court reflected the ambivalence of the justices, executive and congressional leadership, and the vast majority of Americans about dismantling racial segregation in the South."[35] There were practical challenges to the desegregation of schools. For instance, community schools in many places were effectively segregated because the communities themselves were segregated.

But there was also fierce resistance to desegregation.[36] Ten years after *Brown*, only 1 percent of black children in the South attended predominantly white schools.[37] Still, *Brown v. Board of Education* was a momentous decision. Patricia Sullivan writes, "*Brown* was a major turning point in the struggle for civil rights, and it marked the beginning of the most celebrated chapter of the Civil Rights Movement. The decade that followed saw a heightening interplay between Southern blacks striving to realize the promise of *Brown* in the face of 'massive resistance' by Southern whites and the equivocal response of the federal government, unfolding on an increasingly national and international stage."[38]

Civil rights and voting rights acts

In the midst of tensions over desegregation, and less than a year after the assassination of President John F. Kennedy, a civil rights bill was passed. Signed into law by President Lyndon Johnson on July 2, 1964, the Civil Rights Act of 1964 "prohibited discrimination in the workplace, public accommodations, public facilities, and agencies receiving

---

34. Emanuella Grinberg, Sheena Jones, and Amir Vera, "Linda Brown, Woman at the Center of Brown v. Board Case, Dies," CNN, March 26, 2018, https://www.cnn.com/2018/03/26/us/linda-brown-dies/index.html. See also Patricia Sullivan, "Civil Rights Movement," in Appiah and Gates, *Africana*, 446.
35. Sullivan, "Civil Rights Movement," 446.
36. As with earlier arguments for slavery, there were fallacious "biblical" arguments made for segregation. For an account of arguments appealing to the Bible for and against segregation during the period shortly after the *Brown v. Board of Education* decision, see the Southern Baptist ethicist Henlee H. Barnette, *Introducing Christian Ethics* (Nashville: Broadman, 1961), 135–39. Barnette gives evidence of church segregation from his own denomination, citing a study at the time indicating that "of the more than 30,000 Southern Baptist churches in 1958 there were only 14 with Negro members" (141).
37. Sullivan, "Civil Rights Movement," 446. In her survey of the civil rights movement, Sullivan recounts the fierce opposition to desegregation and to voter registration, which led to the murder of a number of leaders in the movement, some of whom were attacked or gunned down in public places.
38. Sullivan, "Civil Rights Movement," 446.

federal funds, and strengthened prohibitions on school segregation and discrimination in voter registration."[39] The bill authorized the attorney general to enforce school integration, and federal funds could be held back from schools that did not comply. In order to try to ensure passage of the bill, the president decided not to include action on voting rights in the 1964 Civil Rights Act. Indeed, none of the civil rights legislations to that point had made it a priority to ensure voting rights and eliminate discrimination.

However, voting rights legislation would come in the following year. A coalition led by Martin Luther King Jr. converged on Selma, Alabama, in January of 1965 with marches aimed at drawing attention to the violence and intimidation that sought to keep black people from voting. The brutality exhibited by police toward demonstrators at the Edmund Pettis Bridge on March 7, 1965, brought nationwide media attention to the issue, and President Johnson moved quickly to pass voting legislation. The Voting Rights Act of 1965 was signed into law by the president on August 6, 1965, giving the federal government more power to prevent discrimination in voter registration and allowing black people greater access to vote than at any time since the end of Reconstruction.[40]

The great civil rights campaigner: Martin Luther King Jr. and his "Letter from a Birmingham Jail"

In the early 1960s, Martin Luther King Jr. emerged as the leading spokesperson for civil rights, due to the fact that he was eloquent and well-educated, a man of courage and vision, and a gifted strategist and organizer who had a conviction that lasting change must come through peaceful protest and nonviolent direct action. In 1963, King helped to organize demonstrations and a boycott of stores in Birmingham, Alabama, one of the most segregated and violent cities in America at that time. The police commissioner Bull Connor was dedicated to maintaining segregation. He obtained a federal court order to stop the protests, which led to the arrest of many, including King and other leaders of the Southern Christian Leadership Conference.[41]

A group of clergy wrote a letter directed to King and others, appealing to "law and order" in addressing racial problems in Alabama. They argued that "honest convictions in racial matters" should be pursued in the courts, and that court decisions "should in the meantime be peacefully observed." Further, they asserted that "responsible citizens" were working on resolving racial problems and that there was an opportunity for a "constructive and realistic" approach

---

39. Library of Congress, "The Civil Rights Act of 1964: A Long Struggle for Freedom," http://www.loc.gov/exhibits/civil-rights-act/civil-rights-act-of-1964.html. See also Sullivan, "Civil Rights Movement," 450.
40. The National Archives, "Congress and the Voting Rights Act of 1965," https://www.archives.gov/legislative/features/voting-rights-1965. See also Sullivan, "Civil Rights Movement," 450. Prior to this legislation, the Twenty-fourth Amendment, passed on January 23, 1964, ended the poll tax, which required voters to pay a tax before voting in national elections, discriminating against the poor and especially aimed at potential black voters.
41. Sullivan, "Civil Rights Movement," 450.

to the problems. They recognized "the natural impatience of people who feel that their hopes are slow in being realized," but they were concerned that the demonstrations in Birmingham were "unwise and untimely." Moreover, they called attention to the fact that the demonstrations were being led by outsiders, and they suggested that racial issues in Birmingham could be addressed better by "citizens of our own metropolitan area, white and Negro," who have better knowledge of the situation. While they decried "hatred and violence" as having no sanction in religion or politics, they also opposed demonstrations—even peaceful ones—that could stir up racial tensions. They concluded by saying that "when rights are consistently denied, a cause should be pressed in the courts and in negotiations among local leaders, and not in the streets. We appeal to both our white and Negro citizenry to observe the principles of law and order and common sense."[42]

It is often the case that even those who are sympathetic with a cause—including people who are not directly experiencing injustice and some who are—express these kinds of concerns. While sympathetic, they do not want to disturb the "peace," and they assert that it is better to wait for changes that will

eventually come. King's response to these pastors became one of his best-known writings, his "Letter from a Birmingham Jail." In it we see King's rationale for the demonstrations in Birmingham and, more generally, his defense of nonviolent direct action, as well as his opposition to segregation.[43]

In his letter, King explains his reasons for coming to Birmingham. To be clear, he didn't simply show up as an outsider. Rather, he says, he came because he was invited to come, because he had organizational ties to local groups through the Southern Christian Leadership Conference, which he served as president. More than that, he came because there was injustice in Birmingham. He could not remain in Atlanta and be unconcerned about injustice in Birmingham because, he states, "injustice anywhere is a threat to justice everywhere." King recognizes the opposition of local clergy to the demonstrations, but wishes they would show equal concern for "the conditions that brought the demonstrations into being." He agrees that the situation is unfortunate, but even more unfortunate is the fact that "the white power structure of this city left the Negro community with no other alternative." Negotiations with the white community and its businesses had tried, for example, to remove humiliating

---

42. The letter from the clergy and King's letter in response can be found in the Stanford Web Archive Portal online, https://swap.stanford.edu/20141218230016/http://mlk-kpp01.stanford.edu/kingweb/popular_requests/frequent-docs/clergy.pdf. For a facsimile of King's letter, as well as other King papers and relevant information from the period, see Stanford University, the Martin Luther King, Jr. Research and Education Institute, okra.stanford.edu/transcription/document_images/undecided/630416-019.pdf.

43. For the citations from the letter that follow, see King, "Letter from Birmingham Jail." My intention in giving some detail to King's letter is to serve as a reminder of the realities of the struggle King and others faced, and to highlight ways in which some things remain the same. Perhaps his writing provides insights concerning some of the racial tensions that exist decades later.

racists signs from stores, but promises were repeatedly made and broken. They realized that nothing would be done without direct action. Concerned about possible violence and retaliation, King organized workshops on nonviolent direct action, and urged participants to engage in peaceful protests, to refuse to retaliate if attacked, and to be prepared to endure jail if necessary.

King agrees that negotiation is the best way forward, and explains that demonstrations were organized so that the issue could no longer be ignored and the resistant majority would be forced to negotiate. He observes that "history is the long and tragic story of the fact that privileged groups seldom give up their privileges voluntarily." Rather, he continues, "we know through painful experience that freedom is never voluntarily given by the oppressor; it must be demanded by the oppressed." Against the assertion that the demonstrations were untimely, and that the protestors needed to be patient, King argues that time itself does not effect change. "For years now," he said, "I have heard the word 'wait!' It rings in the ear of every Negro with a piercing familiarity. This 'wait' has almost always meant 'never.'" In a piercing description of racism and segregation, King writes,

> I guess it is easy for those who have never felt the stinging darts of segregation to say wait. But when you have seen vicious mobs lynch your mothers and fathers at will and drown your sisters and brothers at whim; when you have seen hate filled policemen curse, kick, brutalize, and even kill your black brothers and sisters with impunity; when you see the vast majority of your twenty million Negro brothers smothering in an air-tight cage of poverty in the midst of an affluent society; when you suddenly find your tongue twisted and your speech stammering as you seek to explain to your six-year-old daughter why she can't go to the public amusement park that has just been advertised on television, and see tears welling up in her little eyes when she is told that Funtown is closed to colored children, and see the depressing clouds of inferiority begin to form in her little mental sky, and see her begin to distort her little personality by unconsciously developing a bitterness toward white people; when you have to concoct an answer for a five-year-old son asking in agonizing pathos: "Daddy, why do white people treat colored people so mean?"; when you take a cross country drive and find it necessary to sleep night after night in the uncomfortable corners of your automobile because no motel will accept you; when you are humiliated day in and day out by nagging signs reading "white" men and "colored" . . . when you are harried by day and haunted by night by the fact that you are a Negro . . . then you will understand why we find it difficult to wait.

Asked how he could promote breaking some laws and obedience to others, King advances one of his best-known arguments. Simply put, he says, "there are two types of laws: There are just and there are unjust laws." Further, he argues, in agreement with Saint Augustine, "an unjust law is no law at all."

He explains, "A just law is a man-made code that squares with the moral law or the law of God. An unjust law is a code that is out of harmony with the moral law." In concrete terms, he asserts, "An unjust law is a code that a majority inflicts on a minority that is not binding on itself. This is difference made legal. On the other hand a just law is a code that a majority compels a minority to follow that it is willing to follow itself. This is sameness made legal." As a further example, he says, "An unjust law is a code inflicted upon a minority which that minority had no part in enacting or creating because they did not have the unhampered right to vote." He also gives examples where a law may be "just on its face but unjust in its application." For instance, he writes, "I was arrested Friday on a charge of parading without a permit. Now there is nothing wrong with an ordinance which requires a permit for a parade, but when the ordinance is used to preserve segregation and to deny citizens the First Amendment privilege of peaceful assembly and peaceful protest, then it becomes unjust."

King goes on to argue that a greater obstacle to the "Negro's" freedom is not those who directly oppose them, such as the Ku Klux Klan, but "the white moderate who is more devoted to 'order' than to justice; who prefers a negative peace which is the absence of tension to a positive peace which is the presence of justice." King recognizes that something must be done to change the status quo, and that one of the dangers of doing nothing is to let frustrations grow to the point of violent uprising. King's commitment was to

nonviolent direct action as an alternative to both extremes. White moderates, however well-intentioned, tended to gloss over the problem. King writes, "I guess I should have realized that few members of a race that has oppressed another race can understand or appreciate the deep groans and passionate yearnings of those that have been oppressed and still fewer have the vision to see that injustice must be rooted out by strong, persistent and determined action." He expresses gratitude for a handful of white leaders and churches that demonstrate a commitment to justice, but is disappointment that they are so few. He writes, "I have heard numerous religious leaders of the South call upon their worshippers to comply with a desegregation decision because it is the law, but I have longed to hear white ministers say, 'follow this decree because integration is morally right and the Negro is your brother.' In the midst of blatant injustices inflicted upon the Negro, I have watched white churches stand on the sidelines and merely mouth pious irrelevances and sanctimonious trivialities." King calls on the church to be like the early church, which did not simply reflect its own culture's ideas, principles, and opinions, but transformed society. He expresses hope that the contemporary church can do so as well, and that some have indeed "carved a tunnel of hope through the dark mountain of disappointment."

King's "Letter from a Birmingham Jail" serves as a reminder that the fight for justice is sometimes costly, that well-meaning people may oppose injustice but offer little actual resistance to it, and that often those in the majority or in a privileged position have a difficult time appreciating the depth of struggle experienced by minority groups. It is also a reminder that change does not happen spontaneously, but requires a clear voice and persistent action.[44] King advocated not only active, direct engagement, but also a commitment to nonviolence in the process.

The legacy of racism

Civil rights legislation in the 1950s and 1960s represented hard-won victories over racist laws, policies, and practices. However, having become so deeply engrained in society, in both practices and attitudes, racial prejudice proved difficult to root out. For instance, in housing practices, zoning laws and other policies not only maintained segregation but also led to great disparity between white, increasingly suburban, park-like neighborhoods and predominantly black urban neighborhoods where industry, bars, and nightclubs were permitted.[45] After decades of entrenched practices in housing, schools, churches, and other facilities, informal segregation remains in many areas.[46]

Legislation has not eradicated racial discrimination, let alone racial prejudice.

Issues surrounding race are highly contentious and polarizing. Presuppositions often affect how one interprets data concerning racial justice—for example, whether contemporary problems should be primarily attributed to systemic racism or other causes, and what ought to be done. Whether or not is it possible to identify intentional institutional racism, it is fair to say that there are systemic problems that need to be addressed, and that we ought to come together to make significant efforts to effect change. In housing and economics, past policies segregated black communities, creating generational challenges for mobility and wealth creation. By many economic measures, including employment, wages, poverty, and welfare, African Americans are worse off than whites.[47] There are also educational challenges, with failing school systems that disproportionately affect black communities, which has a long-term impact.[48] The causes of many of these challenges are complex and debated, and there should be open and honest discussion, with

44. For an account of civil rights and other reform movements, and how they work, see Tim Stafford, *Shaking the System: What I Learned from the Great American Reform Movements* (Downers Grove, IL: InterVarsity Press, 2007).

45. For a description of some of the zoning laws and their effects on housing segregation, see Richard Rothstein, *The Color of Law: A Forgotten History of How Our Government Segregated America* (New York: Liveright, 2017). My thanks to one of my students, Michael Matala, for drawing my attention to this resource.

46. For a brief summary of segregation and the legacy of *Plessy v. Ferguson*, see Lily Rothman, "The Long Death of the 'Separate but Equal' Doctrine," *Time*, May 18, 2016, http://time.com/4326692/plessy-ferguson-history-120.

47. It is notable that there is a significant white population that is often overlooked, which closely mirrors the challenges to many urban black communities. Particularly found in large pockets of the Appalachians, their challenges are described by J. D. Vance in *Hillbilly Elegy: A Memoir of a Family and Culture in Crisis* (New York: HarperCollins, 2016).

48. For a survey of a number of injustices disproportionately affecting African Americans, see Glen H. Stassen and David P. Gushee, *Kingdom Ethics: Following Jesus in Contemporary Context* (Downers Grove, IL: InterVarsity Press, 2003), 391–98.

fair consideration of data.[49] For instance, the highly regarded economist Thomas Sowell challenges the attribution of many economic and social inequities in African American communities to the legacy of slavery. Sowell, an African American, offers data to show that many of the statistics related to employment, crime, family structure, and so on were more favorable in the early to middle twentieth century, and actually worsened or remained the same in the decades after civil rights legislation.[50]

A brief look at criminal justice, housing, and education will offer a glimpse into problems faced by African American communities.

Criminal justice

One area that gets a lot of attention in terms of systemic racial injustice is the criminal justice system. As noted earlier, not long after the abolition of slavery, black men were depicted as dangerous criminals. Arrests and convictions could be made without due process or a fair trial, especially when black people were often not allowed to serve on juries.[51] This both encouraged and was reinforced by decades of lynching, where black "suspects" were treated inhumanely, beaten,

burned alive, and hung, often simply with the assumption of guilt on the part of white crowds. They were not presumed innocent or given due process. While lynching eventually came to an end, the idea that black men are dangerous, and the presumption of guilt, persisted. The Equal Justice Initiative report notes that "the Civil Rights Act of 1964, a signature legal achievement of the civil rights movement, contains provisions designed to eliminate discrimination in voting, education, and employment, but it does not address discrimination in criminal justice." Further, the report asserts that "the criminal justice system remains the institution in American life least impacted by the civil rights movement."[52]

The inequities against black men in the criminal justice system can be seen in several ways. For instance, according to the Bureau of Justice Statistics, the likelihood of imprisonment at some point in his life for a white man is one in seventeen; for a black man it is one in three.[53] In 2016, "blacks represented 12% of the U.S. adult population but 33% of the sentenced prison population. Whites accounted for 64% of adults but 30% of prisoners." In terms of the imprisonment rate, in the same year, 2016, "there were

---

49. Causes include the history of racism, including segregation, and the breakdown of the family, which affected African American communities dramatically and especially in recent decades. These and other causes need to be considered carefully, for no significant solution can be formed without an adequate understanding of the causes.
50. See his discussion in "Racial Facts and Fallacies" in Thomas Sowell, *Economic Facts and Fallacies*, 2nd ed. (New York: Basic Books, 2011), 172–205.
51. See details in Equal Justice Initiative, *Lynching in America*, 60–61.
52. Equal Justice Initiative, *Lynching in America*, 61.
53. Thomas P. Bonczar, "Prevalence of Imprisonment in the U.S. Population, 1974–2001," Bureau of Justice Statistics Special Report, August 2003, https://www.bjs.gov/content/pub/pdf/piusp01.pdf, based on 2001 incarceration rates.

1,608 black prisoners for every 100,000 black adults—more than five times the imprisonment rate for whites (274 per 100,000)."[54] These numbers reflect in part a difference in economic status (and thus a difference in legal representation), and a higher crime rate in some urban neighborhoods that are predominantly African American. Yet part of the explanation is racial bias in laws and sentencing. As one advocacy group puts it, "Overall, African Americans are more likely than white Americans to be arrested; once arrested, they are more likely to be convicted; and once convicted, they are more likely to face stiff sentences."[55]

For instance, in the 1980s, tough sentences were adopted to deal with what was called the "crack epidemic." Possession of crack cocaine could carry the same sentence as the possession of one hundred times the amount of powder cocaine, a difference with racial bias. Indeed, a *U.S. News & World Report* article reported that "according to the U.S. Sentencing Commission figures, no class of drug is as racially skewed as crack in terms of numbers of offenses." In 2009, for instance, 79 percent of crack offenders who were sentenced were black, while 10 percent were white. For powder cocaine, 28 percent were black and 17 percent were white.[56] Part of the rationale for tougher sentences for crack cocaine was that it was associated with higher rates of violent crime. However, that disparity could have been addressed by stiffening penalties in cases that involved violent crime. Whether tougher sentences demonstrate direct or indirect racial injustice, it seems to indicate bias in the criminal justice system. Not only was the sentencing skewed, but arrest rates were as well, for according to Jasmine Tyler of the Drug Policy Alliance, while 79 percent of sentenced crack offenders were black, public health data show that two-thirds of users were white or Latino.[57] In 2010, Congress passed the Fair Sentencing Act, which reduced the sentencing disparity between the possession of crack cocaine and powder cocaine.[58]

Housing and education

It is not just criminal justice that has a long history of racial bias. When the Federal Housing Administration was formed in 1934, homeownership—a significant source of wealth creation—was expanded for whites through guaranteed loans. That was not the case for blacks, because the Federal Housing Administration refused to guarantee loans for

---

54. John Gramlich, "The Gap between the Number of Blacks and Whites in Prison Is Shrinking," Pew Research Center, January 12, 2018, http://www.pewresearch.org/fact-tank/2018/01/12/shrinking-gap-between-number-of-blacks-and-whites-in-prison. Similarly, according to the Federal Bureau of Prisons statistics, in the federal prison system, the percentage of black inmates is 37.8 percent. Federal Bureau of Prisons, "Inmate Race," last updated February 15, 2020, https://www.bop.gov/about/statistics/statistics_inmate_race.jsp.

55. From The Sentencing Project, "Criminal Justice Facts," https://www.sentencingproject.org/criminal-justice-facts/.

56. From Danielle Kurtzleben, "Data Show Racial Disparity in Crack Sentencing." *U.S. News & World Report* online, August 3, 2010, https://www.usnews.com/new/articles/2010/08/03/data-show-racial-disparity-in-crack-sentencing.

57. Kurtzleben, "Data Show Racial Disparity in Crack Sentencing."

58. Kurtzleben, "Data Show Racial Disparity in Crack Sentencing." Senator Ron Paul, who supported the bill, said it did not go far enough, calling it the "Slightly Fairer Resentencing Act."

them. The Federal Housing Administration even *graded* neighborhoods, and identified them by color, to indicate where they would and would not back loans.[59] "Redlining" is the name that was later given to this practice, wherein predominantly black neighborhoods were areas where banks would not invest, which not only affected housing but also commercial investments, including grocery stores and other necessities.

Further, zoning laws often prevent the building of apartments and affordable houses in wealthy, predominantly white neighborhoods. These may not be aimed at excluding African Americans (though they may have been in the past), but the effect is that they often do. Income and wealth as much as race determine what neighborhood people live in, shaping patterns of diversity.[60] Studies have shown that racial diversity adversely affects property values, which creates disincentives for changing zoning in a way that would increase diversity.[61] The result is that housing values in wealthy areas increase significantly while in poorer areas they remain flat or even decrease, having an adverse effect on racial minorities. To seek or welcome diversity through a change in certain zoning policies may involve some personal financial loss (or slower gain) for some, but it also creates more opportunity for lower-income people to enjoy the benefits associated with wealthier neighborhoods.

Progress Is Not a Straight Line

Racial disparities and problems are real, and yet there has also been significant progress, which ought not to be discounted. As Ellis Cose put it in the opening of an article in *Newsweek* in 1999, "By a wide array of measures, now is a great time—the best time ever—to be black in America."[62] He writes,

> Black employment and home ownership are up. Murders and violent crimes are down. Reading and math proficiency are climbing. Out-of-wedlock births are at their lowest rate in four decades. Fewer blacks are on welfare than at any point in recent memory. More are in college than at any point in history. And the percentage of black families living below the poverty line is the lowest it has been since the Census Bureau began keeping separate black poverty statistics in 1967. Even for some of the most persistently unfortunate—uneducated black men between 16 and 24—jobs are opening up. . . . More and more blacks have entered the

---

59. See, e.g., Alexis C. Madrigal, "The Racist Housing Policy That Made Your Neighborhood," *The Atlantic*, May 22, 2014, https://www.theatlantic.com/business/archive/2014/05/the-racist-housing-policy-that-made-your-neighborhood/371439.

60. Where there has been significant increase in neighborhood diversity, it is mainly because of a growth in Asian and Hispanic populations, rather than the integration of black and white populations. Dayna Bowen Matthew, Edward Rodrigue, and Richard V. Reeves, "Time for Justice: Tackling Race Inequalities in Health and Housing," *Brookings*, October 19, 2016, https://www.brookings.edu/research/time-for-justice-tackling-race-inequalities-in-health-and-housing.

61. Richard D. Kahlenberg, "The Walls We Won't Tear Down," *New York Times*, August 3, 2017, https://www.nytimes.com/2017/08/03/opinion/sunday/zoning-laws-segregation-income.html.

62. Ellis Cose, "The Good News about Black America," *Newsweek*, June 6, 1999, https://www.newsweek.com/good-news-about-black-america-167404.

realm of the privileged and have offices in (or tantalizingly near to) the corridors of corporate and political power. Some control multimillion-dollar budgets and reside in luxurious communities. They are, by any criteria, living large—walking testaments to the transformative power, to the possibility, of America.[63]

There are African American icons and role models in every sector of American culture, including music, education, television and movies, sports, business, politics (including the first ever African American president), and law (including the Supreme Court), to name a few. These were barely imaginable to many in earlier generations. In terms of politics, which is a significant marker, since politicians not only hold leadership but also influence many segments of society, there has also been progress.[64]

As with many things, racial progress does not move in a straight line. Alongside advances there have been setbacks and reality checks, which serve as a reminder that injustices exist and there is work to be done. Less than a decade after Cose wrote the *Newsweek* article, America elected its first African American president, a very significant sign of progress in race relations in America. Yet, after a giant leap forward, there have been backward steps, and racial tensions heated up in the second decade of the twenty-first century. Further, while Cose emphasized a lot of positive statistics, he also cited a number of negative facts that should not be ignored, including ongoing high rates of unemployment especially for twenty- to twenty-four-year-old black males; a high percentage of black males in certain areas who are either in jail, on parole, or probation; as well as concerns about a lack of progress in education, welfare, income, and the ongoing problem of racism. Cose sums things up by asserting,

> The good news on black America is too clear to deny. In the past few decades, blacks' fortunes and prospects have soared toward the heavens. Blacks have entered virtually every sector of American society and breathed life into Martin Luther King's extraordinary fantasy. . . . The bad news, however, is equally profound, and it can be summed up

---

63. Cose, "Good News about Black America." For more recent statistics on employment, according to the Bureau of Labor Statistics, the unemployment rate for Black or African American dropped from 7.9 percent in July of 2017 to 6.5 percent in August of 2018. US Bureau of Labor Statistics, economic news release, "Table A-2. Employment Status of the Civilian Population by Race, Sex, and Age," last modified February 21, 2020, https://www.bls.gov/news.release/empsit.t02.htm.

64. The progress has been greater in more localized elections. For instance, in 2019 there were only three black senators (compared to zero or one most years since 1965) and no black governors; however, there were fifty-two black members of the US House of Representatives, compared with six in 1964, "putting the share of black House members (12%) on par with the share of blacks in the U.S. population overall for the first time in history." See Anna Brown and Sara Atske, "Blacks Have Made Gains in U.S. Political leadership, but Gaps Remain," Pew Research Center, January 18, 2019, https://www.pewresearch.org/fact-tank/2019/01/18/blacks-have-made-gains-in-u-s-political-leadership-but-gaps-remain; and Ida A. Brudnick and Jennifer E. Manning, "African American Members of the United States Congress: 1870–2018," Congressional Research Service, April 26, 2018, https://fas.org/sgp/crs/misc/RL30378.pdf.

with two simple facts. Despite all the progress of the last several decades, we continue to talk about black America as a place and a people apart. And despite the lip service we pay to the concept of equality, we look with equanimity, even pride, upon a statistical profile of black Americans that, were it of whites, would be a source of horror and consternation. That is not likely to change soon; but until and unless it does, our great nation will never become the country of our finest dreams.[65]

It is possible to focus on either the great progress that has been made or the serious problems that remain to the exclusion of the other. Honesty should compel us to be thankful for the progress that has been made, for we have come a long way as a society. Yet honesty should also compel us to recognize that there is much work to be done to address existing racial disparities and injustices.

Critical Race Theory and the Ongoing Pervasiveness of Racism

Critical race theory developed as a response to a slowing of progress and the persistence of racism following the civil rights movement. Philosophically there are connections between critical race theory and movements representing legal reform, feminism, and

LGBT rights. Critical race theory examines the reality of racism in society, which exists in spite of political and legal measures intended to eliminate it (or at least its overt expression), and in spite of a widespread rejection of racism. Critical race theory recognizes that enlightenment and education do not eliminate racism, contrary to common liberal suppositions. One summary highlights three main arguments made by critical race theory. First, that racism is the normal state of affairs in America—that is, it goes well beyond overt displays by racists groups and symbols; it infuses our institutions, patterns of thought, and actions. Second, systemic racism serves the interests of white people, in various ways privileging whites over nonwhites. Third, the idea of race (particularly positing different races of human beings on the basis of skin color or other physical features) is a social construct created by the white majority to subjugate and maintain power over nonwhites. Further, it is argued, social inequality continues to result from this false construct, advantaging whites and disadvantaging nonwhites.[66]

There has been no shortage of criticism of critical race theory, often because it is marked by opposition to traditional values and property interests, and because it rejects the notion of pursuing things such as neutrality, equal opportunity, and

---

65. Cose, "Good News about Black America."
66. Richard Delgado and Jean Stefancic, *Critical Race Theory: An Introduction*, 3rd ed. (New York: New York University Press, 2017), 8–9. See also, Angela P. Harris, "Critical Race Theory," in *International Encyclopedia of the Social & Behavioral Sciences*, eds. Neil J. Smelser and Paul B. Baltes (Amsterdam: Elsevier, 2012), 5, https://works.bepress.com/angela_harris/17/. Harris comments that, since its main tenets are often challenged, CTR is also "a study of collective denial" (5).

color-blindness.[67] These things are rejected for a number of reasons. In part, it is argued, they ignore the problem of racism and attempt simply to live as though it does not exist, thus perpetuating racism and maintaining the privilege of the majority white population. Insisting on "color-blindness" and "neutrality," and that we should live as if color does not matter, ignores systemic racism, presuming and maintaining a myth that we have moved beyond a racialized society.[68]

Many people resist the view that racism is systemic, arguing that it is mainly a problem of individual expression.[69] Further, in debates about color-blindness and other issues, the two (or more) sides seem not only to be holding different presuppositions but to be talking about different things altogether. For example, many who affirm color-blindness do not mean to pretend as if racism doesn't exist (even, in some cases, systemic racism), or that we should not notice or appreciate our differences. Rather, they mean that we should not treat people differently based on the color of their skin, an extension of the belief that justice should be blind. It is fair to ask whether this represents wishful thinking and not reality, but some such notion is necessary if the very discrimination that critical race theory proponents rightly highlight is to be avoided.

In any case, Christians need not reject some of the claims made by critical race theory, even if it represents an inadequate understanding of the problems it examines, and therefore also inadequate answers, largely due to faulty presuppositions.[70] Critical race theory recognizes that racism is a greater problem than just isolated incidences of prejudice, hatred, and discrimination by individuals. Rather, it is a common human experience and state of affairs, part of a broader enmity between individuals and groups. Yet an adequate description of the problem, and the way forward, will not come from critical race theory, but from Scripture. As Vincent Bacote asserts, we must "turn to Scripture and use categories rooted in creation and redemption in order to have an anthropology that better

---

67. For an early critique of critical race theory, see Daniel Subotnik, "What's Wrong with Critical Race Theory: Reopening the Case for Middle Class Values," *Cornell Journal of Law and Public Policy* 7, no. 3 (Spring 1998): 681–756, https://scholarship.law.cornell.edu/cgi/viewcontent.cgi?article=1238&context=cjlpp; see also Douglas E. Litowitz, "Some Critical Thoughts on Critical Race Theory," *Notre Dame Law Review* 72, no. 2 (1997): 503–29, https://scholarship.law.nd.edu/cgi/viewcontent.cgi?article=1844&context=ndlr.

68. For a brief description of critical race theory and the "problem" of "color-blindness," see Jarvis Williams, "The Cruelty of the Color-Blind Theory of Race in Evangelical Churches," The Witness, March 3, 2016, https://thewitnessbcc.com/cruelty-of-color-blind-theory-in-churches.

69. This includes many white evangelicals, though there are (increasingly) a wide range of views among them. See the significant study of white evangelicals described in Michael O. Emerson and Christian Smith, *Divided by Faith: Evangelical Religion and the Problem of Race in America* (New York: Oxford University Press, 2000). Also an excerpt in Emerson and Smith, "Color-Blinded," *Christianity Today*, October 2, 2000, https://www.christianity-today.com/ct/2000/october2/2.36.html.

70. Anthony B. Bradley underscores a similar problem with wrong presuppositions in black liberation theology in his *Liberating Black Theology: The Bible and the Black Experience in America* (Wheaton, IL: Crossway, 2010), esp. 17–34.

promotes human flourishing and enables us to 'see' better."[71]

A Biblical Perspective on Race, Racism, and Reconciliation

Race Is Not a Black-and-White Issue in Scripture

In Scripture, race does not refer to a people's skin color. What is translated as "human race" in the Psalms (CSB), for instance, is the term for human beings (אָדָם). For example, Psalm 12:1 says,

> Help, LORD, for no faithful one remains;
> the loyal have disappeared from the human race.[72]

In the New Testament, the CSB uses the term "race" ("our race," Acts 7:19; "Abraham's race," Acts 13:26) to translate the term γένος, which means offspring, or family in that context. Γένος can also refer to "species" or "kind" (used for γένος of fish in Matt. 13:47) or nation or people (e.g., the Gentile woman who was a Syrophoenician by γένος in Mark 7:26, or Barnabas, a γένος of Cyprus).

It is understandable that people find identity markers in their kinship line, ethnic group, or nationality, which are often connected to cultural practices. It is less clear that various groups ought to be understood

by categories of race, especially when reduced to "black" and "white," given the many diverse ethnic groups and increasing number of people of "mixed race." The idea of race identified by skin color, and focused on "black" and "white," is a relatively recent (late fifteenth century) social construct with malicious purpose in justifying race-based slavery. Characteristics such as temperament, moral nature, physical abilities, and intelligence were linked to race by skin color; not only were these exaggerated, but they ignored significant differences within ethnic groups and similarities between different ethnic groups.[73] In the nineteenth century, theories of racial hierarchy were advanced with appeal to Darwinian evolution, providing additional rationale for slavery, segregation, and other evil practices and philosophies.[74] As such, critical race theorists are right to call attention to the common use of race as a social construct, largely used (at least initially) to defend white supremacy.

The Creation of All Human Beings in God's Image

While there are good reasons to challenge the use of common racial categories, various terms related to race are deeply ingrained in our vocabulary and used pervasively as a matter of convenience, such as *race relations*,

---

71. Vincent Bacote, "Erasing Race," in *Black Scholars in White Space: New Vistas in African American Studies from the Christian Academy*, ed. Anthony B. Bradley (Eugene, OR: Pickwick, 2015), 134.
72. See also 12:8; 14:2; 21:10; 53:2; 115:16 (CSB); also Prov. 8:31.
73. Bacote, "Erasing Race," 125–26, citing Steve Fenton, *Ethnicity: Racism, Class and Culture* (Lanham, MD: Rowman and Littlefield, 1999), 66.
74. F. W. Bridger, "Race," in *New Dictionary of Christian Ethics and Pastoral Theology*, eds. David J. Atkinson et al. (Downers Grove, IL: InterVarsity Press, 1995), 716–717.

racism, *racial reconciliation*, and so on. It is unlikely that such usage will be discontinued in the near future. Nevertheless, from a biblical point of view, understanding human beings in the commonly used racial categories is a distortion of the creation accounts in Genesis. There it is declared that God created all human beings in his image, distinguished simply as male and female, and together they are given the responsibility to steward what God has created (Gen. 1:26–28). Thus all human beings share a common humanity and dignity as image bearers—we are all sons and daughters of Adam and Eve (Gen. 3:20; cf. Acts 17:26). There is no racial *difference*, let alone *superiority*, in creation—there is no attention drawn to the ethnicity of Adam and Eve.[75] Nations and ethnicities developed with human migration; all human beings and all ethnicities are united by a common ancestry and humanity far more than we are divided by our differences.[76] If we are to overcome racial conflict and prejudice, we "must begin with the habit of seeing each other as made in the image of God; therefore, possessing inestimable, unfathomable dignity and worth."[77]

The Fall and the Sin of Racism

In biblical perspective, the problem described in critical race theory, the problem of racial bias and discrimination, is pervasive because sin is pervasive. The problem, as they recognize, is not limited to overt expressions of racism, such as the use of racial slurs or a white supremacist gathering or displaying symbols of racism. Just as evidence of unfaithfulness in marriage is found in lust and not merely in adultery, so racial enmity is rooted deep in the heart and not merely in overt acts. Prejudice is expressed invisibly in countless ways, not only showing favoritism to those who are like us but also projecting negative attributes to those who are not. Like individuals, groups are often self-centered and self-protective. We tend to resist giving up power, opportunity, and benefits to others because we do not want to lose them. We develop rationales and create arguments to maintain the status quo, even when it is not valid. Blind spots are difficult to uncover, and we are often unaware of our own prejudices.

The Bible indicates with clarity the pervasive and deadly nature of sin—not simply sinful acts by otherwise good people but also acts that stem from a sinful nature. Rather shockingly, not long after sin enters the world, Cain rises up and kills his brother Abel out of envy (Gen. 4). The problem of sin is worse than we want to acknowledge. In what serves as a commentary that sees Cain's struggle as the human struggle, James writes, "What is the source of wars and fights among you? Don't they

---

75. J. Daniel Hays, "What Are We For?," in *The Gospel and Racial Reconciliation*, eds. Russell Moore and Andrew T. Walker, The Gospel for Life Series (Nashville: B&H, 2016), 6.
76. The Human Genome Project has conducted genetic studies that show that human beings share 99.9 percent of the human genome in common. That is, there is no genetic basis for distinguishing different races among human beings. See "Racial Discrimination" in *ESV Study Bible* (Wheaton, IL: Crossway, 2008), 2557. Discussed in Wayne Grudem, *Christian Ethics: An Introduction to Biblical Moral Reasoning* (Wheaton, IL: Crossway, 2018), 642.
77. Thabiti Anyabwile, "What Does the Gospel Say?," in Moore and Walker, *The Gospel and Racial Reconciliation*, 26.

come from your passions that wage war within you? You desire and do not have. You murder and covet and cannot obtain. You fight and wage war" (James 4:1–2). In Genesis, after God's judgment on human wickedness, God prohibits murderous violence on the basis that human beings are made in his image (Gen. 9:5–6). James condemns verbal violence for the same reason—we ought not to curse one another because we are made in God's image (James 3:9). Because of our equal humanity and dignity, God condemns those who oppress and mock the poor and vulnerable; it is an insult to God himself (Prov. 14:31; 17:5).[78] Jesus reveals that it is not only murder but also verbal violence, both of which are rooted in unrighteous anger, that God condemns (Matt. 5:21–22). To oppress or mock others, to use racial slurs, or to see others as inferior is an offense against the God who created all human beings in his image.

We cannot hope to overcome the problem of racial hostilities if we don't recognize the depths of human depravity, including our own hearts, and our need for the radical change brought by the gospel. It is a sad reality that Christians have been prominent among those who have advocated racial bigotry, in direct opposition to biblical teaching, yet often with a "biblical" defense. It is difficult to reconcile the biblical conviction and evangelistic passion of many Christian leaders in the past with their defense of slavery and segregation. R. Albert Mohler, president of the Southern Baptist Theological Seminary, the flagship seminary of the Southern Baptist Convention (SBC), acknowledges the difficulty within the SBC, which was founded in 1845 as a missionary-sending denomination because other national missionary organizations had refused to send out slaveholders as missionaries. That, Mohler asserts, is a devastating indictment of the SBC's founders, and a stain on the SBC, for "it was not only founded by slaveholders; it was founded by men who held to an ideology of racial superiority and who bathed that ideology in scandalous theological argument."[79] Arguments with appeals to theology and the Bible have been used to justify discrimination, laws against "interracial marriages," segregation, and slavery itself, often grounded in a morally vicious claim of racial superiority.[80]

Yet we should not let egregious forms of racism make us blind to hidden forms. Unless we come to terms with more subtle expressions of racial enmity, racism will persist and efforts at reconciliation will be

---

78. Hays, "What Are We For?," 7.
79. R. Albert Mohler Jr., "Conceived in Sin, Called by the Gospel: The Root Cause of the Stain of Racism in the Southern Baptist Convention," in *Removing the Stain of Racism from the Southern Baptist Convention: Diverse African American and White Perspectives*, eds. Jarvis J. Williams and Kevin M. Jones (Nashville: B&H Academic, 2017), 3. See also the extensive report from Southern Baptist Theological Seminary, "Report on Slavery and Racism in the History of the Southern Baptist Theological Seminary," December 2018, http://www.sbts.edu/wp-content/uploads/2018/12/Racism-and-the-Legacy-of-Slavery-Report-v4.pdf.
80. See, e.g., the brief discussion in John Stott, *Issues Facing Christians Today*, 4th ed. (Grand Rapids: Zondervan, 2006), chap. 10.

hampered.[81] Thabiti Anyabwile asserts that "if we don't take sin seriously, we will be tempted to think that racism, racial animosity, prejudice, and bigotry are justifiable in some measure or eradicable by education alone. You cannot educate people out of racism, racial hatred, and animosity."[82] We need a much deeper and more transformational change, one that comes only when someone is washed, sanctified, and justified "in the name of the Lord Jesus Christ and by the Spirit of our God" (1 Cor. 6:11). Various cultural and ethnic differences are a cause for celebration, not division or prejudice. Those who confess God as the one true God and Creator, and Jesus Christ as Savior and Lord, ought to seek unity, grounded in our common humanity in the image of God and the reconciling work of Jesus on the cross.[83]

Excursus: Slavery in the Bible and in the Ancient Near East

What about slavery in the Bible? How should we understand it, and particularly the reality that slavery is not simply condemned outright? Is there an implication that slavery is not necessarily evil, or that slavery in America could have been defended biblically?

In the ancient world, the institution of slavery was widespread and unquestioned. In the first century AD, about 20 percent of people were slaves, and in Italy it was closer to a third of all people. Ancient slavery had some things in common with the American (and European) slave trade, but also some significant differences. People became slaves in many ways—"as a result of capture in war, default on a debt, inability to support and 'voluntarily' selling oneself, being sold as a child by destitute parents, birth to slave parents, conviction of a crime, or kidnapping and piracy. Slavery cut across races and nationalities."[84] Economies in the ancient world were often built on slave labor for agriculture, mining and building projects, although caring for slaves could be expensive, so many landowners leased their land out to slaves as tenant farmers.[85] The majority of people captured in war were settled in land set aside for them, so that they could work on their own and pay taxes.[86]

Some slaves were used in the gladiatorial games for gruesome "entertainment." Some served as craftsmen, and many as civil and domestic servants. Often slaves had significant responsibilities for managing children and households, and were considered

---

81. We may disagree about particular examples, and there are a great many difficulties, including self-deception and plausible deniability, since, like lust, racial animus often remains invisible. We do well to recognize the broader point and reflect on ways that our sinful desire may indeed be expressed in racial prejudice.

82. Anyabwile, "What Does the Gospel Say?," 28.

83. Cf. Joy Jittaun Moore, "Race," in *Dictionary of Scripture and Ethics*, eds. Joel B. Green et al. (Grand Rapids: Baker Academic, 2011), 654.

84. James A. Brooks, "Slave, Servant," in *Illustrated Bible Dictionary*, eds. Chad Brand, Charles Draper, and Archie England (Nashville: Holman Reference, 2003), 1511. See also Muhammad A. Dandamayev, "Slavery: Ancient Near East, Old Testament," in *Anchor Bible Dictionary*, ed. David Noel Freedman (New York: Doubleday, 1992), 6:59.

85. Dandamayev, "Slavery," 60; see also Brooks, "Slave, Servant," 1511.

86. Dandamayev, "Slavery," 60.

to be part of the household. Slaves had no rights but, with the exception of those who did hard labor, were often treated well and fared better than many free persons. In the first millennium AD, some slaves "owned land, houses, and considerable amounts of movable property," and "actively partici-pated in all spheres of economic activity."[87] Slaves were also able to gain their freedom. Masters often freed their slaves, frequently in their will, and slaves could earn and save money and buy their freedom.[88]

Slavery in the Old Testament

Though the Bible is sometimes portrayed as supporting slavery, and was used in defense of the American slave trade, its laws largely aim at the humane treatment of slaves/ser-vants, with provisions for their freedom.[89] Indeed, as one scholar puts it, "We have in the Bible the first appeals in world literature to treat slaves as human beings for their own sake and not just in the interests of their masters."[90] The Decalogue commands that household slaves be given rest on the Sab-bath (Exod. 20:10; Deut. 5:14). If a man in hardship sold himself to a master, he was to be treated as a hired servant and he was to be released in the year of Jubilee (Lev. 25:39–40). If an Israelite was sold into slavery in Israel because they were financially desti-tute, they were to be freed after six years of service (Exod. 21:2; cf. Deut. 15:12). When a

slave was released, he was to be given plenty of provisions of food and drink and live-stock (Deut. 15:13–14). These things appear, in part, to be a way of giving someone a second chance who failed economically, in-cluding perhaps the opportunity to be men-tored so that it would not happen again.[91] If a man was married when he became a slave, he could take his wife out with him (v. 3). If his master gave him a wife and they had children, they would stay with the master when the slave was freed (v. 4). However, if the slave chose to stay with his wife and chil-dren, he could do so by becoming his mas-ter's slave permanently (vv. 5–6). Israelites were to remember how God had blessed and provided for them, and they were to provide for others. Just as God had freed them from slavery in Egypt, they were to free their slaves (vv. 14–15). In addition, a slave or servant could be redeemed and freed at any time by a relative (Lev. 25:47–55). Masters were not to treat their slaves harshly. If a slave was struck and permanently harmed physically, he was to be released (Exod. 21:26–27).

Slavery in the New Testament world

Scott Bartchy asserts that slavery in the first-century Greco-Roman world was sig-nificantly different from slavery in the New World during the seventeenth through nine-teenth centuries. Significant distinguishing features include the following:

---

87. Dandamayev, "Slavery," 61.
88. Brooks, "Slave, Servant," 1511.
89. See Brooks, "Slave, Servant," 1511.
90. Dandamayev, "Slavery," 65.
91. See John Frame, *Doctrine of the Christian Life* (Phillipsburg, NJ: P&R, 2008), 657, esp. n5.

Racial factors played no role; education was greatly encouraged (some slaves were better educated than their owners) and enhanced a slave's value; many slaves carried out sensitive and highly responsible social functions; slaves could own property (including other slaves!); their religious and culture traditions were the same as those of the freeborn; no laws prohibited public assembly of slaves; and (perhaps above all) the majority of urban and domestic slaves could legitimately anticipate being emancipated by the age of 30.[92]

Moreover, in a world in which abject poverty was very common,[93] many people sold themselves into slavery to pay off debts, to reduce economic hardship and gain security, and to gain status and even Roman citizenship (as many freed slaves were granted).[94] Among the distinguishing features listed above, it is perhaps most significant that first-century slavery was not based on race, and that slavery was not a permanent condition for many slaves. Indeed, by gaining Roman citizenship, freed slaves had opportunities and privileges of all citizens: "In contrast to the fact that in the New World skin color often continued to identify the children of slaves and ex-slaves for many generations, freedmen and women in the Roman Empire easily blended into the general population within one generation."[95] It is difficult to overstate not only the cruel immorality of race-based slavery but also the continuation for generations of prejudice and racism resulting from an institutionalized judgment that a group of persons was considered to be inferior based on the color of their skin.

In the New Testament, slaves were instructed to obey their masters with a willing spirit (Eph. 6:5–8; Col. 3:22–25; 1 Tim. 6:1–2; 1 Pet. 2:18–21). Paul tells slaves that they need not be concerned about seeking their freedom, though if they have the opportunity to do so, they could (1 Cor. 7:20–22). The New Testament authors do not reject slavery outright, perhaps because of the various types of slavery and the good standing that many slaves had within their household. Yet masters are required to treat their slaves well and not threaten them (Eph. 6:9; Col. 4:1), and kidnapping and the slave trade are condemned (1 Tim. 1:10). Most significantly, and radically, slaves and freemen are equal in standing before God and in receiving the gospel (Gal. 3:28). The impact of this is seen in Philemon, where Paul encourages Philemon to receive his servant Onesimus back as a brother in Christ, and not merely as a bondservant (v. 16).

---

92. S. Scott Bartchy, "Slavery: New Testament," in Freedman, *Anchor Bible Dictionary*, 6:66. It must be pointed out that not all slaves had equal opportunities. For instance, those who were made slaves by the courts as convicted criminals would be forced into hard labor, and worked to death, or they may have been forced to become gladiators and fight to the death (Bartchy, "Slavery," 70).

93. For a description of poverty in the Greco-Roman world, with statistical evidence, see Bruce W. Longenecker, *Remembering the Poor: Paul, Poverty, and the Greco-Roman World* (Grand Rapids: Eerdmans, 2010).

94. Bartchy, "Slavery," 67.

95. Bartchy, "Slavery," 72.

Jesus's parable of the merciful slave (Matt. 18:23–34) may be understood with the background of debt slavery, with significant implications for master-slave relations, even manumission. Those whose heavenly father has forgiven sins that they could never atone for are warned not to be like the unmerciful slave. After having been forgiven debt he could have never repaid, the unmerciful slave refused to forgive a small debt that someone owed him. Having been freed by our heavenly Father, how could Jesus's followers continue to enslave one another? In the Lord's Prayer, Jesus teaches his disciples to ask God to

> forgive us our debts,
> as we also have forgiven our debtors. (Matt. 6:12)

Reconciliation in Christ: Implications for Racial Reconciliation and Diversity

In recent decades, there has been much discussion of racial reconciliation by evangelicals. Yet, due to challenges that remain, including reaching an understanding of what reconciliation means—beyond simply a promotion of diversity—some have grown weary of all the talk and little tangible progress.[96] The work of reconciliation is difficult, and often those who most need to change their ways do not recognize what is wrong.

What does reconciliation—and diversity—look like in biblical perspective?

John Stott develops a biblical foundation for ethnic diversity and reconciliation from Paul's address to the Athenians in Acts 17. Athens was a bustling city in the ancient world, a center for ideas and trade, and of "ethnic, cultural and religious pluralism."[97] Stott understands several of Paul's assertions to be relevant to ethnic diversity. First, Paul proclaims that God created everything and he is Lord over everything (Acts 17:24), including human life. Paul asserts, "From one man he has made every nationality to live over the whole earth," and "in him we live and move and have our being" and "we are also his offspring" (vv. 26–28). Paul applies these truths to demonstrate the ignorance and culpability of idolatry, yet, Stott argues, "he could equally well have deduced from it the folly and evil of racism, for if he is the God of all human beings, this will affect our attitude to them as well as to him."[98] As indicated earlier, all human beings share a common origin and are members of one race. We are all equal in creation, and therefore equal in dignity and worth.

Second, Stott asserts that "Paul proclaimed the importance of ethnic and cultural diversity, affirming that God is the God of history."[99] In God's providence, he determined that human beings should "live

96. For instance, see Edward Gilbreath, *Reconciliation Blues: A Black Evangelical's Inside View of White Christianity* (Downers Grove, IL: InterVarsity Press, 2006). See also Taelor Gray, "Hostages to Homogeny: Why I'm Done with 'Racial Reconciliation,'" The Witness, February 9, 2016, https://thewitnessbcc.com/why-im-done-with-racial-reconciliation/.
97. Stott, *Issues Facing Christians Today*, 287.
98. Stott, *Issues Facing Christians Today*, 287.
99. Stott, *Issues Facing Christians Today*, 288.

over the whole earth" (v. 26). This likely al-
ludes to the creation command for human
beings to multiply and fill the earth. Stott
notes that "such dispersal under God's
blessing inevitably resulted in the development of distinctive cultures."[100] Differences
naturally develop due to differences in climate, habitats, food, and so on, as well as
natural physical boundaries within which
people develop shared experiences different
from other groups.

Third, Stott makes the important point
that recognizing and celebrating ethnic diversity does not require or imply that we embrace
religious diversity. In Acts 17 Paul attests to
Jesus's resurrection and proclaims the need
for repentance because God's judgment is
coming. Christians are called to love all people
and to recognize their dignity, while rejecting
idolatry and attesting to the truth that there is
one Lord and Savior, Jesus Christ.[101]

Finally, Stott notes, by implication here
(and explicitly in his letters) Paul proclaims
that "Jesus died and rose to create a new
and reconciled community, his church."[102]
Christians are scattered among the nations, and rightly have a certain national
loyalty, but fundamentally our loyalty is to
Jesus Christ and his one church. This does
not mean that belonging to the one church
"obliterates our nationality, any more than it
does our masculinity or femininity. It means

rather that, while our ethnic, national, social and sexual distinctions remain, they
no longer divide us. They have been tran-
scended in the unity of the family of God
(Galatians 3:28)."[103] People from various
ethnicities tend to make their ethnicity a—
even the—central marker of their identity,
perhaps after family identity. But for those
who find their primary identity in Christ, all
else is secondary, including ethnicity. They
are one in Christ, his brothers and sisters,
so that even their relationships with their
biological family are secondary if there is
a conflict between the two (Mark 3:35 and
parallels; cf. Mark 10:30). Therefore, we
should consider ourselves to be united to
other believers of different ethnicities, and
identify more closely with them than we do
with unbelievers who share our ethnicity.[104]
Jarvis Williams argues that "genuine, sincere, Christlike love for brothers and sisters
in Christ that transcends one's love for and
allegiance to one's race and ethnic traditions
is the essence of what it means to live out
racial reconciliation."[105] Our churches ought
to reflect ethnic diversity, in order to reflect
the richness of God's creation and salvation.

Reconciliation to God and to one another
Just as all human beings are created by God
in his image with equal dignity and worth,
so God's reconciling and pursuing love is

100. Stott, *Issues Facing Christians Today*, 288.
101. Stott, *Issues Facing Christians Today*, 288.
102. Stott, *Issues Facing Christians Today*, 288.
103. Stott, *Issues Facing Christians Today*, 288.
104. Cf. Hays, "What Are We For?," 20.
105. Jarvis J. Williams, *One New Man: The Cross and Racial Reconciliation in Pauline Theology* (Nashville: B&H Aca-
    demic, 2010), 137.

extended to all. The promise in Genesis is that through Abram and his descendants God would bless all people on earth (Gen. 12:3). That promise is ultimately fulfilled in Jesus through his atoning death on the cross. Jesus commissions his disciples to be his witnesses, making disciples not only among the Jews but among people to the ends of the earth (Matt. 28:18–20; Acts 1:8). The book of Acts tells how the apostle Paul is appointed as a messenger to the Gentiles and how the gospel is brought to the Gentiles throughout the Roman world (Acts 22:21; cf. Acts 28:28; Gal. 2:8; Col. 1:6).

All those who place their faith in Jesus are his brothers and sisters, and are children of God. Indeed, as Paul says to the Galatians, "There is no Jew or Greek, slave or free, male and female; since you are all one in Christ Jesus" (Gal. 3:28; cf. Col. 3:11). On the cross, Jesus broke down "the dividing wall of hostility" that separated Jew and Gentile, "so that he might create in Himself one new man from the two, resulting in peace. He did this so that he might reconcile both to God in one body through the cross by which he put the hostility to death" (Eph. 2:14–16). Jesus's death on the cross makes possible the reconciliation of sinners to God and to one another in one body. What is true for Jews and Gentiles—those divided by both religious and ethnic difference—is true for believers from all ethnic backgrounds.

To extend and experience this kind of reconciliation, this radical change, requires that we fully identify with Jesus's death. We are raised with Jesus because we have died to sin and our life is now hidden in his (Col. 3:1–4). So we are to put to death those things that belong to our worldly nature (v. 5). We should recognize that, apart from Christ, we walked and lived in these things, including lust, evil desire, anger, wrath, malice, and slander (vv. 5–8). To overcome these things, and to be united with one another in Christ (v. 11), we must put off the old self and put on the new self (vv. 9–10). That is, we must appropriate what God has made possible by the power of the gospel and the indwelling of the Holy Spirit. Therefore, as Anyabwile asserts, "You cannot be a Christian renewed in the image of God and be indifferent or opposed to reconciliation in the body of Christ." Reconciliation, between Greek and Jew, circumcision and uncircumcision, barbarian, Scythian, slave, and free (v. 11), and between believers of different ethnicities "is not something that merely flows out of the cross as a secondary or tertiary application; this is what the cross produces."[106]

The unity produced by genuine reconciliation cannot simply be something we talk about in the abstract. It is concrete. Jesus commands his followers to love one another (John 13:34; 15:12). The New Testament writers develop this in concrete ways. We are to "love one another deeply as brothers and sisters" and "outdo one another in showing honor" (Rom. 12:10). We ought not to provoke one another or envy one another (Gal. 5:26). We ought to encourage one another (1 Thess. 4:18), and be

---

106. Anyabwile, "What Does the Gospel Say?," 33.

hospitable to one another (1 Pet. 4:9). We are to accept one another (Eph. 4:2), and "be kind and compassionate to one another, forgiving one another, just as God also forgave you in Christ" (Eph. 4:32).

Racial unity in the church has often proved to be difficult. Pursuing unity and reconciliation is not exactly the same thing as pursuing diversity, for it is possible to achieve diversity without unity or reconciliation. The pursuit of unity and reconciliation in the church involves loving one another as Christ loved us (John 15:12; Eph. 5:2).[107] Jesus's love was costly, and so is ours. It can be difficult to love those who are different from us, and it is difficult to take the time to listen to and learn from one another, and to be in relationship with one another. When it comes to justice, politics, and various contentious issues, the divide among racial lines—among believers and unbelievers alike—highlights the difficulties.

Broken relationships are caused by sin, but the gospel makes possible the restoration of relationships—with God and one another. Yet there is work to be done, for "positionally, we are restored with one another, but practically we have to deal with the breakdowns that impede our attempts at reconciliation."[108] In practical terms, the different responses of Christians, along racial lines, to cases of police brutality and the killing of African Americans has exposed racial tensions and created a significant barrier to unity. Many white Christians appear to be insensitive or indifferent to the concerns of their black brothers and sisters, and many black Christians have reached a point of apathy or exhaustion when it comes to talk of reconciliation.[109]

The church and racial diversity

It has often been said that Sunday morning is the most segregated time in America, as Christians gather to worship one God in predominantly white and predominantly black (and predominantly Hispanic or Chinese or Korean, etc.) congregations. The explanations for this are varied: in part, people like to gather with others of similar interests and worship styles; also, congregations often simply reflect the demographics of their neighborhood; yet there is a deep problem that the people of God lack unity even in worship.

Should the church actively seek to be diverse? Is a lack of diversity a mark of unfaithfulness to the gospel? How should we respond to a certain church-growth strategy that asserts that it is easier to reach people of a particular ethnicity or group if your church primarily represents that group?[110]

---

107. Trillia Newbell, "How Should the Christian Live?" in Moore and Walker, *The Gospel and Racial Reconciliation*, 51–52.

108. Eric Mason, "How Should the Church Engage?," in Moore and Walker, *The Gospel and Racial Reconciliation*, 57.

109. Mason, "How Should the Church Engage?," 58–59. See also the essays by Anthony B. Bradley in his *Black and Tired: Essays on Race, Politics, Culture, and International Development* (Eugene, OR: Wipf & Stock, 2011).

110. One classic text on church growth affirms that "people like to become Christians without crossing racial, linguistic, or class barriers. This principle states an undeniable fact." Donald A. McGavran, *Understanding Church Growth*, ed. C. Peter Wagner, 3rd ed. (Grand Rapids: Eerdmans, 1990), 163. This is what McGavran calls the

Whether a church may grow faster if it is homogeneous, the question is, What does faithfulness look like in a church's outreach and diversity? There are many reasons why churches ought to be diverse.

- A diverse church reminds us that we are all God's children, brothers and sisters of one another, equally made in his image and thus equal in our humanity and dignity.
- A diverse church is a picture of the kingdom of heaven, which consists of people from all tongues and ethnic groups, united by a common salvation and worship of the one true God (Rev. 7:9–10).
- A diverse church demonstrates the reality of the gospel and its power to break down barriers. If the dividing wall between Jews and Gentiles was broken down so that they are one (Eph. 2:14; cf. Acts 10, 15; Gal. 2:15–21), then surely different groups of Gentiles can be one. How can a people united by the gospel be divided in our worship and fellowship? This is crucial, for while our world seeks to embrace diversity, Jesus's death on the cross is ultimately the only true path to reconciliation to God and to one another.[111] The gospel of reconciliation is stripped of its power if those who are

reconciled to God are not reconciled to one another. Sadly, sometimes the world is more successful at achieving diversity, though it must do so by force of law and through external pressure. Christians, by the grace of God and through the power of the Holy Spirit, possess immeasurably greater resources for achieving true unity. Yet sadly it remains elusive. Richard Hays writes that "the New Testament makes a compelling case for the church to live as a community that transcends racial and ethnic differences. Insofar as the church lives the reality of this vision, it has a powerful effect in society; insofar as it fails to live this reality, it compromises the truth of the gospel. The continuing racial separatism of America's churches . . . is a disturbing sign of unfaithfulness that can only reinforce the racial tensions abroad in our culture." He concludes that if the church is to be a light to the nations, then "ethnic division within the church becomes nothing other than a denial of the truth of the gospel. That is why racism is heresy. One of the church's most urgent pragmatic tasks . . . is to form communities that seek reconciliation across ethnic and racial lines."[112]

- A diverse church is also, usually, representative of a whole community, not just

---

Homogeneous Unit Principle. Often such a principle is advocated not as an ideal, but simply as a matter of fact that churches and other groups grow more quickly with less diversity. In any case, it raises questions about what outreach in a community ought to look like.

111. This point is made clearly by Williams in *One New Man*.

112. Richard B. Hays, *The Moral Vision of the New Testament: Cross, Community, New Creation; A Contemporary Introduction to New Testament Ethics* (San Francisco: HarperSanFrancisco, 1996), 441.

a slice of a community. A diverse church will often include more diverse perspectives on life, contemporary issues, and even applying the Word of God. It requires that we listen to one another and empathize with those whose life experiences are different from our own. This in turn requires a humility to consider how Scripture may be understood or applied faithfully in ways we have not considered because of our limited experiences. As a result, we will reach more diverse people more effectively, and it will help us to resist having our church practices be conformed to one cultural pattern. A church that experiences greater unity-in-diversity may help us to understand the gospel more fully.

These things and more suggest that diversity is to be preferred over a pragmatic understanding of church growth. Should we conclude that a church that is not diverse is not faithful? That answer to that question is nuanced, for it may indeed mean that, but not necessarily. We ought not to make diversity a *primary* marker of gospel fidelity, for there may be a number of reasons that our church is not diverse. It may be that we live in a community (not just a neighborhood) that is not at all diverse. It may be that there are reasons that people belonging to a minority group choose to worship and congregate together on their own. This may not be ideal, but (especially in the short run), it may not reflect unfaithfulness. Further, diversity in itself is not sufficient, and it is not necessarily a mark of faithfulness. It is not

enough, for instance, to try to make ethnic minorities feel welcomed in white churches, for we should not have *white churches*. If we seek diversity at a superficial level (perhaps putting diverse people in the seats but not in genuine fellowship or in positions of influence), whether for virtue-signaling, or because it is in *our* best interest, it is not out of love for God or neighbor, or an understanding of the gospel. On the other hand, if a church resists diversity (because of prejudice, discomfort, or whatever reason), such exclusion may be a mark of unfaithfulness.

Barriers to reconciliation and unity

The call for reconciliation and unity in the body of Christ is common. The desire for reconciliation and unity may be sincere. Yet actual reconciliation and unity is difficult, for many reasons. In general terms, we are often slow to listen to one another, quick to speak and defend our own point of view, and quick to anger when we feel accused or we feel that we are not listened to (James 1:19).

Majority group challenges. For the majority group, there may be ignorance or indifference to the experience of those who suffer discrimination and prejudice on a regular basis. In addition, the majority may feel that it is sufficient to admit past faults (especially the faults of people in the past), without recognizing ongoing—perhaps more subtle but yet real—patterns of racism, discrimination, and prejudice. It is tempting to focus on progress alone, and to urge everyone to "move on" without adequately grappling with problems—past and present. For instance, those in the majority group may assert that they have repented of past sins, and that genuine forgiveness means not bringing up those past sins, especially the sins of our forebears, as evidence of guilt. That may be true, and yet they may not recognize ongoing consequences of previous systemic sinful practices or the necessity of assurances that ongoing injustices will be condemned. By analogy, someone may genuinely forgive their spouse for infidelity, and yet they are not in the same relational situation as someone whose spouse has always been faithful. There may be forgiveness, and yet the damage done by past sinful patterns may require certain assurances and different relational patterns (we may call them compensatory behaviors) that are different from those in a relationship that has not had to endure infidelity.

Many people in the majority group do not harbor racial prejudice or hatred, and it can be difficult for them to understand the complaints leveled against them. It is easy to become defensive and frustrated when it seems that charges of racism are aimed at virtually everyone who is white. Yet even those who are not guilty of racial hostility need to be willing to examine blind spots, and to listen to others with sympathy and grace. We need to recognize that our sinfulness (and blind spots) are often worse than we think, and it is easy to overlook our own biases or insensitivities, or to emphasize the faults of others. It is all too easy to become defensive, and to protect our own

reputation, along with our own rights and privileges against various threats, sometimes at the expense of others. We consider our own motives to be sincere, and refuse to consider or simply cannot imagine that a claim of injustice that implicates us could be legitimate. We may be content with having a few relationships with those who are "other" as evidence of reconciliation, without seeing any need to address structural problems.

As difficult as reconciliation may be in personal relationships, it can be even more difficult when it comes to groups where vested interests and long-held values are challenged. Especially within the larger culture, but also within the Christian community, we ought to consider at least the possibility that our explanations of the problems are incomplete, if not wrong. Reinhold Niebuhr wrote, "All human groups are essentially predatory and tend to hold desperately to their privileges against the pressure of the underprivileged who demand a fairer share of the blessings. All human groups are essentially proud and find that pride very convenient because it seems to justify their special privileges and to explain the sad state of the underprivileged. It is this combination of selfishness and pride that makes the problems of group relationships so difficult."[113]

Minority group challenges. The focus of the challenges here has been on the majority group, but there are challenges that

---

113. Reinhold Niebuhr, *Love and Justice* (Cleveland: The World, 1967), 122.

arise within the minority group as well.[114] It is all too easy to read sinful motives into other people's behavior, whether or not they are intended or actual. Sweeping charges of racism, whether there is evidence of actual racism, is a barrier to reconciliation, as is attributing any problem or conflict to racism or racist motivations. When some people within a victimized group identify so fully with maintaining an ideology of victimization, reconciliation becomes virtually impossible.[115] As with anyone, there can be blind spots, wrong allegiances, sinful motivations and desires, and it can be easy to overlook one's own biases and to emphasize the faults of others.

Conclusion: Moving Forward

Racism and prejudice are deeply rooted problems, and political and legal proposals are often highly charged and controversial. Multifaceted and sometimes invisible problems are difficult to solve. The following are some suggestions for breaking down barriers and to work against racism and prejudice and for genuine diversity, especially among the people of God.[116]

- We need to be honest about our history in our culture and in the church.
- We may not all agree on where responsibility lies, and what changes need to be made, but white Christians can (1) recognize both the history of racism and the lasting negative consequences of it; (2) reject clearly all racism of the past and present; (3) listen to those who feel marginalized; (4) mourn with those who mourn and express genuine, deep sorrow for the hurts that our black friends' experience; (5) refuse to use or listen to racial jokes or insults or stereotypes, and rebuke others when they do.
- As Christians, we ought to speak to issues such as mass incarceration, education, income, employment, fractured families, and so on. These are issues that disproportionately affect our black and poor populations. While cause and effect are not always clear, we should agree that these are issues of justice that need to be remedied. We may have disagreements about how to address them, and sometimes these matters can be very complex and difficult even to assess.[117] We ought

114. One reason for less emphasis on the minority group challenges here is that I do not write from an insider's perspective, though I have sought to listen to those insiders who speak to these issues.
115. See, Bradley, *Liberating Black Theology*, 19–22. Bradley comments, "Many blacks, infused with victimology, wield self-righteous indignation in the service of exposing the inadequacies of the 'other' (e.g., white person) rather than finding a way forward" (20).
116. For some of these, and others, see Williams, *One New Man*, 133136. Also Williams and Jones, *Removing the Stain of Racism from the Southern Baptist Convention*; and Matthew J. Hall and D. A. Horton, "What Does the Culture Say?," in Moore and Walker, *The Gospel and Racial Reconciliation*, 69–90.
117. As a case in point, D. A. Horton, a pastor in Los Angeles County, underscores one very practical problem, citing various studies that show that "low-income communities of color have 50 percent fewer grocery stores within the radius of their neighborhoods than their higher income, predominately white counterparts. . . . There is 20 percent less produce available; and what is available is 30 percent more expensive." Hall and Horton, "What Does the Culture Say?," 85–86. This is a problem that needs some creative solution. Yet the problem, and thus the solution, may not be as straightforward or based on racial prejudice as it first seems. For an explanation of some of the

to reach across racial and political divides and pursue genuine solutions.

- Evangelicals ought to give adequate attention to the outworking of salvation, not only in terms of evangelism, but also in terms of attention to injustices, including systemic injustices, and social needs. This is part of the mission of the church.[118] In his critique of black liberation theology, Anthony Bradley argues that black theology wrongly focuses on social action without attention to evangelism and personal holiness, yet he rightly notes that "redemptive mission without social compassion and justice is biblically deficient."[119] Good works are "ignited by the love of God."[120]

- To pursue genuine diversity, unity and reconciliation in the church requires that we not only welcome visitors of diverse ethnic backgrounds, but that we are ready to make them full members and participants in our congregations, and to place qualified individuals in positions of leadership and influence. This may cause some discomfort, raising questions about things like worship style, and how we preach and teach and evangelize and disciple people. Change and difference are often uncomfortable.

- In theological education, we ought to recruit and hire qualified minorities in leadership and faculty roles, to influence the institution and to draw additional minority students and faculty. At the same time, avoid "token" hiring, which is patronizing and fails to address issues at the heart of the problem.

- We should seek ways to improve educational opportunities where they are inadequate.

- We should build friendships with people of diverse ethnic backgrounds. It is important for white people to try to hear and empathize with the experience of minorities. Admittedly, it is impossible to know exactly what it is like to experience life as a minority, but it is possible to gain greater understanding. Bacote writes that a common experience of African American people among their white friends is that "normative whiteness" blinds white people and keeps them from really knowing or understanding the experience of African Americans in white culture.[121] A starting point for some white people may be just to ask an African American friend to relate their experience.

- We ought to read books, articles, and blogs by diverse authors, especially by trustworthy Christian authors from different backgrounds, to see things from a new perspective, even if we

---

complex economic factors, see the highly regarded African American economist Thomas Sowell, *Economic Facts and Fallacies*, 2nd ed. (New York: Basic Books, 2011), esp. chap. 6.

118. Christopher J. H. Wright draws attention to this in *The Mission of God: Unlocking the Bible's Grand Narrative* (Downers Grove, IL: IVP Academic, 2006), 287.
119. Bradley, *Liberating Black Theology*, 190.
120. Bradley, *Liberating Black Theology*, 191.
121. Bacote, "Erasing Race," 124–25.

ultimately disagree. Those in positions of influence and leadership, and in the majority, especially need to strive to hear minority voices.

- We should work together to find ways to heal families in general, and specifically within the African American community. The family is a gift from God, and its destruction is the reason for countless social and economic problems. The family needs to be restored not simply for those reasons, but for the glory of God.
- We ought to resist referring to churches as "black churches" and "white churches," even if the churches in question are not diverse. It subtly reinforces the legitimacy of *segregated congregations* (that juxtaposition of terms ought to get our attention!).
- We should make racism within the church a matter of church discipline. As Jarvis Williams writes, "Pastors and church members who understand the reconciling power of the gospel would also speak against all forms of racism in the church, would discipline their members for practicing racism, just as they would discipline them for committing sexual sin."[122]

Paul writes to the Colossians, "Therefore, as God's chosen ones, holy and dearly loved, put on compassion, kindness, humility, gentleness, and patience, bearing with one another and forgiving one another if anyone has a grievance against another. Just as the Lord has forgiven you, so you are also to forgive. Above all, put on love, which is the perfect bond of unity" (Col. 3:12–14). Biblical exhortations to reconciliation, unity, and love find no differentiation in race. Christians are those whose primary identity is in Christ, who have been bought at the immeasurable price of Jesus's own life as an atonement for our sins, which reconciles us to God and one another. Our reconciliation and unity with one another, and our love for one another, are clear indicators that we are united to Christ. We anticipate the time when there will be "a vast multitude from every nation, tribe, people, and language, which no one could number, standing before the throne and before the Lamb. They were clothed in white robes with palm branches in their hands" (Rev. 7:9). In that day there will be no pretense of racial superiority. As we seek to remove the stain of racism here and now, we look forward to that day when, robed in white and washed by the blood of the Lamb, every stain of racism will be removed.[123]

---

122. Williams, *One New Man*, 138.
123. Cf. Williams and Jones, *Removing the Stain of Racism from the Southern Baptist Convention*.

Select Resources

Appiah, Kwame Anthony, and Henry Louis Gates Jr., eds. *Africana: The Encyclopedia of the African and African American Experience.* New York: Basic Civitas Books, 1999.

Bacote, Vincent. "Erasing Race." In *Black Scholars in White Space: New Vistas in African American Studies from the Christian Academy,* edited by Anthony B. Bradley, 123–38. Eugene, OR: Pickwick, 2015.

Bradley, Anthony B. *Liberating Black Theology: The Bible and the Black Experience in America.* Wheaton, IL: Crossway, 2010.

Emerson, Michael O., and Christian Smith. *Divided by Faith: Evangelical Religion and the Problem of Race in America.* New York: Oxford University Press, 2000.

Moore, Russell, and Andrew T. Walker, eds. *The Gospel and Racial Reconciliation.* The Gospel for Life Series. Nashville: B&H, 2016.

Stafford, Tim. *Shaking the System: What I Learned from the Great American Reform Movements.* Downers Grove, IL: InterVarsity Press, 2007.

Williams, Jarvis J. *One New Man: The Cross and Racial Reconciliation in Pauline Theology.* Nashville: B&H Academic, 2010.

Williams, Jarvis J., and Kevin M. Jones, eds. *Removing the Stain of Racism from the Southern Baptist Convention: Diverse African American and White Perspectives.* Nashville: B&H Academic, 2017.

CHAPTER 17

CREATION CARE

Then God said, "Let us make man in our image, according to our likeness. They will rule the fish of the sea, the birds of the sky, the livestock, the whole earth, and the creatures that crawl on the earth." So God created man in his own image; he created him in the image of God; he created them male and female. God blessed them, and God said to them, "Be fruitful, multiply, fill the earth, and subdue it. Rule the fish of the sea, the birds of the sky, and every creature that crawls on the earth."—Genesis 1:26–28

The Lord God took the man and placed him in the garden of Eden to work it and watch over it.—Genesis 2:15

The earth is the Lord's, and all it contains, the world, and those who dwell in it. For He has founded it upon the seas and established it upon the rivers.—Psalm 24:1–2 NASB

For everything was created by him, in heaven and on earth, the visible and the invisible, whether thrones or dominions or rulers or authorities—all things have been created through him and for him.—Colossians 1:16

Introduction

Genesis 1:26–28 has significant implications for creation care and environmental ethics. But are those implications positive or negative for the environment? Some take them to be negative. In a widely published and influential article from 1967, historian Lynn White lays much of the blame on Christianity for what he calls "our ecological crisis." He describes Christianity as the most anthropocentric religion in history, stemming from "the Christian axiom that nature has no reason for existence save to serve man."[1] In particular, White indicates that the biblical teaching that human beings are created in the image of God and are given the command to subdue and rule the earth is a major reason for our ecological crisis. He asserts that the negative influence of Christian doctrine is widely felt, saying, "Both our present science and our present technology are so tinctured with orthodox Christian arrogance towards nature that no solution for our ecological crisis can be expected from them alone."[2]

White raised questions more than a half century ago that are at the forefront of contemporary science, politics, and ethics: what is the nature, extent, and cause of our environmental problems? Is it correct that Christianity is to blame, and is Christianity anthropocentric? Where will the solutions to the crisis be found? Some who have found fault with Christianity and a Western worldview for environmental problems have turned to "Eastern" religion and worldviews, which they believe honor (or even worship) nature, thus preserving and protecting it. However, such a view is misleading on both counts. Even though the West has had a track record on the environment that can be criticized, Scripture (as we will see) has a high regard for what God has created and over which human beings have been given stewardship. Further, nations that have been shaped by Eastern religion, rather than simply preserving and protecting nature, have engaged in many actions that are destructive of the environment.[3]

A survey of Scripture that attends to its teaching on creation will demonstrate that while the problems are complex, the criticism brought by White and others is misplaced. Biblical Christianity is neither the anthropocentric religion that White claims, nor is it the root cause of environmental problems. That is not to say that Christians are without fault with respect to destructive

---

1. Lynn White Jr., "The Historical Roots of Our Ecological Crisis," *Science* 155 (1967): 1207. The influence of White's essay is significant enough that it is almost obligatory to cite it, whatever one's view of environmental problems. As one article states, "Within just a few years of its publication, the article was already considered a 'classic'; and over time it would elicit dozens of responses, be frequently reprinted in textbooks, and become standard reading in a wide array of university environmental courses." From Michael Paul Nelson and Thomas J. Sauer, "The Long Reach of Lynn White Jr.'s 'The Historical Roots of Our Ecologic Crisis,'" *Ecology and Evolution*, December 13, 2016, https://natureecoevocommunity.nature.com/users/24738-michael-paul-nelson/posts/14041-the-long-reach-of-lynn-white-jr-s-the-historical-roots-of-our-ecologic-crisis.
2. White, "Historical Roots," 1207.
3. See the account in J. R. McNeill, *Something New Under the Sun: An Environmental History of the Twentieth-Century World* (New York: Norton, 2000).

attitudes and acts toward nature. However, as Douglas and Jonathan Moo assert, "There is good evidence that the rise of humanism and loss of robust belief in a personal, creating God in the last few centuries have fostered a mechanistic way of thinking about the world that has had dramatically unfortunate consequences for the health of God's creation."[4] Similarly, Alister McGrath asserts, "Lynn White is completely right when he argues that human self-centeredness is the root of our ecological crisis, but quite wrong when he asserts that Christianity is the most anthropocentric religion the world has ever seen. The most self-centered religion in history is the secular creed of twentieth-century Western culture, whose roots lie in the Enlightenment of the eighteenth century and whose foundation belief is that humanity is the arbiter of all ideas and values."[5]

These responses represent a better explanation of the problem, even if many Christians have adopted much of the secular mechanistic worldview, or its implications, and then cited Scripture to defend their actions and desires. The answer is thus not to abandon biblical faith, but to reexamine the Bible for true wisdom and guidance concerning our understanding of and actions toward God's creation, and to reject the secular mechanistic worldview.

In the discussion of environmental ethics, various terms are used, which communicate certain important points but which also have potential to miscommunicate.[6] *Nature* rightly refers to the natural world, but it is also ambiguous and can be used in a way that deifies nature, or that sees "nature" in a metaphysical sense as mechanistic, existing apart from God. *Environment* is often used to refer to the natural world that we inhabit, which includes the interconnections that exist and on which we depend. However, it is also used either anthropocentrically (signifying especially that which supports human life) or ecocentrically (that which is good in and of itself, apart from human beings or God).

It may be more helpful, then, to refer to *creation*, for it draws attention to the Creator, and *creation care*, which indicates both that we care *about* and that we care *for* creation. On the other hand, *creation* can refer to the whole of the universe, far beyond the reach, or even sight (let alone the touch), of human beings. When we talk about what human beings have responsibility and care for, it is

---

4. Douglas J. Moo and Jonathan A. Moo, *Creation Care: A Biblical Theology of the Natural World*, Biblical Theology for Life (Grand Rapids: Zondervan, 2018), 26. They cite Erazim Kohák, who writes, "Both in principle and as a matter of historic fact, alienation sets in when humans lose their awareness of the presence of God and persuade themselves to view the cosmos no longer as a creation, endowed with value in the order of being, a purpose in the order of time and a moral sense in the order of eternity, but as a cosmic accident, meaningless and mechanical." Erazim Kohák, *The Embers and the Stars: A Philosophical Enquiry into the Moral Sense of Nature* (Chicago: University of Chicago Press, 1984), 183.

5. Alister McGrath, *The Reenchantment of Nature: The Denial of Religion and the Ecological Crisis* (New York: Doubleday, 2002), 54.

6. See the discussion by Moo and Moo in *Creation Care*, 24–26.

the earth and its immediate atmosphere (at least for now), and even a good deal of the earth is still beyond human touch. Nevertheless, *creation* is perhaps the most suitable term, and unless otherwise indicated, it will be used to refer to the earth and its habitation. At times *nature* and *environment* or *environmental ethics* will be used roughly synonymously, depending on the context of the discussion.

Reasons for Caring about Creation Care

There are many reasons why Christians especially ought to give attention to creation care, and to consider environmental ethics to be an important issue.[7] For one thing, it is a central issue and concern of our day. Christians therefore ought to be thinking about it and be informed at least at a basic level about something that so many people care about. Second, it is deeply connected to the creation mandate given by God to human beings, and thus part of human stewardship to which Christians bear witness. From the creation accounts in Genesis 1–2, we ought to be able to articulate something of why God created, the charge he gave to human beings, and how it relates to environmental ethics. We need to reflect on both human freedom and limitations pertaining to the charge to be fruitful, to multiply, to

fill the earth, and to subdue and rule over the earth. Third, it is important to consider what Scripture teaches about God's attitude toward creation and our care for it as caretakers, not owners. Finally, the earth is the habitat not only for human beings but for other creatures as well, and human beings have the responsibility to manage it well for our own sake, for our descendants, and for other creatures.

Environmental Concerns

Many concerns are raised about the environment and its future. The most prominent concern, and one that relates to many of the others, is global warming or climate change, including the degree to which the change is anthropogenic (i.e., caused by human actions), the severity of its effects, and what should be done about it. Related concerns include rise in sea level, overpopulation and the earth's "carrying capacity," biodiversity loss and species extinction, deforestation, air and water pollution, human consumption and waste, and sustainable farming, to name a few.[8] Among those who raise environmental concerns, there are different alarm levels. Some warn of catastrophic effects of climate change, and urge immediate and significant action to reduce those effects.[9] Others are skeptical of dire predictions of catastrophic effects, without denying that

---

7. Moo and Moo, *Creation Care*, 26–27.

8. This chapter will not seek to examine or evaluate the scientific claims. For a sampling of articles discussing environmental concerns, see the *Economist* magazine online under the heading "Environmental Problems and Protection," https://www.economist.com/topics/environmental-problems-and-protection. For a survey of environmental concerns from two biblical scholars, see Moo and Moo, *Creation Care*, 195–220.

9. Perhaps one of the best-known sources of this kind is the film *An Inconvenient Truth*, released in 2006, produced by former United States Senator vice-president and presidential candidate Al Gore. More recently, Representative

there is warming and that human beings are responsible for some of it.[10]

Evangelical responses to the issue of climate change are also mixed, despite frequent headlines claiming that evangelicals don't care about climate change.[11] There may be some truth to that at a popular level, though it should be noted that there is a wide range of views among Americans in general, not just evangelicals. For instance, in a 2016 poll on climate change sponsored by Yale and George Mason Universities, 45 percent of respondents answered either that they were "alarmed" (17 percent) or "concerned" (28

Alexandria Ocasio-Cortez, a sponsor of proposed legislation called the Green New Deal, said that she and other young Americans are afraid that "the world is going to end in 12 years if we don't address climate change." See William Cummings, "'The World Is Going to End in 12 Years if We Don't Address Climate Change,' Ocasio-Cortez says," *USA Today*, January 22, 2019, https://www.usatoday.com/story/news/politics/onpolitics/2019/01/22/ocasio-cortez-climate-change-alarm/2642481002. On the Green New Deal, see Lisa Friedman, "What Is the Green New Deal? A Climate Proposal, Explained, *The New York Times*, February 21, 2019, https://www.nytimes.com/2019/02/21/climate/green-new-deal-questions-answers.html.

Others express urgent concern as well, and highlight some of the problems listed above, such as the United Nation's Intergovernmental Panel on Climate Change (IPCC) and the environmental group Greenpeace. Information from the IPCC can be accessed at http://www.ipcc.ch/; information from Greenpeace can be accessed at https://www.greenpeace.org/international.

10. For instance, Jay Richards addresses four key questions on global warming. First, is the planet warming? He offers evidence that indicates that there is a slight warming trend. Second, is human activity causing the warming? He offers evidence that points to multiple causes, and argues that we don't know exactly. Third, is warming bad? Rather than being catastrophic, Richards (and others) argue that along with the negative effects there are positive effects, e.g., significantly more people die from cold than from heat each year, and such things at least need to be taken into account. Fourth, would the policies that are advocated (e.g., in the Kyoto or Paris recommendations) make a significant difference? Richards appeals to the official estimates to argue that it would not make much difference, but would cost an enormous amount of money that could be spent more effectively elsewhere. See Jay W. Richards, *Money, Greed, and God: Why Capitalism Is the Solution and Not the Problem* (San Francisco: HarperOne, 2009), 197–99.

One of the most prominent skeptics is Bjørn Lomborg, a Danish scholar and former member of Greenpeace who writes and speaks on environmental economics. He does not deny climate change, but argues that things are not as catastrophic as climate alarmists say, that many of the very expensive "solutions" would do little if anything to change the problem, and that there are much better alternatives to solve the biggest problems we face. For instance, one of his recommendations is heavy investment into green energy research and development. His books include *The Skeptical Environmentalist: Measuring the Real State of the World* (Cambridge: Cambridge University Press, 2001), and *Cool It: The Skeptical Environmentalist's Guide to Global Warming* (New York: Vintage, 2010).

11. For instance, Lisa Vox, "Why Don't Christian Conservatives Worry about Climate Change? God," *Washington Post*, June 2, 2017, https://www.washingtonpost.com/posteverything/wp/2017/06/02/why-dont-christian-conservatives-worry-about-climate-change-god; Ethan Sacks, "The Gospel of Climate Change: Green Pastors Bringing Environmentalism to Evangelicals," NBC News, April 22, 2018, https://www.nbcnews.com/news/religion/climate-change-schism-evangelical-christians-divided-human-role-global-warming-n865081; at one point this article contrasts the "faithful who trust scientists' warnings that the earth is in danger from human-caused climate change, and the vast majority of evangelicals who are left cold by the concept." David Gibson, "Politics, Culture, or Theology? Why Evangelicals Back Trump on Global Warming," *Religion News Service*, June 9, 2017, https://religionnews.com/2017/06/09/politics-culture-or-theology-why-evangelicals-back-trump-on-global-warming. Sometimes the attention is focused on white evangelicals, e.g., Sarah Pulliam Bailey, "Why So Many White Evangelicals in Trump's Base Are Deeply Skeptical of Climate Change," *Washington Post*, June 2, 2017, https://www.washingtonpost.com/news/acts-of-faith/wp/2017/06/02/why-so-many-white-evangelicals-in-trumps-base-are-deeply-skeptical-of-climate-change; Steve Hanley, "Why White Evangelicals Don't Care about Climate Change," CleanTechnica, April 5, 2018, https://cleantechnica.com/2018/04/05/why-white-evangelicals-dont-care-about-climate-change.

percent), 34 percent said that they were "cautious" (27 percent) or "disengaged" (7 percent), and 21 percent were either "doubtful" (11 percent) or "dismissive" (10 percent).[12]

Evangelicals who are engaged on the issue of climate change represent views from "alarmed" to "cautious."[13] One prominent group that can be considered "alarmed" is the Evangelical Climate Initiative, as indicated in their statement, "Climate Change: An Evangelical Call to Action." This document makes four claims. First, that human-induced climate change is real. Second, that the consequences of climate change will be significant, and will hit the poor the hardest. Third, that Christian moral convictions demand our response to the climate change problem. And fourth, that the need to act now is urgent and that governments, businesses, churches, and individuals all have a role to play in addressing climate change—starting now.[14]

Other evangelicals nuance or contest the assertion that climate change is primarily caused by human beings and is catastrophic. Take, for example, the Cornwall Alliance for the Stewardship of Creation, in its document, "The Cornwall Declaration On Environmental Stewardship." They do not deny that global warming has occurred over the past

thirty years or more, but they assert a number of points that challenge the prevailing views. For instance, while they acknowledge that global warming has occurred, they question the assertion that humans are the cause of *most* of the global warming that has occurred. Therefore, they argue that it is doubtful that a reduction in carbon dioxide emissions will significantly mitigate global warming since, they assert, current warming is due in part to regular cycles. Further, they challenge the view that global warming is likely to have catastrophic consequences. They also argue that the effects of proposed actions would have the greatest adverse consequences for the poor, who rely on relatively cheap energy now to rise out of poverty.[15]

In spite of heated debates and sometimes vitriolic language, it should be noted that there are reasonable people who take different positions on the causes of, effects of, and solutions to global warming. While there may not be agreement on many points, it is worth pointing out that there is agreement on some key issues, such as affirming the goodness of God's creation, human responsibility to be good stewards of the earth, and a moral mandate to care especially for the poor who may be most affected by policies.[16]

---

12. Connie Roser-Renouf et al., "Global Warming's Six Americas and the Election, 2016," Yale Program on Climate Communication, July 12, 2016, http://climatecommunication.yale.edu/publications/six-americas-2016-election.
13. I am using "cautious" here differently from the way the Yale/George Mason survey used it. They included among the "cautious" those who "have thought little about the issue and see it as having little personal relevance."
14. "Statement of the Evangelical Climate Initiative," http://www.christiansandclimate.org/statement.
15. For these and many other points, see the arguments of the Cornwall Alliance at https://cornwallalliance.org.
16. It seems to me to be a significant error that in *Kingdom Ethics: Following Jesus in Contemporary Context* (Downers Grove, IL: InterVarsity Press, 2003), 435–37, Glen Stassen and David Gushee label Calvin Beisner's view as an anthropocentric utilitarian approach, particularly considering that most evangelicals, including Beisner no doubt, reject utilitarianism, judging it to be unbiblical.

Problems with Crisis Motivation

One of the problems with the catastrophic claims as a motivator for action, quite apart from challenges to the claims themselves, relates to their effect. While they are undoubtedly used to spur immediate and significant actions, they often do just the opposite: If people are convinced that a catastrophe is imminent, then what is the use of changing behavior, dealing with greed and idolatries, and adopting necessary virtues?[17] Why not, rather, eat and drink, for tomorrow we die (1 Cor. 15:32)? Of course, we need to face facts. We would be foolish not to recognize a crisis when a crisis occurs, and adjust our behavior. While the *Titanic* was sinking, only a fool would have continued to feast and insist on making the most of their fine dining experience. Yet, if the message is that there is a catastrophic crisis that cannot be undone, it is difficult to motivate people to change behavior. Further, it is by no means clear to some who examine the facts that they point to a catastrophic scenario. It is certainly not unprecedented historically for a "crisis" to be announced and used as a catalyst to solve problems by "any means necessary" in order to establish the power of one ideology over another.

Crisis motivation has its dangers, but ignoring or denying all claims of significant environmental degradation has problems as well. In some cases, it simply reflects a view that environmental issues are really not very important, particularly compared to "more pressing" issues, such as evangelism, matters of life and death in abortion and euthanasia, and so on. Yet relegating issues of environmental concern to the periphery threatens to sideline a significant matter of Christian discipleship, witness, and leadership, failing to consider carefully the charge to be stewards of God's creation. Further, it wrongly separates certain core convictions, such as evangelism, from ethical actions. Finally, it unnecessarily alienates those who care for the natural world, and fails to model faithfulness to them, and thus may also alienate them from the Triune God.[18]

Environmental Ethics

Before turning to a survey of Scripture, we will briefly look at approaches to environmental ethics, which tends to be driven by one of three broad perspectives: anthropocentrism, biocentrism, and theocentrism.[19]

Anthropocentric Approaches

Anthropocentric approaches place humanity at the center of reality, and understand the universe primarily in terms of "human values and human interests."[20] There may be concern for the environment, since the environment sustains human

---

17. Cf. Mark Liederbach and Seth Bible, *True North: Christ, the Gospel, and Creation Care* (Nashville: B&H, 2012), 22–23.
18. For the development of some of these themes, see Liederbach and Bible, *True North*, 24–26.
19. For a discussion of these approaches, see Richard A. Young, *Healing the Earth: A Theocentric Perspective on Environmental Problems and Their Solutions* (Nashville: Broadman & Holman, 1994), especially 115–33. Also, Steven Bouma-Prediger, *For the Beauty of the Earth: A Christian Vision for Creation Care*, 2nd ed. (Grand Rapids: Baker Academic, 2010), esp. 111–29; and Stassen and Gushee, *Kingdom Ethics*, 435–40.
20. Young, *Healing the Earth*, 116.

beings, and "often the short-term interests of humanity and almost always our long-term interests coincide with the well-being of the rest of creation."[21] Even the term *environment* is often used in an anthropocentric way, as Douglas and Jonathan Moo point out. We refer to our "work environment" or to sewer and waste removal as "environmental services," or we think of the earth first as the *human* environment. In such cases, its use "implies that human beings are at the center of things: the created world is important only inasmuch as it is the place *we* inhabit."[22] Appeals to Scripture focus on the idea that God has given human beings dominion over creation, which we are to subdue for human benefit (Gen. 1:26–28).

Anthropocentric views connect at certain points with biblical teaching. However, they fall short for at least two reasons. One is that God, not humanity, is of ultimate value and all things exist for God's glory. Second, related to that, while nature serves human interests, "Scripture affirms that it is also valuable irrespective of any usefulness to humans. The natural world is valuable," we should insist, "simply because God made it and sustains it and loves it."[23] This will be developed in the survey of Scripture below.

Biocentric Approaches

Biocentric approaches, including the deep ecology movement, "give no special status to human beings, considering them just one species among others on earth."[24] Rather, as Richard Young describes it, all of nature is "the ultimate reference point for all meaning, purpose, values, and ethics," and exists not for the sake of human benefit but "for the sake of the whole."[25] All creatures share equal intrinsic value with human beings. If human beings have certain unique traits, other creatures have their own unique traits. All creatures are interdependent, together constituting a whole living organism, a view espoused in the popular and influential "Gaia hypothesis" by James Lovelock.[26] Often biocentric approaches adopt a pantheistic spirituality, with connections to the New Age movement and Eastern mysticism. An approach similar to but broader than the biocentric approach is the ecocentric approach, which gives attention not only to all living organisms but also to ecosystems and habitats.[27]

Among the weaknesses of biocentrism, the ultimate one is that it is inadequate because it places biological life "at the center of things," in contrast to the biblical perspective that "God lies at the center of things, not life."[28]

21. Stassen and Gushee, *Kingdom Ethics*, 435.
22. Moo and Moo, *Creation Care*, 25.
23. Bouma-Prediger, *For the Beauty of the Earth*, 120.
24. Stassen and Gushee, *Kingdom Ethics*, 437. On deep ecology, see, e.g., Bill Devall and George Sessions, *Deep Ecology: Living as if Nature Mattered* (Salt Lake City, UT: Gibbs Smith, 1985); and *Deep Ecology for the 21st Century: Readings on the Philosophy and Practice of the New Environmentalism*, ed. George Sessions (Boston: Shambhala, 1995).
25. Young, *Healing the Earth*, 124.
26. James E. Lovelock, *Gaia* (New York: Oxford University Press, 1979).
27. This view, and the authors who defend it, is discussed by Liederbach and Bible, *True North*, 14.
28. Bouma-Prediger, *For the Beauty of the Earth*, 123.

Theocentric Approaches

Theocentric approaches are wide-ranging, but share a rejection of both the anthropocentric and biocentric approaches to the environment. Instead, theocentrism teaches that "God is the center of the universe and that He alone is the Source and Upholder of meaning, purpose, values, and ethics, as well as the unifying principle of the cosmos. Everything finds existence, value, purpose, and meaning in the infinite and transcendent God."[29] God is separate from creation and God, not creation, is eternal. As Steven Bouma-Prediger puts it, "God is the measure of all things, not humans. God is the ultimate good, not life. God is the beginning and the end, not earth."[30] Human beings have special value, but all of creation is valuable. Some forms of theocentrism hold things in common with anthropocentrism, because "human interests and responsibilities are central," and yet they are theocentric in that everything is created by God and for God/Christ (see Col. 1:16). Further, the mandate to rule over creation is also a mandate to care for creation.[31] This perspective, as well as the others, will be examined further in the survey of biblical texts below.

A Survey of Key Biblical Texts for Creation Care

Some may think that theology and ethics have little to do with the relationship between human beings and the nonhuman creation. The storyline of the Bible has to do with the relationship between God and his image bearers, especially focused on human sin and alienation from God, God's redeeming love and provision of reconciliation through Jesus's death on the cross for sin, and resurrection to new life. Often our moral interests are concerned primarily with our relationship to God and one another. The Decalogue, the center of the Mosaic law, concerns human relationships to God and other human beings. Further, the two most important commands, Jesus says, are to love God completely and to love our neighbor as ourselves (Matt. 22:37–40). At one level, it may be possible to conclude that nonhuman creation is considered significant mainly because of its instrumental value in serving human needs. Does the Bible have much at all to say about environmentalism or creation care? In fact it does, as the following survey of biblical texts will demonstrate. Indeed, as Richard Young asserts, "The Christian Scriptures, when interpreted through a theocentric perspective, offer the most satisfying analysis and realistic solution of the environmental problem."[32]

A Development of Creation Care from Key Old Testament Texts

Genesis 1–2

Genesis 1–2 is foundational for the biblical doctrine of creation. It is often appealed to by

---

29. Young, *Healing the Earth*, 128.
30. Bouma-Prediger, *For the Beauty of the Earth*, 112.
31. Stassen and Gushee, *Kingdom Ethics*, 439.
32. Young, *Healing the Earth*, 260.

evangelicals to challenge the theory of evolution, or to develop a theology of marriage
and sexuality. It has not often been mined for
a theology of creation care or environmental
ethics.[33] It is important to see that this text
is foundational to an understanding of environmental ethics and creation care. The following draws out some of the key relevant
points and their implications.

First, everything that God has made
is ordered to his purposes and is good. In
Genesis 1 there is a pattern of creating and
filling. On the first three days, God creates
light and darkness (day one, vv. 3–5), the expanse of the sea and sky (day two, vv. 6–8),
and the land and sea with its vegetation (day
three, vv. 9–13). On the next three days,
God fills the "light" and "darkness" with
lights—the sun, moon, and stars (day four,
vv. 14–19)—he fills the sea and sky with sea
creatures and birds of the sky (day five, vv.
20–23), and he fills the land with all kinds of
living creatures, including humankind (day
six, vv. 24–31). Everything is ordered, and
nothing is by accident—God has created everything just as he intended, and he sees that
each thing is good (vv. 4, 10, 12, 18, 21, 25),
and that everything together is very good (v.
31). The implications of this are straightforward. We ought to marvel at God's handiwork, which should cultivate praise to God
(see Ps. 19:1–6; 97:6; 104). God delights in

what he has created, and we ought to as well.
Creation serves human needs, but all things
are not created simply to serve human needs
(see Ps. 104). God creates and attests that
what he has created is good, even before and
apart from the creation of human beings.
His creation has value in and of itself: "The
value of the rest of creation is not dependent
on what we think about it or merely on its
apparent usefulness to human beings."[34]

Second, human beings are lofty creatures, made in God's image (Gen. 1:27) and
given the charge to "be fruitful, multiply, fill
the earth, and subdue it. Rule the fish of the
sea, the birds of the sky, and every creature
that crawls on the earth" (v. 28). So human
beings are distinct from other creatures, and
have a unique role and authority in creation.
At the same time, we are frail and finite
creatures, and we need to know our place
if we are to rule not as gods but as God's
image bearers. God is Creator, and the earth
is his, not ours (Ps. 24:1). We are caretakers,
not owners. What it means to subdue and
rule will be explored briefly below. The point
here is simply that even as the creation accounts assert that human beings are unique
in creation, and are given authority over
what God has made, the accounts also cultivate humility. For we are creatures too,
dependent on God for life and breath and
fruitfulness; we are made from dust (Gen.

---

33. For a survey of twenty major evangelical theology textbooks written after 1970, examining whether there is any
    development of an environmental ethic or ecological concerns in the treatments of the doctrines of creation and
    atonement, see John Jefferson Davis, "Ecological 'Blind Spots' in the Structure and Content of Recent Evangelical
    Systematic Theologies," *Journal of the Evangelical Theological Society* 43, no. 2 (June 2000): 273–86. While such
    concerns are not completely absent, they are relatively minor. Davis asserts that the doctrines of creation and the
    atonement have significant implications for ecological concerns.
34. Moo and Moo, *Creation Care*, 51.

2:7), and thus very much on the creature side of the Creator/creature divide![35] Understanding these truths is crucial if we are to understand how to rule well, and to care for what God has made.

Third, the authority to subdue and rule (or have dominion, ESV, NASB, NIV) should be understood as an authority to carry out God's purposes for humankind and for creation. The significance of Genesis 1:26–28 cannot be overstated. These verses have been the focus of countless book, articles, and sermons; here we will barely scratch the surface, but several important points stand out that relate to our concern for creation. One is that, while there is much that can be said about what it means to be made in God's image, part of its significance here is that we are "to reflect his sovereignty throughout the earth. This responsibility to reflect God's rule entails a particular relationship with God, with each other, and with the earth." We are to look to God if "we are to rule as God would have us rule," and "if we are to reflect him and his purposes in how we live and reign."[36] As God's image bearers, we ought to emulate God's own rule over creation, to serve God's interests. We read that God created grass and herbs and fruit trees, each "after its kind" (Gen. 1:11–12), and every living creature in water and sky and on the earth "after their kind" (1:21, 24, 25). He designed each

according to his purposes, to reproduce and be fruitful, to fill the earth. That means that we should not only delight in what God has made, but we ought to seek to protect, preserve, and care for what God has made, including the creatures of air, land, and sea over which we rule.

What does it mean to subdue and to rule? The terms that appear in Genesis 1:28 have been interpreted to be a significant cause of environmental problems because, it is charged, they sanction the destruction of the earth for human benefit.[37] The two terms in Hebrew are כָּבַשׁ and רָדָה, translated "subdue" and "rule" or "have dominion." Where used elsewhere in the Old Testament, כָּבַשׁ means to conquer (Num. 32:22, 29; 2 Sam. 8:11; Zech. 9:15) or bring under subjection (1 Chron. 22:18; 2 Chron. 28:10). רָדָה is used to refer to God's rule over the earth (Ps. 72:8; 110:2), a nation's rule over another nation (Lev. 26:17; Neh. 9:28; Ezek. 29:15), or a leader's rule over a people (2 Chron. 8:10).[38]

While these terms could be (mis)understood in a way that gives human beings the right to subdue and rule harshly, that is hardly a proper interpretation in the context of Genesis 1–2. It is true that כָּבַשׁ (subdue) is a strong word that often has the connotation of force or subjugation—for example, to subdue an enemy. Douglas and Jonathan Moo argue that "the most relevant parallels

---

35. Moo and Moo, *Creation Care*, 71.
36. Moo and Moo, *Creation Care*, 74.
37. As noted earlier, a seminal and very influential essay along these lines is that of White, "Historical Roots." See Francis A. Schaeffer and Udo Middelmann, *Pollution and the Death of Man* (Wheaton, IL: Crossway, 1970), for a reprint of the article and a response.
38. For a discussion of these and other uses of the term, see Liederbach and Bible, *True North*, 67–68; also Young, *Healing the Earth*, 161–63.

in the Hebrew Bible, where 'land' or 'earth' is the object of the subduing, are in the context of the conquest of the land of Canaan, 'when the land is subdued before the Lord' (Num. 32:22, 29; cf. Josh. 18:1; 1 Chron. 22:18)." It is suggestive here that "Israel 'subdued' the land by fighting against the enemies of God so that God's people could inhabit it as God intended." With respect to Genesis 1, perhaps "subdue" indicates "at a minimum the active work of bringing the earth under the appropriate rule of those who bear God's image."[39]

The complementary account of creation in Genesis 2 indicates something of what is included in subduing the earth. There the man is placed in the garden to "work it" (עָבַד, also "to cultivate" [NASB] or "to serve") and to "watch over it" (שָׁמַר, also "to keep" [ESV, NASB] or "to take care of" [NIV] or "to protect") (Gen. 2:15). Scholars have recognized that the garden is portrayed as a sort of temple, and it is instructive that the same two words, עָבַד and שָׁמַר, are used in Numbers "to describe the service of the Levitical priests in the tabernacle (3:7; 8:26; 18:7)."[40] These two words, then, indicate that human beings have been given the task to work or serve, and to keep or take care of the world that God has given us dominion over as a service to God.

Mark Liederbach and Seth Bible, in their contribution to the discussion of the significance of עָבַד and שָׁמַר in Genesis 2:15, suggest that, in the context of a theocentric creation account, a better translation of the two

terms is "to worship and obey."[41] This represents a possible meaning of the terms, and it highlights the intimate communion with God that human beings are created to enjoy, as well as the sense that creation functions as a temple of sorts. These terms also highlight the fact that human beings are called to glorify God in all that we do, in this case by serving God and his creation. However, it seems to me that translating עָבַד and שָׁמַר as "worship and obey" actually runs the risk of obscuring the direct meaning of the text, that human beings are to cultivate and keep the garden, and in so doing, we worship and obey God. They recognize and make this point, but prefer to call attention to the ultimate purpose that human beings are called to. It is proper to keep that ultimate purpose—to obey, glorify, and worship God— before us at all times. But we also need to attend to the specific means by which we are given to do so, and in Genesis 2:15, that is by fulfilling what God placed the man and the woman in the garden to do—namely, to cultivate and to keep. In the extreme, it would be possible to answer every question about our vocations that we are called to worship and obey, but that obscures the specific context by which we do so.

To subdue is to cultivate and to keep as a means of serving God and neighbor, and to develop creation for the purposes God made it, which includes serving human needs and purposes (Gen. 1:29). To cultivate the soil,

---

39.   Moo and Moo, *Creation Care*, 76.
40.   Moo and Moo, *Creation Care*, 78. Cf. Liederbach and Bible, *True North*, 60–66.
41.   Liederbach and Bible, *True North*, 64.

to harvest crops or fruit from trees, to cut down trees or make bricks to build houses, to clear brush to make a path for walking, and to build automobiles, computers, and cell phones, each represents a way of subduing the earth (and of course there are countless examples). We would not normally consider these violent activities, but they do require a certain amount of force. And, of course, after the curse of sin, where even the ground itself is cursed, it is only with sweat and toil that it will yield produce (Gen. 3:17–19), requiring a sort of conquest. That is not violence done to creation, but the toilsome work required to produce.

The other term of significance, רָדָה (rule), need not have negative connotations, as in an oppressive rule. As indicated above, it can refer to God's own rule (Ps. 72:8; 110:2), which serves as the paradigm for the kind of rule given to humankind. Just as a government official's God-given authority (Rom. 13:1–6) to rule over a people is to be used for their good, and not as an excuse to oppress, so the rule of human beings over the earth and its creatures is to be a benevolent one. As God's representatives, created in his image, human beings are stewards of a creation that God delights in, and human authority is delegated, not an unlimited authority to do whatever we please.[42] So Vern Poythress asserts that "man does not have a boundless, arbitrary freedom to exploit the things placed under him. He is ultimately a steward who must answer to God for how he uses the gifts and privileges that God gives him." He notes that "God cares for his creation; he does not exploit it. Man must imitate God." Therefore, the "rule" or "dominion" in Genesis 1:28 should be understood "as a thoughtful, caring dominion, a dominion expressing God's goodness and care, and not a heartless, brutal, crushing dominion. Genesis 1–2 repudiates the sinful perversion of dominion into destructive exploitation."[43] It is to exercise authority "toward the preservation of, and fuller realization of, creation's goodness."[44]

In summary, Genesis 1–2 does not give human beings license to destroy the earth and to do with it whatever we like, but to subdue and rule it according to God's purposes. That certainly includes benefits for human beings, but it is much more than that. God created everything, and he delights in what he created, and we ought to delight in his creation as well. As Creator, everything belongs to God, and human beings are best thought of as stewards or caretakers of creation, under God's authority and rule.[45]

Genesis 3

A brief word on this text will be made here, and followed up with a comment on

---

42. Cf. James A. Nash, *Loving Nature: Ecological Integrity and Christian Responsibility* (Nashville: Abingdon, 1991), 104.
43. Vern S. Poythress, *Redeeming Science: A God-Centered Approach* (Wheaton, IL: Crossway, 2006), 150. See also the discussion in Liederbach and Bible, *True North*, 69–72.
44. Michael A. Bullmore, "The Four Most Important Biblical Passages for a Christian Environmental Ethic," *Trinity Journal* 19, no. 2 (1998): 150.
45. For a discussion of stewardship, including its advantages and disadvantages as a term for creation care, see Moo and Moo, *Creation Care*, 180–84.

Romans 8 below. In Genesis 3, there is an account of the curses brought because of the sin of Adam and Eve. The serpent is cursed (vv. 14–15), the woman is cursed (v. 16), and the man is cursed (vv. 17–19). In the curse against the man, there is a sense in which the destiny of human beings and nature are intertwined, and that the sin of the man, who willed to disobey God, results in a curse on nature as well.[46] God declares to Adam,

> The ground is cursed because of you.
> You will eat from it by means of painful labor all the days of your life.
> It will produce thorns and thistles for you, and you will eat the plants of the field.
> You will eat bread by the sweat of your brow until you return to the ground,
> since you were taken from it.
> For you are dust,
> and you will return to dust. (Gen. 3:17–19)

At one level, this curse is directed at the man, for whom the work of cultivating and keeping the garden will become toilsome. Yet it also results in *the travail of nature*, which groans because of human sin, as Paul speaks to in Romans 8:20–23.[47] And, as we will see, the restoration of creation is interconnected with the redemption of the children of God.

Genesis 9:8–17

This text is part of what is known as the Noahic covenant—God's promise to Noah after the devastating flood never again to destroy the earth with a flood. It is called the Noahic covenant because God addresses Noah and his family directly (Gen. 9:1, 8, 17; also v. 12). Also, God here tells Noah and his family that every living creature will be food for them, in addition to the green plants that God gave human beings for food originally (v. 3). In addition, God provides protection for human lives by requiring the death penalty for anyone who sheds human blood (vv. 5–6). Further, God repeats the blessing of fruitfulness to Noah's family that is originally given in creation (Gen. 1:28), no doubt a great encouragement to the few human survivors of the cataclysmic event. And finally, God declares a covenant with Noah's family and their descendants never again to destroy the earth by flood.

This covenant is important for understanding creation care. Indeed, Michael Bullmore asserts that this text is one of the "four most important biblical passages for a Christian Environmentalism." Bullmore suggests that it may be better to designate it as "the Creation covenant, for the covenant is made not only with Noah's family (and their descendants), but with *every*

---

46. Carl F. H. Henry notes that "from the creation account onward the Bible boldly correlates the fortunes of the cosmos with those of man." Carl F. H. Henry, *God, Revelation, and Authority*, vol. 2, *God Who Speaks and Shows: Fifteen Theses, Part One* (Waco, TX: Word, 1976), 101.

47. Cf. H. Paul Santmire, *The Travail of Nature: The Ambiguous Ecological Promise of Christian Theology* (Minneapolis: Fortress, 1985). Santmire's book is a significant contribution to the discussion, although I would argue that it is not that Christian theology is ambiguous, as the subtitle indicates, but that the travail of nature is caused by human sin (which includes in some cases the misappropriation of Christian theology).

living creature.[48] He notes that the essence of these ten verses can be stated in this way: "God has established an everlasting covenant with all living creatures of every kind wherein he has promised never again to destroy them by the waters of a flood." The repetition in this passage is striking: "In the space of these ten verses there are eight occurrences of the word 'covenant,' three references to the 'sign' of the rainbow, and three repetitions of the promise to 'never again destroy by flood.'"[49] Further, and of particular interest for our present purposes, is the repetition with which God declares his covenant to be not only with Noah and the human race, but also with every creature:

Then God said to Noah and his sons with him, "Understand that I am establishing my covenant with you and your descendants after you, and *with every living creature that is with you—birds, livestock, and all wildlife of the earth* that are with you—*all the animals of the earth that came out of the ark.* I establish my covenant with you that never again will *every creature* be wiped out by floodwaters; there will never again be a flood to destroy *the earth.*"

And God said, "This is the sign of the covenant I am making between me and you and *every living creature with you*, a covenant for all future generations: I have placed my bow in the clouds, and it will be a sign of the covenant between me and *the earth.* Whenever I form clouds over the earth and the bow appears in the clouds, I will remember my covenant between me and you and *all the living creatures*: water will never again become a flood to destroy *every creature.* The bow will be in the clouds, and I will look at it and remember the permanent covenant between God and *all the living creatures on earth.*" God said to Noah, "This is the sign of the covenant that I have established between me and *every creature on earth.*" (Gen. 9:8–17, emphasis added)

Just as God took great care to preserve the creatures from the flood by having Noah build the ark, so in his covenant he promises never to destroy them again. The interconnected destiny of nature with human beings is stated again. In creation, all creatures are in some way under the godly rule and responsible care of human beings. In the fall, the earth itself experiences the consequences of human sin. In the flood, terror and death is visited on every creature because of human sin. In Genesis 9, God's covenant never to destroy the earth again by flood is made with human beings and every creature on earth. And, though it is not clear exactly what it means, it anticipates that the future destiny of creation is linked with the redemption of human beings (Rom. 8:20–23), as God declares this covenant to be a "permanent covenant" (v. 16).[50]

---

48. Bullmore, "Four Most Important Biblical Passages," 157.
49. Bullmore, "Four Most Important Biblical Passages," 157.
50. Bullmore, "Four Most Important Biblical Passages," 158.

Exodus 20:8–11; Deuteronomy 5:12–15; 25:4; Proverbs 12:10

Although it is common to think that the Decalogue only deals with relations between God and human beings, the fourth commandment includes a reference to animals. In Exodus, the command to rest on the Sabbath day says, "you must not do any work—you, your son or daughter, your male or female servant, *your livestock*, or the resident alien who is within your city gates" (Exod. 20:10). In Deuteronomy, the wording is expanded slightly, saying, "Do not do any work—you, your son or daughter, your male or female slave, *your ox or donkey, any of your livestock*, or the resident alien who lives within your city gates, so that your male and female slaves may rest as you do" (Deut. 5:14). It is not simply that animals are to be given rest so that human beings can rest, as though it would be acceptable, if possible, to have animals work as long as human beings did not have to. Rather, animals are to be given rest because it is part of caring for them. The law also makes provision to care for an ox when it says, "Do not muzzle an ox while it treads out grain" (Deut. 25:4). The care for animals is significant enough that it is a proverbial mark of the righteous person: "The righteous cares about his animal's health" (Prov. 12:10). These texts articulate a principle that can be deduced from the creation accounts. Since God created all creatures, and delights in them, then part of ruling over them includes caring for their needs. The naming of animals (Gen. 2:19–20) indicates Adam's authority over

them, but it also suggests that he would have to know and care for the animals in order to name them. It is significant, too, that in the beginning God did not give animals to human beings for food, indicating an original relationship of harmony. Only after the flood is that relationship said to be one in which animals fear and dread human beings, and that God then gives them for food (Gen. 9:2–3).

It is difficult to develop a complete ethics of animal care from the few references we have in Scripture. For instance, we do not see, as some advocates would demand, animal "rights" in the same sense as human rights. That is, there is not an inalienable right to life, and there is a definite distinction between humans and animals in status and treatment. They may be used for food, yet animals should be protected from abuse and treated with care. We ought to delight in them as God does.

Deuteronomy 8:7–10; 20:19–20

These texts show both that God has placed within creation things that human beings will discover by subduing the earth for human benefit, and yet that to subdue is not the same as to destroy. Deuteronomy 8:7–10 details the blessing of the land that God has given to Israel. Included in it is the statement that it is "a land whose rocks are iron and from whose hills you will mine copper" (v. 9). This is no license for ravaging the earth, but it does affirm that part of subduing is "mining" the earth for things that are of benefit to human beings (and other creatures).

Deuteronomy 20:19–20 also contributes to our understanding. It says, "When you lay siege to a city for a long time, fighting against it in order to capture it, do not destroy its trees by putting an ax to them, because you can get food from them. Do not cut them down. Are trees of the field human, to come under siege by you? But you may destroy the trees that you know do not produce food. You may cut them down to build siege works against the city that is waging war against you, until it falls." This text has notable features. First, it distinguishes between fruit-producing trees and those that don't produce fruit, when wood is needed for human purposes, such as battle against an enemy. Second, in the midst of warfare, Israel is commanded to preserve fruit trees, because they provide food for human beings. They would normally need no such reminder, dependent as they were on the land and its produce. Yet in the heat of war, when "people forget everything except immediate human ambitions," God's command serves an important reminder that the environment is not to be destroyed. "Concession is made to cut down some trees (v. 20)," Andrew Cameron writes, "but this command highlights the way no human project justifies wholesale environmental destruction."[51]

Psalm 19:1–6; 97:6; Isaiah 6:3; Romans 1:20

Psalm 19:1 affirms,

> The heavens declare the glory of God,
> and the expanse proclaims the work of his hands.

Similarly, Psalm 97:6 states,

> The heavens proclaim his righteousness;
> all the peoples see his glory.

In Isaiah's vision of the Lord on his throne, he declares,

> Holy, holy, holy is the LORD of Armies;
> his glory fills the whole earth. (Isa. 6:3)

This may testify not only to the magnificence of God's glory but also (consistent with the Psalms) that the earth reflects God's glory.[52] Creation does not simply indicate that there is a God, but it tells us something about God, if we are not blinded by our sin. So Paul says that God has shown himself in creation: "For his invisible attributes, that is, his eternal power and divine nature, have been clearly seen since the creation of the world, being understood through what he has made. As a result, people are without excuse" (Rom. 1:20).

---

51. Andrew J. B. Cameron, *Joined-Up Life: A Christian Account of How Ethics Works* (Nottingham, UK: Inter-Varsity Press, 2011), 265.
52. Hilary Marlow, *Biblical Prophets and Contemporary Environmental Ethics* (Oxford: Oxford University Press, 2009), 237. Marlow notes that the noun מְלֹא (fullness) is used, possibly suggesting that "the fullness of all the earth is his glory." Cited in Moo and Moo, *Creation Care*, 58.

These are a few examples of biblical texts that declare that God's creation testifies not only to the fact that God exists (that should be obvious enough!) but also to something about God, particularly his glory. Psalm 19, in fact, affirms two major sources of knowledge of God: the general knowledge of God revealed in creation (vv. 1–6) and the particular, perfect knowledge of God's will revealed in Scripture (vv. 7–11). Douglas and Jonathan Moo suggest two apologetic principles that may be derived from the truth that creation testifies to God. First, as we speak of the goodness of God's work in creation, it may resonate with unbelievers. They note that, in the New Testament, there are only two occasions recorded when the gospel is preached to people who are not familiar with the Old Testament. Interestingly, on both occasions the preaching of the gospel begins with reference to creation.[53] In Acts 14, when the people in Lystra observe that Paul healed a lame man, they conclude that Paul and Barnabas are gods (vv. 8–12). Paul and Barnabas then tear their clothes and shout,

> People! Why are you doing these things? We are people also, just like you, and we are proclaiming good news to you, that you turn from these worthless things to the living God, who made the heaven, the earth, the sea, and everything in them. In past generations he allowed all the nations to go their own way, although he did not leave himself without a witness, since he did what is good by giving you rain from heaven and fruitful

seasons and filling you with food and your hearts with joy. (vv. 15–17)

Also, in the familiar text from Acts 17, when Paul sees the altar to an unknown god, he tells them, "What you worship in ignorance, this I proclaim to you. The God who made the world and everything in it—he is Lord of heaven and earth—does not live in shrines made by hands" (vv. 23–24). He calls them to repentance, declaring that God has provided proof of his judgment through Jesus (vv. 30–31).

The second apologetic principle that we may derive from the knowledge of God in creation, according to the authors, concerns how believers treat what God has made. If we are cavalier and careless in how we live and treat God's creation, not only do we prove to be unfaithful stewards, but we "have also profoundly hindered our witness to the glory of God in Christ."[54] It is a tragedy that so many people love creation but don't know the Creator. It is also a tragedy that they sometimes observe that those who claim to know and love the Creator care little for his creation.

Psalm 24:1; 50:10–12; 89:11; 115:16

The Psalms assert the obvious deduction from the reality that God created the heavens and the earth, that it all belongs to God. Psalm 24:1 makes this point clearly:

> The earth and everything in it,
> the world and its inhabitants,
> belong to the LORD.

---

53. Moo and Moo, *Creation Care*, 59–60.
54. Moo and Moo, *Creation Care*, 60.

Similarly, Psalm 50:10–12 says,

> Every animal of the forest is mine,
> the cattle on a thousand hills.
> I know every bird of the mountains,
> and the creatures of the field are mine.
> If I were hungry, I would not tell you,
> for the world and everything in it is mine.

God may grant human beings the right of sub-ownership and use, but everything is clearly his, not ours. Psalm 89:11 says,

> The heavens are yours; the earth also is yours.
> The world and everything in it—you founded them.

Psalm 115:16 qualifies this slightly, saying,

> The heavens are the Lord's,
> but the earth he has given to the human race.

It is given to human beings to steward by subduing and ruling, but it belongs to God. Because the earth and everything in it was created by God and belongs to God, it is not ours simply to do with as we please. We are responsible, even as we use it, to care for it wisely.

Psalm 104

As we have seen already, the Psalms contain numerous passages for reflection on the significance of creation and implications for human stewardship. No psalm contributes more to the discussion than Psalm 104. As an affirmation of God's handiwork in creation, Psalm 104 not only reflects the creation account in Genesis 1 but also builds on it by describing God's intimate relationship with what he has created, including his sustaining care. As such, "it brings the reader to a more heightened awareness of the response appropriate to the foundational truth it declares."[55]

Psalm 104 begins and ends with praise to God the Creator:

> My soul, bless the Lord!
> Lord my God, you are very great;
> you are clothed with majesty and splendor. . . .
> May the glory of the Lord endure forever;
> may the Lord rejoice in his works. . . .
> I will sing to the Lord all my life;
> I will sing praise to my God while I live.
> May my meditation be pleasing to him;
> I will rejoice in the Lord. . . .
> My soul, bless the Lord!
> Hallelujah! (vv. 1, 31, 33–35)

Reflection on creation should thus cause us to praise God, for "creation continually bears witness to the perfections of God and promotes in man praise toward God."[56] The psalmist describes the majestic work of creation, reflecting Genesis 1 (Ps. 104:1–9), and the wisdom with which everything was made, providing habitats and sustenance for all creatures. He provides water for every wild beast and the birds of the sky (vv.

55. Bullmore, "Four Most Important Biblical Passages," 143.
56. Bullmore, "Four Most Important Biblical Passages," 143.

10–12). He makes grass grow for cattle (v. 14). He provides trees for the birds to make their nests (v. 17), high mountains for wild goats and cliffs for hyraxes (v. 18). Even the prey for lions is provided from God (v. 21)! He provides food for the creatures of the sea as well (v. 27). If God cares for all that he has made, human beings should too, as part of human rule and dominion.

The praise evoked is not simply or even primarily because of God's care for human beings. It is easy to think of creation as made for human consumption, use, and enjoyment. This psalm does recognize God's provisions for human beings, affirming that God

> provides crops for man to cultivate,
> producing food from the earth,
> wine that makes human hearts glad—
> making his face shine with oil—
> and bread that sustains human hearts. (vv. 14–15)

Yet we may ask whether creation has a reason for being apart from a service to human beings.[57] It seems that a central point of this psalm is to assert that it does.

While God has made human beings in his own image, and given human beings a unique and distinct role in creation, this psalm directs us away from an anthropocentric view of the world. Not everything is made to serve human beings! The center of the psalm gives the chief cause of praise:

> How countless are your works, LORD!
> In wisdom you have made them all;
> the earth is full of your creatures. (v. 24)

Indeed, the psalmist describes creatures in places where human beings do not dwell, and that humans never see. The sea is vast and wide, teeming with creatures beyond number (v. 25). Intriguingly, one of the creatures of the sea is "Leviathan, which you formed to play there" (v. 26). Many things in creation serve no purpose for human beings, yet God delights in them, and creates them for his delight. Indeed, "the earth and all things in it belong to God by virtue of his creative work, and all things find their reason for being fundamentally in relation to him."[58] This theocentric view of creation can serve to "rescue us from the greed or indifference that so easily invade an anthropocentric view."[59]

Creation Care in the New Testament?

The Psalms, and the Old Testament in general, have much to contribute to environmental ethics and creation care. What about the New Testament? It might be tempting to think that the New Testament is not concerned at all about creation care, and instead is focused on human salvation and reconciliation with God and other human beings. Indeed, it might be portrayed as having an indifferent or even callous posture toward creation, based on a view that it will all be

---

57. Bullmore, "Four Most Important Biblical Passages," 144.
58. Bullmore, "Four Most Important Biblical Passages," 143.
59. Bullmore, "Four Most Important Biblical Passages," 147.

destroyed anyway, giving way to the establishment of a new creation.

Admittedly, fewer New Testament passages discuss creation, but we should be careful not to conclude that it is therefore indifferent about creation. As a general point, we ought to assume that the New Testament is consistent with the Old Testament, and that it affirms what the Old Testament affirms unless it clearly indicates otherwise. Some may assert that it does indeed indicate otherwise, but that view will be challenged here. First, Jesus appeals to nature in his teaching, and affirms God's care for what he has created. Second, the New Testament asserts a theocentric perspective on creation, for everything is made by Jesus and for him, not merely for humankind. Third, Paul indicates that the creation itself awaits redemption and renewal, not destruction. Fourth, the view that the New Testament teaches that the earth will be destroyed in the end is likely not the best understanding of some passages that are difficult to interpret. Each of these points will be made looking briefly at New Testament texts.

Matthew 6:26, 28–30

In these verses from the Sermon on the Mount Jesus encourages his listeners not to worry about food and clothing. God feeds the birds of the air and clothes the grass of the field. Will he not take care of human beings, who are of more value than these? If human beings are much more valuable to God than these things, some might conclude that these things are of little value to God. However, that would miss Jesus's

point, that God created the birds and the grass, and he cares for what he has created. He delights even to adorn the lilies of the field to out shine Solomon's "glory" (v. 29)! If God cares about these things, we should care about them. We ought to stop and see the beauty of God's creation and the great care with which he created—and then appreciate even how much more he cares for human beings!

John 1:1–3; Colossians 1:15–17 (cf. 1 Corinthians 8:6)

In a clear allusion to the creation account in Genesis, the Gospel of John begins by declaring Jesus's divine nature, and that Jesus was the agent of creation. It reads, "In the beginning was the Word, and the Word was with God, and the Word was God. He was with God in the beginning. All things were created through him, and apart from him not one thing was created that has been created" (John 1:1–3). In Colossians 1:16–17, Paul affirms and expands what John says about Jesus when he asserts that

> everything was created by him . . .
> all things have been created through him
>   and for him.
> He is before all things,
> and by him all things hold together. (cf. 1
>   Cor. 8:6)

Here we see that Jesus not only created all things but also sustains all things. Jesus would delight in the lilies of the field, which he created by his own power and wisdom! He would recognize his own provision in feeding the birds of the air, or providing a place of shelter and rest for foxes and birds (Matt. 8:20)—highlighting the ironic reality that the one who provided for every creature has no place to lay his own head! Moreover, in Colossians Paul expresses a theocentric—or more particularly, a Christocentric—perspective of creation: everything was created for Jesus, not merely for the use of human beings.

Romans 1:22–25

It is proper, if we know God and love God, to love and delight in what God has created.[60] On the other hand, the love of nature should never become the worship of nature, which is a sign and consequence of rejecting the knowledge of God. This is part of the case that Paul makes against those "who by their unrighteousness suppress the truth" (Rom. 1:18). As we have seen, creation points to God and his nature, so that those who reject the truth are without excuse (v. 20). Paul exposes the senselessness and foolishness of refusing to recognize God as Creator and to glorify him (vv. 21–22). Those who suppress the truth are given over to moral impurity (v. 24). To show the foolishness of human sin, Paul uses the language of exchange, for human beings are made to worship, and if we do not worship God we will worship something else. Therefore, he says, "Claiming to be wise, they became fools and exchanged the glory of the immortal God for images resembling mortal man, birds, four-footed animals, and reptiles. . . . They exchanged the truth of God for a lie, and worshiped and served what has been created instead of the Creator, who is praised forever" (vv. 22–23, 25). What was true in Paul's day is true in ours, for some who reject God see nature itself as godlike, to be viewed with the reverence and awe that is reserved for God alone.[61] A true knowledge of and love for God will lead neither to the destruction of nature nor the worship of nature.

Romans 8:18–23; Colossians 1:20

We have seen already that human sin had significant consequences for nature itself.[62] Paul makes this point in Romans 8:18–23. The "whole creation has been groaning together with labor pains until now" (v. 22) because it "was subjected to futility—not willingly, but because of him who subjected it" (v. 20).[63] Creation refers to nonhuman

---

60. Cf. Young, *Healing the Earth*, 212.
61. One well-known example of this view is found in Lovelock, *Gaia*.
62. In addition to Gen. 3, this is seen in the promises to Israel of blessing for their obedience, where the animals and land will be blessed as well (e.g., Deut. 7:12–14; 11:15), and curses for disobedience, which fall on creatures and the land (Deut. 28:15–68). It is also a theme in the Prophets, where the land and creatures suffer and mourn because of Israel's sin (Isa. 24:4–7; Jer. 4:23–28; 9:12–14; 12:4, 10–11; Hosea 4:1–3). For some development of this, see Moo and Moo, *Creation Care*, 99–113.
63. The subjection must be by God, but it also must be because of human sin. Here is an echo of the pronouncement made by God in Genesis 3:27: "the ground is cursed because of you." So, Douglas and Jonathan Moo write, "who is the 'one who subjected' creation? Given that the subjection was done on the basis of the hope that creation would then come to share in the freedom and glory of the children of God, it can be none other than God himself. He alone would have the power both to condemn creation to its present state and to ensure its glorious future. Yet,

creation,[64] which has been subject to futility by God because of human sin, causing it to groan. It is striking that the connection between human beings and the rest of creation is not just in the bondage of sin but in the liberation of redemption as well. The central message of the text has to do with the liberation of the children of God, who are currently suffering, but will be glorified (v. 18), so we now grown while we eagerly await the redemption of our bodies (v. 23). Yet, surprisingly, Paul asserts that the redemption of the children of God will mean freedom from bondage for the rest of creation: "Creation eagerly waits with anticipation for God's sons to be revealed" (v. 19) because "creation itself will also be set free from the bondage to decay into the glorious freedom of God's children" (v. 21). Creation was made to glorify God, but having been subjected to futility, it has been kept from fully realizing the purposes for which God made it. However, with the redemption of the children of God, creation will be set free and "will enjoy a glorious renewal of its ability to be as it was created to be."[65] All creation is included in the hope of the gospel and the consequent freedom from bondage!

Colossians speaks to this point as well. Paul declares that *everything* "in heaven and on earth" was created by Jesus, through Jesus, and for Jesus, and is sustained by Jesus (Col. 1:16–17). Then he says:

> God was pleased to have
> all his fullness dwell in him,
> and through him to reconcile
> *everything* to himself,
> *whether things on earth or things in heaven,*
> by making peace
> through his blood, shed on the cross. (vv. 19–20, emphasis added)

Usually the language of reconciliation refers to the relationship between God and human beings. In this text, however, it is not likely that "everything" (or "all things") refers only to human beings. Rather, the reconciliation of everything in verse 20 corresponds to the creation of everything in verse 15. Douglas and Jonathan Moo comment that it is likely "that the description of God's reconciling all things to himself here is a way of claiming that God will ultimately bring everything in the universe into its appropriate relationship with himself." They conclude that according to Colossians 1:15–20, "Nothing in the universe falls outside of the scope of God's creative and redemptive work in Christ."[66] This is a reminder that God cares for and has a lasting purpose for his creation. If God delights in everything that he has created—both the human and nonhuman

---

if we ask *how* God subjected creation to futility, we find that the only answer can be that God subjected creation to futility by subjecting creation to Adam and to all of humankind. In giving humankind dominion over creation, creation's fate became linked to ours." Moo and Moo, *Creation Care*, 109.

64. See Thomas R. Schreiner, *Romans*, Baker Exegetical Commentary on the New Testament (Grand Rapids: Baker, 1998), 435.

65. Bullmore, "Four Most Important Biblical Passages," 159.

66. Moo and Moo, *Creation Care*, 142.

creation—and will one day liberate the non-human creation from bondage, should we not care about and for all of creation? It will not simply be destroyed when the children of God are revealed. Or will it? Some passages in the New Testament, in particular 2 Peter 3:10, have been interpreted to say that this world will be destroyed ("burned up"). Is that what it teaches?

2 Peter 3:10–13

In the NASB, this text reads (emphasis added),

> But the day of the Lord will come like a thief, in which *the heavens will pass away with a roar* and *the elements will be destroyed with intense heat*, and *the earth and its works will be burned up.*
>
> Since *all these things are to be destroyed in this way,* what sort of people ought you to be in holy conduct and godliness, looking for and hastening the coming of the day of God, because of which *the heavens will be destroyed by burning,* and *the elements will melt with intense heat!* But according to His promise we are looking for new heavens and a new earth, in which righteousness dwells.

The King James and Revised Versions are very similar in wording. It is not too surprising if readers conclude that Peter is declaring that the earth will be destroyed.

Further, some might conclude that if the earth will be destroyed one day, why worry too much about its preservation now?[67] How should we interpret and respond to this text?

To begin with, it should be said that if the earth is one day to be destroyed, it does not follow that we should not concern ourselves with preserving it now. First, because it would be God's prerogative to destroy what he has made, not ours. By analogy, if God determined to destroy Nineveh for their rebellion, it would not give any human authority the right to destroy it on their own terms. Second, by another analogy, it would be like saying that since our body will decay and face death, it doesn't matter what we do with it now. For now, we are responsible to take care of our body, and for now, we are responsible to take care of the earth.

Furthermore, the NASB, and other versions that indicate that the earth will be utterly destroyed and burned up, may not offer the best translation. One of the terms in question in 2 Peter 3:10 is εὑρεθήσεται, translated "burned up." The NIV says that "the earth and everything done in it will be laid bare." The HCSB says that "the earth and the works on it will be disclosed." Thomas Schreiner states that a literal translation reads that "the earth and the works in it shall be found," with εὑρεθήσεται translated "shall be found"[68] (the exclamation

---

67. Some have argued that the eschatological view of the present creation in dispensationalism and premillennialism leads to a disregard for environmental concerns. Examples noted by John Jefferson Davis include Al Truesdale, "Last Things First: The Impact of Eschatology on Ecology," *Perspectives on Science and Christian Faith* 46, no. 2 (1994): 116–22; and Thomas Finger, *Evangelicals, Eschatology, and the Environment* (Wynnewood, PA: Evangelical Environmental Network, 1998). See Davis, "Ecological 'Blind Spots,'" 274n8.
68. Thomas R. Schreiner, *1, 2 Peter, Jude*, New American Commentary 37 (Nashville: Broadman & Holman, 2003), 385.

eureka comes from this Greek term, "to find"). This is, admittedly, a strange and difficult sentence. Because it seems to be an obscure expression, there are textual variations that are apparently based on scribal conjecture, and challenges for scholars interpreting the phrase.

The "day of the Lord" (v. 10) is an Old Testament expression that is "often used to refer to God's judgment and salvation," and in the New Testament it refers to the day of Christ."[69] Peter's emphasis here is that the day of the Lord will come suddenly ("like a thief"), so we must be prepared for the return of Christ and the judgment. Verse 10 says that "the elements will burn" (CSB; NASB: "the elements will be destroyed with intense heat"), so some translators determine that εὑρεθήσεται refers to the destruction in the judgment, and they conclude that the earth and its works will be burned up (cf. v. 7).

However, if "shall be found" is a better translation, it should first be asked whether that makes sense. It may be that Peter does not mean to indicate that the earth will be burned up, but that something will be found out. That is, when the day of the Lord comes, there will be a judgment, when the refiner's fire will destroy the works of ungodliness (cf. v. 7), and "the earth and the works on it" will be found out (NIV: "laid bare"; HCSB: "disclosed"), meaning that

the works of humankind will be exposed by God in the judgment.[70] This is consistent with Old Testament use of judgment language. Isaiah, for instance, "very often uses the imagery of fire to refer to God's judgment (Isa. 1:31; 4:4; 5:24; 9:5, 19; 10:16–17; 26:11; 27:4; 29:6; 30:27–33; 31:9; 33:11, 14–15; 47:14; see also, e.g., Nah. 1:6; Zeph. 1:18; 3:8; Mal. 4:1)."[71] Peter may well be drawing from these Old Testament references, where "apocalyptic-style prophecy features vivid references to physical destruction in order to convey the terrifying reality of God's intervention to judge a sinful and rebellious world."[72] It therefore ties together Peter's references to God's judgment and the day of the Lord (v. 10): "There will be no hiding from God on that great day: all will be 'laid bare' before God so that he might judge fairly and equitably."[73]

So Christopher Wright asserts that "the purpose of the conflagration described in these verses is not the *obliteration of the cosmos itself* but rather *the purging of the sinful world order we live in*, through the consuming destruction of all that is evil within creation, so as to establish the new creation." Interestingly, Peter compares the destruction of God's final judgment by fire in these verses with that of the flood in Genesis (2 Pet. 3:6–7), where the devastation was not a final destruction of the physical world,

---

69. Schreiner, *1, 2 Peter, Jude*, 383.
70. Liederbach and Bible, *True North*, 124, argue for this interpretation.
71. Moo and Moo, *Creation Care*, 159.
72. Moo and Moo, *Creation Care*, 159.
73. Moo and Moo, *Creation Care*, 157. See their discussion of the contested term εὑρεθήσεται in v. 10, "laid bare" vs. "burned up," 156–61.

but a judgment on human sin. As Wright puts it, "A world of wickedness was wiped out in the flood, but the world as God's creation was preserved. Similarly, by analogy, the world of all evil and wickedness in creation will be wiped out in God's cataclysmic judgment, but the creation itself will be renewed as the dwelling place of God with redeemed humanity."[74] The emphasis in verses 11–12 is consistent with this view. Because of the anticipated judgment, which could come at any time, we ought to live "in holy conduct and godliness" as we wait, for evil works will be burned up.

We thus need not understand this text to contradict Romans 8. Taken together we see a vision of the future when the children of God will be glorified, sin and evil will be judged and vanquished, and the earth will be renewed so that it can fulfill the purposes for which God created it. It is unlikely that Peter is claiming that the earth will be destroyed. It is, further, a terrible application of this passage to reach the conclusion that, according to Peter, we can destroy the earth (or even act indifferently toward it).

Summary and Implications Drawn from Biblical Teaching

God delights in what he has made, for it is good. Creation, therefore, does not merely have instrumental value as it serves human needs. Rather, "the heavens declare the glory of God, and the expanse proclaims the work of his hands" (Ps. 19:1) whether human beings observe it or not. Human beings cannot see all of the heavens, yet the heavens declare the glory of God. Human beings cannot see all of the beauty in the depths of the sea, yet Psalm 148:7 declares,

> Praise the LORD from the earth,
> all sea monsters and ocean depths.

The wildflowers, trees, and various animals that we pass by virtually every day are not there by accident, but are adorned by God with splendor (Luke 12:27), and God knows and enjoys them whether human beings observe them or not. Thus John Piper asserts that creation doesn't serve only to testify about God's glory to human beings: "Creation praises God by simply being what it was created to be in all its incredible variety. And since most of the creation is beyond the awareness of mankind (in the reaches of space, and in the heights of mountains and at the bottom of the sea) it wasn't created merely to serve purposes that have to do with us. It was created for the enjoyment of God."[75] Similarly, John Jefferson Davis asserts that while plants have instrumental value in serving as food for human beings and animals, "prior to any such use plants have intrinsic value because they are God's

---

74. Christopher J. H. Wright, *The Mission of God: Unlocking the Bible's Grand Narrative* (Downers Grove, IL: IVP Academic, 2006), 209.
75. John Piper, *The Pleasures of God: Meditations on God's Delight in Being God* (Colorado Springs: Multnomah, 2012), 90.

creations that reflect his glory and are the objects of his delight."[76]

Human beings, as God's image bearers, have been given the task of subduing and ruling God's world in accordance with God's design. It is the role of a steward, caretaker, or manager. Thus we ought to love and delight in what God has made—and take time to notice and enjoy the splendidly adorned flowers of the field, as God does! By God's gracious calling, we are permitted, and even commanded, to develop the earth for human benefit. This highlights the fact that human beings both rule over the earth and yet are dependent on it and intimately involved with it every day. We need clean air and water to flourish. We depend on the soil and the crops that we grow in the soil. Much of our leisure time is spent exploring and enjoying our natural environment. In short, "we all engage with creation all the time."[77]

Human beings are uniquely able to have dominion over and subdue the earth. Indeed, in our subduing we are able to do amazing things: create medicine from nature, build cities and coordinate supply lines for millions of human beings and their needs, develop energy from a wide variety of natural resources, increase crop efficiency and distribution to feed billions of people, domesticate and care for animals, to name a few things. Yet we remain embedded in creation and dependent on it, and often we do damage to our natural environment. As noted earlier, Christians and a Christian worldview are sometimes accused of being a major cause of environmental problems. While we have seen that such criticisms are not well founded, it should not surprise us that human beings, Christians included, go beyond a good use to an abuse of creation, and that some cite the biblical text to defend their abuse. As Andrew Cameron writes, "Rapacity can easily use Christian slogans."[78]

There is sometimes a tension between environmental activists and Christians. The reasons for this are complex, intersecting with political affiliation, views on science versus religion, and especially worldview issues, particularly belief in a Creator God or the denial of God's existence. Indeed, Davis suggests that part of the reason that conservative evangelicals are sometimes ambivalent about environmental concerns is due to "the association of prominent streams of the environmental movement with 'New Age' and eastern religions, liberal Protestant theologies, feminism, and opposition to free-market capitalism."[79] Yet we ought to recognize converging interests and common ground in our common humanity and our common dependence on and love for creation. After discussing God's care for and delight in his creation, including things about which human beings are quite unaware, Cameron notes that "we see an echo of this character in the delight

76. John Jefferson Davis, *Evangelical Ethics: Issues Facing the Church Today*, 4th ed. (Phillipsburg, NJ: P&R, 2015), 266.
77. Cameron, *Joined-Up Life*, 261.
78. Cameron, *Joined-Up Life*, 262.
79. Davis, "Ecological 'Blind Spots,'" 274.

of the scientist, the wilderness activist or the zookeeper."[80] We may learn awe-inspiring things about God's creation from them, be attentive when they call us to protect or preserve some part of creation, and may point them back to the God whose handiwork they observe and in which they delight. We may also demonstrate our care for the natural environment, though it is differently grounded and motivated. We surely should not simply assert a human right to consume and use created goods unchecked.

A General Approach to Creation Care and Environmental Ethics

If we are to subdue and rule properly, to cultivate and keep the part of creation over which God has made human beings responsible, what basic attitude should we have toward the "garden" and the "wilderness"? Several approaches may be considered:[81]

- *Preservation* seeks to maintain natural habitats, to preserve them from significant human development (if humans are there at all, there is some development), as in the case of the National Park System in the United States (which has been called America's best idea[82]), as well as various preserves, sanctuaries, wetlands, and wilderness.[83]
- *Restoration* seeks to facilitate a return to a "pristine" state of nature or wilderness in dedicated areas. This may not entail the undoing of a developed area. It may simply mean an attempt to restore a natural previous state that has been disturbed, for example, by development

80. Cameron, *Joined-Up Life*, 265.
81. See *Kairos Journal*, "Four Environmentalisms," https://kairosjournal.org/document.aspx?DocumentID=9752&QuadrantID=4&CategoryID=11&TopicID=44&L=1.
82. National Park Service, "America's Best Idea Today," https://www.nps.gov/americasbestidea. The National Park System covers over 84 million acres. It includes sixty national parks, including Yellowstone National Park, the nation's (and world's) first national park, established by Congress on March 1, 1872. Information from https://www.nps.gov/aboutus/index.htm. Yellowstone National Park alone is over 2.2 million acres (larger than Rhode Island and Delaware combined). Information on Yellowstone from National Park Service, "Park Facts," https://www.nps.gov/yell/planyourvisit/parkfacts.htm.
83. The US National Wilderness Preservation System "includes more than 700 areas in 44 states, totaling more than 107 million acres." Montana Wilderness Association, "What Is Wilderness," http://wildmontana.org/discover-the-wild/what-is-wilderness. In the Wilderness Act of 1964, Public Law 88–577 (16 U.S.C. 1131–1136) 88th Congress (Second Session, September 3, 1964), 891, https://www.govinfo.gov/content/pkg/STATUTE-78/pdf/STATUTE-78-Pg890.pdf, "wilderness" is defined in this way (note that point 2 evidences an anthropocentric perspective!): "(c) A wilderness, in contrast with those areas where man and his works dominate the landscape, is hereby recognized as an area where the earth and its community of life are untrammeled by man, where man himself is a visitor who does not remain. An area of wilderness is further defined to mean in this Act an area of undeveloped Federal land retaining its primeval character and influence, without permanent improvements or human habitation, which is protected and managed so as to preserve its natural conditions and which (1) generally appears to have been affected primarily by the forces of nature, with the imprint of man's work substantially unnoticeable; (2) has outstanding opportunities for solitude or a primitive and unconfined type of recreation; (3) has at least five thousand acres of land or is of sufficient size as to make practicable its preservation and use in an unimpaired condition; and (4) may also contain ecological, geological, or other features of scientific, educational, scenic, or historical value."

around the area, or by the removal of certain species of animals or the habitat in which they thrive. The American Prairie Reserve in Montana is an example of a large restoration project.[84]

- *Conservation* is an approach to nature that seeks to use nature wisely, to manage it carefully for human benefit.[85]

Each of these has a certain appeal and can be defended from a biblical worldview perspective, and each may be part of an overarching approach to environmental ethics and creation care. Conservation is consistent with meeting the needs of human beings in the present and the future, and with the call to sustainability that is made with increasing urgency. Preservation and restoration, if pursued along with conservation, give attention to the beauty of God's creation and to the protection of nonhuman creation and habitats that exhibit a stewardship over what God has made. Further, they remind us that creation does not exist solely for human benefit.

There are tensions between those who hold different views of the environment, especially between those who seek to preserve or restore nature and those who seek to develop it for human benefit. Often, but not always, preservation and restoration are understood to be hostile toward development. Some environmentalist consider development to be almost entirely negative, and understand the "pristine" wilderness to be the goal to pursue as far as possible.

Conservation and development need not be seen as merely anthropocentric. The biblical picture is one in which God delights in and values what he has created, appointing human beings to steward it well, in large measure for human benefit. As "sub-creators," human beings are given to subdue the earth in a godly way, which includes developing the wilderness into useful gardens, among other things. It is not a permit to degrade and destroy, but to develop in a manner that both respects and protects what God has made and benefits human beings. It includes developing technologies for human well-being (technology need not be destructive of nature), mining the earth to produce goods, developing beneficial medicines from plants, and caring for God's world in the process. Douglas and Jonathan Moo, who urge restraint and care for creation, recognize that "both conservation and development are integral aspects of human 'rule' of the earth," and that "it takes considerable

---

84. The American Prairie Reserve is an attempt to create "the largest nature reserve in the continental United States" by an innovative nonprofit model that seeks to purchase private lands and connect them to public lands to create a vast area that will total over 3 million acres. Among other things, it seeks to restore natural migration patterns of animals that were once prominent on these lands in Montana. Information is take from the American Prairie Reserve website, https://www.americanprairie.org.

85. Bouma-Prediger, *For the Beauty of the Earth*, 120. Bouma-Prediger notes that conservation is often derided by environmentalists, as it is anthropocentric, though he sees it as better than alternatives that are destructive of nature and its resources.

wisdom to determine which is best in any given situation."[86]

Conclusion

While I have not dealt with many of the contentious issues raised in contemporary environmental ethics, I have sought to give a broad biblical perspective on creation and human relation to it. I would like to end with an issue that may not be the most contentious or central issue for environmental ethics, but it draws attention to what I would argue are virtues and vices that have an effect on the environment, and may be applied to a range of issues.

One of the things that is highlighted by environmentalists is the waste that human beings generate. Recycling, repackaging, reusable containers, and innovative products made from "waste" are various means that are commended as part of environmental friendly habits. In response, some see all these things as unnecessary or excessive and burdensome on the consumer, given the cost or effort, alternatives, and so on. Further, they may add, we are not in danger of running out of space used for garbage dumps. All of that may be true (though the problem of plastic and other garbage ending up in the oceans is a significant one).[87] Yet, one of the things that such waste calls attention to

that Christians ought to be concerned about is the pattern of mass consumption that we have been trained to think is good. In the spirit of *homoeconomicus*, we are told that if it is good for "the economy," often in the short run at that, it must be good. We ought to think carefully about ways that we can conserve rather than consume, so that we are not driven by a gluttonous use of material things, and so set an example as stewards of what God has given us to use well, for others to see.

We are accustomed to buying much more than we can consume. We live in such luxury that our food spoils and we think nothing of it, but simply throw it away. Restaurants fill garbage bins with food that customers leave, even after paying handsomely for it. According to the Food and Agriculture Organization of the United Nations, "Roughly one third of the food produced in the world for human consumption every year—approximately 1.3 billion tonnes—gets lost or wasted."[88] In poor countries, the waste is generally due to a lack of refrigeration, or food that spoils on the way from the farm to the market. Very little is thrown away by consumers. Those issues of waste can be largely solved by technological improvements. By contrast, "In wealthy countries, especially in the United States and

---

86. Moo and Moo, *Creation Care*, 193. See also Ron Elsdon, *Green Theology: Biblical Perspectives on Caring for Creation* (Tunbridge Wells, UK: Monarch, 1992), cited by Moo and Moo.

87. One team of scientists that attempted to inventory the amount of plastic in the Pacific Ocean between California and Hawaii, in an area known as the Great Pacific Garbage Patch, estimated the total area to be three times the size of France. Chris Mooney, "Plastic within the Great Pacific Garbage Patch Is 'Increasing Exponentially,' Scientists Find," *Washington Post*, March 22, 2018, https://www.washingtonpost.com/news/energy-environment/wp/2018/03/22/plastic-within-the-great-pacific-garbage-patch-is-increasing-exponentially-scientists-find.

88. https://www.save-food.org/en/Projects/Studies/Global_food_losses_and_food_waste.

Canada, around 40 percent of wasted food is thrown out by consumers."[89]

In this context, consider John's telling of the feeding of the five thousand (John 6:1–14). The crowd ate as much as they wanted (v. 11). Then John says that when the crowd was full, Jesus told his disciples, "Collect the leftovers so that nothing is wasted" (v. 12). This is striking, for Jesus could multiply the loaves and the fish endlessly; there is no scarcity. Yet, as Douglas and Jonathan Moo comment, "Even in a context of overflowing, apparently limitless abundance, the gifts of God's creation are not to be disdained, left to rot, or wasted."[90] It seems fair to say, then, that with our abundance, "even if we faced no crisis in our use and distribution of resources . . . we would all the same be called as God's people to a carefulness and appropriate restraint that reflects our appreciation of the goodness both of our own limited creatureliness and of the gifts God provides."[91]

This, it seems to me, is applicable to our use of food and other consumer goods, as well as the use of energy and natural resources. Whether or not a change in our energy-consumption habits will have a direct effect on something like climate change, it is an issue for how we steward our lives and resources. And if we steward them well, it seems fair to say that we will have a more positive, or less negative, impact on our environment and will demonstrate a more godly care for creation.

---

89. Somini Sengupta, "How Much Food Do We Waste? Probably More Than You Think," *The New York Times*, December 12, 2017, https://www.nytimes.com/2017/12/12/climate/food-waste-emissions.html. The reason much more food is thrown out in wealthy countries, not surprisingly, is because it costs relatively little, especially as a percentage of income, and we buy more than we can eat. So, Sengupta reports, the United States wastes more than $160 billion in food each year.
90. Moo and Moo, *Creation Care*, 122–23.
91. Moo and Moo, *Creation Care*, 123.

Select Resources

Bouma-Prediger, Steven. *For the Beauty of the Earth: A Christian Vision for Creation Care.* 2nd ed. Grand Rapids: Baker Academic, 2010.

Bullmore, Michael A. "The Four Most Important Biblical Passages for a Christian Environmental Ethic." *Trinity Journal* 19, no. 2 (1998): 139–62.

Davis, John Jefferson. "Ecological 'Blind Spots' in the Structure and Content of Recent Evangelical Systematic Theologies." *Journal of the Evangelical Theological Society* 43, no. 2 (June 2000): 273–86.

Liederbach, Mark, and Seth Bible. *True North: Christ, the Gospel, and Creation Care.* Nashville: B&H, 2012.

McGrath, Alister. *The Reenchantment of Nature: The Denial of Religion and the Ecological Crisis.* New York: Doubleday, 2002.

Moo, Douglas J., and Jonathan A. Moo. *Creation Care: A Biblical Theology of the Natural World.* Biblical Theology for Life. Grand Rapids: Zondervan, 2018.

Santmire, H. Paul. *The Travail of Nature: The Ambiguous Ecological Promise of Christian Theology.* Minneapolis: Fortress, 1985.

Schaeffer, Francis A., and Udo Middelmann. *Pollution and the Death of Man.* Wheaton, IL: Crossway, 1970.

Toly, Noah J., and Daniel I. Block, eds. *Keeping God's Earth: The Global Environment in Biblical Perspective.* Downers Grove, IL: IVP Academic, 2010.

Young, Richard A. *Healing the Earth: A Theocentric Perspective on Environmental Problems and Their Solutions.* Nashville: B&H, 1994.

Index

H

I

M

N